Sample Mean

$$\overline{X} = \frac{\Sigma X}{N}$$

(4.1)

Sample Variance

$$s^2 = \frac{SS}{N-1} \quad \text{where } SS = \Sigma X^2 - \frac{(\Sigma X)^2}{N} = \Sigma(X - \overline{X})^2$$

(4.8)

Sample Standard Deviation

$$s = \sqrt{\frac{\Sigma X^2 - \frac{(\Sigma X)^2}{N}}{N-1}}$$

(4.13)

Standard Score to Locate a Single Score

Population

$$z = \frac{X - \mu}{\sigma}$$

(5.1)

Sample

$$z = \frac{X - \overline{X}}{s}$$

(5.2)

Correlation

$$\text{Cov}_{XY} = \frac{SP}{N-1} = \frac{\Sigma(X - \overline{X})(Y - \overline{Y})}{N-1}$$

(6.2)

$$r_{XY} = \frac{\text{Cov}_{XY}}{s_X s_Y}$$

(6.7)

Regression

$$Y' = a + bX \quad \text{where } b = \frac{SP}{SS_x} \text{ and } a = \overline{Y} - b\overline{X}$$

(7.1)

$$s_{Y-Y'} = \sqrt{\frac{\Sigma(Y - Y')^2}{N-2}}$$

(7.8)

Combination of n Events Considered r at a Time

$$_nC_r = \frac{n!}{(n-r)!r!}$$

(8.1)

$$_nC_r \, p^r \, q^{(n-r)}$$

(8.3)

Continued on inside back cover.

Application of Statistics in Behavioral Research

Student:

To help you make the most of your study time and improve your grades, we have developed the following supplement designed to accompany May/Masson/Hunter: *Application of Statistics in Behavorial Research:*

•Study Guide, by Richard May, Michael Hunter, and Barbara Jean Jameson
0-06-044310-3

You can order a copy at your local bookstore or call Harper & Row directly at 1-800-638-3030.

Application of Statistics in Behavioral Research

Richard B. May
University of Victoria

Michael E. J. Masson
University of Victoria

Michael A. Hunter
University of Victoria

HARPER & ROW, PUBLISHERS, New York
Grand Rapids   Philadelphia   St. Louis   San Francisco
London   Singapore   Sydney   Tokyo

Sponsoring Editor: Laura Pearson
Project Editor: Paula Cousin
Art Direction/Cover Coordinator: Heather A. Ziegler
Cover Design: Circa 86
Production: William Lane

APPLICATION OF STATISTICS IN BEHAVIORAL RESEARCH

Library of Congress Cataloging-in-Publication Data

May, Richard B.
    Application of statistics in behavioral research / Richard B. May.
  Michael E.J. Masson. Michael A. Hunter.
        p. cm.
    Includes bibliographical references.
    ISBN 0-06-044311-1
    1. Psychology—Statistical methods.   2. Social sciences—
Statistical methods.   I. Masson, Michael E. J.   II. Hunter,
Michael A.   III. Title.
    BF39.M39   1989
    300'.72—dc20   89-38265
                                                                        CIP

89 90 91 92 9 8 7 6 5 4 3 2 1

Contents

Preface

This textbook treats statistical analysis as a tool to help evaluate empirical research. Too many students think that taking a course in statistics means memorizing formulas and doing computations. Although some exposure to formulas and computations is needed, our major goal is to help students think more clearly about research problems that include statistical analysis.

Mathematically, we have taken a rather informal approach requiring a limited background in high-school algebra. The students will find that practicing with formulas and concepts is more important than having sophisticated mathematical skills. Each chapter contains illustrative problems, with solutions supplied in the text, and example problems to solve at the end of the chapter. Solutions to the end-of-chapter problems are found in Appendix II. These problems provide a formal way to practice applying concepts and formulas. Additional problems are available in the *Study and Computing Guide* that accompanies this textbook. With the exception of Chapter 1, the problems use hypothetical data.

Correlation and Regression. Many introductory statistics textbooks treat the topics of correlation and regression **separately** from other topics. After these topics are presented as part of descriptive methods, little mention is made of them. We believe it is important to relate these topics to statistical tests in the second half of the book. Thus, you will find the point biserial correlation (r_{pb}), and other correlations, mentioned in Chapter 11 and Chapters 13 through 18.

Description and Inference. Like most textbooks in statistics, this book includes chapters on descriptive methods followed by others on statistical tests used to help make inferences about data. Our treatment of descriptive statistics is similar to that of other textbooks. Our handling of statistical testing includes conventional material, but with more emphasis on interpretation of results. The focus on interpretation comes from two sources. First, we found that many students have difficulty writing interpretative statements about the results of their statistical computations. Second, through our studies we have found that students need to learn how to distinguish between interpretations that follow from random sampling of subjects from a population and random assignment of subjects (obtained by any means) to different treatment conditions.

The standard presentation of hypothesis testing uses a statistical theory or model with assumptions that are seldom met. The alert reader will notice the discrepancy between statistical theory in a textbook (assume that subjects are randomly sampled) and statistical procedures actually followed in practice (use a nonrandom sample of available subjects). To resolve this discrepancy, Chapter 9, "Hypothesis Testing: Random Assignment," and Chapter 10, "Hypothesis Testing: Random Sampling," introduce two models for statistical testing. Chapter 11 gives a comparison of these models; both models are mentioned where appropriate in the remaining chapters.

Most applications of statistical testing (for example, t and F tests) involve methods based on statistical ideas that assume subjects are randomly sampled. In theory, these tests assess a hypothesis about population parameters (for example, they may use a sample mean to estimate a population mean). When random sampling is not actually used, these methods neither test a hypothesis about population parameters nor do they lead to interpretations about the generality of sample results in a population. Therefore, computing t tests and F tests does not necessarily lead to statements about generality. We agree that researchers should use these tests when samples are not randomly taken. However, we also feel that appropriate interpretation will follow from the type of random process actually used rather than from the type of test computed.

When a researcher uses an available sample (nonrandom), the hypothesis is about the independence of treatments and data. If, for example, the data are not systematic, the values of the data are independent of the treatment conditions. If systematic differences in group behavior are found and subjects were randomly assigned to treatments, the most likely interpretation is that the treatments caused the differences in behavior. The distinctions between random sampling and random assignment, and their associated interpretations of generality and cause, are repeatedly treated in our chapters on hypothesis testing, as well as in later chapters of the book.

Part Four, "Advanced Research Designs," deals with analysis of variance for one-factor designs with independent groups, multiple comparisons, factorial designs, and single-factor designs for dependent samples. If you have the time to deal with these topics, you will find that we have related them to correlation and random assignment tests.

Part Five, "Tests with Frequencies and Ranks" illustrates chi-square tests of goodness-of-fit, independence, and homogeneity, and rank tests of two or more independent or dependent groups. Throughout the chapters in Part Five, we maintain our themes of presenting correlation indices corresponding to each test statistic and of differentiating between random sampling and randomization interpretations of results.

SUPPLEMENTARY MATERIAL

Study and Computing Guide: Written by Richard B. May, Michael A. Hunter, and Barbara Jameson of the University of Victoria, this softcover supplement provides a way for students to review the major ideas presented in the textbook. Each chapter includes (a) a brief review of the text, (b) example examination questions, and (c) problems to solve. There are appendices on the use of the computer programs for computational problems.

Microcomputer Software. The computer program NPSTAT (May, Masson, and Hunter, 1989) was written to illustrate computation of randomization tests and compare the results with normal curve tests such as t and F. Use of the program requires very little prior experience with computer programs or statistical analysis. This program should be especially useful as a supplement to Chapters 9, 11, 13, 16, 17, and 18.

Instructor's Manual. This supplement, written by the text authors, includes a chapter-by-chapter introduction on the rationale for the way material is treated in the text. It also indicates sections of each chapter that may be omitted without disrupting the flow of the text. Example examination questions are given for each chapter. An appendix explains basic features of the computer program NPSTAT.

ACKNOWLEDGMENTS

We acknowledge the support of John Miller of Harper & Row who provided advice and encouragement through all phases of the project. Many helpful comments were made by those who reviewed the manuscript:

Timothy Ansley, University of Iowa

Arthur Aron, Santa Clara University

Phillip Bersh, Temple University

Robert Bowman, University of Wisconsin

Jim Campbell, Carelton University

Richard L. Cook, University of Colorado

Daniel Coulombe, University of Ottawa

James Erickson, University of Texas at Arlington

Alfred E. Hall, College of Wooster

James Juola, University of Kansas

Eric Knowles, University of Arkansas

Thomas Nygren, Ohio State University

James Pate, Georgia State University

Robert Strahan, Iowa State University

Lois Tetrick, Wayne State University

Benjamin Wallace, Cleveland State University

Charles Weiss, College of the Holy Cross

Arnold Well, University of Massachusetts-Amherst

The authors are grateful to the literary executor of the late Sir Ronald A. Fisher, F. R. S., Dr. Frank Yates, F. R. S., and to Longman Group Ltd (London) for permission to adapt Table III from *Statistical Tables for Biological, Agricultural and Medical Research* (6th edition, 1974).

Finally, this book is dedicated to those people who, for us, are significant well beyond the .05 level: Marj, Ruby, and Louie; Debbie, Jacquie, and Will; Shelly, Bill, and Mary.

Richard B. May
Michael E. J. Masson
Michael A. Hunter

Chapter 1

General Introduction

1.1   WHAT ARE WE DOING?

Human beings maintain a high level of curiosity and exploratory behavior throughout their lives. Beginning in infancy and early childhood with looking, touching, and asking simple questions, our exploratory behavior eventually develops into sophisticated problem solving and scientific reasoning.

Fortunately for exhausted parents, young children often accept fanciful explanations to their questions based on their parents' authority. Teeth fall out to satisfy tooth fairies, being good is important because Santa Claus likes and rewards good children, and so on. Adults, too, rely heavily on the voice of authority to inform them about important issues, for example, while reading a newspaper. For instance, Box 1.1 contains a typical newspaper story that describes the relationship between personality traits and brain chemicals.

But adults also begin to acquire the skills needed to evaluate on their own the plausibility and accuracy of answers to their questions. In this book we present techniques for evaluating the plausibility and accuracy of answers to questions asked by behavioral researchers.

Research Objectives

An important goal of scientific research is to establish new and valid knowledge. One way to do so, known as the *method of authority*, is to rely on existing information. This approach may be used to solve a current problem or to provide a new interpretation of existing information that leads to a new contribution. In the Middle Ages, this was the only acceptable form of learning—except that knowledge was not provided by research results but by some supernatural authority. In Box 1.2 we present a description of an episode that clearly illustrates the powerful grip faith in supernatural authority had over human inquiry. With the evolution of the scientific method, more and more knowledge was provided by humans. The problem, however, was that if knowledge came from a human and not directly from God, it was subject to human fallibility.

As a result, when attempting to do experiments on a problem, experts may differ in their beliefs about whether a particular method is correct or about how to interpret some result. Disagreement of this kind leads to skepticism about the validity of the results produced by other researchers. Rather than accepting new research results without question, experts in a field critically evaluate new results and the methods that produced them.

A second way of establishing new knowledge, the *empirical method*, is to produce new results through some kind of scientific experiment. A simple form of this approach is seen in the proposal made by the unfortunate young friar in Box 1.2. This example also provides a clear indication of when a new experiment is called for: when existing authorities fail to provide a valid answer to the problem. In many cases new experiments are prompted by the development of new ideas or *hypotheses* about some issue (e.g., how to re-

Box 1.1   **Personality Linked to Brain Chemical**

© 1987 *THE WASHINGTON POST*

The personality difference between extroverts and introverts may be related to a chemical difference in their brains, a study at Stanford University Medical Center suggests.

Extroverts—outgoing and talkative people—tend to have higher levels of the brain chemical dopamine than introverted people do, researchers found.

The Stanford study, published in *Psychiatry Research,* is one of the first to link a chemical in the brain to a normal personality trait. It provides a "first clue" to understanding the neurochemistry behind personality variations and could shed light on the chemical basis of such behavioral problems as social withdrawal and drug addiction, said Dr. Roy King, assistant professor of psychiatry and behavioral sciences.

The study was based on measurements of dopamine in the cerebrospinal fluid, the liquid that bathes the brain, in 16 male patients being treated at Stanford for depression.

All 16 had completed the Eysenck Personality Inventory, a psychological test that distinguishes extroverts from introverts. The dopamine level was significantly higher in the more extroverted patients.

The researchers, including scientists from Stanford, Boston College and the National Institute of Mental Health, cautioned that further research on non-depressed patients is needed before the results can be generalized.

Reprinted with permission of the *Los Angeles Times–Washington Post* News Service.

duce stress-induced headaches by using relaxation techniques). These hypotheses are based on existing knowledge but represent new extensions developed through reasoning or insight. If the hypotheses truly are new, it is most unlikely that any evidence relevant to their validity exists. It is at this stage that a researcher will design an experiment to test the hypotheses.

Research studies often are designed to provide an objective test of hypotheses, and it is this type of research that we emphasize in this book. No matter how strongly a researcher believes that a hypothesis is true, a well-designed experiment will provide a fair evaluation. It can even lead to the conclusion that the hypothesis is incorrect. When other scientists evaluate the research, they are concerned with the validity of the results and the method by which they were obtained. Ideally, the researcher's degree of conviction about the truth of a hypothesis is irrelevant.

An example of the empirical method is presented in Box 1.3. The issue in this study was how to induce relaxation to relieve headache. One possibil-

Box 1.2 **An Early Method for Acquiring Knowledge**

In the year of our Lord 1432, there arose a grievous quarrel among the brethren over the number of teeth in the mouth of a horse. For thirteen days the disputation raged without ceasing. All the ancient books and chronicles were fetched out, and wonderful and ponderous erudition, such as was never before heard of in this region, was made manifest. At the beginning of the fourteenth day, a youthful friar of goodly bearing asked his learned superiors for permission to add a word, and straightway, to the wonderment of the disputants, whose deep wisdom he sore vexed, he beseeched them to unbend in a manner coarse and unheard-of, and to look in the open mouth of a horse and find the answer to their questionings. At this, their dignity being grievously hurt, they waxed exceedingly wroth; and joining in a mighty uproar, they flew upon him and smote his hip and thigh, and caste him out forthwith. For, said they, surely Satan hath tempted his bold neophyte to declare unholy and unheard-of ways of finding truth contrary to all the teachings of the fathers. After many days of grievous strife the dove of peace sat on the assembly, and they as one man, declaring the problem to be an everlasting mystery because of a grievous dearth of historical and theological evidence thereof, so ordered the same writ down.

—Sir Francis Bacon

Reprinted from C.E.K. Mees, Scientific thought and social reconstruction, *Sigma Xi Quarterly, 22* (1934), 13–24.

ity would be to use biofeedback techniques that provide feedback concerning the level of relaxation. Another would be to allow people to listen to soothing music. But are these techniques better than giving headache sufferers no training, and if they are, which is more effective? The results of the study provide some useful answers.

Did you notice the statement in Box 1.3 that summarized one of the experiment's important results? "Results indicated that both groups suffered less from headaches after training than did a group of people who received no training." This statement is based on some kind of measurement of the reported *amount* of suffering by subjects in the study and on a comparison of the reported amounts of suffering in the different groups.

The procedures used to compare behaviors such as reported amount of suffering are essential tools that a researcher uses in analyzing the results of an experiment, and they are called *statistics*. Understanding which statistics are applicable in specific situations, how they are computed, and how they should be interpreted is critical for enabling you to evaluate results produced by others and to make sense of results that you will obtain if you do research of your own.

Box 1.3　## Music Hath Charms to Soothe a Throbbing Head

Migraine headaches can be exquisitely painful and are often stubbornly resistant to treatment, both medical and psychological. The precise cause of migraines is uncertain, but stress is often involved. It follows that one way of reducing migraine pain is to relax. But what is the best way to induce relaxation?

Psychologist Jane Lapp conducted an experiment that suggests that music may be the answer. In her study, migraine sufferers received relaxation training in combination with either biofeedback or music. In the biofeedback group, special equipment let individuals know when they were relaxed. In the music group, individuals imagined tranquil scenes while listening to a medley of popular tunes. Training lasted five weeks, and consisted of two 30-minute sessions each week.

The migraine sufferers kept a record of the number, intensity and duration of headaches they had each day during training and for one-week periods approximately one month and one year after training. Results indicated that both groups suffered less from headaches after training than did a group of people who received no training. Overall, the results were better for the music group than for the biofeedback group, especially at the one-year follow-up. "At one year," Lapp says, "the music group had only one-sixth as many headaches as they had before training, and those headaches were less severe and ended more quickly." Lapp also found that some people in the music group were able to end a developing headache before it got a good start.

Lapp is not sure why music aided relaxation so well. She notes that there is some evidence that listening to music releases endorphins, the body's natural pain-killers. And since listening to music does not require the sort of cumbersome equipment of biofeedback, music listeners could practice more often. Some of those in the music group also found that incidental music heard during the day reminded them to relax.

Headache pain can have all sorts of causes, including tumors, so Lapp advises chronic headache sufferers to see their physician. If, however, tension is the culprit, sufferers may want to put on some soft music and relax.

Reprinted with permission from *Psychology Today,* copyright © 1987 (PT Partners, L.P.).

1.2 WHAT ARE STATISTICS?

Statistical procedures can be organized into groups consisting of related items. It is helpful to know this organization so that the similarities between different statistics can be readily seen. Another advantage is that the organizational scheme provides clues about which statistics should be used under certain circumstances. A fundamental distinction that can be made is between statistics that are used to summarize a set of measurements, **descrip-**

Box 1.4 **National DWI Data Questioned by Study**

WASHINGTON (AP)—National statistics on drunken driving and fatal accidents are inaccurate because police let most surviving drivers leave the scene without being tested for alcohol abuse, according to a study issued Sunday.

The report by the Crime Control Institute, a non-profit research organization of law enforcement officials, also found that many drunken drivers in fatal accidents escape prosecution because they are not given a blood-alcohol test.

Various studies have shown that drivers are most likely to be tested if they show visible signs of intoxication. The new study points out the "varying ability of people to 'hold their liquor' " and says the shot of adrenalin that accompanies an accident can have a rapid sobering effect.

Of the 32,000 drivers who survived accidents involving deaths in1984, more than 75 percent left the scene without being tested for alcohol abuse, the report said. More than 25 percent of the 25,582 drivers who were killed in accidents were not tested for blood alcohol concentration. Overall, only 45 percent of all drivers in fatal accidents are tested for alcohol abuse.

Statistics on drunken driving deaths "have lulled us into a false belief that we always detect drunk driving as a cause of fatal accidents," said Lawrence Sherman, president of the Crime Control Institute. "The truth is that we are hardly even trying."

Reprinted with permission from the Associated Press (1986).

---

tive statistics, and those that are used to examine inferences that might be drawn from the measurements, **inferential statistics.**

Descriptive Statistics

The most important purpose of descriptive statistics is to provide a summary of a set of **data.** Data consist of a set of scores or measurements obtained from a collection of individuals. Descriptive statistics frequently appear in newspapers and magazines and on television and radio broadcasts. Box 1.4 provides an example of descriptive statistics associated with automobile accidents. The report reveals that many drivers involved in fatal auto accidents are not tested for level of alcohol in the bloodstream. The accuracy of the U.S. Department of Transportation's estimate of the percentage of traffic fatalities that involve drunken drivers depends on the assumption that all of the untested drivers were sober. Do you think this is a valid assumption?

DATA: A set of scores or measurements obtained from a collection of individuals.

DESCRIPTIVE STATISTICS: Procedures used to summarize a set of data.

Another example of a descriptive statistic is your class's average score on an examination. This statistic is a summary of how well the class, taken as a whole, performed on the test. Descriptive statistics are of great importance in the analysis of scientific data and often are the first kind of statistic that a researcher examines. As will be seen in the next few chapters, they provide important information about many aspects of a set of data.

Inferential Statistics

The importance of a set of data lies in the new knowledge and conclusion or *inferences* that it supports. For example, the study of extroverts and introverts that appears in Box 1.1 found that extroverts had higher levels of dopamine in their cerebrospinal fluid. The researchers inferred from this result that the personality difference between extroverted and introverted people may be related to dopamine level in the brain.

INFERENTIAL STATISTICS: Procedures that allow inferences to be made from a set of data.

Different kinds of inferences can be made from a set of data, and only some of them can be supported through the use of inferential statistics. Other inferences depend on nonstatistical arguments. We illustrate the use of inferential statistics and other arguments in the context of three different kinds of inference: (1) systematic effects, (2) causal effects, and (3) generalization.

Systematic and Random Effects

Many empirical studies are designed to do more than just measure a single behavior (e.g., administer an intelligence test) and report a set of descriptive statistics. Rather, they are intended to determine whether behavior is *related* to some environmental factor or characteristic of the individuals being studied. For example, in the study of relaxation and headaches, the issue was whether the amount of reported pain would be related to the relaxation technique used.

The objective of determining whether behavior is related to some factor requires the behavior to be measured under different conditions (e.g., obtaining pain reports from people trained in relaxation methods and from people not so trained). Inferential statistics are then used to determine whether behavior varies systematically from one condition to another (e.g., people in the relaxation group report fewer headaches than those in the control group).

For example, Box 1.5 presents a study in which intellectual achievement scores varied with type of day-care: a special kind of day-care center or a standard community day-care facility. On the average, scores were higher for children who attended the special day-care center. The inference we might wish to draw here is that intellectual development is systematically related to the day-care environment.

Box 1.5   ## Good Grades for Day-Care

Though young children born into poverty are more likely to score lower on intelligence tests than are their middle-class peers, good day-care can make a big difference. Not only can it lessen the detrimental effects of poverty on children, it may also enhance their intellectual growth.

Psychologist Margaret Burchinal and colleagues recruited 124 low-income children and randomly assigned some of them to research-based, high quality day-care from infancy until they entered kindergarten. The others attended varying amounts of "good day-care" (meeting federal guidelines) in the community.

Using two standard tests of child development and a basic IQ test, the researchers compared the intellectual achievement of the children at various times from 6 months through their 54th month. As expected, those who attended the research day-care outscored the community day-care group on average, even the community kids who got just as many hours of day-care. The children who packed in the fewest hours of day-care (six or fewer months) scored much lower than the other community groups.

Burchinal and colleagues looked not only at the children's level of achievement, but also at patterns of growth and decline. Here they found that "high quality, cognitively oriented day-care prevented the marked decline in IQ scores exhibited in the . . . community group." Interestingly, children who attended little or no day-care scored worse over time than did the others.

Reprinted with permission from *Psychology Today,* copyright © 1987 (PT Partners, L.P.).

An alternative possibility, however, is that the type of day-care experience is not related to intellectual development and that the difference in average scores occurred by chance. These two alternatives (systematic versus random variation in scores across conditions) exist because children were **randomly assigned** to either the special day-care class or to a regular community facility (see the second paragraph in Box 1.5).

Random assignment means that each child had an equal probability of being assigned to either of the day-care conditions and that the assignment of each child was independent of the assignment of any other child. For example, Joey's assignment to the special day-care class had no bearing on whether his best friend, Mikey, would be assigned to that class; they each had an equal and independent opportunity to be assigned to the class. In Box 1.6 we describe a procedure that can be used to assign subjects randomly to different conditions.

RANDOM ASSIGNMENT: Each subject has an equal and independent probability of being assigned to each condition in an experiment.

Box 1.6 # Using the Random Number Table

The table of random numbers, Table A in Appendix III, can be used for tasks such as random assignment of subjects to conditions. Each position in the table is occupied by a single digit that was randomly selected from the values zero through nine. To use the table for randomly assigning subjects to conditions, each condition is to be associated with an equal number of arbitrarily chosen digits. For example, in a study with two conditions, A and B, condition A might be associated with even digits (0, 2, 4, 6, and 8) and condition B with odd digits (1, 3, 5, 7, and 9). Then for each subject a digit is randomly selected from the table, and the subject is assigned to the corresponding condition. Here is a procedure for randomly selecting digits from the table.

1. Place the tip of a pencil at some point in the table without looking and determine which two digits are closest to the point. These digits represent the row from which your first digit will be selected. Repeat this process until you have a valid row number (e.g., 07) and ignore any attempts that produce invalid numbers (e.g., 82).

2. Repeat step 1 to obtain the column number for the first digit. In counting column numbers treat each one-digit column as a whole column.

3. Enter the table at the row and column position determined in steps 1 and 2. This is the first random digit. Obtain other digits by reading down the page. When you reach the bottom of the page, move to the top of the next column and continue down until you have obtained enough digits. If the page is exhausted before you have found enough digits, continue by going back to step 1.

If the number of conditions does not allow an even division of the ten digits (e.g., three conditions), some of the digits can be omitted, and if they are selected randomly from the table they will be ignored. If random numbers consisting of two or more digits are required, treat the entry point defined by steps 1 and 2 as the first digit of the first random number. The remaining digits for the first number are those to the right. The second random number begins immediately below the first, and so on. Ignore any values that are outside the range you have defined.

EXAMPLE

We have six subjects and wish to randomly assign three to condition A and three to condition B. Equal numbers of subjects are to be assigned to each condition, so once a condition is filled any further selection of its digits is ignored. We decide that even digits are associated with condition A and odd digits with condition B. (1) The first placement of the pencil yields 78, so it is ignored (the table has fewer than 78 rows). The second yields 22. (2) The third produces 38. Therefore, the entry point in the table for the first random digit is row 22, column 38. (3) The digit is 3, so the first subject is assigned to condition B. Moving down the page, the next digits are 5 (subject 2 to condition B), 4 (subject 3 to condition A), 5 (subject 4 to condition B—this condition is now filled), 3 (ignore further odd digits), 7 (ignore), 4 (subject 5 to condition A), 5 (ignore), 3 (ignore), 8 (subject 6 to condition A).

The differences between the two day-care groups, then, could have been due to the "luck of the draw"—more of the bright children might have been assigned randomly to the special day-care condition. Inferential statistics can be used to determine whether the random effect explanation is likely to be correct. If it is not likely to be correct, we are justified in concluding that the type of day-care experience is indeed related to intellectual development.

Cause and Effect

Once inferential statistics have been used to reach the conclusion that a systematic effect is present, we can draw one more inference if we have used random assignment. That is, the systematic effect is a *causal* one. This means that differences in the conditions under which behavior was measured caused scores to vary systematically across conditions. In the day-care study, for example, we can conclude that differences in the quality of the programs *caused* intellectual achievement scores to be higher in the special day-care program than in the regular day-care program.

Random assignment allows us to make a causal inference because it virtually ensures that no factor other than differences in conditions could have caused scores to vary across conditions. To see this point more clearly, consider a case in which random assignment was not used, the personality study in Box 1.1. In that study subjects were not randomly assigned to dopamine conditions. They came to the researchers with their level of dopamine already determined by some factor(s) unknown to the researchers (e.g., genetic background or environmental experience).

The study found that those with more dopamine were more extroverted, so it was inferred that the two factors are systematically related. But we cannot be sure that high dopamine level *caused* higher levels of extroversion. It could be that some unknown genetic or environmental factor responsible for producing high dopamine levels also was responsible for producing a high level of extroversion. If so, there may be no causal link between dopamine and extroversion, even though there is a systematic relationship between them (e.g., both are high or low because of the influence exerted by the unknown factor). What would you have been able to infer had similar results been obtained after subjects were randomly assigned to conditions in which the researchers were able to create high or low dopamine levels at will?

The distinction between the day-care and personality studies can be summarized by examining the left side of Figure 1.1, which shows the stages involved in statistical analysis and the requirements for making a causal inference. The key to making a causal inference is the use of random *assignment* of subjects to conditions. The day-care study described in Box 1.5 used random assignment, so we can conclude that the systematic relationship between day-care experience and intellectual achievement is a causal one. The personality study in Box 1.1, however, did not involve random assignment of

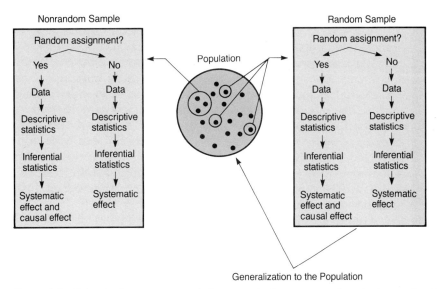

Figure 1.1 Schematic summary of the association among descriptive and inferential statistics, random sampling and random assignment, and types of inferences about relationships between variables.

subjects to the level of dopamine, so we can conclude only that there is a systematic relationship between the level of dopamine and extroversion.

Generalization

Once a researcher has established a new result, there may be some concern about whether there are grounds for claiming that the result would hold if other subjects were tested. For example, the personality study in Box 1.1 found a relationship between extroversion and dopamine level in male patients being treated for depression at Stanford University. Since depressed females and nondepressed subjects were not included in the study, do we have any way of knowing that the result would hold for such people (see the last paragraph of Box 1.1)? Would the results even generalize to other depressed males who are treated at Stanford but who did not take part in the study?

To clarify this issue, we need to make a distinction between the particular set of subjects whose scores are obtained in a study and the larger set of individuals to whom we might wish to generalize the results. The larger set of individuals is called a **population.** Ideally, we would like to obtain scores for each member of a population, but this task is typically impossible because of a population's immense size (e.g., all adults in North America). The compromise made by researchers is to obtain scores from only some of the individuals in the population, and this set of individuals is referred to as a **sample.** Once a result has been found with a sample, an attempt may be made to generalize to some related population.

POPULATION: The entire collection of individuals whose behavior might be measured.

SAMPLE: A subset of a population of individuals.

In the personality study in Box 1.1 the sample consisted of depressed males. The researchers appeared to consider it a sample from a population of depressed patients because they were not willing to generalize to nondepressed patients. On the other hand, the day-care study described in Box 1.5 involved a sample of children from low-income families, and no other distinguishing features are mentioned. Here one might wish to argue that the findings could be generalized to the population of children from low-income families in North America.

Arguments about generalizing results can be made both on statistical and on nonstatistical grounds. Nonstatistical arguments for generalization are based on a comparison of the characteristics of the subjects who were tested and of the population to which generalization is claimed to be valid.

For example, it might seem reasonable to claim that the relationship between dopamine and extroversion found in the depressed males being treated at Stanford would be true of other depressed patients, including females. Arguments against this view would claim that those depressed males in the original sample differ from other depressed patients in a manner related to the characteristics that were measured. With no further information about the individuals included in the sample or about members of the population to which we might generalize our results, making the generalization is a matter of *faith*—our willingness to believe that the sample is representative of the population.

A much stronger argument in favor of making a generalization can be based on inferential statistics used in conjunction with a special procedure— that is, designating the population to which one wishes to generalize, then testing a sample of individuals from that population. The critical step in this procedure involves the selection of individuals from the population by a form of *random sampling*.

There are a number of techniques for obtaining a random sample from a population, but the fundamental criteria are (1) that each member of the population has an equal chance of being included in the sample, and (2) that the selection of any one member of the population is independent of the selection of any other member. The second aspect of random sampling, independence, means that when one individual is sampled, inclusion of that individual has no bearing on who else (e.g., that person's friend) will also be included. A researcher who tries to increase the number of people in a study by inviting participants to bring along their friends is not working with a random sample.

When a random sample from a population is obtained, inferential statistics can be used to determine the probability that some systematic or causal effect found in the sample would be obtained if the whole population were tested. Unlike claims of generalization based on arguments about similarities between members of a sample and a target population, claims based on inferential statistics and random sampling are not open to counterarguments. For this reason random sampling should be used whenever it is feasible.

Figure 1.1 presents a summary of the distinction among the three kinds of inference discussed here: (1) systematic effects, (2) causal effects, and (3) generalization to a population. In making these inferences, two types of randomness are important. One type is random assignment, which forms the basis for inferring causality. The second type is random sampling from a population. It allows generalization of results from a sample to the population from which the sample was randomly drawn. Had the studies described in Boxes 1.1 and 1.5 involved random samples, we could have discussed them by using the stages outlined on the right side of Figure 1.1. Notice that the only difference would have been that we could include the final step of generalizing the obtained causal (day-care study) or systematic (personality study) effect to the population on which the sample was based.

1.3   THEORY AND PRACTICE

Many of the statistical procedures presented in this book are based on a set of theoretical assumptions. For example, many of the inferential statistics used to make inferences from a sample to a population were developed for situations where, among other things, the sample was randomly selected from the population.

When we apply statistical analyses to data, or when we evaluate the results of analyses presented by other researchers, we need to be aware of the assumptions underlying the analyses. Awareness of assumptions is necessary if we are to select the appropriate analysis to use and if we are to detect those instances when other researchers have applied analyses even though the assumptions have not been satisfied. A common example occurs when a researcher does not randomly sample from a population but depends instead on some convenient means of recruiting locally available volunteers. The researcher then submits the obtained data to statistical procedures that are based on the assumption that scores were taken from randomly sampled subjects.

The use of a statistical procedure in a situation that violates one or more of its assumptions often is due to practical considerations. Obtaining a random sample of human subjects is virtually impossible for most research studies. There would be serious logistic problems for researchers in Boston, for instance, who want to test in their laboratory a random sample of North American infants that included babies residing in Flagstaff, Arizona, or Vancouver, Canada. There also would be ethical problems if the parents of a randomly sampled baby did not wish to have their child take part in the study.

When it is likely that the use of a statistical test in a certain situation is going to involve violation of its assumptions, a researcher has four options.

One option is to adhere rigidly to assumptions, using a statistical procedure only when exactly appropriate, and not conduct the kinds of research that lead to violation of some statistical assumption. Along with many diligent researchers throughout the world, we reject this option as an unacceptable obstacle to scientific progress. A second, equally extreme, option is to ignore completely the assumptions of a statistical procedure and to risk making significant errors by using the procedure indiscriminantly. This approach also is an unacceptable one.

A third and preferable solution is to search for an alternative statistic that is based on assumptions that can be satisfied. For example, this is a reasonable approach in situations where the sample is not a random one. In many of these instances the objective is to show that, at least for those subjects in the sample, some factor (e.g., type of relaxation technique) affects subjects' scores on some measure (e.g., severity or frequency of headaches). Making the claim that the effect would hold for some larger population of individuals is much less important.[1] In these cases, inferential statistics of the type described in the previous section on *systematic and random effects* could be used instead of those described in the section on *generalization*.

We also advocate a fourth approach to the problem of violation of assumptions—using a statistical procedure even though one or more of its assumptions have not been satisfied. This approach is acceptable when it can be demonstrated that the results of the statistical test are not strongly influenced by violation of the assumption(s) in question. A number of the statistical tests in later chapters have this property.

1.4   STATISTICS IN BEHAVIORAL RESEARCH

In this book we emphasize statistical aspects of behavioral research, but you should realize that other considerations are important in the design and execution of research. You should also understand how statistics fit into the larger framework of behavioral research. There is a standard series of stages that describe the procedures involved, only some of which include statistical computations. All stages, however, can be tied in some way to statistical issues.

The first stage consists of the development of a *conceptual hypothesis*, which might claim that some factor influences scores on a test. This hypothesis might be generated from a new theory based on a review of previous research. The second stage is a statement of the conceptual hypothesis in terms of a *statistical hypothesis*. This step requires detailed specification of the kinds of behavior and subjects that are of interest, how behavior will be measured, and how the obtained results will be analyzed. This is one point in a research project at which consideration of relevant statistical procedures

---

[1] A useful discussion of this point may be found in an article by Mook (1983).

is essential. A common error among novice researchers is to wait until after the data have been collected before considering how they will be analyzed. This error can lead to catastrophes, such as being unable to analyze the data in a manner that will address the original conceptual hypothesis.

The third stage is data collection (i.e., measuring the relevant behavior of a sample of subjects). The fourth stage once again involves statistics and consists of applying appropriate analyses to the data. In this stage a decision, or *statistical conclusion*, is reached concerning the statistical hypothesis developed in the second stage.

In the fifth stage a researcher uses the statistical conclusion and other information to produce a *conceptual conclusion*, which determines whether the results favor the original conceptual hypothesis or some alternative conceptual hypothesis. It is important to keep in mind that considerations of how the data were collected enter into this judgment as well. For example, statistical analysis of a set of data may indicate that, on the average, neurotic subjects given a drug show more improvement than those not given a drug, supporting the conceptual hypothesis that the drug causes reduced neurotic behavior. But it could be that differential treatment of the two groups of subjects (e.g., subjects given a drug require special treatment such as an injection or pill) rather than the presence of the drug in the bloodstream produced the observed effect. Problems such as these are best solved by ensuring that subjects in different groups are treated as similarly as possible (e.g., the group not given the drug is administered some neutral substance instead).

The final stage of a research project is the preparation and distribution of a report of the work. This may take a number of different forms, such as publication as a journal article or presentation at a professional convention. Communication of research results is a critical aspect of advancing scientific knowledge. It allows researchers in a field to keep up to date on the most recent findings and to examine the details of a research project to understand exactly how the results were produced and to determine whether the conclusions were appropriate.

The research study described in Box 1.7 shows each of the stages we have described. The initial conceptual hypothesis in this study, based on observation of certain artists and writers, was that alcohol consumption may improve creativity (stage 1). It was decided to have subjects take a creativity test after consuming an alcoholic drink and after a nonalcoholic drink. The statistical hypothesis (not directly stated in this summary of the research) was that, on the average, subjects would obtain higher scores after taking a drink of alcohol (stage 2). Data were collected by testing each subject in two conditions, one with alcohol and one without (stage 3).

The initial statistical analysis indicated that alcohol did not, on the average, lead to higher creativity scores (stage 4). At this point the researcher discovered an interesting but unexpected trend in the data. The trend was confirmed by another statistical analysis that was not originally planned. It was found that consuming alcohol improved creativity among those with low scores when sober and reduced creativity among subjects who had high scores

---

Box 1.7 ## Creative Spirits

What would happen if the Earth were enshrouded in fog, and only people's feet were visible? How about if clouds had strings attached to them, hanging down to Earth?

If you have no idea, or simply can't imagine such silly scenes, a shot of vodka might start the creative flow. But if you've already begun to make a list of possibilities, you should probably avoid the local pub.

Many have made the claim that alcohol and creativity go together, based on the observation that a good number of famous artists and writers rarely knew a dry day. To study the link between alcohol and creativity, psychologist Geoff Lowe rounded up a group of 32 moderate social drinkers, aged 18 to 30. Each person attended two sessions spaced a week apart, drinking a glass of water and tonic during one session and a mix of vodka and tonic at the other.

Lowe gave the alcohol 20 minutes to take effect and used a Breathalyzer to gauge the drinkers' levels of intoxication. He then administered a standard creativity test, to which half the group gave written responses and half gave oral answers. The test included questions such as the hypothetical situations mentioned above, and it also required people to think of new ones for ordinary objects.

Lowe found that alcohol didn't much affect the creativity of these people, except that those who wrote their answers were a little less creative than those who verbalized them.

Another look at the findings, however, did uncover an interesting difference: Those low on creativity after a water and tonic saw things in a much more creative light with a dose of alcohol. Yet their counterparts who fared well when sober lost a good deal of the creative touch when moderately drunk.

Lowe concludes that in the less creative people, a moderate dose of alcohol removed the inhibitions they may have felt when sober, whereas the reverse occurred in the more creative people. "They were operating at an optimum level before they drank, so a shot of vodka harmed their performance," he says.

when sober. From these unanticipated results the researcher drew the conceptual conclusion that alcohol reduced the inhibitions of less creative people but apparently had the opposite effect on more creative people (stage 5). As for communicating the results of the project (stage 6), researcher Geoff Lowe presented these findings at a meeting of the British Psychological Society.

Several features of the study in Box 1.7 are noteworthy. First, although statistical analyses were conducted at only one stage, statistical considerations were important at other stages as well, both in the planning of the study and in the development of the final conceptual conclusions. Second, deriving a statistical hypothesis from a conceptual hypothesis requires detailed decisions about how behavior will be measured and under what conditions. Third, statistical analyses are used not only in a *confirmatory* role—as in determining whether the original statistical hypothesis is correct—but also in an *exploratory* role. When the researcher noticed an unexpected pattern in the data, new conceptual and statistical hypotheses were developed and tested with the data that had already been collected.

Exploratory analysis of data makes it possible for researchers to make new and unanticipated discoveries. The problem, however, is that exploratory analyses can be triggered by some aspect of the data that is spurious and might not appear if the study were repeated. Therefore, it is necessary to *replicate* such effects in further studies before placing very much confidence in them.[2]

Finally, you should notice that the development of a conceptual conclusion requires many considerations beyond the statistical conclusion. In the creativity study, for example, the researcher claimed that alcohol influenced creativity by altering a subject's inhibitions. This claim could not be based entirely on the data collected in the study since there was no direct measure of the level of inhibition. The conclusion must have been based on other knowledge or assumptions about the effect of alcohol on inhibition.

1.5 LOOKING AHEAD

In the remainder of this chapter we provide a brief discussion of what you will encounter in later chapters and some suggestions on how to approach the task of studying the kind of material presented here. We also offer some suggestions concerning the use of calculators and computers in association with reading this textbook.

Parts of This Book

The first part of this book (Chapters 2 through 5) is an introduction to descriptive statistics that are used to summarize data based on the measurement of a single aspect of behavior (e.g., scores obtained by a sample of subjects on an intelligence test). The second part of the book (Chapters 6 and 7) emphasizes descriptive statistics that are used to measure the relationship between two different aspects of behavior in a single sample of subjects (e.g.,

---

[2]In fact, there is reason to believe that the unanticipated results obtained in the study described in Box 1.7 were spurious and would not be replicated. People who obtain higher scores on a test may have done so partly because their true score has been overestimated. When tested a second time it is unlikely that the overestimate will be as large, resulting in a lower score. Similarly, people with lower scores on the first test may have been underestimated, and when they are retested the underestimate is not likely to be as large. This phenomenon is related to the concept of *reliability,* which is discussed in Chapter 2.

intelligence and creativity). In the third part (Chapters 8 through 12) we introduce the concepts of probability and inferential statistics and show how they are used in making decisions about hypotheses. In the fourth part of the book (Chapters 13 through 16) we discuss more advanced research designs and the inferential statistics that are commonly used with them. The final part of the book (Chapters 17 and 18) explains statistical techniques that are based on fewer assumptions than those presented in the third part. Some of these procedures can be applied to the kind of data for which statistics in the third part of the book are not appropriate.

Study Strategies

Many people approach the subject of statistics with a great deal of reluctance and even fear. Our experience has been that this anxiety arises, for the most part, from concern that the subject requires extensive knowledge of mathematics. For an introductory course in behavioral science statistics this belief is unfounded. Skill with basic arithmetic and a working knowledge of high school algebra are all that are necessary to understand the concepts we present. A few new mathematical concepts are introduced as necessary, but in a simplified manner. For those who lack confidence in their skill at algebra, a brief review and associated exercises are provided in Appendix I.

In studying the material associated with this book it is advisable to remember that the concepts we introduce are arranged in a hierarchical manner. That is, it is necessary to master the concepts presented in the early part of the book before attempting to understand later material. This requirement is a consequence of the way in which the concepts are organized. Students who are used to dealing with courses that can be separated into independent areas will find that study techniques used for these courses may be unsuccessful here. If you have an unresolved difficulty with one chapter, you are certain to have related problems in some later chapter—and by that time it may be too late to correct the difficulty. Therefore, we strongly suggest that you achieve a clear understanding of the material in each chapter before you move on to the next.

Learning about statistics also involves a form of *skill learning*. Not only are you required to learn new ideas but you will also have to learn to apply them by following a specific series of operations or steps. As with any skill, learning to do this one properly will require practice, and there will be no proper substitute for practice. Further, it is very important to understand thoroughly what you are doing when you practice performing a statistical computation. Through this kind of "intelligent" practice you will begin to gain clearer insight into how statistical procedures behave and how their results are influenced by particular aspects of the data—aspects that you may learn to recognize in raw data even before carrying out an analysis. Questions at the end of chapters and a study guide are available to assist you in this activity.

Calculators and Computers

You may be wondering why, in this age of technology, you are asked to learn about statistical procedures. Can't you simply give the data to a computer and have it produce the answers? After reading this chapter you should have some clues about why statistical analysis is not so simple. Think about the various stages of research in which consideration of statistical analysis plays a significant role, and recall the issue of practical compromises that often have to be made when applying statistical procedures to real data. Even today, no computer is able to take care of these problems for you. Although the computer can carry out the computation, you must decide which procedure to use and you must make sense of the result. Part of this skill depends on a clear understanding of what is computed when a statistical procedure is carried out.

There is no doubt, however, that your skill development will be greatly assisted by the use of calculators and computers. For simple problems with small amounts of data, you can do most of the statistics presented in this book with a hand-held calculator. We recommend one that has the following features: a square root key, a squaring key, and at least one memory. This list of features should reassure you that you will not be required to perform esoteric mathematical procedures. In addition, practice at using a computer package to carry out statistical procedures can be quite valuable. One use of the computer is to check work that you have done by hand or with a calculator. You should be able to consult with your instructor to determine which computer packages are available in your area.

SUMMARY

The purpose of this book is to help you develop skills that will enable you to evaluate statistical aspects of research in the behavioral sciences and that will serve as a foundation for more advanced learning that may help you carry out research of your own. Two general classes of statistical techniques are presented in this book. Descriptive statistics are used to summarize a few critical features of a set of data. Inferential statistics are used to guide inferences about whether the effect of some factor on a measurement of behavior (1) is systematic, (2) is causal, and (3) can be generalized from the sample of subjects who were tested to a much larger population of individuals. Such inferences also depend on nonstatistical arguments and the appropriate design of experiments.

The practical use of a statistical procedure often demands a violation of one or more of the assumptions on which the procedure is based. We advocate finding an alternative statistic or using the statistic even though some assumptions are violated. When the latter course is chosen, it is advisable to seek evidence that violation of the assumption(s) is not likely to have a strong influence on the outcome of the statistical analysis. Statistical considerations are important in research not only at the time statistical analysis is carried out but also when a study is designed: They can influence the way in which data are collected. Further, statistical analyses can play a role in testing the validity of conceptual hypotheses generated at the outset of a project as well as in an exploratory manner to follow up unexpected trends that appear in the data.

KEY WORDS

data	sample
descriptive statistics	random sampling
inferential statistics	statistical assumptions
systematic effects	conceptual hypothesis
random assignment	statistical hypothesis
cause and effect	statistical conclusion
generalization	conceptual conclusion
population	

PROBLEMS

1 What is one method of authority that many North American adults rely on nearly every day?

2 For each of the following examples, indicate whether only a descriptive statistic would be involved or whether an inferential statistic would also be used.
   (a) The average score obtained on a test of extroversion-introversion by a group of depressed clients visiting a clinic.
   (b) A group of laboratory rats given a diet that included a new chemical substitute for sugar had a higher rate of cancer than a group of rats not given the chemical.
   (c) Randomly selected voters are asked for whom they cast their ballot as they leave the polling place.
   (d) The percentage of students in a school's most recent graduating class who went on to college.

3 A magazine has decided to measure its readership's attitude toward the magazine's plan to adopt a ban on advertisements for alcoholic beverages. A set of 500 names is randomly selected from the list of the magazine's subscribers and each person is sent a questionnaire. Identify the population and the sample involved in this example. Suppose only 25 percent of the people who were sent the questionnaire mailed back a response. Would you consider those people who responded a random sample of the magazine's readership? Why or why not? If not, of what population would the respondents be a random sample?

4 Make up an example of a research study concerning whether behavior is systematically related to some factor.

5 Make up an example of a research study to establish a causal relationship between a behavior and some factor.

6 Make up an example of a research study to make a statistically based generalization of the study's results to a large population.

7 The instructor of one of the three introductory psychology classes at a university performs a demonstration in class one day in which each student attempts to answer a set of 10 questions on the history of psychology. The answers for 20 randomly selected students are selected for analysis. Inferential statistics could be used to generalize these results to what population of students? To what larger population might the results be generalized only on the basis of the argument that the sample is similar to that population?

8 Use the random number table in Appendix III to randomly assign a set of 15 subjects to three groups of 5 subjects each.

9 Use the same table to draw a random sample of 10 one-digit numbers in the range 0–9. Now draw a random sample of 10 three-digit numbers in the range 001–500.

10 For the study in Box 1.3 identify the conceptual hypothesis, the statistical hypothesis, the statistical conclusion, and the conceptual conclusion. Do the same for the study in Box 1.5.

ONE

Describing Data for a Single Variable

*T*he examples of research described in Chapter 1 have a number of important features in common. One of the more important ones is the fact that they each involve collection of some kind of information or *data*. In behavioral research, data collection requires that a researcher measure some aspect of behavior, such as frequency of reported headaches, amount of creativity, or intelligence. The chapters in Part One introduce concepts associated with the measurement of behavior (Chapter 2) and techniques used in presenting the results of these measurements (Chapter 3). For example, an important tool used in describing a set of data is the *frequency distribution*. A frequency distribution provides information about the number of individuals who obtained a particular score on a behavioral measure. Later chapters in this Part deal with *descriptive statistics*—methods of summarizing critical aspects such as averages and variability (Chapter 4).

The final chapter in this section (Chapter 5) introduces the *normal distribution* which can be used to model the frequency distribution of many kinds of behavioral data. We show how this model is used to explore various aspects of behavioral data, such as detecting individuals who obtain unexpectedly deviant scores or predicting how many individuals in a sample will obtain scores that exceed some criterion value. This distribution is also used to develop many of the statistical concepts that appear in later chapters of the book, particularly those dealing with *inferential statistics.*

The concepts and formulas presented in Chapters 2–5 serve not only to introduce the topic of descriptive statistics, but also they form the foundation upon which inferential statistics are based. Therefore, it is essential that you fully understand the concepts covered here. Try not to be deceived by the apparent familiarity of some terms used in this part. The notion of an *average,* for example, is likely to be familiar to you. But you will find that this concept can be defined in different ways and that each has a specialized use.

Chapter 2

Variables and Measurement

2.1 VARIABLES

The word *variable* is a label applied to a characteristic of people or objects that can have different values from one person to another or one object to another. Some researchers examine features of behavior that can vary from person to person. Often they are also interested in variation in the traits of subjects (e.g., age, sex, nationality) or features of the environment in which the behavior takes place. Sometimes they are interested in how these characteristics change over time. Properties of behaviors, traits, and environments that can vary, and their changes over time, are called **variables.** Theoretically, any characteristic, whether psychological or physical, can be a variable as long as variations in the characteristic are believed to exist.

VARIABLES: Properties of people or environments that take on different values.

We deal with variables in both general and specific ways. At the conceptual (or theoretical) level, a variable is a general abstraction with a rather vague meaning. That is, we use abstract terms to refer to characteristics of people and environments. For example, intelligence and memory are characteristics treated as variables at the conceptual level. We could generate a theoretical hypothesis that there is a relationship between these variables, such as the amount of intelligence is related to the ability to remember things. Conceptual variables like intelligence and memory are rather vague and might be measured in many different ways. Thus, simply saying that intelligence is related to memory is of limited value to an empirical researcher. To test this relationship it is necessary to specify how each concept is to be measured.

When dealing with a variable at a concrete level we are more specific and tell how the variable is measured in a particular case. Specifying how a conceptual variable is measured is often referred to as providing a *research definition* or an *operational definition,* which translates an abstract concept into something specific. The word *operational* refers to the method used to measure the concept. Thus a *measurement operation* can be defined by telling how the conceptual variable is measured.

An example of the relationship between conceptual variables and their research definitions is outlined in Table 2.1. As is implied in this table, intelligence might be measured by counting the correctly answered items on a standardized IQ test like the Weschler Adult Intelligence Scale (WAIS). Memory might be measured by the number of words a person correctly recalls after studying a list of nouns. Once the concepts have been defined, we can state the specific research hypothesis relating the variables: that scores on the WAIS are related to the number of nouns correctly recalled. Thus, a research definition tells how variables are measured in a specific situation. Consider an alternative way of measuring the conceptual variables intelli-

Table 2.1 SUMMARY OF RELATIONSHIP BETWEEN CONCEPTS AND SCORES

Level of analysis	Variables being related		
	Variable 1		Variable 2
Conceptual hypothesis	Intelligence	is related to	memory.
	↓		↓
Measurement	Number of correct items on WAIS		Number of nouns correctly recalled
	↓		↓
Research hypothesis	WAIS score	is related to	recall score.

gence and memory. Intelligence could be measured by the Stanford-Binet test and memory by the number of words identified on a multiple-choice recognition test. The conceptual hypothesis would be the same as before but the research hypothesis would now be that scores on the Stanford-Binet are related to scores on a recognition test.

In practice we deal with a variable when the act of measurement results in categories or scores that take on different values, that is, when they vary. Uppercase letters such as X or Y are commonly used to represent a variable as a whole, and an individual value of the variable is represented by the letter with a subscript. For instance, we might have three IQ scores, 100, 105, and 120. The entire set of scores can be referred to as X. The first number in the set (100) will be called X_1, the second number (105) is X_2, and so on. The symbol X_i is used to refer to any single score without specifying which one.

Characteristics that are the same across either people or objects are called *constants*. If we were to study the behavior of both males and females, the gender of the subject could be treated as a variable. If we studied only males or only females, the gender of the subject would be treated as a constant. Researchers often "hold variables constant." For instance, in testing the relationship between intelligence and memory, the subjects might all be tested in the same room and at the same time of day. Thus, test room and time of day would be treated as constants, and intelligence and memory would be treated as variables. Alternatively, the range of IQ scores could be restricted so that IQ was treated as a constant, and time of day could be systematically varied. To illustrate, the range of IQ scores could be limited to values between 100 and 105 (relatively constant). Then some of the subjects with scores in this range could be given a memory test in the morning and others in the evening (variable).

2.2 INDEPENDENT AND DEPENDENT VARIABLES

In research design and statistical analysis we distinguish between independent variables and dependent variables. The *dependent variable* is the characteristic that the researcher is interested in accounting for, predicting, or explaining. In psychology and education it is typically the behavior of subjects.

An *independent variable* is the feature of a study that is used to predict or explain variations in the dependent variable. In general, variations in the environment are used to account for variations in behavior. A specific example is the relationship between amount of study time (independent variable) and amount remembered (dependent variable). We might expect that the greater the amount of study time, the greater would be the amount remembered.

Independent variables are given that name because they are controlled by the researcher independently of other variables. The researcher can often decide what stimulus conditions will be used to account for the behavior of interest. The type of control exercised by the researcher leads to a distinction between two types of independent variables: manipulated and measured.

Manipulated independent variables are those that allow the researcher to determine the value of the variable that the subject will experience. Generally, manipulated variables are environmental factors such as amount or type of treatment, for example, the type of training or the amount of a drug given to a subject. Variables that can be given or applied to subjects are often manipulated by randomly assigning each subject to different treatment conditions or levels of the independent variable. By random assignment we mean that each subject has the same independent chance of being given one or the other of the treatments. Assignment of a particular subject to a specific treatment does not influence the assignment of a different subject to the same treatment or a different treatment.

The importance of random assignment is that it strengthens the argument that variation in the dependent variable is due to ("caused by") variation in the independent variable. If the treatments are not randomly assigned, it is difficult to determine whether performance differences are determined by the treatment or some other difference in the groups of subjects.

For example, suppose you wanted to study the effects of the amount of alcohol on driving behavior. You might randomly assign drivers to conditions in which they received 0 ounces or 8 ounces of alcohol before being given a driving test. The group receiving 0 ounces would be the control group, and the group receiving 8 ounces would be the treatment group. Amount of alcohol would serve as the independent variable, and scores on the driving test would serve as the dependent variable. Other features of the situation, such as the car driven during the test, would be held constant.

Alternatively, you might randomly order the presentation of two or more stimuli to one set of subjects. For example, one group of subjects could take a driving test after consuming 0 ounces of alcohol on one day and take the same test after consuming 8 ounces of alcohol on another day. The order in which the two treatments were given could be randomly determined for each subject.

If subjects are not randomly associated with treatments, the results of a study may be confounded and difficult to interpret unambiguously. For example, males could be given 0 ounces of alcohol and females 8 ounces. In this case differences in average performance could be due either to gender differences or to treatment differences. Thus such a nonrandom manipulation would confound treatments and gender differences. Typically, this problem is minimized by random assignment of subjects to treatments.

Many behavioral studies involve the use of variables that cannot be manipulated, such as age and sex of subject. Sometimes called *measured independent variables*,[1] they can be controlled indirectly by the researcher. Although they cannot be literally assigned to individuals, individuals with specific values of interest to the researcher can be selected and other individuals ignored. Examples include traits such as the age or socioeconomic status of the subjects being tested. Of course you cannot randomly assign subjects to age groups since age is a measured trait not under your direct control. However, you would be using age as a measured independent variable if you selected specific age groups for study (e.g., group 1 = 25–35 years and group 2 = 65–75 years). The purpose would be to see if the age groups differ systematically on some dependent variable (e.g., memory of a shopping list). Since people cannot be randomly assigned to age groups, interpretation of the relationship becomes more difficult than when the independent variable is manipulated with randomization. It is difficult to argue that variation in the measured independent variable caused the variation in the dependent variable. For example, the older people may also vary in other ways, such as having had less formal education. Regardless, we can still describe the relationship between such variables as age and memory.

Table 2.2 gives a few examples of the relationships between dependent variables and both manipulated and measured independent variables. Typically, the empirical study of all these relationships would be called experiments because the word *experiment* is generally used loosely; that is, it applies to any empirical study whether the independent variable is manipulated or not. In either context the goal of empirical research is to see how variations in the independent variable are related to variations in the dependent variable. We want to know if the relationship is systematic or not, and if it is systematic we want to specify details of the relationship. More will be said about this topic in later chapters.

---

[1]Measured independent variables are called by various names by different workers, including *traits, subject variables, organismic, personological, classification, individual difference variables*, or *nonmanipulated factors*.

Table 2.2 EXAMPLES OF RELATIONSHIPS BETWEEN INDEPENDENT AND DEPENDENT VARIABLES FOR MANIPULATED AND MEASURED INDEPENDENT VARIABLES [The Relationships Are Stated at Both the Conceptual (1) and the Operational (2) Levels.]

Manipulated Independent Variables

A1. Partial reinforcement leads to greater resistance to extinction than continuous reinforcement.

A2. When reinforcement is no longer given, subjects trained with 50 percent reinforcement will make more responses than those trained with 100 percent reinforcement.

B1. Stimulus complexity affects choice responses in children.

B2. Children are more likely to choose a card with 12 colored squares than one with 4 colored squares.

Measured Independent Variables

C1. There are age differences in the memory of adults.

C2. Older adults (65–75) will remember fewer words from a study list than younger adults (25–35).

D1. There are gender differences in physical aggression.

D2. Boys hit or push their peers more often than girls.

2.3   MEASUREMENT: THEORY AND PRACTICE

When we specify how a variable is **measured** we use rules for assigning numbers to different levels of a variable. The meaning of the numbers will depend on what rules are used. The most basic rule is to assign different numbers for different values of a variable. If subjects take a test consisting of ten questions and answer five items correctly, they are assigned a score of 5. If they have eight correct answers, they receive a score of 8, and so on.

MEASUREMENT: Assignment of numbers to levels of a variable according to rules.

We can also assign numbers to an independent variable, whether it is a measured trait or a manipulated stimulus. For example, we might study the effects of sleep deprivation on the performance of some task. If we randomly assigned subjects to conditions in which they were measured after 0, 24, or 48 hours of sleep deprivation, the numbers 0, 24, and 48 would designate measures of the treatment condition, or independent variable.

Different sets of rules for assigning numbers define different "scales" of measurement. Although researchers disagree about how important particular scales of measurement are in the execution and interpretation of statistical analyses, many of them have relied on the distinctions emphasized by S. S. Stevens (1951). Stevens was probably the most notable psychologist to believe that differences in **measurement scales** have important implications for statistical analysis. He defined four scales that are familiar to most behavioral researchers: nominal, ordinal, interval, and ratio.

MEASUREMENT SCALE: A set of rules for assigning numbers to levels of a variable.

Nominal or Categorical Measures

Sometimes we simply classify environments, subjects, or behaviors into categories. We can do so by using either words or numbers as category labels, but when numbers are used they do not have the usual quantitative meaning associated with them. In this situation we are using *nominal* measurement, which is sometimes called qualitative or categorical measurement. It is frequently the presence or absence of a quality that is important, not the amount.

Consider a hypothetical experiment in which freshmen are randomly assigned to one of three conditions. One-third are required to take a "regular," or traditional English course; one-third are required to take a "novel," or new, course; and the other third do not take an English course at all. These three treatments are measured on a nominal scale since we have only generated categories. As is quite common in this sort of situation, words (not numbers) are used as category names. If group numbers were used (such as regular = 1, novel = 2, none = 3), the assignment of a given number to a particular group would be arbitrary.

The goal of our hypothetical study is to determine the effect of these English-course treatments on subsequent academic performance. We could classify each student according to whether or not he or she passed all courses or failed at least one course before graduating. Thus we can measure the dependent variable by classification according to the question "Did the student fail?" The only measurement rule here is that if what is being measured (failing) has a certain characteristic, it gets one number (e.g., yes = 1) and if it has a different characteristic it gets a different number (e.g., no = 0). We might call this an "identity" rule because things that are identical with respect to the characteristic of interest are placed in the same category. As indicated in Table 2.3, nominal data can be summarized by counting how many people fall into each stimulus and response category. Although the

Table 2.3 NUMBER OF STUDENTS FAILING

Type of program	Did the student fail?		
	Yes	No	Total
Regular	50	450	500
Novel	50	450	500
None	200	300	500
Total	300	1200	1500

Box 2.1   ## On the Abuse of Nominal "Numbers"

The Dominion Bureau of Statistics in Canada (now called Statistics Canada) keeps records of the diagnoses of hospital patients. A different number code is used for each diagnosis. For example, any patient with epilepsy may be assigned the number 353, any patient with polio may be assigned the number 344, and the patient with schizophrenia may be assigned the number 300.

In making up the reports for the Bureau of Statistics, the job of translating the diagnosis into the number code is left to stenographers and clerks. The stenographer goes through the patient's file, locates the diagnosis, finds the appropriate number code in the Bureau of Statistics Handbook, and enters the number code as the patient's diagnosis. However, since doctors do disagree about diagnoses, and since patients often see several doctors, the stenographer faces the problem of several diagnoses in a given patient's file. We would assume that in such an instance she would consult a physician to find out what the real diagnosis is. But the stenographer in one particular hospital used her own judgment. . . . Our stenographer finds that a patient has two diagnoses, one of which can be assigned the code number 308 (suspect brain tumor) and the other which can be assigned the code number 300 (schizophrenia). Being most ingenious, she simply adds the two numbers together (300 + 308 = 608), takes the average by dividing by two, and assigns the patient the code number 304, which happens to stand for senile. Thus:

$$\frac{1 \text{ schizophrenia} + 1 \text{ tumor}}{2} = 1 \text{ senile}$$

With this approach, we have a 24-year-old male patient who has been diagnosed as "brain tumor" (308) by one psychiatrist and "schizophrenic" (300) by another psychiatrist and who ends up with the diagnosis "senile," or old age (304)—an ailment not frequently found in 24-year-olds.

N. Agnew and S. Pyke, *The Science Game: An Introduction to Research in the Behavioral Sciences,* 2d ed., © 1978, pp. 110–111. Adapted by permission of Prentice-Hall, Inc., Englewood Cliffs, NJ.

"score" for each individual was either a 1 or a 0, we use frequency counts (totals) to summarize the data.

When the numbers 1 and 0 are used in this way they do not indicate amount of anything, and the assignment of numbers could be reversed without loss of meaning (0 = no and 1 = yes). Because numbers used in a nominal way do not represent amount, common arithmetic functions should not be performed with them. See Box 2.1 for an inappropriate use of arithmetic with nominal data.

Quantitative Scales

The simplest quantitative scale is an *ordinal* scale, in which behaviors or stimuli are rank ordered. The symbols > (greater than) and < (less than) can be used to indicate rank order. For instance, the expression $A > B$ means that person or object A has more of some property than person or object B. As an example, we might rank order preference for different musical compositions by saying, "I like tune A better than tune B and tune B better than tune C" $(A > B > C)$.

When numbers are used to rank order things, different numbers indicate that what is being measured has more or less of a characteristic than does a behavior or stimulus assigned some other number. An ordinal scale does not indicate how much more or less of the characteristic is present, only that there are different amounts of it. How runners finish a race is an example of measuring with an ordinal scale: $1 =$ first, $2 =$ second, $3 =$ third, and so on. The numbers 1, 2, and 3 tell us only the rank order in which the runners crossed the finish line. They do not imply anything about the amount of time between the runners at the finish.

As shown in Table 2.4, an *interval* scale of measurement has the properties of both nominal scale (identity) and ordinal scale (identity and rank order) but with additional information. Here the difference between two points on the scale, an interval, is meaningful. For example, the concept "temperature" is commonly measured on an interval scale. Numbers representing temperature in degrees carry rank order information such as $25 > 20 > 15 > 10$, where 25 degrees is a higher temperature than 20 degrees, and so on. Furthermore, the difference between two temperature values such as 10 and 15 degrees has the same physical temperature meaning as the difference between 20 and 25 degrees. That is, $15 - 10$ equals $25 - 20$, and they both equal a 5-degree difference in temperature.

Let us reconsider the example of ranking runners as they finish a race. These ranks could be converted to interval scores if we used a stopwatch or similar timing device. Suppose, for example, that after the race had begun you discovered that the timer had not started. If you turn the timer on at an arbitrary point during the race, the running-time scores for each participant

Table 2.4 CHARACTERISTICS OF STEVENS'S FOUR
MEASUREMENT SCALES

Scale of measurement	Scale property			
	Identity	Order of magnitude	Equal intervals	Absolute zero
Nominal	Yes	No	No	No
Ordinal	Yes	Yes	No	No
Interval	Yes	Yes	Yes	No
Ratio	Yes	Yes	Yes	Yes

will not have meaning in terms of absolute value; however, you can still measure the difference between any two runners at the finish line.

Let the time scores for the three fastest runners be 40, 80, and 120 seconds. Of course the total times would be these values plus the time that lapsed before the timer was turned on, a value that is not known. Nevertheless, we could conclude that the difference (interval) between runners 3 and 2 (120 − 80 = 40 seconds) was equal to the difference between runners 2 and 1 (80 − 40 = 40 seconds). We would not, however, be able to say that the second-place runner (80 seconds) took twice as much time as the first-place runner (40 seconds). Similarly, when measuring temperature on a Fahrenheit scale we would not be able to say that 20 degrees is twice as warm as 10 degrees. That sort of statement implies that the scale has a meaningful natural or absolute zero point. The zero points that have been used here are arbitrary and relative, not absolute. Intervals or distances between subjects or events are being measured, not absolute amounts.

Table 2.4 shows that a *ratio* scale has all the properties of an interval scale, with the addition of a true or absolute zero. An absolute zero point means that the characteristic being measured is absent. For example, before a race starts the measure of running time is absolute zero; and if the timer was started promptly when the race began, the running-time scores would have absolute meaning. Thus, our example of measuring runners in a race leads to an interval scale if the timer starts during the race and to a ratio scale if it starts at the beginning of the race. If the delay between the start of the race and onset of the timer were 100 seconds, our ratio scale values would be 40 + 100 = 140, 80 + 100 = 180, and 120 + 100 = 220. With this scale it makes sense to ask if the first-place runner (140) was twice as fast as the second-place runner (180), and we can easily see that this was not the case (180 is not twice 140).

Another characteristic that can be measured by either interval or ratio scales is temperature. The temperature example (discussed previously with interval scales) did not involve a ratio scale because 0 degrees Celsius and 0 degrees Fahrenheit do not correspond to the absence of temperature. As illustrated in Table 2.5, these zero points are relative; 0 degrees Celsius is the same as 32 degrees Fahrenheit. This table also illustrates that temperature can be measured by the Kelvin scale, where absolute zero has the equivalent of −273 Celsius (0 degrees Celsius is +273 Kelvin). For comparison, Table 2.5 also gives brief examples of all four common measurement scales.

In Table 2.6 we illustrate how all four of these scales can be applied to the same underlying concept, "marathon performance." You should notice that the questions asked about marathon performance in Table 2.6 vary somewhat, depending on which scale is used. For example, if you were a novice runner you might be interested in whether or not you could complete the run, and your behavior would simply be classified as 1 = yes (complete) or 2 = no (incomplete). On the other hand, if you were a world class runner, you might be interested in the ratio measure, the absolute number of minutes to finish.

Table 2.5 **SCHEMATIC EXAMPLES OF FOUR MEASUREMENT SCALES**

Nominal (categories)

Trait names	1 = Male	2 = Female
Behavior names	1 = Pass	2 = Fail

Ordinal (ranks)

	1	<	2	<	3
Trait names	Sophomore	<	Junior	<	Senior
Behavior names	Dislike	<	Neutral	<	Like

Interval	− 355	32	50	68	degrees Fahrenheit
(scores)					
	− 273	0	10	20	degrees Celsius
	0	273	283	293	degrees Kelvin
Ratio					
(scores)		4	8	12	length in inches
	0	10.1	20.2	30.3	length in centimeters

Using Measurement in Behavioral Research

Different statistical techniques have been developed for dealing with the results of research using different scales of measurement, and most widely used statistical testing procedures have been developed for scales of at least interval measurement. Thus, in this text we will focus mostly on common techniques for analysis of data assumed to be measured on interval and ratio scales. Less emphasis will be given to dependent variables measured at nominal and ordinal levels (Chapters 17 and 18). Our task is also simplified by the fact that there are few occasions when a researcher might need to distinguish between interval and ratio scales.

Table 2.6 **APPLICATION OF STEVENS'S FOUR SCALES TO THE SAME UNDERLYING VARIABLE OR CONSTRUCT (The Conceptual Dependent Variable Is "Marathon Performance." Data Are for Five Runners: A, B, C, D, and E.)**

Scale	Form of data	Question asked	Example values
Nominal	Frequencies (f)	Did they finish?	ABC = Yes, DE = No f (Yes) = 3, f (No) = 2
Ordinal	Ranks	Order at finish	A = 1, B = 2, C = 3
Interval	Scores	Minutes behind #1	A = 0, B = 10, C = 12
Ratio	Scores	Total time (min.)	A = 160, B = 170, C = 172

There are, however, some problems associated with measurement. Some behavioral scores resemble an interval scale, but it is not clear that numerically equal intervals have equal meaning. Numerous paper-and-pencil tests of psychological attributes fall into this category. Examples include instruments designed to assess anxiety, aggression, affiliation, extroversion, and IQ. Although behavioral measures such as IQ scores may not consist of interval scales, they are often treated *as if* they did. This procedure is particularly acceptable when the scale has received a lot of use and is well standardized (e.g., the WAIS and the Stanford-Binet scale). When less is known about a scale, assuming that it has interval qualities is more controversial.

Since many measurements in the behavioral sciences cannot be proved to have much more than an ordinal relationship to the underlying property being measured, there can be a problem in matching the appropriate statistical technique to a given set of data. There are two schools of thought here. One is represented by statistical measurement purists like Stevens (1951), who claim that the choice of a statistical procedure is closely tied to the scale of measurement. The alternative approach approves of using interval-ratio procedures on other types of data. This approach distinguishes between the mechanics of using a statistical procedure and the interpretation of the results. According to this line of thinking, any procedure might be used with any data, provided it is accompanied by appropriate interpretation. Our approach in this book is consistent with the second point of view. The details of this controversy are beyond the scope of the present discussion but are touched on briefly in later chapters, for example, Chapters 17 and 18.[2]

2.4   CONTINUITY, LIMITS, AND ROUNDING

It is common to distinguish between *continuous* and *discrete* (or discontinuous) quantitative variables. A discrete variable can take on only specific values, such as the number of children in a family (1, 2, 3, etc.). It is not possible to have meaningful values between these discrete numbers since there is no such thing as a fractional person. You might wish to say that the average number of children in a collection of families is 2.4, but the value assigned any given family would be a whole number.

Examples of continuous variables include weight, length, and chronological time. Theoretically, these variables can take on any value within a defined range. By that we mean that an infinite number of possible values might fall between any two values of a continuously measured variable. The reported values of these variables are limited only by the precision of our measuring system. For instance, time might be measured in years, days, sec-

---

[2]The following will introduce the interested reader to details of this controversy: Anderson (1961), Binder (1984), Gaito (1986), and Lord (1953).

onds, or milliseconds, depending on the requirements of the researcher. In practice, measurements of continuous variables are discrete because of the limitations of our measuring procedures. We assume, however, that these discrete values are really estimates of a continuous characteristic.

Real Limits

Because measuring continuous variables results in a **reported value** or apparent value that is an estimate of the real value, we specify an interval in which the real score must lie. The **real limits** of a continuous measurement are the reported value plus and minus one-half of the interval unit being used. For instance, you might measure the number of seconds it takes a person to perform a task and report the result to the nearest second, such as 14 seconds. In this case whole seconds are the interval units being used, and you should assume that the true score is between 13.5 and 14.5 seconds. If the original measurement had been precise to the nearest tenth of a second, such as 13.8 seconds, the real limits would be in hundredths, 13.75 to 13.85.

REPORTED VALUE: An estimate of the unknown real value.

REAL LIMITS: The reported value plus or minus one-half an interval unit.

Rounding

The measured values of a discrete variable will often (but not always) be whole numbers as long as we are only counting, adding, or subtracting them. When we divide either discrete or continuous numbers, the quotient (resulting answer) will often not be a whole number. For instance, if we divide 10 by 3 the answer could be 3.3 or 3.333 or 3.333333. The quotient could have as many numbers to the right of the decimal as we desire, but clearly at some point we will round off the number.

This leads to two questions: First, to how many decimal places do you carry the answer? Second, how do you deal with the last number in the series? Because there are no universally accepted answers to these questions, you might ask your instructor about his or her preference in addition to reading our suggested ways of dealing with these problems.

When you divide one number by another, we recommend that the quotient be **rounded** to two more places than were in the original data. Thus, if you divide the number 10 by 3 the result would be reported to two places to the right of the decimal (3.33). If you divide 10.3 by 3, the result would be carried to three places (3.433). With some computational problems you will need to carry out a series of arithmetic operations, such as add, divide, add, divide, and so on. In those cases (1) round the intermediate results at not less than three places more than the original data, and (2) round the final answer to two places more than the original data.

Table 2.7   EXAMPLE APPLICATIONS OF ROUNDING RULES

Example	Dividend	Divisor	Quotient (6 places)	Rounded answer
A	.025	3	.008333	.00833
B	.7	9	.077777	.078
C	8	3	2.666666	2.67
D	10.6	7	1.514285	1.514
E	110	7	15.714286	15.71
F	15	8	1.875000	1.88
G	5	8	.625000	.62

ROUNDING: The result has two more places than the raw data.

Many calculations will be made with the aid of a pocket calculator or computer that will carry four or more digits to the right of the decimal. In these cases it is often wise to let serial computations be carried to the default limit of the machine (e.g., four to eight places) and simply round off the final answer at two more places than the raw data.

Given that we know how many places will be involved in the final answer, we still have the problem of dealing with the final digit, that is, rounding off. We recommend the following rule. If the number beyond your last reported digit is 6 or larger, increase that digit to the next higher number (e.g., 2.666 becomes 2.67). If the number is less than 5, do not change the last digit (e.g., 2.334 becomes 2.33). If the last digit is 5, round up if the prior digit is odd (e.g., 3.335 becomes 3.34) and round down if it is even (e.g., 3.445 becomes 3.44). Table 2.7 provides several applications of these rules.

2.5   RELIABILITY AND VALIDITY OF MEASURES

So far we have found that measurement involves using rules to assign numbers to levels of variables. This may seem like a simple notion but in practice it can be difficult because merely performing a measurement operation does not ensure that a variable has been accurately and meaningfully represented. In fact, measurement never perfectly represents a variable but, instead, always contains some amount of error. The results of measurement operations are always regarded, then, as approximations or estimates of true scores. For example, we assume that a specific IQ score derived from a standardized IQ test is only an estimate of an individual's intelligence. It may be affected by other factors such as the person's physical or mental state at the time of testing or by specific test questions.

Because measurements only estimate true values, it is useful to specify criteria for judging how good those estimates are. To do so we need to distinguish between two types of errors that jeopardize the quality of measurements: random error and systematic error.

Two Types of Error

Unbiased and chance variation in scores because of uncontrolled or unknown factors constitutes random error, which includes many factors. Among them are temporary environmental states (e.g., noise level or temperature) as well as fluctuations in motivation and attention of both the person being measured and the person performing the measurement. Of course, we do everything we can to minimize the amount of random error even though it cannot be eliminated entirely.

Systematic error consists of systematic but irrelevant portions of a measurement. Scores are often good estimates of the variable they are supposed to measure, but in addition, they inadvertently measure other variables. This portion of the observed score is sometimes called systematic error and may result from several factors. For example, chronic test anxiety, speed of responding, writing skill, and the like can contribute to an observed behavioral score in a systematic way.

The quality of measurement is judged by two criteria: *reliability*, which has to do with the amount of random error, and *validity*, which has to do with the amount of systematic error. You will see that reliability is considered the more basic criterion of measurement because without high reliability, measurements cannot achieve high validity.

Reliability

Reliability can be equated with the amount of random error. Scores that are highly reliable have little random error. In general we assume that any observed score (X_o) consists of at least two parts. One part represents the true score (X_t) and the other, random error (X_{re}). Thus, X_o equals X_t plus X_{re}. A high degree of reliability means that X_{re} is close to zero. Random error is unbiased, which means that it contributes to overestimates of true scores as much as it contributes to underestimates of them.

The nature of random error is illustrated in Figure 2.1. Assume that a child was given an IQ test on three occasions. If we rule out intervening brain damage or the like, the true score will be constant from test to test but the observed score will probably fluctuate. For the example in Figure 2.1, the observed scores differ (93, 85, 92), but the true score is stable (90). Thus, the component of the observed score that has varied is the degree of random error, which is an index of the reliability of the test. In general, a measure of behavior that has a small amount of random error is more reliable than one with a larger amount of random error.

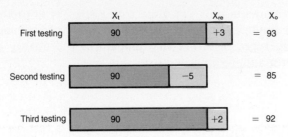

Figure 2.1 Example of how a true score (X_t) and random error (X_{re}) combine to generate an observed score (X_o).

We never know the value of a true score, so we do not know how much error is involved. Generally, we can estimate both the true score and the degree of error. In practice, the reliability of psychological tests is often estimated by measuring several individuals on two occasions. A measurement procedure that provides the same relative rank ordering of observed scores on each testing is considered to be more reliable than one in which the rank orders change from session to session. Thus, even if the scores from all individuals change across sessions (e.g., everyone gets better with practice), the person who scored highest on the first testing should also be near the highest on each later test, and the person who scored lowest at first should remain at approximately that ranking on later tests. When rank orders are similar across tests, it implies that the measures are reliable because a small amount of random error leads to little change from test to test. If the magnitude of error is large, there is greater variation from test to test.

Table 2.8 shows reliability for two measurement procedures, one with high reliability and one with low reliability. For this example, suppose that we have administered a standardized IQ test to six children identified by the

Table 2.8   RELATIONSHIP OF RELIABILITY TO SIZE AND DISTRIBUTION OF RANDOM ERROR, X_{re}
[Form A Has Smaller Amounts of X_{re} (± 1 to ± 3) than Form B (± 4 to ± 12).]

| Subj. ID | True score | Form A | | | | Form B | | | |
| | | Time 1 | | Time 2 | | Time 1 | | Time 2 | |
	X_t	$+X_{re}$	$= X_o$	$+X_{re}$	$= X_o$	$+X_{re}$	$= X_o$	$+X_{re}$	$= X_o$
A	124	+1	125	−2	122	+4	128	−8	116
B	120	−2	118	+1	121	−8	112	+4	124
C	116	+3	119	−3	113	+12	128	−12	104
D	112	−1	111	+3	115	−4	108	+12	124
E	108	+2	110	−1	107	+8	116	+8	116
F	104	−3	101	+2	106	−12	92	−4	100

letters A through F in column 1 of the table. The test is available in two alternate forms, A and B. Each form of the test is administered twice, form A at times 1 and 2 and form B at times 1 and 2. The true scores are listed in column 2; the following columns show the error score and observed score for each testing with each of the two forms. The sum of the error scores is zero, which we assume to be true when large numbers of measurements are obtained. Across many measurements the sum of our overestimates and underestimates will approach zero. This is one reason why a test based on many items is often more reliable than a test based on relatively few items.

Notice in Table 2.8 that the magnitude of the error scores is much smaller with form A (± 1, ± 2, ± 3) than with form B (± 4, ± 8, ± 12). A major consequence of this difference is that the relative rank order of the observed scores is affected differently for the forms across the two tests. For example, with form A the rank order of observed scores is very similar when obtained at time 1 and at time 2. This stable rank order implies that form A has high reliability. Alternatively, when error scores are large, as with form B, the rank order of observed scores from the two test sessions is very different. Thus we find that form A is more reliable than form B in these hypothetical data. It is important to remember that a low amount of random error in measurement is equated with high reliability in scores.

Validity

Although reliability is necessary, it is seldom sufficient for evaluating the quality of scores. Once we have established that a measuring procedure is reasonably reliable, we then turn to the question of what the resulting scores mean. This is the question of validity. *Does the measurement actually estimate the type of characteristic it is supposed to estimate?* Unfortunately, this criterion is more difficult to deal with than reliability.

To illustrate, a so-called intelligence test might give consistent scores when repeatedly used on the same individuals, but it might be measuring something in addition to, or different from, that which the researcher believes is intelligence. That is, the score may have high reliability but low validity. To illustrate this point, Figure 2.2 provides an example of two people

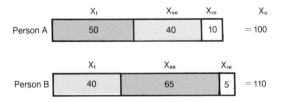

Figure 2.2 Example of how a true score of interest (X_t) combines with other systematic scores (X_{se}) and random error (X_{re}) to generate an observed score (X_o).

given the same test; person A has a score of 100 and person B has a score of 110. In each case the portion of the total score associated with random error is small (10 units for person A and 5 units for person B). Thus, the test has relatively good reliability.

The hypothetical true scores for persons A and B have been partitioned into that part that is of interest, X_t (e.g., intelligence), and systematic error, X_{se} (e.g., test-taking skill), which is irrelevant to the researcher. The test can be considered to have low validity because a large proportion of each total score is systematically associated with the irrelevant behavior, X_{se}. Since the test is allegedly designed to measure only the relevant behavior X_t, and this behavior accounts for not more than 50 percent of the total score, it has low validity. Generally, observed scores resulting from valid measurement include a smaller proportion of irrelevant factors than scores resulting from invalid methods of measurement.

SUMMARY

In this chapter we introduced several very basic notions that underlie much of the material covered in the remaining chapters. Variables are characteristics that take on different values. They are treated at both a general conceptual level and a specific operational level. Measurement is the operation that defines the specific way of dealing with a variable. An operational definition of a variable tells how it is measured.

There are two broad categories of variables: independent variables (both manipulated stimuli and measured traits) and dependent variables (e.g., behaviors). The next several chapters deal with ways of statistically summarizing and describing measures of behavior. Later chapters deal with research design and the comparison of sets of scores associated with groups of subjects representing different treatments or traits.

Measurement was defined as the assignment of numbers to levels of a variable according to rules. In describing data, we are sensitive to different types of data derived from different measurement scales. The emphasis in this textbook is on variables measured as scores (interval and ratio measures). With scores we need guidelines for rounding both the results of measurement and arithmetic operations like dividing. Generally the results of computations will have two more digits to the right of the decimal than raw data.

Finally, it was noted that measurements are evaluated in terms of their reliability and validity. Reliability is equated with amount of random error and validity is equated with amount of systematic error. Although these concepts can be given much more detailed treatment than is provided here, it is important to distinguish between measurement accuracy (reliability) and meaning (validity).

KEY WORDS

conceptual variable   nominal scale

operational definition   ordinal scale

dependent variable   interval scale

manipulated variable   ratio scale

trait variable   reported value

measurement   real limits

measurement scale   rounding

categorical measures   reliability

quantitative measures   validity

PROBLEMS

1 For each item indicate whether it is a variable or a constant.
   (a) Examination scores from a particular class
   (b) Maximum possible score on a final examination
   (c) Legal drinking age in California
   (d) Ages of members of a graduating class

2 For each of the following items decide whether (1) the key terms are both conceptual variables, (2) the key terms are both ways of measuring concepts (operational definitions), or (3) one term can be the operational definition of the other.
   (a) What is the relationship between intelligence and IQ?
   (b) How might memory and learning be related?
   (c) What is the relationship between grade point average and academic ability?
   (d) How are number correct and reaction time related?

3 For each of these terms decide whether it is more likely to be used as a conceptual variable or as a measure of a variable.
   (a) intelligence   (f) reaction time
   (b) learning   (g) percent correct
   (c) grade point average   (h) mental quickness
   (d) memory   (i) academic ability
   (e) IQ

4 Suppose a study was done to estimate the effects of different teaching methods on children's reading. Assume that 60 first-grade children were randomly divided into two groups of 30 and that one group was taught by the "whole word" method and the other group was taught by the "phonics" method. After six months of experience with these methods, the children were given a standardized reading test.
   (a) What was the dependent variable? - what you're looking for (scores)
   (b) What was the independent variable? - constants.
   (c) Was the independent variable manipulated or measured?

5 Assume that 800 students taking an introductory course in psychology were asked whether they were predominantly right-handed, predominantly left-handed, or used both hands equally. From among those not indicating equal use, 20 right-handers and 20 left-handers were randomly selected and administered a reaction time task.
   (a) What was the independent variable?
   (b) What was the dependent variable?
   (c) Was the independent variable manipulated or measured?

6 Identify the scale of measurement for each of the following measures (nominal, ordinal, interval-ratio).
   (a) Number of hours to write an essay *ord, int.*
   (b) A vote for Smith for president - *nom.*
   (c) Military ranks (private, corporal, sergeant) - *ord.*
   (d) Percentage correct on an examination - *int - rat.*
   (e) Letter grades (A, B, C, D, F) assigned for course work - *ord.*

7 Is the number of chairs in a classroom continuous or discrete? Is the number of seconds taken to complete an examination continuous or discrete?

8 For the following variables, scales of measurement, and reported values, what are the real limits of these values?

Variable	Units	Reported value
(a) Reaction time	1/100 sec.	.67
(b) Score on a test	percentage	82

9 Round the following data so there are two numbers to the right of the decimal in the reported value.
   (a) 2.05489
   (b) 199.996
   (c) 4.9750
   (d) 1.0059
   (e) 37.6666
   (f) 16.6259

10 Assume that you have three target rifles that you want to assess for reliability and validity. One hundred bullets are fired from each rifle under standardized conditions. For rifle A the pattern of "hits" is randomly scattered over the entire 30 cm by 30 cm target, including a few just beyond the largest target circle. For rifle B the pattern of hits is a condensed random pattern within 5 cm of the bull's-eye. The pattern for rifle C is condensed like that of rifle B, but the apparent center of the hits is about 6 cm to the left of the bull's-eye.
   (a) Which rifle(s) would you classify as reliable?
   (b) Which rifle(s) would you classify as valid in accuracy?

11 Is it possible to have high reliability of a measure that has low validity? Is it possible to have high validity of a measure that has low reliability?

Chapter 3

Tables and Graphs to Display Data

3.1   INTRODUCTION

Researchers generally deal with a set of several observations. The total set of observations is called data, and a single frequency or score is a datum. Data are rarely very interesting or even meaningful until they are systematically organized and summarized. These are the major functions of descriptive statistics, to organize and summarize data.

Methods for describing data are discussed for three reasons. First, they are sometimes used in reports of research, although the methods in this chapter are more likely to appear in reports of surveys and polls than in experimental studies. Second, researchers often examine their data with these methods before performing other analyses. They do so to get a general impression of the nature of their data and to ensure that the data are appropriate for the statistical method that is to be applied. Third, these methods are used to help explain various statistical testing procedures presented in later chapters (e.g., Chapters 9 through 11).

Using descriptive statistics has sometimes been likened to bringing order out of chaos. Consider, for example, the information in Table 3.1. Here we find the results of a hypothetical survey of senior psychology majors who indicated they planned to obtain an advanced degree in psychology. They were asked to indicate their expected area of specialization. It is not very easy to get an overall picture of data when they are presented in an array like that in Table 3.1. Therefore, it is useful to impose some kind of organization on the data that will help summarize their major features. Good organization will help the researcher efficiently identify important characteristics of a data set.

3.2   ORGANIZATION: THE DATA MATRIX

The data listed in Table 3.1 are for a small survey. Typically, there would be both more subjects and more responses, as well as more information about the subjects. For example, the survey may involve people at more than one

Table 3.1 **RESPONSES ABOUT PLANNED SPECIALIZATION**

Counseling	Counseling	Clinical	Experimental
Experimental	Clinical	Social	Clinical
Clinical	Experimental	Clinical	Social
Counseling	Clinical	Clinical	Counseling
Counseling	Experimental	Experimental	Clinical
Clinical	Counseling	Counseling	Clinical
Clinical	Experimental	Clinical	Social
Experimental	Experimental	Experimental	Clinical
Social	Clinical	Counseling	Experimental
Clinical	Social	Clinical	Social

school and very likely would include both male and female respondents. School and gender information are not easily recorded in the arrangement of Table 3.1. A common and more efficient way to organize such information is to build a *data matrix*.

The matrix is a rectangular table in which the vertical lines are called *columns* and the horizontal lines are called *rows*. The columns and rows meet to form *cells*, where the information of interest is recorded. It is common for some columns to contain numbers identifying the subjects and other columns to contain their responses. Typically, each row represents a subject, with all information for a given subject in a single row.

Table 3.2 shows an outline of a data matrix for a hypothetical survey of senior psychology majors and their intended specialization. The first column in the matrix contains subject identification numbers. The subjects are identified by numbers for three reasons. First, data are usually confidential and using numbers protects the identity of the subject. Second, the researcher rarely needs to know more than the number recorded in the data matrix. If more information is required, a separate record is kept that identifies the subject number with the subject's name and other personal information. Third, the matrix will probably be entered into a computer for analysis, which is more efficiently done with numbers than with letters.

The other columns of the data matrix contain additional information about the characteristics of the subject and the dependent variable (response of interest). Column 2 identifies the school that each subject attends, and

Table 3.2 OUTLINE OF A DATA MATRIX FOR DATA FROM A SURVEY OF SENIOR PSYCHOLOGY MAJORS

Column Headings ⟶ Subject	School	Gender*	Response[†]
First subject school 1 ⟶ 01	1	1	1
02	1	2	4
03	1	1	2
.	.	.	.
.	.	.	.
.	.	.	.
39	1	2	3
Last subject school 1 ⟶ 40	1	1	2
First subject school 2 ⟶ 41	2	1	1
42	2	2	4
.	.	.	.
.	.	.	.
.	.	.	.
75	2	2	1
Last subject school 2 ⟶ 76	2	1	3

*1 = male, 2 = female.

[†]1 = clinical, 2 = counseling, 3 = experimental, 4 = social.

column 3 identifies the subject's gender. Like the name of the subject, these columns contain *coded* information: School 1 is coded as 1 and school 2 is coded as 2. Similarly, gender can be coded as male = 1 and female = 2. Finally, the responses of the subjects are coded and located in column 4 (1 = clinical, 2 = counseling, 3 = experimental, 4 = social).

3.3 TABLES FOR QUALITATIVE DATA

While inspecting the data in Tables 3.1 and 3.2 it may have occurred to you that a useful summary would involve counting how many responses fall into each of several response categories, that is, how many people selected each speciality. Doing so amounts to building a **frequency distribution.** The first step in building a frequency distribution is to identify the names of each category—clinical, counseling, experimental, social. The category names are then listed in a column, as shown in Table 3.3. Since the response variable "speciality" is measured on a nominal scale, the category names can be listed in any order. The categories in Table 3.3 are listed alphabetically. Finally, the number of responses falling into each category are tallied by making a slash (/), indicating each time the response occurred, and they are summarized as a frequency.

FREQUENCY DISTRIBUTION: A summary of a set of data showing the frequency of items in each category or class.

The result of this procedure, as illustrated in Table 3.3, is a tabular frequency distribution, or *frequency table.* The tally marks can be omitted since they are only used as an intermediate step to help ensure accuracy of the frequency counts. Note that the frequency column in Table 3.3 includes the sum of the frequencies (16 + 8 + 10 + 6 = 40) as a check that no responses were mistakenly included or omitted. If you start with 40 responses, as in Table 3.1, the sum of the frequencies in Table 3.3 should be 40.

Table 3.3 SUMMARY OF DATA IN TABLE 3.1 SHOWING TALLIES, FREQUENCY DISTRIBUTION, AND RELATIVE FREQUENCY DISTRIBUTION

Category	Tally	Frequency f	Relative frequency
Clinical	N̷ N̷ N̷ I	16	.40
Counseling	N̷ III	8	.20
Experimental	N̷ N̷	10	.25
Social	N̷ I	6	.15
Total		40	100

The final column in Table 3.3 gives a **relative frequency** distribution. Relative frequencies are proportions or percentages that correspond to the raw frequencies. A frequency (f) is converted to a proportion when it is divided by the total number of cases (N): proportion $= f/N$. For example, when $f = 16$ and $N = 40$, the proportion is $16/40 = .40$. A proportion, such as .40, is converted to a percentage when multiplied by 100: $.40(100) = 40$ percent.

RELATIVE FREQUENCIES:

$$\text{proportion} = \frac{\text{frequency in a category}}{\text{total number of cases}} = \frac{f}{N}$$

$$\text{percentage} = \text{proportion}(100) = \%$$

The meaning of a frequency is tied to the total number of cases being considered. For this reason relative values like proportions and percentages are especially useful when comparing data from different distributions where those distributions are based on unequal numbers of cases. Suppose, as suggested in Table 3.2, that your survey of psychology majors at two schools had 40 responses at one school and 36 responses at the other. A frequency count of 16 people expecting to specialize in clinical psychology at one school could not be compared directly to the count of 16 observed at the second school. Rather, it is necessary to know the total number of people surveyed at each school so that relative frequencies can be compared. With 36 students responding in the second school, a frequency of 16 people expecting to be clinicians would represent $(16/36)100 = 44$ percent of the total, which is greater than the 40 percent expecting to be clinicians in the first school.

3.4 GRAPHS FOR QUALITATIVE DATA

There are many ways to present data graphically, only a few of which will be mentioned in this chapter.[1] In a graphic figure of a frequency distribution the response categories are represented along the horizontal axis (or X-axis) and their frequency or relative frequency is represented along the vertical axis (or Y-axis).

The *bar graph* is one useful way to summarize graphically the information in a frequency distribution of qualitative data. Figure 3.1 is a bar graph of the data in Table 3.3. In addition to placing response categories on the X-

---

[1]Many details on the construction and use of graphic figures are spelled out in the *Publication Manual of the American Psychological Association* (1983).

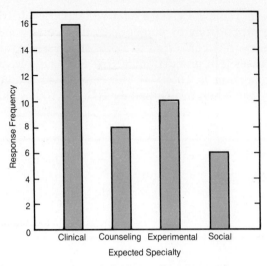

Figure 3.1   Bar graph giving frequency of expected specialities for 40 students.

axis and frequencies on the Y-axis, a few other features of this figure should be noted.

1. The width of the bars is constant.
2. The bars have been separated by an arbitrary (but constant) distance to make the figure easier to read, and so the reader does not assume that the data are continuous.
3. Each axis is labeled in two ways.
   a) The overall name of the variable being represented is the verbal label for the axis. For example, on the X-axis we have "X = Expected Specialities," and on the Y-axis we have "Y = Frequency of Responses."
   b) The possible values of both X and Y are given with convenient numerical units or category names. For example, to label the data in Table 3.3, let the X-axis values be the names of response categories (clinical, counseling, etc.) and the Y-axis values frequencies of occurrence for each category (2, 4 . . . 16).
4. There is a "figure caption" that appears at the *foot* of the figure below the label of the X-axis.

Figure 3.2 is a variation of Figure 3.1, with the starting place on the Y-axis changed from 0 to 6. The purpose in altering the figure was to save space (Figure 3.2 is smaller than Figure 3.1). Although this is a desirable goal, it can lead to perceptual distortion of the results. For example, in Figure 3.1 the number of social responses appears to be about three-fourths the number of experimental responses. On the other hand, in Figure 3.2 the number of social responses appears to be about one-third the experimental responses. This per-

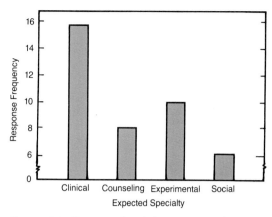

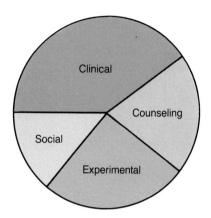

Figure 3.2 Bar graph giving expected specialities in Figure 3.1, with Y-axis starting at $f = 6$.

Figure 3.3 Pie chart of expected specialities.

ceptual problem suggests that, when convenient, the Y-axis on bar graphs of frequency distributions should begin at the value of zero.

An alternative way of summarizing qualitative data from a frequency distribution is the *pie chart*. This format is especially useful when relative frequencies are reported. The relative frequencies from Table 3.3 are shown in a pie chart in Figure 3.3. The figure consists of a circle divided into parts, and the size of each part is proportionate to the relative frequency represented. An advantage of the pie chart over the bar graph is that the same visual impression is generated regardless of the size of the circle.

3.5 TABLES FOR QUANTITATIVE DATA

Quantitative data (e.g., scores from variables measured on interval and ratio scales) present problems similar to those associated with nominal data. It is not particularly easy to understand the major features of data when they are presented in a haphazard array like that in Table 3.4. Therefore, we will organize them into a frequency distribution. Although the numbers in Table 3.4 are hypothetical data, it might be helpful to think of them as examination scores. In what follows we will use these scores several times to illustrate different ways of organizing and summarizing quantitative data.

Table 3.4 **AN ARRAY OF HYPOTHETICAL EXAMINATION SCORES**

73	71	77	78	74	78	83	64	73	79	83
70	55	88	82	68	72	66	95	56	71	80
67	70	77	85	64	53	57	60	67	61	87
62	76	73	72	50	74	68	62	63	83	70

As before, we can begin the analysis by listing the data. The difference in this case is that instead of responses in qualitative categories we now have quantitative score values. A useful way to begin is to identify the highest score (95) and lowest score (50) and then to make a list of all possible score values that could fall between these extremes. This format has been followed in Table 3.5. The table shows that after an ordered list of possible scores was made, the frequency of occurrence of each obtained score was tallied. Finally, the tally marks for each score were counted and summarized by expressing the frequency as a number. As with the frequency distribution for qualitative data, the frequency column in Table 3.5 includes the total number of scores as a check that no scores have been accidentally included or omitted.

The organization of data in Table 3.5 makes it very easy to identify the highest and lowest scores. It also facilitates getting other information, such as the fact that relatively few people had extreme scores either at the upper or lower end of the distribution. This kind of organization, given in a frequency table, provides better understanding of the data without sacrificing any information. Of course there are a lot of details in this table! Counting only the X scores and the frequency counts, we find 92 entries in Table 3.5. If the range of possible score values were larger, the table could become quite cumbersome. Thus, we need both the type of organization and summary given in Table 3.5 and a way of condensing the data summary further.

Outliers

Sometimes a set of data contains one or more scores that do not appear to belong with the others. Such deviant scores are often called *outliers*. There is no general rule for deciding when a score should be considered an outlier other than the fact that it is an extreme score and separated from other scores

Table 3.5 FREQUENCY TABLE SHOWING POSSIBLE SCORES (X), TALLY MARKS (t), AND FREQUENCY COUNTS (f) FOR DATA IN TABLE 3.4

X	t	f	X	t	f	X	t	f	X	t	f
95	/	1	83	///	3	71	//	2	59		0
94		0	82	/	1	70	///	3	58		0
93		0	81		0	69		0	57	/	1
92		0	80	/	1	68	//	2	56	/	1
91		0	79	/	1	67	//	2	55	/	1
90		0	78	//	2	66	/	1	54		0
89		0	77	//	2	65		0	53	/	1
88	/	1	76	/	1	64	//	2	52		0
87	/	1	75		0	63	/	1	51		0
86		0	74	//	2	62	//	2	50	/	1
85	/	1	73	///	3	61	/	1			
84		0	72		2	60		1		Total = 44	

by several possible score values. It is up to the individual researcher to decide whether a given score is sufficiently deviant to be given special treatment.

Consider, for example, how you would have built a frequency table for the data in Table 3.5 if one of the scores had been very deviant from all other scores. For instance, if one score had a value of 10 and the next lowest score was 50, the frequency table could include all the possible score values from 10 through 95, with no scores tallied for values of 11 through 49. This arrangement would lead to a substantial waste of space, and the guidelines previously presented do not suggest how to deal efficiently with this problem. One solution is to list the one (or more) deviant score(s) separately beside the distribution. A second solution is to exclude outliers from the frequency distribution and mention the values of these scores and the fact that they were excluded. Another approach is to carry out data analysis with and without the outliers and report both analyses. Regardless of which solution is used, it is important that the data be inspected by some method such as a frequency distribution to determine whether there are scores that might be considered outliers.

3.6 GROUPED FREQUENCY DISTRIBUTIONS

When the number of possible score values is small, the frequency distribution of raw scores is a useful way to display data. Often, as in the example used here, the range of score values is much larger than the number of different observed scores. In cases like this it is often useful to condense the data by combining adjacent score values into groups. A grouping of possible score values is called a *class interval* and is characterized by its size, that is, the range of possible score values in the interval.

Grouping scores by class intervals leads to a *grouped frequency distribution*, which has two advantages: A large amount of data can be summarized in a relatively small space, and the major features are easy to distinguish. A disadvantage is that some information is lost. For instance, the interval 75–79 might contain six observed scores, but after grouping you would not know the precise values of the scores within this interval unless you went back to the raw data. This trade-off between usefulness and precision is common in data analysis. To get rid of the cumbersome problem of dealing with many raw scores, it is necessary to sacrifice some precision.

Both the number and size of the class intervals will differ from one data set to another. When constructing a grouped frequency distribution most people keep the number of intervals between 5 and 20, and the size of these intervals is often 3, 5, or some multiple of 5. (If the size of the interval is an odd number, the midpoint of the interval will be a whole number.) Even when one is working with these suggested values, the exact number of intervals and the size of the intervals will be a matter of judgment for each researcher.

Table 3.6 displays a grouped frequency distribution of the data in Table 3.5 by using ten intervals each consisting of five units. Although the number and size of class intervals can be determined by trial and error, some guidelines used to construct this table are given in Box 3.1.

Relative Distributions

In addition to class intervals and frequencies, Table 3.6 contains relative frequency distributions. Recall that relative frequencies are proportions or percentages of the raw frequencies. A frequency (f) is converted to a proportion when it is divided by the total number of cases (N); proportion $= f/N$. For example, when $f = 12$ and $N = 44$, the proportion is $12/44 = .2727$. A proportion, such as .2727, is converted to a percentage when multiplied by 100: $.2727(100) = 27.27$ percent.

You should recall that relative values like proportions and percentages are especially useful when comparing data from different distributions where those distributions are based on unequal numbers of cases. Suppose, for example, that the first five columns of data in Table 3.4 represent scores from 20 female students and the remaining columns represent data from 24 male students. Would a score of say, 65, have the same meaning in each of these subgroups? This question is somewhat difficult to answer from the inspection of either raw frequency counts or grouped distributions, but it is easy to answer with relative scores. If you carry out a percentage analysis on these two subgroups, you will find that 33.33 percent [8/24(100)] of the males scored below a raw score of 65 but only 20 percent [4/20(100)] of the females scored that low.

Table 3.6 GROUPED FREQUENCY AND RELATIVE FREQUENCY DISTRIBUTIONS BASED ON DATA IN TABLE 3.5

Class interval	f	Relative frequency	
		Proportion	Percentage
95–99	1	.0227	2.27
90–94	0	.0000	0.00
85–89	3	.0682	6.82
80–84	5	.1136	11.36
75–79	6	.1364	13.64
70–74	12	.2727	27.27
65–69	5	.1136	11.36
60–64	7	.1591	15.91
55–59	3	.0682	6.82
50–54	2	.0455	4.55
Total	44	1.0000	100.00

Box 3.1   # Guidelines That Can Be Used to Construct a Grouped Frequency Distribution

1. Class intervals should not overlap; any given score can be placed into only one interval.

2. All intervals should be the same size.

3. *Interval width:* A reasonable width or size for intervals can be determined by the following method:
   a) Identify the highest and lowest scores.
   b) Excluding outliers, subtract the lowest score from the highest and add 1 (i.e., $95 - 50 + 1 = 46$).
   c) Divide the result by the desired number of intervals, that is, $46/10 = 4.6$. Round the result to the nearest whole number. Thus, with ten intervals and our example data, we have intervals of five units each.

4. Make the lower limit of the lowest interval a multiple of the interval size (e.g., a multiple of five).

5. Ignoring outliers, take the lowest score in the data set (50) and add the interval size minus 1: $50 + (5 - 1) = 54$. This defines the lowest class interval size, 50–54.

6. The next higher class interval begins with the first possible score value above the lowest class interval, for example, 55–59.

7. Rank order the several class intervals, for example, from lowest to highest, and assign obtained score frequencies to appropriate intervals.

8. As with all tables, frequency tables should have a verbal descriptive title that appears at the *top,* above the column headings.

Cumulative Distributions

In Table 3.7 class intervals and their real limits are listed in columns 1 and 2. The grouped frequency distribution is listed in column 3 and the cumulative distributions in columns 4 and 5. The cumulated frequency data in column 4 were obtained in the following manner. Cumulating began with the frequencies in the lowest class interval, that is, $f = 2$. This frequency value was added to the frequency in the next highest interval, $2 + 3 = 5$, and recorded in the column called "Cumulative Frequency." Then this result was added to the frequency in the next higher interval, $5 + 7 = 12$, and so on until the cumulative answer was 44, the total number of observed scores. The cumulative percentages (column 5) were obtained by dividing each of the values in the cumulative frequency column by 44 and multiplying the answer

Table 3.7 GROUPED CUMULATIVE FREQUENCY
DISTRIBUTIONS BASED ON TABLE 3.5

Class interval	Real limits	f	Cumulative frequency	Cumulative percentage
95–99	94.5–99.5	1	44	100.00
90–94	89.5–94.5	0	43	97.73
85–89	84.5–89.5	3	43	97.73
80–84	79.5–84.5	5	40	90.91
75–79	74.5–79.5	6	35	79.55
70–74	69.5–74.5	12	29	65.91
65–69	64.5–69.5	5	17	38.64
60–64	59.5–64.5	7	12	27.28
55–59	54.5–59.5	3	5	11.37
50–54	49.5–54.5	2	2	4.55

by 100. For example, 44/44(100) = 100 percent, 43/44(100) = 98 percent, and so on.

Cumulative information provides an alternative form of data description. With the cumulative distribution it is possible to determine quickly, for example, that 80 percent of the scores are less than the real limit, 79.5, or that 27 percent of the scores are less than 64.5. This distribution also facilitates obtaining certain types of information like the midpoint of the distribution. The midpoint is the score value that divides the data set into two equal parts, with 50 percent of the obtained scores above and below that point. The midpoint of the scores summarized in Table 3.7 is located in the class interval 70–74. This interval can be determined from the cumulative percentage column, where it can be seen that 66 percent of the scores lie below 74.5 and 39 percent lie below the score of 69.5. Thus, the midpoint must lie somewhere between the real limits of 69.5 and 74.5.

3.7 PERCENTILES

The concept of percentile is a useful way of describing the meaning of a score in a distribution because it provides information about the relative standing of a score in the distribution. Any set of scores can be divided into 100 equal parts, called percentiles or **percentile points.** Each of the parts has a specific value on the raw score measurement scale. A percentile point is not a score, although it may be numerically equal to a score. It has a particular proportion or percentage of all cases falling below it.

PERCENTILE POINT: A score value on a measurement scale below which a specified proportion of cases fall.

Suppose that for the 44 examination scores in Table 3.5, you want to determine what score value corresponds to the twenty-fifth percentile point. To do so you first multiply the desired percentile point (P) by the total number of cases in the distribution (N):

$$P(N) = .25(44) = 11$$

Therefore, 11 cases fall at a point equal to or less than the twenty-fifth percentile value. Inspecting the frequency distribution of raw scores in Table 3.5, we can obtain the corresponding raw score value. We begin at the lowest score in the distribution and count observed scores until the desired number (11) is obtained. For these data, the score value of 64 occupies the twenty-fifth percentile point.

This example is not quite as simple as it may seem because there are two scores with the value of 64. It is necessary to separate these two scores so that one is equal to or below the desired point (the eleventh score) and one is above that point (the twelfth score). It may be necessary to partition a set of tied scores into two parts, those above the desired percentile point and those equal to or below that point. A convenient way to approach the problem is to divide the whole set of scores into three parts, those below the desired interval, those in the interval, and those above the interval.

Consider another example, one with three tied scores. Suppose we want to know what score corresponds to the fifty-ninth percentile point. First we find the number of scores below that point: $P(N) = .59(44) = 26$. Referring to Table 3.5 we find that the score twenty-sixth from the bottom of the raw score distribution has a value of 73. This number tells us that the desired percentile point lies between the real limits of 72.5 and 73.5.

As shown in Table 3.8, 24 scores fall below the interval containing the fifty-ninth percentile and there are three scores in this interval. We must decide where in the interval to place the fifty-ninth percentile point. Since 24 cases are below the interval and we want 26 cases, we consider two of the three cases in the interval to be equal to or less than the fifty-ninth percentile point.

$$\frac{\text{number of cases needed}}{\text{number of cases in interval}} = \frac{2}{3} = .67$$

This proportion, (.67), represents the distance into the interval we have to go to reach the fifth-ninth percentile point. Adding that proportion to the lower

Table 3.8 **PARTITIONING SCORES TO FIND A PERCENTILE POINT**

Interval	f
Above 73.5	17
72.5 to 73.5	3
Below 72.5	24
Total	44

limit of the interval gives 72.5 + .67 = 73.17, which is the fifty-ninth percentile point.

This method of dividing a set of tied scores uses an estimation procedure known as *linear interpolation*. The procedure assumes that scores within an interval are evenly distributed over the range of values in that interval.

Now you know how to compute the score value (percentile point) corresponding to a given percentile. Consider that the question can be reversed. You can also ask what is the **percentile rank** corresponding to a known score.

PERCENTILE RANK: The percentage of cases at or below a given point (a given percentile).

Assume that you are given the score value of $X = 80$ and want to know what percentage of all scores are at or below that value. Begin with the lowest score in the distribution and count the subjects with scores up to and including 80. In Table 3.5 we find that 36 scores fall into this category: $f(X \leq 80) = 36$. The next step involves dividing this value (36) by the total number of scores (44). Therefore we have $36/44 = 81.82$, which is the percentile rank when $X = 80$.

With tied scores we can use linear interpolation to estimate the percentile rank. Suppose the known score is 70 and we wish to find the corresponding percentile rank. Table 3.9 shows that by counting you can determine that 17 of the 44 scores (38.64 percent) are below the interval containing this score and that 3 (6.82 percent) are in the interval.

Assuming that the scores are equally distributed in the interval, one-half should lie above the midpoint and one-half below the midpoint. Therefore, we add half of the 6.82 percent within the interval to the 38.64 percent known to be below the interval. Since half of 6.82 is 3.41 [(.5)(6.82) = 3.41], we add 3.41 percent to 38.64 percent. This yields the percentile rank (*PR*) of 42.05 for a score of 70.

$$PR = \% \text{ below} + (\% \text{ within})(\text{fraction needed})$$

$$= 38.64\% \quad + (6.82\%)(.5)$$

$$= 38.64\% \quad + 3.41\% = 42.05$$

Table 3.9   **PARTITIONING SCORES TO FIND A PERCENTILE RANK**

Interval	f	Percentage
Above 70.5	24	54.54
69.5 to 70.5	3	6.82
Below 69.5	17	38.64
Total	44	100.00

Table 3.10   STEM-AND-LEAF DISPLAYS OF DATA IN TABLE 3.4

Stem (leading)	Leaf (trailing)	Stem (leading)	Leaf (trailing)
9	5	9.	5
8	02333578	9*	
7	000112233344677889	8.	578
6	012234467788	8*	02333
5	13567	7.	677889
		7*	000112233344
		6.	67788
		6*	0122344
		5.	567
		5*	13

3.8   STEM-AND-LEAF DISPLAYS

Frequency distributions can be cumbersome and wasteful of space. As an alternative, John Tukey (1977) developed the *stem-and-leaf* display, which provides a form of data summary without loss of information. Consider our example of examination scores that consist of two-digit numbers. A stem-and-leaf display can be constructed by letting the first (left-most) digit of each score represent the stem or vertical axis of the display.[2] The last or trailing digits of scores form the leaves of the display. For data in Table 3.5 the first, or leading, digits are 5, 6, 7, 8, and 9; the trailing digits are 0–9 inclusive. These data have been used to generate a stem-and-leaf display in Table 3.10.

Two forms of the display are presented. On the left half of Table 3.10 is a "bare bones" stem-and-leaf display. The first entry represents the obtained score of 95 in Table 3.5; the number 9 forms the stem and 5 forms the leaf. The second entry has a stem of 8 and a leaf of 02333578. This entry represents all scores between 80 and 89: 80, 82, 83, 83, 85, 87, 88. This display has the drawback of being too coarse for some purposes.

In the right half of Table 3.10 is a variation that uses class intervals of size 5. Here we split the stem so that 5* represents the interval 50–54 and 5. (read 5 dot) represents the interval 55–59. This version of the stem-and-leaf display provides a closer approximation to the grouped frequency distribution given in Table 3.5, although either version of the display could be used, depending on the needs of the researcher.

Both frequency distributions and stem-and-leaf displays are useful in showing the difference in scores from two samples, such as an experimental group that received a specific treatment and a control group that did not. Table 3.11 illustrates this point with data from Table 3.4. The data for the

---

[2]The first digit will not always be the stem. Rather, the stem will depend on your data. In a collection of three-digit IQ scores, for example, the first two digits could serve as the stem.

Table 3.11   CONTRASTING AN EXPERIMENTAL
GROUP (*E*) AND A CONTROL GROUP (*C*)

Frequency distribution			Stem-and-leaf display		
Interval	*E*	*C*	*E*-leaf	Stem	*C*-leaf
95–99	1	0	5	9.	
90–94	0	0		9*	
85–89	1	2	8	8.	57
80–84	4	1	3320	8*	3
75–79	4	2	9887	7.	67
70–74	7	5	4332110	7*	00234
65–69	2	3	86	6.	778
60–64	1	6	4	6*	012234
55–59	2	1	65	5.	7
50–54	0	2		5*	03

experimental group came from the upper two rows of scores in Table 3.4, and the data for the control group came from the lower two rows. It is relatively easy to see in Table 3.11 that these two sets of data are distributed differently. The scores for the experimental group are concentrated in the interval 70–84, whereas those from the control group are concentrated in the interval 60–74.

3.9   GRAPHS FOR QUANTITATIVE DATA

Two of the many ways to summarize quantitative data graphically are the histogram and the frequency polygon. A *histogram* is a graph for quantitative data. It consists of a set of adjacent rectangles where the height of each rectangle depends on the frequency of events (or relative frequency such as percentage) in a class interval. The width of the rectangle corresponds to the upper and lower limits of that class interval, and each rectangle has the same width. Figure 3.4 illustrates the use of this definition of a histogram and the guidelines that follow. The data came from Table 3.7.

In constructing graphic figures, using guidelines or conventions promotes the consistency of the presentation across data sets. They also make construction of the display easier for the researcher as well as reading the display easier for the researcher's audience.

1. Like qualitative data, the score values are represented on the X-axis and their frequency of occurrence on the Y-axis.
2. Where convenient, the intersection of these two axes should be the zero point on both the *X* and *Y* scales. Note that in Figure 3.4 the X-axis is broken near the zero point, which indicates that the values of some possible scores are not represented in the figure. Since our

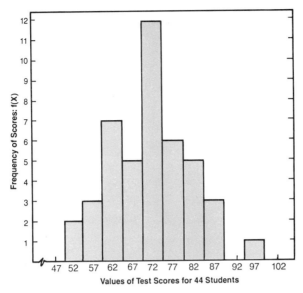

Figure 3.4 Histogram: Examination scores for 44 students.
Data are from Table 3.7, column 2.

data set in Table 3.7 has no values between 0 and 49, it would be a waste of space to include these values on the X-axis. When a set of score values is omitted from a display, it is important to let the reader know it (e.g., by a break in the axis).

3. To give consistency and minimize distortions, the Y-axis (ordinate) is often made to be about three-quarters the length of the X-axis (abscissa).

4. Each axis is labeled in two ways. On the abscissa we have "X = Values of Test Scores," and on the ordinate we have "Y = Frequency of Scores." The possible values of both X and Y are given with convenient numerical units. To label the data from Table 3.7, we let the X-axis values be the midpoints of class intervals, 52, 57 . . . 97, and the Y-axis values are frequencies of occurrence for each class interval, 1, 2 . . . 12.

5. As is the case with tables, figures are given a verbal descriptive title called a "caption." Unlike titles for tables, figure captions appear at the foot of the figure below the label of the X-axis.

The *frequency polygon* is a commonly used variation of the histogram for numerical scores. Figure 3.5 shows a frequency polygon for the data presented as a histogram in Figure 3.4. In each case the midpoints of the class intervals have been given on the X-axis and the frequency of observed scores is given on the Y-axis. The difference between the histogram and the frequency polygon is that the height of the frequency above the X-axis is now represented as a *point* above the midpoint of each interval. In Figure 3.5 these several

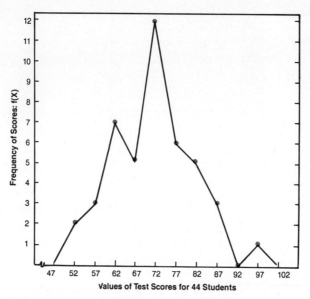

Figure 3.5 Frequency polygon: Examination scores for 44 students.

points have been connected by straight lines. Thus, frequency polygons differ from histograms in that straight lines instead of adjacent bars are used to show the relation between levels of the X variable and their frequencies. These polygons are especially useful when the number of score values is large and a histogram of the data would be perceptually cluttered.

3.10 CHARACTERISTICS OF DISTRIBUTIONS

Graphic displays of data are widely used and can have many different shapes. However, some families of distributions are so common that they are easily recognized and have special names. These names are part of the jargon that researchers use to communicate their expected and observed findings. They form a handy way of conveying the gist of a message about a data set in only a word or two.

Of special interest is a theoretical distribution that often approximates data distributions and is also used to develop procedures for statistical inference later in this book. This is the "bell-shaped" normal distribution.[3] Normal distributions are unimodal and symmetrical. By *unimodal* we mean that there is only one major peak in the distribution. If there are two major peaks, the distribution is referred to as *bimodal*. (The two major peaks do not have

---

[3]The distribution is sometimes called the "Gaussian" distribution after C. F. Gauss (1777–1855). According to Bell (1937), Gauss was one of the three greatest mathematicians of all time. The other two were Archimedes and Newton.

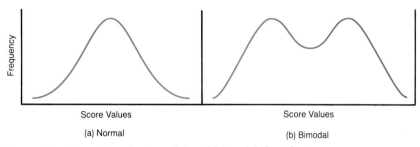

Figure 3.6 Examples of unimodal and bimodal distributions.

to be exactly the same height.) By *symmetrical* we mean that you could ver-
tically fold the distribution in half at the midpoint of the X-axis and the two
halves would perfectly overlap. Figure 3.6(a) illustrates a normal distribution,
which is both unimodal and symmetrical. It has a concentration of scores
near the middle of the distribution and relatively few scores at the extreme
ends, that is, in the "tails." The distribution in Figure 3.6(b) is also symmetrical, but since it is bimodal, it is not a normal distribution.

Skewness

The notion of skewness is related to the symmetry of a distribution of scores.
A perfectly symmetrical distribution has zero skewness. In Figure 3.7 there
are two distributions with quite different directions of skew. Although they
are unimodal, they are not symmetrical. The majority of scores in these distributions are concentrated around a particular value, but a few of them are
unusually far from the majority. These few scores generate skew in one tail
of the distribution. When these scores have higher values than the majority,
the distribution is said to be *positively skewed.* When they have lower values
than the majority, the distribution is *negatively skewed.* To illustrate,
skewed distributions of scores have often been found when people's response
time is measured. In tasks with this dependent variable the subjects typically
are asked to respond on several occasions. Most of the time their response
time is relatively brief, such as less than one-half second. But occasionally
the signal to respond leads to a delay of a second or more. These relatively

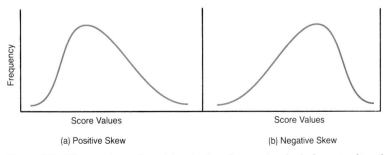

Figure 3.7 Illustration of positive (+) and negative (−) skew in distributions.

rare delayed responses tend to make the total distribution of time scores positively skewed.

Two features of skew should be noted. First, although there is a formula by which the amount of skew can be computed for a given set of data, the quantity is rarely computed in behavioral research. Much more frequently, verbal labels are used to describe a set of data generally as having positive or negative skew. Second, it is often necessary to have a large data set to get a reasonable estimate of skew.

SUMMARY

In this chapter we have illustrated several common methods used to display data in tables and graphs. The first step in summarizing a set of data is to place them into a data matrix. The matrix contains information about subjects (their identity, gender, etc.) and their observed responses. In the data matrix this information is coded as numbers.

Frequency distributions are created by listing the possible data values and the number of times each data value is actually observed. With quantitative data sometimes the number of possible score values between the highest and lowest observed scores is much greater than the amount of scores in the data set. In these cases frequency distributions based on groups of score values called class intervals are used, rather than individual score values.

The response frequency associated with each score value or class interval may also be reported as relative frequencies (i.e., proportions or percentages). Relative values are particularly useful when comparing responses from samples of different sizes. Percentiles are useful in describing the relative standing of a score in a distribution. Given a percentile of interest you can find the score value that divides the measurement scale into two parts, one corresponding to values above the percentile and one corresponding to those equal to or less than the percentile. Similarly, when given a score value, you may find the corresponding percentile rank.

Stem-and-leaf displays are a relatively new form of data summary that are similar to histograms. They are useful because they preserve more information about the raw data than do grouped frequency distributions but are just as easily interpreted as a histogram or frequency polygon.

Graphic displays of qualitative data can be produced by using bar graphs and pie charts, in which each score value is represented as a bar or as a wedge-shaped section of a circle. Histograms and frequency polygons are used to display quantitative data. In a histogram, each bar represents a score value or a class interval. In a frequency polygon, score values or class intervals are represented by a single point and the points from each value or interval are connected by straight lines.

Distributions of data are often described with words comparing them to a normal distribution. Normal distributions are symmetrical and unimodal (one major peak). Deviations from normal can refer to lack of symmetry such as positive skew and negative skew.

KEY WORDS

data matrix	cumulative distribution
frequency distribution	percentile point
relative frequency	linear interpolation
proportion	percentile rank
percentage	stem-and-leaf display
bar graph	histogram
pie chart	frequency polygon
outlier	normal distribution
class interval	negative skew
grouped frequency distribution	positive skew

PROBLEMS

1 From the data that follow
(a) Construct a grouped frequency table with class intervals of size 3.
(b) How many intervals are in this grouped distribution?
(c) Would you verbally describe this distribution as roughly normal, positively skewed, or negatively skewed?

31	37	32	22	31	36	33	38
35	34	26	33	39	30	29	35
29	21	37	24	32	19	36	16
36	33	31	30	34	38	34	36

2 Construct a cumulative percentage distribution for the data in problem 1.

3 A class of 122 students was asked to evaluate their textbook on a five-point scale: (a) much better than average, (b) somewhat better than average, (c) neither better nor worse than average, (d) somewhat worse than average, and (e) much worse than average. The number of students selecting each alternative was $a = 11$, $b = 25$, $c = 50$, $d = 25$, and $e = 11$.
(a) What scale of measurement was used in this study?
(b) Generate a frequency table of these data.
(c) Verbally describe the general shape of this distribution.

4 Distinguish between a bar graph and a frequency polygon.

5 For the set of data in problem 1, generate a stem-and-leaf display.

6 For the raw data in problem 1, what is the percentile rank corresponding to the scores (a) 30 and (b) 36?

7 For the raw data in problem 1, what is the raw score value corresponding to the percentile rank of (a) 90 and (b) 40?

8 What scale of measurement is represented by percentiles (nominal, ordinal, interval, ratio)?

Chapter 4

Central Tendency and Variability

4.1   INTRODUCTION

Before reading a novel or going to see a movie we often try to obtain some kind of summary or review to help us decide whether it is interesting enough to spend time and money on it. Similarly, it is important to be able to summarize a set of data so that its main features can be understood and readily communicated to others. A frequency distribution often does not present the key information in a form that is useful for evaluating a set of data. For example, we might want to compare the performance of male and female schoolchildren on a test of spatial skill (e.g., the ability to mentally visualize three-dimensional objects). It could be cumbersome to describe the differences between boys and girls in terms of the shapes of the two distributions of scores. A better approach might be to compare the average score for each group.

In fact, it is very common for researchers to summarize data sets by providing some measure of *average* or *central tendency*. This is a single numerical value that is meant to represent the typical score in the data set. Of course, not all scores are necessarily the same, but the average value is, in a sense, representative of the scores. After all, the purpose of a summary is not to present all information, just a core idea. Scores in a data set may be quite different from what we take as the central tendency, so it is also important to provide in our summary some indication of the size of this difference—that is, the extent to which the scores *vary* from one another or from the central tendency. In this chapter we will discuss these two aspects of summarizing data sets—central tendency and the degree to which scores vary from the central tendency. In each case we will consider data sets that represent whole populations (which is very rare in practice but important in developing statistical theory) and data sets that represent samples drawn from populations (the typical situation in research studies).

4.2   CENTRAL TENDENCY

Measures of central tendency provide an estimate of the "typical" score in a distribution. Each of the three measures we consider can be defined, in some sense, as the center of a distribution of scores. For this reason we have chosen to use the term *central tendency* rather than *average.*

Mode

One way of defining central tendency is in terms of the most frequently occurring value. This value is called the **mode** and is "central" only in the sense that more scores in the data set take on this value than any other value. Suppose that a group of six clients attending a weight-loss clinic report the following scores, representing the number of times during the past week that they consumed food other than at regular meals: 8, 6, 20, 6, 6, 8. In this case the mode is 6, although 6 is the smallest value in the data set. Note that the mode is the most frequently occurring value, *not* the frequency with which the value occurs—three times in this case.

MODE: The most frequently occurring value in a distribution of scores.

No arithmetic computation is needed beyond counting the number of times each value occurs. Thus computation of the mode can be carried out even when a nominal measurement scale is used. For example, if the six clients attending the weight-loss clinic were classified according to gender, with a score of 1 assigned to males and 2 assigned to females, we might have the following data: 2, 2, 1, 2, 2, 1. In this case the mode would be 2 (female).

The fact that the mode is the most frequently occurring value means that when a set of data is presented in the form of a frequency polygon, the mode is the score value that corresponds to the peak of the distribution (see Figure 4.1). If the polygon is based on class intervals, the mode is the midpoint of the interval with the highest frequency of scores.

In some cases a distribution may have two values that occur with very high (but not necessarily equal) frequency. Distributions of this type are said to be *bimodal*, indicating that there are two modes. This form might occur when two distinct groups of subjects, having different modes on a variable, are included in the same data set. For example, Figure 4.2 presents hypothetical distributions of scores for accountants and for architects on a test of spatial ability. The effect of combining these two distributions is also shown, and it is clear that two peaks emerge, producing a bimodal frequency polygon.

Things get a bit out of hand when more than two values claim the title of mode. When a distribution has more than two modes, the mode no longer offers a clear impression of the central tendency of the distribution. It is even possible that all values in a set of data will occur with equal frequency. In these cases we say that there is no mode.

Median

A second measure of central tendency is the **median,** the value above and below which no more than 50 percent of the scores in the distribution fall.

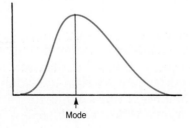

Figure 4.1 Frequency polygon, with the mode indicated by a vertical line. The mode is the value that corresponds to the peak of the frequency polygon.

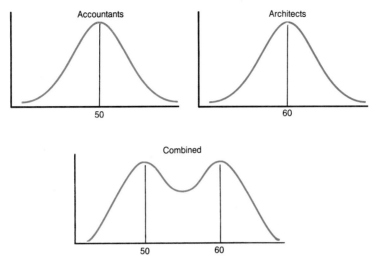

Figure 4.2 Hypothetical frequency polygons representing scores on a spatial ability test for accountants and architects. Combining the two distributions results in a bimodal distribution.

In this sense, the median is in the "middle" of a distribution and is the fiftieth percentile (see Chapter 3). To find the median of a set of scores we begin by ordering the scores from lowest to highest. Consider the following fictional data representing scores on a test of mental stress given to seven people just after they broke up with a romantic partner (higher score indicates more stress): 5, 9, 3, 2, 4, 8, 2. Ordering these scores yields 2, 2, 3, 4, 5, 8, 9. The median is 4, the middle score in this distribution. Notice that calculation of the median requires ordering the scores from lowest to highest, which means that the variable must be quantitative.

MEDIAN: The value above and below which no more than 50 percent of the scores in a distribution fall.

Computation of the median is slightly different when there is an even number of scores in a data set because no single value lies at the middle of the distribution. Then the median is taken as the midpoint between the two middle scores. Assume that an eighth person is given the test of mental stress and obtains a score of 6. The ordered scores now are 2, 2, 3, 4, 5, 6, 8, 9. The two middle scores are 4 and 5, and the midpoint between them is equal to their sum divided by 2. So we have $(4 + 5)/2 = 4.50$ for the median of the eight scores on the stress test.

The median represents the point that would cut in half the area under a frequency polygon, as illustrated in Figure 4.3, because the area under a frequency polygon falling within a given range of values corresponds to the

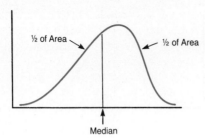

Figure 4.3 Frequency polygon, with the median indicated by a vertical line. The median is the value that divides the area under the polygon into two equal portions.

number of observed scores in that range. In a set of 100 scores, for instance, 50 of the scores would be above and 50 would be below the median. In the frequency polygon the area representing the lower 50 scores would equal half of the area under the polygon, and the area representing the upper 50 scores would equal the other half of the total polygon area. This point will be developed more fully in the next chapter.

Mean

There are several different kinds of means, but in this book we will emphasize the **arithmetic mean.** The arithmetic mean is what most people usually associate with the concept of average, and it is computed by adding all the scores in a data set and then dividing the resulting total by the number of scores in the set. Consider the following set of ten scores on the mental stress test: 2, 2, 3, 4, 4, 4, 5, 6, 6, 9. These scores would have a mean of

$$\frac{2 + 2 + 3 + 4 + 4 + 4 + 5 + 6 + 6 + 9}{10} = \frac{45}{10} = 4.50$$

Because computation of the mean requires adding all the scores, they must be based on a quantitative variable in order for this operation to be meaningful.

MEAN: The sum of scores in a distribution divided by the number of scores.

When we are dealing with a set of scores representing a sample that has been drawn from a population, the symbol for the mean is $\overline{X}$ (pronounced *X-bar*). Characteristics of samples, such as $\overline{X}$, are called *statistics*. On those occasions (rare in actual practice) when we are dealing with a set of scores that represents a whole population, we use the Greek letter μ (pronounced *mew*) to represent the mean of the population. Characteristics of a population are called *parameters*. We often use sample statistics such as $\overline{X}$ to estimate population parameters such as μ.

A specific formula is used to define the mean. This formula introduces another Greek letter, this one representing the arithmetic operation of addition. The uppercase Greek letter sigma, Σ, is used to indicate that a series of numbers is to be added. But how do we know which series of numbers to add? Typically we wish to add the numbers of a set of data that represent scores on some variable, X. To indicate this operation, we write ΣX. Then if we want the mean of the set of scores, we just divide the result of this summation by the number of scores (represented by the letter N). Putting these two steps together provides the formula for the mean:

$$\overline{X} = \frac{\Sigma X}{N} \qquad (4.1)$$

By comparing the parts of this formula to the calculation of the mean mental stress ratings previously given, you can clearly see how the formula works. The symbols ΣX represent summing the stress score of each person to obtain a total; then dividing by N produces the mean.

$$\overline{X} = \frac{\Sigma X}{N} = \frac{2 + 2 + 3 + 4 + 4 + 4 + 5 + 6 + 6 + 9}{10} = 4.50$$

Guidelines for using Σ to specify addition are presented in Appendix I.

When we want to discuss a set of data that represents scores from a whole population, we use the Greek letter μ, rather than $\overline{X}$, to represent the mean. The formula for calculating μ is the same as for calculating $\overline{X}$:

$$\mu = \frac{\Sigma X}{N} \qquad (4.2)$$

The mean represents the *central* tendency of a distribution in a very important sense. Suppose we were to consider a wooden beam with a number of score values marked at equal intervals, as in Figure 4.4(a). Now we place blocks of equal size and weight, representing individual scores, at the appropriate locations on the wooden beam. This step has been taken in Figure 4.4(a) for the ten mental stress scores given earlier. Once the blocks corresponding to the scores have been placed on the beam, the mean is that point along the beam at which a fulcrum must be placed in order to balance the beam perfectly (assuming the beam has no weight itself).

This interpretation of the mean has two important implications. First, the mean is very sensitive to the presence of even a single extreme score. For instance, imagine what would happen in Figure 4.4 if the person who obtained a score of 5 had actually scored 10. This score would cause the beam to tip over to the right, as shown in Figure 4.4(b). To balance it we would have to move the fulcrum in that direction. Its exact location would correspond to the new mean (50/10 = 5.00), as shown in Figure 4.4(c).

Second, what happens when we consider scores in terms of their distance from the mean? Each score's distance can be expressed as the difference between it and the mean, $X - \overline{X}$, and is called a *deviation score*. Some scores will be above the mean, producing positive deviation scores, and others will be below the mean, yielding negative deviation scores. Since the mean is the

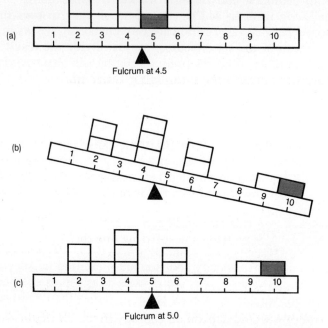

Figure 4.4 A set of rating scores is placed along a balance beam. The beam can be balanced if the fulcrum is placed at the point corresponding to the mean (a). Changing a score to a more extreme value will cause an imbalance (b), unless the fulcrum is moved to the new mean (c).

balance point, the total of the positive deviations will balance the total of the negative deviations. So when we add all the deviation scores in a data set we get zero. For instance, from the data shown in Figure 4.4(c) we have

$$\Sigma(X - \overline{X}) = (2 - 5) + (2 - 5) + (3 - 5) + (4 - 5) + (4 - 5) +$$
$$(4 - 5) + (6 - 5) + (6 - 5) + (9 - 5) + (10 - 5)$$

$$= (-3) + (-3) + (-2) + (-1) + (-1) + (-1) + 1 + 1 + 4 + 5$$

$$= 0$$

In fact, no matter what set of scores we use, if we find the difference between each one and the mean, and then add these deviation scores, we will get zero (within the limits of rounding error) every time. The algebraic proof of this claim is shown in Proof 4.1 at the end of this chapter. (In general, algebraic proofs are shown at the end of the chapter.)

The mean has another important characteristic, and it also has to do with deviation scores. If we square the deviation scores before summing them, we will not get zero because there are no negative values. The resulting sum of squared deviations will, however, be smaller than the result that would be obtained had the deviation scores been based on any other value other than the mean. For example, consider the set of three mental stress scores 2, 3, and 7, which has a mean of 4. The sum of squared deviation scores (based on the mean) would be

$$\Sigma(X - \overline{X})^2 = (2 - 4)^2 + (3 - 4)^2 + (7 - 4)^2 = 14$$

If we calculate deviation scores from any other number, say, the median, which is 3 in this case, we would get a result that is greater than 14:

$$\Sigma(X - 3)^2 = (2 - 3)^2 + (3 - 3)^2 + (7 - 3)^2 = 17$$

Using this set of data, try computing the sum of squared deviations from other values that are not equal to the mean. In each case you will obtain a value that is greater than 14. In fact, the larger the difference between the mean and the value you choose, the larger will be the sum of squared deviations.

The importance of this fact will become apparent in Chapter 7, where we consider issues such as plotting a best-fitting line through a set of data points. For now consider the following problem. Suppose your task is to predict with as little error as possible the number of between-meal snacks eaten in the past week by randomly selected members of the weight-loss clinic. What would be your best prediction for each member?

That prediction would depend on the way in which we measure error. An important measure of error that will be used in Chapter 7 is the square of the difference between a prediction and the actual score. If you predicted five snacks for one of the clients and that person's actual number of snacks was only three, the amount of error would be $(3 - 5)^2 = 4$. If you knew the mean number of snacks for the entire group of clients, for each randomly selected client you should predict the mean. Over many such predictions the sum of squared differences between the predictions and actual scores will be minimized if the mean is predicted each time. The algebraic proof that the sum of squared deviation scores is minimized when deviations are based on the mean rather than any other value is shown in Proof 4.2 at the end of the chapter.

Comparing Measures of Central Tendency

There are a number of common situations in which all three measures of central tendency are very similar to one another. These situations arise when the distribution of scores is symmetrical and unimodal [see Figure 4.5(a)]. When a distribution is skewed, however, there are systematic differences among the three measures, as shown in Figure 4.5. In the case of a positive skew, where there are a few extremely high scores, the mean will occur at a point nearer to the skew (and so will have a higher value) than either the median or mode. It is as though the few extreme scores draw the mean toward them (recall the balance beam analogy described earlier). The mode, as usual, is found at the peak of the distribution. The median, which divides

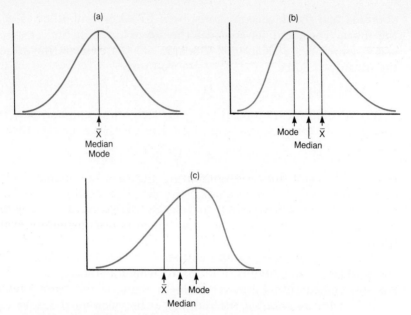

Figure 4.5 Frequency polygons showing the position of the mean, median, and mode for normal (a); positively skewed (b); and negatively skewed (c) distributions.

the area under the distribution into two equal halves, falls between the mean and the mode. A similar pattern occurs with a negatively skewed distribution, with the mean drawn toward the low end of the distribution by the few extremely low scores. In this case the mean will have a lower value than either the median or the mode.

We will be emphasizing the mean in later chapters of this book, but there are situations in which one of the other two measures might be preferred. One instance is when the distribution of scores is *open-ended*. That is, the exact value of a number of scores is not known, but it is known that they are extreme outliers. As an example, consider a study in which a researcher is measuring the time required for grade 9 students to solve algebra problems. In some cases a student may never be able to reach a solution, and it is not possible to assign a valid score. We do know, however, that the score is rather high. In this case we could not compute the mean for the entire sample of subjects because some scores would be unknown. But we could compute the median very easily by ordering the scores, placing the unknown values at the upper end of the distribution.

Another situation in which computation of the mean is not feasible arises when data are based on a qualitative variable. In these cases we cannot even quantitatively order the scores, so the mode is the only possible measure of central tendency. For instance, we might want to find out what kind of computers grade school children were exposed to in their homes. Each child who comes from a home in which a computer is used would receive a score indicating the manufacturer of the computer (e.g., 1 = Apple, 2 = Commodore, 3 = IBM). Since the numbers are assigned arbitrarily to manufacturers, they have no quantitative meaning. All we can do is determine how many scores of each value occur. The most frequently occurring value is the mode.

4.3 VARIABILITY

A very important limitation in using a measure of central tendency to summarize a set of scores is the fact that the measure may not be very representative of the scores. For example, consider the problem faced by the president of a university students' organization who is responsible for evaluating students' opinions on the desirability of allowing a fast-food chain to open a restaurant on campus. A sample of students has been asked to give an opinion, and each has provided a rating in which a score of 1 indicates that the idea is completely unacceptable and a score of 10 means that the plan is highly acceptable. For the sake of simplicity, suppose that only five students were sampled. If the ratings were 5, 5, 6, 6, 6, the mean rating would be 5.6, indicating that the students considered the plan to be moderately acceptable.

But suppose that the five scores turned out to be 2, 3, 3, 10, 10. Again the mean is 5.6, but there is something quite different about these two sets of scores. In the first case, there is general agreement among the students' opinions, and the mean is quite representative of their ratings. In the second case, however, the mean is not similar to any of the obtained scores. In fact, there is clearly a polarization of opinion—students feel strongly one way or another, and there is no general agreement. These two patterns of responses have very different implications for what the president should do. In the first case either accepting or rejecting the chain's proposal probably would not cause too much trouble. In the second case it is virtually certain that no matter which decision is made, part of the student body will be very displeased.

This example provides a hint about another kind of information that a summary of a set of scores should contain—an assessment of the representativeness of the measure of central tendency. A measure of representativeness typically gauges how different individual scores are from one another. If the scores are very similar, the measure of central tendency will be representative. But if the scores are very different from one another, we should be aware that the measure of central tendency may not be very close to many of the actual scores. This is the concept of *variability*, and it represents a method of summarizing the extent to which scores are clustered closely together or are widely scattered. Although there are a number of different ways of measuring this aspect of a set of data, each one depends on measuring distances between scores.

Range

The simplest measure of variability is the *range,* which is calculated by finding the difference between the highest and lowest scores in a distribution.

$$\text{range} = X_{\text{highest}} - X_{\text{lowest}} \tag{4.3}$$

According to this measure, the more discrepant the highest and lowest scores, the more the scores in the distribution vary. Obtaining the highest and lowest scores in a distribution and finding the distance between them (subtraction) implies that the data are measured on at least an interval scale.

In the two cases on student opinion just described, different amounts of variability are intuitively apparent in the data. In the first case the scores are tightly bunched and there is low variability, whereas in the second case there is much more variability. The values of the range in these two cases reflect this discrepancy, as the range in the first case is $6 - 5 = 1$ and in the second case it is $10 - 2 = 8$.

But there are a number of problems with the range as a measure of variability. The most obvious is that it takes into account only the two most extreme scores, and different amounts of variability among intermediate scores are not reflected. The range also is very sensitive to the presence of a single aberrant score in a distribution. For example, suppose that in the sample of student ratings you obtained nothing but 5s and 6s, except for one student who gave the proposal a rating of 10. The presence of this person in the sample would produce a range of 5 instead of 1.

Finally, in some instances we are interested in using the data from a sample to provide an estimate of the nature of a larger population from which the sample was drawn. When the range is calculated from a sample, it is a very poor estimate of the range of an entire population because it changes dramatically with sample size. Larger samples are more likely to include extreme scores and therefore are more likely to produce larger estimates of the range. This is a very undesirable property for a sample statistic that is supposed to provide an accurate estimation of a population parameter.

Variance

The measure of variability that we will consider next has none of the disadvantages associated with the range and also gets at the heart of one of the major issues of variability—the representativeness of the measure of central tendency. The mean of a set of scores is considered to be representative to the extent that many scores in the set are close to the mean. A useful method of measuring representativeness is based on deviation scores, which are obtained by finding the difference between each raw score and the mean $(X - \overline{X})$. It should be apparent that the size of the deviation scores provides information about how well the mean represents the raw scores. Summing the deviation scores to get a single statistic, however, would not be useful because, as you may recall, the sum of deviation scores is zero. A method removing the negative signs is needed.

This removal can be accomplished by squaring each deviation score. The mean of a set of squared deviation scores is called the **variance.** The symbol for the variance of a population is the lowercase Greek letter sigma raised to the second power, σ^2, indicating that deviations from the mean are squared.

$$\sigma^2 = \frac{\Sigma(X - \mu)^2}{N} \tag{4.4}$$

From this formula you should be able to see that the variance can be conceptualized as the mean of squared deviations from the mean. In fact, variance is sometimes called the *mean square.* For the sake of convenience, the sum of squared deviations from the mean (the numerator of Formula 4.4) is referred to as the *sum of squares*, which is symbolized in formulas by *SS.* Thus, an alternative version of Formula 4.4 would be Formula 4.5.

$$\sigma^2 = \frac{SS}{N} \tag{4.5}$$

VARIANCE: The mean of squared deviations from the mean.

Recall from our introduction to the mean that in a task involving prediction of a score value drawn at random from a set of scores, the prediction error was minimized by predicting a value equal to the mean. This effect was true when the prediction error was defined as the sum of squared deviations from the mean. Another interpretation of the variance, then, is the mean of squared error associated with using the mean as a predictor.

Biased and Unbiased Statistics

When we are working with a sample randomly drawn from a population, one goal in calculating the variance of the scores in the sample is to obtain an estimate of the population variance. One method of doing so is to use a revised version of Formula 4.4 in which the symbol S^2 represents the variance of a sample.

$$S^2 = \frac{\Sigma(X - \overline{X})^2}{N} \tag{4.6}$$

Unfortunately, if we were to use Formula 4.6 to find the variance of a sample, it is likely that we would *underestimate* the population variance. To see why, consider a population consisting of just three scores: 1, 2, and 3. In this case the population mean is 2 and the population variance is .67.

Now suppose that we were to draw a random sample of two scores and compute the variance of the sample as an estimate of the population variance. In drawing the sample, we will first draw one score, then put it back into the data set before drawing a second score. Thus it will be possible to draw a sample consisting of two equal scores. This procedure is known as *sampling with replacement*. What result might we expect to get, on the average, across all the possible samples of size 2? Table 4.1 shows all the possible combination of scores that could be included in these samples and the mean and variance (computed from Formula 4.6) for each.

Notice that for some of the samples the mean is equal to the population mean and that for other samples the mean is a bit less or a bit more than the population mean. The mean value of the sample means, however, is equal to the proportion mean. When the mean value of a sample statistic is equal to the corresponding population parameter, we say that the sample statistic (in this case $\overline{X}$) is an *unbiased* estimate of the population parameter. This is a highly desirable property for a statistic to have since we would not want to use a statistic that on the average produces an estimate of a population parameter that is too large or too small.

Is the sample variance computed from Formula 4.6 an unbiased estimate of the population variance? In Table 4.1 you can see that for a majority of the samples the variance is less than the actual population variance. Further, the mean of the sample variances, taken across all possible samples, is .33. But the real population variance is .67, so it is clear that on the average we will underestimate σ^2 if we compute the sample variance with S^2.

In fact, for any population the mean of the variance estimates (based on Formula 4.6) provided by all possible samples of size N is

$$\frac{N-1}{N}\sigma^2$$

Formula 4.6 produces a *biased* estimate of the population variance in the sense that on the average it will be an underestimate. In the case of samples

Table 4.1   MEAN AND VARIANCE FOR ALL
POSSIBLE SAMPLES FROM A
POPULATION CONSISTING OF
THREE SCORES

Sample	Mean	Variance (using N)	Variance (using $N - 1$)
1 1	1.0	0.00	0.00
1 2	1.5	0.25	0.50
1 3	2.0	1.00	2.00
2 1	1.5	0.25	0.50
2 2	2.0	0.00	0.00
2 3	2.5	0.25	0.50
3 1	2.0	1.00	2.00
3 2	2.5	0.25	0.50
3 3	3.0	0.00	0.00
Mean =	2.0	0.33	0.67

Box 4.1   **Alteration of Formula 4.6 to Produce an Unbiased Estimate of Population Variance**

In this box we understand the equal sign to mean that, *on the average,* the left-hand term will equal the right-hand term.

$$S^2 = \frac{N-1}{N}\sigma^2$$

$$\frac{N}{N-1} \cdot \frac{\Sigma(X-\overline{X})^2}{N} = \frac{N}{N-1} \cdot \frac{N-1}{N}\sigma^2 \qquad \text{(multiply both sides of the equation by } N/N-1)$$

$$\frac{\Sigma(X-\overline{X})^2}{N-1} = \sigma^2 \qquad \text{(cancel where appropriate)}$$

---

of size 2, there is quite a discrepancy between the mean of the estimates of the population variance and its actual value—the mean of our estimates of the population variance is only half what it should be:

$$\frac{N-1}{N} = \frac{2-1}{2} = \frac{1}{2}$$

The problem is less serious with larger sample sizes, but still it exists. The mean of sample estimates of variance is too small by a factor of $(N-1)/N$. We can solve the problem by multiplying the original computation of sample variance (Formula 4.6) by the reciprocal of $(N-1)/N$ to increase our estimate by the appropriate amount. This step yields Formula 4.7, an unbiased estimate of σ^2 (see Box 4.1).

$$s^2 = \frac{\Sigma(X-\overline{X})^2}{N-1} \tag{4.7}$$

When this formula is used to calculate the sample variance, we get an unbiased estimate of the population variance, as shown in Table 4.1. Unless stated otherwise, whenever the variance is computed in examples used in this book, the value $N-1$ will be used as in Formula 4.7.

To understand why Formula 4.6 produces a biased estimate of the population variance, examine Table 4.1 once again. Notice that when a sample consists of extreme scores from the same end of the distribution (e.g., both scores are 1 or both are 3), the sample variance is quite small (zero). This result occurs because $\overline{X}$, used to compute the sample variance, depends on which scores are included in the sample.

When the population variance is computed by using the population mean, however, the extreme raw scores produce very large deviation scores.

Table 4.2   COMPUTATION OF SAMPLE VARIANCE BY
USING DEVIATION FROM A POPULATION
MEAN RATHER THAN FROM A SAMPLE
MEAN

Sample	μ	Sum of squared deviations	Variance (using N)
1 1	2.0	$(1 - 2)^2 + (1 - 2)^2 = 2$	$2/2 = 1.00$
1 2	2.0	$(1 - 2)^2 + (2 - 2)^2 = 1$	$1/2 = 0.50$
1 3	2.0	$(1 - 2)^2 + (3 - 2)^2 = 2$	$2/2 = 1.00$
2 1	2.0	$(2 - 2)^2 + (1 - 2)^2 = 1$	$1/2 = 0.50$
2 2	2.0	$(2 - 2)^2 + (2 - 2)^2 = 0$	$0/2 = 0.00$
2 3	2.0	$(2 - 2)^2 + (3 - 2)^2 = 1$	$1/2 = 0.50$
3 1	2.0	$(3 - 2)^2 + (1 - 2)^2 = 2$	$2/2 = 1.00$
3 2	2.0	$(3 - 2)^2 + (2 - 2)^2 = 1$	$1/2 = 0.50$
3 3	2.0	$(3 - 2)^2 + (3 - 2)^2 = 2$	$2/2 = 1.00$

Mean $= 0.67$

To see this effect, suppose we did not have to estimate the population mean but had μ available to compute the variance in each sample. Table 4.2 shows what would be the sum of squared deviations from μ and what would be the estimated population variance (with N as the denominator) for each sample of size 2. You can see that the mean estimate of the population variance, based on all possible samples, would be equal to the actual population variance. Thus, we have an unbiased estimate of the population variance by using N rather than $N - 1$ in the denominator, as long as we can base the sum of squared deviations on μ instead of $\overline{X}$. Typically, of course, we will not know the value of μ and so we must estimate it by using $\overline{X}$. It is the use of this estimated value of the population mean that produces the bias associated with Formula 4.6.

Degrees of Freedom

Each score that is included in a sample is free to take on any value, under the constraint that it is randomly sampled from a population. Each freely varying score in a sample is considered to be a *degree of freedom*. When a sample statistic is computed as an estimate of a population parameter by using the N scores in the sample, we say that the statistic is based on N degrees of freedom. Computation of some parameter estimates, however, required that we first obtain an estimate of some other parameter. Each of these preliminary parameter estimates places a constraint on the computation of the subsequent parameter estimate that uses up 1 degree of freedom. Therefore, some sample statistics are based on fewer than N degrees of freedom.

For example, when the sample statistic $\overline{X}$ is computed by using the N scores in a sample, there are N degrees of freedom. Computation of the sample variance, however, is based on N deviation scores $(X - \overline{X})$ and so requires the sample mean to be calculated first. Because this operation will cost 1 degree of freedom, the sample variance is based on $N - 1$ degrees of freedom. To see why, notice that not all of the deviation scores in a sample are free to vary because they must sum to zero. Thus when the variance is computed, only $N - 1$ of the deviations are free to vary. Once these deviations have been entered into the computation, the remaining deviation is fixed. For instance, suppose four scores are randomly drawn from a population. To compute the sample variance we first obtain the mean and then the deviation scores. Suppose that the first three deviation scores are -3, $+2$, and -4. The fourth deviation score must equal $+5$ in order for the four deviation scores to sum to zero. Thus, only the first three were free to take on any value.

To see more clearly why a degree of freedom is lost in using $\overline{X}$ as an estimate of μ in computing the sample variance, notice what would happen if μ were known. There would be no need to estimate $\overline{X}$ and the sample variance could be computed by using deviations based on μ instead of $\overline{X}$. In this case each of the deviations $(X - \mu)$ would be free to vary because there is no constraint on what will be the sum of a set of sample deviation scores based on μ. An unbiased estimate of σ^2 could be obtained by dividing the sum of these squared deviations by N, as shown in Table 4.2.

The term $N - 1$ in Formula 4.7 now takes on an additional meaning, that of degrees of freedom. We can view the computation of the variance as the sum of squared deviations from the mean, divided by degrees of freedom. In the case of the population variance, this concept is captured by Formula 4.5. For the sample variance we have Formula 4.8.

$$s^2 = \frac{SS}{N - 1} \tag{4.8}$$

Moreover, we can replace the term $N - 1$, which represents degrees of freedom, by the symbol *df*.

$$s^2 = \frac{SS}{df} \tag{4.9}$$

Computational Formula for Variance

Formula 4.7 (along with Formulas 4.8 and 4.9) is considered a *definitional* formula for variance since it directly represents the definition of variance as the mean of squared deviations from the mean. But in applications of Formula 4.7 you will find that it can be cumbersome to calculate each squared deviation, especially when the mean is an unwieldy number like 12.62. Furthermore, often it is the case that the mean used in Formula 4.7 has been rounded. The result is that the computation of each deviation score will include a small amount of error. For these reasons an alternative formula, arithmetically equivalent to 4.7, is more frequently used to calculate the variance. This formula is easier to use, eliminates rounding error introduced by using $\overline{X}$ to calculate each deviation score, and provides the same answer as Formula

4.7 (except for possible differences due to rounding error). Since one of its purposes is to ease the process of computation, it is called a *computational formula*.

$$s^2 = \frac{\Sigma X^2 - \dfrac{(\Sigma X)^2}{N}}{N - 1} \tag{4.10}$$

The proof that 4.7 and 4.10 are equivalent formulas is shown in Proof 4.3. The proof consists of showing that the two different expressions for the sum of squares are equivalent. It follows from this proof that we can apply a similar computational formula for the population variance.

$$\sigma^2 = \frac{\Sigma X^2 - \dfrac{(\Sigma X)^2}{N}}{N} \tag{4.11}$$

In using the computational formula for the variance it is essential that you make a distinction between ΣX^2 and $(\Sigma X)^2$. The first term involves squaring each raw score, then summing these squared values. The second term instructs you first to sum the raw scores and then to square the total. These two procedures yield different results, so do not confuse them. If you ever obtain a negative value for the variance while using a computational formula, it means that you have failed to apply these procedures properly. An application of the formulas for the sample variance (4.7 and 4.10) is shown in Box 4.2.

Standard Deviation

There is a problem with the variance as a measure of variability, and this problem stems from the fact that it is based on the average *squared* deviation from the mean. The deviations are squared, so the relevant unit of measurement is squared as well. For example, if the variable being measured were seconds required to solve a problem, deviations from the mean would also be measured in seconds. When we square these deviations to produce the variance, however, the unit of measurement becomes *seconds squared*. It would be much better to be able to deal with seconds rather than seconds squared. We can do so by taking the square root of the variance, which returns the measurement to the original units (seconds in our example). The square root of the variance is called the *standard deviation*, and we symbolize it in the case of a population with σ. The sample standard deviation is represented by the letter *s*. The definitional and computational formulas for the population and sample variance (Formulas 4.4, 4.5, 4.7, 4.8, 4.9, 4.10, and 4.11) are changed into formulas for the standard deviation by adding a square root sign. The definitional formula for the sample standard deviation is

$$s = \sqrt{\frac{\Sigma(X - \overline{X})^2}{N - 1}} \tag{4.12}$$

Box 4.2   **Example Application of Formulas for the Sample Variance**

Consider the data obtained in a sample of students' opinions concerning the fast-food restaurant. The ratings are 2, 3, 3, 10, and 10. The mean for these ratings is 5.60. We can use Formula 4.7 to compute the sample variance in the following way:

$$s^2 = \frac{(2 - 5.6)^2 + (3 - 5.6)^2 + (3 - 5.6)^2 + (10 - 5.6)^2 + (10 - 5.6)^2}{5 - 1}$$

$$= \frac{12.96 + 6.76 + 6.76 + 19.36 + 19.36}{4} = 16.30$$

Alternatively, we can apply Formula 4.10 by using the following procedure:

X	X^2
2	4
3	9
3	9
10	100
10	100
$\Sigma X = 28$	$\Sigma X^2 = 222$

$$s^2 = \frac{222 - \dfrac{(28)^2}{5}}{5 - 1} = \frac{222 - 156.8}{4} = 16.30$$

and the computational formula is

$$s = \sqrt{\frac{\Sigma X^2 - \dfrac{(\Sigma X)^2}{N}}{N - 1}} \tag{4.13}$$

Working from the example computation given in Box 4.2, we have a sample variance of 16.30 for the ratings obtained from students. The standard deviation would be

$$\sqrt{16.30} = 4.04$$

Both variance and standard deviation are measures of average distance between the mean and the scores in a distribution. The advantage of the standard deviation is that it is a measure of distance in the original units of measurement. The standard deviation of 4.04, for example, refers to 4.04 rating points. We can then use the standard deviation as a unit of measurement.

For example, suppose that a normal distribution of IQ scores has a mean of 100 and a standard deviation of 15. A score of 130 is 30 IQ points from the

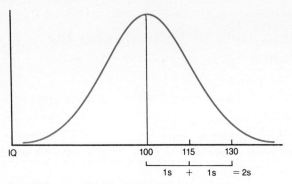

Figure 4.6 A hypothetical distribution of IQ scores showing the distance between an IQ score and the mean in terms of standard deviations. In this distribution each standard deviation is equivalent to 15 IQ points.

mean. This distance could also be expressed in terms of how many standard deviations there are between the score of 130 and the mean of 100. The answer is 2 standard deviations, since there are 15 points in a single standard deviation (see Figure 4.6). The standard deviation does not have a very simple, intuitive meaning beyond the notion of a measure of distance from the mean. But we will add more meaning to this concept in the next chapter when we consider its role in dealing with the normal distribution. Another computational example involving the mean, variance, and standard deviation is presented in Box 4.3.

4.4 TRANSFORMED SCORES

A researcher occasionally is interested in transforming a set of scores in some simple manner. For example, data may be collected as the number of items correctly answered on a test, but the researcher wishes to express the scores in terms of the percentage correct. In this situation the transformation consists of dividing each raw score by the maximum possible score and then multiplying by 100. Now suppose that you are reading an article in which the mean and standard deviation for a group of subjects are given in terms of the number of items correct. It might be useful to have this summary in terms of percentages, perhaps for the purpose of comparing the data with other studies that have reported data as percentages. Fortunately, the mean, standard deviation, and variance change in predictable ways when simple transformations are applied to raw data. Therefore, given the total number of items on the test, you could easily compute the mean and standard deviation in terms of the percentage correct rather than the number correct.

First, consider how the mean, variance, and standard deviation are affected when a constant is added to each score. (Note that the constant could be less than zero, so this operation amounts to subtracting a value.) The mean changes by an amount equal to the constant, whereas the variance and

Box 4.3　**Example Application of Computational Formulas for Sample Mean, Variance, and Standard Deviation**

Suppose that a group of seven clients visiting a clinic for the treatment of depression are asked to keep track during the next week of the number of times they encountered events that were sufficiently humorous to make them laugh. The scores for these clients were 0, 0, 2, 3, 3, 6, and 12.

To compute the mean, variance, and standard deviation by using computational formulas, we begin by obtaining some preliminary values.

$$\Sigma X = 0 + 0 + 2 + 3 + 3 + 6 + 12 = 26$$

$$\Sigma X^2 = 0^2 + 0^2 + 2^2 + 3^2 + 3^2 + 6^2 + 12^2$$

$$= 0 + 0 + 4 + 9 + 9 + 36 + 144 = 202$$

$$N = 7$$

These values can be used to compute the desired descriptive statistics. Formula 4.1 is used for the mean, and Formula 4.10 is used for the variance.

$$\overline{X} = \frac{26}{7} = 3.71$$

$$s^2 = \frac{202 - \frac{(26)^2}{7}}{7 - 1} = \frac{202 - 96.57}{6} = 17.57$$

$$s = \sqrt{17.57} = 4.19$$

standard deviation are not changed. For example, suppose that a constant of 2 were added to each of the five rating scores given in Box 4.2. The new mean would be

$$\overline{X} = \frac{(2 + 2) + (3 + 2) + (3 + 2) + (10 + 2) + (10 + 2)}{5} = 7.60,$$

and the new variance would be

$$\frac{(4 - 7.6)^2 + (5 - 7.6)^2 + (5 - 7.6)^2 + (12 - 7.6)^2 + (12 - 7.6)^2}{4}$$

$$= 16.30.$$

You should be able to see that adding the constant increased the original mean by an amount equal to the constant, and that the variance (and, hence, the standard deviation) was not changed at all. In fact, this is always the result when a constant is added to each and every score in a distribution. The proof of this claim is presented in Proof 4.4.

Now consider what happens when each score in a distribution is multiplied by a constant. (Note that division by a constant is the same as multiplication by the reciprocal of the constant, so if each score were divided by 2 an equivalent result would be obtained by multiplying each score by 1/2.) The mean of the transformed scores will be equal to the mean of the raw scores multiplied by the constant. The variance will be equal to the variance of the raw scores multiplied by the constant squared, and the standard deviation will be equal to the standard deviation of the raw scores multiplied by the absolute value of the constant. If the students' ratings from Box 4.2 each were multiplied by 2, the new mean would be

$$\frac{4 + 6 + 6 + 20 + 20}{5} = 11.20$$

and the new variance would be

$$\frac{(4 - 11.2)^2 + (6 - 11.2)^2 + (6 - 11.2)^2 + (20 - 11.2)^2 + (20 - 11.2)^2}{4}$$

$$= 65.20.$$

The new standard deviation would then be 8.07. Multiplying each score by the constant of 2 produced a new mean that is twice the size of the original mean—that is, the new mean is equal to the constant times the old mean. The standard deviation was changed in almost the same way; the new standard deviation is equal to the old standard deviation times the absolute value of the constant. The new variance is equal to the old variance times the constant squared. The proof that these changes will always occur regardless of the value of the constant is shown in Proof 4.5.

SUMMARY

The major concepts introduced in this chapter involve methods of summarizing large data sets in terms of two important characteristics: central tendency and variability. A measure of central tendency is used to summarize, in a single number, the most typical or representative value in a distribution. Three measures of central tendency were introduced, and each is applicable under certain circumstances. The most commonly used measure is the mean, and in later chapters we devote a great deal of attention to more sophisticated statistical procedures involving the mean.

The degree to which the measure of central tendency is representative of a set of scores is indicated by measures of variability. All of the measures discussed in this chapter are based on the distance between scores and should be interpreted in this manner. The most important methods of measuring variability involve computing squared deviations from the mean. The mean of the squared deviations from the mean is the variance. The standard deviation is the square root of the variance and is useful because it measures variability in terms of original units of measurement rather than squared units. Both the variance and standard deviation can be represented by definitional and computational formulas. Definitional formulas serve as a reminder of the meaning of a quantity, but computational formulas are easier to apply in practice and it is recommended that these be used whenever possible.

The mean, variance, and standard deviation behave in a predictable manner when scores in a data set are transformed in simple ways, such as adding or multiplying by a constant. They are used in the development of most of the statistical analyses to be introduced in later chapters.

KEY WORDS

central tendency	biased estimate
mode	unbiased estimate
bimodal	mean square
median	sum of squares
mean	degrees of freedom
deviation score	standard deviation
open-ended distribution	definitional formula
variability	computational formula
range	transformed score
variance	

PROBLEMS

1 Working with the following set of scores, obtain mean, median, and mode: 3, 5, 3, 6, 8, 1, 3, 4, 2, 2, 4, 5, 6, 7, 5, 9, 5, 7, 7, 5, 6, 4, 5, 5, 4, 6, 4.

2 Plot a frequency polygon of the data given in Problem 1. Use raw score values rather than class interval midpoints on the X-axis. Draw vertical lines on the polygon to indicate the position of each of the three measures of central tendency.

3 Repeat Problems 1 and 2 for the following data set: 11, 5, 9, 3, 5, 3, 7, 6, 4, 3, 3, 1, 8, 12, 4, 2, 2, 4, 3, 2, 10, 4, 1, 3, 4, 5. For which data set were the measures of central tendency more similar to one another? Why do the three measures agree with one another more in one data set than in the other?

4 Carry out the following steps by using these data: 9, 2, 12, 8, 4. (a) Find the mean and median. (b) Calculate $\Sigma(X - \overline{X})$. (c) Find $\Sigma(X - \overline{X})^2$ and $\Sigma(X - \text{Median})^2$ and determine which of these two values is smaller.

5 For each of the two data sets that follow, calculate the range, variance, and standard deviation. Assume that these data represent samples, not populations.

Set A: 8, 12, 3, 9, 8, 13, 2, 14, 15, 4, 9, 16, 8, 1, 5, 9
Set B: 12, 5, 1, 4, 16, 13, 13, 1, 4, 5, 12, 16, 4, 13, 16, 1

The two data sets differ in amount of variability. Which measures of variability are more sensitive to this difference?

6 Using the random number table in Appendix III, randomly draw five samples, each consisting of four single-digit numbers. Once you have five samples of size 4, select five more samples, each consisting of ten randomly drawn single-digit numbers. For each sample, obtain the range and variance. For samples of size 4, obtain the mean value for range and the mean value for variance. Do the same for samples of size 10. Take note of how much the mean value of the range changes as you go from samples of size 4 to samples of size 10. Compare this change with the change observed in the mean value of variance as the sample size increases. Which measure of variability appears to change more as the sample size increases?

7 For the following data obtain the variance, first using the definitional formula for sample variance, then using the computational formula: 12, 9, 15, 6, 4, 7. Are your answers the same? If not, why not?

8 Recall that the standard deviation is a measure of distance in terms of the original units of measurement. Suppose that the following data represent a sample of IQ scores: 107, 104, 100, 102, 108, 103. Find the mean IQ score and the standard deviation for this sample; then determine how many of the scores in the sample are more than 1 standard deviation above the mean. How many scores are no more than 1 standard deviation away from (above or below) the mean?

9 What would a set of scores with variance equal to zero be like?

10 Find the mean and standard deviation of the following sample of data: 10, 3, 13, 9, 5. Transform these scores by subtracting a constant so that the mean of the transformed scores will be zero. Is this constant equal to one of the statistics that you computed from the original scores? List the new scores and find their standard deviation. Is it different from the standard deviation of the original scores? Now transform these scores by dividing by a constant so that the standard deviation of the new scores will be equal to 1. Is the constant equal to one of the statistics that you computed from the original scores?

PROOFS

Proof 4.1 PROOF THAT THE SUM OF DEVIATION SCORES IN ANY DATA SET IS ZERO

$$\Sigma(X - \overline{X}) = \Sigma X - \Sigma \overline{X} = \Sigma X - N\overline{X} = \Sigma X - N\frac{\Sigma X}{N}$$

$$= \Sigma X - \Sigma X = 0$$

Proof 4.2 PROOF THAT $\Sigma(X - v)^2$ IS MINIMIZED WHEN $v = \overline{X}$.

Our goal is to show that if any value other than $\overline{X}$ (represented by $\overline{X} + c$, where c is any nonzero value) is used in the formula $\Sigma(X - \overline{X})^2$, the sum of squares will be greater than when $\overline{X}$ is used. Therefore, we need to show that

$$\Sigma(X - \overline{X})^2 < \Sigma[X - (\overline{X} + c)]^2$$

We begin with the formula on the right side of the inequality and show how it can be changed to make more easily a comparison with the left side of the inequality.

$$\Sigma[X - (\overline{X} + c)]^2 = \Sigma[X - \overline{X} - c]^2 = \Sigma[(X - \overline{X}) - c]^2$$

$$= \Sigma[(X - \overline{X})^2 - 2(X - \overline{X})c + c^2] = \Sigma(X - \overline{X})^2 - \Sigma2(X - \overline{X})c + \Sigma c^2$$

$$= \Sigma(X - \overline{X})^2 - 2c\Sigma(X - \overline{X}) + \Sigma c^2 = \Sigma(X - \overline{X})^2 - 2c\Sigma(X - \overline{X}) + Nc^2$$

$$= \Sigma(X - \overline{X})^2 - 2c(0) + Nc^2 = \Sigma(X - \overline{X})^2 + Nc^2$$

You can now see that the value we have just derived must always be larger than $\Sigma(X - \overline{X})^2$ since Nc^2 will always be greater than zero, even when c is negative, because c is squared. So no matter which value we pick, if it is even a tiny bit different from $\overline{X}$, the sum of squared deviations will be greater than what would be obtained by using $\overline{X}$. In fact, the larger the absolute value of c, the greater will be the sum of squared deviations from $\overline{X} + c$.

Proof 4.3 PROOF THAT FORMULAS 4.7 AND 4.10 ARE ARITHMETICALLY EQUIVALENT

Since both formulas have the term $N - 1$ in the denominator, it is not necessary to work with this part of the formulas. All we need do is show that the numerator (sum of squares) is the same in the two cases. We begin with our definitional formula for the sum of squares and show that the computational formula can be derived from it.

$$\Sigma(X - \overline{X})^2 = \Sigma(X^2 - 2X\overline{X} + \overline{X}^2)$$

$$= \Sigma X^2 - \Sigma2X\overline{X} + \Sigma\overline{X}^2 = \Sigma X^2 - 2\overline{X}\Sigma X + \Sigma\overline{X}^2$$

$$= \Sigma X^2 - 2\overline{X}\Sigma X + N\overline{X}^2 = \Sigma X^2 - 2\overline{X}N\overline{X} + N\overline{X}^2$$

$$= \Sigma X^2 - 2N\overline{X}^2 + N\overline{X}^2 = \Sigma X^2 - N\overline{X}^2$$

$$= \Sigma X^2 - N\frac{(\Sigma X)^2}{N^2}$$

$$= \Sigma X^2 - \frac{(\Sigma X)^2}{N}$$

Proof 4.4 THE EFFECTS OF ADDING A CONSTANT TO EACH SCORE ON THE MEAN, VARIANCE, AND STANDARD DEVIATION

We can represent the addition of a constant to each X score by writing $X + c$, where c represents the constant. The formula for the mean of these new scores can then be rewritten by using $X + c$ instead of X and simplified.

$$\frac{\Sigma(X + c)}{N} = \frac{\Sigma X + \Sigma c}{N} = \frac{\Sigma X + Nc}{N} = \frac{\Sigma X}{N} + \frac{Nc}{N} = \frac{\Sigma X}{N} + c = \overline{X} + c$$

With the new mean available we can rewrite and simplify the expression for the variance of the transformed scores.

$$\frac{\Sigma[(X + c) - (\overline{X} + c)]^2}{N - 1} = \frac{\Sigma(X + c - \overline{X} - c)^2}{N - 1}$$

$$= \frac{\Sigma(X - \overline{X} + c - c)^2}{N - 1} = \frac{\Sigma(X - \overline{X})^2}{N - 1}$$

Since the variance is unchanged, the standard deviation will also be unaffected by adding a constant to each score.

Proof 4.5   THE EFFECTS OF MULTIPLYING EACH SCORE BY A CONSTANT ON THE MEAN, VARIANCE, AND STANDARD DEVIATION

We can represent the multiplication of each X score by a constant by writing Xc, where c represents the constant. The formula for the mean of these new scores can then be rewritten by using Xc instead of X and simplified.

$$\frac{\Sigma(Xc)}{N} = \frac{c\Sigma X}{N} = c\overline{X}$$

With the new mean available we can rewrite and simplify the expression for the variance of the transformed scores.

$$\frac{\Sigma(Xc - \overline{X}c)^2}{N - 1} = \frac{\Sigma c^2(X - \overline{X})^2}{N - 1}$$

$$= \frac{c^2\Sigma(X - \overline{X})^2}{N - 1} = c^2\frac{\Sigma(X - \overline{X})^2}{N - 1}$$

$$= c^2 s^2$$

Since the standard deviation is the square root of the variance, the new standard deviation will be equal to cs, the constant times the old standard deviation.

Chapter 5

Standardized Scores and the Normal Distribution

5.1   INTRODUCTION

When we try to evaluate some characteristic of a new object or event we usually do so by comparing it to some other similar objects or events with which we are already familiar. For example, suppose you have just finished reading Tolstoy's novel *The Cossacks* and someone were to ask you how well you liked it. A meaningful answer, at least to someone familiar with Tolstoy's work, might be "more than *Anna Karenina* but not as much as *War and Peace.*"

Interpreting the value of someone's score on a variable depends on a very similar process. When an executive of a company makes a decision about whether to hire a new employee, the applicant's score on some psychological test may be considered. The raw score is not very informative by itself, but the executive's knowledge of how well previous applicants have scored on the test provides a useful guideline in evaluating the applicant's potential. If the applicant's score is very high in comparison to previous applicants' scores, the executive might be wise to hire that applicant. In this chapter we consider a method of describing a score in relation to other scores in a distribution. In addition, we consider a special application of this method that can be used when a set of scores forms a bell-shaped distribution.

5.2   STANDARDIZED SCORES

An individual's raw score is not meaningful unless we have some kind of background against which it can be compared. When a student is told that he or she received 42 points on an examination, very little information has been conveyed. A score of 42 will take on much more meaning when we are told that the maximum possible score was 50. That is, the student received 84 percent of the possible points. To the student who is well acquainted with grading procedures, this test score is very encouraging; scores of this magnitude typically are not obtained by many students and so are rewarded with high letter grades. The key idea here is that because of past experience we assume that 84 percent is a good score. But it is entirely possible that the test was very easy and that most students obtained scores higher than 84 percent. For example, the student would not be in a very desirable position if the class mean were 97 percent. In this case, the score of 84 percent takes on quite a different meaning.

To avoid possible ambiguities or to overcome the complete absence of background information about scores on a variable, it often is desirable to transform raw scores into a more informative measure. Transforming scores into percentages will not do, as the previous example demonstrates. Further, there are many circumstances in which transforming scores to a percentage of some total is not meaningful (e.g., when measuring time required to perform some task). One useful transformation involves converting raw scores into percentile ranks, as we did in Chapter 3. In this chapter we will discuss a more general approach that involves transforming raw scores into *standardized scores.* This is a more general method because, as we demonstrate later in this chapter, under certain circumstances standardized scores can be easily used to obtain percentile ranks.

There are a number of methods of producing standardized scores, but they are fundamentally similar and the end products provide exactly the same information. A standardized score tells us immediately how far a score is above or below the mean of the set of scores from which it was taken (e.g., class of students).

z-scores

A very important standardized score, one that will appear again in later chapters, is the **z-score.** This standardized score is so prominent in statistics that it is often referred to as a *standard score.* The *z*-score, like all standardized scores, is based on comparing a raw score, X, to the mean, $\overline{X}$, of the set of scores from which the raw score was taken. Specifically, the *z*-score is a measure of distance between a raw score and the relevant mean, expressed in standard deviation units.

To calculate a *z*-score from a raw score, we begin by subtracting the mean from the raw score to produce a deviation score. A deviation score is a measure, in raw score units, of a raw score's distance from the mean. The deviation score is converted into standard deviation units by dividing it by the number of raw score points in a standard deviation.

As an example, suppose that a computer microchip manufacturing company administers a psychological test to all job applicants. The mean score of the applicants who have taken the test since it was first used is 60, and the standard deviation of these raw scores is 8 ($\mu = 60$, $\sigma = 8$). From the company's point of view a higher score indicates a more desirable psychological profile than a lower score. The applicant currently under consideration obtained a score of 72. This score is 12 points above the mean ($72 - 60 = 12$). If we were to express this distance in standard deviations instead of raw score points, we would have $12/8 = 1.50$, since there are 8 points in each standard deviation. We can now say that the applicant's score is 1.5 standard deviations above the mean. The *z*-score, then, is 1.50. The formula that symbolizes these steps, assuming that we are working with a population of scores, is

$$z = \frac{X - \mu}{\sigma} \tag{5.1}$$

We can use Formula 5.1 to transform the raw score of 72 into a *z*-score as follows:

$$z = \frac{72 - 60}{8} = \frac{12}{8} = 1.50$$

In cases where we are working with a sample drawn from a population, the formula for the z-score transformation is

$$z = \frac{X - \overline{X}}{s} \tag{5.2}$$

---

z-SCORE: A standard score that expresses the distance between a raw score and the mean of a distribution in standard deviation units.

Now consider an applicant who obtains a score of 46 on the psychological test. This applicant's z-score can be computed as follows:

$$z = \frac{46 - 60}{8} = \frac{-14}{8} = -1.75$$

The second applicant's score is further from the mean (1.75 standard deviations) than the first applicant's score (1.50 standard deviations), but the negative value indicates that it is below the mean. The z-score, then, provides information about how far an individual's score is from the mean, and the sign indicates whether the score is above or below the mean. Which of the following two people is more likely to be hired: someone with a z-score of −0.50 or someone with a z-score of −2.00?

Not only can we use Formulas 5.1 or 5.2 to transform a raw score into a z-score, but given a z-score, we can also use them to find out a person's raw score. For example, consider the z-score of −.50 just given. How would we go about finding this person's raw score?

We know that the raw score is .50 standard deviations below the mean. This distance can be converted to a measurement in raw score units by multiplying the measurement in standard deviation units (−.50) by the number of raw score points in each standard deviation (8). This operation produces −4, indicating that the raw score is 4 raw score points below the mean. Since the mean is 60, and the raw score is 4 points below that, the raw score must be 60 − 4 = 56.

These steps can be summarized by altering Formulas 5.1 and 5.2 to produce formulas that allow us to find a raw score from a z-score. For a population, the formula is

$$X = \mu + \sigma(z) \tag{5.3}$$

and for a sample the formula is

$$X = \overline{X} + s(z). \tag{5.4}$$

The steps involved in generating Formula 5.4 are shown in Proof 5.1 at the end of this chapter. Exactly the same steps would be used to generate Formula 5.3.

A Distribution of z-scores

One could transform each and every raw score in a distribution into a z-score by using Formula 5.2 (or Formula 5.1 in the case of a population of scores). The set of z-scores produced by this process would have a number of important characteristics. In fact, these characteristics would hold for any complete distribution of z-scores.

First, the mean of any distribution of z-scores is zero. Second, the variance and standard deviation of any distribution of z-scores is 1. These two facts are proven in Proof 5.2. Finally, the distribution of z-scores will have exactly the same shape as the distribution of raw scores from which they were derived. For example, if a set of raw scores forms a negatively skewed distribution, the corresponding z-scores will form a distribution with the same negative skew. The preservation of the shape of the distribution raw scores that occurs when z-scores are computed is demonstrated with a small set of scores in Box 5.1.

The shape of the raw score distribution is preserved because the transformation of raw scores to z-scores has three important properties. One is that two equivalent raw scores will have equivalent z-scores. This result must occur because the same formula is applied to all raw scores. Second, if one raw score is greater than another, its z-score will be greater than the other's. This effect results from the fact that for given values of $\overline{X}$ and s (or μ and σ), Formula 5.2 (or Formula 5.1) will produce larger z-scores for larger X values.

Finally, the z-score transformation maintains equal intervals that are present among the raw scores. For example, notice that the difference between the following two pairs of raw scores is the same—the members of each pair are separated by equal intervals, namely, 4 raw score points.

$$X_1 = 17, X_2 = 13 \qquad X_3 = 9, X_4 = 5$$

$$X_1 - X_2 = 17 - 13 = 4 \qquad X_3 - X_4 = 9 - 5 = 4$$

We will convert these raw scores to z-scores, letting $\overline{X} = 12$ and $s = 5$. The intervals between the members of each pair of z-scores are equal, just as the intervals between the corresponding raw scores are equal.

$$z_1 = 1.00, z_2 = 0.20 \qquad z_3 = -0.60, z_4 = -1.40$$

$$z_1 - z_2 = 1.00 - 0.20 = 0.80 \qquad z_3 - z_4 = -0.60 - (-1.40)$$

$$= 0.80$$

Other Standardized Scores

The use of z-scores provides a ready interpretation of an individual's standing with respect to a known reference group. A problem with z-scores in some practical applications, however, is the fact that there are positive and negative values. For example, imagine if we expressed scores on an intelligence test in terms of z-scores and assigned those people who scored below the

Box 5.1

Demonstration that Distribution of z-scores Follows the Distribution of the Original Raw Scores

A set of ten raw scores and their corresponding z-scores are listed below. To the right are frequency polygons based on (1) the raw scores and (2) the resulting z-scores. Notice that the negative skew present in the distribution of raw scores appears in the distribution of z-scores as well.

X	$X - \overline{X}$	z
1	-3	-1.92
2	-2	-1.28
3	-1	-0.64
4	0	0.00
4	0	0.00
5	1	0.64
5	1	0.64
5	1	0.64
5	1	0.64
6	2	1.28

$\overline{X} = 4$
$s = 1.56$

You should verify that $\overline{X}_z = 0$ and that $s_z = 1$, within a small amount of rounding error.

mean a negative value! For this reason many standardized test scores, including intelligence tests and admissions tests such as the Scholastic Aptitude Test (SAT) and the Graduate Record Examination (GRE), are expressed by a standardized score that is slightly different from the z-score.

These standardized scores are set up so that the mean and standard deviation will be equal to arbitrarily chosen values. In the case of some intelligence tests, for example, a mean of 100 and a standard deviation of 15 have been chosen. For the SAT and GRE a mean of 500 and a standard deviation of 100 are used. A set of standardized scores with an arbitrary mean and standard deviation can be obtained by first converting each individual's raw score to a z-score, producing a distribution with a mean of zero and a standard deviation of 1. Suppose we wanted to produce a mean of 100 and a standard deviation of 15 from these z-scores. Recall that multiplying each score in a set by a constant will produce a new set of scores with a standard deviation equal to the original standard deviation times the constant. If we multiply each member of a set of z-scores by 15, the standard deviation of the resulting scores will be $1(15) = 15$.

We now want to produce a mean of 100. First, what has happened to the mean of the scores as a result of multiplying each z-score by 15? Remember that under these circumstances the new mean is equal to the previous mean times the constant: $0(15) = 0$. So the mean is still zero. If we wish to set the mean at 100, we need only add a constant of 100 to each score (recall that this operation produces a mean that is equal to the previous mean plus the constant). The addition of a constant does not change the standard deviation, so we now have a set of scores that has a mean of 100 and a standard deviation of 15. In summary, this result was accomplished by multiplying each person's z-score by 15, then adding 100. In general, to obtain a standardized score for each member of a population, such that the set of standardized scores has a desired mean (μ') and standard deviation (σ'), we apply the following formula:

$$\text{standardized score} = z(\sigma') + \mu' \tag{5.5}$$

In the case of a sample of scores, the formula for obtaining standardized scores with a desired mean $(\overline{X}')$ and standard deviation (s') is

$$\text{standardized score} = z(s') + \overline{X}' \tag{5.6}$$

If someone were to obtain a raw score on our intelligence test that was 2 standard deviations above the mean (i.e., $z = 2.00$), this person would have a standardized intelligence score of $15(2) + 100 = 130$.

You should note that transformations obtained through Formula 5.5 or Formula 5.6 behave just like z-score transformations, in that the frequency polygon of the resulting standardized scores will have the same shape as the frequency polygon of the original raw scores.

5.3   NORMAL DISTRIBUTION AND z-SCORES

About 100 years ago Sir Francis Galton (1889) noted that many naturally occurring physical and psychological variables form distributions that are shaped very much like the bell-shaped normal distribution.[1] This observation contributed to the development of a large number of statistical procedures designed for use when the distribution of data is approximately normal. It is important to realize that in practice data rarely, if ever, follow precisely the

---

[1]For a recent discussion of Galton's data, see Johnson et al. (1985).

normal distribution. Often, however, scores are sufficiently close to the normal distribution for us to apply statistical procedures intended for normal distributions without sacrificing much accuracy.

Standard Normal Distribution

Each distribution of scores that is approximately normal in shape can be transformed, just by changing the raw scores to *z*-scores, into a special normal distribution that we refer to as the *standard normal distribution.* Consider what would happen if each member of a normally distributed set of raw scores were converted to a *z*-score. As shown earlier, the new set of scores would have a mean of zero, a standard deviation of 1, and would be normally distributed. The normal distribution that would be produced by this set of *z*-scores is presented in Figure 5.1.

Now consider a different set of normally distributed scores, and suppose that each score is converted to a *z*-score. Again we would have a normal distribution with a mean of zero and a standard deviation equal to 1. This distribution of *z*-scores also would approximate the normal distribution shown in Figure 5.1.

In fact, *any* normally distributed set of raw scores that is converted to *z*-scores will produce this same distribution. For this reason, a normal distribution with a mean of zero and a standard deviation of 1 is called the standard normal distribution. The standard normal distribution has a number of properties that inform us about the proportion or number of individuals in a distribution who obtain scores within specific ranges of *z*-score values. To understand how this distribution works, it is necessary to have a clear idea of the relationship between the area under a histogram or frequency polygon and the proportion of scores in the distribution.

Area Under Histograms and Frequency Polygons

When histograms and frequency polygons were introduced in Chapter 3, we showed that the height of the figure at any *X* value or interval represented

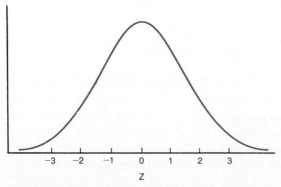

Figure 5.1   The standard normal distribution produced by transforming any set of normally distributed scores into *z*-scores.

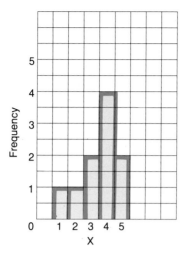

Figure 5.2 Histogram for a set of ten scores, with background grid to calculate area.

the number of scores equal to that value or in the interval. The area enclosed under a histogram or frequency polygon can also represent frequency.

For example, consider the histogram in Figure 5.2, based on the following ten scores: 1, 2, 3, 3, 4, 4, 4, 4, 5, 5. Using the background grid in this figure you can see that the total area covered by the histogram is 20 square units. Furthermore, notice that the bar representing the value of 1 occupies 2 square units, the bar for 2 is 2 square units, the bar for 3 is 4 square units, and so on. In Table 5.1 we show that the proportion of a histogram's total area that is occupied by a bar is equal to the proportion of scores in the distribution that have the value represented by the bar.

It is also true that if we consider two or more values, the same general principle holds. So, for example, if we consider the proportion of the histogram area occupied by the bars representing scores of 3 and 4, we have 12 square units out of a total of 20, which is a proportion of .60. Since there are

Table 5.1 PROPORTIONS OF AREA UNDER THE HISTOGRAM IN FIGURE 5.1 AND CORRESPONDING PROPORTIONS OF SCORES IN THE DATA SET

X	Area in square units	Proportion	Frequency of score	Proportion
1	2	2/20 = .10	1	1/10 = .10
2	2	2/20 = .10	1	1/10 = .10
3	4	4/20 = .20	2	2/10 = .20
4	8	8/20 = .40	4	4/10 = .40
5	4	4/20 = .20	2	2/10 = .20
	___		___	
Total = 20			Total = 10	

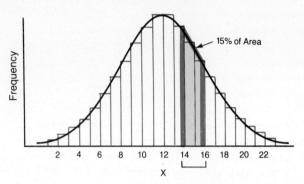

Figure 5.3 Frequency polygon approximated by a series of thin bars. The shaded area represents 15 percent of the scores in the distribution.

six individuals with scores of 3 or 4, the relevant proportion of scores is 6/10 = .60.

The principle we have just introduced also holds for frequency polygons. To see this relationship it is necessary only to consider the polygon as made up of a series of very thin bars. This procedure provides a good approximation to a smooth polygon, as shown in Figure 5.3. In this case we have shaded an area (including a number of bars) that is equivalent to .15 of the total area under the polygon. Thus, 15 percent of the scores in the distribution are in the range indicated on the X-axis.

5.4 z-SCORES AND AREAS OF THE NORMAL DISTRIBUTION

In general, the proportion of area under a histogram or frequency polygon that lies within some interval is equal to the proportion of scores in the distribution that lies within that interval. This fact brings us to the issue of why we cannot consider the height of the theoretical normal distribution to be equal to the frequency of the corresponding value of X. The normal distribution is based on the assumption that the underlying variable is *continuous*, which means that theoretically each score could be measured to an arbitrary degree of precision. For example, in measuring time taken for subjects to read a page of text it would be possible to get measurements precise to the nearest second, millisecond (1/1000 second), or beyond.

With such precise measurements it is quite unlikely that even one person in the distribution would obtain a score exactly equal to, for example, 48.00000 seconds. Therefore, we do not treat the height of a distribution based on a continuous variable as the frequency of the corresponding X value. Instead, the height of the distribution at any point is called *density*, and it is closely related to the relative frequency of scores in some interval centered at X. The greater the density, the greater the proportion of scores in the distribution falling in that interval.

For instance, suppose we have a normal distribution of time (measured to the nearest second) taken by high school students to read a page of text. The height of the distribution of reading times at the point where $X = 48$ seconds does not represent the number or proportion of scores equal to 48. Rather, the height of the distribution at that point is related to the proportion of scores in the distribution that is in any small interval centered on that point, such as 47.5 to 48.5.

This relationship is illustrated in Figure 5.4. Notice that the highest point of the distribution is at $X = 60$ and that a one-second interval centered on 60 (59.5 to 60.5) has been shaded. This interval clearly occupies more area under the curve than does the one centered on $X = 48$ (i.e., it has greater density), even though both intervals are of equal width. We can conclude that the greater the density associated with an X value, the greater the proportion of the distribution that falls into an interval centered on that value.

Area and z-scores

The normal distribution follows a very precise mathematical function, so we can specify accurately the proportion of scores that lies within specific regions of the distribution. It is best to define these regions in terms of z-scores because any set of normally distributed data can be transformed to the standard normal distribution.

According to the mathematical definition of the normal distribution, 50 percent of the scores in the distribution fall above the mean ($z = 0$) and 50 percent are below the mean. The definition also specifies that .3413, or 34.13 percent, of the scores in a normal distribution fall between the mean and 1 standard deviation above the mean (i.e., between z-scores of 0.00 and 1.00). The normal distribution is symmetrical, so it should be no surprise that another .3413 of the scores lies between the mean and 1 standard deviation

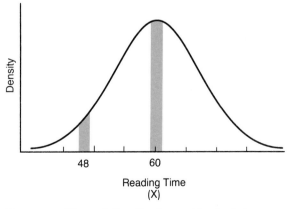

Figure 5.4 Normal distribution, with shaded areas representing density for two different X values.

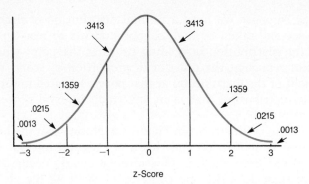

Figure 5.5 Frequency polygon for a set of normally distributed scores, with areas corresponding to whole-value z-scores.

below the mean (z-scores of 0.00 and −1.00). These areas and a few others are illustrated in Figure 5.5.

The approximate areas lying between each pair of whole-number z-scores can serve as reasonable benchmarks for quick evaluations of z-scores. For example, about 34 percent of scores are between z-scores of 0 and 1 or 0 and −1, about 14 percent are between z-scores of 1 and 2 or −1 and −2, and so on.

Converting any approximately normal distribution of raw scores to z-scores will produce a distribution that is very much like that in Figure 5.5— even for distributions based on discrete rather than continuous variables. Therefore, the facts illustrated in Figure 5.5 will hold for *all* such distributions, and those facts give us a powerful analytic tool. To make full use of this tool, however, we must have information about regions defined by any z-score, not just z-scores with integer values.

This information is provided in Table B in Appendix III. Table B consists of groups of three columns of numbers. The first column in each group represents the values of a series of z-scores beginning with 0.00 and increasing by increments of .01.

In the second column of Table B are values indicating the proportion of area under the normal curve that falls between the mean and the z-score given in the first column. For example, the z-score of 0.00 is, of course, the mean, so none of the area (.0000) lies between the mean and this z-score. For a z-score of 0.50, .1915 of the area under the normal curve falls between it and the mean; for a z-score of 1.00, .3413 of the area falls between the mean and this point (also shown in Figure 5.5).

The third column in the group represents the proportion of area that lies beyond the z-score (between the z-score and the nearest tail of the distribution). For a z-score of 0.00, half of the distribution (.5000) lies beyond, whereas for a z-score of 0.50, .3085 of the area falls beyond. Figure 5.6(a) indicates the areas represented by the columns of Table B for a z-score of 0.50.

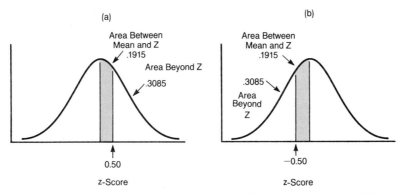

Figure 5.6   Areas under the standard normal distribution defined by z-scores of 0.50 and −0.50.

You should notice that for any z-score, the area between the mean and z (column 3) and the area beyond z (column 4) sum to .5000. This result occurs because these two sections account for all of the area under the distribution that falls on one side of the mean. The other half of the distribution falls on the other side of the mean.

You will not find any negative z-scores in Table B. The reason is that the normal distribution is symmetrical, so whatever holds for a positive z-score also will be true for a negative z-score. In the case of the column representing the area beyond a z-score, however, remember that the term *beyond* refers to the region between the z-score and the *nearest* tail of the distribution. In the case of a positive z-score, it means the area to the right of z, and in the case of a negative z-score, it means the area to the left of z. These features are illustrated in Figures 5.6(a) and (b), where relevant areas for z-scores of 0.50 and −0.50 are shown.

Using Scores to Find Areas

When a set of scores approximates the normal distribution, we can use Table B to find information about proportions of scores that fall within specific ranges of score values. You should keep in mind, however, that the accuracy of this information depends on how well the distribution of raw data fits the normal distribution.

To use Table B we must assume that each of the raw scores is transformed into a z-score to produce the standard normal distribution. Suppose, for example, that applicants for jobs at the microchip company mentioned at the beginning of this chapter obtained scores on the psychological test that were normally distributed, as shown in Figure 5.7, with a mean of 60 and a standard deviation of 8. In Figure 5.7 we show the raw scores that correspond to the mean and to 1, 2, or 3 standard deviations above and below the mean. If all scores were transformed to z-scores, we would have a new normal dis-

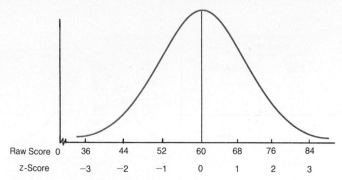

Figure 5.7 Normally distributed scores on a psychological test, with raw scores and corresponding z-scores.

tribution with z-score values instead of raw score values, as shown in Figure 5.7. This is the standard normal distribution.

We can now use the fact that our transformed test scores follow the standard normal distribution to determine the proportion of the area under the distribution that falls within certain score values. For example, suppose that a job applicant, John Diode, obtains a score of 72 on the test. It is easy to find the proportion of applicants who obtained scores between the mean of 60 and this applicant's score of 72. We need only express the applicant's raw score as a z-score and use Table B to find the proportion of scores between the mean and that z-score. A raw score of 72 corresponds to a z-score of

$$\frac{72 - 60}{8} = 1.50.$$

Table B informs us that .4332 of the distribution falls between the mean and the z-score of 1.50 (or raw score of 72). In addition, we can readily find the proportion of applicants (scores in the distribution) that exceed a z-score of 1.50. Table B indicates that .0668 of the applicants obtained higher scores than did Mr. Diode. These regions of the distribution are shown in Figure 5.8(a). We can also find the proportion of applicants who scored below Mr. Diode, leading directly to Mr. Diode's percentile rank. Note that the whole area under the distribution is equal to 1. Since .0668 of the area is above Mr. Diode's score, 1 − .0668 = .9332, or 93.32 percent of the scores are below his, yielding a percentile rank of 93.32. This is quite a good standing and the company may well offer him a job.

It should be apparent that lower z-scores will be associated with lower percentile ranks. For example, an applicant who obtains a score of 50 on the microchip company's test has a z-score of

$$\frac{50 - 60}{8} = \frac{-10}{8} = -1.25$$

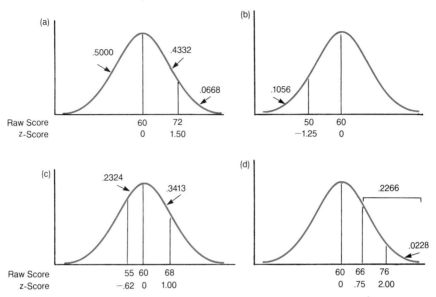

Figure 5.8 Diagrams for problems involving the standard normal distribution when the task is to determine areas from scores.

To determine the percentile rank, we begin (as we always should when working with problems involving the standard normal distribution) by producing a diagram of the situation, as shown in Figure 5.8(b). The area that is of interest is the part of the distribution that is below the z-score of -1.25. In Table B, this is the area *beyond* a z-score of 1.25 (i.e., between z and the nearest tail of the distribution), or .1056 of the distribution. Thus, the applicant's percentile rank is only 10.56.

Areas Defined by Two z-scores

The standard normal distribution also can be used to find the proportion of scores that fall in regions defined by two different score values. For example, we may want to know the proportion of job applicants who obtain test scores between 55 and 68. To handle problems of this type, we construct a diagram representing the area in which we are interested. Figure 5.8(c) shows this area. The z-scores that correspond to the two raw score values are

$$\frac{55 - 60}{8} = \frac{-5}{8} = -0.62 \quad \text{and} \quad \frac{68 - 60}{8} = \frac{8}{8} = 1.00$$

The critical area clearly consists of two parts, the area between the mean and a z of -0.62, and the area between the mean and a z of 1.00. From Table B we find that these two areas are .2324 and .3413, respectively. The total area, then, is equal to the sum of these two parts, .5737.

Consider one more example of this type. Our task is to find the proportion of applicants who obtained scores in the range of 66 to 76. The corresponding z-scores are

$$\frac{66 - 60}{8} = \frac{6}{8} = 0.75 \quad \text{and} \quad \frac{76 - 60}{8} = \frac{16}{8} = 2.00$$

respectively. A diagram of this situation is shown in Figure 5.8(d). This time the area of interest is one section of the distribution that lies to the right of the mean. One way to find this area is to determine the area beyond the z of 0.75 (.2266 according to Table B). This area includes the area of interest, plus the area beyond the z of 2.00 (.0228 according to Table B). Therefore, the area of interest must be the difference between the area beyond $z = 0.75$ and the area beyond $z = 2.00$: $.2266 - .0228 = .2038$.

You should make careful note of the fact that we used z-scores to obtain areas, then subtracted the smaller area from the larger to find the final answer. We would not get a sensible answer if we made the mistake of subtracting z-scores. The problem could also have been handled by working with areas between the mean and the z-scores. Try this approach, but be sure to begin with a diagram.

Interpreting Proportions of Area

In problems of the type we have just introduced, there are a number of different forms your answer can take. The most direct form, dictated by the nature of Table B, is to answer in terms of proportion of scores in a distribution. These proportions, however, can easily be converted to other kinds of values, such as percentages. Recall that conversion of a proportion to a percentage requires you to multiply the proportion by 100. It is also possible to convert the proportion into the *number* of scores in a distribution, just by multiplying the proportion by the total number of scores in the distribution. For instance, in the microchip company example, we showed that .2038 of the applicants obtained scores between 66 and 76. If the total number of applicants taking the test were 138, the number of applicants obtaining scores in this range would be .2038(138) = 28.12, or 28 people. Remember that there may not be exactly 28 people with scores in this range since the test scores might not follow the normal distribution exactly. But if the distribution is closely approximated by the normal, we have a very good estimate.

Finally, the proportions can be considered as probabilities. For example, .2038 of the applicants obtained scores between 66 and 76. So if we were to draw one applicant at random from the set of 138 applicants who took the test, the probability that the applicant would have a score in the range of 66 to 76 would be .2038. That is, the proportion of area in a distribution can be directly translated into the probability of randomly selecting a member of the distribution from that area.

Using Areas to Find Scores

When a normal distribution is involved, Table B can be used to determine raw score values that correspond to particular areas of the distribution. Going back to the microchip company, suppose we wanted to establish a criterion to use in offering jobs to applicants. Specifically, the company decides to offer jobs to those people who obtain scores in the top 10 percent of the distribution. What would be the minimum raw score needed in order to get a job offer? As usual we begin with a diagram of the situation, as shown in Figure 5.9(a).

The vertical line has been placed so that an area that appears to be about 10 percent of the distribution lies beyond it. Our task is to discover the raw score value of this position. An intermediate step, made necessary by the fact that Table B deals with z-scores rather than raw scores, is to find the z-score that corresponds to this position. By converting the z-score to a raw score, we will have completed the task. The first step, then, is to find the value of the z-score that has 10 percent of the distribution beyond it. We can do so by searching the "Area Beyond z" column of Table B for the value .1000 (the proportion that corresponds to 10 percent). The closest we can come to .1000 is .1003, which corresponds to a z-score of 1.28. The raw score equivalent, using Formula 5.3 and the mean and standard deviation of the test scores of the microchip applicants, is $X = 60 + 8(1.28) = 70.24$.

Another example of this sort of procedure involves obtaining raw score values that correspond to percentile ranks. For example, suppose we wanted

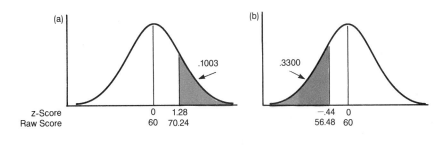

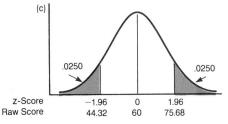

Figure 5.9 Diagrams for problems involving the standard normal distribution when the task is to determine scores from areas.

to find the raw score that corresponded to a percentile rank of 33. This means that we want to find the raw score below which .3300 of the distribution falls. This situation is shown in Figure 5.9(b). To determine the raw score we need to search the column in Table B labeled "Area Beyond z" for the value .3300. This search will produce an exact match at a z-score of 0.44. We are at a point below the mean, so this z-score is to be interpreted as -0.44. According to Formula 5.3 the raw score that corresponds to $z = -0.44$ is $X = 60 + 8(-0.44) = 56.48$.

As a final example, consider the following situation. It may be the case that the microchip company is a little concerned about individuals who obtain extreme scores (be they high or low) on a psychological test. They might want to use the test to eliminate those applicants who obtain extreme scores. All others may be considered for further screening. Suppose that the company decides to reject immediately those applicants who obtain the most extreme scores. In all, 5 percent of the applicants are to be rejected on this basis. This 5 percent is to be equally divided between applicants with very high scores and applicants with very low scores. Thus, anyone with a score falling in the upper 2.5 percent or lower 2.5 percent of the distribution will be rejected. The task is to find the raw score values that correspond to these cutoffs.

This situation is shown in Figure 5.9(c). The first step is to find the z-score such that .0250 of the area falls beyond it. The answer is 1.96. For the lower end of the distribution, of course, it is -1.96. The raw score values that are represented by these z-scores can be found by using Formula 5.3. For the upper cutoff we have $X = 60 + 8(1.96) = 75.68$, and for the lower boundary we have $X = 60 + 8(-1.96) = 44.32$. So anyone with a score that falls outside the range of 44.32 to 75.68 will be rejected automatically. If only whole numbers are possible on this test, values should be rounded to produce a range of 44 to 76.

SUMMARY

Transforming raw scores into standardized scores is a useful means of providing critical information about an individual's score. A standardized score indicates whether an individual obtained a score that was above or below the mean of the distribution, and also how far the score was from the mean. In the case of z-scores, this distance is expressed in standard deviation units.

Many naturally occurring variables approximately follow the normal distribution. When scores on a variable of this type are transformed into z-scores, the resulting distribution is approximated by the standard normal distribution. Specific areas of the standard normal distribution fall within known z-score values. This information can be used to accomplish tasks such as finding percentile ranks and setting raw score cutoff values that correspond to particular proportions of a distribution.

In later chapters we make frequent use of the concept of transforming raw data into values that can be used to determine areas under normal and other distributions. For this reason it is very important that you clearly understand the procedures involved in making use of the standard normal distribution.

KEY WORDS

z-score

standard score

area under a distribution

standard normal distribution

density

PROBLEMS

1 For the following sample of scores, find the mean and standard deviation: 6, 6, 6, 7, 7, 7, 7, 7, 8, 8, 8, 9, 9, 10, 11, 12. Convert each raw score into a z-score. Compute the mean and standard deviation of the z-scores. Plot a frequency polygon for the raw scores and another for the z-scores. Compare the two polygons.

2 A sample of scores has a mean of 23 and a standard deviation of 12. Suppose that each score is now transformed into a z-score. For each of the following z-scores, find the corresponding raw score.
(a) −1.30, (b) 0, (c) 2.75, (d) 0.05, (e) −0.70, (f) 1.00

3 For a sample of scores the mean is 75, and a raw score of 80 corresponds to a z-score of 0.80. What is the standard deviation of the sample of raw scores?

4 A researcher is working on the development of a standardized test of vocabulary for schoolchildren. A large sample of children have taken the test and produced a mean raw score of 42 items correct with a standard deviation of 18 items. The researcher decides to standardize so that the standardized score mean is 50 and the standard deviation is 10. What would be the standardized score equivalent of the following raw scores?
(a) 30, (b) 42, (c) 60, (d) 20, (e) 70

5 Use the grid areas in the following histogram to find the proportion of scores in the distribution that are greater than 8.

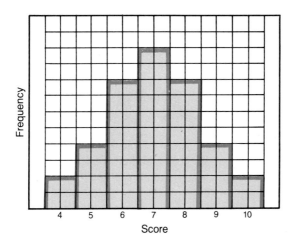

6 Given the following information based on just two members of a sample, determine the mean and standard deviation of the whole sample. One member of the sample has a raw score of 50 and a corresponding z-score of 1.00. Another member has a raw score of 56 and a z-score of 2.00. (Hint: Draw a diagram of the distribution, including the location of these two scores and the mean. The shape of the distribution does not matter.)

7 Assume that scores on the vocabulary test discussed in problem 4 are normally distributed. What is the percentile rank for a raw score of 56? For a standard score of 56? What standard score corresponds to the thirtieth percentile? What raw score corresponds to the eightieth percentile?

8 A sample of 500 television viewers produces an approximately normal distribution of scores on a test measuring ability to recall the content of a television commercial. A score consists of the percentage of the commercial's content that a viewer was able to recall. The mean score was 30 percent, and the standard deviation was 8 percent.
   (a) What proportion of the sample of viewers was able to recall more than half of the commercial's content?
   (b) How many viewers in the sample recalled between 20 percent and 25 percent of the content of the commercial? Give your answer to the nearest whole number.
   (c) What percentage of the viewers recalled between 20 percent and 40 percent of the commercial?
   (d) How many viewers recalled 32 percent of the content? Give your answer to the nearest whole number. (Hint: A score of 32 percent has real limits of 31.5 percent to 32.5 percent. Anyone with a recall percentage in this interval will be assigned a score of 32 percent.)

9 A consulting firm carries out an evaluation of two samples of commercials in the manner described in problem 8. One sample consists of humorous commercials, and the other consists of nonhumorous commercials. Each commercial is assigned a score equal to the mean percentage of the content that was recalled by a group of television viewers. The distribution of scores for the humorous commercials is normal, with a mean of 45 and a standard deviation of 12. The nonhumorous commercials also have a normal distribution, with a mean of 28 and a standard deviation of 10. Draw a frequency polygon for each distribution, using just one set of axes so that the distributions overlap. Draw vertical lines indicating the location and value of the mean for each distribution.
   (a) What percentage of the humorous commercials is better recalled than the average nonhumorous commercial?
   (b) What percentage of the nonhumorous commercials is better remembered than the average humorous commercial?
   (c) If you were a manufacturer, what would these results indicate concerning the type of commercial you would use to promote your product?

10 A flight training school run by the armed forces to select new recruits uses a training simulator to evaluate the potential of cadets. Only cadets who score in the top 30 percent on this test will be selected. Furthermore, those in the top 5 percent will be offered the chance to train for positions as test pilots for new fighter aircraft. Finally, only those cadets who score in the top 70 percent on the test will be offered the chance to remain in this branch of the armed forces. Assuming that scores on the test are normally distributed and that the mean score is 23.8, with a

standard deviation of 6.0, find the raw score cutoffs for each of the categories described.

11 A large university class in social psychology has a discussion on the topic of littering. One student claims that most people who take food out of fast-food restaurants place the wrappers and sundry leftovers in trash bins. A general discussion ensues in which different opinions are expressed. The instructor decides to have the class carry out an empirical test: Each of the students goes to the local fast-food restaurant to observe the behavior of ten people who buy a take-out item and leave on foot with it. Each student reports how many of the ten people dropped some litter rather than placing all of it into trash bins. The scores reported by the class members are normally distributed, with a mean of 5.40 and a standard deviation of 1.49. Within what range did the middle 90 percent of the distribution of scores fall? The middle 99 percent? The student who argued that people rarely litter reported that of the ten people he observed, only one littered. Is there any reason to suspect that he may have faked his data?

PROOFS

Proof 5.1 DERIVATION OF A METHOD OF OBTAINING A RAW SCORE FROM A z-SCORE

Beginning with the formula for a z-score, we can solve for X, the raw score, by using basic rules of algebra. This operation produces a formula for finding the raw score when we know the corresponding z-score and the mean and standard deviation of the distribution.

$$z = \frac{X - \overline{X}}{s}$$

$$s(z) = X - \overline{X}$$

$$\overline{X} + s(z) = X$$

Proof 5.2 PROOF THAT A SET OF z-SCORES HAS $\overline{X} = 0$ AND $s = s^2 = 1$

The following proofs hold for z-scores based on a sample or on a population. The proofs are shown for the sample version of the z-score formula, but they can be extended for the case of populations by substituting μ for $\overline{X}$, σ for s, and N for $N - 1$.

We begin by showing that the mean of a set of z-scores will be equal to zero.

$$\overline{X}_z = \frac{\Sigma z}{N} = \frac{\Sigma \dfrac{X - \overline{X}}{s}}{N} = \frac{\Sigma \dfrac{1}{s}(X - \overline{X})}{N}$$

$$= \frac{\dfrac{1}{s}\Sigma(X - \overline{X})}{N} = \frac{\dfrac{1}{s}(0)}{N} = 0$$

Next we show that the variance and therefore the standard deviation of a set of z-scores is equal to 1.

$$s_z^2 = \frac{\Sigma(z - \overline{X}_z)^2}{N - 1} = \frac{\Sigma z^2}{N - 1}$$

$$= \frac{\Sigma \frac{(X - \overline{X})^2}{s^2}}{N - 1} = \frac{\frac{1}{s^2}\Sigma(X - \overline{X})^2}{N - 1}$$

$$= \frac{1}{s^2} \cdot \frac{\Sigma(X - \overline{X})^2}{N - 1} = \frac{1}{s^2}s^2 = 1$$

TWO

Describing Bivariate Distributions

INTRODUCTION

Previous chapters presented methods for describing a single variable, that is, for describing *univariate* distributions. Yet most research is designed to investigate two or more variables, in which case we are interested in describing the *relationship* among variables. In Chapters 6 and 7 we present methods for describing the relationship between *two* variables, that is, for describing *bivariate* distributions. Figure II.1 is an example of a bivariate distribution of two psychology midterm exams taken by 14 students. These scores are also listed in Table II.1. Each point in Figure II.1 corresponds to a pair of scores, one pair for each student. An inspection of these points sug-

Table II.1 **SCORES ON TWO PSYCHOLOGY MIDTERM EXAMS FOR 14 COLLEGE STUDENTS**

Student	Midterm A	Midterm B
1	21	16
2	23	18
3	26	22
4	25	24
5	22	20
6	24	22
7	23	22
8	25	26
9	26	28
10	27	28
11	21	18
12	27	30
13	24	24
14	22	18
Mean	24.00	23.00
Standard deviation	2.08	4.15

gests that students who score high on one exam tend to score high on the other. When this result occurs we say there is a *positive* relationship between scores on the two exams. If the scores on one exam had decreased as the scores on the other increased, we would say there was a *negative* relationship.

Some examples of research questions that focus on the relationship between two variables follow:

1. Is high school grade point average related to college grade point average?
2. Is age related to memory performance?
3. Is intelligence measured in infancy related to intelligence measured in elementary school?
4. Is social competence related to social popularity?
5. Is type of reinforcement schedule related to rate of learning?

In Chapters 6 and 7 we are particularly interested in the extent to which bivariate distributions can be summarized by a straight line. The task is to describe how strongly two variables are related, to indicate whether the relationship is positive or negative, and to describe in mathematical terms the characteristics of the line that best captures that relationship. This task is accomplished by using the techniques of correlation (Chapter 6) and regression (Chapter 7).

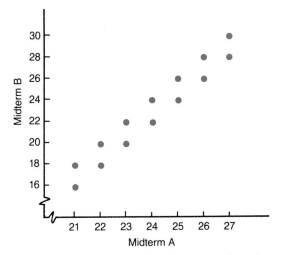

Figure II.1 Scatterplot of midterm A and midterm B scores.

SIMILARITIES BETWEEN UNIVARIATE AND BIVARIATE DISTRIBUTIONS

Students are often convinced that univariate statistics and bivariate statistics are totally different entities. In truth, they have much in common, and we point out some of their similarities here in order to introduce linear correlation and regression. Later, in Chapters 6 and 7, we describe specifically how to compute and interpret correlation and regression statistics, but even then we emphasize that understanding the statistics of bivariate distributions requires nothing more difficult than understanding means and variances.

A summary of some of the similarities between univariate and bivariate statistics appears in Box II.1. As you can see, there are few new concepts (but lots of terminology) needed to grasp the essential ideas in the analysis of bivariate distributions. Let us look a little closer.

Recall from Chapter 4 that the sample mean $(\overline{X})$ can be interpreted as the single value that best predicts the scores in a univariate distribution. It is chosen as the value about which the sum of squared deviations is minimized (see Chapter 4, Section 4.2). Given the scores on only one of the midterm exams in Table II.1, the best predictor of *any* individual's score is the mean score. For example, given the scores only on midterm B, the best predicted score for any individual would be 22.0 $(\overline{X})$.

This interpretation of the mean is important because it can help us understand a key topic in bivariate statistics, namely, the regression line (i.e., the line in Figure II.1). The regression line is the line that best predicts the scores in a bivariate distribution. In fact, the regression line can be thought of as a *moving mean*, the line that connects the means of one variable cal-

Box II.1   **Similarities Between the Statistics of Univariate Distributions and the Statistics of Bivariate Distributions**

Univariate Distributions

Polygon   visual display of univariate distribution

Mean   value that best predicts scores in a univariate distribution

Variance   error associated with using the mean as a predictor

Standard deviation   square root of the variance

Standard score   relative standing of a score in a univariate distribution

Bivariate Distributions

Scatterplot   visual display of bivariate distribution

Regression line   line that best predicts scores in a bivariate distribution

Variance of estimate   error associated with using the regression line as a predictor

Standard error of estimate   square root of the variance of estimate

Correlation   relative standing of a score in one distribution given the relative standing of a score in another distribution

culated across separate values of a second variable. Moreover, it is derived by using exactly the same statistical criterion used to obtain the mean. It is the line about which the sum of squared deviations is minimized. Thus, given scores on both midterm A and midterm B, as in Table II.1, the best predictor of an individual's midterm B score would not be the overall mean but instead would *depend* on the individual's midterm A score. The best predicted score on midterm B would be 19.0 for individuals who scored 22.0 on midterm A, 27.0 for individuals who scored 26.0 on midterm A, and so on.

The analogy between univariate and bivariate statistics goes further. Consider the variance of a set of scores. Recall that the variance is an average of the squared deviations of scores from the mean and that it can be interpreted as the amount of error associated with using the mean as a predictor (see Chapter 4, Section 4.3). Similarly there is usually some error associated with using the regression line as a predictor (you will have noticed that none of the points in Figure II.1 fall precisely on the regression line). In this case the amount of error is equivalent to finding the variance of one variable across the fixed values of another variable and then averaging. It is called the *variance of estimate*. The square root of the variance is the standard deviation. Analogously, the square root of the variance of estimate is called the *standard error of estimate*.

Finally, recall that a standard score (*z*-score) indicates the relative standing of a score in a univariate distribution. More precisely, it indicates how far above or below the mean an individual's score is in standard deviation units. An analogous statistic for bivariate distributions is the correlation coefficient. It indicates the extent to which the relative standings on two variables (the *z*-scores on two variables) are the same, that is, are co-related.

Try to keep these analogies in mind. Soon you will see that a thread of unity runs through most statistical procedures, which once noticed, will greatly simplify the learning process.

Chapter
6

Correlation

6.1 VISUAL DISPLAYS OF BIVARIATE FREQUENCY DISTRIBUTIONS

Correlation methods assess the relationship between two variables. An *essential* first step in examining the relationship between two variables is to visualize it in a table or graph. Table 6.1 is a *bivariate frequency table* of hypothetical scores on two intelligence tests for 100 individuals. The univariate frequency distribution of one intelligence test is shown along the bottom of the table, and that of the other test, along the left side of the table. Traditionally the variable represented by values along the bottom is called the *X* variable, and the variable represented by values along the left side, the *Y* variable. When distinguishing between an independent and a dependent variable makes sense, *X* is reserved for the independent variable and *Y* for the dependent variable. When no such distinction is obvious, as in the present example, which variable is designated as *X* or *Y* is irrelevant.

Table 6.1 BIVARIATE FREQUENCY TABLE OF SCORES ON TWO INTELLIGENCE TESTS FOR 100 INDIVIDUALS

Test B	f	30	35	40	45	50	55	60	65	70	Conditional test A means
120	3							|	|	|	65.0
115	5						|	||	|	|	62.0
110	12				|	|	||||	|||	||	|	57.9
105	18				|	||	||||||	|||||	|||	|	52.8
100	24			||	|||||	||||| |||||	|||||	||			50.0
95	18		|	|||	|||||	||||||	||	|			47.2
90	12	|	||	|||	||||	|	|				42.1
85	5	|	|	||	|						38.0
80	3	|	|	|							35.0
Test A		30	35	40	45	50	55	60	65	70	
f		3	5	12	18	24	18	12	5	3	
Conditional test B means		85.0	88.0	92.5	96.7	100.0	103.3	107.5	112.0	115.0	

Each position in the body of the table is called a "cell" and denotes a particular paired score on the two tests. Data are entered into the body of the table as follows: First move along the bottom until an individual's score on test A is found. Then move up the left side of the table until that individual's score on test B is found. At the intersection of the test A column and the test B row is the cell for that particular paired score. Place a slash mark in the cell. Repeat this procedure for each individual, and, finally, add up the slash marks in each cell. The end result of this procedure is shown in Table 6.2.

From Table 6.2 we can better appreciate the nature of bivariate distributions. We can see that each column is really a univariate frequency distribution of test B scores for each fixed value of test A. For example, the first column shows that the three individuals who each scored 30 on test A, scored 80, 85, and 90 on test B. Similarly, each row is really a univariate frequency distribution of test A scores for each fixed value of test B. The first row shows that the three individuals who each scored 120 on test B, scored 60, 65 and 70 on test A. Thus, a bivariate frequency distribution is nothing more than a series of univariate frequency distributions of one variable across, or *conditional* on, constant values of a second variable. We call such distributions **conditional frequency distributions,** and at its most fundamental level, the analysis of bivariate data turns out to involve nothing more than a comparison of the univariate statistics (e.g., the means) of these conditional distributions. If the means differ, as in Table 6.2 (e.g., $85.0 \neq 88.0 \neq 92.5 \ldots \neq 115.0$), we say there is a relationship between the two variables. If they are the same, we say the two variables are not related. This point warrants emphasizing: Nothing more is involved in the analysis of relationships than determining whether conditional distributions are the same or different.

Table 6.2 BIVARIATE FREQUENCY TABLE OF SCORES ON TWO INTELLIGENCE TESTS FOR 100 INDIVIDUALS

Test B	f	30	35	40	45	50	55	60	65	70	Conditional test A means
120	3							1	1	1	65.0
115	5						1	2	1	1	62.0
110	12				1	1	4	3	2	1	57.9
105	18			1	2	6	5	3	1		52.8
100	24			2	5	10	5	2			50.0
95	18		1	3	5	6	2	1			47.2
90	12	1	2	3	4	1	1				42.1
85	5	1	1	2	1						38.0
80	3	1	1	1							35.0
Test A		30	35	40	45	50	55	60	65	70	
f		3	5	12	18	24	18	12	5	3	
Conditional test B means		85.0	88.0	92.5	96.7	100.0	103.3	107.5	112.0	115.0	

CONDITIONAL FREQUENCY DISTRIBUTION: The univariate frequency distribution of one variable at some constant value of a second variable.

Although bivariate frequency tables allow us to better understand the meaning of a relationship between two variables, the most common reason for visually displaying bivariate frequency distributions is to determine the shape of the relationship, usually by constructing a **scatterplot.** The basic format of a scatterplot is shown in Figure 6.1. The values of the X variable are placed along the horizontal or X-axis in X variable units, and the values of Y are placed along the vertical or Y-axis in Y variable units.

SCATTERPLOT: A graphic description of a bivariate distribution in which scores are plotted on two variables for each subject.

Notice that representing X and Y uses up both dimensions of the graph. How then do we represent frequencies without leaving the page and entering the third dimension? There are two solutions to this problem. In one the frequencies are placed in the body of the scatterplot, as was done in Figure 6.2 with the data from Table 6.1. Such scatterplots are common output from statistical analysis packages like SPSS$_X$ and MINITAB.

The other, and by far most common, solution is to represent each distinct joint observation as a dot on the scatterplot and to ignore the frequency information. This procedure may seem a bit drastic, but in fact little is lost from the purpose of graphing bivariate data, namely, seeing the shape of a relationship between two variables. (Also, when graphing continuous variables there usually are relatively few overlapping dots, in which case ignoring

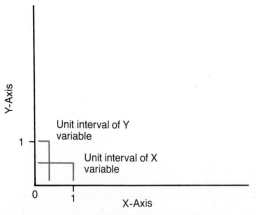

Figure 6.1 Basic format of a scatterplot.

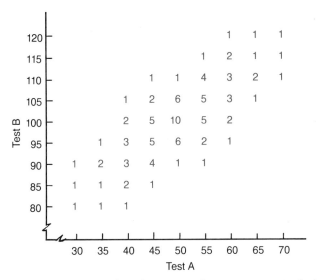

Figure 6.2 Scatterplot of test A and test B scores, including frequency information.

frequency information produces only minor distortion of the data.) Figure 6.3 is a scatterplot of the intelligence test data in which dots are used to represent paired observations. Plotting the dots is accomplished by drawing a line perpendicular to the X-axis from an individual's *X* score, and to the Y-axis from an individual's *Y* score, and placing a dot at the intersection of these two perpendicular lines. This procedure is illustrated for one paired observation in Figure 6.3. As you can see, Figure 6.3 does not show that ten individuals scored 50 on test A and 100 on test B. Nevertheless, it does clearly show

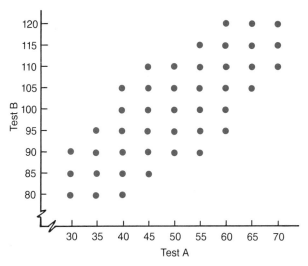

Figure 6.3 Scatterplots of test A and test B scores, without frequency information.

that an increase in test A scores is accompanied by a general increase in test B scores. This is evidence of a positive linear relationship between test A and test B scores.

6.2   TYPES OF RELATIONSHIPS BETWEEN TWO VARIABLES

In Figure 6.4 scatterplots show various types of relationships, which may be linear or curvilinear, positive or negative, strong or weak. In a **linear relationship** the dots tend to swarm around a straight line. A positive linear relationship is shown when the line runs upward from the bottom left of the plot to the upper right, whereas a negative linear relationship is shown when the line runs downward from the upper left of the plot to the bottom right. Dots tightly clustered around the line, whether positive or negative, indicate a stronger relationship, whereas a weaker relationship is indicated by more loosely clustered dots. In a curvilinear relationship the dots tend to swarm around a curved line, either close to it (a strong relationship) or dispersed around it (a weak relationship).

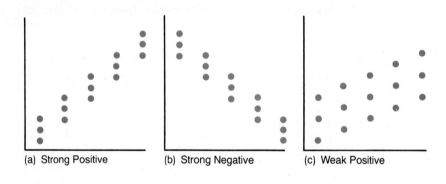

(a) Strong Positive   (b) Strong Negative   (c) Weak Positive

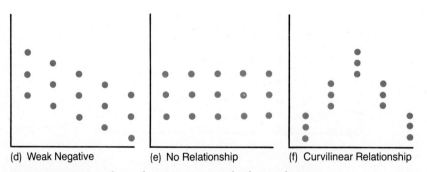

(d) Weak Negative   (e) No Relationship   (f) Curvilinear Relationship

Figure 6.4 Scatterplots of various types of relationships.

LINEAR RELATIONSHIP: A relationship between two variables in which the relationship is best described by a straight line. A positive linear relationship occurs when increases in one variable are accompanied by increases in another variable. A negative linear relationship occurs when increases in one variable are accompanied by decreases in another variable.

By and large, most relationships between psychological variables are linear or very close to linear. This is not to deny that curvilinear relationships exist or to suggest they are not important. Indeed, some very important relationships, such as those between degree of motivation and performance on a wide variety of motor and intellectual tasks, are consistently curvilinear. We briefly deal with such relationships in the next chapter. However, because linear correlation is a good representation of the relationship between most psychological variables, we discuss it in detail. We begin by presenting the *Pearson product-moment correlation coefficient* for describing the linear relationship between two relatively continuous variables, each measured on interval or approximately interval scales. Then we present variants of the *Pearson* correlation for describing relationships between variables that are measured on nominal and ordinal scales.

6.3   PEARSON PRODUCT-MOMENT CORRELATION

The Pearson product-moment correlation coefficient is the most frequently used of all measures of linear relationship. It is referred to simply as the **correlation coefficient,** or more simply by the symbol, r, with subscripts identifying which variables are being correlated. For example r_{xy} is used to represent the correlation between variables X and Y, although it is common practice when there are only two variables to use r without subscripts. However, when describing the bivariate distributions among several variables, the subscripts become important for distinguishing which pairs are being correlated. If there are five variables, r_{13} would represent the correlation between variables 1 and 3, r_{25} would be used for variables 2 and 5, and so on.

CORRELATION COEFFICIENT: A statistical description of the magnitude and direction of the linear relationship between two variables.

The data in Table 6.3 will help put the correlation coefficient into context. These data are hypothetical scores representing sociometric popularity and social competence for 20 kindergarten children. Sociometric popularity was measured by presenting the children with photographs of their classmates and having them assign each picture to one of three boxes on which were drawn cartoons of faces. A happy face, indicating that a classmate was

Table 6.3   DATA FOR COMPUTING THE PEARSON CORRELATION COEFFICIENT BETWEEN THE SOCIAL
POPULARITY (X) AND SOCIAL COMPETENCE (Y) SCORES OF 20 CHILDREN

Child	X	Y	$(X - \bar{X})$	$(Y - \bar{Y})$	z_X	z_Y	$(X - \bar{X})(Y - \bar{Y})$	$z_X z_Y$	X^2	Y^2	XY
1	2.5	15	0.37	1.5	0.82	0.41	0.56	0.34	6.25	225	37.5
2	1.9	11	−0.24	−2.5	−0.53	−0.68	0.60	0.36	3.61	121	20.9
3	1.8	13	−0.34	−0.5	−0.76	−0.14	0.17	0.11	3.24	169	23.4
4	1.9	9	−0.24	−4.5	−0.53	−1.23	1.08	0.65	3.61	81	17.1
5	2.7	16	0.57	2.5	1.27	0.68	1.43	0.86	7.29	256	43.2
6	2.2	14	0.06	0.5	0.13	0.14	0.03	0.02	4.84	196	30.8
7	2.0	16	−0.14	2.5	−0.31	0.68	−0.35	−0.21	4.00	256	32.0
8	2.0	15	−0.14	1.5	−0.31	0.41	−0.21	−0.13	4.00	225	30.0
9	2.8	14	0.67	0.5	1.49	0.14	0.34	0.21	7.84	196	39.2
10	2.7	20	0.57	6.5	1.27	1.78	3.71	2.26	7.29	400	54.0
11	2.1	11	−0.04	−2.5	−0.08	−0.68	0.10	0.05	4.41	121	23.1
12	2.9	17	0.77	3.5	1.71	0.96	2.70	1.64	8.41	289	49.3
13	1.6	9	−0.54	−4.5	−1.20	−1.23	2.43	1.48	2.56	81	14.4
14	2.5	19	0.37	5.5	0.82	1.51	2.04	1.24	6.25	361	47.5
15	1.7	12	−0.44	−1.5	−0.98	−0.41	0.66	0.40	2.89	144	20.4
16	1.7	8	−0.44	−5.5	−0.98	−1.51	2.42	1.48	2.89	64	13.6
17	2.3	15	0.17	1.5	0.38	0.41	0.26	0.16	5.29	225	34.5
18	1.5	10	−0.64	−3.5	−1.42	−0.96	2.24	1.36	2.25	100	15.0
19	2.4	18	0.27	4.5	0.60	1.23	1.22	0.74	5.76	324	43.2
20	1.5	8	−0.64	−5.5	−1.42	−1.51	3.52	2.14	2.25	64	12.0
Sums	42.7	270					24.95	15.16	94.93	3898	601.1

$\bar{X}$ = 2.14, S_X = .45 $\bar{Y}$ = 13.50, S_Y = 3.65

liked a lot, was assigned a score of 3; a neutral face, indicating that a classmate was liked an average amount, was assigned a score of 2; and a sad face,
indicating that a classmate was not liked, was assigned a score of 1. Each
child's popularity score represents the average rating by members of his or
her class. Social competence was measured by having the kindergarten
teacher complete for each child a questionnaire concerning his or her prosocial behavior with other children (e.g., politeness, sharing toys, or taking
turns in games). High scores suggest high social competence.

These data are plotted in Figure 6.5. Clearly there is a positive, approximately linear relationship between popularity and social competence. The
most popular children tend to show more prosocial behavior than do less
popular children. Moreover, because the dots cluster quite tightly together,
this relationship appears to be relatively strong.

How are we to capture this impression in a single descriptive statistic?
An immediate problem arises from the fact that popularity and competence
are measured in different units. Child 1's popularity score is 2.5 and his or
her social competence score is 15. Is he or she more popular than competent,

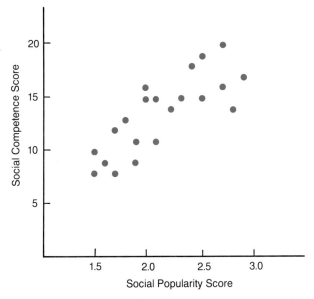

Figure 6.5 Scatterplot of social popularity and social competence data.

more competent than popular, or equivalent on both? Obviously we cannot tell directly from the child's raw data. The solution is to transform each of the scores into deviations from their respective means, $X - \overline{X}$ and $Y - \overline{Y}$. From these deviation scores we can tell if a child is above average on both variables, below average on both, or above on one but below on the other. Thus, the *first* step in producing the Pearson correlation is to transform scores on both variables for each child into deviation scores. These results are shown in columns 3 and 4 of Table 6.3, where you can see that child 1 is above average both in popularity and in social competence.

The *second* step is to multiply together the deviation scores on each variable for each child:

$$(X - \overline{X})(Y - \overline{Y})$$

To see why we take this step, notice that children who are above average in both variables have two positive deviation scores, and children who are below average in both variables have two negative deviation scores. In both cases when we multiply deviation scores the result will be positive. In contrast, children who are above average on one variable but below average on the other will produce negative numbers when their deviation scores are multiplied. Thus, products of deviation scores indicate whether individuals' scores on two variables deviate from their respective means in the same direction (positive products) or in the opposite direction (negative products). Products of deviation scores appear in column 7 of Table 6.3.

The Covariance

The *third* step in deriving the correlation coefficient is to average the multiplied deviation scores to produce a quantity called the **covariance** (Cov_{XY}).

$$\text{Cov}_{XY} = \frac{\Sigma(X - \overline{X})(Y - \overline{Y})}{N - 1} \qquad (6.1)$$

The numerator of this formula specifies summing the deviation score products over all individuals. It is symbolized by the expression *SP*, meaning *sum of products*, and Formula 6.1 can be written as

$$\text{Cov}_{XY} = \frac{SP}{N - 1} = \frac{\Sigma(X - \overline{X})(Y - \overline{Y})}{N - 1} \qquad (6.2)$$

Notice that we obtain the average by dividing *SP* by $N - 1$, the degrees of freedom, rather than by *N*, the number of subjects.

COVARIANCE: The average of the cross products of deviation scores.

The *covariance* is a measure of the extent to which two variables correspondingly vary, or co-vary, from their respective means across an entire group. If cross products are consistently positive across individuals, their average, the covariance, will be positive; if they are consistently negative, the covariance will be negative; and if some cross products are positive and some negative, the covariance will be close to zero.

Formulas 6.1 and 6.2 are useful for conceptualizing the covariance. However, for computational purposes an alternative formula is

$$\text{Cov}_{XY} = \frac{\Sigma XY - \dfrac{\Sigma X \Sigma Y}{N}}{N - 1} \qquad (6.3)$$

For the data in Table 6.3 the covariance computed by using Formulas 6.1 and 6.2 is

$$\Sigma(X - \overline{X})(Y - \overline{Y}) = 24.95; \; N - 1 = 19$$

$$\text{Cov}_{XY} = \frac{24.95}{19} = 1.31$$

and using Formula 6.3, it is

$$\Sigma XY = 601.1; \; \Sigma X \Sigma Y = 11529.0$$

$$\text{Cov}_{XY} = \frac{601.1 - \dfrac{11529}{20}}{19} = 1.30$$

The slight difference between the two values is due to rounding error.

Although in some respects the equations used to compute the covariance are unique, notice that they are actually very similar to the equations used to compute the variance. If the Ys in the preceding equations were changed to Xs, the result would be the variance of X (S_X^2).

$$\text{Cov}_{XX} = \frac{\Sigma(X - \overline{X})(X - \overline{X})}{N - 1} = \frac{\Sigma(X - \overline{X})^2}{N - 1}$$

$$= S_X^2$$

$$\text{Cov}_{XX} = \frac{\Sigma XX - \frac{\Sigma X \Sigma X}{N}}{N - 1} = \frac{\Sigma X^2 - \frac{(\Sigma X)^2}{N}}{N - 1}$$

$$= S_X^2$$

Of course, if the Xs were changed to Ys, the result would be the variance of Y (S_Y^2). Thus the variance is the covariance of a variable with itself.

One other similarity is worth noting. Recall that the variance can be defined as the *sum of squares (SS)* divided by degrees of freedom *(df)*

$$S_X^2 = \frac{SS_X}{df}$$

A similar definition holds for the covariance, only in this case it is the *sum of products (SP)* divided by degrees of freedom, as shown in Formula 6.4.

$$\text{Cov}_{XY} = \frac{SP_{XY}}{df} \tag{6.4}$$

It should be clear to you that the sign of the covariance is immediately meaningful. It tells you directly whether the relationship is positive or negative. Unfortunately, the size of the covariance does not offer such clear meaning. From the value of 1.30 previously computed, we cannot tell if the relationship is strong or weak. The problem with the covariance is that its size is partly dependent on the nature of the units used to measure each variable. For example, multiplying all of the scores on both variables by 2.0 would change the covariance to a value of 5.20. Yet such an arbitrary change in scale does not change the strength of the relationship. Thus, the *fourth* step in deriving the correlation coefficient is to transform the covariance to a scale that directly conveys information about the strength of the relationship between two variables regardless of the units originally used to measure them.

The Covariance of z-scores—The Correlation Coefficient

One way in which this transformation can be accomplished is by dividing the deviation scores of X and Y by their standard deviations to produce z_X and z_Y scores for each subject. In this way both variables will be transformed to the same standard deviation units of measurement, regardless of the units originally used to measure each variable. If the covariance of those z-scores is computed, the result is the Pearson correlation coefficient.

$$\text{Cov}_{z_X z_Y} = \frac{\Sigma(z_X - \bar{z_X})(z_Y - \bar{z_Y})}{N - 1}$$

$$= \frac{\Sigma(z_X - 0)(z_Y - 0)}{N - 1} \tag{6.5}$$

$$= \frac{\Sigma z_X z_Y}{N - 1} = r_{XY}$$

Thus, the correlation coefficient can be defined as the covariance of z_X and z_Y scores. The z-score equivalents for the popularity and competence data are shown in columns 5 and 6 of Table 6.3, and their products appear in column 8. Using Formula 6.5, the correlation coefficient equals

$$\frac{\Sigma z_X z_Y}{N - 1} = \frac{15.16}{19} = .80$$

You will notice that the signs of the covariance and the correlation coefficient agree. This will always be true. However, their sizes differ, which is usually true. Unlike the covariance, which has no limits on its size, the correlation coefficient will always range from -1.0 to 1.0. A correlation of -1.0 indicates a perfect negative relationship, 1.0 indicates a perfect positive relationship, and 0.0 indicates no linear relationship between variables.

Understanding why the limits of the correlation coefficient are ± 1.0 is not difficult and can help clarify its meaning. The maximum positive value of r will occur when *for each individual z-scores have the same sign and exactly the same value:* $z_X = z_Y$ for each individual. When z-scores have exactly the same value their covariance equals their variance.

When $z_X = z_Y$

$$\text{Cov}_{z_X z_Y} = S_{z_X}{}^2 = S_{z_Y}{}^2$$

$$= r_{XY}$$

In Chapter 5 the variance of any set of z-scores was shown to equal 1.0. Therefore, when all individuals have identical pairs of z-scores the covariance of those scores, the correlation coefficient, equals a maximum value of 1.0. Similarly, when pairs of z-scores are the same for all individuals but are opposite in sign, their covariance also equals their variance but takes on a negative value. In this case r reaches a minimum value of -1.0.

Values between -1.0 and 1.0 reflect varying degrees of dissimilarity between z-scores, a value of zero indicating that pairs of z-scores are sometimes the same and sometimes opposite but that on the average the two kinds of pairs cancel each other out. Thus, you can see that r describes the relationship between two variables by indexing the extent to which standard scores from one univariate distribution have the same value and sign as standard scores from another univariate distribution. The value of $r = .80$, found in the example previously presented, indicates that *on the average* standard scores on social popularity are quite similar in sign and size to standard scores on social competence.

Computational Formulas for r

Formula 6.5 is useful for conceptualizing the correlation coefficient. However, converting all of the scores in a data set into z-scores is a tedious business. Fortunately, as shown in Proof 6.1, there is an equivalent way to transform the covariance into r that does not involve converting raw scores into z-scores, that is, by dividing the covariance between X and Y by the product of their standard deviations.

$$r_{XY} = \frac{\text{Cov}_{XY}}{S_X S_Y} \qquad (6.6)$$

For the data in Table 6.3 the covariance is 1.30, the standard deviation of X is 0.45, the standard deviation of Y is 3.65, and using Formula 6.6 we find

$$r_{XY} = \frac{1.30}{(0.45)(3.65)} = .80$$

the same value as was found by using Formula 6.5.

Several computational formulas for the correlation can be derived from Formula 6.6. The most common one is based on the following algebraic equivalence:

$$r_{XY} = \frac{\text{Cov}_{XY}}{S_X S_Y} = \frac{\dfrac{SP_{XY}}{N-1}}{\sqrt{\dfrac{SS_X}{N-1} \cdot \dfrac{SS_Y}{N-1}}}$$

Since $N - 1$ terms cancel, this equation can be simplified to Formula 6.7.

$$r_{XY} = \frac{SP_{XY}}{\sqrt{SS_X SS_Y}} \qquad (6.7)$$

Inserting computational formulas for SP, SS_X, and SS_Y gives

$$r_{XY} = \frac{\Sigma XY - \dfrac{(\Sigma X)(\Sigma Y)}{N}}{\sqrt{\Sigma X^2 - \dfrac{(\Sigma X)^2}{N} \cdot \Sigma Y^2 - \dfrac{(\Sigma Y)^2}{N}}} \qquad (6.8)$$

which after multiplying both numerator and denominator by N becomes

$$r_{XY} = \frac{N\Sigma XY - (\Sigma X)(\Sigma Y)}{\sqrt{[N\Sigma X^2 - (\Sigma X)^2][N\Sigma Y^2 - (\Sigma Y)^2]}} \qquad (6.9)$$

The advantage of Formulas 6.8 and 6.9 is that no prior computation of means and standard deviations is required; they are *raw score* formulas. Applying them to the data in Table 6.3 we have

$$\Sigma XY = 601.1, \; \Sigma X \Sigma Y = 11529, \; \Sigma X^2 = 94.93, \; (\Sigma X)^2 = 1823.29,$$

$$\Sigma Y^2 = 3898, \; (\Sigma Y)^2 = 72900$$

And using Formula 6.8,

$$r_{XY} = \frac{601.1 - \dfrac{11529}{20}}{\sqrt{94.93 - \dfrac{1823.29}{20} \cdot 3898 - \dfrac{72900}{20}}}$$

$$= .80$$

Formula 6.9 produces

$$r_{XY} = \frac{20(601.1) - 11529}{\sqrt{20(94.93) - 1823.29 \cdot 20(3898) - 72900}}$$

$$= .80$$

Of course, no matter how r is computed, its meaning remains the same. We now turn to an expanded discussion of its meaning.

6.4   INTERPRETING THE CORRELATION COEFFICIENT

We have emphasized that the correlation coefficient summarizes information about the direction and extent of a relationship between two variables. Although this information is fundamental, there is more to interpreting correlation coefficients than merely noting their sign and size.

A Second Correlation—r_{YX}

All of the discussion has been focused on the correlation between X and Y (r_{XY}). Intuitively it would seem that the direction and degree of the relationship between two variables should be the same regardless of whether the relationship is described in terms of X with Y or Y with X. This intuition is correct; r_{XY} does equal r_{YX}, as can easily be seen from the z-score formula for r.

$$r_{XY} = \frac{\Sigma z_X z_Y}{N - 1}$$

$$r_{YX} = \frac{\Sigma z_Y z_X}{N - 1}$$

Since $\Sigma z_X z_Y = \Sigma z_Y z_X$, $r_{XY} = r_{YX}$.

Interpreting the Size of r

It is often difficult to decide what values of r indicate low, moderate, or high degrees of relationship. Obviously this decision involves the size of r, but it also involves some familiarity with the particular variables under study as well as with the particular context in which the correlation is being used. If an intelligence test were given to a group of individuals and then given again to the same individuals two weeks later, the correlation between the two sets of scores would indicate the reliability of the test. In this context a high value of r would be expected, with values in the .70s considered barely acceptable. In contrast, exploratory research into the relationship between cognitive development and emotional maturity would judge correlations in the .40s as high. Such variables are expected to interrelate in complex ways with many other variables, but not highly with any one variable in particular.

The size of r is also at issue when we want to compare two correlation coefficients. It is tempting to believe that $r = .80$ is twice the size of $r = .40$. Such comparative statements assume that the values of r form a ratio scale of measurement. They do not. The correlation scale is ordinal, not ratio, or even interval. However, values of the correlation squared (r^2) *do* form a ratio scale, and therefore legitimate statements can be made about how much bigger one r^2 value is compared to another. We will have much more to say about r^2 in Chapter 7, where it will be much easier to understand in the context of linear regression. For now notice that $r = .80$ really represents *four* times the strength of relationship as $r = .40$ because $.80^2 = .64$ is four times larger than $.40^2 = .16$.

Linearity

The Pearson correlation measures the direction and degree of *linear* relationship. Therefore, a low value of r does not necessarily mean that two variables are totally unrelated. It could be that they are related, even very strongly related, but as shown in Figure 6.6, in a curvilinear fashion. This figure depicts the relationship between stimulus information and attention. Low levels of stimulus information are usually considered boring and elicit low levels of attention. As information increases so does attention, up to some optimal level of information, where attention is at its highest. Beyond the optimal level there is too much information to be processed and attention drops off. Consider applying the Pearson correlation in this situation. In the first half of the distribution, information and attention simultaneously increase and the product of their z-scores will be positive. In the second half, attention decreases as information increases and the product of the z-scores will be negative. Taken over the entire distribution, the average of all the products of the z-scores will produce a correlation close to 0.0. Thus you can see that a correlation close to 0.0 does not have to mean that there is no relationship between two variables; rather it can mean that there is no *linear* relationship between them. Potential confusion about the meaning of low correlations can

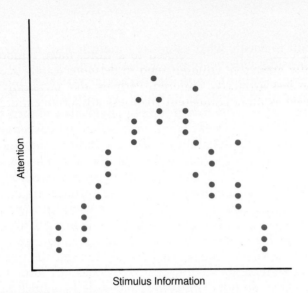

Figure 6.6 Example of curvilinear relationship.

be avoided simply by examining bivariate distributions in scatterplots before proceeding with correlational analyses.

Correlation and Conditional Distributions

We have emphasized that bivariate statistics are an extension of univariate statistics. In particular, bivariate statistics involve comparing the univariate distributions of one variable across different values of a second variable—they compare *conditional* distributions. The correlation coefficient can be interpreted within this framework. If r_{XY} is relatively large, it indicates that across fixed values of X the mean Y scores differ. Further, because r describes linear relationships, those conditional means not only differ but also fall approximately along a straight line. Similarly, across fixed values of Y, the mean X scores differ and form approximately a straight line.

Correlation and Causality

Although the correlation coefficient describes the degree of linear relationship between two variables, it does not necessarily indicate whether one caused the other. A correlation between social popularity and social competence does not mean that high popularity has caused children to be more socially competent, whereas less popular children, not having the same opportunity to practice their social skills, are therefore less socially competent. It is equally plausible that social competence determines one's popularity. Which of these is the correct explanation cannot be determined on the basis of a correlation coefficient.

Moreover, it is possible that neither explanation is the correct one. Instead, the correlation between popularity and competence might be caused by the fact that each of them is related to a third, more remote variable. Perhaps physically attractive children tend to be more readily accepted into peer groups than less attractive children. Perhaps, too, physically attractive children are judged as more competent than less attractive children on a variety of characteristics, including social competence. Thus, physical attractiveness may lead directly to both popularity and judged competence and indirectly to a relationship between them, but popularity and competence by themselves might not be causally related at all.

The temptation to infer causation on the basis of correlation is strong, particularly when one of the variables in a relationship cannot cause the other. There is a correlation between smoking and cancer that is undoubtedly not due to cancer causing smoking. Yet the possibility that some other variable accounts for this correlation exists and cannot be ignored. It could be that some unmeasured predisposition leads both to smoking and to cancer. The only certain way to untangle causation from correlation is to follow the finding of a correlation with a controlled study in which one of the variables is manipulated. In the case of smoking, at least two groups of individuals, comparable on all other characteristics except that one group smokes and the other does not, would have to be compared on their incidence of cancer. Of course such an experiment would be unethical with humans, although animal experiments of this type have essentially determined that smoking can cause cancer.

6.5 FACTORS THAT AFFECT THE CORRELATION COEFFICIENT

Sample Characteristics

We have already seen that the shape of a relationship can affect the size of r. The size of r can also be influenced by characteristics of the sample on which it is based.

For example, if a sample is selected in which the range of values on either or both of two variables is restricted, the value of the correlation between those variables will typically underestimate the value in the population.[1] Suppose for the moment that the 20 children on whom we have social popularity and social competence scores are a population of interest. Their scatterplot is reproduced in Figure 6.7. Now suppose that only children with average popularity are sampled. The range of scores on both variables would be restricted relative to the population, as shown in Figure 6.7, and the correlation would be only .50 instead of .80.

---

[1]Restricting the range of X or Y may overestimate the Pearson r when the restriction truncates a curvilinear relationship to produce a linear relationship.

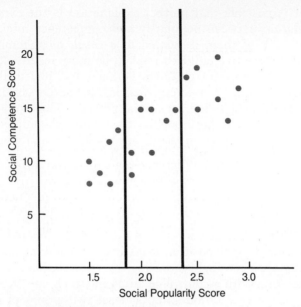

Figure 6.7 Replication of Figure 6.5, including the effects of restriction of range.

Intuitively this result makes sense; discriminating among individuals who differ a little is much harder than discriminating among individuals who differ a lot. It also makes sense when we inspect Formula 6.6 for *r*. Looking at the denominator, we can see that as the range is restricted on either or both variables, the variance (and hence the standard deviation) tends toward zero. Thus, the formula for *r* becomes undefined because we are dividing by zero.

In Figure 6.7 the selected group of children is less variable on both *X* and *Y* than is the population as a whole. Of course, this problem would arise if the scores of only unpopular or only popular children were included in a sample.

The same rationale that explains why restriction of range decreases *r* also explains why using only *extreme groups* tends to inflate *r*. If children average in popularity or competence were excluded from a sample, the correlation computed on the remaining relatively unpopular and relatively popular children would be larger than the population correlation. For example, if only children with popularity scores less than 1.8 and greater than 2.3 are included in the sample, the correlation is .85. This result is due to omitting children whose scores are near the mean, resulting in increased covariance and, thus, a higher *r*.

Thus, correlations based on extreme groups, or on groups that restrict the range on one or both variables, must be interpreted with caution. Such correlations may accurately discriminate among individuals in the particular sample under investigation, but they may either underestimate or overestimate the relationship in the population.

Combining Populations

One must also be careful when a correlation between two variables is based on two samples, each representing a distinct population. One reason is that the population correlations may differ, so that combining samples may produce a single correlation uncharacteristic of either taken separately. Figure 6.8(a) shows how combining a sample in which the correlation is positive with a sample in which the correlation is negative produces an overall correlation close to zero.

A second reason is that the population means may differ on one or both of the variables, and these mean differences can affect the correlation. Figures 6.8(b) and 6.8(c) show how samples from populations in which the correlation is the same, but in which the means differ, combine to produce an r that is larger, 6.8(b), or smaller, 6.8(c), than would be the case for either considered alone. Figures 6.8(d), 6.8(e), and 6.8(f) show how combining samples that dif-

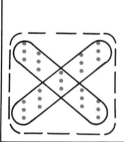

(a) Combining positive and negative relationships to produce no relationship

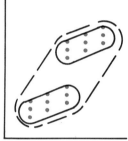

(b) Combining two weak positive relationships to produce a stronger positive relationship

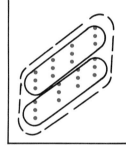

(c) Combining two strong positive relationships to produce a weaker positive relationship

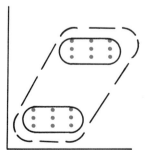

(d) Combining two groups in which there is no relationship to produce a positive relationship

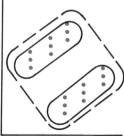

(e) Combining two positive relationships to produce a negative relationship

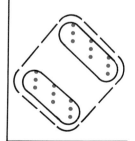

(f) Combining two negative relationships to produce a positive relationship

Figure 6.8 Effects of combining different populations into single correlation coefficients.

fer in mean values can entirely misrepresent the relationship that exists in each separate sample.

Of course, we should not be surprised that mean differences between samples can so drastically affect the correlation coefficient. After all, r indicates whether conditional distributions are the same or different, and by definition, groups with different Y means across different values of X (or vice versa) have different conditional distributions. The problems associated with combining samples can usually be alleviated by carefully examining scatterplots before computing correlations. If groups are found that have different mean values or that differ in direction and strength of relationship, correlations should be computed separately for each group.

6.6   ALTERNATIVE CORRELATION COEFFICIENTS

On many occasions researchers are interested in describing relationships between variables that are measured on nominal or ordinal scales. Correlation coefficients between such variables are given special names to distinguish them from one another and from r used with interval scales. There are also special computational formulas for each of them, but we emphasize at the outset that these formulas are merely algebraic manipulations of the now familiar Pearson correlation. Three of these correlations follow.

Correlating Ordinal Data

When two variables are each measured on an ordinal scale they can be correlated by using the *Spearman rank correlation*. Often ordinal data are collected because interval or ratio data are not needed or not possible. Other times, interval or ratio data are transformed to ranks because the original data are markedly skewed.

To transform data into ranks,

1. List the original scores in order from smallest to largest
2. Assign a rank (first, second, etc.) to each score in the ordered list
3. When tied scores occur, compute the average of their ranks and assign that average to each score

This procedure is illustrated with the following data: 4 1 3 4 1 9 4. Ordered from smallest to largest the scores are 1 1 3 4 4 4 9. Assigning ranks to this ordered list produces 1 2 3 4 5 6 7. Because the first two scores are tied, each is assigned the average of their ranks: $(1 + 2)/2 = 1.5$. Similarly the three values of 4 would be assigned their average rank, $(4 + 5 + 6)/3 = 5$, and the final rank ordering would be 1.5 1.5 3 5 5 5 7.

Table 6.4 DATA FOR COMPUTING THE SPEARMAN CORRELATION BETWEEN RANKED POPULARITY AND COMPETENCE SCORES

| Original data | | Ranks | | | |
X (popularity)	Y (competence)	X	Y	D	D^2
1.5	10	1.5	5.0	−3.5	12.25
1.5	8	1.5	1.5	0.0	0.00
1.6	9	3.0	3.5	−0.5	0.25
1.7	12	4.5	8.0	−3.5	12.25
1.7	8	4.5	1.5	3.0	9.00
1.8	13	6.0	9.0	−3.0	9.00
1.9	11	7.5	6.5	1.0	1.00
1.9	9	7.5	3.5	4.0	16.00
2.0	16	9.5	15.5	−6.0	36.00
2.0	15	9.5	13.0	−3.5	12.25
2.1	11	11.0	6.5	4.5	20.25
2.2	14	12.0	10.5	1.5	2.25
2.3	15	13.0	13.0	0.0	0.00
2.4	18	14.0	18.0	−4.0	16.00
2.5	15	15.5	13.0	2.5	6.25
2.5	19	15.5	19.0	−3.5	12.25
2.7	16	17.5	15.5	2.0	4.00
2.7	20	17.5	20.0	−2.5	6.25
2.8	14	19.0	10.5	8.5	72.25
2.9	17	20.0	17.0	3.0	9.00

Using ranked data,

$$\Sigma X = 210 \qquad \Sigma Y = 210 \qquad \Sigma D^2 = 256.5$$

$$\Sigma X^2 = 2867 \qquad \Sigma Y^2 = 2865.5$$

$$\Sigma XY = 2738 \qquad \Sigma X \Sigma Y = 44100$$

$$(\Sigma X)^2 = 44100 \qquad (\Sigma Y)^2 = 44100$$

Table 6.4 presents ranked scores for the childrens' popularity and competence data. Calculating the Pearson correlation on these ranked data by using Formula 6.9, we obtain

$$\Sigma X^2 = 2867, (\Sigma X)^2 = 44100, \Sigma Y^2 = 2856.5, (\Sigma Y)^2 = 44100,$$

$$\Sigma XY = 2738, \Sigma X \Sigma Y = 44100,$$

and

$$r_s = \frac{20(2738) - 44100}{\sqrt{[20(2867) - 44100][20(2856.5) - 44100]}} = .80$$

To emphasize that this correlation is used with ranked data we label it r_s instead of r. The subscript s refers to A. B. Spearman, who developed the following simplified formula:

$$r_s = 1 - \frac{6\Sigma D^2}{N(N^2 - 1)} \qquad (6.10)$$

in which D represents the difference between the two ranks for each subject, as shown in Table 6.4. Using this alternative formula we find

$$r_s = 1 - \frac{6(256.5)}{20(400 - 1)} = .81$$

which is nearly the same result found by using the standard formula for the Pearson r. The reason for the discrepancy is that there are tied ranks in Table 6.4. The standard formula for the Pearson correlation and the Spearman rank correlation will produce identical values only when there are no tied ranks. We recommend using the standard formula for three reasons: First, nothing new need be learned. Second, it avoids false notions that something different is being done or that a different statistic is required for correlating ranked data compared to interval data. Finally, when tied scores occur, the standard formula is actually easier to use than the supposedly simplified alternative version. With ties, the alternative version should itself be altered by a very cumbersome correction procedure, and thus any benefits of simplification vanish. In contrast, the standard formula for the Pearson r gives an accurate correlation between ranks even when ties occur.

Correlating a Dichotomous Variable with an Interval Variable

Often in research one of the variables of interest is measured on an interval scale and the other is dichotomous (has only two values). Most often the dichotomous variable indicates group membership, such as male/female, employed/unemployed, agree/disagree, and experimental group/control group. At other times a continuous variable is dichotomized. An example of this procedure would be to find the median of childrens' social competence scores and then to classify all those children above the median in a group labeled "high" social competence, and those below the median in a second group labeled "low" social competence.

Whether the dichotomy occurs naturally or is constructed, a dichotomous variable can be correlated with an interval variable merely by scoring the two levels of the dichotomous variable as 0 and 1 and calculating a Pearson r. The resulting correlation is called a *point-biserial* correlation to indicate the nature of the variables.[2] The symbol for the point-biserial correlation is r_{pb}.

---

[2] A statistic sometimes used when a continuous variable is dichotomized and then correlated with an interval variable is called the *biserial* correlation coefficient. We have not presented the biserial correlation because its validity depends on strong normality assumptions, and in fact is very rarely used in practice.

Using 1 and 0 as scores is an arbitrary decision. Any two numbers could be used without affecting the resulting correlation. We use 0 and 1 simply because these values make calculations easier. Also, which level of the dichotomous variable is assigned to 0 or 1 is arbitrary. If it denotes gender, we could use 0 for males and 1 for females or vice versa.

An example of using r_{pb} appears in Table 6.5. The hypothetical data represent the relationship between type of reinforcement schedule (continuous reinforcement = 0, variable reinforcement = 1) and persistence of a response (number of trials necessary to extinguish a learned response). The resulting value of .64 indicates that on the average more trials are necessary to extinguish a response learned under variable reinforcement compared to continuous reinforcement. In other words, the means of the two conditional distributions differ. In Chapter 11 we see that there is a direct correspondence between r_{pb} and statistical tests of the difference between two means.

Notice that had we chosen to assign 1 to the continuous reinforcement condition and 0 to the variable reinforcement condition, the interpretation of the results would remain the same but the sign of r_{pb} would have been negative.

Table 6.5   **EXAMPLE DATA FOR CALCULATING** r_{pb}
(Continuous Reinforcement = 0, Variable Reinforcement = 1. Trials Refer to the Number of Trials Necessary to Extinguish a Learned Response.)

	Reinforcement			
Subject	Condition	Trials		
1	0	6	$\Sigma X = 10$	$\Sigma Y = 163$
2	0	5		
3	0	6	$\Sigma X^2 = 10$	$\Sigma Y^2 = 1445$
4	0	7		
5	0	8	$(\Sigma X)^2 = 100$	$(\Sigma Y)^2 = 26569$
6	0	5		
7	0	9	$\Sigma XY = 97$	$\Sigma X \Sigma Y = 1630$
8	0	6		
9	0	6	$r_{pb} = .64$	
10	0	7		
11	1	10		
12	1	12		
13	1	9		
14	1	8		
15	1	12		
16	1	6		
17	1	14		
18	1	9		
19	1	10		
20	1	7		

Table 6.6 EXAMPLE DATA FOR CALCULATING PHI (ϕ)
(For Family Stability: Parents Divorced = 0, Parents
Not Divorced = 1. For Maintenance of a Relationship:
Subject Divorced = 0, Subject Not Divorced = 1.)

Subject	Family stability	Relationship maintenance		
1	0	0	$\Sigma X = 10$	$\Sigma Y = 12$
2	0	1		
3	0	1	$\Sigma X^2 = 10$	$\Sigma Y^2 = 12$
4	0	0	$(\Sigma X)^2 = 100$	$(\Sigma Y)^2 = 144$
5	0	1		
6	0	0	$\Sigma XY = 7$	$\Sigma X\Sigma Y = 120$
7	0	0		
8	0	0	$\phi = .20$	
9	0	1		
10	0	1		
11	1	0		
12	1	1		
13	1	1		
14	1	0		
15	1	1		
16	1	1		
17	1	1		
18	1	0		
19	1	1		
20	1	1		

Correlating Two Dichotomous Variables

When two dichotomous variables are correlated by using the Pearson r, the result is denoted by the Greek letter ϕ (phi). To illustrate, suppose we were interested in the relationship between family stability and subsequent ability to maintain an intimate relationship. We might sample a group of individuals and score them according to whether their parents had divorced (coded 0) or not (coded 1) and whether they themselves were divorced (coded 0) or not (coded 1). Table 6.6 gives such data for a sample of 20 individuals. Using the standard formula for the Pearson r on these data, we obtain a value of .20. It indicates a slight tendency for individuals whose parents are divorced to themselves be divorced.

6.7   THE CORRELATION MATRIX

Most studies reported in the contemporary psychological literature are concerned with interrelationships among several variables rather than between only two variables. Thus, several correlation coefficients are reported, usually in a **correlation matrix.** An example of a correlation matrix showing the interrelationships among four variables, X_1, X_2, X_3, and X_4, appears in the left panel of Table 6.7.

CORRELATION MATRIX: A table containing the correlations between several pairs of variables.

The variable names are placed along the top and left side of the matrix. The body of the matrix contains correlations among corresponding variables. Thus, finding X_1 on the left side of the matrix and scanning to the right, you can locate the correlations between X_1 and each of the other variables, that is, r_{11}, r_{12}, r_{13}, and r_{14}. A similar procedure for each of X_2, X_3, and X_4 will locate the correlations between all possible pairs of variables.

Notice that the diagonal of the matrix stretching from the top left to the bottom right contains all 1.0s because any variable correlates perfectly with itself. Also notice that the correlations above the diagonal are the mirror image of those below the diagonal because $r_{12} = r_{21}$, $r_{13} = r_{31}$, and so on. The most common form of a correlation matrix excludes the diagonal of 1.0s and reports only those correlations that appear either above or below the diagonal. The right panel of Table 6.7 illustrates such a matrix.

Table 6.7 CORRELATION MATRIX AMONG FOUR VARIABLES
(The Matrix on the Left Includes Correlation Among All Possible Pairs. The Matrix on the Right Is the Most Common Way of Reporting a Correlation Matrix.)

	X_1	X_2	X_3	X_4		X_2	X_3	X_4
X_1	1.00	r_{12}	r_{13}	r_{14}	X_1	r_{12}	r_{13}	r_{14}
X_2	r_{21}	1.00	r_{23}	r_{24}	X_2		r_{23}	r_{24}
X_3	r_{31}	r_{32}	1.00	r_{34}	X_3			r_{34}
X_4	r_{41}	r_{42}	r_{43}	1.00				

	Drug	Memory	Intelligence	Impression
Drug	1.00	.39	.00	.30
Memory	.39	1.00	.60	.01
Intelligence	.00	.60	1.00	−.43
Impression	.30	.01	−.43	1.00

	Memory	Intelligence	Impression
Drug	.39	.00	.30
Memory		.60	.01
Intelligence			−.43

Assume that an experimenter gave either a placebo or a drug expected to benefit memory to a group of 20 elderly adults every day for 60 days. At the end of that time the adults were given a memory test and a standardized IQ test and asked for their subjective impression of whether their memory had improved or not. The hypothetical data are presented in problem 19 at the end of this chapter. The complete correlation matrix, showing all possible intercorrelations among the four variables, and the more common form of reporting such a matrix are shown in the middle and bottom panels of Table 6.7.

SUMMARY

In this chapter we considered some ways of describing the relationship between two variables. In particular we discussed ways of plotting bivariate distributions and of calculating and interpreting the Pearson correlation coefficient. The Pearson r, which describes the direction and degree of linear relationship between two variables, can be used with two interval variables (r), two ordinal variables (r_S), a dichotomous variable and an interval variable (r_{pb}), and two dichotomous variables (ϕ).

Throughout the chapter we have emphasized the general concept of what a relationship between two variables means. If you visualize a bivariate frequency distribution as a set of univariate frequency distributions (called conditional distributions), a relationship between two variables exists if those conditional distributions have different means. A *linear* relationship exists if the means of those conditional distributions not only differ but also approximate a straight line. However, a word of caution is appropriate here. With sample data, some differences between means of conditional distributions may be merely sampling fluctuations. Procedures for deciding whether differences among the means of conditional distributions of a sample reflect "real" differences in a population, or are due merely to sampling fluctuations, are explored in later chapters.

KEY WORDS

bivariate distribution	sum of products
conditional frequency distribution	covariance
linear relationship	r^2
correlation coefficient	restriction of range
curvilinear relationship	correlation and causation
positive relationship	Spearman's correlation
negative relationship	point-biserial correlation
scatterplot	phi
Pearson correlation	correlation matrix

PROBLEMS

(Answer items 1–10 with true or false.)

1 A correlation of .70 indicates a stronger relationship than does a correlation of $-.70$.

2 A correlation of 0.0 always indicates no relationship between two variables.

3 If $r = 1.0$ and an individual's z_X score is 2.0, that individual's z_Y score must also be 2.0.

4 If $r = .75$ and an individual's z_X score is 2.0, that individual's z_Y score must be 1.5.

5 If the conditional means of X fall exactly along a straight line, the correlation will be 1.0.

6 If the correlation between two variables is $-.60$ and you doubled the raw values on X, the correlation would remain the same.

7 A correlation of .70 indicates approximately twice as strong a relationship as does a correlation of .50.

8 The values of r computed by using the standard Pearson r equation and the special equation for r_S on the same ranked data are always the same.

9 A nonzero correlation indicates the extent to which conditional means differ and fall along a straight line.

10 You could use the Pearson correlation to index the relationship between different levels of an experimental treatment variable and a dependent variable.

11 What is a scatterplot? Draw scatterplots representing positive and negative linear relationships, curvilinear relationships, and no relationship.

12 Explain how to interpret the sign and size of a correlation coefficient.

13 How do restriction of range and combining groups affect the correlation coefficient?

14 For what kinds of data are the Pearson, point-biserial, phi, and Spearman correlations appropriate?

15 What does the general concept of a relationship mean in terms of conditional distributions? How must the means of conditional distributions be ordered before the Pearson correlation is an appropriate index of relationship?

16 A professor was interested in the possible linear relationship between the average number of hours students spend studying per week and their grade point average (GPA). A random sample of ten students produced the following data:

Student	X Hours Studied	Y GPA	xy	x^2	y^2
1	8	2.3	18.4	64	5.29
2	15	3.0	45	225	9.0
3	15	1.5	22.5	225	2.25
4	14	2.8	39.2	196	7.84
5	19	3.2	60.8	361	10.24
6	13	2.7	35.1	169	7.29
7	17	2.2	37.4	289	4.84
8	17	2.5	42.5	289	6.25
9	20	4.0	80.	400	16.0
10	19	3.7	70.3	361	13.69

Plot the data in a scatterplot. Compute the covariance by using the conceptual formula and by using the computational formula. Compute the Pearson correlation by using the z-score formula and by using one of the computational formulas. Is there a relationship between the two variables? Do you think this correlation accurately reflects the relationship you would find in the general population if everyone went to college? Why or why not? If you randomly selected another student who studied 16 hours per week, what would you expect his or her standardized (z-score) GPA to be?

17 Rank order both variables in Problem 16 and compute r_S.

18 Dichotomize the data in Problem 16 into the five students who studied the least and the five students who studied the most. Compute the point-biserial correlation between the dichotomized variable and GPA. How should you interpret the sign of your answer? Can you change the sign without changing the interpretation of your results? How?

19 Using the following data, calculate the correlations shown in Table 6.7. Use the appropriate labels for each of these correlations.

Subject	Drug type 0 = placebo 1 = drug	Memory test	IQ	Impression better = 1 or not = 0
1	0	8	100	0
2	0	7	95	1
3	0	8	105	0
4	0	10	110	0
5	0	7	90	1
6	0	12	120	0
7	0	11	125	0
8	0	10	115	0
9	0	12	90	1
10	0	7	100	1
11	1	9	100	0
12	1	8	95	1
13	1	10	105	1
14	1	12	90	1
15	1	14	110	1
16	1	12	120	0
17	1	15	125	1
18	1	13	115	1
19	1	7	90	1
20	1	11	100	0

20 Interpret the results from the previous problem.

PROOFS

Proof 6.1 PROOF THAT THE COVARIANCE BETWEEN z-SCORES IS EQUAL TO THE COVARIANCE BETWEEN RAW SCORES DIVIDED BY THE PRODUCT OF THEIR STANDARD DEVIATIONS

$$r_{XY} = \frac{\Sigma z_X z_Y}{N - 1} \qquad \text{by Formula 6.5}$$

$$= \frac{1}{N - 1}\Sigma z_X z_Y \qquad \text{rearranging terms}$$

$$= \frac{1}{N - 1}\Sigma \frac{X - \overline{X}}{S_X} \cdot \frac{Y - \overline{Y}}{S_Y} \qquad \text{substitution}$$

$$= \frac{\dfrac{\Sigma(X - \overline{X})(Y - \overline{Y})}{N - 1}}{S_X S_Y} \qquad \text{rearranging terms}$$

$$= \frac{\text{Cov}_{XY}}{S_X S_Y} \qquad \text{substitution}$$

Chapter
7

Regression and Prediction

7.1　INTRODUCTION

In Chapter 6 we dealt with linear correlation, a procedure for describing the degree and direction (positive or negative) of the linear relationship between two variables. The focus of this chapter is on using the concepts of linear correlation to develop the concepts of **linear regression.** Linear regression is a procedure for describing, in mathematical terms, the characteristics of the line that best captures the relationship between two variables. There are two important pieces of information that result from this procedure. First, we can use the regression line to predict individuals' scores on one variable from knowledge of their scores on another variable. Second, we can estimate how accurate our predictions are likely to be.

LINEAR REGRESSION:　A statistical procedure for predicting one variable from another variable by using a linear prediction rule.

We begin our discussion with an example that illustrates the basic concepts of linear regression. Then we turn to the more technical aspects of regression.

7.2　CONCEPTS OF PREDICTION

Figure 7.1 presents a scatterplot of hypothetical scores on two midterm exams taken by 12 students. Notice that there is a relatively strong, but not perfect, positive correlation between the two sets of scores ($r = .78$). Now suppose that one student in the class had obtained a score of 20 on the first midterm but, because of illness, was unable to take the second midterm. What prediction could we make about that student's performance on the second midterm?

For illustrative purposes let us start by ignoring the correlation between the two exams and predicting the student's score only on the basis of other students' performance on the second midterm. In this case our best prediction would be the class mean on the second midterm ($\overline{Y} = 15.42$) because the mean is the value about which the sum of squared deviations between it and all other scores in the distribution is minimized. Moreover, we can estimate the average amount of error in our prediction by computing the class standard deviation ($s_Y = 3.58$). Recall that the standard deviation is a measure of the amount of error associated with using the mean as a predictor.[1]

Let us now predict the student's score by taking into account the correlation between the two exams. Figure 7.1 displays that correlation by plotting

---

[1]See Chapter 5, Section 5.3.

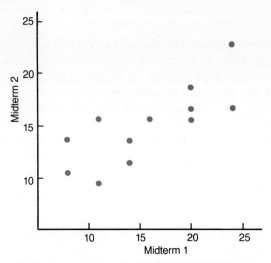

Figure 7.1   Scatterplot of hypothetical scores on two midterm exams.

midterm 2 scores against midterm 1 scores. Referring to Figure 7.1, we locate a score of 20 on the *X* axis. The values directly above are the second midterm scores of those students who obtained 20 on the first midterm, the same score obtained by our ailing student. These values represent the distribution of second midterm scores conditional on having scored 20 on the first midterm. The mean of that conditional distribution (17.33) is the best **predicted score** on midterm 2 for any student who scored 20 on the first midterm.

Clearly the prediction based on the correlation between the two exams (17.33) is different from the prediction that ignored that correlation (15.42). But is it more accurate? The answer is yes because the standard deviation of the conditional distribution (1.53) is smaller than the overall class standard deviation (3.58). That is, the actual midterm 2 scores for students who scored 20 on midterm 1 are closer, on the average, to the mean of their conditional distribution than to the overall class mean. The preceding comparison between using and not using the correlation to predict the midterm 2 score of a student who obtained a score of 20 on midterm 1 is summarized as follows:

	Predicted score	Prediction error
Ignoring correlation	15.42	3.58
Using correlation	17.33	1.53

In sum, when there is a correlation between two variables, we can use that information to make predictions from one variable to another that are more accurate than predictions that do not take the correlation into account. Next we want to derive a mathematical procedure that is akin to the procedure just described for making predictions from correlated data.

PREDICTED SCORE: The predicted value of one variable for a given value of another variable.

7.3   LINEAR RELATIONSHIPS

Figure 7.2 is a reproduction of Figure 7.1, with the means of each of the conditional distributions of second midterm scores connected to produce a prediction, or regression, line. You can see that this particular regression line is quite jagged and constitutes a very complex curve. If we were to derive a mathematical formula for describing this curve it would be extremely complicated. However, looking at the means of the conditional distributions, it appears that they fall *approximately* on a straight line. A simpler description, and undoubtedly a more reasonable one, is that the relationship is linear in the whole population of students. However, because each conditional mean is estimated from only a small sample of students, the relationship deviates from a straight line because of sampling fluctuation. Consequently, when a relationship is approximately linear (indicated by a sizable Pearson correlation), we adopt a straight-line model and use it to derive a relatively simple mathematical equation for the relationship.

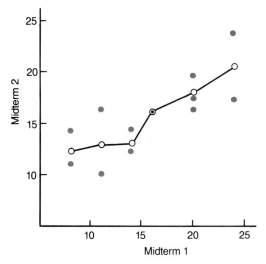

Figure 7.2   Regression line joining the conditional means of midterm 2 scores for each distinct value of midterm 1.

You should note that because we are adopting a linear model to describe relationships that may not be precisely linear in a particular sample of individuals, predictions based on this model will not necessarily equal conditional means, as they did in the previous illustration. Predictions from a linear model are, in fact, *estimates* of conditional means based on the assumption that the relationship between two variables is precisely linear in an entire population of individuals.

In the section to follow we will consider the mathematical characteristics of straight lines where all points fall precisely on the line, that is, where the linear relationship is perfect. Although perfect linear relationships are rare in behavioral research, examining them first will help you understand procedures for mathematically describing imperfect linear relationships.

The Formula for a Straight Line

The formula for a straight line expresses a relationship between two variables. Any straight line has the general formula of

$$Y = a + bX \tag{7.1}$$

This equation states that for any value of variable X, the value of variable Y that is paired with it on a straight line can be found by multiplying X by a constant value, b, and adding a second constant value, a, to that product. In this general equation, b is the *slope* of the line. Its value indicates how much Y will change for a one-unit change (increase or decrease) in X. In symbols, given any two points on a line (X_1, Y_1) and (X_2, Y_2) the slope of the line is given as

$$b = \frac{Y_2 - Y_1}{X_2 - X_1}$$

The value of a indicates the value of Y when X is zero. Because the value of Y when $X = 0$ is found on a graph where the line intercepts the Y-axis, a is called the *Y intercept*.

To illustrate the properties of Formula 7.1, suppose you resolved to get fit in the upcoming year and decided that the best way to do so was to join a local fitness club. However, before joining the club you need to estimate whether you can afford the expense. Assume that the fitness club charges a yearly membership fee of $50 and a session fee of $2 for each time you work out. From this information you can use a linear equation to compute how much keeping fit will cost you per year.

yearly cost = $50 (membership fee) + $2 (session fee) × no. of workouts

$$Y = \$50 + \$2(X)$$

Clearly, because of the membership fee, it will cost you $50 per year even if you never work out at all. Thus, in this example the yearly cost (Y), when the number of workouts (X) is zero, is equal to 50. Therefore, $a = 50$. For every additional workout (for each unit increment in X), your yearly cost (Y) will increase by $2. Therefore, $b = 2$.

By placing any value for number of workouts into this equation, you can compute the corresponding yearly cost. For example, if you want to know how much working out once a week for a year would cost (52 workouts), your answer would be

$$Y = \$50 + \$2(52)$$

$$= \$50 + \$104$$

$$= \$154$$

Figure 7.3 shows a graph of the relationship described by the equation $Y = 50 + 2(X)$. From it you can see at a glance whether you can afford the expense of using the club some specific number of times.

You should notice several things about Figure 7.3. First, the relationship described is indeed a straight line. Second, the line intercepts the Y-axis at 50, the value of a. Third, there is a positive slope to the line—it increases from the lower left to the upper right—because b has a positive value ($+2$). Linear relationships can also have a negative slope, which would be indicated by a negative value of b. For example, in some localities the relationship between car accidents and car insurance is negative. For each additional year of accident-free driving the cost of car insurance goes down. Finally, you should notice that Figure 7.3 illustrates a perfect linear relationship. That is, all points fall exactly on the line. As we mentioned earlier, in behavioral research the relationship between two variables is rarely perfectly linear. Nonetheless, it is possible to determine a linear equation like Formula 7.1 that will allow us to approximate, or predict, values of Y for different values of X. The procedure for determining the linear equation for an imperfect lin-

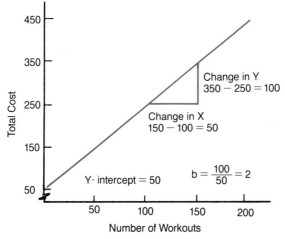

Figure 7.3 A perfect linear relationship described by $Y = 50 + 2(X)$.

ear relationship amounts to determining the values of *a* and *b* for the line that best approximates the relationship. The procedure is called linear regression.

7.4 LINEAR REGRESSION: THE CRITERION OF LEAST SQUARES

We now know the general formula for a straight line. How can we use it to produce the regression line plotted in Figure 7.4? The first thing to notice is that no single linear equation can be found that reproduces exactly the values of *Y* from their corresponding values of *X*. The reason, of course, is that the data in Figure 7.4 are not perfectly linear. To reflect this fact, when the general formula for a straight line is used to describe imperfect linear relationships, it is slightly altered to read

$$Y' = a + bX \tag{7.2}$$

Where *Y'* (pronounced Y prime) refers to the *predicted* value of *Y*.

The basic problem facing us is that any number of lines could be fit to these data, each having different values of *a* and *b*, and therefore, each producing different predicted values of *Y*. We need a criterion for deciding which of these many lines is in some sense the best line. The criterion chosen is the same criterion used to select the mean as the central location of a univariate distribution, namely, the *criterion of least squares*. Recall that the criterion of least squares specifies the mean as the "best" central location of a univariate distribution because it is the point about which the sum of squared deviations is minimized. That is, the mean is chosen so that $\Sigma(X -$

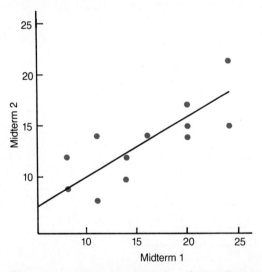

Figure 7.4 Linear regression line for predicting midterm 2 scores from midterm 1 scores.

$\overline{X})^2$ is a minimum. Similarly, the criterion of least squares specifies the "best" central location of a bivariate distribution (assuming a linear relationship) as the line about which the sum of squared deviations between it and the actual Y values is minimized. That is, the regression line is chosen so that $\Sigma(Y - Y')^2$ is a minimum.

The regression line drawn in Figure 7.4 was derived by using the least squares criterion. For each value of X, the predicted value of Y is located on the regression line. The sum of squared deviations between actual Y values and corresponding Y' values predicted from this line are smaller than the sum of squared deviations between obtained Y values and Y' values predicted from any other line. The obvious question at this point is, how did we arrive at this line? The answer is that we determined the values of a and b that satisfied the least squares criterion. How we determined those values is the topic of the next section.

7.5   DETERMINING THE REGRESSION COEFFICIENTS

The values of the Y intercept, a, and the slope, b, that describe the line that best fits the data in the least squares sense are defined as

$$b = r_{XY}\frac{s_Y}{s_X} \tag{7.3}$$

$$a = \overline{Y} - b\overline{X} = \overline{Y} - r_{XY}\frac{s_Y}{s_X}\overline{X} \tag{7.4}$$

From Formulas 7.2, 7.3, and 7.4 we can derive a formula for computing Y'.

$$Y' = \qquad a \qquad + \qquad bX$$

$$Y' = [\overline{Y} - r_{XY}\frac{s_Y}{s_X}\overline{X}] + [r_{XY}\frac{s_Y}{s_X}X]$$

which by rearranging terms becomes

$$Y' = \overline{Y} + r_{XY}\frac{s_Y}{s_X}(X - \overline{X}) = \overline{Y} + b(X - \overline{X}) \tag{7.5}$$

Focusing for a moment only on the slope of the best fitting line (Formula 7.3), you can see that its value depends partly on r. (See Proof 7.1.) Now looking at Formula 7.5, you can see that when r is 0.0, the slope is zero and the resulting predicted value of Y is $\overline{Y}$ for all values of X.

$$Y' = \overline{Y} + 0\frac{s_Y}{s_X}(X - \overline{X})$$

$$Y' = \overline{Y} + 0 = \overline{Y}$$

For example, if the correlation were zero between the two midterm exams discussed earlier, regardless of which X value is placed in Formula 7.5, the predicted score on midterm 2 would be the mean of $Y = 15.42$.

As the absolute value of r increases so does the absolute value of the slope, and predicted Y values increasingly deviate from $\overline{Y}$ as each value of X deviates from $\overline{X}$. With a perfect correlation, the predicted value of Y deviates from $\overline{Y}$ precisely as much as the corresponding value of X deviates from $\overline{X}$ (relative to their respective standard deviations), and therefore, Y is precisely predictable from X. This relationship between correlation and prediction can be seen most clearly by translating Formula 7.5 into standard score terms:

$$Y' = \overline{Y} + r_{XY}\frac{s_Y}{s_X}(X - \overline{X})$$

$$Y' - \overline{Y} = r_{XY}\frac{s_Y}{s_X}(X - \overline{X})$$

$$\frac{Y' - \overline{Y}}{s_Y} = r_{XY}\frac{(X - \overline{X})}{s_X}$$

$$z_{Y'} = r_{XY}z_X \tag{7.6}$$

Formula 7.6 shows that when raw scores are transformed into standard scores, $r = b$ and the predicted values of Y in standard score units $(z_{Y'})$ is equal to r times the standard score value of $X(z_X)$. The relation between correlation and regression is an important one and will be touched on throughout this chapter. Now, however, it is time to use the information learned to this point to show how we arrived at the regression line in Figure 7.4.

Table 7.1 reproduces the data plotted in Figure 7.4. We will use it to compute the **regression coefficients** (Formulas 7.3 and 7.4), produce regression formulas for predicting Y (Formulas 7.2 and 7.5), and show how to plot the regression line.

REGRESSION COEFFICIENTS: The values of a and b derived by using the least squares criterion to determine a best fitting line.

Included in Table 7.1 are the values of r_{XY}, s_X, s_Y, $\overline{X}$, and $\overline{Y}$, all the information we need to compute the regression coefficients. Thus,

$$b = r_{XY}\frac{s_Y}{s_X} = .78\frac{3.57}{5.73} = .485$$

Table 7.1 COMPUTING REGRESSION STATISTICS
ON TWO MIDTERM EXAMS
(Midterm 1, *X*, is used to predict midterm 2, *Y*.)

Student	Midterm 1 (X)	Midterm 2 (Y)
1	8	11
2	8	14
3	11	10
4	11	16
5	14	12
6	14	14
7	16	16
8	20	16
9	20	17
10	20	19
11	24	17
12	24	23
Mean	15.8	15.4
Standard deviation	5.7	3.6
r = .78		

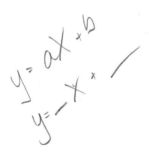

and

$$a = \overline{Y} - b(\overline{X}) = 15.42 - .485(15.83) = 7.75$$

Putting these values for *a* and *b* into Formula 7.2, we find that

$$Y' = a + bX = 7.75 + .485(X)$$

If we use Formula 7.5 instead,

$$Y' = \overline{Y} + b(X - \overline{X}) = 15.42 + .485(X - 15.83)$$

Either formula will produce the same predicted *Y* scores, and therefore, the same regression line. The advantage of Formula 7.2 is that it literally describes the mathematical characteristics (the values of *a* and *b*) of the regression line for predicting *Y*. Thus, it is usually used for descriptive purposes. However, to actually compute *Y'* values it is easier to use Formula 7.5 because computation of *a* is unnecessary.

To construct our regression line for predicting *Y* from *X* all we need to do is take two values of *X* (since a straight line is completely determined by two points), enter them into either Formula 7.2 or Formula 7.5, and compute two values of *Y'*. We then place these two paired scores, (X_1, Y'_1) and (X_2, Y'_2), on a scatterplot and join the points with a line.

Here is an example of computing *Y'* values by using both Formula 7.2 and Formula 7.5. The chosen values of *X* (midterm 1 scores) are 11 and 20.

X value	Formula 7.2 for Y'	Formula 7.5 for Y'
X = 11	Y' = 7.74 + .485(11) = 13.10	Y' = 15.42 + .485(11 − 15.83) = 13.10
X = 20	Y' = 7.74 + .485(20) = 17.44	Y' = 15.42 + .485(20 − 15.83) = 17.44

You can see that both formulas produce the same values of Y'.

Referring to Figure 7.4, locate the values of 11 and 20 on the X-axis. Moving up perpendicularly from these scores to the regression line, you will find that the values of 13.1 and 17.44 fall on the line. Any other value of Y' can be found by looking at the regression line or by using either Formula 7.2 or Formula 7.5. What are the Y' values associated with X values of 8 and 24?

7.6 PREDICTION ERROR

Although the regression line provides the best prediction of Y values from known X values, rarely do predicted values (Y's) actually equal obtained values (Ys). In fact, only when the correlation between X and Y is perfect will Y and corresponding Y' values equal one another. In all other cases there will be some deviation between Y and Y', in which case we say there is some amount of **prediction error** associated with the regression line. By estimating the magnitude of this prediction error we can then evaluate how well the regression line fits the data. This evaluation takes the form of comparing the prediction error associated with the regression line to the error associated with using the sample mean as a predictor. The smaller the prediction error of the regression line relative to the prediction error of the mean, the better the regression line fits the data. Let us now develop this idea a little further.

PREDICTION ERROR: The average difference between predicted scores and obtained scores.

Variance Error and Standard Error of Estimate

Consider developing a predictor of students' midterm 2 scores without benefit of knowing their midterm 1 scores. In this case we could not use the regression line based on the correlation between midterms. Instead, we would have to use as our predictor the class mean on midterm 2 because it is our best least squares predictor when no other information is available. The prediction errors associated with using $\overline{Y}$ to predict Y are the $Y - \overline{Y}$ values for each student. The prediction error for student 10 is indicated in Figure 7.5 by

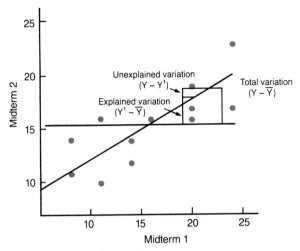

Figure 7.5 Scatterplot of midterm exam scores showing (a) the line representing the overall mean of midterm 2 across distinct values of midterm 1, (b) the linear regression of midterm 2 on midterm 1, (c) the total deviation scores $(Y - \overline{Y})$, (d) the unexplained deviation scores, $(Y - Y')$, and (e) explained deviation scores $(Y' - \overline{Y})$.

the vertical distance between the student's observed Y value and the line representing the value of $\overline{Y}$ across all values of X. The average prediction error associated with the mean is the sample variance,

$$s_Y^2 = \frac{SS_Y}{df} = \frac{\Sigma(Y - \overline{Y})^2}{N - 1}$$

or the sample standard deviation,

$$s_Y = \sqrt{\frac{SS_Y}{df}} = \sqrt{\frac{\Sigma(Y - \overline{Y})^2}{N - 1}}$$

Now let us use the regression line for our predictions. The prediction errors associated with using X to predict Y are the $Y - Y'$ values for each student, an example of which is shown for student 10 in Figure 7.5. The average prediction error associated with the regression line is conceptually equivalent to the sample variance and is computed as

$$s_{Y-Y'}^2 = \frac{SS_{Y-Y'}}{df} = \frac{\Sigma(Y - Y')^2}{N - 2} \tag{7.7}$$

This statistic is called the *variance error of estimate* or *residual variance*. Its square root is called the **standard error of estimate**:

$$s_{Y-Y'} = \sqrt{\frac{SS_{Y-Y'}}{df}} = \sqrt{\frac{\Sigma(Y - Y')^2}{N - 2}} \tag{7.8}$$

STANDARD ERROR OF ESTIMATE: The standard deviation of the prediction errors in linear regression.

The degrees of freedom for the variance error of estimate and the standard error of estimate are $N - 2$. Recall from our discussion of variance in Chapter 4 that the degrees of freedom for a particular statistic are equal to the number of observations (N) minus the number of parameters that have to be estimated to compute that statistic. In the case of the sample variance, 1 degree of freedom is lost because one parameter, the population mean, has to be estimated from the sample data to compute the sum of squared errors from the mean. Therefore, the degrees of freedom for the sample variance are $N - 1$, where N is the total number of observations and 1 is the number of parameters estimated. In the case of the variance error of estimate, two parameters, a and b, must be estimated from the sample data to compute the sum of squared errors from the regression line. For this reason the degrees of freedom for the variance estimate of error are $N - 2$. The variance error of estimate and the standard error of estimate computed from Table 7.2 are

$$s^2_{Y-Y'} = \frac{54.46}{10} = 5.45$$

$$s_{Y-Y'} = \sqrt{5.45} = 2.33$$

These values are smaller than the obtained sample variance and standard deviation, indicating that the regression line is a better predictor than the class mean.

Predictor	Variance error	Standard error
$\overline{Y}$	$s_Y = 12.81$	$s_Y = 3.58$
Regression line	$s^2_{Y-Y'} = 5.45$	$s_{Y-Y'} = 2.33$

Prediction Error and Correlation

Estimating prediction error by using Formulas 7.7 and 7.8 involves calculating Y', then subtracting it from Y and squaring the result for every observation, a tedious task that only the most vigilant of us can accomplish without computation error. Fortunately there is an easier way. With some algebraic manipulation, the numerator of Formula 7.7 can be rewritten as

$$SS_{Y-Y'} = SS_Y(1 - r^2) \tag{7.9}$$

which, when expressed in variance terms instead of sums of squares, becomes

$$s^2_{Y-Y'} = s_Y^2(1 - r^2)\frac{N - 1}{N - 2} \tag{7.10}$$

Table 7.2 EXAMPLE DATA FOR COMPUTING REGRESSION STATISTICS ON MIDTERM 1 (X) AND MIDTERM 2 (Y) SCORES

Student	Midterm 1 (X)	Midterm 2 (Y)	Estimate (Y')	Error ($Y - Y'$)	Error^2 ($Y - Y'$)^2
1	8	11	11.59	-0.59	0.34
2	8	14	11.59	2.41	5.81
3	11	10	13.05	-3.05	9.25
4	11	16	13.05	2.95	8.69
5	14	12	14.52	-2.52	6.35
6	14	14	14.52	-0.52	0.27
7	16	16	15.50	0.50	0.25
8	20	16	17.45	-1.45	2.10
9	20	17	17.45	-0.45	0.20
10	20	19	17.45	1.55	2.41
11	24	17	19.41	-2.42	5.81
12	24	23	19.41	3.59	12.89

$s_Y^2 = 12.82$ $SS_Y = 140.92$

$s_Y = 3.58$ $SS_{Y'} = 86.46$

$s_{Y-Y'}^2 = 5.46$ $SS_{Y-Y'} = 54.46$

$s_{Y-Y'} = 2.33$

$r_{XY} = .78$

When N is large, the ratio of $N - 1$ to $N - 2$ approaches 1, and the formula for the variance error of estimate is simplified to

$$s_{Y-Y'}^2 = s_Y^2(1 - r^2) \tag{7.11}$$

Taking the square root of the variance error of estimate produces the standard error of estimate,

$$s_{Y-Y'} = s_Y \sqrt{(1 - r^2)\frac{N - 1}{N - 2}} \tag{7.12}$$

which with large samples can be simplified to

$$s_{Y-Y'} = s_Y \sqrt{(1 - r^2)} \tag{7.13}$$

The variance error of estimate from Formulas 7.10 and 7.11 is

$$s_{Y-Y'}^2 = 12.81(1 - .78^2)\frac{11}{10} = 5.45$$

$$s_{Y-Y'}^2 = 12.81(1 - .78^2) = 4.96$$

The standard error of estimate is simply the square root of each of these quantities, that is, 2.33 and 2.23, respectively. With the term $N - 1/N - 2$

included, the correlation formulas agree exactly with the raw score formulas. Without it, the variance error of estimate and standard error of estimate are underestimated, a result you should keep in mind because Formulas 7.11 and 7.13 are frequently used in practice, sometimes erroneously when sample sizes are small.

From these formulas you can easily see the range of possible values for the prediction error associated with the regression line. When the correlation is zero, the prediction error associated with the regression line is essentially equal to the prediction error associated with the mean. That is,

$$s_{Y-Y'}^2 = s_Y^2(1 - 0)\frac{N - 1}{N - 2} \approx s_Y^2$$

This result should make sense if you remember that when $r = 0$, $Y' = \overline{Y}$ for all values of X. Thus, the prediction errors, $Y - Y'$, will equal $Y - \overline{Y}$, and the maximum value of $s_{Y-Y'}^2$ must be s_Y^2.

In contrast, when the correlation is 1.0 or -1.0, all of the data fall precisely on the regression line and there is no prediction error:

$$s_{Y-Y'}^2 = s_Y^2(1 - 1)\frac{N - 1}{N - 2} = 0$$

Again, this should make sense because if $r = 1.0$, $Y' = Y$ for all values of X, and therefore, the prediction errors, $Y - Y'$, will attain their minimum value of zero.

It should now be apparent that regression and correlation are closely related concepts and that both are related to the concept of variation. We now examine certain aspects of these relationships in order to shed additional light on the interpretation of correlation and regression statistics.

Regression and Variation

Consider once again Figure 7.5. We have already seen that the deviations, $Y - \overline{Y}$, represent error associated with using the sample mean as a predictor of Y. The value of $Y - \overline{Y}$ is called a *total deviation score*. For example, the total deviation score on Y for student 10 in Table 7.2 is

$$Y - \overline{Y} = 19.00 - 15.42 = 3.58$$

If we square each total deviation score and sum, we obtain SS_Y, which in regression analysis we call the *total variation in* Y. It is the amount of variation in Y that exists without considering the relationship between Y and X. In Table 7.2, $SS_Y = 140.92$.

We have also seen that the deviations $(Y - Y')$ represent error associated with using the regression line as a predictor of Y. The value of $Y - Y'$ is called the *unpredictable deviation score*. Student 10's unpredictable deviation score on Y is

$$Y - Y' = 19.00 - 17.45 = 1.55$$

If we square each of these deviations and sum, we obtain $SS_{Y-Y'}$, which we call the *unpredictable variation in Y*. It is the amount of variation in Y that remains after we consider the relationship between Y and X. In Table 7.2 $SS_{Y-Y'} = 54.46$.

Now let us look at a deviation we have not previously mentioned: $Y' - \overline{Y}$. From Figure 7.5 it is apparent that the deviations $(Y' - \overline{Y})$ are the differences between the regression line and the line representing $\overline{Y}$ across all values of X. What do these deviations mean? They are most easily understood by referring back to Formula 7.5:

$$Y' = \overline{Y} \qquad + r_{XY}\frac{s_Y}{s_X}(X - \overline{X})$$

Y' = mean of Y + predictable deviation

This formula shows that the predicted value of Y consists of two parts: $\overline{Y}$ and a deviation score $(X - \overline{X})$ scaled to reflect the predictability of Y from X $[r_{XY}(s_Y/s_X)]$. When $\overline{Y}$ is subtracted from both sides of Formula 7.5, we find that $Y' - \overline{Y}$ is equal to the portion of predictable deviation:

$$Y' - \overline{Y} \qquad = r_{XY}\frac{s_Y}{s_X}(X - \overline{X})$$

Y' − mean of Y = predictable deviation

Thus, the value of $Y' - \overline{Y}$ is called the *predictable deviation score*, which for student 10 is

$$Y' - \overline{Y} = 17.45 - 15.42 = 2.03$$

When this predictable deviation is squared and summed over subjects, the result is $SS_{Y'}$, which is called the *predictable variation in Y*.

Thus we have three types of deviation scores and three corresponding sources of variation.

Deviation score	Source of variation
$Y - \overline{Y}$ = total deviation	SS_Y = total variation in Y
$Y' - \overline{Y}$ = predictable deviation	$SS_{Y'}$ = predictable variation in Y
$Y - Y'$ = unpredictable deviation	$SS_{Y-Y'}$ = unpredictable variation in Y

Moreover, a relationship exists among the three types of deviation scores such that

$$Y - \overline{Y} = Y' - \overline{Y} \qquad\qquad + Y - Y'$$

total deviation = predictable deviation + unpredictable deviation

Using student 10's data, for example, you can see that

$$Y - \overline{Y} = Y' - \overline{Y} + Y - Y'$$

$$3.58 = 2.03 \quad + 1.55$$

Similarly, the relationship among the three sources of variation is

$$SS_Y = SS_{Y'} + SS_{Y-Y'} \tag{7.14}$$

total variation = predicted variation + unpredicted variation

In Table 7.2, $SS_Y = 140.92$, $SS_{Y'} = 86.46$, $SS_{Y-Y'} = 54.46$, and you can see that $140.92 = 86.46 + 54.46$.

The importance of Formula 7.14 is twofold. First, it forms the basis for interpreting the "quality" of a particular regression analysis directly in terms of predictable and unpredictable variation. Second, each of the components on the right-hand side of Formula 7.14 can be expressed in terms of r. Therefore, correlation can also be interpreted in terms of predictable and unpredictable variation. We first consider regression and variation.

Because the total variation in Y can be partitioned into predictable and unpredictable components, we can evaluate the accuracy of prediction by looking at the ratio of predicted variation to total variation. Conversely, we can evaluate the error of prediction by looking at the ratio of unpredicted variation to total variation. Dividing both sides of Formula 7.14 by SS_Y, we find

$$\frac{SS_Y}{SS_Y} = \frac{SS_{Y'}}{SS_Y} + \frac{SS_{Y-Y'}}{SS_Y}$$

$$1 = \frac{SS_{Y'}}{SS_Y} + \frac{SS_{Y-Y'}}{SS_Y}$$

The ratio $SS_{Y'}/SS_y$ is the *proportion* of the total variation in Y that is predictable from X. Similarly, the ratio $SS_{Y-Y'}/SS_Y$ is the *proportion* of the total variation in Y that is unpredictable from X. Using the example data illustrated in Table 7.2, we find these proportions to be

$$\frac{SS_{Y'}}{SS_Y} = \frac{86.46}{140.92} = .61 \qquad \frac{SS_{Y-Y'}}{SS_Y} = \frac{54.46}{140.92} = .39$$

Thus, .61 of the total variation in Y, or 61 percent of that variation, is predictable from our knowledge of X, and 39 percent is unpredictable from X.

Since the predictable and unpredictable proportions of variation must add up to 1.0 (see Formula 7.14), it follows that as one of them approaches 1.0 the other must approach zero. Clearly, the only way in which the predictable proportion of Y variation can be 1.0 is if the predictable variation is equal to the total variation. Similarly, the only way in which the unpredictable proportion of Y can be 1.0 is if the unpredictable variation is equal to the total variation. Thus, with perfect prediction, all the variation in Y is predictable and $SS_{Y'} = SS_Y$. With no predictability from X to Y, none of the variation in Y is predictable and $SS_{Y-Y'} = SS_Y$.

Correlation and Variation—The Coefficients of Nondetermination and Determination

To this point all of the SS values have been computed directly from obtained Y scores, predicted Y scores, and error scores. Fortunately, you might have noticed that one of the components in Formula 7.14, the unpredictable variation, can be expressed in terms of r, or more precisely, r^2. Earlier we showed that

$$SS_{Y-Y'} = SS_Y(1 - r^2) \tag{7.9}$$

If $SS_Y(1 - r^2)$ is the *amount* of unpredictable variation in Y, the corresponding *proportion* of unpredictable variation is

$$\frac{SS_{Y-Y'}}{SS_Y} = \frac{SS_Y(1 - r^2)}{SS_Y} = 1 - r^2 \tag{7.15}$$

This value, $1 - r^2$, is called the **coefficient of nondetermination** because it is the proportion of Y score variation that is *not* determined or predicted from X.

What about the variation in Y that is predictable? Intuitively, if the unpredictable variation can be expressed in terms of r, so too should the predictable variation. In fact, this intuition is correct. Combining Formulas 7.9 and 7.14, we obtain

$$SS_Y = SS_{Y'} + SS_Y(1 - r^2)$$

Rearranging terms, we have

$$SS_{Y'} = SS_Y - SS_Y(1 - r^2)$$

$$= SS_Y(1 - 1 + r^2)$$

$$= SS_Y(r^2)$$

Thus, the *amount* of variation in Y that is predictable from X is $SS_Y(r^2)$, and the corresponding *proportion* of predictable variation is

$$\frac{SS_{Y'}}{SS_Y} = \frac{SS_Y(r^2)}{SS_Y} = r^2 \tag{7.16}$$

The value of r^2 is called the **coefficient of determination** because it is the proportion of variation in Y that *is* determined or predicted by X.

Earlier we worked out proportions of predicted and unpredicted variation by using the sums of squares formulas. Using Formulas 7.15 and 7.16 with the midterm data, we find that

$$r^2 = .78^2 = .61$$

and

$$1 - r^2 = 1 - .61 = .39$$

exactly the same values as before.

In sum, r^2 has a very important interpretation in regression analysis. Its value indicates what proportions of variation in Y are partitioned into predictable variation (equal to r^2) and unpredictable variation (equal to $1 - r^2$).

COEFFICIENT OF NONDETERMINATION: The proportion of total variance in one variable that is not predictable from another variable. It is equal to $(1 - r^2)$.

COEFFICIENT OF DETERMINATION: The proportion of total variance in one variable that is predictable from another variable. It is equal to r^2.

7.7 A FINAL EXAMPLE

Social popularity and social competence data were used in Chapter 6 to illustrate the correlation coefficient. These data are shown again in Table 7.3 and will be used as a final example of the regression concepts covered in this chapter. In this example social popularity will be the predictor variable (X) and social competence will be the predicted variable (Y). Extracting the summary statistics necessary to compute a and b and to describe the regression equation, we have

Social popularity (X)	Social competence (Y)
$\overline{X} = 2.14$	$\overline{Y} = 13.50$
$s_X = .45$	$s_Y = 3.65$
$r_{XY} = .80$	

The values of the slope, b, and the intercept, a, can be computed by using Formulas 7.3 and 7.4

$$b = .80\frac{3.65}{.45} = 6.55 \qquad a = 13.50 - 6.55(2.14) = -.48$$

From Formula 7.2, the regression equation is

$$Y' = -.48 + 6.55(X)$$

By entering each X value into this equation or by using Formula 7.5, you can reproduce the predicted Y values (Y') shown in Table 7.3.

The regression line for predicting social competence from social popularity is shown in Figure 7.6. Clearly, not all of the data points fall precisely on the regression line, which you would expect because the correlation between these two variables is not perfect. Each deviation $(Y - Y')$ is a prediction error, and the average prediction error can be computed as either the variance error of estimate or the standard error of estimate. These values

Table 7.3 REGRESSION ANALYSIS OF SOCIAL POPULARITY (X) AND SOCIAL COMPETENCE (Y) DATA

Popularity (X)	Competence (Y)	Estimate (Y')	Error ($Y - Y'$)	Error^2 ($Y - Y'$)^2
2.5	15	15.89	−0.89	0.79
1.9	11	11.96	−0.96	0.92
1.8	13	11.31	1.69	2.86
1.9	9	11.96	−2.96	8.76
2.7	16	17.20	−1.20	1.22
2.2	14	13.93	0.07	0.01
2.0	16	12.62	3.38	11.42
2.0	15	12.62	2.38	5.66
2.8	14	17.85	−3.85	14.82
2.7	20	17.20	2.80	7.84
2.1	11	13.27	−2.27	5.15
2.9	17	18.51	−1.51	2.28
1.6	9	10.00	−1.00	1.00
2.5	19	15.89	3.11	9.67
1.7	12	10.65	1.35	1.82
1.7	8	10.65	−2.65	7.02
2.3	15	14.58	0.42	0.18
1.5	10	9.34	0.66	0.43
2.4	18	15.24	2.76	7.62
1.5	8	9.34	−1.34	1.80

$SS_Y = 252.99$ $SS_{Y'} = 161.36$ $SS_{Y-Y'} = 91.63$

$\overline{X} = 2.14$ $\overline{Y} = 13.50$ $s^2_{Y-Y'} = 5.09$ $s_{Y-Y'} = 2.26$

$s_x^2 = 0.20$ $s_Y^2 = 13.32$ $s_{Y'}^2 = 8.49$ $r_{XY} = .80$

$s_x = 0.45$ $s_Y = 3.65$

were computed in Table 7.3 by using Formulas 7.7 and 7.8. They can also be found by using Formulas 7.10 or 7.12:

$$s_{Y-Y'}^2 = 13.32(1 - .80^2)\frac{19}{20} \qquad s_{Y-Y'} = 3.65\,(1 - .80^2)\frac{19}{20}$$

$$= 5.06 \qquad\qquad\qquad = 2.25$$

The slight difference between these values and those appearing in Table 7.3 is due to rounding error.

The value of $SS_{Y-Y'}$ represents the amount of total social competence variability that is not predictable from social popularity. Dividing that value by the total variation in Y, SS_Y, produces the proportion of total social competence variation that is not predictable from social popularity:

$$\frac{91.63}{252.99} = .36$$

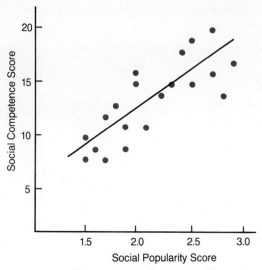

Figure 7.6 The regression line for predicting social competence (Y) from social popularity (X).

This proportion is equal to $1 - r^2 = 1 - .80^2 = .36$, the value of the coefficient of nondetermination.

The amount of social competence variation that *is* predictable from social popularity is $SS_{Y'}$, which from Table 7.3 is seen to be equal to 161.36. The ratio of $SS_{Y'}$ to SS_Y produces the coefficient of determination, r^2:

$$\frac{161.36}{252.99} = .64$$

which indeed is the value of r^2: $.80^2 = .64$. Thus, .64 of the total variation in social competence is predictable from social popularity. Of course, this result does not mean that .64 of the variability in social competence is *caused* by variability in social popularity. These are correlational data, and as you recall from Chapter 6, correlation does not necessarily mean causation.

7.8 A SECOND REGRESSION LINE: PREDICTING *X* FROM *Y*

The discussion to this point has been concerned with predicting Y scores from X scores. Predictions also can be made in the other direction. That is, we can predict X scores from Y scores. To do so we again invoke the criterion of least squares, only this time the regression line is chosen such that

$$\Sigma(X - X')^2 = minimum$$

The formulas for predicting X from Y are the same as all of the previous formulas except that Xs and Ys are interchanged. For example, the regression line coefficients for predicting X from Y are

$$b = r_{XY}\frac{s_X}{s_Y}$$

$$a = \overline{X} - b(\overline{Y})$$

whereas we saw previously that the regression coefficients for predicting Y from X were

$$b = r_{XY}\frac{s_Y}{s_X}$$

$$a = \overline{Y} - b(\overline{X})$$

Notice that in contrast to r, where correlating X with Y produces the same result as correlating Y with X, the regression coefficients for predicting X from Y are not the same as the regression coefficients for predicting Y from X. Earlier we found that the values of a and b for predicting Y from X were

$$b = .78\frac{3.57}{5.73} = .485 \qquad a = 15.42 - .485(15.83) = 7.74$$

For predicting X from Y the values of a and b are quite different:

$$b = .78\frac{5.73}{3.57} = 1.257 \qquad a = 15.83 - 1.257(15.42) = -3.55$$

Of course, because the values of a and b are different for predicting X from Y, the formula for the regression line also is different:

$$X' = a + b(Y) = -3.55 + 1.257(Y)$$

instead of

$$Y' = a + b(X) = 7.75 + .485(X)$$

Figure 7.7 illustrates the regression lines for predicting X from Y (dashed line) and Y from X (solid line). Notice that minimizing the sum of square deviations between X and X' involves minimizing the *horizontal* distances between the regression line for predicting X from Y and the Y-axis. Contrast this result with Figure 7.5, in which predicting Y from X minimized the *vertical* distances between the regression line and the X-axis.

Clearly, the two regression lines shown in Figure 7.7 are different. This will be the case whenever r is less than 1.0 or -1.0. When $r = 0.0$, the regression line for predicting Y from X will be a horizontal line through the value of $\overline{Y}$, whereas the regression line for predicting X from Y will be a vertical line through the value of $\overline{X}$. Thus, when $r = 0.0$, the two regression lines are perpendicular, one predicting $\overline{Y}$ from all values of X and the other predicting $\overline{X}$ from all values of Y.

When $r = 1.0$ or -1.0 all data points are perfectly predictable, whether predicting X from Y or Y from X. Thus, only when the correlation between X and Y is perfect do the two regression lines coincide.

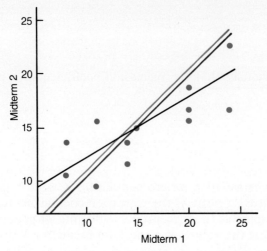

Figure 7.7 The regression lines for predicting (1) midterm 2 from midterm 1 and (2) midterm 1 from midterm 2.

7.9   NONLINEAR RELATIONSHIPS

We have repeatedly pointed out that the correlation and regression procedures discussed in Chapters 6 and 7 are useful only for describing *linear* relationships. For the sake of completeness and to familiarize you with a procedure you will see again in Chapter 13 on analyses of variance, we end this chapter by presenting a descriptive measure of *nonlinear* relationships.

Figure 7.8 is an illustration of a hypothetical nonlinear relationship be-

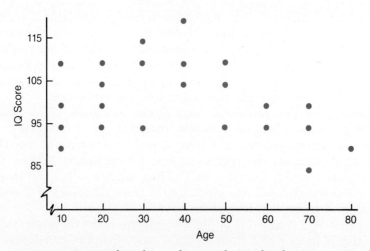

Figure 7.8 Scatterplot of a nonlinear relationship between age and IQ.

tween age (X) and IQ (Y). These data are also shown in Table 7.4. It is clear from these illustrations that IQ scores rise until age 40 and then decline.

A measure of the *total* relationship, both linear and nonlinear between two variables is called *eta²*, i.e., η^2, or the *correlation ratio*. Formula 7.17 gives the correlation ratio

$$\eta^2 = 1 - \frac{SS_{Y-Y'}}{SS_Y} \tag{7.17}$$

The expression SS_Y is not new. It is the sum of squared deviations of obtained Y scores from the overall mean of Y scores—what we earlier called the total variation in Y. The other expression, $SS_{Y-Y'}$ has the same form and, in fact, a similar meaning as our earlier expression for unpredictable variation in Y. However, it differs from that earlier expression in that each Y' value equals a conditional mean rather than a value predicted from a linear regression line. Thus, $SS_{Y-Y'}$ is the sum of squared deviations of obtained Y scores from their respective conditional distribution means. It is typically called the sum of squares within conditional distributions, or in shortened form, the *sum of squares within*. It is denoted by SS_{within}.

You can see in Figure 7.8 and Table 7.4 that for each age group there is a conditional distribution of IQ scores. The SS_{within} is calculated by finding the squared deviation of each Y value from its corresponding conditional mean and then summing all of the squared deviations. For example, the squared deviations for 10-year-olds are

$$(90 - 99)^2 = 81.00$$

$$(95 - 99)^2 = 16.00$$

$$(100 - 99)^2 = 1.00$$

Table 7.4 **EXAMPLE DATA FOR CALCULATING *eta²* BETWEEN AGE (X) AND IQ (Y)**

			Age					
	10	20	30	40	50	60	70	80
	90	95	95	105	95	95	85	90
	95	100	110	110	105	100	95	
IQ	100	105	115	120	110		100	
	100	110						
	110							
Means	99.00	102.50	106.67	111.67	103.33	97.50	93.33	90.00

Overall $\overline{Y}$ = 101.46

SS_Y = 1723.92

SS_{within} = 923.73

$$(100 - 99)^2 = 1.00$$

$$(110 - 99)^2 = 121.00$$

This process is continued for each distinct value of X. Finally, all of the squared deviations are summed to produce

$$SS_{within} = 923.73$$

The value of SS_Y is found in the usual way and equals 1723.92. Thus

$$\eta^2 = 1 - \frac{923.73}{1723.92}$$

$$= .46$$

The correlation ratio should be interpreted similarly to r^2. The ratio SS_{within}/SS_Y is the proportion of Y variation that is *not* predictable from X. The correlation ratio is 1 minus that proportion, and therefore, like r^2, is the proportion of Y variation that *is* predictable from X. Moreover, the correlation ratio equals *all* the variation in Y that is predictable from X, both from linear and nonlinear regression. Thus, eta^2 will always be larger than r^2, unless there is a perfect linear relationship between X and Y, in which case $eta^2 = r^2$. A measure of the degree of the nonlinear and *only* the nonlinear relationship between X and Y would be the difference $eta^2 - r^2$.

Finally, like all correlation indices, eta^2 does not necessarily imply causality. In the present example, although age accounts for 46 percent of the variation in IQ, it clearly cannot cause IQ. A more likely interpretation is that some factor that is correlated with age, such as years of education, accounts for the variation in IQ.

SUMMARY

In this chapter we extended the concepts of correlation to develop the concepts of regression. When a linear correlation exists between two variables, it is always possible to produce a linear equation of the form $Y' = a + b(X)$ that predicts the values of one of the variables from values of the other variable. The criterion for determining the constants a (the y intercept) and b (the slope) in the regression equation is called the criterion of least squares. This technique minimizes the errors of prediction, which are summarized by the variance error of estimate $(s_{Y-Y'}^2)$ or its square root, the standard error of estimate $(s_{Y-Y'})$. In addition, the accuracy of prediction can be expressed in terms of the variability in one variable that is predicted from another variable. We found that the proportion of total variation in one variable that is predictable from another is equal to r^2. Conversely, the proportion of total variation in one variable that is not predictable from another is equal to $1 -$

r^2. We also found that either variable in a correlated pair can be used to predict the other, although the regression constants and error estimates will be different, depending on which variable is used as the predictor. Finally we discuss eta^2, a measure similar in meaning to r^2 but which indexes the total extent of relationship, both linear and nonlinear, between two variables.

KEY WORDS

prediction	variance error of estimate
linear prediction	standard error of estimate
linear regression	predicted variation
regression coefficients	unpredicted variation
slope	coefficient of nondetermination
intercept	coefficient of determination
predicted score	eta^2
prediction error	

PROBLEMS

(Answer items 1–10 with true or false.)

1 If the correlation coefficient is negative, the slope of the regression line must be positive.

2 If two variables are perfectly linearly related, the slope of the regression line must equal -1 or 1.

3 The least squares method is used to determine the regression line that minimizes the variance of the actual Y values from the regression line.

4 The total sum of squares is equal to the sum of squared prediction scores plus the sum of squared error scores.

5 The variance of Y is equal to the variance of predicted scores plus the variance error of estimate.

6 The variance error of estimate is equal to the residual variance.

7 If the correlation between X and Y is .50, the predicted value of z_Y corresponding to $z_X = 2.0$ is 1.0.

8 If the correlation between X and Y is .50, the predicted value of Y corresponding to $X = 2$ is 1.0.

9 For the estimated regression line $Y' = 4 - 5(X)$, the correlation coefficient is less than zero.

10 If $SS_Y = 20$ and $SS_{Y-Y'} = 15$, the coefficient of determination equals .20.

11 The following data were collected regarding the hourly salaries and grade point averages (GPA) for students who graduated with a B.A. in psychology:

GPA X	Salary Y
2.5	$18
2.7	17
2.8	20
3.0	24
3.2	22
3.5	26
3.5	24
3.7	30

(a) Produce a scatterplot for these data with GPA as the X variable.
(b) Draw a straight line through the data to approximate a linear relationship between GPA and salary.
(c) Compute the least squares regression coefficients, a and b, and describe the regression line.
(d) Predict the monthly salary of students with GPAs of 2.9, 3.3, and 3.6.
(e) Use Formula 7.5 to predict the salaries for each actual GPA; then compute the $Y - Y'$ values for each student.
(f) Compute SS_Y, $SS_{Y'}$, and $SS_{Y-Y'}$.
(g) Compute the variance error of estimate and the standard error of estimate by using Formulas 7.7, 7.8, 7.10, and 7.12.
(h) Compute the coefficients of determination and nondetermination. Comment on the strength of the relationship.

PROOFS

Proof 7.1 SOME TEXTBOOKS DEFINE THE SLOPE AS Cov_{XY}/s_X^2. THE FOLLOWING PROOF SHOWS THE EQUIVALENCE OF THIS FORMULA AND FORMULA 7.3:

$$r_{XY}\frac{s_Y}{s_X} = \frac{Cov_{XY}}{s_X s_Y} \cdot \frac{s_Y}{s_X} \qquad \text{by definition of } r_{XY}$$

$$= \frac{Cov_{XY}}{s_X^2} \qquad \begin{array}{l}\text{by cancellation of } s_Y \text{ in the} \\ \text{numerator and denominator and} \\ \text{multiplication of the two } s_X \\ \text{terms in the denominator}\end{array}$$

Hypothesis Testing and Statistical Inference

*I*n Chapters 2 to 7, methods were introduced that can be used to quantify and organize sample data. These methods provide a meaningful description of scores on a variable or of relationships between variables. Tables, graphs, and descriptive statistics (e.g., means and variances) all are ways of reducing a potentially confusing welter of numbers into a more succinct description of a sample. In the next series of chapters we discuss another major application of statistics, namely, *hypothesis testing* and statistical *inference*. This application uses the information from a sample to make inferences (1) about relationships between variables or (2) about the characteristics of the population from which the sample was drawn.

For example, consider an experiment in which ten laboratory rats are randomly assigned to one of two maze-learning conditions, with five animals in each condition. In all respects the rats are treated the same, except that one group is injected with a special protein-synthesizing drug believed to enhance memory, and the other group is injected with a placebo (a neutral substance that does not affect bodily functions). It is found that the mean learning score for rats in the protein group is higher than the mean in the placebo group. Should we conclude that the protein injection caused learning scores to improve in the rats tested in this experiment? Or is it likely that rats who were more capable of learning mazes (regardless of what substance was injected) happened, just by chance, to be assigned to the protein group and the less capable animals were assigned to the placebo group? The fact that rats were randomly assigned to conditions allows us to use statistics that estimate the probability of the observed outcome. If the probability is very small that the outcome of the random assignment alone could have produced the observed difference between means, we should conclude that the protein injection contributed to the difference.

As a second example, consider a case in which we want to know whether male and female schoolchildren in some population (e.g., school district or city) differ in their ability to read. Rather than testing all children in the population we could take a sample of males and females and test only those children. Some of the statistics to be introduced in this part of the book are based on the assumption that the sample is drawn *randomly*, that is, that each child in the population has an equal chance of being included in the sample. Furthermore, random sampling involves independent selection of individuals, so selection of one individual for inclusion in the sample has no bearing on which of the remaining individuals will be included.

Suppose that the mean reading score for females turns out to be greater than the mean for males in our sample. Could we conclude that, on the average, females *in the population* are better readers than males? Or is it likely that the observed difference between sample means could have occurred even though population means do not differ? Random sampling permits us to use statistics that provide an estimate of this likelihood.

These examples are intended not only as instances of the kinds of inferences drawn on the basis of research results but also as an indication of the importance of understanding the principles of probability. Chapter 8 is devoted exclusively to introducing the concepts of randomness and probability. Once these ideas are clearly understood, the concepts underlying the statistical techniques described in later chapters can be readily grasped. We present two classes of inferential statistics, one for cases in which individuals are either randomly assigned to conditions or experience different conditions in some randomly determined order, and one for cases in which samples are drawn randomly from populations.

Chapter 8

Probability and the Binomial Distribution

8.1   INTRODUCTION

Every day we experience a large number of situations that, from our perspective, have unpredictable outcomes. For example, when walking along a crowded downtown sidewalk you might "chance" upon someone you know but did not expect to see in that location. The person just seemed to turn up. The mystery of events with unpredictable outcomes (usually those more exciting than walking down a sidewalk), along with the possibility of gaining instant wealth, may be among the primary motivations drawing many gamblers to their chosen games of chance. Each card that is dealt, each spin of the roulette wheel, and each drawing of a lottery number has associated with it an important aspect of randomness: The exact outcome of the event cannot be predicted in advance.

This would seem very shaky ground on which to build the foundation of successful gambling houses and lottery schemes. But there is another critical characteristic of randomness that makes these enterprises remarkably successful for the gambling houses and lottery organizers and rather costly for the vast majority of gamblers. Although an individual event, or *trial*, may have an unpredictable outcome, there is a predictable pattern of results that will almost certainly be obtained over a long series of trials (e.g., plays in a game of chance).

Consider a very simple game consisting of the flip of a fair coin. You and an opponent each wager one dollar on the outcome of the coin flip—heads or tails. Assuming that it is a fair coin, we cannot know for certain what will be the outcome of the flip, but we do know that either outcome has an equal **probability** of occurring. By the phrase "probability of obtaining a result" we mean the proportion of equally likely outcomes of the trial that produces the result. In the case of flipping a fair coin, each of two outcomes is equally likely, heads or tails. So the probability of obtaining heads is 1/2, or .5.

Knowledge of the probability of obtaining a result on a single trial allows us to determine the proportion of times a result should occur over many trials. For example, if the coin-flipping game is played over a long series of trials, a predictable pattern will emerge. Each side of the coin will appear approximately equally often, and neither player will be very far ahead or behind. There is no guarantee that one specific player will be ahead in the long run. This pattern, combined with the fact that it is not a very elaborate and exciting game, are why you will not find this game being played in casinos.

Lotteries and gambling casinos use only those systems and games that ensure an advantage over the gambler *in the long run*. That is, in the long run the gambler would lose more times than he or she would win, ensuring that the casino would make money. Since there are so many gamblers, many of whom play many times, casinos and lottery organizers need only be concerned with long-term patterns. These patterns are predictable, as we will demonstrate in this chapter.

8.2   PROBABILITY MADE SIMPLE

As with concepts such as intelligence, learning, or personality, probability can be defined in various ways. The definition that we use is based on the notion of proportion, or *relative frequency*. Recall from Chapter 3 that the relative frequency of a *score* is obtained by dividing the frequency of that score by the total number of scores. Similarly, the probability of a trial producing a particular result (e.g., a coin flip yielding heads or drawing an ace from a deck of 52 playing cards) can be defined as the number of equally likely and *mutually exclusive* outcomes that fit the result, divided by the total number of possible, equally likely, and mutually exclusive outcomes. *Equally likely* means that in the long run each of the possible outcomes will occur with approximately equal frequency.

PROBABILITY: The proportion of equally likely and mutually exclusive outcomes of a trial that produce a result of interest.

By **mutually exclusive** we mean that no more than one of the outcomes can be produced by a single trial. For example, the toss of a coin cannot produce both heads and tails—when one outcome occurs, the other(s) cannot. The aspects of probability covered in this chapter may be applied to any problem that meets this definition of probability.

MUTUALLY EXCLUSIVE: Outcomes of a trial are mutually exclusive if the occurrence of one outcome precludes the occurrence of the other outcomes.

Consider a simple example. If you were to take an examination consisting of a single true-false question, what would be the probability of guessing the correct answer? Most people respond with something like "50-50" or "one-half" or ".5," and they would be correct. How do people come to that kind of conclusion? There are three steps involved in arriving at the answer: (1) Specify the total number of outcomes that are equally likely and mutually exclusive, (2) specify the number of outcomes that fit the result of interest, and (3) generate a ratio of these two frequencies. The total number of mutually exclusive outcomes in our true-false example is two, "right" and "wrong." The number of outcomes that fit the result (being right) is one. We can now define the probability (let us call it p) of being right by guessing on a single true-false question as

$$p = \frac{\text{number of outcomes that fit the result}}{\text{total number of outcomes}} = \frac{1}{2} = .5$$

The probability value also can be viewed as the relative frequency with which a result is expected to occur over many trials. In the case of a test consisting of many true-false items and a student who guesses on each one, we would expect the student to get about .5, or 1/2, of the items correct.

As a second example, suppose that someone had a jar containing three $20 bills and a single $1 bill. You are given the opportunity to draw one bill from the jar without looking. What would be the probability of choosing a $20 bill? There are four outcomes in all, and three (the $20 bills) fit the result of interest, so the probability would be

$$p = \frac{\text{number of outcomes that fit the result}}{\text{total number of outcomes}} = \frac{3}{4} = .75$$

We will sometimes express the probability of a result as $p(R)$, where R stands for some description of the result. In the case of drawing bills from a jar, the probability of drawing a $20 bill could be written as $p(\$20) = .75$.

Some very important facts about probability follow from our definition. One is that the lowest possible probability of obtaining a result of interest occurs when no outcomes fit, yielding a probability of zero (e.g., the probability of drawing a joker from a deck of cards after all jokers have been removed). Similarly, the highest possible probability of obtaining a result of interest is when all of the possible outcomes of a trial fit the result (e.g., the probability of obtaining heads or tails when flipping a coin). We can summarize these observations by noting that the probability of a result, p, will take on some value in this range: $0 \leq p \leq 1$.

8.3 ADDITION RULE

In some situations we must find the probability that any one of a number of possible results will occur, where each result consists of a set of outcomes. For instance, suppose we have an ordinary deck of 52 playing cards and want to compute the probability of randomly drawing a single card that is either an ace or a king. In this case there are two results of interest: ace or king. There are four aces in the deck (ace of hearts, ace of diamonds, ace of clubs, ace of spades), so there are four outcomes that fit the result of drawing an ace. Because all cards are equally likely to be drawn, the probability of obtaining this result is 4/52, or .077. Similarly, the probability that the draw will result in a king is .077. Now what is the probability of drawing *either* an ace *or* a king?

One way to handle this problem would be to follow the three steps outlined in our definition of probability. First, find the total number of possible outcomes. In the present case there are 52. Next, determine the number of outcomes that fit either of the results of interest, ace or king. There are eight cards that meet this requirement (four aces and four kings). The ratio of these two frequencies is 8/52, or .154, and is the probability of obtaining either an ace or a king when randomly drawing a single card from a deck.

Alternatively, we could have solved this problem by first finding the probability of occurrence for each of the two results of interest (ace, king) and then adding these probabilities together:

Result: ace   king

Probability: 4/52 + 4/52 = 8/52 = .154

This procedure is based on a rule known as the **addition rule** of probability. This rule states that on a single trial, the probability of obtaining any one of a set of possible results based on mutually exclusive outcomes is equal to the sum of the individual probabilities of each result. This rule holds because in the act of adding the individual probabilities we have tallied the number of outcomes that fit each result of interest, as required by step 2 in our computation of probability.

ADDITION RULE: The probability of obtaining any one of a number of mutually exclusive results is equal to the sum of the probabilities of the individual results: $p(A$ or B or C or . . .$) = p(A) + p(B) + p(C) + . . .$

It is no surprise that the same answer is found when we use the addition rule as when we count all the outcomes that fit the results of interest and divide by the total number of outcomes. The two methods are two different procedures for accomplishing the same thing. In finding the probability of drawing an ace or a king we could use either approach:

Addition rule: 4/52 + 4/52 = 8/52 = .154

Count outcomes: (4 + 4)/52 = 8/52 = .154

This form of the addition rule does not apply, however, when the outcomes that fit the results of interest are not all mutually exclusive. This situation might occur, for example, when we want to determine the probability of drawing an ace or a heart. Notice that one outcome fits both of the results of interest (ace of hearts), which violates the restriction that all outcomes be mutually exclusive. The addition rule can be adjusted to handle such cases, but this is not necessary for any of the concepts introduced in this book.[1]

The addition rule is useful, then, for situations in which probabilities of results consisting of mutually exclusive outcomes are known and we wish to

---

[1]The general form of the addition rule does not include the restriction that results must be mutually exclusive. In this version the probability of obtaining any one of a number of results is the sum of their individual probabilities minus the probability of their joint occurrence. For example, the probability of drawing an ace or a heart from a deck of cards would be $p(A$ or $H) = 4/52 + 13/52 - 1/52$. There is one outcome that represents the joint occurrence of the two results (the ace of hearts), and the probability of drawing that card is 1/52.

find the probability of a trial producing one or another of the results. For instance, consider the example from the introduction to Part Three, the reading ability of male and female children. Suppose that the population of reading ability scores for males is normally distributed. What is the probability of randomly sampling from that population a score that is 2 or more standard deviations above or below the population mean?

Figure 8.1 illustrates this situation, the shaded regions indicating the results of interest (2 or more standard deviations above or below the mean). Using the properties of the standard normal distribution learned in Chapter 5, we can determine the probability of drawing a score from each of these regions. According to Table B in Appendix III, each region occupies .0228 of the total area under the curve. Therefore, there is a .0228 probability of randomly selecting a score from the region 2 or more standard deviations below the mean and a .0228 probability of drawing a score from the area 2 or more standard deviations above the mean. (Recall from Chapter 5 that the proportion of area under a frequency distribution corresponds to the proportion of scores in that region.) These two results consist of mutually exclusive outcomes (a score in one region cannot also be in the other), so the addition rule can be applied. Thus, the probability of randomly selecting a member of the population that is in either of these two regions is .0228 + .0228 = .0456.

One could just count outcomes to find the probability of obtaining any one of a number of mutually exclusive results, so you might wonder why the additional rule is useful. There are occasions when we might know the probabilities of a number of mutually exclusive results for a trial, without knowing how many outcomes are in each result or how many possible outcomes exist. The sampling problem described in the previous paragraph is an example of this situation. The addition rule allows problems of this type to be solved without knowing the number of scores in the population or the number of scores that fit each of the results.

One more important implication of the addition rule is that when a trial consists of mutually exclusive outcomes, the sum of the probabilities of all

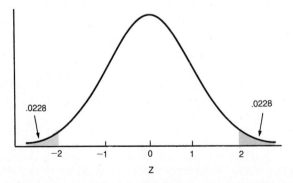

Figure 8.1 Areas of the standard normal distribution representing 2 or more standard deviations below the mean and 2 or more standard deviations above the mean.

the outcomes is equal to 1: $\Sigma p = 1$. For example, in the case of rolling a die (singular for *dice*), each of the six outcomes has a probability of 1/6. When all are summed together we have $1/6 + 1/6 + 1/6 + 1/6 + 1/6 + 1/6 = 6/6 = 1$.

8.4   MULTIPLICATION RULE

Some statistical problems require calculation of the probability of results based on a group of trials, where each trial has its own set of possible outcomes and the trials are *independent* of one another. Trials are independent when the outcome of the trial has no influence on the outcome of the other trials. Examples include rolling two dice or flipping a coin five times in a row. In these cases each die or coin toss represents an **independent trial.** That is, the outcome of the roll of the first die tells us nothing about how the second roll will turn out, and the outcome of the first coin flip does not permit us to predict the outcome of the next.

INDEPENDENT TRIALS: The outcome of one trial has no influence on the outcome of another trial.

To illustrate, consider a psychic who claims to be able to predict the outcome of a series of two coin flips. We will work under the assumption that the psychic has no special power. That is, his predictions are unrelated to what actually occurs. What is the probability that he will make a correct prediction on the first flip and again on the second? We begin by finding the number of possible sequences of outcomes associated with two coin flips. Figure 8.2 shows that there are four possible sequences. Each of the sequences are equally likely to occur because each of the outcomes in a sequence is equally likely. The psychic must choose just one of these sequences, only

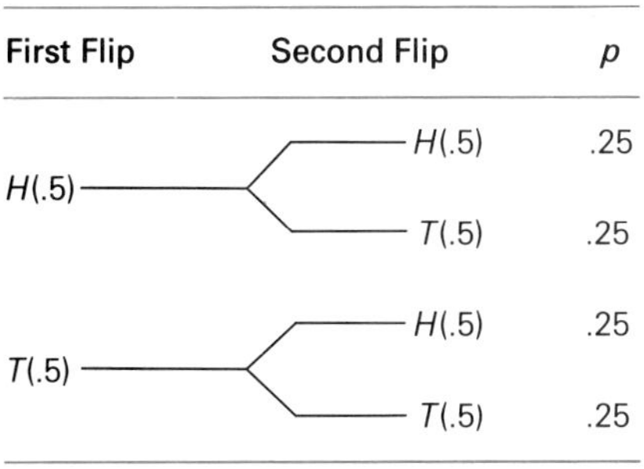

First Flip	Second Flip	p
H(.5)	H(.5)	.25
	T(.5)	.25
T(.5)	H(.5)	.25
	T(.5)	.25

Figure 8.2   Possible outcomes of a series of two flips of a fair coin. H = heads; T = tails.

one of which will turn out to be correct. Therefore, the probability of predicting the correct sequence will be the ratio of the number of correct sequences (one) to the total number of sequences (four), which is 1/4, or .25.

Now consider what would happen if the psychic were to make predictions about a series of three coin flips. What is the probability of being correct on all three? Start by determining the total number of possible sequences. The first flip has two possible outcomes, and each of these could be paired with the two possible outcomes on the second flip, as shown in Figure 8.3. Each of these four sets of outcomes could be combined with either of the two outcomes on the third flip, making a total of eight possible sequences of outcomes. Only one of these sequences will occur, so the probability of choosing the one that occurs is 1/8, or .125.

Each of these two problems could have been solved with a different approach, called the **multiplication rule** of probability. This rule states that the probability of obtaining a set of results involving a number of independent trials (e.g., flipping coins or rolling dice) can be found by multiplying the individual probabilities of each result. In the case of making correct predictions about two consecutive coin flips, we have the probability of a correct prediction on the first flip multiplied by the probability of a correct prediction on the second flip: $1/2(1/2) = 1/4 = .25$.

MULTIPLICATION RULE: The probability of obtaining a set of results from a group of independent trials is equal to the product of the probability of the individual results: $p(A \text{ and } B \text{ and } C \ldots) = p(A)p(B)p(C). \ldots$

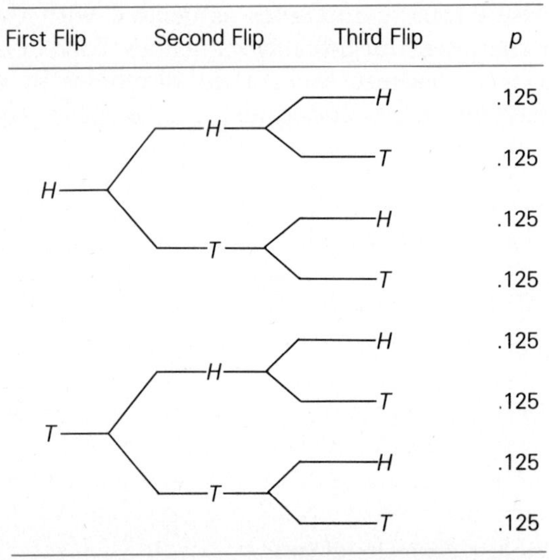

First Flip	Second Flip	Third Flip	p
H	H	H	.125
		T	.125
	T	H	.125
		T	.125
T	H	H	.125
		T	.125
	T	H	.125
		T	.125

Figure 8.3 Possible outcomes of a series of three flips of a fair coin. H = heads; T = tails.

As with the addition rule, the multiplication rule represents a different way of counting the total number of possible outcomes and the outcomes that fit the result of interest. Multiplication represents the fact that in determining the total number of outcomes, each possible outcome of one trial could be combined with any one of the possible outcomes of the other trial (as shown in Figures 8.2 and 8.3), and each of these combinations could then be combined with any one of the possible outcomes of the third trial, and so on.

The multiplication rule will also work for groups of trials that each consist of more than just two possible outcomes. Suppose, for example, that our psychic were asked to predict the result of rolling two dice. We will assume that one is red and the other white, and the psychic is to predict what will turn up on each one when they are rolled together. If the psychic's predictions are unrelated to what actually happens when the dice are rolled, there is a 1/6, or .167, probability of being correct on any single die. What would be the probability of a correct prediction on both dice? The multiplication rule tells us to multiply the probability of a correct prediction by itself twice to represent two occurrences of a correct prediction: $1/6(1/6) = 1/36 = .028$. This answer can be verified by examining Figure 8.4, which presents the 36 possible sets of outcomes produced by rolling two dice. Only one of the sets will actually occur, so there is only a 1/36 probability that the psychic will select the correct one.

The multiplication rule can be applied to sampling from populations as well. For example, suppose that the population of reading ability scores for male children and the population of scores for female children both have normal distributions. A single score is randomly drawn from each population, with each selection independent of the other. What is the probability that the sample will consist of a score for a male that is below its population mean and a score for a female that is above its population mean? In any normal distribution half of the members are above the mean and half are below, so the two individual results each have a probability of .5. The multiplication rule states that the probability of two independent events producing a specific sequence of results can be found by multiplying the individual probabilities of those results: $.5(.5) = .25$.

An additional example of the multiplication rule is a case in which a sample of four scores is drawn from the distribution of male scores. To simplify this example we will assume that sampling is done *with replacement;* that is, after the first score is drawn, it is put back into the population before the next score is drawn. On any draw, then, each member of a population of N scores will have a probability of $1/N$ of being chosen. When sampling is done *without replacement,* however, once a score is drawn it is not returned to the population. The number of scores remaining in the population decreases with each draw, so the probability of drawing any specific score changes from one draw to the next: $1/N$ on the first draw, $1/(N - 1)$ on the second, $1/(N - 2)$ on the third, and so on.

When sampling is done with replacement, then, what is the probability that all four scores will be less than or equal to the mean of the distribution? We know that the probability of drawing a single score less than or equal to

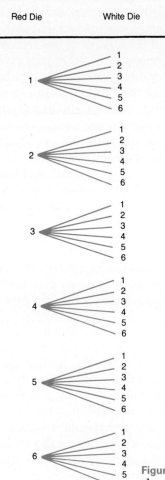

Red Die	White Die

Figure 8.4   Thirty-six possible outcomes in the roll of two dice.

the mean of a normal distribution is .5. The multiplication rule indicates that the probability of obtaining four such outcomes in a set of four independent trials would be .5(.5)(.5)(.5) = .0625.

One further application of the multiplication rule is demonstrated in Box 8.1. The multiplication rule can be altered to accommodate situations involving trials that are not independent, but for our purposes there is no need to deal with that version of the rule.

8.5   WHEN BOTH RULES APPLY

Up to this point we have learned two important rules of probability. The addition rule states that the probability of a single trial producing any one of a number of mutually exclusive outcomes is equal to the sum of the proba-

Box 8.1   # The Multiplication Rule and Methods of Contraception

One source of information available to people making choices among methods of contraception is the probability of preventing pregnancy in a one-year period. For example, one method might have a prevention probability of .95 and another a probability of .98. It may appear that these two methods differ very little in their effectiveness, suggesting that other factors (e.g., cost or convenience) may be more likely to affect one's choice. But before ignoring the small difference in annual probability of prevention, consider the long-term differences. If we assume that each year represents an independent trial and that the probability of remaining free of pregnancy in any given year is .95 with one method and .98 with the other, what is the probability of remaining free of pregnancy for 15 years with each of these methods?

The multiplication rule allows us to answer this question because each year represents an independent trial. The probability of having no pregnancies in a 15-year period by using the first method is equal to .95 multiplied by itself 15 times, or $(.95)^{15}$. This figure is equal to .463—so there is a better than 50 percent chance of having at least one pregnancy in a 15-year period. For the second method, the probability of having no pregnancies in 15 years is $(.98)^{15}$, which is equal to .739.

Clearly, there is a noticeable difference in the long-term effectiveness of these two methods.

bilities of the individual outcomes. The multiplication rule states that the probability of a set of independent trials producing a specific set of outcomes can be obtained by multiplying the probabilities of the individual outcomes. There are important situations that call for application of both of these rules. One example is when the task is to find the probability of obtaining *any one* of a number of different sets of outcomes based on a group of independent trials. The multiplication rule can be used to find the probability for each set of outcomes; then the addition rule is used to find the probability of obtaining any one of the sets.

For instance, recall the psychic's attempt to predict the outcome of two coin flips. We used the multiplication rule to determine the probability of correct predictions on both flips under the assumption that the psychic's predictions were not related to the actual outcomes of the coin flips. In this case there was only one outcome set of interest to us. But what if we had been given the task of determining the probability of making one correct prediction on two coin flips? In this case there are two outcome sets of interest: a correct prediction followed by an incorrect one, or an incorrect prediction followed by a correct one. The probability of obtaining the first set (correct then incorrect) would be .5(.5) = .25. The other set (incorrect then correct) would have a probability of .5(.5) = .25. Therefore, the probability of making exactly one correct prediction would be the probability of obtaining one *or* the other of the two sets that produce one correct prediction. The two sets consist of mutually exclusive outcomes, so according to the addition rule we have only to add the probabilities of each set to find the probability of obtaining any one of them: $.25 + .25 = .5$.

Consider the case in which the psychic is asked to make predictions for a series of three coin flips. To find the probability of making exactly one correct prediction, we first need to list the sets of outcomes that fit the pattern; then we can compute each of their probabilities and add them. There are three such sets: correct, incorrect, incorrect; incorrect, correct, incorrect; and incorrect, incorrect, correct. Each one has a probability of $.5(.5)(.5) = .125$. Therefore, the probability that any one of them will occur is $.125 + .125 + .125 = .375$.

The probability of one correct prediction in rolling two dice (e.g., a red one and a white one) can also be found with this procedure. Two sets of outcomes fit the pattern: correct on red and incorrect on white or incorrect on red and correct on white. The probability of the first set is $1/6(5/6) = 5/36 = .139$, and the probability of the second is $5/6(1/6) = 5/36 = .139$. The probability of obtaining either one (i.e., the probability of one correct prediction) would be $.139 + .139 = .278$.

We can summarize the steps involved in using the multiplication and addition rules together as follows: First, determine the number of outcome sets that fit the desired pattern. Second, compute the probability of each outcome set by using the multiplication rule. Third, find the probability of obtaining any one of the outcome sets by using the addition rule.

Unfortunately, with larger groups of trials, such as predictions about the outcome of a series of 10 coin flips, the number of sets of outcomes that fit the required pattern can grow very large. For example, in the coin-flipping task there are 252 sequences of correct and incorrect predictions that produce the pattern of exactly 5 correct predictions in 10 attempts. One of the patterns would be 5 correct predictions in a row followed by 5 incorrect ones; another would be 5 incorrect predictions, then 5 correct ones; and there are 250 others. Each one of these sequences would be equally likely—$(.5)^{10}$. For a series of 20 attempts, there are 184,756 sequences that yield 10 correct predictions! It clearly would be an onerous task to list all of the possible sequences in order to find out how many fit the required pattern, so a different approach is needed.

Combinations

The solution to this problem is to use a system of counting based on the concept of **combination.** This concept refers to unique subgroups of objects that can be formed from a larger group of objects. For example, consider a set of four pets: a rabbit, dog, cat, and bird. One could form several unique combinations or subgroups of two pets from this set of four. Suppose we designate the four pets by using the first letter of their names. We can see that there are six unique combinations of two pets each: RD, RC, RB, DC, DB, and CB. Note that we are interested only in the identity of the pets in each combination, not the order in which we mention them. Thus, RD and DR represent the same combination and would not be counted twice.

Now consider a case of predicting the outcome of coin flips. Suppose that 1, 2, 3, and 4 represent the four flips. There are six possible combinations of two correct predictions in a set of four flips: correct on the first and second flips, correct on the first and third, and so on.

COMBINATION: A unique subgroup of objects formed from a (usually) larger group.

There is a formula for computing the number of unique combinations of r objects that can be selected from a set of n objects:

$$_nC_r = \frac{n!}{(n-r)!r!} \tag{8.1}$$

The term $n!$ designates an operation known as *factorial*, in which we find the factorial of some integer, n, by multiplying together all the integers from n down to 1: $n(n-1)(n-2)\ldots(1)$. For example, the factorial of 4 would be $4! = 4(3)(2)(1) = 24$. The term $4!$ would be read as "four factorial." The value of $0!$ is defined to be 1, which prevents division by zero. In our example of forming combinations of two objects from a set of four, we would have

$$_4C_2 = \frac{4!}{(4-2)!2!} = \frac{4(3)(2)(1)}{2(1)(2)(1)} = \frac{24}{4} = 6$$

We can now apply this formula to the problem of determining how many different sets of outcomes fit a specified result for a group of independent trials. For example, in the case of the psychic's prediction of the outcomes of two coin flips, we found that two different sets of outcomes fit the result of one correct response. Formula 8.1 can be used to produce the same conclusion. In this case we are interested in how many combinations of one object (the correct prediction) can be drawn from a set of two objects (first and second prediction). This problem could be computed as

$$_2C_1 = \frac{2!}{(2-1)!1!} = 2$$

Similarly, for the case of one correct response in three attempts we would have

$$_3C_1 = \frac{3!}{(3-1)!1!} = 3$$

which is consistent with what we found earlier. We can also verify the claim that there are 252 combinations of five correct and five incorrect predictions in ten attempts:

$$_{10}C_5 = \frac{10!}{(10-5)!5!} = 252$$

Try using Formula 8.1 to determine how many different combinations of 10 objects can be selected from a set of 20 objects.

We now have a method of determining how many different sets of outcomes fit a specific result (e.g., one correct prediction in three attempts). This is the first step in our use of the multiplication and addition rules to compute the probability of obtaining any one of the sets of outcomes that fit the result of interest. The second step is to find the probability of each outcome set. For a group of identical trials (e.g., coin flips), each of the outcome sets that yield a specific number of outcomes of interest (e.g., five correct predictions in ten attempts) has an equal probability. This statement is true because each set contains the same number of trials that produce an outcome of interest (e.g., a correct prediction by the psychic) and the same number that do not produce the outcome (e.g., an incorrect prediction). To compute the probability of each set of outcomes, we multiply the same probability values together, but in different orders.

This reasoning can be seen clearly in such an example as having a psychic predict the outcome of three rolls of a die. If we consider outcome sets that lead to two correct predictions, we see that there are three: correct, correct, incorrect; correct, incorrect, correct; incorrect, correct, correct. Assuming that the psychic's predictions are not related to the outcomes of the rolls, the probabilities of these three outcome sets, respectively, are

$$1/6(1/6)(5/6) = 5/216 = .023$$

$$1/6(5/6)(1/6) = 5/216 = .023$$

$$5/6(1/6)(1/6) = 5/216 = .023$$

The calculation of the probability of outcome sets such as these can be expressed with the following general formula:

$$p^r q^{(n-r)} \tag{8.2}$$

where p is the probability of a trial producing the outcome of interest (e.g., a correct prediction), q is the probability of not producing that outcome, n is the total number of trials, and r is the number of trials that produce the outcome of interest.

We have shown how to find the number of outcome sets that meet some criterion (e.g., one correct prediction) and how to compute the probability of obtaining each set. The final step is to figure the probability of obtaining any one of these outcome sets by using the addition rule. This probability is obtained by computing the sum of the individual probabilities of the outcome sets (.023 + .023 + .023 = .069). The act of summing a number of identical values is equivalent to multiplying the value by the number of times it occurs in the addition operation. Thus, summing .023 to itself three times will produce the same result as multiplying .023 by three. Thus, we can make our three-step procedure even easier for cases in which each outcome set that fits the pattern of interest is equally probable. First, find the number of relevant outcome sets by using the combinations formula. Second, find the probability of obtaining a specific set by using Formula 8.2. Finally, multiply the two results together. These steps are summarized in Formula 8.3:

$$_nC_rp^rq^{(n-r)} \tag{8.3}$$

The term $_nC_r$ represents the number of outcome sets that will produce r occurrences of the outcome of interest (e.g., a correct prediction) in a set of n trials. The term $p^rq^{(n-r)}$ represents the probability of each of the $_nC_r$ sets.

Next we will try some examples involving Formula 8.3. For the first one suppose that we flip a fair coin eight times. What is the probability that we will obtain five heads? The probability of a head (p) is .5, the probability of not getting a head (q) is .5, there are eight trials in all $(n = 8)$, and we are interested in sets of outcomes where five trials produce a head $(r = 5)$. Applying Formula 8.3, we have

$$_8C_5(.5)^5(.5)^{(8-5)} = 56(.031)(.125) = .219$$

Now suppose that we ask our psychic to predict the suit (heart, diamond, club, spade) of a card randomly drawn from a deck of 52 cards. The psychic is asked to make a prediction on each of five trials; the card drawn on each trial is put back and the deck is reshuffled at the end of each trial (this step ensures sampling with replacement). If the predictions are not influenced by the upcoming result of the card draw, what is the probability that the psychic will be correct on four trials? In this case the probability is .25 that he will be correct on any one trial and .75 that he will not be correct, so $p = .25$ and $q = .75$. In addition, $n = 5$ and $r = 4$. By Formula 8.3 we have

$$_5C_4(.25)^4(.75)^{(5-4)} = 5(.004)(.75) = .015$$

Use Formula 8.3 to find the probability that, in the absence of any special power, the psychic could predict correctly the outcome of all five trials.

8.6   THE BINOMIAL PROBABILITY DISTRIBUTION

In any situation involving a group of independent trials (e.g., predictions about the outcomes of a series of coin tosses), we can compute the probability of obtaining any particular frequency of occurrence of a specific outcome (e.g., six correct predictions in ten tosses). For example, in ten coin tosses we could obtain anywhere from zero to ten correct predictions. Formula 8.3 could be used to find the probability of each of these results. We have done this computation under the assumption that predictions are not influenced by the outcome of the trial. The probability of obtaining a given number correct in a series of ten two-alternative choices is shown in Table 8.1. Note that it is quite unlikely that someone would obtain an extreme score like zero or 10 if his or her predictions were not related to the outcomes of the trials. On the other hand a score like 5 would occur with a probability of about .25.

Table 8.1

Number correct	Probability
0	.0010
1	.0098
2	.0439
3	.1172
4	.2051
5	.2461
6	.2051
7	.1172
8	.0439
9	.0098
10	.0010

The distribution in Table 8.1 is called a **binomial probability distribution.** The name indicates that it is a distribution of probabilities, and the term *binomial* refers to the fact that it is based on trials that consist of outcomes that may be assigned to two classes: outcomes of interest versus all other outcomes. In the case of predicting the result of coin flips, the classes of outcomes would be correct versus incorrect predictions.

BINOMIAL PROBABILITY DISTRIBUTION: A distribution of the probability of each possible number of outcomes of interest in a group of independent trials where each trial has two possible classes of outcomes.

The binomial probability distribution can be useful for answering questions of the sort introduced in this chapter. In addition, it can make finding solutions to even more complicated problems rather easy. Consider the problem of finding the probability that a psychic without special power could make *eight or more* correct predictions in a series of ten coin tosses. Scores of 8, 9, or 10 correct would all be considered results of interest. The probability of obtaining each of these three results can be found by using the binomial probability distribution. Then we can use the addition rule to determine the probability that any one of these three different results will be obtained. The addition rule is applicable because the three results (eight, nine, or ten correct) are mutually exclusive. Taking the probabilities from Table 8.1 we have .0439 + .0098 + .0010 = .0547.

Notice that it is quite unlikely that someone would be able to get eight or more predictions correct in ten attempts if they were not truly psychic. If a psychic were able to score in this range, what would you conclude? Would you consider it a fluke or would you believe the psychic has some special power? Use Table 8.1 to find the probability of making more than eight or fewer than two correct predictions in the absence of special psychic power (answer: .0216). How likely would one be to make four, five, or six correct predictions (answer: .6563)?

Fortunately, binomial probability distributions have been worked out for cases involving many different values of n (number of trials). Table C in Appendix III provides the distributions for the values of n from 5 through 24 with $p = .5$. In each distribution the probability of obtaining each possible value of r (number of trials that produce an outcome of interest) is given. We will examine the task of predicting the outcomes of a series of ten coin tosses in the absence of any psychic power. The probability, p, of being correct on a single trial is .5. According to Formula 8.3 the probability of making seven correct predictions would be

$$_{10}C_7(.5)^7(.5)^{(10-7)} = 120(.0078125)(.125) = .1172$$

which is consistent with the entry in Table 8.1. This probability value can also be found in the appropriate location in Table C.

We also can use Table C to obtain the probability that the number of correct predictions will fall within a certain range, for example, *at least* 12 correct out of 15 predictions on the coin-flipping task. The relevant values of number correct (12, 13, 14, and 15) represent mutually exclusive results, so by the addition rule the probability of obtaining any one of them is the sum of their individual probabilities. The probability of obtaining each result is available in Table C. The number of independent events is 15 and the probability of a correct prediction on any toss is .5, so the relevant probabilities are

$$p(12, 13, 14, \text{ or } 15) = p(12) + p(13) + p(14) + p(15)$$

$$= .0139 + .0032 + .0005 + .0000 = .0176$$

A similar problem is solved in Box 8.2.

Normal Approximation to the Binomial Distribution

Table C is appropriate for situations involving up to 24 independent trials when the probability of a trial producing the outcome of interest is .5. For cases in which the probability is different from .5, other sources may be consulted for tables of the binomial probability distribution (e.g., Beyer, 1968; Pagano, 1986). What about cases involving more than 24 trials? A solution to this problem is based on the fact that when the probability of any event producing the outcome of interest is .5., the shape of the binomial distribution is unimodal and symmetrical. You can see this result by examining the probabilities in Table C.

Further, with a larger number of independent trials, the shape of the binomial probability distribution is more closely approximated by the normal distribution, even when p is not equal to .5. The normal distribution is a better approximation, however, the closer p is to .5 and the more independent trials there are. The advantage of the similarity between the binomial and

Box 8.2   # The Binomial Distribution and Wine Tasting

Suppose that a vintner has developed a method of producing an inexpensive wine that imitates the taste of an expensive wine. He claims that wine-tasting experts cannot tell the difference between his wine and the much more expensive vintage that it is intended to imitate. To test the claim, a group of 20 experienced wine tasters are asked to taste two unmarked wine samples. One is the expensive vintage and the other is the imitation. The tasters are asked to decide which of the two samples is genuine, even if they must make a guess. If the experts are unable to tell the difference between the two samples, what is the probability that 16 or more of the 20 experts will correctly identify the expensive wine?

In this problem the 20 experts are considered independent trials because we assume that each one is asked to make a decision on his or her own, without consulting colleagues. If none of the experts can truly distinguish the authentic wine, for each expert there is a .5 probability that the correct wine will be selected. Therefore, we have 20 independent binomial trials, where the outcome of interest is the selection of the correct wine. The probability of at least 16 experts making the correct choice can be computed from Table C in Appendix III, with $n = 20$ and $p = .5$. Notice that the task is to find the probability of obtaining any one of a number of results (16 or more). Each of the different results is mutually exclusive, so the probability of obtaining any one of them is the sum of their individual probabilities. From Table C we have

$$p(16) + p(17) + p(18) + p(19) + p(20) =$$

$$.0046 + .0011 + .0002 + .0000 + .0000 = .0059$$

If 16 or more experts did successfully identify the expensive wine, what would you conclude about the vintner's claim?

the normal distributions is that we can use facts about the normal distribution to estimate the probability of obtaining certain kinds of results with a large series of independent trials. All we need is the mean and standard deviation of the distribution; then we can convert the result to a z-score.

The mean and standard deviation of any binomial distribution (regardless of the value of p) are given in Formulas 8.4 and 8.5.

$$\mu = np \tag{8.4}$$

$$\sigma = \sqrt{npq} \tag{8.5}$$

For example, with 50 independent trials and $p = .5$, the mean number of events that will yield the outcome of interest is 50(.5), or 25. The standard deviation of this binomial distribution is $\sqrt{50(.5)(.5)}$, or 3.54. In the case of 50 flips of a fair coin, for instance, we expect to obtain 25 heads. But we also know that some other result might occur. If we performed many sets of 50 flips and computed the number of heads for each set, we would expect the mean number of heads to be 25 and the standard deviation to be 3.54.

We can use the mean and standard deviation of the binomial to compute a z-score for any result (i.e., number of trials that produce the outcome of interest). Table B in Appendix III can then be consulted to estimate the probability of obtaining any range of results. In using the normal distribution to estimate binomial probabilities we need to remember that the normal distribution is to be used for continuous variables, whereas the number of trials that produce an outcome of interest is a discrete variable. To compensate for this discrepancy we must treat results as though they were based on a continuous variable. This means that when we wish to find the area of the normal distribution that lies above or below some value we must work with the real limits of that value. When finding the area at or above a value we use its lower real limit, and when finding the area at or below a value we use its upper real limit.

For example, if we use the normal distribution to estimate the probability of someone correctly predicting the outcome of 40 or more coin tosses in a sequence of 50 tosses, we would use the real limit of 39.5. This limit will include all of the normal distribution associated with an outcome of 40 (i.e., 39.5 to 40.5). Similarly, if we were interested in the probability of someone being correct on 40 or fewer tosses, we would use the real limit of 40.5.

To transform a result into a z-score we use the following formula where r_{RL} is the appropriate real limit of the result.

$$z = \frac{r_{RL} - np}{\sqrt{npq}} \qquad (8.6)$$

For example, we will do the problem in Box 8.2 using the normal distribution as an approximation to the binomial distribution. Given the information in Box 8.2, the mean for the distribution is 20(.5) or 10, and the standard deviation is $\sqrt{20(.5)(.5)}$ or 2.24. The probability of obtaining 16 or more correct responses can be obtained by computing the z-score for 16 correct, then finding the proportion of area under the normal distribution that lies beyond that value of z. For 16 or more correct selections the appropriate real limit is 15.5. To estimate the probability of obtaining 16 or more correct selections we will compute the area under the normal distribution that is greater than this real limit, which means that the area includes 16. The diagram for this situation is shown in Figure 8.5.

$$z = \frac{15.5 - 10}{2.24} = 2.46$$

Table B indicates that .0069 of the normal distribution is beyond a z-score of 2.46, so our estimate of the probability of 16 or more experts selecting the more expensive wine by guessing is .0069. This value is similar to the more accurate one (.0059) computed in Box 8.2 with Table C. We did not obtain identical answers because the binomial distribution is not exactly normal, especially with small numbers of trials. But with larger numbers of indepen-

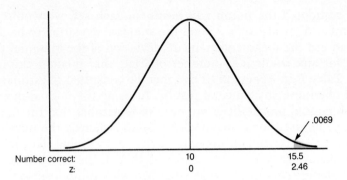

| Number correct: | 10 | 15.5 |
| z: | 0 | 2.46 |

Figure 8.5 Using the normal distribution to estimate the probability of 16 or more outcomes of interest in a group of 20 binomial trials.

dent trials, the approximation improves and using the normal distribution to solve binomial probability problems is even more accurate. For example, suppose we had tested 60 wine experts. The exact probability (obtained by using Formula 8.3) of, say, 37 or more of them choosing the more expensive wine if they are just guessing ($p = .5$) is .0462. The estimate obtained by using the normal distribution is .0465.

In general, when the total number of trials is listed in a table, you should use the probabilities given there. When the total number exceeds the number listed in the table, probabilities generated from the normal distribution should be used.

SUMMARY

In this chapter we have presented some important concepts of probability in preparation for a more detailed analysis of statistical inference. Probability was defined as the proportion of outcomes of interest relative to the total number of equally likely outcomes that a trial can produce. Procedures for simplifying the calculation of probabilities were described, including the addition and multiplication rules of probability. The two rules can be used together in cases involving outcomes of a group of independent trials. The concept of combinations (different ways of forming subsets of a larger group of objects) is important in helping to determine how many different outcome sets in a group of independent trials can produce a specific result of interest.

We also introduced the binomial probability distribution. This distribution is very useful in finding the probability of obtaining a particular number of occurrences of an outcome over a set of trials (e.g., how many times a head will turn up in five tosses of a coin). For cases involving many independent trials the normal distribution can be used to obtain reasonably accurate estimates of probabilities.

KEY WORDS

random	multiplication rule
trial	sampling with replacement
probability	sampling without replacement
equally likely	factorial
mutually exclusive	combination
addition rule	binomial probability distribution
independent trials	

PROBLEMS

1 Which of the following sets of outcomes represent mutually exclusive outcomes?
   (a) Obtaining a two or a spade in drawing a single card from a deck
   (b) Rolling a 4 or a 5 on a single die
   (c) Randomly drawing a male or a female from a population of university students
   (d) Randomly drawing a male or someone over 20 years of age from a population of university students
   (e) Randomly assigning a subject to the experimental condition or to the control condition in an experiment

2 Which of the following sets of trials are independent?
   (a) Rolling three dice
   (b) Five tosses of a coin that is biased to frequently turn up tails
   (c) In an experiment involving twins, randomly assigning one member of each pair to one condition and the other member to the other condition
   (d) Randomly assigning each member of a group of subjects to one of two conditions in an experiment

3 In using the binomial probability distribution, what do each of the following elements represent: n, r, p, and q?

4 A social scientist is planning to take a random sample of college students in a survey of opinions about which one of three new proposed programs should be funded (engineering, medical school, law school). The numbers of students enrolled in each of the university's divisions follows, classified by undergraduate or graduate student standing.

Division	Undergraduate	Graduate
Science	358	104
Arts	483	182
Education	136	52
Fine arts	73	19

What is the probability that the first student sampled from this population is (a) an undergraduate, (b) a graduate student, (c) a fine arts student, (d) an arts or science student, (e) an education student, (f) an education graduate student, (g) a science student or a graduate student?

5 A psychologist interested in studying gambling behavior sets up a game of chance involving the numbers 1 through 50. On each play of the game any one of the numbers can occur with equal probability. Each of the odd numbers on the betting board is green and each of the even numbers is blue. On each play of the game the player is given an opportunity to choose one of two possible bets. For each pair of bets listed intuitively decide which one you think is more likely to result in a win; then find the probability of each bet to see how well you have done.
   (a) (i) A blue number
        (ii) A number greater than 20
   (b) (i) A green number less than 10
        (ii) A blue number in the range of 8 to 20, inclusive
   (c) (i) An even number divisible by 3
        (ii) A green number divisible by 3
   (d) (i) The number that came up on the most recent play
        (ii) A specific number of your choice other than the previous winner

6 Suppose the game in problem 5 were made a little more interesting by basing the bets on the outcome of two consecutive plays. For each of the bets that follow, make an intuitive judgment about which would be more likely to result in a win; then compute the probability of a win in each case.
   (a) (i) An odd number on the first play and an even number on the second play
        (ii) An odd number on both plays
   (b) (i) A green number greater than 40, then a blue number
        (ii) A blue number greater than 25 on both plays
   (c) (i) Obtaining the number 16 on both plays
        (ii) Obtaining a 4 on the first play and a 12 on the second play

7 A therapist is attempting to cure a compulsive gambler of her attachment to the game of roulette. In this game the player can place a bet on any one of 36 numbers, half of which are black and half of which are red. The wheel contains compartments numbered 1 through 36 and two additional compartments numbered 0 and 00 on which players may not place bets. The roulette ball may land, with equal probability, in any of the 38 compartments. If the player bets on a black (or red) number and wins, she wins an amount equal to the original wager. The therapist's task is to convince the gambler that in the long run she is bound to lose money by making such bets. To help the therapist, determine the probability that betting on a color will produce a win. Over the course of 1000 plays how many times (to the nearest whole number) would you expect the gambler to win? Assuming that one dollar is bet on each play, what would be the expected net gain or loss with this number of wins?

8 A job applicant is given a skills test involving 12 true-false items. If the applicant simply guesses on each item, how many different sequences of answers would produce a score of exactly 8 correct? What is the probability of obtaining any one of these sequences? Based on these two answers, what would be the probability of obtaining exactly 8 correct by guessing? What would be the probability of obtaining exactly 5 correct?

9 In an experiment on infant visual perception, infants are shown two simultaneously available displays. One is a complex pattern of black and white stripes and the other is a black square on a white background. The experimenter records which of the two displays is viewed for a longer time period. Eight infants are tested. It is found that seven of the infants spend more time viewing the striped

pattern. Suppose we assume that infants actually have no preference for striped over square patterns and should be equally likely to look at either pattern for a longer time. What is the probability of obtaining the reported results?

10 A psychologist studying intuitive decision making offers subjects in an experiment the choice between two possible bets involving the toss of a fair coin. For each pair of bets listed, intuitively decide which one you think is more likely to result in a win; then compute the probability of each by using Formula 8.3. Check your answers by consulting Table C in Appendix III.

   (a) (i) Obtaining 4 heads on 10 tosses
      (ii) Obtaining 8 heads on 20 tosses
   (b) (i) Obtaining 6 or more heads on 8 tosses
      (ii) Obtaining 11 or more heads on 16 tosses

11 Two competing soft drink companies agree to have a research company conduct an independent survey to find out once and for all which brand of cola is preferred by more consumers. A sample of 100 cola drinkers is obtained by visiting supermarkets and asking customers to sample two unmarked containers of cola. Each customer is asked to decide which one he or she prefers. People who indicate no preference are replaced. The research company is working under the assumption that the two colas are liked by equal numbers of people in the population. Based on this assumption, what is the probability that a particular person in the sample will prefer brand A? Use the normal distribution to estimate the probability that 60 or more people in the sample of 100 will prefer brand A. What is the probability that either one of the brands will be preferred by 60 or more people?

Chapter 9

Hypothesis Testing: Random Assignment

9.1 INTRODUCTION

Reports of research can give the impression that the results of a study were more clear-cut than was actually the case. The reported summary statements rarely reflect the ambiguity that may exist in data. If the results of research were very clear-cut or obvious, we could confine statistical analysis primarily to the descriptive procedures given in the first few chapters. The additional procedures developed here and in the next several chapters are needed because raw data and descriptive statistics are often difficult to interpret.

Consider the example of an alleged psychic making predictions about the outcome of coin flips. If the psychic predicted the outcome of 100 flips of a coin and was correct on all 100 predictions, we would be inclined to conclude that some kind of special ability had been demonstrated. If only 50 of 100 predictions were correct, we might conclude that he did not possess any special power and that his predictions were unrelated to the actual outcomes of the coin flips. However, if we actually tested such a person, the number of correct predictions might not be near either 100 percent or 50 percent. What would we conclude if, say, 72 percent of the predictions were correct? Is 72 percent correct likely to occur just by chance or does the psychic have some special power?

A similar problem occurs when the average behavior of groups of subjects is compared. For example, 12 aggressive young boys could be randomly assigned to two groups of 6 subjects (where "randomly" means that each subject had the same probability of being assigned to either group and the assignments were made independently). One group (experimental) is given a treatment intended to reduce aggressive behavior, such as receiving instruction about how unrealistic are the heroes of violent television programs. The other group (control) receives instruction on some neutral topic. Both groups are later rated on aggressiveness by their peers. Table 9.1 presents ratings for these subjects for three hypothetical outcomes of such an experiment.

In outcome 1 all six ratings in the experimental group are smaller than all six scores in the control group. If this outcome actually were observed, it might be possible for the researcher to decide immediately that the differences between the groups were not a chance outcome of the random assignment of the subjects to conditions. Instead, it might be concluded that the outcome was produced because receiving the special instruction decreased aggressiveness. In outcome 2 we find that the two groups performed in exactly the same way. This is an instance in which the researcher would have grounds to conclude that the experimental treatment did not reduce aggressiveness.

Neither of these outcomes is typical of what actually occurs in most research. Rather, something like outcome 3 is more likely. Here you can see that, on the average, the experimental group obtained lower aggressiveness ratings than the control group. Therefore, you might be inclined to say that exposure to the special instruction about violent television heroes caused the subjects to reduce their aggressive behavior. Inspection of the raw data, how-

Table 9.1   EXAMPLE OUTCOMES OF AN EXPERIMENT IN WHICH TWO SETS OF
DATA ARE CLEARLY DIFFERENT (OUTCOME 1), THE SETS ARE CLEARLY
THE SAME (OUTCOME 2), OR THE DIFFERENCE IS AMBIGUOUS
(OUTCOME 3)

	Outcome 1		Outcome 2		Outcome 3	
	Experimental	Control	Experimental	Control	Experimental	Control
	1	7	4	4	3	3
	2	8	5	5	4	4
	3	9	6	6	5	5
	4	10	7	7	6	9
	5	11	8	8	7	10
	6	12	9	9	8	11
Sum	21	57	39	39	33	42
$\overline{X}$	3.5	9.5	6.5	6.5	5.5	7.0

ever, reveals that half of the subjects in each group had the same ratings (3,
4, 5). This fact suggests that perhaps the special instruction did not reduce
aggressiveness, and that purely by chance the process of random assignment
placed the boys who were more aggressive in the control condition. Thus,
inspection of the raw data and means leads to a dilemma. How can the researcher decide about the effect of the special instruction with results like
those in outcome 3?

The answer is that we need a set of guidelines or standards that researchers can apply objectively to data. The most widely used procedure for evaluating data by statistical criteria is called *hypothesis testing*. It involves defining a hypothesis (an expectation about how a study should turn out) and then
testing it by collecting data. An important part of the test consists of assuming that the hypothesis is true (e.g., the psychic's predictions about coin flips
are independent of the outcome of the coin flips). Working under this assumption, we then determine whether the results of the study are unlikely
to have occurred. If the results are not unlikely (i.e., typical of what would
be expected if the hypothesis were true), we have no reason to claim that the
hypothesis is false (e.g., the psychic's predictions are correct on about half
the trials). But if the obtained results turn out to be unlikely, we should
conclude that the hypothesis is not valid (e.g., the psychic's predictions are
correct on nearly all of the trials).

There are two systems of hypothesis testing that are used in different
research contexts. One system, discussed in the next chapter and depicted on
the right side of Figure 1.1, is based on the assumption that subjects were
randomly selected from a population. The other system is described in this
chapter and is summarized in the first column on the left side of Figure 1.1.
It is appropriate for studies in which subjects have not been randomly sampled but some form of random assignment has been used (e.g., subjects are
randomly assigned to conditions). In each of these two chapters we show how

to determine the probability of obtaining the observed results under the assumption that some hypothesis is true.

9.2 RANDOMNESS AND STATISTICAL HYPOTHESES

The Null Hypothesis

At the outset of most research projects the researcher has a set of expectations, called hypotheses, concerning how the results should turn out. One hypothesis is that the data represent a chance outcome of some random events.

For example, in the case of the self-proclaimed psychic discussed earlier, one hypothesis is that he does not possess psychic power and that his responses are independent of the actual outcomes of the events. To test this idea we could have the psychic make a series of predictions about the outcomes of coin flips. On each trial the psychic makes a prediction and we randomly assign an outcome (heads or tails) by tossing a coin. This assignment is random in the sense that each trial has the same probability of being assigned a head or tail and the outcome on one trial is independent of the outcome on any other trial.

The actual predictions of the psychic are compared with the randomly assigned outcomes. If his predictions are independent of the outcomes of our random assignments, any prediction is equally likely to be correct or incorrect. This statement is true because on each trial it is just as likely for the outcome of our random assignment to match the prediction as it is for the outcome not to match it. Thus, the hypothesis assumes that the psychic's predictions are not related to the outcome that we assign to each trial. This hypothesis is called the *null hypothesis* and is designated H_0.

H_0: Each of the psychic's predictions is independent of the actual outcome of the trial.

To assess the psychic's performance we could count the number of trials on which correct predictions were made. Under the null hypothesis the psychic would be equally likely to be correct or incorrect on any given trial, so we would expect him to be correct on half of the trials. His actual performance might deviate from 50 percent correct, but according to H_0 this deviation is due only to the chance outcome of our random assignments of outcomes to trials.

The Alternative Hypothesis

The null hypothesis that the results of a study are determined by the chance outcome of some random process can be contrasted with an *alternative hypothesis*. According to this hypothesis the results of the study are due to some nonrandom, systematic effect. For the example of the psychic, an alternative hypothesis is that his prediction will be influenced by the outcome of the upcoming coin flip.

> H_1: The psychic's predictions are not independent of the actual outcomes of the trials.

This form of hypothesis is called a **nondirectional alternative hypothesis.** It says that something systematic will influence the data so that the observed measure of behavior will depart significantly from what is expected by chance. But we are not certain how the result will differ from chance. For example, it does not specify whether the psychic will be more or less than 50 percent accurate.

NONDIRECTIONAL ALTERNATIVE HYPOTHESIS: The observed outcome will differ in an unspecified way from the outcome expected under the null hypothesis.

The alternative, H_1, can be more specific. It can include a statement about how the observed outcome will differ from what is expected by chance. In the case of the psychic, for example, H_1 might state that the number of correct predictions will be greater than the number expected by chance. If the psychic has special power we probably can assume that it will allow him to be *more* accurate than chance. For the study of aggressive boys, we might assume that revealing the unrealistic nature of television characters would reduce the tendency for children to imitate those "heroes." This effect would *reduce* aggression among boys who were in that treatment group, so H_1 might state that the specially instructed group should, on the average, obtain *lower* aggression scores than the control group. In these cases the researcher specifies the *direction* of the outcome, so H_1 is referred to as a **directional alternative hypothesis.**

DIRECTIONAL ALTERNATIVE HYPOTHESIS: The observed outcome will differ in a specified direction from the outcome expected under the null hypothesis.

9.3   EVALUATING THE NULL HYPOTHESIS

Once the null and alternative hypotheses have been established, the next step is to obtain data that will allow us to decide which one is correct. They cannot both be true. The strategy followed is to assume that the null hypothesis is true until you have evidence that it is false. If such evidence is obtained, we conclude that the alternative hypothesis is true.

The evidence used in making this decision is based on determining whether the observed result of a study is among the least likely outcomes that the study *could have produced* under the assumption that H_0 is true.

For example, in our study of the psychic we would assume that his predictions are independent of our random assignment of heads and tails. Then we would figure out which of the possible outcomes of the study would be least likely (e.g., 16 correct in 16 predictions, 15 correct in 16 predictions, etc.). Finally, we would conduct the study and determine whether the actual number of correct predictions is among the set of least likely results.

Notice that we do not determine which outcomes are unlikely under the assumption that the alternative hypothesis is true. The reason is that H_1 does not specify the *degree* to which scores are dependent on the random assignment that is made. For example, we cannot specify how much the psychic's correct predictions should differ from 50 percent, so we cannot compute probabilities from H_1.

If the observed result is among those that are least likely under the null hypothesis, we have two options. One is to decide that we obtained a highly improbable result (a fluke) and that the null hypothesis is true. You can see that if we always made this decision we would not get anywhere. No matter how the study turned out, no matter how unlikely the result, we could say that it was a fluke and maintain our claim that the null hypothesis is true.

For this reason, researchers choose a different option. When an obtained result is unlikely under the assumption that H_0 is true, they infer not that the result is improbable but that H_0 is not true. The obtained result is assumed to be typical of what would happen if the *alternative* rather than the null hypothesis were true. Under these circumstances, the null hypothesis is rejected in favor of the alternative hypothesis, and we say that we have obtained a **statistically significant** result.

STATISTICALLY SIGNIFICANT: The observed outcome is among the most unlikely outcomes expected on the basis of H_0, leading to rejection of H_0.

When the null hypothesis is *not* rejected in favor of the alternative, we say that we have obtained a *nonsignificant* result. The obtained result is interpreted to represent a likely outcome when the null hypothesis is true. Under that circumstance we would *fail to reject*, or *retain*, the null hypothesis. For reasons discussed later in this chapter and in Chapter 12, we do not claim that the null hypothesis *must* be true.

Setting the Decision Criterion

In our discussion of significant results, we used phrases such as "unlikely" and "least likely." Of course, this kind of vagueness is not desirable. We need to provide a specific definition of the concept of unlikely. Remember that our approach to evaluating the result of a study is to determine whether it is among the set of least likely results that could have been produced if H_0 were true. This approach allows a number of results to be considered unlikely, and the occurrence of any one of them will lead to the rejection of H_0. Therefore it will be necessary to construct the set of "least likely" outcomes so that the probability of obtaining *any* member of the set is very small.

We construct the set of least likely outcomes by selecting the most extreme or unlikely outcome, then the next most unlikely outcome, and so on. We continue adding outcomes to the set until the probability of obtaining any one of them reaches some limit or criterion. These outcomes are mutually exclusive, so by the addition rule from Chapter 8, the probability of obtaining any one of them is equal to the sum of their individual probabilities. The set of least likely results defined in this manner is known as the **region of rejection.** If the observed result falls in this region, we conclude that an improbable result has been obtained and we reject H_0.

REGION OF REJECTION: The set of least likely, most extreme possible outcomes of a study that are consistent with the alternative hypothesis.

The question is, what limit should be placed on the size of the region of rejection? The limit is determined by the probability of obtaining any one of the outcomes in the region, and a commonly used limit or criterion is .05. That is, the sum of the individual probabilities of the least likely outcomes is allowed to be no more than .05.[1]

Establishing the Region of Rejection

To demonstrate how a region of rejection is constructed when random assignment is used in a study, we will work with the example of the psychic. In this case H_0 states that the psychic's predictions are independent of the random assignment of heads and tails that we happened to use. The psychic's predictions would have been the same no matter which sequence of heads and tails we happened to obtain when flipping the coin. So let us look at how accurate the psychic would be under various random assignments (outcomes of our coin flips). In Table 9.2 we show a set of predictions made by the psychic in 16 trials. The other columns show possible random assignments that we *might* have made by flipping the coin. Notice that different assignments sometimes lead to different results in the number of correct predictions.

It is possible to compute the probability of any given number of correct predictions (e.g., 15 correct) by considering how many different random as-

---

[1]The .05 criterion was not intended by early statisticians to be rigidly and universally used in all types of research. It was customarily used by Sir Ronald Fisher and others in making statistical decisions, but Fisher himself said that strict use of .05 as a criterion is "absurdly academic." An interesting summary of the issue may be found in Feinstein (1985, pp. 398–399).

Table 9.2 SOME POSSIBLE RANDOM ASSIGNMENTS
          OF COIN TOSS OUTCOMES TO TRIALS

Trial	Observed predictions*	Some possible random assignments				
		A	B	C	D	E
1	H	H	T	H	H	T
2	H	H	H	T	H	H
3	T	T	T	T	H	T
4	H	H	H	H	H	H
5	T	T	T	T	T	T
6	T	T	T	T	T	H
7	T	T	T	T	T	H
8	H	H	H	H	T	T
9	T	T	T	T	T	T
10	H	H	H	H	H	H
11	T	T	T	T	H	T
12	H	H	H	H	H	H
13	T	T	T	T	T	H
14	H	H	H	H	H	T
15	H	H	H	H	T	T
16	T	T	T	T	T	H
Correct predictions =		16	15	15	12	9

*Predictions were made by a hypothetical psychic.

signments lead to that outcome and the probability of obtaining each of those assignments. On any given trial the probability of obtaining a random assignment (heads or tails) that matches the psychic's prediction is .5 and the probability of obtaining one that does not match is also .5. So, following Formula 8.2, over n trials the probability of obtaining one specific sequence of r correct and $n - r$ incorrect predictions would be $(.5)^r(.5)^{(n-r)}$.

Next consider how many random assignments would produce each possible number of correct predictions. Examination of Table 9.2 indicates that only one assignment would produce exactly 16 correct predictions. How many random assignments would produce 15 correct? Two are shown in Table 9.2, but there are more. In general, the number of random assignments that would lead to r correct predictions in n attempts could be found by using Formula 8.1, the formula for combinations:

$$_nC_r = \frac{n!}{(n-r)!r!}$$
(8.1)

Each of the random assignments that produce a given number of correct predictions is mutually exclusive. Thus we can use the addition rule to find the probability of obtaining any one of the relevant assignments. That is, we can sum their individual probabilities. Each assignment is equally likely to occur, so we can express the sum of the probabilities as the product of the number of assignments and the probability of one assignment:

$$_nC_r(.5)^r(.5)^{(n-r)}$$

This formula, of course, fits Formula 8.3 and can be used to compute values in the binomial probability distribution. Table 9.3 presents the binomial probability distribution for the case of 16 trials. The probabilities listed in the second column were obtained from Formula 8.3 and also match those in Table C in Appendix III, except that the values in Table C provide only four decimal places of accuracy. The reason that the probabilities of various outcomes match those in Table C is that in this study the random assignment on each trial can be considered a binomial event. We are, therefore, conducting a binomial test, just as in Chapter 8.

The probabilities in Table 9.3 indicate which outcomes are least likely. To construct the region of rejection we first decide which outcomes are compatible with the alternative hypothesis. If we reject H_0, the evidence must be consistent with H_1. The selection of least likely outcomes depends on whether H_1 is directional or nondirectional. In the case of the psychic, the nondirectional alternative hypothesis is that the psychic's predictions are not independent of the outcome of the random assignment of coin tosses. This H_1 allows us to consider unlikely outcomes in which the psychic made either very many or very few correct predictions. Thus, unlikely outcomes from

Table 9.3   PROBABILITY OF CORRECT PREDICTIONS IN A SET OF 16 TRIALS

Correct predictions	Probability	Cumulative probability	
		Directional H_1	Nondirectional H_1
0	.0000152	1.0000000	.0000152
1	.0002441	.9999838	.0002593
2	.0018310	.9997397	.0020903
3	.0085449	.9979087	.0106352
4	.0277709	.9893638	.0384061
5	.0666503	.9615929	.1050564
6	.1221923	.8949426	.2272487
7	.1745605	.7727503	.4018092
8	.1963806	.5981898	—
9	.1745605	.4018092	.4018092
10	.1221923	.2272487	.2272487
11	.0666503	.1050564	.1050564
12	.0277709	.0384061	.0384061
13	.0085449	.0106352	.0106352
14	.0018310	.0020903	.0020903
15	.0002441	.0002593	.0002593
16	.0000152	.0000152	.0000152

either end, or tail, of the distribution of outcomes allow rejection. For this reason, nondirectional alternative hypotheses are sometimes called *two-tailed*.

A directional H_1, in which it was claimed that the psychic can make accurate predictions, would allow us to consider only those unlikely outcomes in which the psychic made very many correct predictions. The region of rejection in this case would be confined to one end, or tail, of the distribution of possible outcomes, so directional alternative hypotheses are sometimes called *one-tailed*.

We will first build a region of rejection for the case of a directional H_1: The psychic should be *more* accurate than expected by H_0. The criterion will be .05, which means that the probability of obtaining any of the least likely outcomes in the region must be no greater than .05. To build the region of rejection we start at the least likely outcome (16 correct), then add the next least likely outcome, then the next, and so on until .05 is exceeded.

The cumulative probabilities shown in the third column of Table 9.3 indicate that we can include the outcomes of 16, 15, 14, 13, or 12 correct: $p(16$–12 correct$) = .0384$. Including 11 correct would make the probability of obtaining a result in the region of rejection greater than .05, so that result cannot be included: $p(16$–11 correct$) = .1051$. The region of rejection for this example, then, is 16–12 correct predictions. If H_0 is true the probability of obtaining any result in that region is .0384. If one of these outcomes were obtained, we would reject H_0 and conclude that the psychic's predictions were related to the outcome of the coin tosses. The region of rejection for this case is also shown in Figure 9.1, which displays the binomial probability distribution in the form of a histogram.

If H_1 had been nondirectional (i.e., the psychic's predictions are not independent of the outcome of the random assignment), the region of rejection would have included the least likely outcomes from both ends of the binomial distribution. In building the region of rejection we would first include the most extreme outcome from each end of the distribution (16 and 0 correct), then the next most extreme outcome from each end, and so on. We would continue until adding in the next pair of outcomes would cause the cumulative probability to exceed the criterion.

In Table 9.3 we show in the last column the cumulative probability, working in from both ends. The region of rejection is built symmetrically by using both extreme ends of the distribution, so half of the extreme outcomes will be in one end and the other half will be in the other end. The probability of obtaining an outcome in either end must be no greater than the criterion we have set, such as .05. Therefore, the sum of the cumulative probabilities from both ends of the distribution must be no greater than the criterion. When the outcomes of 16 and 0 correct are included in the region of rejection, the probability of obtaining either result is $.0000152 + .0000152 = .0000304$. Clearly, this is lower than the criterion of .05, so we try to include the next pair of extreme outcomes, 15 and 1 correct. Doing so brings the cumulative probability from both ends up to $.0002593 + .0002593 = .0005186$.

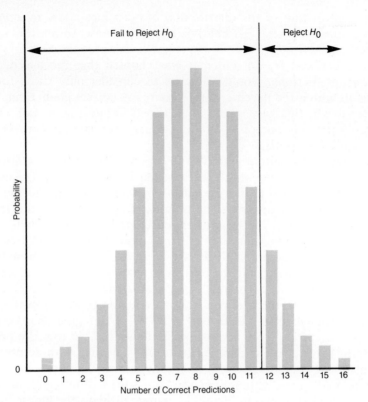

Figure 9.1 Probability distribution for predictions of the heads-tails outcome of 16 coin flips. The region of rejection is shown for a directional alternative hypothesis.

We can keep including pairs of extreme outcomes in this manner until we get to 13 and 3. This is the last pair we can include in the region of rejection because including the next pair, 12 and 4, would make the total cumulative probability greater than .05. If it is not possible to include both members of the next most extreme pair, neither can be added. The region of rejection must be symmetrical because the alternative hypothesis is nondirectional and no preference can be given to one end of the distribution over the other. In this example, then, the region of rejection consists of 16–13 and 0–3 correct predictions. This region is shown in Figure 9.2, which presents the probability distribution as a histogram.

Region of Rejection and the Alternative Hypothesis

A comparison of Figures 9.1 and 9.2 reveals something important about the choice of a directional or nondirectional alternative hypothesis. When a directional H_1 can be specified, all of the unlikely outcomes in the region of rejection are in one end of the distribution. This fact usually means that the region of rejection with a directional alternative hypothesis includes some

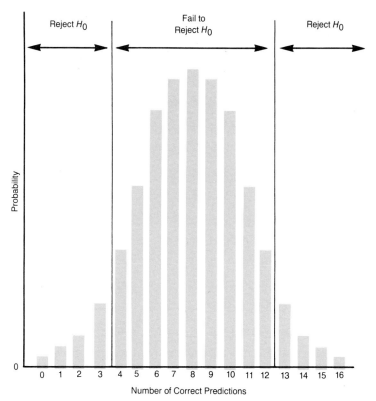

Figure 9.2 Probability distribution for predictions of the heads-tails outcome of 16 coin flips. The region of rejection is shown for a nondirectional alternative hypothesis.

less extreme outcomes that would not be included had a nondirectional H_1 been used. In the present example, a directional H_1 includes the outcome of 12 correct, but a nondirectional H_1 does not. Thus, rejection of the null hypothesis does not require as extreme a result when a directional alternative hypothesis is used.

Researchers typically try to reject H_0, so if there is good reason to use a directional H_1 they will do so. The advantage is that the obtained results do not have to be as extreme to be considered statistically significant. The disadvantage of using a directional H_1, however, is that if an extreme result is found that comes from the opposite end of the distribution (e.g., very few correct predictions), the researcher is not justified in rejecting the null hypothesis because the obtained result is not consistent with the alternative hypothesis—it is not in the region of rejection. Consequently, a researcher must be very confident in the expected direction of the effect to use a directional alternative hypothesis.

A situation in which a directional alternative hypothesis can be appropriate involves having substantial background information about the topic being studied. Generally the availability of this information means that prior research of a similar nature has been reported and that there is a theoretical framework that makes a directional prediction. If this kind of justification is made and the researchers use a directional hypothesis, they must be willing to retain H_0 even if the results turn out to be strongly in the opposite direction. For example, you might make a directional prediction that older subjects will perform better than younger subjects, perhaps because they have more relevant experience. You then compare people 65–75 years with those 25–35 years and find that the younger people do *substantially* better. With a directional hypothesis favoring older subjects, you would fail to reject the null hypothesis.

Another caution regarding the region of rejection and the binomial test is presented in Box 9.1.

9.4 DECISION MAKING AND DECISION ERROR

In using hypothesis testing to help evaluate research outcomes the researcher acts as a decision maker, the decision being whether or not to reject the null hypothesis. Because the decision is based on probability, not certainty, it is possible that whichever hypothesis is settled on, H_0 or H_1, a decision error may occur. For example, even though the obtained result allows rejection of H_0, it could be that H_0 is true and the result *was* a fluke. Table 9.4 summarizes the relationship between decisions made by the researcher and the "truth" of the hypothesis in the "real world."

The decision matrix in Table 9.4 shows that rejecting H_0 when it is false leads to a correct decision. The alternative hypothesis is then correctly accepted. On the other hand, rejecting H_0 when it is actually true leads to a mistake. This mistake is called a **Type I error.** The probability of a Type I error is equal to our predetermined decision criterion (e.g., .05) and is called α (alpha). Our decision criterion determines the value of alpha because it represents the probability of obtaining any one of a set of unlikely results, under the assumption that H_0 *is true.* A Type I error can be committed only if the H_0 is true and we obtain an unlikely result.

A Type I error consists of deciding that a systematic relationship between variables was responsible for producing the observed result, when in fact

Table 9.4 **POSSIBLE CONSEQUENCES OF A STATISTICAL DECISION**

Decision	True hypothesis	
	Null (H_0)	Alternative (H_1)
Reject H_0	Type I error	Correct
Not reject H_0	Correct	Type II error

Box 9.1   # A Caution in Using the Binomial Test

When a directional alternative hypothesis was used in our experiment with the psychic, we found that if 12 or more of the 16 predictions were correct we could reject the null hypothesis. Twelve out of 16 happens to represent 75 percent of the trials. Does this mean that in any application of the binomial test where 75 percent or more of the trials produces the outcome of interest we can reject H_0—assuming the probability of a trial producing the outcome of interest is .5 and $\alpha = .05$—and a directional H_1?

To answer this question consider the same percentage (75 percent) with a different number of trials. For example, 6 out of 8 is also a case in which 75 percent of the predictions are correct. Is the outcome in this case also statistically significant with $\alpha = .05$? Inspection of Table C in Appendix III shows that under the null hypothesis the probability of 6 or more correct predictions would be .1445. Clearly, the region of rejection could not include all of these outcomes if α is to be kept below .05.

$$p(\text{at least 6 correct predictions}) = p(6/8) + p(7/8) + p(8/8)$$
$$= .1094 + .0312 + .0039$$
$$= .1445$$

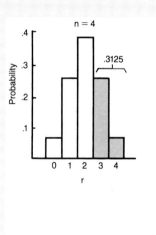

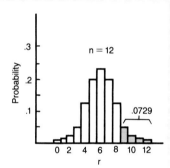

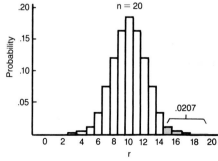

> The reason we cannot rely on a constant value like 75 percent to represent the boundary of the region of rejection is that the binomial probability distribution varies with the number of independent events. This fact is illustrated in the diagram on page 213, where the probability distributions for 4, 12, and 20 events are presented. The probability of at least 75 percent of the events producing the outcome of interest is indicated in each case. The binomial probability distribution changes with the number of events, so we need to know what the distribution is like for each different number of events. That is the purpose of Table C.

there is no systematic relationship. When we mistakenly reject H_0 the decision is sometimes called a "false alarm" because it tells people that something happened, a systematic relationship was observed, when it was actually an outcome due to unsystematic factors.

TYPE I ERROR: Rejection of the null hypothesis when it is true: $p(\text{Type I error}) = \alpha$.

Consider the nature of a Type I error in our example of a psychic predicting the outcome of coin flips. Given $\alpha = .05$, we reject H_0 if we observe 12 or more correct predictions in 16 attempts (assuming a directional H_1). We could, in fact, observe these outcomes even though the null is true. According to Table 9.3, the probability of obtaining 12 or more correct predictions when H_0 is true would be .0384.

Given 12 out of 16 correct predictions and a decision to reject H_0, how do you know whether you have made an error? The answer is that, on the basis of this single set of data, you do *not* know. If H_0 is true, it is unlikely that repeating the data collection will lead to rejecting H_0 again. Further sets of data should lead to frequencies of correct predictions that are closer to 8 out of 16 correct than 12 or more correct. Eight correct is what we would expect if H_0 were true (predictions are independent of the outcome of each trial) because this figure represents 50 percent correct and the probability of a correct prediction on any single trial is .5.

If the null hypothesis actually is false, further replications should lead to more than 8 out of 16 correct predictions most of the time. In short, the best check on whether a correct decision has been made is to repeat the study under similar circumstances. Replication is a good way to check the accuracy of our decision to reject H_0, but it still does not produce absolute certainty that we are correct. It simply increases our degree of confidence in the conclusion drawn.

On the other hand, when the researcher mistakenly fails to reject H_0 a **Type II error** is made. The probability of a Type II error is called β (beta). The error consists of not rejecting H_0 even though it is false. Sometimes a Type II error is referred to as a "miss" because there is a systematic relationship between, say, the psychic's predictions and the outcomes of the coin flips; but because this relationship was not strongly expressed in our particular study, we could conclude that there is no evidence for a systematic relationship.

TYPE II ERROR: Failure to reject H_0 when it is false: $p(\text{Type II error}) = \beta$.

In setting a decision criterion we need to take into account both Type I and Type II errors. Consider what happens if, instead of setting alpha at .05, we use a very strict criterion for our definition of highly unlikely, say .001. In our test of psychic ability what kind of result would we have to obtain to reject the null hypothesis that the psychic's predictions were independent of the outcomes of the coin flips? The answer is in Table 9.3, where we find that with $\alpha = .001$, and a directional H_1, the psychic has to be correct on at least 15 of the 16 trials. This is a demanding performance, and even if our subject were psychic it is possible that he could not do quite that well. Therefore, using a criterion of .001 increases the risk of failing to reject a false H_0. Assuming that other aspects of the study are unchanged, decreasing α causes an increase in β. Avoiding the use of α values that are much less than .05 helps to reduce Type II error probability.

To acknowledge the possibility that a Type I error is being made when rejecting H_0, researchers typically include a statement of the probability of making such an error when H_0 is true. Assuming α is .05, this statement usually takes the form $p < .05$. For a different value of α, a different value is used in place of .05, such as $p < .01$.

Note that the probability statement expresses the probability that the observed result or one more extreme would be obtained *if H_0 were true.* It does *not* represent the probability that H_0 is true, given the present result. Either H_0 is true or not. It does not make sense to speak of "the probability that H_0 is true."

When the outcome of a study is not in the region of rejection, we fail to reject the null hypothesis and claim that we obtained a nonsignificant outcome. We use the term "fail to reject" rather than "accept" the null hypothesis because from a statistical point of view it seldom makes sense to accept H_0.

There are many possible reasons for a nonsignificant outcome. One, of course, is that the outcome might really be due to random factors, and failing to reject H_0 was a correct decision. Alternatively, it could be that not enough subjects or trials were tested to detect that H_0 is false. Or the observed data may have been obtained by an unreliable method, so a specific observed value, such as 10 correct predictions in 16 attempts, does not provide an accurate estimate of a subject's true ability. For one reason or another, then, the observed result may not be accurate.

Typically, when our observed results prevent us from rejecting H_0, we "suspend judgment," meaning that we retain both H_0 and H_1 as possible true statements. We can adopt the position that although the present data do not support the alternative hypothesis, it might be supported in subsequent tests. We suspend judgment pending access to additional data. In Boxes 9.2 and 9.3 we present two further examples of testing hypotheses with the binomial test.

In addition to using Table C in Appendix III or the normal approximation to the binomial distribution, a computer package made available with this book, NPSTAT, can be used to find probabilities associated with binomial events. NPSTAT computes the probability of obtaining the observed result or one more extreme, under either a directional or nondirectional H_1.

Box 9.2   ## A Preference for Complexity

A researcher decides to test the claim that young children prefer to view stimuli that are complex rather than simple. To do so the researcher creates a complex stimulus consisting of a card with 12 differently colored squares and a simple stimulus consisting of a card with just four differently colored squares. The researcher visits a preschool to test 24 children with these two stimuli. Each child is presented with the two stimuli arranged side by side, and the child is asked to indicate which card he or she likes better by pointing to the card on the right or the one on the left. For each child the researcher randomly assigns one card to the left and the other to the right.

The null hypothesis is that each child's choice of the right or left card is independent of the random assignment made by the researcher—the child would have chosen that side regardless of which card had been assigned there. That is, the choice is not influenced by the complexity of the stimulus. The alternative hypothesis is directional and claims that children should be more likely to choose the complex stimulus. This is the original claim for which the researcher wants to find evidence.

H_0: Each child's choice of left or right stimulus is independent of the nature of the stimulus assigned to that position.

H_1: Children have a preference for the complex stimulus.

The researcher decides that it is important to avoid making a Type I error, so an α level of .01 is chosen. The next step is to determine which possible outcomes of the study are the least likely. The possible outcomes of the study are the possible random assignments of cards to the left and right positions. The set of *unlikely* possible outcomes will consist of just enough outcomes so that the probability of obtaining any one of them is no greater than α (.01), under the assumption that H_0 is true. If H_0 were true, each child's choice would be the same, regardless of the outcome of the researcher's random assignment of the two cards to left and right positions. Therefore, we can assume that the probability that any one child will select the complex card is .5 because there is a .5 probability that card will be assigned to the side the child was about to choose.

Now we can find the probability of obtaining the most extreme result that is consistent with the alternative hypothesis: For all 24 children the complex card is randomly assigned to the side that the child was about to select. This is a binomial problem in which $n = 24$ (there are 24 independent random assignments—one for each child), $r = 24$ (all assignments produce the outcome of interest), and $p = .5$ (there is a .5 probability of an assignment producing the outcome of interest). Table C in Appendix III indicates that the probability of the most extreme result is .0000, to four decimal places of accuracy. This number does not exceed .01, so we can try to include the next most extreme outcome, which is the random assignment of the complex card to the side chosen by exactly 23 children. Once again, the probability is .0000, so we can continue to include less extreme outcomes. In fact, we can include all outcomes from 24 to 19. Assuming H_0 is true, the probability of obtaining any one of these results is .0032, the sum of the individual probabilities of the 6 outcomes in the set.

We cannot include the outcome of 18 assignments of the complex card to the chosen side because the probability of obtaining any one of the outcomes in the range 24 to 18 is .0112, which exceeds the value set for α. Therefore, the region of rejection is 24 to 19 children selecting the complex card. If the researcher finds that the number of children selecting the complex card falls in this range, the null hypothesis would be rejected and it would be concluded that children prefer complex stimuli. On the other hand, if fewer than 19 children select the complex stimulus, the null hypothesis cannot be rejected and the researcher cannot make a firm conclusion concerning the children's preference for complexity. Notice that because a directional H_1 was used, even if very few children had selected the complex stimulus, indicating a preference for simplicity, the researcher could not reject H_0.

Box 9.3   Tasting the Difference

A soft-drink company decides that it is going to alter the taste of its cola and launch a major advertising campaign announcing the change in an attempt to gain an advantage over its main competitor. Company executives, however, want convincing evidence that people familiar with the taste of the regular cola will be able to tell that the new cola has a new taste. Marketing researchers decide to visit a local supermarket and ask 100 people who claim to regularly drink their cola to taste two cola samples. One sample is the old cola and the other sample is the new cola. The people are asked to indicate which sample tastes like the regular cola, the first one they taste or the second one. For each person tested, the researchers randomly assign the old or the new cola to be tasted first.

The null hypothesis is that each person's selection (first or second sample) is independent of which cola was randomly assigned to the selected sample. That is, it is assumed under H_0, that people cannot distinguish the new and old tastes, so their decision is based on some other unknown factor. The alternative hypothesis is that people can distinguish the tastes, so their selection will not be independent of the random assignment. It is decided to use a nondirectional alternative hypothesis just in case people can distinguish the tastes but have a tendency to claim that the *new* cola tastes like the regular product. The alternative hypothesis, then, is that the selection a person makes is influenced by which cola was assigned to that sample.

H_0: Each subject's selection is independent of the random assignment made by the researchers.

H_1: For at least some subjects the selection is influenced by the outcome of the random assignment.

The researchers decide to set the value of α to .05. The binomial test can be used here because the study consists of a set of 100 independent binomial events (random assignment of the old or the new cola to the sample that eventually is selected by the person being tested). Under H_0 it is assumed that each person's choice (first or second sample) would be unaffected by which cola the researchers randomly assigned to be that sample. Therefore, the probability, under H_0, that the old cola will be assigned to the sample that the person was about to select is .5.

To construct the region of rejection, we need to consider the most extreme outcomes from each end of the binomial distribution because H_1 is nondirectional. These two outcomes would be all 100 random assignments resulting in the old cola being assigned to the selected sample and none of the 100 assignments resulting in selection of the old cola. The next most extreme outcomes would be 99 or 1 assignment resulting in the old cola being selected, and so on. We cannot use Table C in Appendix III to compute the probability of obtaining these outcomes because that table contains values for cases involving up to only 24 independent events. But we can use the normal approximation to the binomial distribution that was introduced in Chapter 8. Recall that when *n* is large and *p* is .5, we can treat the binomial as a normal distribution with a mean of *np* and a standard deviation of $\sqrt{npq}$.

In the present study we have a mean of $100(.5) = 50$ and a standard deviation of $\sqrt{100(.5)(.5)} = 5$. We can use Table B in Appendix III to determine the probability of obtaining various sets of outcomes expressed as *z*-scores. For example, examining the column headed "Area Beyond *z*" in Table B, we find that the probability of obtaining an outcome with a *z*-score of 1.96 or greater is .0250. The distribution is symmetrical, so we can infer that the probability of obtaining a result with a *z*-score of -1.96 or less also is .0250 (see the diagram on page 219). Therefore, there is a .05 probability of obtaining an outcome in either of these extremes. This probability is equal to α, so we have our region of rejection. The *z*-scores of 1.96 and -1.96 can be converted to raw scores by using Formula 5.3.

$$X = \mu + (\sigma)(z)$$

$$X = 50 + (5)(1.96) = 59.8 \qquad X = 50 + (5)(-1.96) = 40.2$$

Thus, if the researchers find that 59.8 or more people in the sample select the old cola, they can reject H_0 and conclude that people can correctly identify the old cola's taste. If 40.2 or fewer select the old cola, H_0 can be rejected, but the researchers would have to conclude that people mistakenly believe the new cola tastes more like the old one. Finally, if the number of people selecting the old cola is between 59.8 and 40.2, the researchers could not reject H_0.

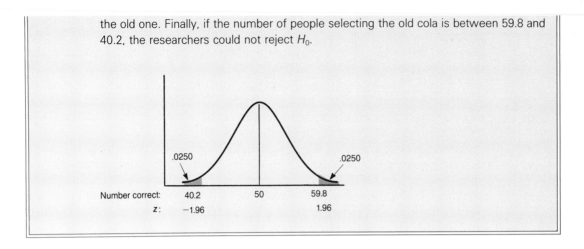

Number correct:	40.2	50	59.8
z:	−1.96		1.96

9.5 TESTING HYPOTHESES ABOUT TWO SETS OF SCORES

So far we have discussed testing hypotheses about binomial data, but often the data of interest will be numerical scores. In these cases the observed score for each individual can take on any of several possible values, such as number correct on an aptitude test or number of seconds taken to complete a task. The general method of testing hypotheses with this type of data is the same as with binomial data. It still is necessary to specify H_0, H_1, and α. Furthermore, the same sort of method for constructing the region of rejection can be used in this context.

We will consider an example based on a hypothetical sample of aggressive young boys. They are randomly assigned to one of two treatment conditions. In the experimental condition they are shown how the violent television heroes with whom they identify are unrealistic. Boys assigned to the control condition are given instruction on some neutral topic. A few weeks after this training, an aggressiveness rating is obtained for each boy based on information obtained by interviewing his peers. The null hypothesis is that, for this sample of subjects, the outcome of a subject's assignment to a treatment condition has no influence on the aggressiveness rating that the subject receives. The alternative hypothesis claims that assignment to the experimental treatment will *reduce* aggressiveness. This is a directional H_1.

H_0: Aggressiveness scores are independent of the treatment conditions to which subjects are assigned.

H_1: Aggressiveness scores are reduced as a result of assignment to the experimental condition.

The null hypothesis implies that no matter how a subject's random assignment turned out, he would have obtained the same aggressiveness score. We will find it convenient to compare the scores in each condition by summarizing them with a descriptive statistic such as the mean. We can then compare the mean aggressiveness score for each condition. It is likely that they will differ, but H_0 claims that the difference is due only to the outcome of the random assignment: Subjects with higher scores happened to be assigned to the same condition. A different random assignment would produce a different result. Further, rather extreme differences between condition means would be unlikely to occur under H_0 because very few of the equally likely random assignments could produce them.

If we were to find that the difference between condition means is among the most extreme, and therefore unlikely, outcomes possible under H_0, we should reject the null. This is the same logic we followed in using the binomial test. Now, however, we are not dealing with binomial events, so we need a different method of determining the region of rejection. The approach in cases in which subjects are randomly assigned to conditions is to use a *randomization test*, which involves listing all possible random assignments of subjects to conditions. The list tells us all the different ways the experiment *could* have turned out if H_0 were true. We can then examine the difference between the means associated with each outcome to determine which outcomes produce the most extreme differences between means.

The region of rejection is defined as the set of most extreme outcomes that represent a proportion, equal to α, of the entire set of possible outcomes. Thus, the probability under H_0 of obtaining a random assignment that yields one of the most extreme differences between condition means is equal to α. If the observed outcome belongs to this set, we reject H_0. The reasoning here is that if scores are unaffected by the condition to which subjects are assigned, there is a very small probability of obtaining any one of the results that represents an extreme difference between condition means. If such a result is obtained, we do not wish to conclude that a fluke occurred and that H_0 is true. Rather, we conclude that H_0 is false and that assignment to conditions did have an influence on the scores.

Computing the Randomization Test

To see how the randomization test works, suppose that a sample of six boys was used, with three randomly assigned to the experimental condition and three to the control condition. Further, let the hypothetical aggressiveness ratings equal 1, 2, 3, 4, 5, and 6. For the moment we will assume that we do not know to which condition each score belongs. There are 20 ways that these six scores might have been assigned randomly to the two groups. Table 9.5 provides a listing of these assignments. You can determine how many possible assignments there are without making a complete list if you compute the combination of six scores taken three at a time: $_6C_3 = 6!/(6 - 3)!3! = 20$.

Table 9.5 shows that for each possible random assignment of the six scores we have taken the value of $\overline{X}$ for each group. Group 1 is the control condition and group 2 the experimental condition. The difference between

Table 9.5 ALL POSSIBLE ARRANGEMENTS OF SIX AGGRESSIVENESS
RATINGS INTO TWO GROUPS (G1 AND G2)

Arrangements	G1	G2	$\overline{X}_1 - \overline{X}_2$ = Difference
1	1,2,3	4,5,6	2.00 − 5.00 = −3.00
2	1,2,4	3,5,6	2.33 − 4.67 = −2.34
3	1,3,4	2,5,6	2.67 − 4.33 = −1.66
4	1,2,5	3,4,6	2.67 − 4.33 = −1.66
5	1,2,6	3,4,5	3.00 − 4.00 = −1.00
6	1,3,5	2,4,6	3.00 − 4.00 = −1.00
7	2,3,4	1,5,6	3.00 − 4.00 = −1.00
8	1,3,6	2,4,5	3.33 − 3.67 = −0.33
9	1,4,5	2,3,6	3.33 − 3.67 = −0.33
10	2,3,5	1,4,6	3.33 − 3.67 = −0.33
11	2,3,6	1,4,5	3.67 − 3.33 = +0.33
12	2,4,5	1,3,6	3.67 − 3.33 = +0.33
13	1,4,6	2,3,5	3.67 − 3.33 = +0.33
14	1,5,6	2,3,4	4.00 − 3.00 = +1.00
15	2,4,6	1,3,5	4.00 − 3.00 = +1.00
16	3,4,5	1,2,6	4.00 − 3.00 = +1.00
17	2,5,6	1,3,4	4.33 − 2.67 = +1.66
18	3,4,6	1,2,5	4.33 − 2.67 = +1.66
19	3,5,6	1,2,4	4.67 − 2.33 = +2.34
20	4,5,6	1,2,3	5.00 − 2.00 = +3.00

the means of each group has been calculated and listed in the final column
on the right. Notice that most of the 20 differences are not unique. For example, three arrangements have a difference between means of +1.00. We
will refer to a set of outcomes having the same difference between means as
a *class* of outcomes.

Each individual outcome in Table 9.5 has one chance in 20 of occurring
if H_0 is true (1/20 = .05), and classes of outcomes have a probability equal to
the sum of probabilities of their individual members. Table 9.6 shows that
the 20 outcomes can be collapsed into 10 classes, and the probabilities of
individual outcomes have been summed to obtain probabilities for classes of
outcomes. The table illustrates that with α = .05 and a directional hypothesis, there is only one case in which H_0 can be rejected. This is the most
extreme possible outcome, where the mean of the control group is greater
than the mean of the experimental group by 3.00 rating points. Thus, the
region of rejection in this example contains only one outcome.

Now we inspect the actual data and see how the six ratings are distributed in the two groups. Assume that the scores in group 1 (control) are 3, 5,
6 ($\overline{X}_1$ = 4.67), and the scores in group 2 (experimental) are 1, 2, 4 ($\overline{X}_2$ = 2.33).
This outcome leads to an obtained difference in the mean rating of 4.67 −
2.33 = 2.34. Since our obtained difference of 2.34 rating points is not as

Table 9.6   TEN POSSIBLE ARRANGEMENT CLASSES FOR THE DATA IN TABLE 9.5

Outcome $(\overline{X}_1 - \overline{X})_2$	Frequency (f)	Probability (p)	Cumulative Probability (cum p)	
−3.00	1	.05	1.00	
−2.34	1	.05	.95	
−1.66	2	.10	.90	
−1.00	3	.15	.80	
−0.33	3	.15	.65	
+0.33	3	.15	.50	Region of
+1.00	3	.15	.35	rejection with
+1.66	2	.10	.20	$\alpha = .05$ and
+2.34	1	.05	.10	a directional
+3.00	1	.05	.05	← hypothesis
Sum 0.00	20	1.00		

extreme as the 3.00 points in the region of rejection, we fail to reject H_0. We can summarize the outcome of this statistical test as follows:

$$\overline{X}_1 - \overline{X}_2 \text{ (critical)} = 3.00$$

$$\overline{X}_1 - \overline{X}_2 \text{ (observed)} = 2.34$$

Decision: Fail to reject H_0

We further illustrate statistical testing for the two-group case by repeating the aggressiveness study. The same null hypothesis, directional alternative hypothesis, and α level will be used. In the replication, the major difference is that there will be four subjects assigned to the experimental condition and four assigned to the control condition. Suppose that the ratings were 1, 2, 3, 4, 5, 6, 7, 8. With eight subjects randomly divided into two groups of four, there are $_8C_4 = 8!/(8 - 4)!4! = 70$ possible arrangements of the eight scores.

Rather than list all 70 possible arrangement, we can examine the frequency distribution based on the null hypothesis by listing the outcome classes and their probabilities in Table 9.7. As in the previous example, each of the outcomes has an equal chance of occurring if H_0 is true. Therefore, each outcome has 1 chance in 70 of being observed ($1/70 = .014$).

The most extreme possible case favoring the alternative hypothesis of lower aggressiveness ratings in the experimental group arises from the four highest ratings, 5, 6, 7, 8, occurring in the control group ($\overline{X}_1 = 6.5$) and the four lowest ratings, 1, 2, 3, 4, occurring in the experimental group ($\overline{X}_2 = 2.5$). Thus, the largest possible difference between means is $6.5 - 2.5 = 4.0$, and the probability of this outcome occurring is .014 if H_0 is true.

The region of rejection is built by including successively less extreme outcomes. Outcomes are included until the sum of their probabilities

Table 9.7 OUTCOME CLASSES OF POSSIBLE ARRANGEMENTS
FOR TWO GROUPS OF FOUR SCORES

$\overline{X}_1 - \overline{X}_2$	f	p	cum p	
−4.00	1	.0143	1.0001*	
−3.50	1	.0143	.9858	
−3.00	2	.0286	.9715	
−2.50	3	.0429	.9429	
−2.00	5	.0714	.9000	
−1.50	5	.0714	.8286	
−1.00	7	.1000	.7572	
− .50	7	.1000	.6572	
.00	8	.1143	.5572	
+ .50	7	.1000	.4429	
+1.00	7	.1000	.3429	
+1.50	5	.0714	.2429	
+2.00	5	.0714	.1715	
+2.50	3	.0429	.1001	
+3.00	2	.0286	.0572	
+3.50	1	.0143	.0286	} Region of
+4.00	1	.0143	.0143	} rejection
Sum 0.00	70	1.0001*		

*This value is not 1.0000 because of rounding error.

reaches, but does not exceed, the predetermined $\alpha = .05$. As shown in Table 9.7, with a directional alternative hypothesis two outcomes are in the region of rejection, $\overline{X}_1 - \overline{X}_2 = 4.00$ and $\overline{X}_1 - \overline{X}_2 = 3.50$. When H_0 is true, the probability of obtaining either of these outcomes is .0286:

$$p(4.00) + p(3.50) = .0143 + .0143 = .0286$$

If we were to include the next most extreme outcome (+3.00 points), the sum of the probabilities would exceed α, our decision criterion:

$$p(4.00) + p(3.50) + p(3.00) = .0143 + .0143 + .0276 = .0572$$

Thus, only differences in means that consist of higher ratings in the control group by 3.50 or more points are in the region of rejection.

Assume that the ratings obtained by subjects in the control group were 4, 6, 7, 8 ($\overline{X}_1 = 6.25$) and those in the experimental group were 1, 2, 3, 5 ($\overline{X}_2 = 2.75$). These data lead to a difference in mean errors of $6.25 - 2.75 = 3.50$. Therefore, we reject H_0 for these example data:

$$\overline{X}_1 - \overline{X}_2 \text{ (critical)} = 3.50$$

$$\overline{X}_1 - \overline{X}_2 \text{ (observed)} = 3.50$$

Decision: Reject H_0

We then conclude that for subjects in this sample, aggressiveness ratings were not independent of the outcome of assignment to conditions, but that exposure to the experimental treatment was associated with lower aggression ratings. We also can conclude that the treatment applied in the experimental condition *caused* the reduction in aggressive behavior.

Interpreting Results

You should notice that in the last example, when the null hypothesis was rejected, we made two different inferences. One was that the rating obtained by each subject was not independent of the treatment condition to which the subject was assigned. That is, aggressiveness ratings were in some way related to the treatment received.

The second inference, based on the fact that the subjects had been randomly assigned to the two conditions, is that the relationship between treatment and aggressiveness rating is causal. In other words, we can infer that some difference in the way subjects were treated in the experimental versus the control conditions *caused* the observed difference in mean aggressiveness ratings.

A causal inference is warranted because random assignment minimizes the chance that some characteristic of the subjects will be systematically related to group membership. For example, consider what might have occurred had random assignment not been used. Suppose the first four boys to be tested were assigned to the control group and the last four given the experimental treatment. The early arrivals might have been more strongly encouraged to take part in the study because of particularly high aggressiveness in their behavior. If higher aggressiveness is observed in the control group, it may be due to this bias in assignment to conditions. Without random assignment, then, the composition of the two groups may differ for reasons unrelated to the treatment that is administered.

Repeated Measures Design

Experiments sometimes are carried out by a procedure that calls for each subject to be tested under two or more different conditions. This is referred to as a *repeated measures* design because the subjects are measured more than once. Random assignment is used to determine the order in which treatments will be administered to each subject. The randomization test can then be used to determine whether the observed results are among the least likely under the null hypothesis.

For example, a researcher might study the influence of hypnosis on the ability to remember the details of a staged crime. After watching a simulated crime, the subjects are questioned under two different conditions about what they saw. In one condition they are in a waking state and in the other they are hypnotized. For each subject we randomly determine whether questions will be asked first while the subject is in a normal waking state or in a hypnotic state. The null hypothesis is that the accuracy of the subject's answers on the first and second tests will be independent of the state in which he or she is tested.

H_0: Question-answering accuracy is independent of the randomly assigned condition under which testing is done.

Under the assumption that H_0 is true we can determine the set of outcome classes and the most extreme, least likely outcomes, just as we did in Tables 9.5 and 9.6 for two groups of different subjects. In the case of repeated measures, however, the different outcomes represent the random assignment of subjects to specific treatment orders. A simple example involving only three subjects is shown in Tables 9.8 and 9.9. Scores represent the number of questions answered correctly. In Table 9.8 we show the hypothetical scores obtained on each of two testing occasions, time 1 ($t1$) and time 2 ($t2$). For now we do not need to know the treatment order to which each subject was assigned. In Table 9.9 we show all possible outcomes of these random assignments. Each subject has a pair of scores, and the different random assignments refer to which condition is to be tested first. Under H_0 a subject's two scores will be the same regardless of which treatment is administered at each time.

Table 9.9 shows that there are eight possible outcomes of the three random assignments (one assignment per subject). In general, with two conditions and n subjects, the number of possible assignments is 2^n. With only three subjects, $2^n = 2^3 = 8$, so that even the most extreme outcomes (-2.34 or $+2.34$) have a 1/8, or .125, probability of occurring. This figure is much larger than conventional values of α. Clearly, a larger sample of subjects is required to obtain a reasonable test of the null hypothesis.

Suppose that four additional subjects were tested, making a total of seven in all. The scores obtained at time 1 and time 2 for each subject are shown in Table 9.10. Under H_0, these scores are independent of the conditions under which they were obtained. In this case there are 2^7, or 128, possible outcomes of the random assignment of subjects to treatment order. Rather than showing all 128 arrangements of data, as in Table 9.9, we present a list of outcome classes and frequencies in Table 9.11. Each outcome class represents a particular difference between condition means. The frequency indicates how many different outcomes of the random assignment procedure produce that differ-

Table 9.8   QUESTION-ANSWERING SCORES

Subject	Time of Test	
	$t1$	$t2$
1	4	8
2	6	5
3	7	9

Table 9.9   POSSIBLE OUTCOMES OF RANDOM ASSIGNMENT OF TREATMENT
CONDITIONS TO TESTING TIMES ($t1$ AND $t2$)

	Outcome 1			Outcome 5	
Subject	Waking	Hypnotized	Subject	Waking	Hypnotized
1	($t1$) 4	($t2$) 8	1	($t1$) 4	($t2$) 8
2	($t1$) 6	($t2$) 5	2	($t2$) 5	($t1$) 6
3	($t1$) 7	($t2$) 9	3	($t2$) 9	($t1$) 7
	$\overline{X}$ 5.67	7.33		$\overline{X}$ 6.00	7.00
	$\overline{X}_w - \overline{X}_h = -1.66$			$\overline{X}_w - \overline{X}_h = -1.00$	

	Outcome 2			Outcome 6	
Subject	Waking	Hypnotized	Subject	Waking	Hypnotized
1	($t2$) 8	($t1$) 4	1	($t2$) 8	($t1$) 4
2	($t1$) 6	($t2$) 5	2	($t1$) 6	($t2$) 5
3	($t1$) 7	($t2$) 9	3	($t2$) 9	($t1$) 7
	$\overline{X}$ 7.00	6.00		$\overline{X}$ 7.67	5.33
	$\overline{X}_w - \overline{X}_h = 1.00$			$\overline{X}_w - \overline{X}_h = 2.34$	

	Outcome 3			Outcome 7	
Subject	Waking	Hypnotized	Subject	Waking	Hypnotized
1	($t1$) 4	($t2$) 8	1	($t2$) 8	($t1$) 4
2	($t2$) 5	($t1$) 6	2	($t2$) 5	($t1$) 6
3	($t1$) 7	($t2$) 9	3	($t1$) 7	($t2$) 9
	$\overline{X}$ 5.33	7.67		$\overline{X}$ 6.67	6.33
	$\overline{X}_w - \overline{X}_h = -2.34$			$\overline{X}_w - \overline{X}_h = 0.34$	

	Outcome 4			Outcome 8	
Subject	Waking	Hypnotized	Subject	Waking	Hypnotized
1	($t1$) 4	($t2$) 8	1	($t2$) 8	($t1$) 4
2	($t1$) 6	($t2$) 5	2	($t2$) 5	($t1$) 6
3	($t2$) 9	($t1$) 7	3	($t2$) 9	($t1$) 7
	$\overline{X}$ 6.33	6.67		$\overline{X}$ 7.33	5.67
	$\overline{X}_w - \overline{X}_h = -0.34$			$\overline{X}_w - \overline{X}_h = 1.66$	

ence. As in Table 9.7 for the case of two groups of subjects, we also show the
probability of obtaining a result in each of the outcome classes and the cumulative probabilities. In this case we assume a nondirectional H_1, so the
probabilities are accumulated from both ends of the distribution.

H_1: Question-answering accuracy is related to the condition under
which questions are asked.

Table 9.10 QUESTION-ANSWERING SCORES

Subject	Time of Test	
	t1	t2
1	4	8
2	6	5
3	7	9
4	2	3
5	12	10
6	14	11
7	13	15

With α set at .05, the region of rejection for a nondirectional H_1 consists of a difference between the means that is ≤ -1.86 or ≥ 1.86. If H_0 is true, the probability of obtaining a random assignment that produces a difference between the condition means that lies in the region of rejection is .0234 + .0234 = .0468. The region of rejection could not include the next less extreme outcomes (+1.57 and −1.57) because they would raise the cumulative probability to .1092, which exceeds α.

Now we can examine the observed means, shown in Table 9.12, and com-

Table 9.11 POSSIBLE OUTCOMES OF RANDOM ASSIGNMENT OF TREATMENT ORDER FOR SEVEN SUBJECTS AND TWO TREATMENTS

$\overline{X}_1 - \overline{X}_2$	f	p	cum p
−2.14	1	.0078	.0078
−1.86	2	.0156	.0234
−1.57	4	.0312	.0546
−1.29	7	.0547	.1093
−1.00	9	.0703	.1796
−0.71	12	.0938	.2734
−0.43	14	.1094	.3828
−0.14	15	.1172	.5000
0.14	15	.1172	.5000
0.43	14	.1094	.3828
0.71	12	.0938	.2734
1.00	9	.0703	.1796
1.29	7	.0547	.1093
1.57	4	.0312	.0546
1.86	2	.0156	.0234
2.14	1	.0078	.0078
Sum	128	1.0000	

Table 9.12   ACTUAL OUTCOME OF RANDOM
ASSIGNMENT OF TREATMENT ORDERS
FOR DATA SHOWN IN TABLE 9.10

Subject	Waking	Hypnotized
1	(t1) 4	(t2) 8
2	(t2) 5	(t1) 6
3	(t1) 7	(t2) 9
4	(t1) 2	(t2) 3
5	(t1) 12	(t2) 10
6	(t2) 11	(t1) 14
7	(t2) 15	(t1) 13
	$\overline{X}$ 8.00	9.00
	$\overline{X}_w - \overline{X}_h = -1.00$	

pare their difference with the region of rejection. The means for the two conditions differ by only -1.00. This outcome does not fall in the region of rejection, so we would not reject H_0.

$$\overline{X}_1 - \overline{X}_2 \text{ (critical): } \leq -1.86 \text{ or } \geq 1.86$$

$$\overline{X}_1 - \overline{X}_2 \text{ (observed)} = -1.00$$

Decision: Fail to reject H_0

Our conclusion is that the study provided no evidence that, for the subjects included in the sample, hypnosis influences the ability to recall details of a crime.

9.6   COMPUTATIONAL PRACTICALITY

Randomization tests can be used with larger numbers of both subjects and treatment conditions than we have demonstrated. When the computations are carried out by hand the method becomes very time-consuming as the number of cases is increased. For example, with ten subjects assigned randomly to two groups with five subjects per group, there are 252 possible random arrangements of the ten scores $[_{10}C_5 = 10!/(10 - 5)!5! = 252]$. If the number of subjects per group is five and the number of groups is three, there are 756,756 possible arrangements.[2]

Many research projects involve more subjects than these examples and

---

[2] In general, the number of possible random assignments of subjects to conditions in a study involving a total of N subjects and k conditions is given by $N!/(n_1!)(n_2!) \ldots (n_k!)$, where n_i represents the number of subjects assigned to group i.

often involve more groups, so an alternative method for determining probabilities is needed. This requirement explains why randomization tests, developed early in this century, did not become engrained in the set of statistical tools taught and used in behavioral research. The emergence of powerful computer systems, however, has provided a highly accessible means of conducting randomization tests. For example, Edgington (1987) has published a number of computer programs for such tests. In addition, the NPSTAT program that we have made available with this textbook can easily be used to perform randomization tests. In Chapter 11 we provide examples of the application of this program to cases involving two groups of scores.

SUMMARY

In this chapter we presented some fundamental ideas that are widely used to help make inferences about sets of data. The method involves setting a null hypothesis, H_0, that there is no systematic relationship between variables (e.g., group membership and scores on a test), and an alternative hypothesis, H_1, that a systematic relationship exists. To decide which of these two hypotheses is supported by the observed data, a set of possible outcomes is identified and a region of rejection is defined. The criterion defining this region, often .05, specifies those outcomes that lead to rejection of H_0. If the obtained result does not fall into this region, we fail to reject H_0.

If we reject H_0 when it is true, we make a Type I error. Conversely, if we fail to reject H_0 when it is false, we make a Type II error. Finally, directional versus nondirectional alternative hypotheses were defined. With a directional, or one-tailed alternative, all the region of rejection is located in one end of the distribution of possible outcomes. But with a nondirectional, or two-tailed alternative, half the region is located in each end of the distribution.

These hypothesis-testing concepts were applied to two types of data collection problem: (1) one set of binomial data where the experimenter performed some type of random assignment (e.g., outcomes of coin flips to trials) and (b) two sets of scores where the experimenter performed some type of random assignment (e.g., subjects to conditions). In each case, rejection of the null hypothesis led to the inference that for subjects in the sample there was a systematic relationship between two variables (e.g., outcome of coin toss and psychic's prediction; type of treatment and aggressiveness rating). A second inference was that the observed relationship was causal (e.g., the experimental treatment caused a reduction in aggressive behavior).

KEY WORDS

null hypothesis	β (beta)
alternative hypothesis	binomial test

statistically significant

region of rejection

Type I error

α (alpha)

Type II error

directional alternative hypothesis

nondirectional alternative hypothesis

randomization test

repeated measures

PROBLEMS

1 Why do researchers use the hypothesis testing procedures discussed in this chapter?

2 If the observed result of a study is in the region of rejection, what decision do you make?

3 If the observed result of a study is not in the region of rejection, what decision do you make?

4 Suppose you carry out a study with $\alpha = .05$ and H_0 is true. What is the probability that your study will produce a result that does *not* allow rejection of H_0?

5 Assume that you were to carry out two studies in which children make a choice between a complex and a simple stimulus card. Let $n = 20$ (the number of children tested) and $\alpha = .05$. The null hypothesis is that a child's choice is independent of the card's complexity, so the child is equally likely to select either card.
   (a) Given that you have a directional alternative hypothesis that children prefer complex stimuli, what is the minimum number of children that must choose the complex card in order for H_0 to be rejected?
   (b) What possible outcomes would be in the region of rejection if you had a nondirectional hypothesis?

6 An automobile manufacturer has developed a new suspension system. It wants to obtain evidence in favor of the claim that the new system provides a noticeable improvement over the old system. A group of 40 volunteers are tested. Each person is given two automobile rides over the same course, once in a car with the old suspension system and once in an identical car equipped with the new system. For each person, the order of testing the old and the new suspension systems is randomly determined. After taking the two rides, each person indicates which one he or she preferred.
   (a) What are the null and alternative hypotheses?
   (b) With $\alpha = .05$, what is the region of rejection for a binomial test? Use the normal approximation to the binomial distribution.
   (c) If 30 people preferred the ride that involved the new suspension system, would H_0 be rejected? What if only 25 preferred the ride with the new system?

7 A professor wants to know if there is a relationship between behavior modification training and amount of verbalization in dyslexic children. He can find only five children who satisfy his criterion of being classified as dyslexic. These five are observed for the amount of verbalization and then are randomly divided into two groups, three children receiving the behavior modification training and two children not receiving the training. The verbalization observations are then repeated for all five children. The amount of improvement in the verbalization score was 3, 4, and 5 for those in the treatment condition and 1 and 2 for those in the no treatment condition.

(a) State the null hypothesis.
(b) State the alternative hypothesis.
(c) Make a list of all outcome classes similar to that in Table 9.6.
(d) If the professor were to set the probability of a Type I error at .05, what is the region of rejection?
(e) Could the professor reject H_0 on the basis of this study?

8 Two methods of relieving headache pain are studied by randomly assigning ten chronic headache sufferers to one of two possible treatment conditions. Five subjects are randomly assigned to a condition involving relaxation training alone, and the others are assigned to a condition based on relaxation training with classical music. After receiving the training, the subjects are asked to keep a record for three months of the frequency with which they have severe headaches. The goal of the study is to find evidence that the use of music with relaxation training increases the effectiveness of the training. The reported frequencies for the subjects in each condition were

  Relaxation alone: 5 6 6 7 8

  Relaxation with music: 2 3 4 5 6

(a) State the null and alternative hypotheses.
(b) The outcome classes of the study, under the assumption that H_0 is true, are shown in the following table.

$\overline{X}_1 - \overline{X}_2$	f	p
−2.8	1	.0040
−2.4	6	.0238
−2.0	8	.0318
−1.6	15	.0595
−1.2	21	.0833
−0.8	28	.1111
−0.4	30	.1190
0.0	34	.1349
0.4	30	.1190
0.8	28	.1111
1.2	21	.0833
1.6	15	.0595
2.0	8	.0318
2.4	6	.0238
2.8	1	.0040

What range of outcomes (values of $\overline{X}_1 - \overline{X}_2$) constitute the region of rejection with $\alpha = .05$.
(c) Does the outcome of the study (the observed value of $\overline{X}_1 - \overline{X}_2$) allow rejection of H_0? On the basis of this result, what conclusion should you draw about the values of using music with relaxation training?

9 A researcher interested in the influence of mood on memory tests a group of seven subjects under two different mood conditions: normal and depressed. For each subject the researcher randomly determines which test condition will be experienced first. A depressed mood is induced when appropriate by having subjects think about sad or depressing events. The number of words recalled from a 20-item list by each

subject under each test condition follows. The researcher has no expectations about whether a depressed mood will improve or harm memory.

Subject	Normal	Depressed
1	16	14
2	13	11
3	18	15
4	15	14
5	10	12
6	16	13
7	12	10

(a) What are the null and alternative hypotheses?
(b) Assuming H_0 is true, the following table lists the possible outcome classes of the study.

$\bar{X}_1 - \bar{X}_2$	f	p
-2.143	1	.0078
-1.857	1	.0078
-1.571	4	.0312
-1.286	6	.0469
-1.000	8	.0625
-0.714	14	.1094
-0.429	13	.1016
-0.143	17	.1328
0.143	17	.1328
0.429	13	.1016
0.714	14	.1094
1.000	8	.0625
1.286	6	.0469
1.571	4	.0312
1.857	1	.0078
2.143	1	.0078

With $\alpha = .05$, what is the region of rejection?
(c) Does the observed result allow rejection of H_0? What do you conclude about the influence of mood on memory?

Chapter 10

Hypothesis Testing: Random Sampling

10.1   INTRODUCTION TO SAMPLING INFERENCE

Statistical tests are used to make inferences based on sample information. The rationale underlying statistical tests and the types of inference based on them are justified according to the type of random procedure a researcher uses to obtain sample information. For example, the rationale underlying the statistical tests outlined in Chapter 9 is based on random assignment. By randomly assigning subjects to treatment groups, potential sources of bias that could lead to systematic differences among groups are controlled, leaving only chance or treatment effects as likely explanations for observed differences among groups. When the probability is low that chance accounted for the difference, H_0 is rejected and we are justified to infer not only that there is a systematic relationship between the variables but also that the relationship is causal.

In this chapter we turn our attention to a second type of statistical inference. Here random *sampling*, rather than random assignment, forms the basis of statistical tests, and inferences concern population characteristics rather than causality. Like random assignment, random sampling is a procedure for controlling bias. In this case, however, the random process controls bias that may lead to systematic differences between the characteristics of a sample and the characteristics of the population from which the sample was selected. When these biases are controlled, we are in a position to make inferences from sample data to a population, a type of inference called **generalization.**

GENERALIZATION: The making of inferences from a sample to a population from which the sample was selected.

We consider two aspects of population inference, (1) hypothesis testing and (2) interval estimation. As in Chapter 9, hypothesis testing involves stating a null and alternative hypothesis, H_0 and H_1. It also involves setting a decision criterion, α, and making a decision based on an observed value of a test statistic. In this chapter, however, hypothesis testing differs from previously discussed procedures in the nature of H_0 and H_1 and in the type of test statistic. When hypothesis testing is used to make population inferences, the goal of the analysis is to determine if the population from which the sample data were selected has some assumed characteristic such as a specific mean value, $\mu = a$ (where a is some specific value). Thus, H_0 and H_1 are written with reference to population parameters. For example,

H_0: $\mu = a$

H_1: $\mu \neq a$.

Because the rationale underlying this type of hypothesis testing is based on random sampling rather than random assignment, the type of test statistics used will differ from randomization tests. Essentially, they are ways to determine whether the observed result is among the least likely that could have occurred in a sample of subjects taken from a population in which H_0 is true. If the observed result is among the least likely, the null hypothesis is rejected. Otherwise, H_0 is not rejected.

The second aspect of population inference, interval estimation, is appropriate whenever we do not know or do not want to assume a specific value for a population characteristic. The goal of interval estimation is to use sample information to estimate a range of values that has some probability of including the population value. For instance, you might use the sample statistic $\overline{X}$ to estimate a range of values that have a certain probability of including μ. As with hypothesis testing about an assumed value of μ, interval estimation is critically dependent on random sampling. Without random sampling we cannot make statistically valid inferences about populations.

10.2   SAMPLING PROCEDURES

Probability Sampling

The best way to test hypotheses or obtain interval estimates about population characteristics is to obtain a sample representative of the population of interest. Representativeness, however, presents a problem. How can you tell if a sample is representative? The answer is that you do *not* know this information for any single sample. Instead, you can use samples drawn randomly. Although any given random sample is unlikely to be representative, samples selected in this way provide a basis for estimating the relationship between the sample and the population sampled. The procedure allows a researcher to specify the probability that the obtained sample comes from a given population.

Random sampling can be conducted in several ways, the most straightforward of which is **simple random sampling.** First we define a population of interest from which we intend to select a sample of size n. We then obtain a simple random sample if each sample of size n has the same probability of being selected. This step is typically accomplished by randomly sampling individual cases in which each case has the same independent probability of being sampled.

SIMPLE RANDOM SAMPLE: A sample of n cases from a population chosen in such a way that each case in the sample has an independent and equal chance of being selected.

To illustrate simple random sampling, suppose that you are asked to determine the average achievement score for the 750 pupils at an elementary school. One reason for doing so could be to describe the population of 750 pupils. Another reason could be that you wish to compare the performance of this population against some criterion, such as the known national average of pupils who have taken the achievement test. If you do not have the resources to measure all 750 pupils, you can test a sample of, say, 30 pupils. A simple random sample could be obtained as follows. First, each pupil is given an identification number from 1 to 750. Then all 750 numbers are written on slips of paper and placed in a container, and 30 of the slips are drawn one at a time.

Another way to obtain a simple random sample of 30 slips from the 750 is to use a table of random numbers such as Table A in Appendix III. In Chapter 1 (Box 1.6) we explained how to use this table to assign subjects randomly to groups. It can be used in a similar way to draw randomly a set of values.

1. Close your eyes and place the tip of a pencil on Table A in Appendix III and determine the two digits closest to the pencil tip. This number is the row from which your first random number will be selected.
2. Repeat step 1 to obtain the column number of your first random number.
3. Enter the table at the row and column position determined by steps 1 and 2. The number at this location is your first random number.
4. From the number determined in step 3, read down successive columns of three-digit numbers between 1 and 750 until enough digits, 30, have been found.

You may wish to refer to Chapter 1, where Box 1.6 contains more details about the use of the random number table.

Several other procedures involve random sampling but place some restriction on the process.[1] The major purpose in restricting the sampling procedure is to help ensure representativeness of a sample that has fewer subjects than might be required in simple random sampling. For example, in *stratified* random sampling, the population is divided into subgroups, or strata, and the criteria for forming the strata are decided by the researcher. Common examples of strata criteria in behavioral research are age, school grade level, family size, and so on. Strata could be formed from age by dividing the population by age measured in decades, 20–29, 30–39, 40–49, and so on. After the strata have been defined, a simple random sample is then taken from each stratum.

In our example of sampling 30 pupils from an elementary school population of 750, a stratified random sample could be selected by taking random samples from each of the grade levels from 1 through 6. This form of sampling is illustrated in the left side of Table 10.1. The advantage of stratified

---

[1]Extensive discussion of these and several other sampling procedures (e.g., cluster, systematic, quota, two-stage) is found in books devoted to this topic by Cochran (1977) and by Kish (1965).

Table 10.1   RANDOM SAMPLING WITH RESTRICTIONS

Strata (grades)	Stratified sampling	Total pupils in population	Proportional sampling
1	5	150	6
2	5	125	5
3	5	100	4
4	5	100	4
5	5	125	5
6	5	150	6
Total	30	750	30

random sampling is that a certain amount of representativeness is ensured. Whereas a simple random sample might omit pupils from a particular grade level, the stratified procedure makes sure that some pupils from each grade will be included. An even more representative sample can be obtained when *proportional* stratification is used. As shown in the right side of Table 10.1, if there were more pupils in grades 1 and 6 than in grades 3 and 4, we would sample proportionally more pupils from the grades with large enrollment and proportionally fewer from other grades.

It is important for the researcher to specify the method used in selecting a sample because the sampling method is critical to the validity of inferences made from a sample to a population. In practice, the population that a researcher intends to sample may not be the one actually sampled. For example, you may wish to sample the children at a particular school but the school principal insists that parental permission must be obtained. Thus, the definition of the population must be changed from children enrolled in the school to children in the school whose parents agree to having their children sampled. In general, researchers need to be sensitive to the restrictions placed on sampling and to report carefully the way in which the sample was selected.

Nonprobability Sampling

In the example of sampling 30 pupils from a school with 750 pupils, selecting a random sample involves several deliberate steps. You might think that it would be easier just to ask the principal of the school to select 30 pupils who she felt were representative of the pupils in the school. That procedure would lead to a *judgmental* sample with unknown sources of bias. With a random sample you typically have a better estimate of representativeness of a sample. Judgmental samples are frequently used in some types of work, such as when television or newspaper reporters select certain politicians for interviews. The quality of a sample taken in this way depends on the judgment of the person doing the sampling, and caution must be used in generalizing from data collected in this fashion.

Another type of nonprobability sample is often called an *available* or *convenience* sample. A common example of this form of sampling occurs when professors ask students to volunteer as subjects in research. The results of this research may or may not generalize to samples that are not volunteers or to samples that are not students. Without random sampling there is no statistically justified way of making inferences about the generality of such results. This does *not* mean that empirical research without random sampling is worthless, just that a statistical argument regarding generality cannot be supported.[2]

10.3   SAMPLING DISTRIBUTION OF THE MEAN

Even when we are able to sample randomly, the obtained sample will still differ from the population in some way. We now examine the nature of these variations.

Consider the case in which you wish to test the null hypothesis that the population from which a sample was drawn randomly has μ equal to a particular value a. To have a valid statistical evaluation of H_0, we need to know the distribution of possible outcomes that could occur when H_0 is true. We can then define a region of rejection consisting of some small percentage of least likely outcomes that will lead to rejection of H_0.

A key concept for the random sampling method of obtaining probabilities is a type of distribution called a theoretical **sampling distribution.** It is a distribution that shows all possible values of some summary statistic and the probability associated with each value. For example, the sampling distribution of the mean shows the probability associated with all possible values of sample means based on samples drawn at random.

SAMPLING DISTRIBUTION: The sampling distribution of a statistic is the probability distribution of that statistic.

This type of distribution can be added to the list of distributions with which you are already familiar. A distribution of all scores in a population is a *population* distribution. If the scores are from a sample, they form a *sample* distribution. If the elements of the distribution are sample statistics like $\overline{X}$, they form a *sampling* distribution.

To illustrate the theoretical sampling distribution of the mean, we describe how a sampling distribution of the mean could be approximated. A

---

[2]A useful discussion of this point may be found in an article by Mook (1983).

Table 10.2   SAMPLING DISTRIBUTION OF THE MEAN
FOR ALL POSSIBLE SAMPLES FROM A
POPULATION OF THREE SCORES

Sample	Scores	$\overline{X}$
A	1,1	1.0
B	1,2	1.5
C	1,3	2.0
D	2,2	2.0
E	2,3	2.5
F	3,3	3.0
G	2,1	1.5
H	3,1	2.0
I	3,2	2.5

specific example of a theoretical sampling distribution is shown in Table 10.2. The table gives the nine possible unique samples of size two (i.e., of two scores each) drawn with replacement from a population of three scores (1, 2, 3). The mean for each possible sample has been computed and listed in column 3 of the table. The frequency distribution of this set of means is shown in Figure 10.1 with possible values of $\overline{X}$ on the X-axis and the frequency of occurrence of these values, $f_{\overline{X}}$, on the Y-axis. Notice that even though the parent population is rectangular in shape (each score occurs an equal number of times), the sampling distribution in Figure 10.1 is unimodal and symmetrical.

Several important features of the sampling distribution of the mean make it important for hypothesis testing. First, if equal-sized random samples of scores are drawn from a normal population, the sampling distribution of the means of those samples will also be normal with the mean equal to μ and the standard deviation equal to $\sigma/\sqrt{N}$. Second, even if the population from which random samples are drawn is *not* normal, the sampling distribution of the mean will often be closely approximated by the normal distribution. This very important result is expressed by a powerful theorem called the **central limit theorem.**

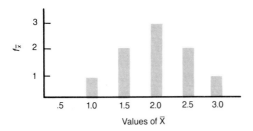

Figure 10.1   Frequency polygon of a sampling distribution of the means in Table 10.3.

CENTRAL LIMIT THEOREM: If random samples of equal size, N, are drawn from a population with mean μ and standard deviation σ, when N is large, the sampling distribution of the mean $\overline{X}$ will be approximately normally distributed with mean μ standard deviation $\sigma/\sqrt{N}$. This approximation holds regardless of the population distribution and becomes more and more accurate as N becomes larger.

The theorem tells us that with a larger sample size (N), the distribution of means of random samples will more closely be approximated by a normal distribution. Moreover, for any N, the mean of the distribution will equal the mean of the population distribution, and the standard deviation of the distribution will equal the population standard deviation divided by the square root of N. We now expand each of these points.

Shape of the Sampling Distribution

If the population distribution from which random samples of scores are drawn is normal, the sampling distribution of means from that population will also be normal for any size N. Furthermore, the sampling distribution of the mean is approximated by the normal distribution regardless of the shape of the population distribution from which the scores were sampled. As illustrated in Figure 10.2, this approximation becomes increasingly correct as the size of the samples on which the means are based increases. For many variables that are more or less normally distributed, samples of as few as 5 or 10 cases provide a sampling distribution that is approximated by the normal distribution. For samples of 30 or more cases, the sampling distribution of means is especially well approximated by the normal distribution.

Mean of the Sampling Distribution

The mean of the sampling distribution of means can be labeled $\mu_{\overline{X}}$. Over many samples, $\mu_{\overline{X}}$ will equal μ, the mean of the population from which the samples were drawn. An example of this idea is presented in Table 10.3 for the nine samples of size two ($N = 2$) given in Table 10.2.

In Table 10.3 the sum of the three individual scores in the population is $1 + 2 + 3 = 6$. Therefore, the value of μ is $6/3 = 2$. As shown in the table, the mean of any given sample depends on the particular scores in that sample, and of course, these vary from sample to sample. Even though the sample means vary from 1.0 to 3.0, the mean of the nine sample means is 2, the same as the mean of the population of three scores.

Researchers often refer to the variability that occurs from sample to sample as *random variation* or *sampling variation*. In this context we can also use the expression *sampling error* to indicate that, by chance, the value of any particular sample statistic will rarely be exactly the same as the population value or parameter. Thus, both raw scores and the statistics that arise

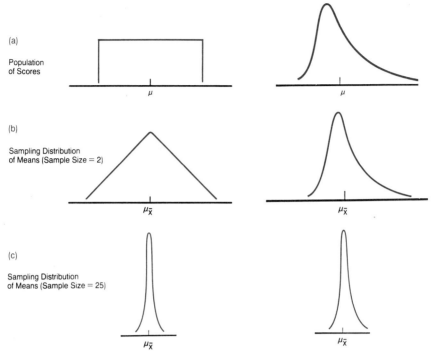

(a)

Population
of Scores

μ

(b)

Sampling Distribution
of Means (Sample Size = 2)

$\mu_{\bar{x}}$

(c)

Sampling Distribution
of Means (Sample Size = 25)

$\mu_{\bar{x}}$

Figure 10.2   Sampling distribution of the mean for different sample sizes.

**Table 10.3   SAMPLING DISTRIBUTION OF THE MEAN AND STANDARD
ERROR OF THE MEAN FOR ALL POSSIBLE SAMPLES FROM A
POPULATION OF THREE SCORES**

Sample	Scores	Means	
A	1,1	1.0	From the raw scores:
B	1,2	1.5	
C	1,3	2.0	$\mu = 6/3 = 2$
D	2,2	2.0	$\sigma = \sqrt{SS_x/N} = \sqrt{2/3} = \underline{.816}$
E	2,3	2.5	
F	3,3	3.0	From the means:
G	2,1	1.5	
H	3,1	2.0	$\mu_{\bar{x}} = 18/9 = 2$
I	3,2	2.5	$\sigma^2\bar{x} = \sigma^2/N$

$$\sigma_{\bar{x}} = \frac{\sigma}{\sqrt{N}} = \frac{.577}{\sqrt{9}} = \underline{.192}$$

from them are estimates of true values and include some amount of random error.

Standard Deviation of the Sampling Distribution

The variance of the sampling distribution is σ^2/N. This division by N, the sample size, indicates that the variability of the sample mean is less than the variability of raw scores. It also implies that with larger sample sizes, the variation in sample means becomes smaller.

When a standard deviation is computed on the means in a sampling distribution, it is computed by dividing the standard deviation of the data by the square root of the sample size, $\sqrt{\sigma^2/N} = \sigma/\sqrt{N}$. The quantity is given a distinct name, **standard error of the mean ($\sigma_{\bar{X}}$)**, which helps to distinguish it from the standard deviation of raw scores (σ_X) and the standard error of estimate discussed earlier.

STANDARD ERROR OF THE MEAN ($\sigma_{\bar{X}}$):   The standard deviation of a sampling distribution of means.

$$\sigma_{\bar{X}} = \sigma/\sqrt{N} \tag{10.1}$$

To summarize, when the sample means are based on small samples, the shape of the sampling distribution of the mean is similar to the shape of the parent population. With a large sample size, the sampling distribution is approximated by the normal distribution. This point is illustrated in Figure 10.2. The implication is that we can use the normal distribution in testing statistical hypotheses about means when *either* (1) the parent population is normal or (2) the sampling distribution of the mean is approximately normal. In either case random sampling is needed to use the distributions we have been discussing. Without random sampling we have no way of knowing whether our sample data can be related to the sampling distribution of the mean. Now we can show how to use the statistical model of random sampling for testing a hypothesis about a mean.

10.4   TESTING THE ONE-SAMPLE CASE WHEN σ IS KNOWN

We can combine what we know about statistical testing with what we know about sampling distributions to generate a region of rejection and carry out a statistical test. Consider testing the null hypothesis, H_0, that the population mean μ has some particular value a.

H_0: $\mu = a$

Suppose that you are interested in comparing the achievement scores at an elementary school with the national norms for the achievement test. According to the manual that accompanies the test, the mean and standard deviation are $\mu = 100$ and $\sigma = 16$. Further assume that there are 750 pupils in the school and you do not have time to test all of them. Consequently, you decide to sample randomly and test 64 of them. The question of interest is whether the population of elementary schoolchildren has a mean with value *a* that is the same, higher, or lower than the value of μ given as the national norm. Given no other information, the null hypothesis is that μ equals 100, and we let the alternative hypothesis be nondirectional, that μ does not equal 100.

$$H_0\!: \mu = 100$$

$$H_1\!: \mu \neq 100$$

We can test this hypothesis by using a sampling distribution of means when H_0 is true and a sample size of 64. If the observed $\overline{X}$ is among the least likely sample means, we will conclude that the null hypothesis should be rejected. The specific procedure for doing so involves using the distribution of a *z*-ratio similar to the standard score (*z*) presented in Chapter 5: $z = (X - \overline{X})/s$.

As before, the *z*-ratio can be used to express distance between observed and expected values in a standard normal distribution. The difference is that here the observed event is some particular value of $\overline{X}$ instead of a raw score, and the expected value is μ instead of $\overline{X}$. The denominator of this ratio is a measure of the variation in the sampling distribution of the mean instead of a raw score distribution. Thus we use the standard error of this distribution. In Formula 10.2, dividing by $\sigma_{\overline{X}}$ expresses the distance $\overline{X} - \mu$ in standard error units.

$$z_{\overline{X}} = \frac{\overline{X} - \mu}{\sigma_{\overline{X}}} \tag{10.2}$$

The results of statistical test ratios, such as the $z_{\overline{X}}$-ratio in Formula 10.2, can be thought of as measures of distance along the X-axis. In standard error units, they tell how much a given outcome deviates from the mean of a distribution. The more the observed value of *z* deviates from the mean of the sampling distribution, the smaller the probability of that value or more extreme values occurring when the null hypothesis is true. If the observed result is among the least likely results defined by the criterion α, H_0 is rejected. This procedure gives a statistical basis to infer that if H_0 is true, an unlikely event has been observed, one that is rare if random factors accounted for the value of $\overline{X}$.

Example of the $z_{\overline{X}}$-test

As an example of the application of the *z*-ratio in Formula 10.2, we use the problem of comparing achievement scores at a given school with the national norms for an achievement test. The null and alternative hypotheses have been defined—H_0: $\mu = 100$, and H_1: $\mu \neq 100$. Finally, we set α at .05 so that with a nondirectional alternative hypothesis the region of rejection is distributed equally in each tail of the null distribution. For α equal to .05, the nondirectional H_1 places half the region (.025 of the distribution) in each tail.

Given this information, we can identify the region of rejection in z units by consulting Table B in Appendix III. We enter the table looking for the area beyond z that equals 2.5 percent (.0250) of the total area in the distribution of the z statistic. Inspection of the table shows that 2.5 percent of the area is in the smaller portion when $z_{\bar{X}} = +1.96$. Of course, that means that 2.5 percent of the total area also lies below $z_{\bar{X}} = -1.96$. Each of these areas is a proportion of the total area in the sampling distribution, and there is a probability of .025 that the obtained result will be in that area.

If the obtained $z_{\bar{X}}$ is greater than $+1.96$ or smaller than -1.96, it has a small probability of occurrence when H_0 is true. Thus, any obtained $z_{\bar{X}}$-value that is more extreme than ± 1.96 will fall in the region of rejection and allow us to reject H_0. The location of these areas and related decisions are shown in Figure 10.3.

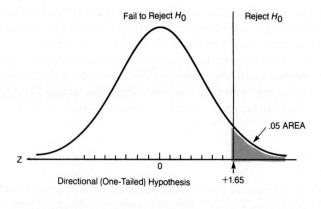

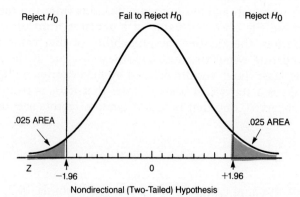

Figure 10.3 Sampling distribution of z, indicating region of rejection when $\alpha/2 = .025$.

Suppose that the sample of 64 pupils turned out to have a mean of 105, $\overline{X} = 105$. We want to know whether this obtained $\overline{X}$ is among the least likely if the null hypothesis is true. Given $\sigma = 16$, we calculate the standard error of the mean by using Formula 10.1: $\sigma_{\overline{X}} = \sigma/\sqrt{N} = 16/\sqrt{64} = 2$. With this information, a $z_{\overline{X}}$-ratio can be formed by using Formula 10.2:

$$z_{\overline{X}} = \frac{105 - 100}{16/\sqrt{64}} = \frac{5}{2} = 2.50$$

This value of $z_{\overline{X}} = 2.50$ tells us that the observed outcome is 2.50 standard deviation units above the mean of the distribution of $z_{\overline{X}}$. Since this value exceeds the predetermined criterion of $z_{\overline{X}} = \pm 1.96$, the null hypothesis can be rejected with $\alpha = .05$ and a nondirectional alternative hypothesis:

$z_{\overline{X}}$ (critical) $= \pm 1.96$

$z_{\overline{X}}$ (obtained) $= +2.50$

Decision: Reject H_0

In reporting this outcome one acceptable format is to include the results of the statistical test in a sentence. Typically the focus of the sentence is that "The sample mean (105) was significantly larger than the hypothesized population mean (100), $z_{\overline{X}} = 2.50$, $p < .05$." The probability statement, $p < .05$, indicates that the observed result is among the least likely outcomes defined by an α of .05. Notice that the probability statement is placed at the end of the sentence, the intent being to support the verbal and descriptive portion of the statement that came first.

When you read technical reports in the research literature you will find that other probability values are frequently reported, such as $p < .01$ or $p < .001$. The reported value does not necessarily represent the alpha level set by the researcher. Rather, it is the smallest conventional value that allows the null to be rejected for a given set of data. Consider that in Table B the probability value associated with the obtained $z_{\overline{X}} = \pm 2.50$ is .006 in each tail of the distribution. Thus, under a nondirectional alternative hypothesis, the probability of obtaining a value equal to or more extreme than ± 2.50 is $2(.006) = .012$. Even though the obtained probability was $p = .012$, we typically do not report the exact value. Instead, we make a statement about the probability of the observed outcome relative to the alpha level set before data collection, $p \leq .05$.

10.5 TESTING THE ONE-SAMPLE CASE WHEN σ IS ESTIMATED

The $z_{\overline{X}}$-ratio in Formula 10.2 is useful when we know both the mean and standard deviation of the population under the null hypothesis. In many applied situations we might assume the value of the population mean but not the value of the population standard deviation, and we must estimate that value. Our best estimate of σ is the sample standard deviation, s, and our best estimate of $\sigma_{\overline{X}}$ is $s_{\overline{X}}$.

$$\sigma_{\overline{X}} = \sigma/\sqrt{N} \text{ is estimated by } s_{\overline{X}} = s/\sqrt{N}$$

To take this estimation into account, we define an alternative ratio that is closely related to the z-ratio in Formula 10.2. The distribution of this new ratio is called the t-distribution and its values can be computed by Formula 10.3. It shares with z the assumption of a normal distribution in the parent population. As you can see, Formula 10.3 is very similar to Formula 10.2:

$$t = \frac{\overline{X} - \mu}{s_{\overline{X}}} \tag{10.3}$$

Degrees of Freedom

The term *degrees of freedom*, *df* (see Chapter 4), will be used repeatedly in connection with the t-ratio and similar ratios. It is defined as the number of "units" or pieces of information on which a statistic is based minus the number of estimated population parameters. Specifically, in the case of the t-ratio for a single sample, $df = N - 1$. This result derives from the fact that in calculating the sample standard deviation it is necessary to estimate the population value of the mean. Making that estimate results in the loss of one degree of freedom. Values of t are typically reported along with their associated value of *df* given in parentheses, $t(df)$.

The Distribution of t When H_0 Is True

Although the distribution of the t-ratio resembles a normal distribution, it is actually somewhat flatter because the value of $s_{\overline{X}}$ is an estimate that varies from sample to sample. This variation leads to greater variability in the values of t than the values of z. As shown in Figure 10.4, the distribution of t changes systematically with its degrees of freedom. Since this distribution depends on the sample size, you can see that it is really not a single distribution but a family of distributions. With a large sample size the t-distribution more closely approximates the standard normal distribution. Consequently, when N is very large, the two ratios (z and t) lead to very similar probability statements. For example, if N is extremely large (approaching infinity), $z \geq 1.645$ and $t(\text{inf}) \geq 1.645$ have the same probability of occurring (.05) when H_0 is true.

The z-ratio and t-ratio can be evaluated in the same general way. The larger the obtained value of the test ratio (z or t), the smaller the probability of observing that value if the null hypothesis is true. One difference between these two ratios comes from the fact that probability of a range of z-ratios is the same regardless of sample size because there is only one standard normal distribution. But with t-ratios, the probability of a given range of values [e.g., $t(df) \geq 2.00$] varies with its degrees of freedom. In practice we rarely know

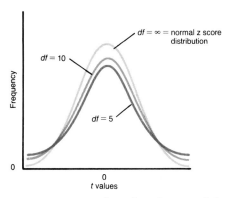

Figure 10.4 Sampling distribution of the *t*-ratio for various *df* values.

the value of the population standard deviation, σ, so the test based on $z_{\bar{x}}$ is of more theoretical than practical interest. In most cases the *t*-ratio is used.

The *t*-table

We evaluate a given *t*-ratio by using a table that is somewhat different from the table of the standard normal distribution (Table B in Appendix III). The major difference is that, as indicated in Figure 10.4 and Table 10.4, there is a

Table 10.4 ABBREVIATED FORM OF THE *t*-TABLE FOR SELECTED VALUES OF *df*

For any given value of *df*, the table shows the values of *t* corresponding to various levels of probability. An obtained *t* is significant at a given probability level if it is equal to or greater than the tabled value.

	Area in *both* tails				
	.20	.10	.05	.02	.01
df					
	Area in *one* tail				
	.10	.05	.025	.01	.005
1	3.078	6.314	12.706	31.821	63.657
2	1.886	2.920	4.303	6.965	9.925
3	1.638	2.353	3.182	4.541	5.841
. . .	. . .	. . .	. . .	. . .	. . .
15	1.341	1.753	2.131	2.602	2.947
. . .	. . .	. . .	. . .	. . .	. . .
30	1.310	1.697	2.042	2.457	2.750
. . .	. . .	. . .	. . .	. . .	. . .
∞	1.282	1.645	1.960	2.326	2.576

family of t-distributions to consider because there is a slightly different distribution for each value of $df = N - 1$. Only t values with a small probability of occurrence under the null hypothesis are of interest. Thus, only these values and their probability of occurrence are recorded in the table. You should examine the t-table, Table D in Appendix III, and become familiar with its use.

Table 10.4 is an abbreviated version of Table D in Appendix III. For each value of $df = N - 1$ in the table, five t values have been selected. The tabled t values are those associated with the more common probabilities reported in hypothesis testing. Because in practice exact probabilities are rarely reported, only the values .10, .05, .025, .01, and .005 are given in the table.[3] Even though it is possible to estimate the exact probability (under H_0) of obtaining $\overline{X}$ or more extreme values, it is not necessary.

Example of the *t*-ratio

As an example of using the t-ratio, assume that we have the same problem as with the $z_{\overline{X}}$-ratio: We wish to see if average achievement scores at an elementary school are higher, the same, or lower than a given value. Thus we still have H_0: $\mu = 100$ and H_1: $\mu \neq 100$. The difference in this case is that we do not know the value of σ. Instead, we will estimate σ with s calculated from the data at hand.

Suppose that five pupils were randomly selected from the population of 750 pupils. They were tested and obtained the following achievement scores: 98, 100, 101, 104, 105. Given this information, the null hypothesis that μ equals 100 can be tested. As shown in Table 10.5, the numerator of the t-ratio is straightforward: $\overline{X} = 508/5 = 101.6$ and $(\overline{X} - \mu) = (101.6 - 100) = 1.6$.

Because the value of the population standard deviation, σ, is not known, the denominator requires a bit more work. To estimate the standard error of the mean, you must first find the sample standard deviation. Table 10.5 shows that for our sample of five scores, the sum of squares = 33.2 and $N - 1 = 4$. Thus, our sample standard deviation is $\sqrt{33.2/4} = 2.881$. The next step is to use this value to obtain the standard error: $s_{\overline{X}} = 2.881/\sqrt{5} = 1.288$. Finally, the t-ratio can be formed: $t(4) = 1.6/1.288 = 1.242$.

$$t(4) = \frac{101.6 - 100}{2.881/\sqrt{5}} = \frac{1.6}{1.288} = 1.242$$

---

[3]Beginning researchers often place too much emphasis on the probability reported with an outcome, particularly when summarizing results from a computer printout. Many computer programs are written to give probabilities to several places, for example, $p = .0442$ or $.008475$. However, the sensitive researcher knows that this degree of precision is rarely, if ever, achieved. The computer value should be rounded to one of the conventional probability levels, such as $p < .05$ or $p < .01$, corresponding either to the alpha level set by the researcher before data collection or the minimal value in the table of critical values.

Table 10.5   **EXAMPLE COMPUTATION OF A ONE-SAMPLE *t*-RATIO**

Given H_0: $\mu = 100$ Sum of Squares $= 51646 - (508^2/5) = 33.2$

H_1: $\mu \neq 100$

$$s = \sqrt{\frac{SS}{N-1}} = \sqrt{\frac{33.2}{4}} = \underline{2.881}$$

$$s_{\overline{X}} = \frac{s}{\sqrt{N}} = \frac{2.881}{\sqrt{5}} = \underline{1.288}$$

Data	X	X^2
	98	9604
	100	10000
	101	10201
	104	10816
	105	11025
Sum	508	51646

$$t(df) = \frac{\overline{X} - \mu}{s_{\overline{X}}}$$

$$t(4) = \frac{101.6 - 100}{1.288} = \underline{1.24}$$

The region of rejection for testing the null hypothesis that μ equals some specific value (e.g., H_0: $\mu = 100$) can be found by inspecting Table D in Appendix III. Before looking at the table, guess what minimal value of t will be called significant for our nondirectional hypothesis. It is reasonable to guess that a value near ± 1.96 is critical since that is the value found when we tested the same hypothesis with the $z_{\overline{X}}$-ratio. Although the critical value of $t(4)$ is not likely to be exactly ± 1.96, would you expect it to be more or less extreme than ± 1.96?

In Table D we find that for $df = N - 1 = 4$, and a nondirectional H_1 with $\alpha = .05$, the region of rejection contains all values of t equal to or more extreme than ± 2.776. Since the obtained t-ratio (1.242) is less than these critical values, the data in this sample do not permit rejection of the null hypothesis:

t(critical) $= \pm 2.776$

t(obtained) $= 1.242$

Decision: Fail to reject H_0

The researcher has two options for reporting this nonsignificant finding. The more detailed statement would be that "The mean from the sample (101.6) was not significantly different from the hypothesized mean (100): $t(4) = 1.24$, $p > .05$." Although this reporting of our t-test outcome is accurate, some workers prefer a less complex format. In reporting an outcome that is not significant, the t value might not be reported at all. That is, the researcher simply reports that the outcome was not significant. Alternatively, a very small value can be reported as $t < 1$ because all values of t between -1 and $+1$ are nonsignificant at any reasonable level of alpha.

A significant value of t is reported in the same manner as a significant value of $z_{\overline{X}}$. For example with $N = 30$ and $t = 10.00$, we would report that

$t(29) = 10.00$, $p < .05$. In this case the probability refers only to the α level set by the researcher. As a courtesy to other researchers who might use a different level of α, $p < .001$ could have been reported because the t value would be in the region of rejection even for $\alpha = .001$.

In general, values of $z_{\overline{X}}$ and t can be thought of as standard deviation unit measures of distance from the mean of a unimodal and symmetrical distribution. The more extreme the value of the test ratio, the smaller the probability of its occurrence under the null hypothesis. We typically hope to find an extreme value of z or t so that the obtained result will be among the .05 or .01 least likely outcomes under the null hypothesis. This result provides a statistical basis for the researcher to reject H_0 and state that a significant outcome has been observed.

10.6 TESTING THE SIGNIFICANCE OF r BY USING t AND z

This section is concerned with whether an obtained correlation coefficient indicates a statistically significant relationship between two variables. We consider two contexts in which this question might be asked. In one case we are concerned with testing the null hypothesis that an obtained r comes from a population in which the population correlation, ρ (spelled *rho* and pronounced *row*), is equal to zero—H_0: $\rho = 0$. In the other case we test the null hypothesis that $\rho = a$, where a can take on any value between -1.00 and $+1.00$.

Does $\rho = 0$?

When the population correlation is assumed to be zero, the sampling distribution of r will be normally distributed; have a mean value equal to zero; and have a standard error, σ_r, that can be estimated by

$$s_r = \sqrt{\frac{1 - r^2}{N - 2}} \tag{10.4}$$

The null hypothesis is that an obtained r comes from this sampling distribution—H_0: $\rho = 0$. The alternative hypothesis is that an obtained r does not come from this sampling distribution. The alternative, H_1, can be stated either directionally, H_1: $\rho > 0$ or $\rho < 0$, or nondirectionally, H_1: $\rho \neq 0$.

The test statistic for evaluating H_0 follows the general format used previously to test hypotheses about a mean. That is, the amount that the obtained r deviates from ρ is transformed into standard error units, s_r. The result of this transformation is an obtained t value. A convenient formula for transforming r to t is the following:

$$t = \frac{r - \rho}{s_r} = \frac{r - 0}{s_r} = \frac{r}{s_r}$$

Substituting Formula 10.4 for s_r into this new formula, we have

$$t(N - 2) = \frac{r}{\sqrt{\dfrac{1 - r^2}{N - 2}}} \qquad (10.5)$$

This t value follows the general t-distribution with $N - 2$ degrees of freedom. Two degrees of freedom are lost because in calculating s_r, we need to estimate the standard deviations of both the X variable (s_X) and the Y variable (s_Y). One degree of freedom is lost for each of these estimates.[4]

As an example of the application of significance testing with r, assume that you have obtained two sets of IQ scores from a class of 32 students, one set at the beginning of an academic term and one set at the end of the term. Suppose the two sets of scores produced a correlation of .70. We want to know whether this correlation suggests a true relationship between these variables, or whether a correlation this size merely reflects sampling error from a population in which the relationship is zero. Although one might expect a positive relationship between two IQ scores, we will test H_0: $\rho = 0$ against the conservative alternative H_1: $\rho \neq 0$, with $\alpha/2 = .05/2 = .025$. Substituting the values of $N = 32$ and $r = .70$ into Formula 10.5 leads to an obtained t value of 5.38:

$$t(30) = \frac{.70}{\sqrt{\dfrac{1 - .49}{32 - 2}}} = \frac{.70}{\sqrt{\dfrac{.51}{30}}} = 5.38$$

This obtained t value is compared with the critical nondirectional value of t listed in Table D for $df = 30$. We use the nondirectional critical value with $\alpha/2 = .025$ because H_1 is nondirectional. In Table D we find the critical value of $t(30)$ is ± 2.042, which is less than the obtained t value of 5.38. Therefore, we reject the null hypothesis that $\rho = 0$.

t(critical) $= \pm 2.042$

t(obtained) $= 5.38$

Decision: Reject H_0

Such a finding indicates that the obtained r value is more deviant from zero than would be expected by sampling error, allowing us to conclude that $r \neq 0$. The validity of this statistical decision depends on having randomly sampled subjects from some clearly defined population.

---

[4]The calculation of s_r involves the use of r (actually r^2), and from $\text{Cov}_{XY}/s_X s_Y$, you can see that the standard deviation of both X and Y are estimated.

Does $\rho = a$?

Although the sampling distribution of r is approximately normal when $\rho = 0$, when ρ is a value other than zero the distribution of r is skewed. Moreover, the amount of skew in the sampling distribution of r varies with the value of ρ, making direct tests on r impossible with the t-ratio or any other test statistic. The solution to this problem is to transform r values into values that are normally distributed regardless of the value of ρ.

This conversion can be done by using Fisher's r to z_r transformation. Sir R. A. Fisher showed that when n is fairly large (50 or more) and when r is transformed by using the rule

$$z_r = \frac{1}{2} \ln \frac{1+r}{1-r} \quad \text{(where } \ln = \text{natural logarithm)} \tag{10.6}$$

resulting z_r values are approximately normally distributed for all values of ρ. The mean of this sampling distribution is z_ρ (the Fisher z-transformation of the population correlation), and the standard error is

$$s_{zr} = \frac{1}{\sqrt{N-3}} \tag{10.7}$$

The z_r values corresponding to various values of r are listed in Table E in Appendix III. This table makes finding values of z_r much easier than using Formula 10.6.

Now that we have defined the relevant distribution we can define the test ratio to be used. The null hypothesis to be tested is that an obtained r comes from a population in which the population parameter, ρ, is equal to some nonzero value (a)—H_0: $\rho = a$. The alternative hypothesis, H_1, is either that $\rho \neq a$ (nondirectional) or that $\rho > a$ or $\rho < a$ (directional H_1). To evaluate H_0 we follow the general procedure of finding the amount that the sample statistic deviates from the population parameter in standard deviation units. In this case we find the amount that z_r deviates from z_ρ in s_{zr} units. The result of this transformation is a z-score that belongs to the standard normal distribution. The z_r values are transformations of r using Formula 10.6. Given this context, the formula for our test statistic can be expressed as

$$z = \frac{z_r - z_\rho}{\dfrac{1}{\sqrt{N-3}}} \tag{10.8}$$

where z_r is the Fisher transformed value of the sample r, z_ρ is the Fisher transformed value of the hypothesized null value of ρ, N is the sample size, and z is the obtained z-score value.

To illustrate this test, consider the correlation of .70 between the two sets of 32 IQ scores described at the beginning of this section. Suppose we wanted to test the null hypothesis that $\rho = .50$ against the directional alternative hypothesis that $\rho > .50$. To carry out the test we transform the sample

r and ρ into Fisher z-scores by using Table E, and we obtain $z_{.70} = .867$ and $z_{.50} = .549$. Recall that the sample size is 32. Substituting these values into Formula 10.8, we find

$$z = \frac{.867 - .549}{\dfrac{1}{\sqrt{32 - 3}}} = \frac{.318}{.186} = 1.71$$

In the unit-normal distribution, a z-score of 1.65 is required to reject H_0 with a directional alternative and $\alpha = .05$. Since the obtained z-score value of 1.71 is greater than the critical value of 1.65, we reject the null hypothesis that $\rho = .50$ and accept the alternative hypothesis that $\rho > .50$:

$z(\text{critical}) \quad = 1.65$

$z(\text{obtained}) = 1.71$

Decision: Reject H_0

Interpretation of Statistical Testing with z and t

The model of significance testing that has been outlined here with the z-distribution and the t-distribution assumes that the scores have been randomly sampled from a specific population of interest. By means of random sampling we use these distributions to construct a valid region of rejection. Without random sampling we cannot safely use the procedures discussed in this chapter. A nonrandom sample may have scores that are not independent of each other (e.g., scores from twins or spouses). Lack of independence can lead to greater similarity among sample scores than is found in the population, and consequently, s becomes an underestimate of σ. In that case we produce an underestimate of $\sigma_{\overline{X}}$ or σ_r and an inflation in the obtained value of t. Thus, when random sampling is not carried out, an obtained probability value of z or t is not a good estimate of the true probability.

10.7   CONFIDENCE INTERVALS

The preceding sections of this chapter describe a general procedure for comparing the value of a sample statistic ($\overline{X}$ or r) with an assumed value of a population parameter (μ or ρ). This hypothesis-testing procedure is one way to make statistical inferences about populations. In this section we consider a related form of statistical inference in which sample information is used to estimate the unknown value of a parameter. The procedure is called *interval estimation*. It involves identifying a *confidence interval*, which is a range of values having a specific probability of including an unknown population parameter. We discuss confidence intervals for estimating the population mean and for estimating the population correlation.

Confidence Intervals for Estimating the Population Mean

Assume that in our hypothetical example of school achievement, we rejected the null hypothesis that the mean achievement score of the local students is equal to the national mean of the test. Our next question might be "What is the value of the local student's population mean?" There are three ways to answer this question. First, we could test all the students in the current year and find the exact value of their population mean. At best, testing all members of a population can be expensive and time-consuming, and sometimes it is impossible. A more realistic procedure would use sample information to estimate the population mean.

Therefore, a second way to answer our question uses the sample mean as an estimate of its population counterpart. This strategy would, in fact, produce the best single-number estimate of the population mean. The problem with using $\overline{X}$ is that it almost certainly will not be exactly equal to μ because of sampling error.

A third way to ask about the value of μ takes into account both the sample mean and sampling error to estimate a range of values that you feel confident will include μ. Such a range of values is called a *confidence interval*. The values marking the boundaries of a confidence interval are called *confidence limits*. The degree of confidence associated with a confidence interval is the *probability* that the interval contains μ within its range, and it is expressed as $100(1 - \alpha)$ percent. If $\alpha = .05$ is the probability that the confidence interval does not contain μ, we have $100(1 - .05) = 95$ percent confidence that the interval does contain μ.

To illustrate how confidence intervals are determined, we begin by considering the sampling distribution of the mean. We know that the sampling distribution of the mean is approximated by the normal distribution with the mean equal to μ, the population mean, and standard deviation equal to $\sigma_{\overline{X}}$, the standard error of the mean. Because the distribution is normal, 95 percent of the values of $\overline{X}$ are expected to fall within the range of -1.96 and $+1.96$ standard errors of μ:

$$p(-1.96 \cdot \sigma_{\overline{X}} \leq \overline{X} - \mu \leq +1.96 \cdot \sigma_{\overline{X}}) = .95$$

It follows that if 95 percent of all sample means randomly drawn from a population lie within 1.96 standard errors to either side of μ, μ will lie within $\overline{X} \pm 1.96$ standard errors 95 percent of the time.

This range of values covering $\overline{X} \pm 1.96\sigma_{\overline{X}}$ is called the 95 percent confidence interval for μ. The center of the interval is $\overline{X}$, and its limits are obtained by multiplying $\sigma_{\overline{X}}$ by the nondirectional critical value of z at $\alpha = .05$. If we want to increase our confidence to 99 percent, we multiply $\sigma_{\overline{X}}$ by the nondirectional critical value of z at $\alpha = .01$. From Table B in Appendix III, we find that this z value is 2.58 (.005 of the distribution is beyond this z), and the 99 percent confidence interval for μ will be $\overline{X} \pm 2.58\sigma_{\overline{X}}$. Notice that the critical value of z for a 99 percent confidence interval (2.58) is larger than the critical value for a 95 percent confidence interval (1.96). As a result, the

99 percent confidence interval will be wider than the 95 percent interval, which is exactly what one would expect from increasing the probability that μ is included in the interval.

In practice we rarely know the value of $\sigma_{\overline{X}}$, so we estimate $\sigma_{\overline{X}}$ from $s_{\overline{X}}$. In this case the center of the 95 percent confidence interval will still be $\overline{X}$, but the limits will be obtained by multiplying $s_{\overline{X}}$ by the nondirectional critical value of $t(df)$ at $\alpha = .05$. Thus, the 95 percent confidence interval for μ when $\sigma_{\overline{X}}$ is not known is equal to $\overline{X} \pm t(df)_{.05/2} \cdot s_{\overline{X}}$.

An Example

As an example of finding confidence intervals for μ, consider the hypothetical achievement scores of five students described earlier. We already know that $\overline{X} = 101.6$, $s_{\overline{X}} = 1.288$, and $df = 4$. All we need to add to find the 95 percent confidence interval is the nondirectional critical value for $t(4)$ at $\alpha = .05$, which, from Table D, is $t(4) = 2.776$. Combining this information, we find that the limits of the 95 percent confidence interval for μ are

$$101.6 - 2.766(1.288) = 98.037 \text{ and}$$

$$101.6 + 2.776(1.288) = 105.163.$$

Thus, we can say that the probability is .95 that the interval of 98.037 to 105.163 includes the mean achievement score of the population from which this random sample of five students was obtained. To find the 99 percent confidence interval, we use Table D to find the nondirectional critical value of $t(4)$ at $\alpha = .01$, which is $t(4) = 4.604$. Then the 99 percent confidence limits are

$$101.6 - 4.604(1.288) = 95.670 \text{ and}$$

$$101.6 + 4.604(1.288) = 107.530$$

Again, notice that increasing the level of confidence leads to increasing the width of the confidence interval.

Interpreting Confidence Intervals

It is important to note that the probability statement associated with confidence intervals refers to the interval, not to the population parameter. It is incorrect to state that the probability is $1 - \alpha$ that μ will be in some range of values. Rather, the correct interpretation is that over all possible random samples of size N, the probability is $1 - \alpha$ that an interval of the form $\overline{X} \pm t_{(.05/2)} \cdot s_{\overline{X}}$ will include μ. So, for example, the following statements about the confidence intervals constructed previously would be *incorrect*.

1. The probability is .95 that μ equals 101.6.
2. The probability is .99 that μ is between 95.670 and 107.530.
3. The probability is .95 that the interval from 98.037 to 105.163, *and only that specific interval*, includes μ.

The problem with the first two statements is that the probability value refers to μ, which does not make sense because the population mean is a particular value; it does not take on a value with some probability. The third statement is incorrect only to the extent that the italicized part is included. Removing that part we are left with the correct statement:

4. The probability is .95 that the interval from 98.037 to 105.163 is a member of a set of similarly constructed intervals that includes μ.

The problem is that statement 4 is often interpreted to mean statement 3, suggesting that the specified confidence limits are the *only* limits that have a .95 probability of including μ. In fact, over repeated random samples of size N many different means and standard deviations would be obtained, and therefore, many confidence intervals having different limits could be constructed. Yet each sample interval has a 95 percent chance of containing μ. Thus a single confidence interval has some probability of containing μ, but the specific limits on the interval have no meaning as absolute limits on μ.

Confidence Intervals for Estimating the Population Correlation

Confidence intervals for estimating ρ by using sample r values are determined in much the same manner as are intervals for estimating μ by using sample means. As before, we begin by considering a sampling distribution, this time the sampling distribution of r. Because we are interested in estimating *any* potential value of ρ, the sampling distribution used is the sampling distribution of z_r.

We know the sampling distribution of z_r is approximately normal, with the mean equal to z_ρ and the standard error equal to $\sigma_{z_r} = 1/\sqrt{N-3}$. Thus, over all possible samples, 95 percent of the transformed sample correlations will lie within 1.96 standard errors to either side of the transformed population correlation, and the limits of the 95 percent confidence interval for z_ρ will be $z_r + 1.96 \cdot s_{z_r}$. Similarly, over all possible samples, 99 percent of the sample correlations will lie within 2.58 standard errors to either side of the transformed population correlation and the 99 percent confidence interval will be $z_r \pm 2.58 \cdot s_{z_r}$.

To illustrate how to construct confidence intervals for ρ, consider the hypothetical IQ data discussed in the section on testing hypotheses about correlations. We know that the sample r is .70 and that the sample size is 32. The steps in constructing a 95 percent confidence interval around this sample correlation are as follows. First, r is transformed to z_r by using Table E in Appendix III. For $r = .70$, z_r is .867. Second, the standard error of z_r is found by computing $1/\sqrt{N-3}$, which is equal to $1/\sqrt{29} = .186$. Third, the 95 percent confidence limits are computed as $.867 - 1.96(.186) = .502$ for the lower limit and $.867 + 1.96(.186) = 1.232$ for the upper limit.

When $z_r = .502$, $r = .46$, and when $z_r = 1.232$, $r = .84$. Thus, we have a confidence level of .95 that the interval from .46 to .84 includes ρ. Notice that the limits of the 95 percent confidence interval are not equally distant from the sample r of .70 because the sampling distribution of r is skewed when $\rho \neq 0$.

10.8   HYPOTHESIS TESTING COMPARED TO INTERVAL ESTIMATION

Although hypothesis testing and interval estimation are conceptualized differently, they are related procedures. In hypothesis testing we focus on the value of a population parameter specified by H_0 (e.g., $\mu = a$) and then determine whether an observed statistic such as $\overline{X}$ was unlikely to have been obtained from such a population. When we define a region of rejection to include values more extreme than $\pm t(df)$ standard errors, we have defined a confidence interval $\mu \pm t(df) \cdot s_{\overline{X}}$. If $\overline{X}$ *is between* $\mu \pm t(df)$ standard errors, we fail to reject H_0, and if it is outside this interval, we reject H_0.

In contrast, interval estimation makes no assumptions about the value of a population parameter. Instead, our knowledge of sampling distributions is used to construct a confidence interval around a sample statistic [e.g., $\overline{X} \pm t(df) \cdot s_{\overline{X}}$]. We are $100(1 - \alpha)$ percent confident that such an interval contains the unknown population parameter.

Notice that the information obtained from these two procedures is closely related. If H_0 is rejected (e.g., reject $\mu = 100$), the confidence interval around the sample statistic, $\overline{X}$, will not include the value 100. Similarly, any hypothesized parameter value falling *outside* the limits of the confidence interval for a sample statistic is a value that would be rejected as a null hypothesis. Any value falling *within* the confidence interval is a value of the parameter that would not be rejected as a null hypothesis. Thus, the limits of a confidence interval around a sample statistic contain all the values of a parameter that would lead us to not reject the null hypothesis.

Given the strong connection between hypothesis testing and interval estimation, you might wonder why we need both procedures. In particular, you might wonder why we use hypothesis testing when the same information, and more, can be obtained from confidence intervals. There are two important reasons.

First, hypothesis testing is possible in many situations in which interval estimation is not possible. For example, later in this book we describe hypothesis testing for analyzing experiments that compare three or more groups. Such comparisons cannot be translated into confidence interval terms.

Second, hypothesis testing and interval estimation are used under different circumstances and for different purposes. The purpose of interval estimation is always to estimate the specified value of a population parameter. For this type of statistical inference to be valid, random sampling from a specified population is critical. It would not make sense to infer the value of a parameter from a sample if nothing were known about the relationship between the population and the sample. An important feature of random samples is that we can determine the extent of representativeness to be expected in the long run. Random samples permit us to estimate how much the sample statistic will vary around a population value.

In contrast, the purpose of hypothesis testing often is not to make inferences about the specific values of population characteristics. For example, when two or more samples are studied (rather than a single sample), the objective of hypothesis testing is usually to determine whether the samples differ relative to one another. The question being asked is about their relative standing rather than their absolute population values. In this context, hypothesis testing can be justified either on the basis of random sampling *or* on the basis of random assignment (using the procedures introduced in Chapter 9).

For both of these reasons—greater flexibility and freedom from the assumption of random sampling—the remainder of this book focuses on hypothesis testing. However, we approach hypothesis testing from both the random sampling and the random assignment points of view.

SUMMARY

This chapter introduced procedures for using sample information to make inferences about the characteristics of populations. For these inferences to have a basis in probability and statistical theory, they must be accompanied by random sampling of the subjects. It was argued that randomly selected samples have advantages over judgmental samples and convenience samples. They permit an unbiased estimate of the amount of error in making inferences.

The sampling distribution of the mean was described as being approximated by the normal distribution with mean $\mu_{\bar{X}} = \mu$ and standard deviation $\sigma_{\bar{X}} = \sigma/\sqrt{N}$. These concepts were then used to form a $z_{\bar{X}}$-ratio testing the null hypothesis H_0: μ = a specified value. For the case in which σ cannot be assumed, a related ratio, the *t*-ratio, was developed. To use the *t*-ratio it is necessary to estimate the population value σ with the sample value *s* taken from the data at hand. The sampling distribution of *t* varies with the number of degrees of freedom (df), where $df = N - 1$.

Other applications of hypothesis testing were illustrated. The Pearson *r* can be tested for significance by converting it to a *t*-ratio (with $df = N - 2$) when the null is that $\rho = 0$. It can be tested by a *z*-ratio when the null is that ρ is some other value.

Confidence intervals for estimating the value of μ or ρ can be obtained by using procedures similar to those involved in hypothesis testing. Finally, the similarities and differences between hypothesis testing and interval estimation were discussed. Interval estimation is critically dependent on random sampling, which is often difficult to carry out in practice.

KEY WORDS

generalization	standard error of the mean $(\sigma_{\bar{x}})$
simple random sample	$z_{\bar{x}}$-ratio
stratified random sample	t-ratio
judgmental sample	degrees of freedom
convenience sample	r to t transformation
sampling distribution	r to z transformation
central limit theorem	confidence intervals

PROBLEMS

1 What two benefits are derived from random sampling of the subjects in an empirical study?

2 Which procedure (random sampling or randomization) is more often used in behavioral research? Which of these procedures is assumed necessary for the statistical tests (z and t) discussed in Chapter 10?

3 Why might you want to sample with a restriction instead of using simple random sampling? Give an example of random sampling "with restriction."

4 What limitations are associated with nonrandom sampling?

5 The principal of a high school is interested in students' attitudes toward a proposed dress code. Each of the 1000 students in the school is assigned a number from 1 to 1000. A random sample of 50 students is selected from a table of random numbers. When the principal's secretary saw the list of 50 students to be interviewed, she pointed out that he had not selected a random sample because 40 of the 50 students were females. Evaluate the secretary's comment.

6 Assume that you have a normally distributed population with $\mu = 500$ and $\sigma = 100$. H_0: $\mu = 500$; H_1: $\mu \neq 500$. What critical values of $z_{\bar{x}}$ are the minimum limits of the region of rejection when $\alpha = .05$? When $\alpha = .01$?

7 Repeat Problem 6 for H_1: $\mu > 500$.

8 Given $\alpha = .025$ and a one-tailed hypothesis, compare the area in the smaller portion of the z-table for $z = 1.960$ with the critical value of t for infinity degrees of freedom.

9 Professor X had difficulty deciding whether to give her class of 110 students a midterm examination. To help her make up her mind, she had her teaching assistant randomly sample eight students and administer a ten-item true-false test. If the mean errors in this sample were significantly better than the mean expected by guessing, there would be no midterm exam. The number of errors made by the eight students on the test was 1, 2, 2, 2, 3, 4, 4, 6.
(a) State the null hypothesis.
(b) State the alternative hypothesis.

(c) Given $\alpha = .05$, carry out a t-test to evaluate H_0. (Determine μ and compute $\overline{X}$, SS, s^2, and $s_{\overline{x}}$.)

(d) Will Professor X give a midterm examination?

10 Assume that you have a random sample of scores with $\overline{X} = 45$ and $s = 10$. The null hypothesis is that $\mu = 50$ and H_1: $\mu \neq 50$. For $\alpha = .05$, compute a t-test and make a decision about H_0 for each of the following sample sizes: (a) $N = 9$, (b) $N = 25$. (c) By comparing the results of these two t-tests, what general statement might you make about the relationship between sample size and statistical significance?

11 A sample of N is drawn at random from a population with a mean μ and variance σ^2. Determine the probabilities with which the following confidence intervals contain μ:

(a) $\overline{X} \pm 1.00 \cdot \sigma/\sqrt{N}$ (c) $\overline{X} \pm 2.58 \cdot \sigma/\sqrt{N}$

(b) $\overline{X} \pm 1.64 \cdot \sigma/\sqrt{N}$ (d) $\overline{X} \pm .675 \cdot \sigma/\sqrt{N}$

12 A sample of 25 persons was randomly drawn from a population with an unknown mean μ. The value of $\overline{X}$ was 106.5 and the value of s^2 was 16. Construct the 95 percent and 99 percent confidence intervals around $\overline{X}$.

13 Construct the 95 percent and 99 percent confidence intervals around r for the following data:

(a) $N = 12$, $r = .36$

(b) $N = 28$, $r = -.65$

(c) $N = 292$, $r = .14$

14 Suppose that a particular 95 percent confidence interval around μ (based on $\overline{X} = 100$, $s^2 = 256$, and $N = 20$) was $100 \pm t(19) \cdot s_{\overline{x}}$. Give two values of μ that would be rejected under the null hypothesis.

Chapter
11

The t-test for Independent and Dependent Means

11.1   INTRODUCTION

Chapter 10 examined statistical tests of single means and correlations. Although research with a single sample is not rare, it is more common for researchers to investigate problems involving at least two samples. In this chapter we discuss variations of the *t*-test for testing hypotheses about two means. These situations are frequently referred to as research designs, where *design* refers to the plan of the study such as whether one or two samples are involved.

First we focus on the **independent samples design** for two samples, in which scores in one sample are independent of the scores in the other sample. This design is useful in answering questions such as "Does the performance of subjects in an experimental group differ in some systematic way from the performance of subjects in a control group?" or "Does the mean from a sample of females differ systematically from the mean from a sample of males?" These questions, and others like them, are frequently asked in behavioral research. A common feature of studies asking this type of question is that there is one score per subject. Thus, the number of subjects equals the number of scores and any given score is independent of every other score.

INDEPENDENT SAMPLES DESIGN: A procedure involving two or more samples of data in which scores in one sample are independent of scores in other samples.

Later in this chapter we deal with the **dependent samples design,** in which scores in one sample are paired with scores in other samples. Typically this pairing means that there is more than one score per subject. For instance, each subject serves in two or more conditions. This design is useful in answering questions such as "Does performance change when subjects are given the same task on more than one occasion?" or "Does performance differ when subjects are tested under two different conditions?" Briefly, in this chapter we deal with the independent samples case and the dependent samples case when there are two samples of scores to compare. In later chapters we extend this treatment to consider each type of research design when there are more than two samples.

DEPENDENT SAMPLES DESIGN: A procedure involving paired scores in two or more samples. Either there is more than one score per subject or the subjects are matched on some criterion.

In what follows, data from each of these research designs are analyzed by two procedures. First they are submitted to analysis by *t*-tests based on the random sampling model developed in Chapter 10. Then the same data are analyzed by the random assignment model developed in Chapter 9. Following the comparison of results by these two procedures we introduce a different criterion for evaluating research outcomes. This criterion is not based on probability. It uses correlation to assess the strength of the relationship between group membership (treatment or trait differences) and the dependent variable.

11.2   HYPOTHESIS TESTING WITH TWO INDEPENDENT SAMPLES

The Null Hypothesis

The typical null hypothesis in the two-sample case is that there is no difference between two population means, μ_1 and μ_2.

$$H_0: \mu_1 - \mu_2 = 0$$

There are two contexts in which we may be interested in comparing independent sample means. One context arises when two random samples are taken from populations known to be different in some way, such as a population of males and a population of females. In this context, when the null hypothesis is rejected we conclude that the two populations sampled have a systematic difference in the characteristic that was measured (e.g., number correct on a test). When we fail to reject H_0, the conclusion is that the populations do not differ systematically on the characteristic that was measured.

The second context in which we compare independent means arises when we randomly sample subjects from a single population. The subjects are then randomly assigned to groups that receive different treatments (e.g., an experimental group and a control group). This manipulation simulates sampling from two hypothetical treatment populations. In this context, when the null hypothesis is rejected we conclude that the difference in group means reflects differences in two populations, an experimental population with mean μ_1 and a control population with mean μ_2. When we fail to reject H_0, the conclusion is that the treatment was not effective and the resulting scores are representative of a single population with mean μ: $\mu_1 = \mu_2 = \mu$.

In each research context we compare an observed difference in sample means, $\overline{X}_1 - \overline{X}_2$, with the difference expected when the null hypothesis is true, $\mu_1 - \mu_2 = 0$. If H_0 is true, the difference in sample means should be small and is the result of sampling variation. If H_0 is false, meaning that the population means are different, the difference between sample means is likely to be large and among the least likely differences expected under the null hypothesis.

The Distribution of Differences Between Means

The logic of testing hypotheses about two sample means is the same as in the one-sample case. First, we assume the null hypothesis is true; then we determine whether the observed difference between means, $\overline{X}_1 - \overline{X}_2$, is among the least likely expected under H_0. The null is rejected if the observed difference between means meets this criterion. To determine whether an observed difference between means is unlikely, we need to compare it to a theoretical *sampling distribution of differences between means*. This is the distribution of differences between all possible pairs of sample means (based on independent random samples of the size used in the study), under the assumption that H_0 is true.

A number of important facts are known about this distribution. First, if the two populations have equal means (as usually is assumed by H_0), the mean of this distribution is zero. Although it is almost certain that any two samples drawn from the populations will have different means, in some cases the mean of the sample from the first population would be larger ($\overline{X}_1 - \overline{X}_2 > 0$) but in other cases the mean of the sample from the second population would be larger ($\overline{X}_1 - \overline{X}_2 < 0$). In the long run (across many pairs of samples), the mean of the differences between means would be zero.

Second, the variance of the sampling distribution of differences between means can be computed easily if the variances of the two populations are known. To demonstrate, we will first note that when a distribution is formed by taking the difference between pairs of values, say X and Y, the distribution has a variance given by Formula 11.1.

$$\sigma^2_{X-Y} = \sigma^2_X + \sigma^2_Y - 2\rho_{XY}\sigma_X\sigma_Y \tag{11.1}$$

In Formula 11.1 ρ represents the correlation between a population of X and Y pairs. In the case of the sampling distribution of differences between means, the X and Y values in Formula 11.1 are replaced by $\overline{X}_1$ and $\overline{X}_2$, and ρ is the correlation between all possible pairs of sample means, giving Formula 11.2.

$$\sigma^2_{\overline{X}_1 - \overline{X}_2} = \sigma^2_{\overline{X}_1} + \sigma^2_{\overline{X}_2} - 2\rho\sigma_{\overline{X}_1}\sigma_{\overline{X}_2} \tag{11.2}$$

Keep in mind that $\sigma^2_{\overline{X}_1}$ and $\sigma^2_{\overline{X}_2}$ are the variances of the sampling distributions of the mean for the individual populations.

If the two samples are drawn independently from their respective populations, there will be no correlation between pairs of means. That is, the value of $\overline{X}_1$ is independent of the value of $\overline{X}_2$. Therefore the value of ρ in Formula 11.2 will be zero, making the last term disappear. The result, shown as Formula 11.3, is that the variance of the distribution of differences between pairs of independent sample means is the sum of the variances of the sampling distribution of the mean for each population.

$$\sigma^2_{\overline{X}_1 - \overline{X}_2} = \sigma^2_{\overline{X}_1} + \sigma^2_{\overline{X}_2} \tag{11.3}$$

A numerical example of the relationship between the variance of the sampling distribution of differences between means and the variance of the sampling distributions of the mean is shown in Table 11.1. The example is based on a hypothetical set of 18 means, where 9 means come from each of two populations. To emphasize that all pairs of samples are independent, the means have been paired so that the correlation between them is zero. (With

Table 11.1   ADDING VARIANCE VALUES FROM
TWO SETS OF UNRELATED MEANS
EQUALS THE VARIANCE OF THE
DIFFERENCE BETWEEN MEANS

Population 1	Population 2	Difference
1	1	0
1	2	−1
1	3	−2
2	1	1
2	2	0
2	3	−1
3	1	2
3	2	1
3	3	0
$\sigma_{\bar{X}}^2$ .667	.667	1.334
μ 2	2	0

From the means in columns 1 and 2:

$$\sigma_{\bar{X}_1 - \bar{X}_2} = \sqrt{.667/9 + .667/9} = .385$$

From the differences in column 3:

$$\sigma_{\bar{X}_{\text{diff.}}} = \sqrt{1.333/9} = .385$$

Note: If you add a constant to the means in one sample, μ_1 no longer equals μ_2 but the sum of column 1 and column 2 variances still equals the variance of the differences in column 3.

many randomly paired means we would expect to find $\rho = 0$.) In Table 11.1 you can see that when the variances of means from each separate population are added, the result is the same as taking the variance of the differences between means: .667 + .667 = 1.334.

The standard deviation of the distribution of differences between means is called the **standard error of the difference between means.** It is the square root of the variance, as shown in Formula 11.4.

$$\sigma_{\bar{X}_1 - \bar{X}_2} = \sqrt{\sigma_{\bar{X}_1}^2 + \sigma_{\bar{X}_2}^2} \tag{11.4}$$

We can replace the symbol for standard error of the mean in Formula 11.4 with its formula to produce another version of the standard error of the difference between means:

$$\sigma_{\bar{X}_1 - \bar{X}_2} = \sqrt{\frac{\sigma_1^2}{n_1} + \frac{\sigma_2^2}{n_2}} \tag{11.5}$$

STANDARD ERROR OF THE DIFFERENCE BETWEEN MEANS: The standard deviation of the sampling distribution based on the differences between means of random
samples drawn from two populations.

The shape, mean, and standard deviation of this sampling distribution are
illustrated in Figure 11.1.

We can use the mean and standard deviation of the sampling distribution
of the difference between means to express the difference between two sample means in standard score form.

$$z = \frac{(\overline{X}_1 - \overline{X}_2) - 0}{\sqrt{\dfrac{\sigma_1^2}{n_1} + \dfrac{\sigma_2^2}{n_2}}} = \frac{\overline{X}_1 - \overline{X}_2}{\sqrt{\dfrac{\sigma_1^2}{n_1} + \dfrac{\sigma_2^2}{n_2}}} \tag{11.6}$$

A third important characteristic of the sampling distribution of differences between means is that it has a normal distribution if the populations
of raw scores are normally distributed. Under these circumstances z values
computed with Formula 11.6 fit the standard normal distribution. This result
allows us to test H_0 by comparing z obtained from a pair of samples to critical
values in the standard normal distribution, just as we did in Chapter 10 with
the one-sample test.

Estimating the Standard Error

In practice we most likely will not know the variances of the two populations, so it is necessary to use the variances of the two samples to obtain
estimates. To maximize the accuracy of the estimate, it is assumed that the
population variances are equal: $\sigma_1^2 = \sigma_2^2 = \sigma^2$. This is referred to as the assumption of *homogeneity of variance*. It allows us to consider the two sam-
ple variances as independent estimates of the population variance. We can
combine the two estimates to form a single, *pooled* estimate of variance. The
pooled estimate, $s_p{}^2$, is expected to be more accurate than either of the individual sample estimates because it is based on more scores.

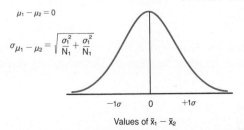

Figure 11.1   Sampling distribution of the difference between means.

To understand how the pooled estimate is formed, recall from Chapter 4 that variance can be written as follows:

$$s^2 = \frac{SS}{df} \tag{4.9}$$

The two sample variances are pooled by adding the sum of squares from each sample and dividing by the sum of the degrees of freedom:

$$s_p{}^2 = \frac{SS_1 + SS_2}{df_1 + df_2} = \frac{SS_1 + SS_2}{(n_1 - 1) + (n_2 - 1)} = \frac{SS_1 + SS_2}{n_1 + n_2 - 2} \tag{11.7}$$

If the sum of squares values are not already available, they can be computed from the raw scores by using Formula 4.10 from Chapter 4. This operation gives us the raw score formula for the pooled variance estimate, where X_1 represents the raw scores from the first sample and X_2 represents the raw scores from the second sample.

$$s_p{}^2 = \frac{\left(\Sigma X_1^2 - \dfrac{(\Sigma X_1)^2}{n_1}\right) + \left(\Sigma X_2^2 - \dfrac{(\Sigma X_2)^2}{n_2}\right)}{n_1 + n_2 - 2} \tag{11.8}$$

Alternatively, the sample variances may already be computed, so we can make use of the fact, easily derived from Formula 4.9, that

$$SS = s^2(df)$$

to produce Formula 11.9 for the pooled estimate of variance:

$$s_p{}^2 = \frac{s_1^2(n_1 - 1) + s_2^2(n_2 - 1)}{n_1 + n_2 - 2} \tag{11.9}$$

The pooled estimate of variance can be used in place of population variance values in Formula 11.5 to produce an estimate of the standard error of the difference between means:

$$s_{\overline{X}_1 - \overline{X}_2} = \sqrt{\frac{s_p{}^2}{n_1} + \frac{s_p{}^2}{n_2}} = \sqrt{s_p{}^2\left(\frac{1}{n_1} + \frac{1}{n_2}\right)} \tag{11.10}$$

Formula 11.11 uses the estimate of standard error (Formula 11.10) in place of the actual standard error in Formula 11.6 to form a *t*-ratio:

$$t = \frac{\overline{X}_1 - \overline{X}_2}{\sqrt{s_p^2\left(\dfrac{1}{n_1} + \dfrac{1}{n_2}\right)}} \tag{11.11}$$

The obtained ratio will not be normally distributed because the estimated standard error will vary from one pair of samples to the next. Instead, as long as the variances are homogeneous, the ratio will be distributed as *t*, with degrees of freedom equal to the combined degrees of freedom used in estimating the standard error $(n_1 + n_2 - 2)$. The t-ratio obtained from a set of data can then be compared to the t-distribution with the appropriate degrees of freedom to determine whether the observed results are among the least likely expected under H_0.

11.3   APPLICATION OF THE t-TEST WITH INDEPENDENT SAMPLES

Suppose that a cognitive psychologist is interested in the effects of word frequency on the ability to recall words from a list. It is possible that high-frequency, or common, words will be remembered differently than low-frequency, or rare, words. Stimulus words can be selected by consulting a book that lists the frequency with which words appear in printed English (e.g., in newspapers, textbooks, and novels). From this book the psychologist draws a list of 20 words that occur more than 100 times per million (high-frequency words) and a list of 20 that occur fewer than 5 times per million (low-frequency words).

To test the effects of word frequency, 16 volunteers are randomly sampled from a list of volunteers in an introductory psychology course. These students are randomly assigned to two groups that study the words for one minute before being asked to write down all the study words they can remember (free recall). One group is given the list of high-frequency words and the other group is given the list of low-frequency words for study and recall.

The behavioral measure here is the number of words correctly recalled during a two-minute test. The obtained scores and subject identification numbers are listed in Table 11.2. This table also includes the squared scores to help in computing the sum of squares *(SS)* for each sample. If the null hypothesis is true, we expect the difference in mean number correct for group 1 (high-frequency words) and group 2 (low-frequency words) to be zero. The alternative hypothesis is that the difference between means will be larger than expected from sampling variation.

H_0: $\mu_1 - \mu_2 = 0$

H_1: $\mu_1 - \mu_2 \neq 0$

As shown in Table 11.2, the mean for the group receiving high-frequency words is 11.125 and the mean for the other group is 8.875. Thus, the numerator of the t-ratio is $11.125 - 8.875 = 2.25$. Table 11.2 also gives a step-by-step computation of the standard error of the difference between means. This computation began with computing the *SS* values for each sample.

$$SS = \Sigma X^2 - \frac{(\Sigma X)^2}{n}$$

$$SS_1 = 1013 - \frac{(89)^2}{8} = 22.875$$

$$SS_2 = 647 - \frac{(71)^2}{8} = 16.875$$

Table 11.2 **NUMBER OF CORRECT SCORES FROM TWO INDEPENDENT SAMPLES**

High frequency			Low frequency		
Subject number	Score X	X^2	Subject number	Score X	X^2
1	13	169	9	10	100
2	9	81	10	9	81
3	12	144	11	8	64
4	14	196	12	10	100
5	10	100	13	11	121
6	11	121	14	8	64
7	9	81	15	9	81
8	11	121	16	6	36
Sum	89	1013		71	647

Numerator of the *t*-ratio:

$$\bar{X}_1 - \bar{X}_2 = (\Sigma X_1/n_1) - (\Sigma X_2/n_2)$$

$$= (89/8) \ - (71/8)$$

$$= 11.125 \ - 8.875 = \underline{2.25}$$

Denominator of the *t*-ratio:

$$s_{\bar{X}_1 - \bar{X}_2} = \sqrt{\frac{SS_1 + SS_2}{n_1 + n_2 - 2}\left(\frac{1}{n_1} + \frac{1}{n_2}\right)}$$

$$= \sqrt{\frac{22.875 + 16.875}{8 + 8 - 2}\left(\frac{1}{8} + \frac{1}{8}\right)}$$

$$= \sqrt{(39.75/14)(.25)} = \underline{.8425}$$

Thus, $t = 2.25/.8425 = 2.67$, with $df = n_1 + n_2 - 2$.
Inspecting Table D in Appendix III, we find $t(14) = \underline{2.67}$, p $< .05$.

These two *SS* values were substituted into Formula 11.7 to obtain the pooled variance, s_p^2. Then s_p^2 was placed into Formula 11.8. As shown in Table 11.2, the result of these computations yielded a standard error of the difference between means equal to .8425. Thus, the *t*-ratio for these data is the ratio $2.25/.8425 = 2.67$. Referring to Table D in Appendix III, we find that with 14 degrees of freedom, $df = 14$, the critical value of $t(14)$ is ± 2.145. The obtained value is greater than the critical table value, and therefore, H_0 is rejected.

$t(\text{critical}) = \pm 2.145$

$t(\text{obtained}) = 2.67$

Decision: Reject H_0

The psychologist might report that "The mean number correct for the high-frequency group (11.13) is significantly greater than the mean for the low-frequency group (8.88), $t(14) = 2.67$, $p < .05$." Most likely, the report would focus on the idea that a statistically significant difference was observed. It would be inferred that chance factors were unlikely to account for the observed outcome. Because our statistical test was based on the fact that subjects had been randomly sampled, its results can be generalized to the population that was sampled, volunteers from that particular introductory class.

As a note of caution, there is no *statistical* basis to argue that a difference this large would also be found in nonvolunteers. On statistical grounds we would not generalize these results to nonvolunteers any more than we would generalize them to students at other schools. The result might be generalized to these other populations on *nonstatistical* grounds, such as reference to similar studies carried out by other researchers.

The most reasonable explanation for the observed difference in behavior of these two groups is that differences between high- and low-frequency words caused the difference in memory performance. This interpretation follows from the random assignment of subjects to the two treatment conditions.

11.4   THE *t*-TEST FOR TWO DEPENDENT SAMPLE MEANS

We now consider using the *t*-ratio to analyze scores from a dependent samples design.[1] Such designs occur when the scores from two samples are in some manner paired or related. One type of dependent samples design is called **repeated measures design.** One form of this design occurs when two types of stimuli are presented to one sample of subjects and their responses to each type of stimulus is recorded. Subjects could, for example, take a memory test twice, once with memory cues and once without memory cues. In another case, the responses of the subjects might be measured under one condition at different times. For instance, you could give a vocabulary test to a sample of children when they are 3 years old and repeat the test when they are 5 years old. In each of these examples a single subject actually contributes two scores.

REPEATED MEASURES DESIGN: The same subjects are tested more than once on the same dependent variable.

---

[1]Several expressions are used to label designs falling in this general category. These expressions include designs that are within subjects, correlated, or involve repeated measures; subjects by treatments; subjects by trials; and subjects as their own controls.

Another type of dependent samples design is called **matched-groups design.** In this type of design different subjects make up each sample, but the subjects are matched on the basis of some shared attribute. Twins, for example, could be randomly assigned so that a different twin was in each of two conditions. Similarly, matched groups could be produced by randomly assigning pairs of individuals with equivalent IQ scores.

MATCHED-GROUPS DESIGN: Each individual in one group is paired with an individual in another group. The pairing is carried out so that the paired individuals are very similar on some specific variable.

In each of these cases two scores are dependent and analyzed as a pair because they came either from the same subject or from two subjects who are treated as being similar. This dependency leads to a somewhat different version of the *t*-test for two samples of data.

The Null Hypothesis

With dependent sets of scores we can test the differences between paired scores. The difference between means is equal to the mean of the difference between paired scores, $\mu_{\overline{D}}$, so our null hypothesis becomes $\mu_1 - \mu_2 = \mu_{\overline{D}} = 0$. That is, if the null hypothesis is true, we expect the difference between means to be zero and the mean of the differences between paired scores to be zero.

Definitional Formula

The *t*-test for dependent samples differs from that for independent samples only in determining $s_{\overline{X}_1 - \overline{X}_2}$ and degrees of freedom. The numerator of the *t*-ratio can be treated as in the case with independent samples. As shown in Formula 11.12, the computation of the standard error of the difference between means must take into account the possible correlation between the paired scores. This correlation has a nonzero value if scores in the two samples can be meaningfully paired. In the dependent samples case such pairs of scores are expected to be correlated because each pair comes from a single subject or from two matched subjects. Formula 11.12 expresses the resulting standard error in terms of sample estimates.

$$s_{\overline{X}_1 - \overline{X}_2} = \sqrt{\frac{s_1^2}{n} + \frac{s_2^2}{n} - \frac{2r_{12}s_1 s_2}{n}} \tag{11.12}$$

The left-hand portion of Formula 11.12 is the standard error given in Formula 11.5. The only difference is that the distinction between n_1 and n_2 is no longer useful because n now refers to the number of pairs of scores. The right-hand portion contains a correlation coefficient, r. When the value of r

in Formula 11.12 is zero, the entire right-hand portion of the formula becomes zero. We then have the formula for the standard error of the difference between means for the independent samples case.

Thus, the standard error used in the dependent samples case is the same as that in the independent samples case but with the correlation between the paired scores taken into account. When the correlation is positive, subtracting the right-hand portion of Formula 11.12 reduces the standard error. The positive correlation implies that when X_1 is large, X_2 will tend to be large, leading to less variability in the mean differences.

Box 11.1 illustrates the computation of standard error terms and t-tests based on independent and dependent samples. When these hypothetical data are assumed to come from independent subjects, the standard error is .559 and the obtained t is not significant: $p > .05$. When the same data are assumed to form meaningful pairs of scores, the standard error is reduced to .250 and the obtained t is significant: $p < .05$.

Computational Formula

When testing the null hypothesis $\mu_{\overline{X}_1 - \overline{X}_2} = 0$, Formula 11.12 involves tedious arithmetic, and in practice a simpler formula is more likely to be used. This formula is based on the difference between paired scores. We take the two scores for a given subject and subtract to get the difference: $X_1 - X_2 = D$. Formula 11.13 shows that the numerator of the t-ratio consists of the mean of these D scores, $\overline{D}$. Formula 11.14 shows that the denominator of this t-ratio is based on the standard deviation of difference scores.

$$t(df) = \frac{\overline{X}_1 - \overline{X}_2}{s_{\overline{D}}} = \frac{\overline{D}}{s_{\overline{D}}} \qquad df = n - 1 \qquad (11.13)$$

$$s_{\overline{D}} = \frac{s_D}{\sqrt{n}} = \frac{\sqrt{\dfrac{SS_D}{n-1}}}{\sqrt{n}} = \sqrt{\frac{SS_D}{n(n-1)}} \qquad (11.14)$$

$$\text{where } SS_D = \Sigma D^2 - \frac{(\Sigma D)^2}{n}$$

The use of Formulas 11.13 and 11.14 is illustrated by our study of word frequency and recall.

11.5   APPLICATION OF THE t-TEST WITH DEPENDENT SAMPLES

Consider a variation of our hypothetical experiment on the relationship between word frequency and the recall of nouns. We have the same conceptual hypothesis as before, namely, that word frequency influences recall. Furthermore, we can use the same stimulus words as in our earlier experiment. The

Box 11.1 **Application of Two Different *t*-test Formulas to One Set of Data**

We are given two samples of data:

Sample 1	Sample 2	Difference
3	1	2
3	2	1
4	3	1
4	3	1
$\overline{X}$ 3.50	2.25	1.25

If we assume that the scores are from eight independent subjects, assume $\rho = 0$ and use Formula 11.10 for the standard error:

$$t(6) = \frac{3.50 - 2.25}{\sqrt{\frac{2.75 + 1.00}{4 + 4 - 2}\left(\frac{1}{4} + \frac{1}{4}\right)}} = \frac{1.25}{.559} = \underline{2.236}$$

$t(6) = 2.236$, $p > .05$, fail to reject H_0

If we assume that the scores are four pairs, take an estimate of ρ ($r = .905$) into account with Formula 11.12:

$$t(3) = \frac{3.50 - 2.25}{\sqrt{\frac{.917}{4} + \frac{.333}{4} - \frac{2(.905)(.957)(.577)}{4}}} = \frac{1.25}{.250} = \underline{5.00}$$

The same result is obtained with Formula 11.14:

$$t(3) = \frac{3.50 - 2.25}{\sqrt{\frac{.75}{4(3)}}} = \frac{1.25}{.250} = \underline{5.00}$$

$t(3) = 5.00$, $p < .05$, reject H_0

difference is that in this experiment we will use a single list of stimulus words.

Words are selected for study by randomly sampling 10 high-frequency words from the 20 in the high-frequency list previously used. Similarly, 10 low-frequency words are selected from the previous list. These 20 words are then randomly placed in a new list for study, with each subject receiving a different random arrangement of the words.

Eight volunteers are randomly selected from the same introductory psychology class used in the previous example. As before, they are given one minute to study the list of words followed by a two-minute recall test. In this study two number-correct scores are calculated for each subject. One score is based on the number of correct high-frequency items out of ten, and the other is based on the number of correct low-frequency items out of ten. The number-correct scores are listed in Table 11.3 along with the subject identification numbers and difference scores.

As shown in Table 11.3, the numerator of the t-ratio can be determined

Table 11.3   NUMBER OF CORRECT SCORES FROM ONE SAMPLE OF SUBJECTS

Subject number	High frequency	Low frequency	Difference D	D^2
1	4	3	+ 1	1
2	3	4	− 1	1
3	5	6	− 1	1
4	2	3	− 1	1
5	4	5	− 1	1
6	5	7	− 2	4
7	3	6	− 3	9
8	4	7	− 3	9
Sum	30	41	−11	27

Numerator of the t-ratio:

$$\bar{X}_1 - \bar{X}_2 = (\Sigma X_1/n_1) - (\Sigma X_2/n_2) \quad \text{or} \quad \bar{D} = \Sigma D/n$$

$$= (30/8) \quad - (41/8) \qquad = -11/8$$

$$= 3.75 \quad - 5.125 \qquad = \underline{-1.375}$$

Denominator of the t-ratio:

$$s_{\bar{D}} = \frac{s_D}{\sqrt{n}} = \frac{\sqrt{\dfrac{SS_D}{n-1}}}{\sqrt{n}} = \sqrt{\frac{SS_D}{n(n-1)}}$$

Where $SS_D = \Sigma D^2 - \dfrac{(\Sigma D)^2}{n} = 27 - \dfrac{(-11)^2}{8} = \underline{11.875}$ (11.14)

$$s_{\bar{D}} = \sqrt{\frac{11.875}{8(7)}} = .460$$

$df = n - 1$, where n is the number of pairs of scores.
Thus, $t(7) = -1.357/.46 = \underline{-2.989}$, $p < .05$.

either in the same fashion as for the independent samples case, $\overline{X}_1 - \overline{X}_2 =$ 3.75 − 5.125 = −1.375, or by taking the mean of the difference scores, $\overline{D} =$ −11/8 = −1.375.

The denominator will be obtained with Formula 11.14 by using the difference scores, D, and squared difference scores, D^2, from the two right-hand columns in Table 11.3. We use the sum of the D-scores and the sum of their squared values to compute the standard error of the difference between dependent sample means, $s_{\overline{D}}$.

$$s_{\overline{D}} = \sqrt{\frac{SS_D}{n(n-1)}} = \sqrt{\frac{11.875}{8(7)}} = .460$$

The step-by-step computations in Table 11.3 show that for these data $s_{\overline{D}}$ is .46. Thus, the t-ratio for these data is −1.375/.46, or −2.989. This t-ratio has $n - 1$ degrees of freedom. That is, df equals the number of *pairs* of scores minus 1. Referring to Table D in Appendix III, we find that with $df = 8 - 1 = 7$, the critical value of $t(7)$ is ±2.365. Our obtained value is more extreme than the critical table value, and we therefore reject H_0, $t(7) = -2.989$, $p < .05$.

t(critical) = ±2.365

t(obtained) = −2.989

Decision: Reject H_0

This statistical decision would lead the researcher to conclude that word frequency has an effect on recall and that low-frequency words are easier to remember than high-frequency words. The conclusion that frequency affects recall agrees with the previous experiment involving independent samples. However, the direction of the outcome is opposite to the previous finding.[2] This result is usually explained as a contrast effect, in which low-frequency words are more likely to stand out when contrasted with high-frequency words than when imbedded in a list of other low-frequency words.

Taken together, these two experiments might suggest that the effects of word frequency depend on the type of research design. With an independent samples design, in which a given subject was exposed to words of only one frequency (either all high or all low frequency), high-frequency words were remembered better. With a dependent samples design, where each subject was exposed to both types of words, the low-frequency items were remembered better. Thus, in this case, the type of outcome is related to the type of design. Such different or opposite findings derived from two types of research

---

[2]This combination of results has actually been reported several times. For example, see Gregg, Montgomery, and Castaño (1980), and May, Cuddy, and Norton (1979).

design occasionally occur in practice.[3] Therefore, careful thought should go into the selection of independent or dependent samples design. In some cases, researchers may plan to carry out two studies, one using each type of design.

11.6   VIOLATION OF STATISTICAL ASSUMPTIONS

Any statistical test has assumptions or formal requirements on which that test is based. We have introduced the following assumptions related to the t-test for independent samples and the t-test for dependent samples: (1) Population variances are homogeneous ($\sigma_1^2 = \sigma_2^2$), (2) the scores come from normally distributed populations, and (3) the scores or pairs of scores are independent (e.g., by random sampling). In general it is wise to be familiar with these assumptions and try not to violate them. In practice, however, it has been found that homogeneity and normality assumptions may be violated to some extent without appreciably affecting the validity of the statistical test's outcome.

Homogeneity of Population Variances

In testing for the difference between means, we assume that other features of the populations are constant, for example, that the distributions are normal and their variances are equal. Both variances are assumed to be estimates of a common population variance. If the two means differ *and* the two variances differ, the test of means can be biased. With unequal variances, the probability of obtaining very different sample means may be higher than the tabled t values, even when the population means are equal. That is, more Type I errors are made than expected, so use of the standard t-distribution may not be valid.

Fortunately, this problem is not serious as long as (1) the two variance estimates, s_1^2 and s_2^2, are based on samples of equal size and (2) the samples are not too small: $n_1 = n_2 \geq 7$ (Ramsey, 1980). If sample sizes are unequal, a rule of thumb is that variance estimates may differ by a ratio of about four to one without introducing substantial bias (Boneau, 1960). That is, one variance estimate can be as much as four times the size of the other estimate and we can still make a valid comparison of the observed t-ratio with the t-distribution.

The major exception to this guideline occurs when the variances are unequal, the sample sizes are unequal (by a ratio of at least two to one), *and* the larger variance occurs in the smaller sample. That is, n_1 is less than n_2 and s_1^2 is greater than s_2^2. When all three of these conditions are present at the same time, it is better to use a statistical test that does not make assump-

---

[3]A clear discussion of this point is given by Grice (1966).

tions about **homogeneity of variance** (see Section 11.7 and Chapter 18). In general, the t-ratio is said to be a **robust** procedure since violation of the assumption of equal variances usually has little effect on our ability to evaluate the observed t-ratio against a region of rejection based on the t-distribution.

HOMOGENEITY OF VARIANCE: In theory, $\sigma_1^2 = \sigma_2^2$. In practice, when sample sizes are equal the assumption can be violated if $n_1 = n_2 \geq 7$.

ROBUST: A statistical test is said to be robust if it gives valid results when its assumptions are violated to some extent.

Normal Population Distributions

The t-test and related tests are based on a formal statistical procedure sometimes called the "normal model." One assumption of the model is that scores come from normally distributed populations. As discussed in Chapter 10, we use the normal distribution in statistical testing when either the parent population is normal or when the sampling distribution of the mean is approximated by the normal distribution. In practice the t-test can be used when parent populations are simply unimodal and more or less symmetrical. We can also use it with data from nonnormal populations because the sampling distribution of the mean is rapidly approximated by the normal distribution as the sample size increases.

Independence of Scores

The most important assumption underlying t-tests for differences between means is that the scores, or pairs of scores, must be independent of each other. Like random assignment to groups, random sampling is a procedure that will lead to independence. Using random sampling, the researcher tries to sample each individual or pair of individuals so that the selection of one case has no bearing on the selection of other cases. In that way each score should be free to take on various values independently of other scores.

Nonrandom sampling can lead to a dependence between scores that may yield a biased statistical test. For example, if a researcher were interested in patterns of child rearing, parents of young children might be sampled. One option is to sample names from a list of parents until the desired number is obtained. Another option is to sample a given parent and, if that person agrees to participate, ask if the spouse will also participate. The second option might require fewer telephone calls but it would also generate a lack of independence in the data. When each parent is contacted independently, the data are more likely to be independent than if spouses of volunteers are systematically selected. Two subjects could be given the same or similar scores for reasons unrelated to the hypothesis being tested. This condition would result in a reduced value of s^2 and, therefore, a reduced value of the standard error for the difference between means. Consequently the observed t-ratio would be inflated.

In practice random sampling is rarely carried out although the t-test is still used. However, comparing obtained t values to the t-distribution based on randomly drawn samples rests on the assumption that subjects were randomly sampled from a population of interest. How can this procedure be justified and what are the implications of using the t-test without satisfying the assumption of random sampling? For instance, how would it have changed our analysis and interpretation if the subjects in the examples used in this chapter (i.e., the two studies on recall and word frequency) had not been randomly sampled? For statistical analysis, the answer is that using the t-test is justified without random sampling but only as an *estimate* of the result that would be obtained by using randomization tests. The relationship between data analysis and interpretation is developed in the next section.

11.7 COMPARISON OF STATISTICAL MODELS

The statistical tests in this book are based on two models. One model attempts to achieve independence through random *sampling,* which formed the basis of Chapters 10 and 11. The other model attempts to achieve independence through random *assignment,* and this model was outlined in Chapter 9. Formally, these models have different assumptions, different methods of computing the probability of a Type I error, and different implications for interpretation of results.[4] Both models assume independence in the data but they use different methods to achieve it, random sampling and random assignment.

With the random sampling model, the method for obtaining a region of rejection involves using a theoretical sampling distribution, such as the t-distribution, and finding the area in the distribution associated with the least likely, most extreme outcomes. With this procedure a valid region of rejection can be specified and the results can be generalized to the specific population that was sampled.

The random assignment model assumes that subjects selected by *any* means were exposed to some randomly determined treatment during the execution of the experiment. In the independent samples case, this assumption

---

[4]One way in which these different assumptions, computing methods, and interpretations can be captured is by recognizing that there are two categories of tests, parametric and nonparametric. Loosely speaking, tests based on random sampling can be considered *parametric* tests, and those based on random assignment can be considered *nonparametric* tests. In the context of this chapter the t-test is a parametric test and the randomization test is a nonparametric test. The distinction between parametric and nonparametric tests is developed further in Part V (Chapters 17 and 18).

typically means that subjects were randomly assigned to different treatment groups. In the dependent samples case, it means that the order of stimulus presentation or the administration of treatments was randomized. A region of rejection is obtained by listing all possible random groupings of the observed scores and selecting the most extreme ones for the alpha level chosen by the researcher. When the observed outcome is among the most extreme outcomes, the significant finding implies that treatment differences caused the observed differences in behavior.

The Independent Samples Case

To compare the two models we can apply the randomization test to the data from the word frequency study, in which independent groups studied either high-frequency or low-frequency words. As discussed in Chapter 9, the test involves using the scores actually obtained to make a list of all possible arrangements, those that might have occurred if the null hypothesis were true. The null hypothesis and the nondirectional alternative hypotheses can be stated as follows. (You should notice that these hypotheses are not stated in terms of population parameters such as μ_1 and μ_2.)

H_0: Number-correct scores are independent of the random assignment to study lists of high- and low-frequency items.

H_1: Number-correct scores are not independent of the random assignment to study lists of high- and low-frequency items.

With this example, using two samples of eight scores each, there are $_{16}C_8 = 12,870$ ways the data could be arranged. Table 11.4 shows the two most extreme possible arrangements of the scores from Table 11.2. They can be compared with the observed arrangement listed in the middle columns of the table.

The problem is to determine if the obtained outcome is in the region of rejection. This region consists of all extreme arrangements whose individual probabilities sum to a value equal to or less than α (e.g., .05). For our nondirectional alternative hypothesis, this sum includes probabilities for outcomes when the high-frequency group has large scores (shown in the left side of Table 11.4) and for when the low-frequency group has large scores (the right side of Table 11.4). Using the computer program NPSTAT, we found that 344 of the 12,870 possible arrangements fall in the region of rejection when α = .05 (172 in each tail). We also found that the obtained arrangement falls in this region. Thus, both the null hypothesis of the t-test ($\mu_1 = \mu_2$) and the null for the randomization test (scores are independent of treatments) can be rejected when α = .05.

Example output from the NPSTAT program is shown in Box 11.2. The descriptive statistics and parametric t-test are shown in the top of the box, and the nonparametric randomization test is shown below. For now, the intervening material on the F-test can be ignored as that test is introduced in Chapter 13.

Table 11.4   EXAMPLE ARRANGEMENTS OF RECALL DATA FOR COMPUTATION
OF A RANDOMIZATION TEST OF INDEPENDENT SAMPLES

Rank: 1 .... ? 12870

Extreme arrangement favoring high frequency		Obtained arrangement		Extreme arrangement favoring low frequency	
High	Low	High	Low	High	Low
14	10	14	11	10	14
13	9	13	10	9	13
12	9	12	10	9	12
11	9	11	9	9	11
11	9	11	9	9	11
11	8	10	8	8	11
10	8	9	8	8	10
10	6	9	6	6	10
ΣX 92	68	89	71	68	92

The Dependent Samples Case

The randomization test can also be applied to paired scores. We will illustrate this use with the data from the word frequency study, in which eight subjects were given a study list of ten high-frequency and ten low-frequency nouns.

The null hypothesis is that the number of words recalled from the list positions occupied by high-frequency words and the number recalled from positions occupied by low-frequency words are independent of the type of word (high or low frequency) that was randomly assigned there. In other words, a subject's scores on high and low items would be the same even if the random assignment had reversed the positions of the two types of words. Either the obtained or the reverse assignment was possible and equally likely for each subject, so for eight subjects there are 2^8, or 256, equally likely outcomes of the random assignment.

Table 11.5 shows the obtained arrangement of data in our experiment and the two most extreme possible outcomes. In each case there are two number-correct scores from each subject. On the left side of the table is a data arrangement suggesting that high-frequency words are remembered better than low-frequency words. The high score is higher than the low score for each subject. On the right side of the table is the opposite extreme outcome. In this case the high score is lower than the low score for each subject.

The problem for the researcher is to determine if the obtained arrangement is in the region of extreme arrangements with probabilities summing to a value equal to or less than α. Since a nondirectional hypothesis is being tested, outcomes from each extreme end of the list of possibilities are considered. The probability of the extreme outcome in the left side of Table 11.5

Box 11.2 **Comparison of Results from a *t*-test and a Randomization Test Applied to Two Independent Samples of Eight Number-Correct Recall Scores (The format and content of this box simulates the results obtained from the program NPSTAT.)**

Descriptive statistics

	N	Mean	Standard deviation	Variance
Group 1	8	11.125	1.808	3.268
Group 2	8	8.875	1.553	2.411

t-test

Difference between means	2.250
Standard error of mean difference	0.843
$t(df = 14)$	2.671
p (2-tailed)	0.01828

F-test (Analysis of Variance)

Source	SS	df	MS	F	p
Between groups	20.250	1	20.250	7.132	0.01828
Within groups	39.750	14	2.839		
Total	60.000	15			

Randomization Test

	1-tailed	2-tailed
Alternative hypothesis		
Number of permutations that meet criterion	172	344
Total number of permutations possible	12870	r12870
Exact probability	0.01336	0.02673

Outcome			Cumulative	Probability
$\overline{X}_1 - \overline{X}_2$	Frequency	Probability	1-tailed	2-tailed
−3.000	3	0.00023	1.00000	0.00023
−2.750	15	0.00117	0.99977	0.00140
−2.500	49	0.00381	0.99860	0.00521
−2.250	105	0.00816	0.99479	0.01336
−2.000	197	0.01531	0.98664	0.02867
−1.750	308	0.02393	0.97133	0.05260
.	.	.	.	.
.	.	.	.	.
.	.	.	.	.
1.750	308	0.02393	0.05260	0.05260
2.000	197	0.01531	0.02867	0.02867
2.250	105	0.00816	0.01336	0.01336
2.500	49	0.00381	0.00521	0.00521
2.750	15	0.00117	0.00140	0.00140
3.000	3	0.00023	0.00023	0.00023

Table 11.5   EXAMPLE ARRANGEMENTS OF RECALL DATA FOR COMPUTATION OF A RANDOMIZATION TEST OF DEPENDENT SAMPLES

Rank: 1 .... ? 256

Subject	Extreme arrangement favoring high frequency		Obtained arrangement		Extreme arrangement favoring low frequency	
	High	Low	High	Low	High	Low
1	7	4	5	7	4	7
2	7	4	5	7	4	7
3	6	4	4	6	4	6
4	6	3	4	6	3	6
5	5	3	4	5	3	5
6	5	3	3	4	3	5
7	5	3	3	3	3	5
8	4	2	2	3	2	4
ΣX	45	26	30	41	26	45

(1/256) and similar outcomes with probabilities summing to 2.5 percent defines half the region of rejection. The probability of the outcome on the right of the table and similar outcomes summing to 2.5 percent defines the other half of the region of rejection.

Using the program NPSTAT we found that the obtained outcome is among the 12 most extreme outcomes of the null frequency distribution (6 outcomes in each tail). You can see that when H_0 is true, the exact probability of our obtained data arrangement is 12/256, or $p = .047$. This result leads to the rejection of H_0, the same decision reached with the t-test for dependent samples.

Table 11.6 provides a comparison of the steps involved in carrying out a statistical test with the normal and randomization models. They can both involve defining H_0 and H_1 and setting the probability of a Type I error, α. The nature of the hypotheses varies between the models. Specifically, the random sampling model tests a hypothesis about two population parameters, μ_1 and μ_2. On the other hand, the randomization test assesses the hypothesis that there is no relationship between scores and the randomly assigned treatment. As shown in Table 11.6, these models also differ in the way the probability value is computed and the way the results are interpreted.

Statistical studies have shown that for many sets of data, using either the random sampling model or the random assignment model leads to the same statistical decision (e.g., Boik, 1987; McHugh, 1963). This result is why researchers are justified in using the normal model when they have not employed random sampling. The relationship between results from the two types of test is important because it is often very difficult to sample randomly

Table 11.6 COMPARISON OF TWO PROCEDURES FOR STATISTICAL TESTING

Random Assignment	Random Sampling
1. H_0: Scores are independent of randomly assigned treatments.	1. H_0: $\mu_1 = \mu_2$.
2. Set a decision criterion, α.	
3. Randomize subjects, stimuli, or orders of stimuli.	3. Randomly sample cases.
4. List all possible outcomes and build a null frequency distribution.	4. Select a test ratio (e.g., t) and its sampling distribution.
5. Identify the region of rejection.	
6. Locate the observed result in the null distribution.	6. Compute the test ratio and find its probability in the t-table.
7. If the obtained value is in the region of rejection, reject H_0.	
8. Support causal inference.	8. Support generality inference.

in practice. It is also important because probability values are generally much easier to compute with the normal model. In other words, for practical reasons researchers want to use the normal (random sampling) model. One justification for doing so without satisfying the assumption of independence through random sampling is that the answer obtained from each method is often about the same. Exceptions to this general statement occur with extreme violations of the assumptions underlying the t-test or when $n_1 < n_2$ and $s_1^2 > s_2^2$.

Therefore, we find that the normal model is routinely used in statistical testing regardless of the presence or absence of random sampling. The region of rejection generally forms a valid criterion to judge the null hypothesis when either random sampling or random assignment to treatments is carried out. You may recall, however, that *two* inferences are often derived from a statistical test. One inference is that there is a systematic relationship between scores and treatment conditions (the null hypothesis can be rejected with α probability of a Type I error when H_0 is true). The other inference depends on which type of random process was carried out.

It should be kept in mind that the randomization procedure and the random sampling procedure evaluate different null hypotheses. The random sampling procedure is concerned with estimating the relationship between population parameters—H_0: $\mu_1 = \mu_2$. The null hypothesis for the randomization procedure is H_0: The values of scores are independent of their random assignment to the two groups. Thus, different interpretations follow from tests based on random sampling and tests based on random assignment. When a researcher does not use random sampling but does use random assignment to groups, the null hypothesis being tested concerns the independence of scores from group membership regardless of the test statistic used to make a statistical decision, that is, *t*-ratio or an exact probability from listing arrangements of data.

As mentioned in Chapter 1 (see Figure 1.1), when random sampling is carried out and a decision is made about H_0, the researcher has a statistical basis to *generalize* the results to the specific population that was sampled. Alternatively, when random assignment is carried out and a decision made about H_0, the researcher has a statistical basis to make an inference about the *cause* of the difference between groups. Occasionally a researcher is in a position both to sample subjects randomly and to assign them randomly to treatments. In that case the researcher has a statistical basis to draw a causal conclusion that can be generalized to the population that was sampled.

To conclude, the statistical basis for generality and causal inference is tied to the type of random process used rather than to the method of determining the region of rejection. Computing a *t*-test does not generate statistical implications about generality unless random sampling was used. (In practice, generality is often based on nonstatistical criteria, such as a logical argument comparing the present outcome with other research on the problem.) Similarly, computing a probability value with a randomization test does not lead to implications about cause and effect unless random assignment was used.

11.8   STRENGTH OF RELATIONSHIP

Conclusions resulting from statistical tests such as the *t*-test help assess a hypothesis about the difference between means. We use the region of rejection to evaluate the null hypothesis, and the smaller the region, the more likely we are to reject H_0. In this sense the magnitude of α is used as an index of reliability, and small α levels imply minimal error in rejecting the null hypothesis.

Frequently, the value of α is incorrectly interpreted as the only index of the statistical importance of a finding. Suppose, for example, that you wish to compare two studies that test the same conceptual hypothesis. The studies could be replications carried out by different researchers. Assume that both studies involved two independent samples (e.g., experimental and control groups) and similar measures of behavior, such as the number of correct responses on a memory test. The outcome in study A is $t(60) = 2.67$, $p < .01$, and the outcome in study B is $t(14) = 2.15$, $p < .05$. Using only this statistical information, you might be more impressed with the outcome of study A than study B because the probability of a Type I error is smaller ($p < .01$ versus $p < .05$).

The problem with this interpretation of statistical testing is that a probability value by itself does not directly indicate the strength of the relationship between the independent variable (e.g., treatments or group membership) and the dependent variable (response we are trying to account for). The strength of the relationship is one of two components in a statistical test.

The other component is the size of the study based on the number of cases that are involved (e.g., number of scores). Increasing either the strength of the relationship or the size of the sample increases the size of the statistical test ratio (e.g., t) and reduces the probability of its occurrence by chance.

Even though study A is significant, with a smaller α than study B, it is possible that study A shows a weaker relationship because the studies differ in size: $df = 60$ in study A, and $df = 14$ in study B. Study A is more impressive in terms of the probability of a Type I error, but study B may be more impressive in terms of the strength of the relationship.

Estimating Percentage of Variation Accounted For

You should recall from Chapter 6 that the strength of relationship between an independent variable and a dependent variable can be determined with a correlation coefficient. Computing this statistic provides the researcher with an important piece of information to use along with a probability in evaluating a research finding.

Independent Samples

We illustrate the strength of relationship measure for two independent samples by using the data from our experiment dealing with word frequency and recall. To do so, the raw data from Table 11.2 have been copied on the right side of Table 11.7. This arrangement of data makes it easy to see that we have two samples of eight scores each. We then generated "condition codes" to identify each raw score with a treatment condition. The actual value of these coding numbers is not important as long as all scores in a given group receive the same code number. Commonly used condition codes are 1 and 0 or $+1$ and -1. In Table 11.7 all scores in the high-frequency condition are coded 1 and those in the low-frequency condition are coded 0.

The result of this coding is shown on the left side of Table 11.7 as two columns of data, group membership (1 or 0) and recall responses (number correct). The correlation between these two sets of data was calculated by using Formula 6.8 for the Pearson correlation coefficient. Remember that the resulting value is referred to as a point-biserial correlation (r_{pb}) simply to remind us that one of the variables being correlated is dichotomous (takes on only two values).

For the data in Table 11.7, r_{pb} is .581. This result gives an index of the strength of the relationship between the word frequency treatment conditions and the recall scores. If desired, this correlation can be tested for statistical significance by using Formula 10.7. But consider what such a test will tell you. It will provide a test of the relationship between the treatment conditions and the recall responses. That is exactly what was obtained by calculation of a t-test in Section 11.4. This point is illustrated at the foot of Table 11.7, where you can see that the t-test for independent sample means gives the same value, $t(14) = 2.67$, as obtained from testing the significance of the point-biserial correlation. Thus, the t-test can be obtained by either

Table 11.7   EXAMPLE CALCULATION OF r_{pb} FOR AN INDEPENDENT
SAMPLES DESIGN
(The Data Are From Table 11.2. Group Codes Are 1 = High
Frequency and 0 = Low Frequency.)

Subject number	Condition code	Recall response	Treatment	
			High frequency	Low frequency
1	1	13	13	10
2	1	9	9	9
3	1	12	12	8
4	1	14	14	10
5	1	10	10	11
6	1	11	11	8
7	1	9	9	9
8	1	11	11	6
9	0	10	$\overline{X}$ 11.125	8.875
10	0	9		
11	0	8	r_{pb} = .581	
12	0	8		
13	0	10	$r_{pb}^2(100)$ = 33.8%	
14	0	11		
15	0	9		
16	0	6		

$$t(14) = \frac{\overline{X}_1 - \overline{X}_2}{s_{\overline{x}_1 - \overline{x}_2}} = \frac{11.125 - 8.875}{.8425} = 2.67 \qquad (11.6)$$

$$t(14) = \frac{r}{\sqrt{\dfrac{1 - r^2}{n - 2}}} = \frac{.581}{\sqrt{\dfrac{.663}{14}}} = 2.67 \qquad (10.5)$$

direct calculation of the ratio or by calculation of a correlation and the conversion of the r value to a t value.

When the value of r is known, Formula 11.15 can be used to calculate
the strength of the relationship in terms of the percentage of variation in
recall responses that is accounted for by variation in word frequency treatments. For the data in Table 11.7, r_{pb} = .581, so the percentage of variation
in the recall scores that can be accounted for by high- versus low-frequency
treatments is

$$r^2(100) = \% \text{ of variation} \qquad (11.15)$$
$$.581^2(100) = 33.8\%$$

The percentage of variation accounted for can be computed without actually calculating the value of the correlation coefficient directly because the
relationship between t and r can be summarized as shown in Formula 11.16:

$$r = \sqrt{\frac{t^2}{t^2 + df}} \quad \text{or} \quad r^2 = \frac{t^2}{t^2 + df} \qquad (11.16)$$

For our example data, $r^2 = 2.67^2/(2.67^2 + 14) = .338$, and $r^2(100) = .338(100) = 33.8$ percent.

Dependent Samples

The same type of assessment of strength of relation can be carried out with data from a dependent samples design. The only problem is that the correlation between paired scores must be taken into account before calculation of r_{pb}. To account for the correlation between paired scores, the data must be adjusted for the amount of variation within each pair of scores. Then we can assess the differences between independent pairs. The adjustment involves subtracting each score within a pair from the average of the two scores for that pair. The procedure is illustrated in Table 11.8, using the raw data from Table 11.3.

Given the adjusted scores, the correlation was computed in the same manner as in the independent samples case. Condition codes were assigned (1 = high frequency and 0 = low frequency) and these were correlated with the adjusted recall scores. For our example data in Table 11.8, $r_{pb} = .75$, and the percentage of explained variation is $.75^2(100) = 56\%$.

To summarize, observed t-ratios and the values of α at which they are significant do not provide a good index of the strength of the relationship between group membership and behavior scores. Therefore it is advisable to report *both* the t-value and the strength of the relationship (r) or the percentage of variation, $r^2(100)$. When evaluating a study, a better decision can be made by using both a significance level (e.g., $\alpha = .05$) and the estimated strength of the relation than by either criterion alone.

Comparison of Studies

Analysis of the percentage of variation accounted for provides a way of comparing the outcomes of different studies separately from the α used in evaluating the null hypothesis. This type of comparison has been made in Table 11.9 for our two experiments involving word frequency and free recall. Although both studies were significant, with $\alpha = .05$, the values of r and percentages of explained variation are quite different.

Unlike Type I error probabilities obtained from hypothesis testing, estimates of the percentage of variation accounted for do not have a conventional criterion for evaluation. They are used in a descriptive fashion. We simply note that in the study involving independent samples, word frequency ac-

Table 11.8 CALCULATION OF PERCENTAGE OF BEHAVIORAL
VARIATION ACCOUNTED FOR BY TREATMENTS
IN A DEPENDENT SAMPLES DESIGN
(The Raw Data Are From Table 11.3.)

Subject number	High frequency	Low frequency	$\overline{X}$	Adjustment $X_1 - \overline{X}$	Adjustment $X_2 - \overline{X}$
1	4	3	3.5	0.5	−0.5
2	3	4	3.5	−0.5	0.5
3	5	6	5.5	−0.5	0.5
4	2	3	2.5	−0.5	0.5
5	4	5	4.5	−0.5	0.5
6	5	7	6.0	−1.0	1.0
7	3	6	4.5	−1.5	1.5
8	4	7	5.5	−1.5	1.5
Sum				−5.5	5.5

Subject	Raw scores	Condition code*	Adjusted scores	
1H	4	1	0.5	
2H	3	1	−0.5	
3H	5	1	−0.5	
4H	2	1	−0.5	
5H	4	1	−0.5	
6H	5	1	−1.0	
7H	3	1	−1.5	
8H	4	1	−1.5	$r_{pb} = .7485$
1L	3	0	−0.5	
2L	4	0	0.5	$r_{pb}^2(100) = 56.0\%$
3L	6	0	0.5	
4L	3	0	0.5	
5L	5	0	0.5	
6L	7	0	1.0	
7L	6	0	1.5	
8L	7	0	1.5	

*1 = high frequency (H); 0 = low frequency (L).

counted for 33.8 percent of the variation in recall scores. In the study with
dependent samples, word frequency accounted for 56 percent of the behavioral variation. We can compare these studies on two statistical criteria. On
the test of significance the two studies have almost the same probability of
Type I error (.0183 and .0203) and are equally impressive by that criterion.
Inspecting the strength of relationship, we could say that the study with dependent samples was more impressive than the study with independent samples. Ideally, the data in a given study will be impressive on both criteria.

Table 11.9 COMPARISON OF OUTCOMES OF TWO EXPERIMENTS
RELATING WORD FREQUENCY TO FREE RECALL

Experiment	t	df	Exact p*	Tabled p	r_{pb}^2	$r_{pb}^2(100)$
Independent	2.67	14	.0183	.02	.581	33.8%
Dependent	−2.99	7	.0203	.05	.748	56.0%

*Obtained by the computer program NPSTAT; these values only have precise meaning if all assumptions underlying the test are satisfied perfectly.

That is, rejecting H_0 has a small probability of a Type I error, and treatments account for a substantial proportion of variation in scores.

SUMMARY

The t-ratio is a useful statistical test for comparing two sample means. It can be used in an independent samples design with one score per subject or in a dependent samples (or matched groups) design with two scores from each subject (or matched pairs).

Assumptions underlying the use of the t-ratio for two samples include (1) homogeneity of variance and (2) normal distributions in the particular populations that were sampled. The t-ratio is a robust statistical procedure with respect to these two assumptions. That is, homogeneity and normality assumptions may be violated to some extent without appreciably affecting the validity of the resulting t value. Another formal assumption is that the scores are independent of each other. When independence is not achieved by random sampling, the t-test may be used as an approximation to the randomization test.

Statistical testing with the t-ratio can lead to three types of inference. When the observed outcome is in the region of rejection, it is inferred that the difference between means results from a systematic relationship between treatments and scores. Additional inferences depend on whether random sampling or random assignment (or both) was actually carried out. With random sampling and rejection of H_0, there is a statistical basis to generalize the results to the specific population that was sampled. With random assignment and rejection of H_0, there is a statistical basis to argue that the treatment caused the observed differences in behavior. Both types of random process may be present in a single study, supporting both generality and causal interpretations.

The statistical conclusion resulting from the use of the t-test provides only one type of information about the observed data. It is used to evaluate the null hypothesis. However, we often want to know not only if H_0 can be rejected but also about the strength of the relationship between the independent and dependent variables. This information can be obtained through the calculation of a correlation between group membership and the behavior scores. The resulting value of r or r^2 is interpreted much like the correlations discussed in Chapter 6.

KEY WORDS

independent samples design

dependent samples design

numerator of the t-ratio

denominator of the t-ratio

standard error of difference between means

homogeneity of variance

robust

repeated measures design

matched-groups design

difference scores

independence of scores

normal model

randomization model

strength of relationship

percentage of variation accounted for

PROBLEMS

1 Informal observation led a counselor to think that when clients arrived late for appointments, males arrived later than females. She decided to test the null hypothesis that there is no sex difference associated with the average time of arrival against the alternative hypothesis that males arrive later.
   (a) Using the notation of hypothesis testing, make a formal statement of H_0 and H_1 for a t-test.
   (b) Lateness of arrival was recorded for all clients in one work week, and the following summary statistics were generated. Carry out a t-test and make a statistical decision. Let $\alpha = .05$. (Hint: See Formula 11.9.)

	Males	Females
n	10	13
$\bar{X}_{Minutes}$	8.22	6.31
s	3.23	2.86

   (c) What type of sampling procedure was used in this study?
   (d) What kinds of statistically based inferences can be drawn from these results?
      (i) Inference about the null hypothesis?
      (ii) Inference about generality?
      (iii) Inference about causal relationship?

2 A cognitive psychologist wanted to know if practice in reading text in a novel format affects retention of information. He made up three 500-word passages for study, two for the practice phase and one for the test phase. One practice passage was text from an encyclopedia. The other was the same text reprinted backward so that it had to be read from right to left rather than from left to right. For the test passage, the text was from the same source but the words were all inverted. The subjects

were 12 volunteers from the psychologist's course in cognitive psychology. Six subjects were randomly assigned to each practice condition (forward versus backward text). Each group had 10 minutes to study the text before taking a 16-question multiple-choice test. They practiced this study and test sequence twice before beginning the test phase of the study. The test phase consisted of one 10-minute study of the inverted text followed by a multiple-choice test on the content of what they had studied. The raw data follow.

NUMBER OF CORRECT ITEMS

Type of practice text	
Forward	Backward
12	10
10	7
14	7
9	9
11	6
10	9

(a) Make a formal statement of H_0 and H_1 for a t-test.
(b) Find the observed value of t.
(c) Given $\alpha = .05$, make a statistical decision.
(d) What causal inference might you make from this study?
(e) What generality inference might you make?

3 A colleague of the psychologist in Problem 2 was asked to comment on the finding. "With only 12 subjects, I am not very impressed with your finding." What two statistical criteria might be used to respond to this criticism?

4 There are 120 third-grade children in a particular elementary school. At the beginning of the school year 10 of them were randomly sampled and given a standardized arithmetic test. The test was repeated at the end of the school year, and the scores for both tests follow. If you let $\alpha = .05$, was there a statistically significant change in their arithmetic performance?

Student	Test 1	Test 2
1	30	32
2	46	45
3	34	40
4	33	34
5	27	25
6	32	39
7	36	36
8	37	41
9	33	38
10	36	32

5 You decide to replicate the study described in Problem 2. This time you give a vocabulary test to all 12 subjects before randomly assigning them to the two treatments. First they are ranked according to vocabulary scores. Then the two subjects with the highest vocabulary scores (ranked 1 and 2) are randomly assigned to treatments, then the next two highest (3 and 4) are randomly assigned, and so on.

(a) Carry out a t-test and make a statistical decision.
(b) What verbal label would you apply to this design?
(c) Why is the value of t here different from that in Problem 2?
(d) Compare the strength of relationship in the two studies dealing with the type of practice text and recognition errors with inverted text (the studies in Problems 2 and 5). Is the same study more impressive by both criteria (alpha level and percentage of variation)?

NUMBER OF CORRECT ITEMS

Rank order on vocabulary	Pair number	Type of practice text	
		Forward	Backward
1	1	12	
2	1		10
3	2		7
4	2	10	
5	3	14	
6	3		9
7	4	11	
8	4		7
9	5		6
10	5	9	
11	6		9
12	6	10	

6 Assume that you have read a research report on a topic of great interest to you. The original finding was reported as a t-test between two independent samples, with $t(120) = 2.00$, $p < .05$. You decide to carry out a replication of the study but have only 30 subjects. The rank order of the sample means is in the same direction in each study (e.g., $\overline{X}_{\text{Experimental}} > \overline{X}_{\text{Control}}$). In your replication you find $t(18) = 1.60$, $p > .05$.

(a) Is the alternative hypothesis in the replication directional or nondirectional?
(b) Is the outcome in the replication significant?
(c) Calculate the correlation between behavior scores and group membership in each study.
(d) Compare the outcomes of the two studies in terms of both the alpha level and correlation and draw a conclusion.

7 In statistical theory, which random procedure (random sampling or random assignment) is assumed necessary for t-tests of two sample means? How can you justify using this test when the theoretically appropriate random method is not used?

8 If you have access to the computer program NPSTAT, complete the following problem. A class of nine students was randomly divided into two groups that received different treatments. They generated the following scores:

Treatment A: 2, 4, 4, 3, 2, 3

Treatment B: 5, 20, 5

(a) Compute a t-test of the difference between means and make a statistical decision about the outcome.
(b) Compute a randomization test to see if the scores are independent of their random assignment to groups and make a statistical decision about the outcome.
(c) Compare the results of these two analyses and suggest a likely reason for the difference.

9 If you have access to the computer program NPSTAT, complete the following problem. A therapist has six clients with similar problems and has them complete a life-stress questionnaire before they begin weekly sessions and again after four sessions. The two scores for each client follow.

Client	Before	After
A	18	12
B	15	13
C	13	14
D	17	9
E	14	10
F	15	10

(a) Compute a t-test of the difference between means and make a statistical decision about the outcome.
(b) Compute a randomization test to see if the scores are independent of their random assignment to groups and make a statistical decision about the outcome.
(c) Compare the results of these two analyses and suggest a likely reason for the difference.

Chapter
12

Power of Statistical Tests

12.1   INTRODUCTION

A researcher's primary objective in testing a null hypothesis usually is to reject it in favor of the alternative hypothesis. You might think that if the null hypothesis were false, a study would be quite likely to produce results that would lead to its rejection. Unfortunately, even a study that is carefully conducted may turn out to have very little chance of producing results that will allow the rejection of a false null hypothesis.

Consider a researcher who wishes to demonstrate that a new method of training people to use a word processing program on a computer will produce more efficient performance than the usual method. In the usual training procedure all features of the program are available for use, even complex ones that a novice need not and should not use during the early stages of training. In the new training method, those features are eliminated from the program. The researcher plans to have one group of 20 secretaries learn to use the editor by the usual method, and another group of 20 will be trained by the revised method. For each group the training task consists of typing a business letter, and the researcher measures how much time is required to complete it. After collecting the data the researcher will test the null hypothesis against a nondirectional alternative hypothesis by computing a t-test with $\alpha = .05$.

Now suppose that we, but not the researcher, happen to know the following facts about the population of secretaries and their ability to learn to use the word processing program by either of these methods. First, we know that, on the average, secretaries using the usual training method take 50 minutes to type the sample letter, but if given the revised method they would take an average of 45 minutes. Second, we know the standard deviation for each method is 12 minutes.

This is, of course, a hypothetical situation because if this knowledge were generally known, it would be available to the researcher and there would be no need to do the study. For now, just imagine that we happen to have access to some magical authority from which this information was obtained. You should immediately see that the researcher's hunch is correct, and you should be rooting for the study to provide evidence in support of it. But in this study the probability of obtaining results that allow rejection of the false null hypothesis is only about .26. That is, in only about 26 out of 100 studies of this kind would the researcher correctly reject the null hypothesis.

In this chapter we show how probabilities of this sort are computed and what they mean. We also explain the two most important applications of this information. One concerns the issue of how studies can be designed to maximize the chances of rejecting a false null hypothesis. The second concerns the interpretation of the results of studies that fail to reject null hypotheses. For example, if the training study failed to reject the null hypothesis, the researcher could not necessarily conclude that the two training methods did not differ. It could be that an existing difference was not detected because the study did not have a high probability of obtaining the required results.

12.2   REJECTING A FALSE NULL HYPOTHESIS

When a null hypothesis is tested one of two possible assertions are true—but not both. One is that the null hypothesis is true, and the other is that the alternative hypothesis is true. In addition, the researcher can make only one of two possible decisions: reject or not reject the null hypothesis. This arrangement was summarized in Table 9.4, and a slightly altered version is shown in Table 12.1.

In Table 12.1 we have included the probability that the results of a study will support a decision (reject or not reject), given that a particular hypothesis is true. Recall from Chapter 9 that when the null hypothesis is true, the researcher wants to ensure that the probability of rejecting the null hypothesis (i.e., making a Type I error) is small. This is done by establishing a region of rejection that occupies a small portion of the appropriate sampling distribution. The relative size of this region is equal to α, the probability of making a Type I error. If the null hypothesis is true, the probability of obtaining a result that falls in this region is α. The probability that the result falls anywhere else, leading to a failure to reject the null hypothesis will be $1 - \alpha$. For example, if α is set at .05 and the null hypothesis is true, the probability that the researcher will obtain a result that favors not rejecting the null hypothesis is .95.

When the null hypothesis is false the correct decision would be to reject it, and failing to do so would be a Type II error. In Table 12.1 we have labeled the probability of making this kind of error β. The probability of correctly rejecting the null hypothesis would then be $1 - \beta$. A special term, **power,** is also used to refer to the probability of correctly rejecting a false null hypothesis. Thus, a powerful study is one in which there is a high probability of rejecting the null hypothesis when it is false.

POWER: The probability of obtaining a result that allows a false null hypothesis to be rejected.

Table 12.1   **SUMMARY OF CONSEQUENCES OF DECIDING TO REJECT OR NOT REJECT THE NULL HYPOTHESIS**

	True hypothesis	
Decision	Null (H_0)	Alternative (H_1)
Reject H_0	Type I error probability = α	Correct probability = $1 - \beta$
Not Reject H_0	Correct probability = $1 - \alpha$	Type II error probability = β

Unlike α, the researcher is not able to set the probability of a Type II error, β, at some specific value because statistical tests are set up to be tests of the assumption that the null hypothesis is *true*. The region of rejection and evaluation of research results are based on that assumption. The values of β and power are determined by a number of factors (e.g., sample size and α), and the researcher has only a limited degree of influence over some of them. It is very important to understand how these factors influence power so that the researcher has the best possible chance of rejecting a null hypothesis when it is false.

12.3 POWER AND THE ONE-SAMPLE TEST

To understand how power is influenced by various factors and how a researcher can control these factors, you first need to understand how power is calculated. We will illustrate this operation by using a simple statistical test: The one-sample test when population variance is known. (This test was described in Chapter 10.) Recall that the null hypothesis states that the mean of a population of scores is equal to some specific value. We will now refer to that value as μ_0, so we now have H_0: $\mu = \mu_0$.

Also recall that a region of rejection is established for the sampling distribution of the mean. The region is defined by assuming that H_0 is true; by setting α to some specified value, such as .05; and by stating an alternative hypothesis. For now we will assume a directional alternative hypothesis— H_1: $\mu > \mu_0$.

Figure 12.1(a) illustrates the region of rejection for the sampling distribution of the mean, assuming that H_0 ($\mu = \mu_0$) is true. In the diagram we show the minimum value of $\overline{X}$ needed to reject the null hypothesis. We refer to this value as the **rejection criterion.** If the observed sample mean is equal to or greater than the rejection criterion, the researcher will reject H_0. In this case the researcher is interested only in sample means that equal or exceed the rejection criterion because the alternative hypothesis is directional and claims that the true value of μ is greater than the value claimed by H_0.

REJECTION CRITERION: The value of a statistic that represents the boundary of the region of rejection.

Now suppose the alternative hypothesis is true, that is, the actual value of the population mean is some value, μ_1, that is greater than the value specified by the null hypothesis, μ_0. The appropriate sampling distribution of the mean, based on the correct value μ_1, appears in Figure 12.1(b). The rejection criterion is unchanged—it *always* is based on the assumption that the null hypothesis is true. But because the actual value of the population mean is μ_1,

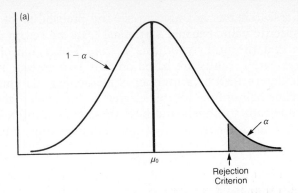

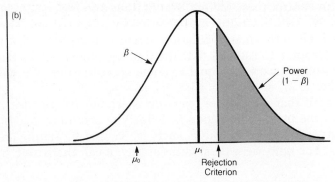

Figure 12.1 Sampling distributions of the mean (a) based on the null hypothesis that $\mu = \mu_0$ and (b) based on the true value of $\mu = \mu_1$.

the true probability of obtaining a sample mean equal to or larger than the rejection criterion is based on the sampling distribution with μ_1 as its mean. In Figure 12.1(b) this region is given the label *power*. This region is less than half the area of the distribution, so it is not very likely that the researcher will obtain a sample mean larger than the rejection criterion. Only a result in this region would allow the researcher to reject correctly the false null hypothesis.

A diagram like Figure 12.1(a) reflects what happens each time a null hypothesis is set up and used to establish a rejection criterion. In addition, when the null hypothesis is false, the true sampling distribution of the mean (from which the researcher's sample mean is drawn) is like the one shown in Figure 12.1(b). Thus, although the sampling distribution of the mean based on H_0 is used to establish a rejection criterion, a different sampling distribution based on H_1, typically with an unknown mean, will determine the actual research result if H_0 is false.

A Numerical Example

We will now work out a numerical example showing how power can be computed. Assume that the population standard deviation is known to be 10 and that the following hypotheses are in effect:

$$H_0: \mu = 50$$

$$H_1: \mu > 50$$

A researcher sets $\alpha = .05$ and draws a random sample of 25 subjects to test the null hypothesis. According to H_0 the appropriate sampling distribution of the mean is the one shown in Figure 12.2(a). The H_1 is directional, so the entire region of rejection is in one tail of the distribution, as shown in the figure, and it occupies .05 of the distribution.

The sampling distribution is normal and σ is given, so we can determine the z-score that corresponds to the rejection criterion quite easily. The z-score will be that value in the distribution beyond which .05 of the scores fall. The critical z-score can be found by turning to Table B in Appendix III

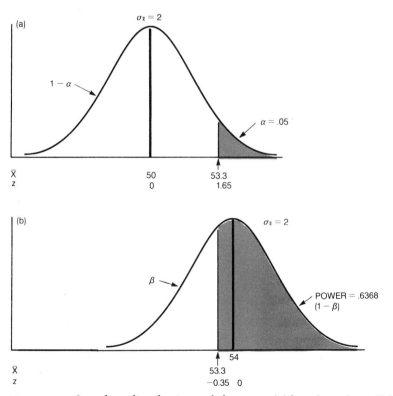

Figure 12.2 Sampling distributions of the mean (a) based on the null hypothesis that $\mu = 50$ and (b) based on the true value of $\mu = 54$.

(representing the standard normal distribution) and searching for the value of α (.0500) in the column labeled "Area Beyond z." No value exactly corresponding to this one can be found, but there are two values equally close to it: .0505 and .0495. We choose to work with .0495 because it will prevent α from exceeding .05. The z-score associated with .0495 is 1.65, and we can use it to figure out the value of the sample mean that corresponds to this position in the distribution. Recall from Chapter 10 that when dealing with a sampling distribution of the mean, z-scores can be expressed as follows:

$$z_{\overline{X}} = \frac{\overline{X} - \mu}{\sigma_{\overline{X}}} \qquad (10.2)$$

In this example $\mu = 50$ and $\sigma_{\overline{X}} = 10/\sqrt{25} = 2$, so we have

$$1.65 = \frac{\overline{X} - 50}{2}$$

We can solve this equation for $\overline{X}$, which represents the rejection criterion. It is the minimum value of the sample mean needed to reject H_0. In general, the solution of Formula 10.2 for $\overline{X}$ takes the form

$$\overline{X} = \mu + \sigma_{\overline{X}}(z_{\overline{X}}) \qquad (12.1)$$

This formula involves the same procedures as those used in computing a raw score from a z-score (Formulas 5.3 and 5.4). In the present example we have

$$\overline{X} = 50 + 2(1.65) = 53.3$$

The rejection criterion, then, is 53.3, as shown in Figure 12.2(a). If the researcher should obtain a sample mean of this size or larger, the null hypothesis will be rejected.

The calculation of the power of a statistical test is based on the assumption that H_0 is false. In the present example, which is based on a directional H_1, this assumption means that power will be computed using a value of the population mean that is greater than 50. Calculating the power of a test consists of finding the probability of obtaining a sample result that meets the rejection criterion established under the assumption that H_0 is true. Remember that such a sample result must be obtained if the researcher is to reject H_0. Now we can ask how likely that event is, given that H_0 is false and that H_1 is true.

Finding this probability requires knowledge of the true value of μ. In practice this is something that we will have to estimate, perhaps from previous research. We will deal with this issue in Section 12.4, but for now suppose that a supernatural authority has informed us, but not the researcher, that the real population mean is 54. We can use this information to create a new sampling distribution of the mean based on a population mean of 54, as shown in Figure 12.2(b). This distribution has the same shape and variability as that based on H_0, but its mean is different. This is the distribution that will determine power: The real probability of obtaining a sample mean that meets the rejection criterion of 53.3.

To compute power we first convert the rejection criterion to a z-score in the context of this new, valid sampling distribution. We then use Table B in Appendix III to find the proportion of the distribution that is equal to or greater than that value. We are interested in sample means that are greater than the rejection criterion because H_1 claims that μ is greater than the value specified by H_0. The z-score can be found by using Formula 10.2:

$$z_{\overline{X}} = \frac{53.3 - 54}{2} = -0.35$$

Table B indicates that .1368 of the distribution falls between this z-score and the mean, and a further .5000 falls beyond the mean. Thus, a total of .1368 + .5000 = .6368 of the possible sample means actually fall above the rejection criterion. This result means that the power of the one-sample test in this study, the probability of drawing a random sample that produces a mean greater than or equal to 53.3, is .6368.

In summary, power is computed by first finding the rejection criterion based on the assumption that H_0 is true. Then we use knowledge of the true value of μ to set up an alternative sampling distribution. That distribution is used to determine the probability of obtaining a sample result that will meet the original rejection criterion, allowing rejection of the false null hypothesis.

12.4 FACTORS AFFECTING POWER

Several aspects of a study contribute to the level of power of the statistical test used in it. Many of these aspects can be affected by decisions that a researcher makes when designing the study. Making the correct decisions can greatly enhance the chances of rejecting a null hypothesis when it is false. We explain how various factors influence power by using the one-sample test as an example.

Effect Size

When developing an alternative hypothesis for a study, no particular value is specified for the population mean; only a range is stated (e.g., $\mu > 50$). The actual value of μ, however, has a very strong influence on power. Look back to Figure 12.1 and imagine what would happen if the true value of the population mean (μ_1) were larger than indicated in the figure. The sampling distribution based on the true population mean—Figure 12.1(b)—would shift further to the right, and therefore more of the area in the distribution would be to the right of the rejection criterion. Thus, power would increase as the difference increased between the true value of the population mean, μ_1, and the value claimed by the null hypothesis, μ_0.

We refer to the difference between the true value of μ and its value under the null hypothesis as **effect size.** Although a researcher typically has no control over effect size in studies involving the one-sample test, experiments involving more than one sample (e.g., different treatments are administered) provide an opportunity for influencing effect size and are discussed later in this chapter.

EFFECT SIZE: The difference between the true value of a population parameter and the value assumed by the null hypothesis.

Effect size generally is expressed in terms of the number of standard deviations separating the hypothesized and true values of a population parameter, such as μ. We use the symbol γ (the Greek letter gamma) to refer to this measure of effect size. For the one-sample case, then, we have the following formula for γ.

$$\gamma = \frac{\mu_1 - \mu_0}{\sigma} \qquad (12.2)$$

In our example with $\mu_1 = 54$, the effect size would be

$$\gamma = \frac{54 - 50}{10} = 0.4$$

To see how effect size influences power, suppose that in the example used for Figure 12.2 the true value of μ were 56, rather than 54. In this case the effect size would be

$$\gamma = \frac{56 - 50}{10} = 0.6$$

rather than 0.4. All other aspects of the example remain unchanged. The true sampling distribution of the mean, with $\mu = 56$, is shown in Figure 12.3. With reference to this distribution, the z-score for the rejection criterion is

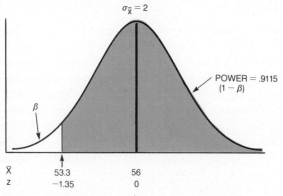

Figure 12.3   Sampling distribution of the mean when the true value of $\mu = 56$.

$$z_{\overline{X}} = \frac{53.3 - 56}{2} = -1.35$$

and the proportion of the distribution that exceeds the rejection criterion (according to Table B) is .4115 + .5000 = .9115. This is a substantial increase over the power (.6368) that would have been achieved had the true population mean been 54. In general, a larger effect size means greater power.

Type I Error Probability

The researcher has the freedom to choose any reasonable value of α. Although conventions adopted by researchers favor .05, there are circumstances that justify the use of higher or lower values of α. For example, when carrying out a pilot study to determine whether a full-scale study might lead to rejection of the null hypothesis, a researcher might set $\alpha = .10$. On the other hand, consider a researcher who tests a drug that may reduce depression but

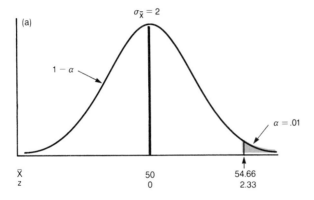

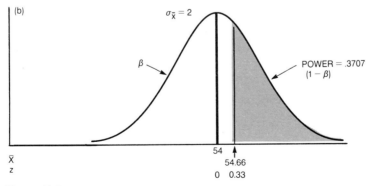

Figure 12.4   Sampling distributions of the mean (a) based on the null hypothesis that $\mu = 50$ and (b) based on the true value of $\mu = 54$. In this case $\alpha = .01$.

has undesirable side effects. The null hypothesis is that the drug has no influence on depression, so it should not be used. Because of the drug's nasty side effects, the researcher would want to be very certain to avoid making a Type I error. Such an error could lead to the drug being used as a treatment for depression even though it did not relieve symptoms while producing unwanted side effects. In this instance α might be set to .01.

The value of α has a strong effect on power because it determines the rejection criterion. The smaller the value of α the more extreme will be the rejection criterion. With a more extreme rejection criterion, it is less likely that a result will be obtained that allows rejection of the null hypothesis even when H_0 is false. This effect is illustrated in Figure 12.4, which is based on the example used with Figure 12.2. For Figure 12.4(a), $\alpha = .01$, and you can see that the region of rejection in this case is smaller than in Figure 12.2(a), where $\alpha = .05$. The more extreme rejection criterion also reduces the region of the true sampling distribution of the mean that allows rejection of the false null hypothesis. In Figure 12.4(b) you can see that the area allowing rejection is only .3707. (You should verify that this value is correct by using Table B and the information in Figure 12.4.) This value of power is much less than the value of .6368, which was obtained with $\alpha = .05$. It should now be clear why researchers do not often use α values that are smaller than .05.

Alternative Hypothesis

In Chapter 9 we explained the advantage of using a directional alternative hypothesis: It allows the entire region of rejection to be placed in one tail of the distribution of possible outcomes of a study. The result is a less extreme rejection criterion and, therefore, greater power. When a nondirectional alternative hypothesis is used, the total region of rejection must be divided in half and each half is assigned to one tail of the distribution. This division is shown in Figure 12.5(a), which is based on the example used to generate Figure 12.2, except that a nondirectional alternative hypothesis ($\mu \neq 50$) is used. The region of rejection in each tail is .025, and the z-scores corresponding to two rejection criteria are -1.96 and $+1.96$. We will continue to suppose that the true value of μ is 54.

Figure 12.5(b) shows that the lower region of rejection is not relevant to our calculation of power because with a true population mean of 54, there is no measurable chance that a sample mean will be that low. The upper rejection criterion is more extreme than when a directional alternative hypothesis was used because this part of the region of rejection is only $\alpha/2$. A smaller region of rejection makes it less likely that a sample mean will fall beyond the rejection criterion. In this instance power is .5319, which is somewhat smaller than the .6368 obtained with a directional alternative hypothesis. In general, using a directional alternative hypothesis will make a test more powerful than using a nondirectional alternative.

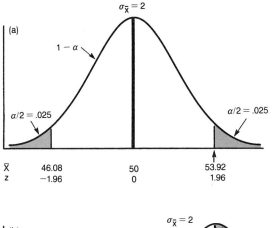

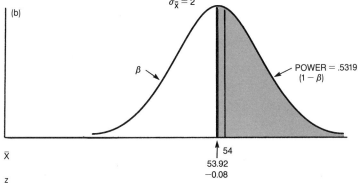

Figure 12.5 Sampling distribution of the mean (a) based on the null hypothesis that $\mu = 50$ and (b) based on the true value of $\mu = 54$. In this case a nondirectional alternative hypothesis is used.

Sample Size and Variability

The power of a test is closely related to the variability of the sampling distribution that is used to determine the rejection criterion. The variability of the sampling distribution depends on sample size and population variability, as shown by the formula for the standard deviation of the sampling distribution of the mean:

$$\sigma_{\overline{X}} = \frac{\sigma}{\sqrt{n}} \qquad (10.1)$$

The researcher selects the size of the sample to be drawn and so has direct control over this factor. There also are certain circumstances, described later in this chapter, in which the researcher can influence the amount of variability in a hypothetical population of scores.

Formula 10.1 indicates that the variability of the sampling distribution of the mean will be smaller with larger sample sizes and with smaller population variability. Smaller variability in the sampling distribution increases power in the one-sample test in the following way. When the z-score equivalent of the rejection criterion is converted to a raw mean value, this value will be closer to μ_0 when $\sigma_{\bar{x}}$ is smaller. You can see how this relationship works by looking at Formula 12.1 (page 300), which is used to make this conversion. Having a less extreme rejection criterion makes it more likely that a sample mean will be obtained that will allow rejection of H_0 when H_1 is true.

The influence of sample size on power is illustrated in Figure 12.6, where we show the sampling distributions of the mean associated with the null hypothesis, Figure 12.6(a), and the true value of μ, Figure 12.6(b). Figure 12.6 is based on the numerical example represented in Figure 12.2, with the exception that the sample size is now assumed to be 100 instead of 25. Notice that this sample size makes the standard error of the mean 1 rather than 2. The result is that the rejection criterion now is 51.65 instead of 53.3, and power is .9906 rather than .6368.

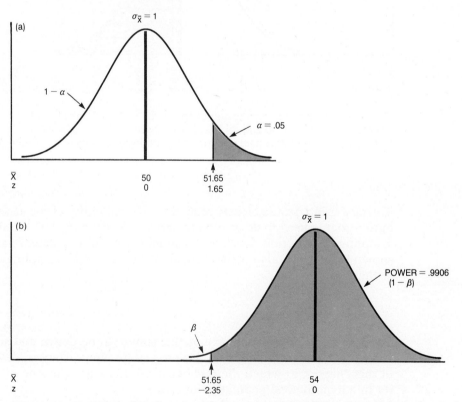

Figure 12.6   Sampling distributions of the mean (a) based on the null hypothesis that $\mu = 50$ and (b) based on the true value of $\mu = 54$. In this case sample size is 100.

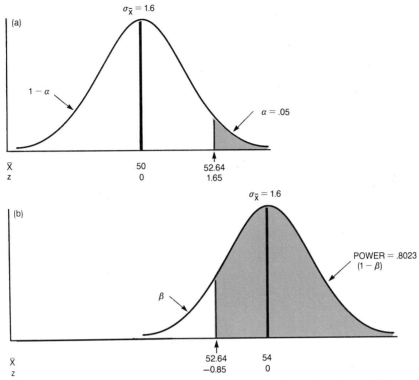

Figure 12.7   Sampling distributions of the mean (a) based on the null hypothesis that $\mu = 50$ and (b) based on the true value of $\mu = 54$. In this case $\sigma = 8$.

Power also is greater when the population variability is smaller, as shown in Figure 12.7. The example used with Figure 12.2 now has been changed so that the population standard deviation is 8 rather than 10. This change in σ makes the standard error of the mean 1.6 instead of 2, and the rejection criterion becomes 52.64 rather than 53.3. In this case power is greater than when a larger population standard deviation was in effect, .8023 versus .6368.

12.5   SIMPLIFIED METHOD FOR ESTIMATING POWER

The process of computing power generally involves computing the area under the sampling distribution associated with a particular statistical test. In the previous section we illustrated this operation through diagrams and the table for the standard normal distribution. This procedure was meant to enable you to see why various factors influence power in the ways they do. Now we will introduce a simpler method for computing power. This procedure involves computing a statistic much like effect size, then looking up the value of that statistic in a table and reading off the value of power that corresponds to it.

We will demonstrate the procedure with the one-sample test and the numerical example introduced with Figure 12.2. In this case, effect size was

$$\gamma = \frac{54 - 50}{10} = \frac{4}{10} = 0.40$$

because the population standard deviation was 10. Effect size can also be expressed in terms of variability in the *sampling distribution of the mean*, rather than variability in the population of raw scores. This transformation is done by replacing the population standard deviation in Formula 12.2 (page 302) with the standard error of the mean (the standard deviation of the sampling distribution). This operation produces the *statistical* effect size, δ (the Greek letter delta), for the one-sample test:

$$\delta = \frac{\mu_1 - \mu_0}{\left(\dfrac{\sigma}{\sqrt{n}}\right)} = \frac{\mu_1 - \mu_0}{\sigma}\sqrt{n} \tag{12.3}$$

Notice that the statistical effect size is equal to effect size multiplied by the square root of the sample size.

The statistical effect size in our example would be

$$\delta = \frac{54 - 50}{10}\sqrt{25} = \frac{4}{10}(5) = 2.00$$

The next step is to find this statistical effect size in Table F in Appendix III and read off the corresponding value of power. In our example we are using a directional alternative hypothesis with $\alpha = .05$. The value of power is found in Table F by reading down the column associated with this α and a directional alternative hypothesis until we reach the δ value of 2.00. The value in Table F is equal to .64, which is very close to the value we computed by using the longer method (.6368). You should try to recompute power with this table for each of the examples that were worked out in Figures 12.3 through 12.7. When you obtain a δ value that does not exactly correspond to one of the values in Table F, choose the value in the table that is closest to it. In addition, in cases where δ is negative, we ignore the sign when finding values in Table F.

12.6 ESTIMATING POWER FOR *t* and *r*

The two methods we have shown for computing power for the one-sample test are based on the assumption that the population standard deviation is known. In this case the value of the standard error of the mean is known, so we can compute *z* values and use the standard normal distribution. As you recall from Chapter 10, however, we usually do not know the population standard deviation but must estimate it from sample data. In Chapter 10 this estimate led to the use of the *t*-distribution so that we could maintain accurate control over Type I error.

For the purposes of computing power when population variability is not known, we will continue to use the procedure introduced in Section 12.5. In the case of the one-sample *t*-test, we would use exactly the procedure previously given. We assume that the sample standard deviation is the best available estimate of the population standard deviation, so we assume $\sigma = s$ and proceed as before.

In using this procedure to compute power when the population variability is unknown, we concede that the estimate of power that we obtain is just that—an *estimate*. This approach is justified because the estimate of power computed with this procedure is sufficiently accurate for most applications. Concern with power is more likely to involve whether or not it is near .7 than whether it is .70 or .75.

The *t*-test for Independent Samples

The power of a *t*-test used to compare the means of two independent samples can be estimated with a procedure similar to that for the one-sample case. There are only two differences. One is that the null and alternative hypotheses now refer to the difference between two population means, μ_1 and μ_2. The other is that the appropriate sampling distribution is the distribution of differences between means. We assume that the population standard deviation is equal to the pooled estimate obtained from the two samples. Once again, this is a simplification that allows us to use Table F in Appendix III because the sampling distribution is normal when the population variability is known.

We express effect size in the two-sample case as the difference between two population means, measured in standard deviations. Under H_0 the difference is zero, but under H_1 it is some other value. The formula for effect size is

$$\gamma = \frac{\mu_1 - \mu_2}{\sigma}$$

To compute power with the simplified procedure we need to obtain a statistical effect size, which requires computation of the standard deviation of the sampling distribution of differences between means. The difference between population means then is expressed in terms of this standard deviation. Assuming equal sample sizes of *n*, the standard error of the difference between means is

$$\sigma_{\overline{X}_1 - \overline{X}_2} = \sqrt{\frac{\sigma^2}{n} + \frac{\sigma^2}{n}} = \sqrt{\frac{2\sigma^2}{n}} = \sigma\sqrt{\frac{2}{n}}$$

so the statistical effect size is

$$\delta = \frac{\mu_1 - \mu_2}{\sigma\sqrt{\dfrac{2}{n}}} = \frac{\mu_1 - \mu_2}{\sigma}\sqrt{\frac{n}{2}} \qquad\qquad (12.4)$$

The statistical effect size is equal to effect size multiplied by the square root of sample size over 2.

For example, consider the study described at the beginning of this chapter. Two samples of 20 secretaries are to be trained on two different versions of a word processing program, and the amount of time taken to type a letter during training will be recorded. The null hypothesis is that the two population means are not different. In this case the two populations are defined by the populations of secretaries who potentially could be trained under each system. The alternative hypothesis is that the two population means differ. We will assume that there is a difference of five minutes between the new and the usual training methods $(45 - 50)$. Suppose that when the data are collected the two samples yield a pooled variance estimate of 144, so we assume that the population standard deviation is the square root of 144, or 12. Thus, the effect size is estimated to be

$$\gamma = \frac{45 - 50}{12} = -0.42$$

The statistical effect size is

$$\delta = \frac{45 - 50}{12}\sqrt{\frac{20}{2}} = -0.42(3.16) = -1.33$$

The δ value in Table F that is closest to 1.33 (we ignore negative signs when using Table F) is 1.30. With a nondirectional alternative hypothesis and $\alpha = .05$, Table F indicates that the power of the t-test in this case would be .26, which is the value stated in the introduction to this chapter.

Unequal Sample Sizes

In studies where the two samples are not of the same size, it is necessary to combine the two sample sizes, n_1 and n_2, to produce a single value that can be used in Formula 12.4 to compute the statistical effect size. This operation is done by obtaining the *harmonic mean* of the two sample sizes. In general, the harmonic mean of a set of k sample sizes is obtained by summing the reciprocals of the sample sizes and dividing the result into k:

$$\bar{n} = \frac{k}{\sum\dfrac{1}{n_i}}$$

In this formula n_i represents the different sample sizes. In the case of two sample sizes of 12 and 18, for example, the harmonic mean sample size would be

$$\bar{n} = \frac{2}{\frac{1}{12} + \frac{1}{18}} = \frac{2}{0.139} = 14.39$$

Although the *t*-test and its power can be computed with unequal sample sizes, a researcher can get maximum power from a *t*-test by using equal sample sizes. In the previous example there was a total of 30 subjects. If they had been divided into two groups of equal size, the value of *n* for the statistical effect size would have been 15 instead of 14.39. Remember that statistical effect size, and therefore power, is larger with a greater *n*. In fact, for a given number of subjects in a two-sample study, the greater the difference in the two sample sizes the smaller will be their harmonic mean, and the smaller will be power.

The *t*-test for Dependent Samples

The procedure for computing the power of the *t*-test for dependent samples is very similar to that for the *t*-test for independent samples. For example, effect size is calculated in exactly the same way. The major difference is that an additional population parameter is involved in the measure of the variability of the sampling distribution of differences between means. Recall from Chapter 11 that the variability of this distribution is smaller when there is a larger correlation between pairs of scores. This relationship was evident in Formula 11.12, which is used to compute the variance of the sampling distribution. Formula 12.5 presents an estimate of the standard deviation of the sampling distribution, based on the assumption that the variances of the two populations of scores are the same.

$$\sigma_{\bar{X}_1 - \bar{X}_2} = \sqrt{\frac{\sigma^2}{n} + \frac{\sigma^2}{n} - \frac{2\rho\sigma^2}{n}} \tag{12.5}$$

The statistical effect size would then be

$$\delta = \frac{\mu_1 - \mu_2}{\sqrt{\frac{\sigma^2}{n} + \frac{\sigma^2}{n} - \frac{2\rho\sigma^2}{n}}} = \frac{\mu_1 - \mu_2}{\sigma} \sqrt{\frac{n}{2(1 - \rho)}} \tag{12.6}$$

Formula 12.6 is very similar to the formula for the statistical effect size for the independent samples *t*-test. The only difference is the presence of $(1 - \rho)$, representing the reduction in variability of the sampling distribution due to the correlation between pairs of scores.

The difficulty in applying Formula 12.6 comes in obtaining information about the value of ρ. In practice this might be done by using the data in the study or in a pilot study. An estimate might be obtained before data are collected by searching the literature for other studies that contain estimates of the correlation. Alternatively, if the dependent variable is based on a standardized test, the published reliability of the test could serve as a good approximation to ρ. The reliability of a test sometimes is based on the correlation between scores obtained by the same individuals who take the test on two different occasions. This procedure is similar to the dependent samples t-test in which the same (or matched) people are measured under two different conditions.

For example, consider a researcher who wants to test the null hypothesis that alcohol has no effect on performance on a standardized test of perceptual-motor coordination. Suppose this test consists of sorting cards into piles according to the visual pattern on each card. Among the test materials is information about the reliability of the test, which has been shown to be .80. Let us assume that the average time to take this test actually is increased from 80 to 85 seconds as a result of consuming an ounce of alcohol. Further, assume that the standard deviation of the population of completion time scores is 16. The effect size in this case would be

$$\gamma = \frac{85 - 80}{16} = 0.31$$

and with a sample size of 20, the statistical effect size would be

$$\delta = \frac{85 - 80}{16}\sqrt{\frac{20}{2(1 - .8)}} = 0.31(7.07) = 2.19$$

The researcher is convinced that alcohol consumption could only be detrimental to task performance and therefore opts for a directional alternative hypothesis. The researcher sets $\alpha = .05$. Looking in Table F in Appendix III with a δ value of 2.20 (the closest we can come to 2.19), we see that the power of this test would be .71.

Now consider what the power would have been had the researcher done the study differently. Suppose that the 20 subjects were assigned randomly to two independent groups of 10. The statistical effect size in this case would be

$$\delta = \frac{85 - 80}{16}\sqrt{\frac{10}{2}} = 0.31(2.24) = 0.69$$

This value is less than 1 and so is not included in Table F. Even if the number of subjects tested were doubled, so that there were 20 subjects in each training condition, the statistical effect size would be

$$\delta = \frac{85 - 80}{16}\sqrt{\frac{20}{2}} = 0.31(3.16) = 0.98$$

The closest value in Table F is 1.00, and the corresponding value of power is only .26. This comparison demonstrates that for a given number of subjects the dependent samples t-test, in which all subjects are exposed to both treatments, is more powerful than the independent samples t-test. A researcher can increase power by selecting the dependent samples design whenever it is feasible to use this method of administering treatments to subjects.

Correlation Coefficient

It is possible to compute the power of the significance test for the Pearson correlation coefficient. We will deal only with the case in which the null hypothesis is $\rho = 0$. If H_0 is false, ρ is some other value. The size of the difference between the true value of the correlation coefficient, ρ_1, and the value specified by H_0, ρ_0, is the effect size.

$$\gamma = \rho_1 - \rho_0$$

There is no need to divide by a standard deviation because computation of the correlation coefficient includes converting raw scores to standard scores.

The standard deviation of the sampling distribution of r can be expressed as $1/\sqrt{n-1}$, where n is the sample size, so the statistical effect size is obtained by Formula 12.7:

$$\delta = (\rho_1 - \rho_0)\sqrt{n-1} \tag{12.7}$$

The value of δ that is obtained with Formula 12.7 can then be used with Table F in Appendix III to determine the power of the significance test for r.

Suppose that a researcher wants to study the relationship between the amount of television viewing and the degree of aggressive behavior exhibited by schoolchildren. Let us say the researcher adopts the null hypothesis that there is no relationship and decides to test it against the alternative hypothesis that there is some linear relationship. A sample of 20 schoolchildren is drawn randomly from a local school district, and each child is measured on the number of hours of weekly television viewing and the level of aggressiveness as rated by the child's teacher. The researcher sets α at .05 for the significance test of r. In this case, we will assume that, unknown to the researcher, the true value of ρ is .40. According to Formula 12.6 the effect size is

$$\gamma = .40 - 0 = .40$$

and the statistical effect size is

$$\delta = (.40 - 0)\sqrt{20 - 1} = .40(4.36) = 1.74$$

Consulting Table F with $\delta = 1.70$ (our best approximation to 1.74) and $\alpha = .05$ with a nondirectional H_1, we find a power of .40.

Randomization Tests

It is not feasible to compute power estimates for randomization tests because there is no simple way to express effect size. But the power of randomization tests is sensitive to the same factors as the power of corresponding random sample tests. Also, in many instances the power of a randomization test is similar to the power of the corresponding random sample test (e.g., Collier & Baker, 1966). Therefore, the power of a randomization test may be estimated by computing the power of the appropriate random sample test.

12.7   POWER IN PRACTICE

We have shown how power can be computed for a number of different significance tests. The explanations we provided were presented in the context of idealized examples in which the true value of the effect size was known and our only objective was to obtain an estimate of power. In practice, however, we never have perfectly reliable information about the true value of effect size. In this section we deal with how estimates of effect size might be obtained.

In addition, there are two very important practical reasons for computing power. The first is that in the course of designing a study, we can take steps to maximize power and we can determine how large a sample size is needed to obtain a given level of power. Second, if the results of a study fail to provide evidence for rejection of the null hypothesis, it is useful to know whether the study had a reasonable chance of producing results that would have allowed rejection. If it turns out that power was very low in a study that failed to reject H_0, there would be grounds to continue being suspicious of H_0.

Estimation of Effect Size

In practice, the true effect size can only be estimated because perfectly reliable information about its value is not available. If it were, there would be no need to do the study. One method of estimating effect size is to review the results of related studies. For example, if a researcher is studying the difference between two different instructional methods, the existing body of data on studies of instructional effects can be consulted. Research reports usually contain information about means and variances that can be used to produce estimates of effect sizes for various instructional methods. These estimates can be used to get an idea of how large the present instructional effect size might be. If the present instructional method is similar to one that has been used before, it should have a similar effect size; if it is assumed to be superior, it should have a larger effect size.

A second procedure is to determine what would be an *important* effect size. It is possible to do a study involving a very large number of subjects that will have an excellent chance of rejecting H_0, even though effect size is extremely small and of no practical importance. For this reason it sometimes is useful to estimate effect size by considering how large an effect would be considered important. For example, suppose that a company is contemplating an aptitude test to help select employees who show promise for high productivity. The test would be administered to each applicant and scores would be considered in selection decisions. If test scores can be shown to be correlated with job performance, the company would be interested in using the test. The company wants to design a study so that the power of the correlation coefficient is high enough to find a significant correlation if one exists. In calculating the power of the test, the company needs to estimate the effect size.

Consider two different cases. In one, the company already has an employee selection procedure that has been shown to have a correlation of .4 with job performance. Under these circumstances the company probably would not consider using a new test that had a weaker correlation with job performance. There would be little point in designing a study so that the correlation coefficient would be powerful enough to detect an effect size as small as .3. An effect of this size would not be important in this case. It is likely that effect sizes of greater than .4 would be considered important. In the second case, a company does not yet have a selection procedure that is correlated with job performance. For this company, detecting a correlation of .3 between an aptitude test and performance might be very important.

In cases where there are no specific indications of how large an effect size should be expected or would be important, one can use guidelines suggested by Cohen (1977). A researcher need only decide which one of three general categories the expected effect size is likely to fit: small, medium, or large. For example, in an experiment designed to test for the effects of different kinds of classroom lighting (florescent versus incandescent) on children's intellectual performance, it seems reasonable to expect only a small effect size. Many factors other than lighting have powerful effects on learning. On the other hand one might expect a large effect size when testing the effects of high doses of alcohol on perceptual-motor coordination.

Cohen (1977) advocated a specific effect size for each of these categories, and that value could be used in computing power. One set of effect sizes was proposed for t-tests and another for tests of the correlation coefficient. For t-tests, a small effect size is taken to be .2, a medium effect size is .5, and a large effect size is .8. For the correlation coefficient small, medium, and large effect sizes are .10, .30, and .50, respectively.

Maximizing Power

The factors that affect power can be influenced to some degree by the researcher. The level of α and the form of the alternative hypothesis are determined by the researcher before carrying out a study. Although both of these factors are primarily governed by conventional rules (e.g., $\alpha = .05$ and a nondirectional H_1), there are circumstances in which a higher α (e.g., a pilot study) or a directional H_1 are warranted.

Variability in a set of scores is difficult to control, but a careful researcher has some means of minimizing variance. Working with a homogeneous sample of subjects (e.g., similar age and educational level) is a first step. Another strategy is to ensure that all subjects are treated in as similar a manner as possible. That is, the methods of administering treatments, if any, and of measuring the variable(s) of interest should be applied in the same way to each subject. For example, the behavior of the researcher who interacts with the subjects should be as uniform as possible from one subject to the next. Variability in the researcher's behavior or the use of different researchers who interact with subjects in different ways will introduce additional variability in scores, which will reduce power.

In studies involving comparison of two different treatments and the use of a two-sample *t*-test (independent or dependent samples), a researcher has some control over effect size. In the operational definition of the independent variable, the researcher specifies how the subjects are to be treated. In general, the greater the difference in the treatments administered, the larger will be the effect size. For instance, suppose that a researcher plans a study to determine whether a drug can reduce the amount of hyperactive behavior in children. The researcher would want to administer a sufficiently high dose of the drug to those subjects in the drug condition to have a chance of creating a large effect size. If the dose is too low, the effect size might be so small as to produce a very low level of power. Furthermore, the use of the dependent samples design generally produces a more powerful *t*-test than the independent samples design.

Sample size is one factor that the researcher has great freedom to determine, with the exception that there usually is some upper limit on how many subjects can be tested. Rather than trying to test as many subjects as possible, however, a researcher can use knowledge about the estimated effect size to determine how large a sample size is needed to attain a particular level of power. This figure is calculated by using the appropriate formula for statistical effect size and solving for *n*.

In the case of the one-sample *t*-test, Formula 12.3 (page 308) shows that the statistical effect size is equal to the effect size multiplied by the square root of the sample size. Solving for *n*, we have

$$n = \frac{\delta^2}{\gamma^2} \qquad (12.8)$$

To determine the sample size required to obtain a given level of power, we consult Table F in Appendix III under the appropriate value for α and type of H_1. The corresponding value for δ is entered in Formula 12.8 along with the estimated effect size, γ.

Consider an example in which a researcher wishes to demonstrate that, on the average, high school students who have taken a special course in preparation for the Scholastic Aptitude Test (SAT) obtain higher scores than the national average score of 500. The null hypothesis is that the average score of the students who have taken the training is equal to the national average. A random sample of students who have taken the training will be drawn and their SAT scores obtained. Then a one-sample *t*-test will be performed to test H_0 against a nondirectional alternative with $\alpha = .05$.

It is assumed that the program is able to produce at least a medium effect size, so according to Cohen's (1977) guidelines the effect size should be .50.

The researcher wants to draw a large enough sample to achieve a power of .80. We can consult Table F to find the statistical effect size that corresponds to this level of power. We first find the value of .80 for a nondirectional H_1 and $\alpha = .05$, then read across to find the corresponding statistical effect size, 2.80. The estimated effect size is .50, so our estimate of the necessary sample size is

$$n = \frac{2.80^2}{.50^2} = 31.36$$

Rounding to the nearest whole number produces a required sample size of 31 students to ensure a power of .80 under the assumptions we have described.

A similar procedure can be used to determine minimum sample sizes for *t*-tests of two means and for the correlation coefficient. In the case of the *t*-test for two independent samples, Formula 12.4 indicates that the statistical effect size is equal to the effect size multiplied by the square root of *n*, divided by 2. Solving for *n* we have

$$n = \frac{2\delta^2}{\gamma^2}$$

For example, suppose that in a study the anticipated effect size is .7 and that $\alpha = .05$ with a nondirectional H_1. We can find the number of subjects required in each of the two samples to achieve a particular level of power, say, .85. Table F in Appendix III shows that for power to equal .85 under the present circumstances, a statistical effect size of 3.00 is needed. The estimated sample size would be

$$n = \frac{2(3.00)^2}{.70^2} = 36.73$$

Rounding produces a demand for 37 subjects in *each* of the two samples.

Now suppose that in the previous example, a *t*-test for two *dependent* samples is to be carried out. We can find the required number of subjects by using Formula 12.6 and solving for *n*:

$$n = \frac{2(1 - \rho)\delta^2}{\gamma^2} \tag{12.9}$$

The only additional information we need to compute the required *n* involves the degree of correlation between scores in the two conditions, ρ. For this example we will assume that $\rho = .3$. From Formula 12.9 we have

$$n = \frac{2(1 - .3)(3.00)^2}{.70^2} = 25.71$$

Thus, a single sample of 26 subjects, each tested under two different conditions, should be used to achieve a power of .85.

For the two kinds of *t*-test, compare the sample sizes required to achieve power of .85. Notice that many fewer subjects are required with the dependent samples test. That test requires only one sample of 26, compared with two samples of 37 each (a total of 74 subjects) required by the independent samples t-test. We see that the dependent samples design requires fewer subjects to achieve the same amount of power as the independent samples design.

To determine the sample size required to achieve a particular level of power when working with the correlation coefficient, we can use Formula 12.7. Solving for n yields

$$n = \frac{\delta^2}{\gamma^2} + 1 \qquad (12.10)$$

Suppose that we wish to do a correlational study to find a significant correlation between two variables with $\alpha = .05$ and a nondirectional H_1. We assume that previous research suggests that the true population correlation is .5 rather than zero, as claimed by H_0. Thus, we believe there is a true effect size of 0.50. How many subjects should be sampled so that power will be .95? Table F indicates that this level of power corresponds to a statistical effect size of 3.60, so using Formula 12.10 we have

$$n = \frac{3.60^2}{.50^2} + 1 = 52.84$$

This result gives $n = 53$ with rounding.

Failing to Reject the Null Hypothesis

When the results of a study lead a researcher to decide that the null hypothesis should not be rejected, there are two possible explanations for the outcome. One is that H_0 is true. The other is that although H_0 is *false*, this particular study produced a set of results that did not allow the rejection of H_0. The second alternative is especially plausible when a study is designed so that the statistical test is not very powerful. When a test has low power, there is a high probability of a Type II error. Therefore, it is very useful to compute power when the results of a study do not allow H_0 to be rejected. If power is found to be low, we know that there is a good chance of obtaining results that would not allow the rejection of H_0. The appropriate conclusion in this case would be that the null hypothesis may or may not be true and a more powerful test should be performed.

On the other hand, if power is found to be high, a different explanation for the nonsignificant results is warranted. The explanation is that effect size (used in computing power) probably is not as large as we had assumed. If we were to recompute power with a smaller effect size, we might find that our statistical test was not so powerful after all, and we might wish to conduct a new and more powerful study. Alternatively, we might find that even when the smallest effect size of any importance is assumed, power still turns out to be high. In this case we would be justified in claiming that the failure to find a significant result is evidence that no effect size of any importance exists.

Consider an example in which a company wishes to assess a new method of training employees to work on an assembly line. A study is designed to measure the time taken to perform some assembly task. Two randomly assigned groups of 20 workers each are tested. One group is given the special training program prior to testing and the other is not. A summary of the results of this hypothetical study is shown in Table 12.2. The researcher finds that the value of t is not significant with $\alpha = .05$ and a nondirectional alternative hypothesis. Before reporting to the company, the researcher decides to find out whether the study was powerful enough to detect an effect that would be large enough to be important to the company.

The researcher works from the company's claim that the training method would have to reduce average assembly time by at least ten seconds to be worth the cost of its implementation. The results of the study can be used to estimate the standard deviation of the population of assembly times. The pooled estimate for σ^2 is 110.5, so the estimate for σ is 10.51. Therefore, the effect size of interest in this case is

$$\gamma = \frac{10}{10.51} = 0.95$$

and the statistical effect size is

$$\delta = 0.95 \sqrt{\frac{20}{2}} = 3.00$$

From Table F in Appendix III we find that a statistical effect size of 3.00 with $\alpha = .05$ and a nondirectional alternative hypothesis yields a power of .85. Therefore, the study had a high level of power to detect an improvement of at least ten seconds. The failure to reject H_0 in this case means that the researcher could reasonably claim that the training method does not produce enough improvement in performance to warrant implementation.

Table 12.2 RESULTS OF A STUDY OF ASSEMBLY TIMES

	Group	
	No training	Training
$\overline{X}$	95.4	91.2
s	11.0	10.0
n	20	20

$s_p^2 = 110.5$ $t = 1.26$

It would not be reasonable for the researcher to claim that the training method produced no improvement at all (i.e., H_0 is true). To see this limitation, suppose that training actually led to an average improvement of four seconds. Would the researcher's study have had a high level of power to detect a difference this small? The effect size would be

$$\gamma = \frac{4}{10.51} = 0.38$$

and the statistical effect size would be

$$\delta = 0.38 \sqrt{\frac{20}{2}} = 1.20$$

Table F shows that in this case power would be only .22. So the study had little chance of finding evidence for such a small effect size. Conceivably, an effect size of at least four seconds exists, and the researcher's study probably would fail to detect it.

SUMMARY

It is possible that even when the null hypothesis is false, a study may fail to produce results that will allow its rejection. As a result, whenever a researcher fails to reject H_0, it is important to interpret the result in terms of how likely the study was to produce a result that would have allowed rejection. We use the term *power* to refer to the rejection of a false H_0 and to the probability that a statistical test will result in such a rejection. A number of factors influence the power of a test. One of the most important is effect size. In a one-sample t-test, effect size refers to the difference between the actual value of μ and the value claimed by H_0. For the two-sample t-test, effect size is the true difference between the two population means, and for the correlation coefficient it is the true value of ρ.

In general, the larger the effect size, the more powerful will be the statistical test. Power is also greater when (1) larger sample sizes are used, (2) larger values of α can be used, (3) a directional alternative hypothesis is used, (4) variability in scores is relatively low, and (5) a two-sample design uses dependent rather than independent samples. When designing a study a researcher has some amount of control over a number of the factors that affect power, particularly sample size and choice of dependent or independent samples designs.

Computing power requires estimates of variability in scores and effect size. These estimates can be obtained from reports of previous research or a pilot study. In addition, an effect size estimate may be based on consideration of how large an effect would be considered important. Estimates of power are particularly useful when nonsignificant results are obtained. When a nonsignificant result is produced by a powerful test of H_0, the researcher has some basis for the claim that, although the true effect may not be zero, it is not likely to be as large as the estimate used in computing power.

KEY WORDS

power	statistical effect size
rejection criterion	harmonic mean
effect size	

PROBLEMS

1 When evaluating a research finding are you more likely to compute power when a finding is significant (reject H_0) or nonsignificant (fail to reject H_0)?

2 In a research report the following expressions are used. In which cases are you likely to want to compute power?
(a) $t < 1$, (b) $t = 12.24$, (c) $p > .10$, (d) $p < .01$

3 Assume that you are planning to carry out a two-sample study. Make a list of the features of the study that you should consider in order to maximize power.

4 In a one-sample study involving 30 subjects, the null hypothesis is that the population mean is 75. The alternative hypothesis is that the population mean is larger than that. Compute the power of the t-test with $\alpha = .05$ and assuming $\sigma = 4.2$ and $\mu = 77$. How many subjects would have to be included in the sample for power to be .95?

5 A statistics instructor places a number on each one of a set of plastic poker chips. The numbers are selected so that the mean value is 80, the standard deviation is 20, and the distribution of values is approximately normal. The chips are placed in a cloth bag and taken to class. Each of the 60 students in the class is asked to test the null hypothesis that the mean of the numbered chips is 80. This test is to be done by having each student select a random sample with replacement of 20 chips and record the values. Then each student carries out a one-sample t-test with a nondirectional alternative hypothesis and $\alpha = .05$. How many of the students do you think will obtain a significant t value?

6 In Problem 5, what would be your answer if the instructor had asked the students to test the null hypothesis that $\mu = 75$ and the alternative hypothesis that $\mu > 75$?

7 Suppose that data from young adults on a test involving memory for spatial locations of objects indicate that, on the average, people can remember the locations of eight objects with a standard deviation of 2. Similar data are to be collected for a random sample of 25 older adults, and a one-sample t-test will be computed to determine whether older people are able to perform at the same level of skill as younger adults. The test will be based on a directional H_1 (older adults cannot remember as much) and $\alpha = .05$. We assume that the value of σ for the older adults is the same as for younger adults.
(a) Draw a diagram reflecting the sampling distribution of the mean for the performance of the older people under the assumption that their mean is equal to

that of the younger people. Draw vertical lines indicating the location of the population mean and the rejection criterion. Write the numerical value for each line at the bottom of the diagram, as was done in Figure 12.2.

(b) Draw another diagram representing the sampling distribution of the mean for the older people under the assumption that their average performance is seven rather than eight items correct. Draw a vertical line representing this population mean and another to represent the rejection criterion, and write in the numerical value of each.

(c) Indicate in the second diagram the region of rejection. Use Table B in Appendix III to find the area in the region of rejection and the area in the remainder of the distribution. What do you conclude to be the probability of a Type II error?

(d) Assuming that the true population mean for older people is 7, what would be the power of a one-sample t-test if the sample consisted of 64 subjects?

8 (a) What is the power of a two-sample t-test to detect a medium effect size (as per Cohen, 1977) with 25 subjects in each condition, $\alpha = .01$, and a nondirectional alternative hypothesis?

(b) How many subjects would be needed in each condition for power to be .70?

(c) If the 50 subjects were used instead in a dependent samples design, what would be the power of the t-test, assuming the correlation between scores in the two conditions is .35?

(d) How many subjects would be needed in the dependent samples design for power to be .85?

9 A researcher plans to compare the effectiveness of two different methods of improving foreign language vocabulary. One method consists of using a foreign word in an English sentence, and the other involves finding an English word that sounds like the foreign word and then forming a mental image of the objects representing the foreign and English words interacting in some way. A group of 60 students is divided randomly into two groups, each group receiving a different method of training. Following training on a set of 50 items, the subjects are given French words and try to recall their English equivalents. Previous research with the second method indicates that on the average it improves performance over rote memorization by about 10 items on a 50-item test. The standard deviation of scores on the test is about 12.

(a) The researcher decides to (i) use a nondirectional H_1, (ii) set $\alpha = .05$, (iii) randomly assign 22 subjects to the sentence method and 38 to the word method, and (iv) compute power by assuming $\sigma = 12$ and $\gamma = 0.8$. Justify or criticize each of these decisions.

(b) Given the decisions listed in part (a), what value for power would the researcher compute for this t-test?

(c) Suppose that the researcher decided to use a dependent samples design and only 30 subjects. Each of the subjects is to study two lists of 50 words, one list with each method. Assuming that the correlation between scores in these two conditions would be $\rho = 0.2$, what would be the power of the dependent sample t-test? If we assume $\rho = .5$, what would be the power of the test? What would be the power if there were no correlation (i.e., $\rho = 0$)? Can you make a general statement about the influence of ρ on the power of a dependent sample t-test?

10 A social psychologist learns that a remote village in northern Canada is scheduled to begin receiving television signals for the first time. This is seen as an opportunity to study the influence of television on social skills among children. The re-

searcher plans to administer a test of social interaction skill to the village's children just prior to the introduction of television signals and again one year later. A dependent samples t-test will be used to test for differences with a nondirectional H_1 and $\alpha = .05$. The measure of social interaction typically produces a raw score standard deviation of 18. Further, it is assumed that the correlation between scores obtained before and after the introduction of television will be about 0.7 (this is the published reliability of the test). But the researcher is not clear about what will be the effect size. Therefore, Cohen's (1977) guidelines are to be used in a power analysis. For each of Cohen's three effect sizes, find the power of the dependent sample t-test for a sample size of 16.

11 What is the power of a test of the null hypothesis that $\rho = 0$ under a nondirectional alternative hypothesis, with $\alpha = .05$, a sample size of 35, and an estimated true ρ of .6? What is the power if $\alpha = .01$?

12 A researcher is interested in finding evidence for a correlation between scores on the Graduate Record Examination (GRE) and later success in graduate school. The GRE scores and graduate school performance ratings for a random sample of 100 people who recently completed graduate school in North America are to be obtained. What is the likelihood that the researcher will find a significant correlation by using a directional alternative hypothesis $(\rho > 0)$ and $\alpha = .01$, assuming that the true correlation is .3? What would be the power if we assumed that the true correlation were only .15? Assuming the true correlation is .15, how many subjects would be needed in the sample for power to be .75?

13 To study the possible influence of physical exercise on mental depression, a researcher randomly assigns 48 volunteers from a depression therapy program to two groups of 24 each. One group receives no special treatment, and the other is asked to increase the average time spent exercising each week by 20 percent. At the end of two months each subject is assessed for level of depression. Scores for the control group produce $\overline{X} = 27$ and $s = 7$, and for the extra exercise group $\overline{X} = 24$ and $s = 6$. The value of t, 1.59, is not significant, with $\alpha = .05$ and a nondirectional H_1.

(a) Using the pooled variance estimate for σ and assuming that there actually is a large effect size of exercise on depression (i.e., $\gamma = .8$), what is the power of this researcher's test?

(b) Based on the outcome of the study, what would you say about the claim that physical exercise has a large effect on depression?

(c) If the claim had been that the effect size was only a small one (i.e., $\gamma = .2$), what would you conclude on the basis of the outcome and the power of this researcher's test?

PART
FOUR

Advanced Research Designs

Although some studies involve comparison of two groups of data, many studies involve more than two groups. The next four chapters deal with research designs having two or more groups of scores. Chapter 13 presents the general case in which any number of independent groups can be compared. The procedure introduced in Chapter 13 is an extension of the t-test of independent means described in Chapter 11. The statistical method, known as analysis of variance (ANOVA), allows the several groups to be compared with a single test.

In some cases ANOVA answers the major question of interest about the relationship among group means. In other cases, more detailed examination of specific pairs of means is required. Chapter 14 deals with different ways in which both planned and unplanned comparisons can be made among several group means.

In Chapter 15 we examine a particular set of planned comparisons that arise when two or more independent variables are treated in a single study. This research design gives rise to a planned comparison called an interaction. Since many behavioral studies include two or more independent variables, their joint effect, or interaction, is an especially important concept.

Finally, Chapter 16 deals with the case in which two or more groups of scores are collected in a dependent groups design. For example, a single set of subjects may be tested under three different treatments or they may be tested three different times with the same treatment. The procedure is an extension of the t-test of dependent samples introduced in Chapter 11.

The statistical tests derived from ANOVA are based in random sampling theory. Often, however, behavioral researchers do not randomly sample but instead, randomly assign subjects to treatments. Therefore, throughout the chapters in this section randomization tests will be discussed as alternatives to more traditional ANOVA procedures.

Chapter 13

Analysis of Variance: One-Factor Designs

13.1   INTRODUCTION

In this chapter and in the next three chapters, we deal with research designs in which two or more groups are compared. The form of the analysis is an extension of the t-test, and the purpose is to decide whether the differences among groups represent random effects or systematic effects. The statistical test involves deciding whether observed differences among samples represent the least likely differences that could occur. If they are among the least likely (e.g., 5 percent or less), we reject the null hypothesis, and if they are not among the least likely, we fail to reject it.

You might ask why we introduce a new procedure to compare more than two means when a series of two-sample t-tests would provide the same information. If you had a study with three means to compare, you could simply use the t-ratio to test three null hypotheses separately: H_0: $\mu_1 = \mu_2$, H_0: $\mu_2 = \mu_3$, H_0: $\mu_1 = \mu_3$.

One problem with a series of t-tests is that the researcher takes multiple opportunities to reject the null hypothesis. When each test has the same criterion, the probability of making a Type I error for the set of comparisons is no longer simply α. Furthermore, as the number of groups being studied increases, the number of possible comparisons increases dramatically. The problem of determining the probability of a Type I error increases as the number and type of comparisons increase. This problem is discussed further in Chapter 14.

A second problem is that each t-test has a different error term. Pooling within-group variation from several groups generally provides a better estimate of the population error than an error term based on only two groups. When the error terms are based on all groups in a study, the comparisons are statistically more powerful.

Basic Terms

We use the word **factor** as a general term that applies to two types of independent variables: manipulated independent variables and measured (or trait) independent variables. A manipulated independent variable involves randomization, either by random assignment of subjects to different treatments (independent samples design) or random ordering of successive treatments (dependent samples design). For example, randomly composed groups might be given different amounts of alcohol (e.g., 0 ounces, 2 ounces, or 4 ounces) before being given a driving test. The implication of this manipulation is that the researcher is in a good position to argue that the alcohol factor *caused* the observed differences in the driving test scores of the several groups.

Measured independent variables involve the classification of subjects into groups according to some feature or trait that the subjects possess. Examples of measured variables that can be treated as factors include such traits as age or IQ of the subject. You might want to study the relationship between mean spelling scores and the grade level of randomly selected schoolchildren. If the children are classified into groups according to their grade (e.g., grades 2, 4, 6, 8), the factor grade in school would be a measured independent variable. With random sampling of subjects, the implication is that observed differences in spelling test scores associated with the grade factor could be *generalized* to the population that was sampled.

FACTOR: An independent variable that can be either a manipulated treatment condition (involving random assignment) or a measured trait (involving classification of subjects into categories).

There are at least two **levels of a factor.** When the independent variable is manipulated, the levels are sometimes called treatment conditions. For the study that randomly assigned subjects to groups receiving different amounts of alcohol, we had one manipulated treatment factor (alcohol) with three levels (treatments 0, 2, 4 ounces). For the example that classified children by grade, we had one classification factor (school grade) with four levels (grades 2, 4, 6, 8).

LEVELS OF A FACTOR: The individual treatments or classification categories that make up the factor.

13.2   COMPARISON OF TWO OR MORE LEVELS OF A FACTOR

As in Chapter 11, we describe two statistical procedures for analysis of group differences. You should recall that the randomization model was designed for situations in which the researcher can randomly assign subjects to treatments or levels of a factor. The normal curve model is designed for cases in which a random process is used in the selection of subjects. Both models can be used when there are two or more levels of a factor.

The Randomization Method

Consider the case in which three levels of a factor lead to three groups of data, a one-factor design with three levels. For this example we will keep the problem relatively simple by having only three subjects randomly assigned to each level of the factor. Thus, our example deals with three groups of three scores each.

Under the assumption of random assignment of subjects to levels, the nine scores might have occurred in any of 1680 possible arrangements, with three subjects in each of three groups.[1] Of course, only one of these 1680 possibilities will be observed in any single experiment. The task of statistical testing is to determine what proportion of the 1680 possibilities yields a summary statistic equal to or larger than the value obtained from one observed arrangement of data.

When we introduced the randomization model in Chapter 9, the summary statistic used was the difference between two means. Here we may have any number of groups and thus need a different statistic, one that takes into account the scores from three or more groups. A useful statistic in this case is based on the square of total scores from each group, T^2 [$T^2 = (\Sigma X)^2$]. Since the groups might vary in size, we use the sample size, n, to weight each squared total, T^2/n. This quantity is computed for each group and the results are added for all groups: $\Sigma(T^2/n)$. Although other statistics besides $\Sigma(T^2/n)$ might be used with the randomization test, we have chosen it because it is also used in the analysis of variance. With either type of test, when the differences between groups are large, the values of $\Sigma(T^2/n)$ are also large.

Assume that our nine hypothetical scores are 1, 2, 3, 4, 5, 6, 7, 8, 9. Table 13.1 gives the distribution of outcomes that could occur with these data when the null hypothesis is true (the null frequency distribution). Note that typically there are several outcomes that have the same value of $\Sigma(T^2/n)$; each outcome may occur in more than one way. Furthermore, the maximum and minimum values of $\Sigma(T^2/n)$ have a smaller frequency of occurrence than most intermediate values. This frequency distribution serves the same function as the sampling distribution of t when the random sampling model is used to assess an outcome with two samples of data. Specifically, the distribution is used to determine the probability of outcomes equal to or larger than the observed outcome.

Let us assume that the observed arrangement of scores is as follows: Group A = 1, 2, 3 ($T = 6$); group B = 4, 5, 7 ($T = 16$); group C = 6, 8, 9 ($T = 23$). We will determine the probability of obtaining $\Sigma(T^2/n)$ for this outcome or larger values of $\Sigma(T^2/n)$ when H_0 is true. First compute the value of the summary statistic for these obtained data:

$$\Sigma(T^2/n) = 6^2/3 + 16^2/3 + 23^2/3$$

$$= 12 \quad + 85.33 + 176.33 = \underline{273.667}$$

Then locate this value in the column labeled "$\Sigma(T^2/n)$" in Table 13.1 and read the corresponding information from the columns on the right. The table

---

[1]Recall from Chapter 8 that the expression $_nC_r$ (Formula 8.1) gives the number of ways that n elements can be combined when considered r at a time. With nine subjects divided into three groups, you first consider how many ways six subjects (two groups) can be taken from nine subjects. Then you find how many ways those six can be assigned to groups of three. Finally you multiply the two results: $(_9C_6)(_6C_3) = (84)(20) = 1680$. A useful alternative formula when there are several samples of equal or unequal size is $N!/(n_1!)(n_2!) \ldots (n_k!)$ or $9!/(3!3!3!) = 1680$.

Table 13.1   DISTRIBUTION OF POSSIBLE
OUTCOMES WITH THREE GROUPS
OF THREE SCORES

$\Sigma(T^2/n)$	f	p	cum p
224.000	12	.00714	1.00000
225.667	108	.06429	.99286
227.000	84	.05000	.92857
227.667	84	.05000	.87857
229.667	180	.10714	.82857
231.000	96	.05714	.72143
233.000	60	.03571	.66429
233.667	144	.08571	.62857
235.667	54	.03214	.54286
237.667	120	.07143	.51071
239.000	96	.05714	.43929
241.667	36	.02143	.38214
243.000	36	.02143	.36071
243.667	72	.04286	.33929
245.667	72	.04286	.29643
249.000	36	.02143	.25357
249.667	60	.03571	.23214
251.000	48	.02857	.19643
253.667	48	.02857	.16786
257.000	12	.00714	.13929
257.667	54	.03214	.13214
259.667	24	.01429	.10000
263.000	24	.01429	.08571
265.667	36	.02143	.07143
267.000	36	.02143	.05000	Region of rejection with alpha of .05
267.667	6	.00357	.02857
269.667	24	.01429	.02500
273.667	12	.00714	.01071
279.000	6	.00357	.00357
Total	1680	1.00000	

shows that there are 12 arrangements of the data, with a summary value of 273.667. Thus, the probability of this specific value of $\Sigma(T^2/n)$ is

$$p(273.667) = 12/1680 = .00714$$

The only possible outcome greater than 273.667 is 279, and this value has a probability of .00357. Thus, the probability of the observed value or larger values is

$$p(273.667 \text{ or larger}) = p(273.667) + p(279)$$
$$= .00714 + .00357 = \underline{.01071}$$

Since the probability of the observed outcome and larger outcomes is less than $\alpha = .05$, we reject H_0, that this arrangement of scores is a random outcome.

A problem with using the randomization model as a statistical test is that the number of possible arrangements increases very rapidly even for small increases in sample size. If we add only one score to each of three groups, so that $n = 4$ ($N = 12$), the total possible arrangements of the 12 scores is 34,650. Without access to a computer program designed to handle this type of testing, the task becomes very tedious. That is one reason why the random sampling model has become so widely used to estimate probabilities that would be obtained with the randomization test. In most circumstances it requires much less computational effort to obtain approximately the same probability value as the randomization test. The computer program NPSTAT computes both normal curve tests and randomization tests for two to eight samples.

The Normal Curve Method

The statistical procedure we use here is known as *analysis of variance*, or ANOVA. Developed by the English statistician Sir Ronald Fisher, it has become one of the most widely used statistical testing techniques in behavioral research. Several variations of the procedure have been developed for different research problems, and in this book we provide only a limited introduction to the topic. This chapter deals with ANOVA for one-factor designs involving independent samples.

The analysis of variance has several similarities to the *t*-ratio discussed earlier. The notions of normal distributions, homogeneous population variances, and random sampling apply as before. When subjects have been randomly sampled, ANOVA can be used with either manipulated or measured factors (or both at the same time; see Chapter 15). When subjects are not randomly sampled, but instead a factor is manipulated through random assignment, ANOVA and the normal curve model are used to obtain a probability that estimates the value expected with the randomization test. In both of these cases the computations are the same, but the type of random process (random sampling or random assignment) affects the interpretation of results (generality or cause).

13.3   THE NULL AND ALTERNATIVE HYPOTHESES

In the analysis of variance, scores from subjects are designated as coming from one of k different populations, where k is the number of levels of a factor. Several populations may be identified by subscripts such as 1, 2, 3, or a, b, c. The means of these populations can then be identified as μ_1, μ_2, and so on up to μ_k. The null hypothesis states that if the populations do not differ on the characteristic being measured, we expect their means to be equal:

$$H_0: \mu_1 = \mu_2 = \mu_3 = \ldots = \mu_k$$

When the group means, which are estimates of the population means, are sufficiently deviant from one another, the null hypothesis is rejected.

When the number of groups exceeds two, the alternative hypothesis is often not very specific. A nonspecific or "omnibus" alternative hypothesis states that the null hypothesis may be false in any of several ways. For example, two means may be the same but both may differ from a third mean, and this difference can occur in different ways:

$$\mu_1 = \mu_2 \neq \mu_3$$

$$\mu_2 = \mu_3 \neq \mu_1$$

$$\mu_3 = \mu_1 \neq \mu_2$$

Therefore, the usual alternative hypothesis is that not all means are equal.

H_1: Not all μs are equal.

More specific alternative hypotheses are not tested in this chapter. They require testing by related methods called multiple comparison procedures, which are dealt with in Chapter 14.

13.4 GENERAL LOGIC OF THE ANALYSIS

To illustrate the general logic used in ANOVA, we use a one-factor study involving three groups and $N = 15$ scores. Subjects were randomly assigned to groups that received different amounts of alcohol (0 ounces, 2 ounces, or 4 ounces). Although the group sizes could be equal, we have let them be unequal: $n_1 = 5$, $n_2 = 4$, and $n_3 = 6$. After consuming the alcohol, the subjects were asked to drive a car while their performance was rated by a police officer. They were assigned pass/fail responses on each of ten tasks (e.g., starting, braking, etc.), and the total number of failed tasks (zero to ten) were recorded for each subject. The data for each group has been plotted as frequency distributions in Figure 13.1. Each of the three groups has a sample mean, $\overline{X}_j$, and the mean of all groups taken together is a *grand mean*, which we label *GM*.

Total Variation

At the foot of Figure 13.1 is a frequency distribution of all 15 scores. It makes sense to consider the amount of variability in these scores taken together because if the null hypothesis is true, the scores from all groups can be considered to come from a single population. The variability here is the deviation

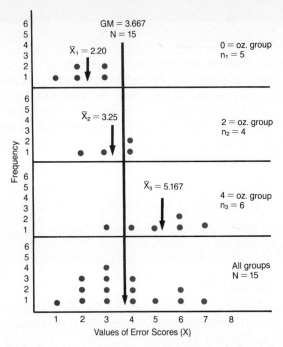

Figure 13.1 Frequency distributions of driving error scores for three groups with means $\bar{X}_1$, $\bar{X}_2$, $\bar{X}_3$, and the total sample of 15 scores with mean *GM*.

of each raw score, *X*, from the grand mean, *GM*. These $X - GM$ deviations represent the *total* amount of variability in our sample scores. When they are squared and summed across all cases, the result is referred to as SS_{total} or SS_t.

Of course the null hypothesis might not be true. We test that possibility by partitioning the total amount of variability into two distinct parts referred to as *within*-group variation and *between*-group variation. As illustrated in Figure 13.2, when the null hypothesis is true, each of the parts will represent variation due to random factors such as sampling error. When the null is not true, part of the between-group variation will be attributed to systematic rather than random differences between groups. Of all the variation in a set of scores, some portion of it can be explained or accounted for by group membership defined by either treatment differences or trait differences.

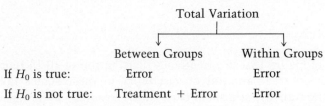

Figure 13.2 Partitioning of total variation into between-group variation and within-group variation.

Explainable variation comes from the effect of the independent variable. Thus, depending on the type of research, the amount of this variation is affected by manipulated treatment differences or measured trait differences related to the dependent variable being measured. For convenience, we use the term *group* to refer to variation of this type, but you should keep in mind that between-group variation refers to effects from either type of independent variable.

Within-Group Variation

As shown in Figure 13.1 subjects within each group have different scores. Their scores vary from one another even though they were all given the same treatment (e.g., they all consumed 4 ounces of alcohol before being tested).

This subject-to-subject variation can be expressed as the deviation of individual scores, X, from the mean of the sample to which the subjects belong, $\overline{X}_j$. These $X - \overline{X}_j$ deviations represent unexplained sources of variation, sometimes referred to as "inherent variation" or "experimental error." When these deviations are squared and summed across all cases, the resulting quantity is called **within-group variation,** and is referred to as SS_{within} or SS_w.

WITHIN-GROUP VARIATION: Variation among the subjects in the same treatment group or the same trait group, $X - \overline{X}_j$. This variation is considered to be error variation independent of between-group variation.

To illustrate the nature of within-group variation, we use two examples. First, consider two identical sets of data, where group 1 scores are 1, 2, 3, and group 2 scores are 1, 2, 3. The mean of each group is $6/3 = 2$. The deviations of each score from this mean are $1 - 2 = -1$, $2 - 2 = 0$, and $3 - 2 = +1$. Of course, the sum of these raw deviations is zero, as it would be for any set of data. The sum of the squared deviations is $(-1)^2 + (0)^2 + (+1)^2 = 2$ for each group.

In our second example, we add a constant of 2 to each score in group 2 to simulate the effect of a treatment factor (raw scores are now 3, 4, 5). Now the within-group variation is based on the following deviations: $3 - 4 = -1$, $4 - 4 = 0$, and $5 - 4 = +1$. Squaring and summing these deviations results in a value of 2, just as in the first case. This exercise shows that the amount of variation of scores within a group is independent of their absolute value. Even if all the scores in one group are larger than all the scores in a second group, the amount of variation within each group can be identical.

As was the case in the two-sample t-ratio, we assume that all populations have the same variance. This is equivalent to assuming that the variation within each sample is an estimate of the common population variance. That is, we assume that $\sigma_1^2 = \sigma_2^2 = \ldots = \sigma_k^2 = \sigma^2$.

In behavioral research an important source of within-group variation is the individual differences in the subjects themselves. Each person who contributes a score has a unique combination of genetic features and behavioral experiences. These factors lead to a certain amount of subject-to-subject variation in scores regardless of the way in which the data are collected.

Another source of within-group variation is the testing environment, which includes the way the researcher presents stimuli, the way the responses are scored, and so on. Even though the researcher attempts to standardize procedures for presenting stimuli and recording responses, some variation in procedure is bound to be present. This combination of genetic and behavioral differences in the subjects and the measurement errors associated with obtaining the scores contributes to within-group variation. Generally, within-group variation is treated as an unexplained variation, or "error variation."

Between-Group Variation

Figure 13.1 also illustrates the relationship between the three group means $(\overline{X}_j)$ and the grand mean (GM). The figure illustrates that each of the group means differs from the grand mean by some amount: $\overline{X}_j - GM$.

When H_0 *is true:* According to the null hypothesis, the deviations of group means from the grand mean will be zero. In practice if H_0 is true, observed deviations of the group means from GM will represent only sampling variation. In that case the independent groups can be thought of as coming from the same population because the groups are drawn from normally distributed populations with equal means and equal variances. Thus, if H_0 is true, the variation in the means can be thought of as another estimate of the population variance, σ^2.

When H_0 *is not true:* If H_0 is not true, the deviation of means represents both the error variation associated with random sampling and the variation associated with treatments (or traits). For example, if the groups were treated differently, some portion of the deviations in group means would be explained by the differential treatment. We refer to this type of variation, $\overline{X}_j - GM$, as **between-group variation.** When we square and sum these deviations, the result is referred to as $SS_{between}$, or SS_b.

BETWEEN-GROUP VARIATION: Variation among the means of two or more groups: $\overline{X}_j - GM$. If H_0 is true it represents error variation. If H_0 is not true, it represents both treatment and error variation.

To illustrate the nature of between-group variation, we use examples like those in the discussion of within-group variation. First, consider two identical examples of data, where group 1 scores = 1, 2, 3, and group 2 scores = 1, 2, 3. Clearly, the within-group variation is the same $(SS_1 = SS_2 = 2)$, and the mean for each group is the same $(\overline{X}_1 = \overline{X}_2 = 2)$. Each group mean is equal to their average, the grand mean: $(\overline{X}_1 + \overline{X}_2)/2 = (2 + 2)/2 = 2$. Thus, the deviations of each mean from the grand mean is zero, so we conclude that there is no appreciable between-group difference and H_0 cannot be rejected.

For our second example, we again add a constant of 2 to each score in group 2 (raw scores $= 3, 4, 5$) to simulate the effect of the treatment factor. This addition makes the mean of group 2 equal to 4 $(\overline{X}_2 = 4)$. With $\overline{X}_1 = 2$ and $\overline{X}_2 = 4$, the grand mean is $(2 + 4)/2 = 3$. Now the deviation of the group 1 mean from the grand mean is $2 - 3 = -1$, and the deviation of the group 2 mean from the grand mean is $4 - 3 = +1$. Squaring and summing these deviations gives $(-1)^2 + (+1)^2 = 1 + 1 = 2$. You can see that changing the value of scores in one group did not change the values of the within-group variation (2 in each case). However, the variation between groups is no longer zero, so it may be possible to reject H_0.

The larger the amount of between-group variation relative to within-group variation, the more this quantity can be attributed to treatment or trait variation. With a measured independent variable, the quantity represents error plus the differences associated with a trait (e.g., grade 2 versus grade 8). With a manipulated independent variable, the quantity represents error plus the effect of differences in treatment (e.g., 0 versus 4 ounces of alcohol). In our study of the effects of alcohol on driving scores, large differences between means in the samples receiving 0, 2, or 4 ounces of alcohol would represent variation in driving behavior explained by the effect of alcohol.

The Test Ratio

The procedure we use here is called analysis of *variance*, where variance is defined by the definition used in earlier chapters. It is a sum of squares (SS) divided by degrees of freedom (df):

$$\text{variance} = \frac{\text{sum of squares}}{\text{degrees of freedom}} = \frac{SS}{df}$$

We compute the SS value for all scores, SS_{total}, and then partition this quantity into two parts representing error variation, SS_{within}, and the error plus group variation, $SS_{between}$. We then divide SS_b and SS_w values by their respective degrees of freedom to obtain variance estimates. In the context of ANOVA, the ratio SS/df is called a *mean square*, or MS, to distinguish it from a variance estimate computed from a single sample.

$$MS_b = \frac{SS_{between}}{df_{between}} \quad \text{and} \quad MS_w = \frac{SS_{within}}{df_{within}}$$

Finally, we take a ratio of these mean squares. The test ratio, MS_b/MS_w, is called F after Sir Ronald Fisher, who developed it.

$$F = \frac{MS_b}{MS_w}$$

If the treatment effect is large relative to the error variation, the *F*-ratio is large (MS_b is substantially larger than MS_w). In that case we may have a statistically significant result. If the treatment effect is small relative to the error variation, the *F*-ratio is small and we may not have a significant result.

13.5   COMPUTATION: PARTITIONING THE SS_{total}

The relationship among SS_t, SS_b, and SS_w can be given at the level of an individual score. To illustrate this point we use the data plotted in Figure 13.1, which are also listed in Table 13.2. We have arbitrarily selected the score of six driving errors from a subject in the group that consumed 4 ounces of alcohol before the driving test (see the third column of data in Table 13.2). This raw score deviates from the grand mean by 2.33 units. The deviation consists of two meaningful components: (1) the difference between the group mean and the grand mean (5.17 − 3.67) and (2) the difference between the raw score and the mean of the group to which the score belongs (6 − 5.17).

$$
\begin{aligned}
\text{total} &= \text{between groups} + \text{within groups} \\
(X - GM) &= (\overline{X}_3 - GM) + (X - \overline{X}_3) \\
(6 - 3.67) &= (5.17 - 3.67) + (6 - 5.17) \\
2.33 &= 1.50 + .83
\end{aligned}
$$

Of course, when we consider several scores in each sample, these deviations

Table 13.2   ERROR SCORES FOR 15 SUBJECTS JUDGED ON THEIR DRIVING PERFORMANCE AFTER CONSUMING DIFFERENT AMOUNTS OF ALCOHOL

	Amount of alcohol						
	0 oz		2 oz		4 oz		
	X	X^2	X	X^2	X	X^2	
	1	1	2	4	3	9	
	2	4	3	9	4	16	
	2	4	4	16	5	25	
	3	9	4	16	6	36	
	3	9			6	36	
					7	49	
T_j	11		13		31		$G = 55$
n_j	5		4		6		$N = 15$
$\overline{X}_j$	2.20		3.25		5.17		$GM = 3.67$
ΣX_j^2		27		45		171	$\Sigma X^2 = 243$

must be squared and summed across all cases, as indicated in the following formulas.

In computing SS values for ANOVA we need to distinguish between the total of scores in a given group, T_j, and the total of all scores, G (G = grand total). We can also distinguish between the mean for a given group, $\overline{X}_j$ (where j can vary from 1 to k), and the grand mean of all scores, GM. Keeping these distinctions in mind, Formula 13.1 is used to define group means, and Formula 13.2 is used to define the grand mean.

$$\overline{X}_j = \frac{T_j}{n_j} \qquad \begin{array}{l} \text{where } T_j = \text{total for the } j\text{th group} \\ \text{where } n_j = \text{number of cases in the } j\text{th group} \end{array} \qquad (13.1)$$

$$GM = \frac{G}{N} \qquad \begin{array}{l} \text{where } G = T_1 + T_2 + \ldots + T_k \\ \text{where } N = n_1 + n_2 + \ldots + n_k \end{array} \qquad (13.2)$$

The SS_{total} is the amount of variation in all the scores taken together. Fortunately, computing SS_t is accomplished with procedures already developed in several earlier chapters. Formula 13.3 provides the familiar formula for the sum of squares. The left side is the definitional form, and the right side is a common computational form.

$$SS = \Sigma(X - \overline{X})^2 = \Sigma X^2 - \frac{(\Sigma X)^2}{N} \qquad (13.3)$$

In the notation of ANOVA, this SS value for all scores taken together is

$$SS_t = \Sigma(X - GM)^2 = \Sigma X^2 - \frac{G^2}{N} \qquad (13.4)$$

The SS_{within}

The amount of variation within any given group is found by Formula 13.5:

$$SS_{wj} = \Sigma(X - \overline{X}_j)^2 = \Sigma X^2 - \frac{T_j^2}{n_j} \qquad (13.5)$$

To obtain the total amount of within-group variation for the study as a whole, it is necessary to pool the SS_{wj} from each of the individual groups.

$$SS_{\text{within}} = SS_{w1} + SS_{w2} + \ldots + SS_{wk} \qquad (13.6)$$

The SS_{between}

The SS_{between} can be computed with Formula 13.7. The left-hand side of this formula gives the definition, and the right-hand side gives the common computational form.

$$SS_b = \Sigma n_j(\overline{X}_j - GM)^2 = \Sigma \frac{T_j^2}{n_j} - \frac{G^2}{N} \qquad (13.7)$$

The computational form on the right side of Formula 13.7 should be familiar to you for two reasons. In general it should be familiar because it is a sum of squares. More specifically, the expression $\Sigma(T_j^2/n_j)$ is the same quantity computed as a summary statistic in our earlier introduction of the randomization model for two or more groups.

The relationship between these three SS values is summarized by Formula 13.8. This formula emphasizes that the total variation in a set of scores can be partitioned into two parts, between group variation (the deviations of group means from the grand mean) and within-group variation (pooled deviations of individual scores from group means).

$$SS_t \quad = \quad SS_b \quad + \quad SS_w$$

$$\text{total} = (\text{treatment} + \text{error}) + \text{error}$$

(13.8)

13.6   COMPUTATIONAL EXAMPLE WITH A MANIPULATED FACTOR

The analysis may be carried out with either the definitional version or the computational version of Formulas 13.4 through 13.7. The definitional formulas provide a better understanding of the meaning of what is being computed, but they can be cumbersome to deal with when using real data sets. Their use is illustrated in Box 13.1 for the driving error scores reported in Table 13.2.

The computational versions of these formulas are especially efficient when performing the analysis by hand. Their use is illustrated as follows, using the same data that were analyzed in Box 13.1 using definitional formulas (for the one-factor study, with 15 subjects randomly assigned to groups receiving different amounts of alcohol). We are given the following null hypothesis, omnibus alternative, and alpha level:

H_0: $\mu_1 = \mu_2 = \mu_3 = \ldots = \mu_k$

H_1: Not all μs are equal

$\alpha = .05$

Application of Computational Formulas

Sum of Squares Total

$$SS_t = \Sigma X^2 - \frac{G^2}{N}$$

$$= (1^2 + 2^2 + \ldots + 7^2) - \frac{55^2}{15}$$

$$= 243 - 201.67 = \underline{41.33}$$

Box 13.1 **Computation of Sums of Squares with Definitional Formulas**

Subject Number	Group ID	X Score	SS_{total} $X - GM$	SS_{total} $(X - GM)^2$	SS_{within} $X - \bar{X}_j$	SS_{within} $(X - \bar{X}_j)^2$
1	0	1	−2.667	7.113	−1.200	1.440
2	0	2	−1.667	2.779	−0.200	.040
3	0	2	−1.667	2.779	−0.200	.040
4	0	3	−0.667	.445	.800	.640
5	0	3	−0.667	.445	.800	.640
Sum					(0)	(2.800)
6	2	2	−1.667	2.779	−1.250	1.560
7	2	3	−0.667	.445	−0.250	.063
8	2	4	.333	.111	.750	.563
9	2	4	.333	.111	.750	.563
Sum					(0)	(2.749)
10	4	3	−0.667	.445	−2.167	4.696
11	4	4	.333	.111	−1.167	1.362
12	4	5	1.333	1.777	−0.167	.028
13	4	6	2.333	5.443	.833	.694
14	4	6	2.333	5.443	.833	.694
15	4	7	3.333	11.109	1.833	3.360
Sum					(0)	(10.834)
Grand total		55	0.000	41.333		(16.383)

$$SS_t = \Sigma(X - GM)^2 = \Sigma(X - 3.667)^2$$

$$= \underline{41.333}$$

$$SS_w = SS_{w1} + SS_{w2} + SS_{w3}$$

$$= 2.800 + 2.749 + 10.834 = \underline{16.383}$$

$$SS_b = \Sigma n_j (\bar{X}_j - GM)^2$$

$$= 5(2.20 - 3.667)^2 + 4(3.25 - 3.667)^2 + 6(5.167 - 3.667)^2$$

$$= 10.756 + .695 + 13.500 = \underline{24.951}$$

Box 13.2　**Simplified Computation of SS_b When Samples Are of Equal Size**

To compute SS_b with equal group sizes, you can sum the squared group totals and then divide *once* by the common group size n. This is more efficient than dividing each squared total by n. As an example, assume we have group totals of 11, 13, and 31 from three groups, where $n = 5$ subjects in each group.

For equal group sizes only:

$$SS_b = \frac{T_1^2 + \ldots + T_k^2}{n} - \frac{G^2}{N}$$

$$= \frac{11^2 + 13^2 + 31^2}{5} - \frac{55^2}{15}$$

$$= \frac{1251}{5} - \frac{3025}{15} = \underline{48.53}$$

For either equal or unequal group sizes:

$$SS_b = \frac{T_1^2}{n_1} + \ldots + \frac{T_k^2}{n_k} - \frac{G^2}{N}$$

$$= \frac{11^2}{5} + \frac{13^2}{5} + \frac{31^2}{5} - \frac{55^2}{15}$$

$$= (24.2 + 33.8 + 192.2) - 201.67$$

$$= 250.2 - 201.67 = \underline{48.53}$$

Sum of Squares Between

$$SS_b = \Sigma\frac{T_j^2}{n_j} - \frac{G^2}{N}$$

$$= \frac{11^2}{5} + \frac{13^2}{4} + \frac{31^2}{6} - \frac{55^2}{15}$$

$$= (24.20 + 42.25 + 160.17) - 201.67$$

$$= 226.62 - 201.67 = \underline{24.95}$$

Box 13.2 gives a shortcut for computing SS_{between} when sample sizes are equal.

Sum of Squares Within

$$SS_w = SS_{w1} + SS_{w2} + SS_{w3}$$

where $SS_{wj} = \Sigma X^2 - \dfrac{T_j^2}{n_j}$

$$SS_{w1} = 27 - 11^2/5 = 27 - 24.2 = 2.8$$

$$SS_{w2} = 45 - 13^2/4 = 45 - 42.25 = 2.75$$

$$SS_{w3} = 171 - 31^2/6 = 171 - 160.17 = 10.83$$

$$SS_w = 2.8 + 2.75 + 10.83 = \underline{16.38}$$

The SS_{within} is a pooled sum of squares that can be obtained either by subtraction or by direct computation. Although subtracting $SS_{between}$ from SS_{total} gives the value of SS_{within}, this method can hide errors made in computing $SS_{between}$ and SS_{total}. Therefore, it is good procedure to compute SS_{within} by direct computation of the variation within each of the k groups, SS_{wj}, and to pool these terms. As you can see from our examples, the two methods yield the same result:

$$SS_w = SS_t - SS_b$$

$$= 41.33 - 24.95 = \underline{16.38}$$

13.7   THE ANOVA SUMMARY TABLE

Once the three basic SS quantities have been computed, they are placed in an ANOVA summary table as illustrated in Table 13.3.

Sources of Variation

The first column in Table 13.3 contains the name of each source of variation computed. The column heading is usually abbreviated "Source." The second column of the ANOVA summary table contains the values of these quantities as previously computed from the data in Table 13.2.

Degrees of Freedom

The third column of Table 13.3 is headed df to indicate the degrees of freedom associated with each source of variation that has been reported. These values are computed by using the same general definition applied in previous cases such as the t-test. A df value is determined by the number of units available minus the number of population parameters estimated. The degrees of freedom associated with each source of variation will be labeled by the

Table 13.3   THE ANOVA SUMMARY TABLE GIVING SOURCES
OF COMPUTATIONS

Source	SS	df	MS	F
Between	$\Sigma(T_j^2/n_j) - (G^2/N)$	$(k - 1)$	SS_b/df_b	MS_b/MS_w
Within	$\Sigma X^2 - (T_j^2/n_j)$	$\Sigma(n_j - 1)$	SS_w/df_w	
Total	$\Sigma X^2 - (G^2/N)$	$(N - 1)$		

THE ANOVA SUMMARY TABLE FOR EXAMPLE DATA

Source	SS	df	MS	F
Between	24.950	2	12.475	9.137
Within	16.383	12	1.365	
Total	41.333	14		

appropriate letter, just as we labeled different values of SS. For example, df_{total} becomes df_t.

For df_{total}, 1 degree of freedom is lost in estimating the grand mean. Thus, the total number of degrees of freedom, df_t, is $N - 1$. For our example,

$$df_t = N - 1$$

$$= 15 - 1 = 14$$

For $df_{between}$, we compute the variability of group means based on the sum of their squared differences from the population mean. Since we need to estimate the population mean with GM, we lose 1 degree of freedom. Therefore,

$$df_b = k - 1$$

$$= 3 - 1 = 2$$

For df_{within}, we compute the variability in each group based on the sum of squared differences from a population mean. In this case we use each group mean as an estimate, and for each of these estimates 1 degree of freedom is lost. Thus, each group has $n - 1$ degrees of freedom. When the variability in each group is pooled to get one estimate of population variability, we also pool the df values from each group.

$$df_w = \Sigma(n_j - 1) = (n_1 - 1) + \ldots + (n_k - 1)$$

$$= (5 - 1) + (4 - 1) + (6 - 1) = 12$$

Box 13.3 **Simplified Computation of df_{within} with Equal Sample Size**

For the df associated with SS_w, you can multiply the number of groups, k, by the number of degrees of freedom in each group, $n - 1$. For three groups of size 5 we have the following:

For equal group sizes only:

$$df_w = k(n - 1)$$

$$= 3(5 - 1) = \underline{12}$$

For either equal or unequal group sizes:

$$df_w = (n_1 - 1) + \ldots + (n_k - 1)$$

$$= (5 - 1) + (5 - 1) + (5 - 1) = (15 - 3) = \underline{12}$$

Box 13.3 gives a short way of obtaining df_w when the groups are all of equal size.

The total $N - 1$ degrees of freedom may be seen as two components associated with SS_b and SS_w:

$$df_t = df_b \quad\quad + df_w$$

$$N - 1 = (k - 1) + [(n_1 - 1) + \ldots + (n_k - 1)]$$

$$14 = 2 \quad\quad + 12$$

Mean Squares

Given values of SS and df, variance estimates have been computed from the ratio $MS = SS/df$, and these figures are entered in column 4 of Table 13.3. Generally, we do not need to compute the MS_{total}. We want to know the size of the treatment variance relative to error variance.

$$MS_{between} = \frac{SS_{between}}{df_{between}} = \text{treatment} + \text{error variance}$$

$$MS_{within} = \frac{SS_{within}}{df_{within}} = \text{error variance}$$

The MS_b represents error variance when H_0 is true and treatment variance plus error variance when H_0 is not true. The MS_w represents error variance both when H_0 is true and when it is not true.

The F-ratio

Our test statistic, F, consists of the treatment variance, MS_b, divided by the pooled error variance, MS_w. For our example data in Table 13.2, this quantity is

$$F = \frac{MS_{\text{between}}}{MS_{\text{within}}} = \frac{12.475}{1.365} = 9.14$$

In general, values of the F-ratio are interpreted in a manner similar to values of z and t. When the treatment effect is relatively large, it results in a large value of F. The larger the value of F, the more likely it is that the null hypothesis will be rejected. To interpret the specific value $F = 9.14$ from our example, it is necessary to consider some features of the F-ratio and its null sampling distribution.

13.8 EVALUATING THE *F*-RATIO

Recall that when H_0 is true, both the numerator (MS_b) and the denominator (MS_w) of the F-ratio are estimates of the same variance. Thus, when H_0 is true we expect the obtained value of the F-ratio to be about 1.00.[2]

Our problem is to decide what "about 1.00" means. Is $F = 1.50$ about 1.00? Is $F = 2.00$ about 1.00? To deal with this problem we need to define the characteristics of the random sampling distribution of F when H_0 is true. This definition has already been partially made when we note that the mean of the distribution is about 1.00.

If MS_b is less than MS_w the F-ratio will have a value of less than 1. The minimum value of F is zero because the ratio is made up of two variances and variances are always positive. Thus, the distribution of possible F-ratios varies from zero through an expected value around 1.00 to some value greater than 1.00. When testing H_0 we are interested in determining whether the obtained F is significantly greater than 1.00.

If MS_b is greater than MS_w, the F-ratio will have a value greater than 1. This is the only situation likely to result in the rejection of H_0.

The F-ratio and Decisions About H_0

When $MS_b < MS_w$, $\quad F < 1.00$, $\quad$ fail to reject H_0.

When $MS_b = MS_w$, $\quad F = 1.00$, $\quad$ fail to reject H_0.

When $MS_b > MS_w$, $\quad F > 1.00$, $\quad$ perhaps reject H_0.

---

[2]We say that the expected value of F (when H_0 is true) is "about" 1.00 for the following reason: This expected value approaches 1.00 as the value of df_w increases. The precise expected value is determined by $df_w/(df_w - 2)$. If $df_w = 20$, the expected value of F is $20/18 = 1.11$. If $df_w = 100$, the expected value of F is 1.02, and so on.

When the null hypothesis is true, most *F*-ratios have values near 1.00 and there is no upper limit to the *F*-ratio. Therefore, the sampling distribution of the *F*-ratio is not symmetrical like the distributions of *z* and *t*. Rather, as shown in Figure 13.3, it is positively skewed.

Like the distribution of *t*, the distribution of *F* is really a family of distributions that vary with degrees of freedom. But with the *F*-ratio we must take into account both the degrees of freedom associated with the numerator, df_b, and the degrees of freedom associated with the denominator, df_w. As an example, consider the *F*-ratio of 9.14 obtained with our data relating amount of alcohol consumed with scores on a driving test, as shown in Table 13.3.

This *F*-ratio can be evaluated by entering Table G in Appendix III, but for the moment we will use an abbreviated version of Table G given in Table 13.4. This version of the *F*-table contains critical values of *F* for cases in which $\alpha = .05$. The table is entered by using two *df* values. The appropriate column entry is determined by $df_b = 2$, and the row entry is determined by $df_w = 12$. In this way we find that the critical table value for *F* with 2 and 12 degrees of freedom is 3.88. For $df = 2,12$ any obtained *F* must be at least 3.88 if H_0 is to be rejected. When H_0 is true there is only a 5 percent chance of obtaining a value as large as 3.88.

Since the obtained value of 9.14 is larger than this critical value, we reject the null hypothesis and accept the alternative. The result could be reported in a sentence such as "There was a systematic relationship between the amount of alcohol consumed and the number of errors on a driving test, $F(2,12) = 9.14$, $p < .05$."

$$F(2,12)(\text{critical}) = 3.88$$

$$F(2,12)(\text{obtained}) = 9.14$$

Decision: Reject H_0

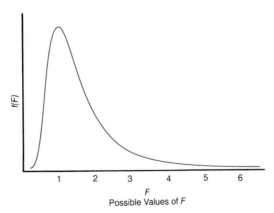

Figure 13.3 A typical *F* distribution, with most values piled up near the value of 1.00 and positive with skew.

Table 13.4   AN ABBREVIATED VERSION OF THE *F*-TABLE, TABLE G IN APPENDIX III
(The Table Gives Critical Values of *F* for α = .05. If an Obtained *F*-value Is
Greater than the Table Value, Reject H_0. Table G Also Includes Values For
α = .01.)

Degrees of freedom: denominator	Degrees of freedom: numerator					
	1	2	3	4	8	12
2	18.51	19.00	19.16	19.25	19.37	19.41
·	·	·	·	·	·	·
·	·	·	·	·	·	·
12	4.75	3.88	3.49	3.26	2.85	2.69
·	·	·	·	·	·	·
·	·	·	·	·	·	·
24	4.26	3.40	3.01	2.78	2.36	2.18
·	·	·	·	·	·	·
·	·	·	·	·	·	·
48	4.04	3.19	2.80	2.56	2.14	1.96
·	·	·	·	·	·	·
·	·	·	·	·	·	·
∞	3.84	2.99	2.60	2.37	1.94	1.75

Because subjects were randomly assigned to treatments, this result can be interpreted to mean that different amounts of alcohol consumption *caused* differences in the driving test scores of the subjects in this particular study. However, since the subjects were not randomly sampled, but simply "available," there is no statistical basis for generalizing the results to other subjects. Therefore, this example involves an application of the normal curve model of statistical testing to a problem in which the randomization model is theoretically more appropriate. You should recall that the practice of using the normal curve model without random sampling is widespread. It is generally considered to be acceptable because the probability value obtained is approximately the same with either model.

To illustrate this point we compare the probability values resulting from the analysis of these 15 scores by each statistical model. Using the randomization model, all possible arrangements of the obtained scores for groups of four, five, and six cases can be listed. For each possible arrangement, the summary statistic $\Sigma(T_j^2/n_j)$ is then computed. These steps will generate a summary statistic for each of 630,630 possible arrangements. Instead of examining all possible arrangements, we use the program NPSTAT to sample randomly 10,000 arrangements. Finally, we find the proportion of randomly selected 10,000 cases that yield a summary statistic equal to or larger than the value from the observed data set. Using the randomization test, we find that the probability of the scores yielding the obtained value of $\Sigma(T^2/n)$ or larger values is .00430. Using the normal curve method and the program NPSTAT, we find that the probability associated with $F(2,12) = 9.14$ is .00388. You can see that the two procedures lead to approximately the same probability value and, consequently, to the same decision about H_0.

Random Processes and Interpretation

It is important to keep in mind that, theoretically, ANOVA tests a null hypothesis about population parameters:

$$H_0: \mu_1 = \mu_2 = \mu_3 = \ldots = \mu_k$$

This hypothesis is tested only when random sampling has actually been carried out. When ANOVA is used without random sampling, it tests the hypothesis

H_0: The scores are independent of the treatments.

Even though the probability of the obtained result is often about the same with ANOVA and the randomization test, interpretation depends on which type of random process was used. Random sampling affects generality interpretation, and random assignment affects causal interpretation.

When neither random sampling nor random assignment is used, the researcher can behave *as if* one of these random processes had been used. That is, ANOVA is applied to the data. If H_0 is rejected, the researcher infers that a systematic outcome has been observed but there is no statistical basis to make either generality or causal inferences. Interpretation is limited because neither sampling bias nor treatment bias were controlled by a random process. This result leads to a situation in which replication of the study is especially important. Until it is established that the systematic result can be repeated, it is questionable how much effort should be spent attempting to interpret it.

13.9   A SECOND EXAMPLE: A TRAIT FACTOR

Now that we have defined the basic concepts of ANOVA with one example, we briefly review them with a second example. Assume that the topic of interest is the spelling performance of children as a function of their grade level in school. Of course, we cannot randomly assign children to grade levels, so we are dealing with a measured (not manipulated) independent variable. Therefore, to give the obtained probability value statistical validity, we randomly sample children from a population such as a particular school district.

We begin by noting the null hypothesis and the alternative hypothesis and selecting a decision criterion (α).

H_0: $\mu_1 = \mu_2 = \mu_3 = \ldots = \mu_k$

H_1: Not all μs are equal

$\alpha = .05$

For this example six children are randomly sampled from each of four grade levels (grades 2, 4, 6, 8) in the school district. Then a 20-word spelling test is administered to all 24 children who were sampled. The number of spelling errors (X) for each child is given in Table 13.5 along with the X^2 values to assist in computing sums of squares.

Just below the raw data in Table 13.5 you will find summary statistics such as totals, T_j, and sample sizes, n_j. At the foot of the table you will find

Table 13.5 SPELLING ERRORS ON A 20-WORD SPELLING TEST

Grade	2		4		6		8		
	X	X^2	X	X^2	X	X^2	X	X^2	
	13	169	10	100	8	64	7	49	
	15	225	10	100	5	25	6	36	
	12	144	13	169	6	36	7	49	
	12	144	9	81	10	100	11	121	
	9	81	7	49	6	36	9	81	
	12	144	11	121	9	81	9	81	
T_j	73		60		44		49		$G = 226$
n_j	6		6		6		6		$N = 24$
$\bar{X}_j$	12.17		10.00		7.33		8.17		$GM = 9.42$
ΣX_j^2		907		620		342		417	$\Sigma X^2 = 2286$

$$SS_{total} = \Sigma X_j^2 - \frac{G^2}{N}$$

$$= (907 + 620 + 342 + 417) - \frac{(73 + 60 + 44 + 49)^2}{24}$$

$$= 2286 - \frac{226^2}{24} = \underline{157.83}$$

$$SS_{between} = \Sigma \frac{T_j^2}{n_j} - \frac{G^2}{N}$$

$$= \frac{73^2 + 60^2 + 44^2 + 49^2}{6} - \frac{226^2}{24} = \underline{82.83}$$

$$SS_{within} = SS_{total} - SS_{between} = 157.83 - 82.83 = \underline{75.00}$$

the computation of the required sums of squares. The SS_t (157.83) has been partitioned into two parts, $SS_b = 82.83$ and $SS_w = 75.00$.

These sums of squares values have been entered into Table 13.6 to help in computing the required F-ratio. Note that the total degrees of freedom $(N - 1 = 23)$ have also been partitioned into two parts and entered into the table. Using these values, we compute the F-ratio: $F = 7.36$.

To evaluate this outcome turn to Table G in Appendix III. The table is entered by using two df values. The column entry is $df_b = 3$, and the row entry is $df_w = 20$. Thus we find that when $\alpha = .05$, the critical table value for F with 3 and 20 degrees of freedom is 3.10. Since the obtained value of 7.36 is larger than this critical value, we reject the null hypothesis and accept the alternative.

$$F(3,20)(\text{critical}) = 3.10$$

$$F(3,20)(\text{obtained}) = 7.36$$

Decision: Reject H_0

A research outcome like this could be reported in a sentence format such as the following: "There was a systematic relationship between spelling scores and grades in school. The children in grade 2 made the most errors $(\overline{X}_2 = 12.17)$ and those in grade 6 made the fewest errors $(\overline{X}_6 = 7.33)$, $F(3,20) = 7.36$, $p < .01$." There are three features to notice in this outcome statement. First, the statistical test information came at the end of the sentence to support the descriptive message, which came first. Second, the F value is accompanied by its degrees of freedom because the ratio cannot be evaluated without these values.

Finally, the α set before the data were collected was .05, but the outcome was reported as $p < .01$. Reporting the smaller value allows readers of the research to evaluate the finding at either the .05 or the .01 level of significance. You should notice that Table G in Appendix III contains two sets of critical values: those that are used when $\alpha = .05$ and those for $\alpha = .01$. According to Table G, with 3 and 20 degrees of freedom, the researcher can reject H_0 at the .05 level if the obtained F is equal to or greater than 3.10. The same hypothesis can be rejected at the .01 level if F is equal to or greater than 4.94. Since the obtained F exceeds both of these values, we can reject H_0 at either level of significance.

Table 13.6 ANOVA ON 24 SPELLING TEST SCORES

Source	SS	df	MS	F	η^2
Between	82.83	3	27.61	7.36	.5248
Within	75.00	20	3.75		
Total	157.83	23			

13.10   PERCENTAGE OF VARIATION

One new piece of information is contained in Table 13.6 that was not contained in Table 13.3; namely, a quantity labeled η^2 has been listed next to the F-ratio. Recall that a probability statement such as $p < .05$ does not provide sufficient information to evaluate a research outcome adequately. A better decision about a finding can be made when the probability value is accompanied by an index of the strength of the relationship between the independent variable and the dependent variable.

We can determine the percentage of SS_t that is associated with variability among the group means. This value can be computed in various ways, and one of the simplest measures of "percentage of variation accounted for" is called *eta squared*, η^2. The η^2 value reported in Table 13.6 describes the percentage of variation in spelling scores that can be accounted for by school grade groupings.

In Chapter 7 η^2 was computed with the following formula:

$$\eta^2 = 1 - \frac{SS_{Y-Y'}}{SS_Y} = 1 - \frac{SS_{\text{error}}}{SS_{\text{total}}} = \frac{SS_{\text{explained}}}{SS_t}$$

In ANOVA the $SS_{\text{explained}}$ is described in a sample by SS_b, and η^2 can be computed by Formula 13.9. This ratio provides an index of the strength of relationship between the dependent variable (spelling scores) and the independent variable (school grade). For the present example it tells us that about 52 percent of the variation in the spelling test scores can be accounted for by the differences in grade level of the children.

$$\eta^2(100) = \frac{SS_b}{SS_t}(100) = \frac{82.83}{157.83}(100) = 52.48 \tag{13.9}$$

Eta squared is useful because it is easy to calculate and it describes the strength of the relationship in the sample tested. If, however, the researcher has randomly sampled subjects and wishes to use the sample data to estimate the strength of the relationship in the parent population, η^2 gives a biased overestimate because SS_b contains both treatment effect and error. An unbiased estimate would remove error from the numerator. Therefore, an alternate measure, *omega squared* (ω^2), is available. In one-factor designs, this ratio can be computed by Formula 13.10:

$$\omega^2(100) = \frac{SS_{\text{between}} - (k-1)MS_{\text{within}}}{SS_{\text{total}} + MS_{\text{within}}}(100) \tag{13.10}$$

For our example analysis in Table 13.6 we have

$$\omega^2(100) = \frac{82.83 - (4-1)(3.75)}{157.83 + 3.75}(100) = 44.30$$

With this particular set of data, $\eta^2 = 52.48$ percent and $\omega^2 = 44.30$ percent, a difference of about 8.2 percent. In general, the difference between these measures of the strength of the relationship becomes smaller as the size of the effect decreases. For example, if $\eta^2 = 8.68$ percent, ω^2 would be about 7.26 percent, a difference of only 1.4 percent. In later chapters we will continue to use the sample description η^2, but in practice some researchers are more likely to report values of ω^2.

13.11 ASSUMPTIONS AND ROBUSTNESS

The analysis of variance is similar to the t-test in that the same assumptions were made in the mathematical derivation of the sampling distribution of the test statistics, t and F. You should recall that these assumptions are

1. The scores within each of the populations are normally distributed.
2. The population variances are equal: $\sigma_1{}^2 = \sigma_2{}^2 = \ldots = \sigma_k{}^2$.
3. The individual observations are independent.

The third assumption may be satisfied by randomly sampling subjects from a specified population. In many cases we cannot randomly sample but may be able to satisfy normality and homogeneity assumptions anyway. In these cases we carry out and interpret the analysis as if we had obtained a random sample. If H_0 were rejected, interpretation would be limited to inferring that a systematic outcome had been observed. The researcher would not have a statistical basis for generalization.

If we had randomly assigned subjects to treatments we would have a reasonable approximation of the probability that would have been obtained with a randomization test. This probability value would be used in judging the null hypothesis and facilitating causal interpretation. Again, the researcher would not have a statistical basis for making statements about the generality of the finding.

In most cases, as long as the independence assumption is met, the F-ratio is robust to the violation of normality and homogeneity assumptions. The sample variances should be similar, but under most circumstances they may vary by a ratio of four to one or more without leading to a biased conclusion. Similarly, with reasonable sample size, the assumption of a normal population distribution rarely presents a problem. Thus for various violations of assumptions, the obtained probability will be a good estimate of the actual probability when the null hypothesis is true and ANOVA assumptions are met.

Although the F-test is generally robust, there is one caution to consider. As with the t-test, there may be problems using F when one sample is larger than another by a ratio of at least two to one and one variance is larger than another by a ratio of at least four to one. If the larger variance happens to fall in the group with the smaller number of scores, the result from the F-test may produce an alpha level several times larger than the stated alpha level. In that case more Type I errors are made than expected, and the probability of the obtained outcome will differ for the F-test and the randomization test.

When this result occurs you should use a randomization test of scores or one of the randomization tests of ranks given in Chapter 18.[3]

13.12   COMPARING THE *t*- AND *F*-RATIOS

In addition to statistical assumptions, there are other similarities between one-factor ANOVA and the two-sample *t*-test discussed in Chapter 11. For example, in both tests the numerator is based on a difference between means and the denominator is based on pooled within-group variance. For the two-sample case, the degrees of freedom for the *t*-test are the same as the degrees of freedom for the MS_w from ANOVA. For example, if we let $n_1 = n_2 = 10$ ($N = 20$), the degrees of freedom for *t* are $n_1 + n_2 - 2 = 18$. With the same research design, the *df* for MS_w is $k(n - 1) = 2(10 - 1) = 18$.

When dealing with two groups, the precise relationship between these statistical test ratios can be expressed as: $t^2 = F$. You can easily verify this relationship by taking a small set of data for two samples and computing each ratio. The relationship between *t* and *F* can also be examined by comparing critical values of these test ratios in Tables D and G in Appendix III.

When $k = 2$, $t^2 = F$

A comparison of the *t*-distribution with the *F*-distribution will show how general (nondirectional) alternative hypotheses operate when one is using the *F*-ratio to assess two groups. To illustrate, Figure 13.4 gives the sampling distribution for each ratio when $k = 2$ and $n_1 = n_2 = 10$ ($df = 18$). The *t*-distribution is symmetrical with a mean of zero, and the *F*-distribution is positively skewed with a mean near 1.00.

Using Table D in Appendix III, with $\alpha = .05$ and a nondirectional alternative hypothesis, we find the critical value of $t(18)$ to be 2.10. This value cuts off $.05/2 = .025$ (2.5 percent) of the area in each tail of the *t*-distribution. As shown in Figure 13.4, the application of *F* to the same situation yields a critical value of $F(1,18) = 4.41$, which cuts off 5 percent of the area in one tail of the *F*-distribution. Notice that in the null distribution for *F*, both possible directional outcomes ($\mu_1 < \mu_2$ and $\mu_1 > \mu_2$) are aggregated in the same tail. In the null distribution of *t* they are in separate tails. Since $2.10^2 = 4.41$, we can see that $t^2 = F$ and the two tests lead to the same conclusion about the null hypothesis.

As noted earlier, when the number of groups is greater than two, the alternative hypothesis is often not very specific. In this chapter we have dealt only with the general alternative, H_1: Not all μs are equal. In the next chapter we deal with more specific hypotheses for multiple group research designs.

---

[3]The statistical program NPSTAT will carry out three tests: ANOVA, randomization test of scores, and randomization test of ranks.

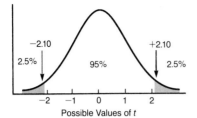

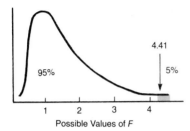

Figure 13.4 A comparison of the distribution of t with $df = 18$ and the distribution of F with $df = 1,18$. Critical values of the test have been selected for $\alpha = .05$ and a nondirectional alternative hypothesis.

In general, with more than two samples we talk about omnibus alternative hypotheses (Chapter 13) versus specific alternatives (Chapter 14) instead of nondirectional and directional alternatives.

13.13 GRAPHING MEANS AND THE MEASUREMENT OF FACTORS

As the number of levels of a factor increases, the more likely it is that the researcher will provide a graphic summary of a significant finding. For example, if you were to sample children in only two grade levels, a description of the outcome could be made by simply reporting the two means in a sentence. If you sample children from four grades, or perhaps eight grades, a graphic figure can be an economical way to communicate the results.

Figure 13.5 provides a graphic figure of the two studies analyzed in this chapter. The figure follows the general guidelines for constructing figures that were outlined in Chapter 3 when dealing with frequency distributions. The values of the dependent variable (mean scores on a driving test and mean scores on a spelling test) are on the Y-axis. The independent variables, amount of alcohol consumed and grade in school, have been placed on the X-axis. Since each of these independent variables was measured on at least an interval scale, the figure was drawn with straight lines connecting the data points. Representing the data in this way implies that levels of the independent variable are ordered on a quantitative scale. It further implies that intervening values, such as 1 or 3 ounces of alcohol, could have been sampled.

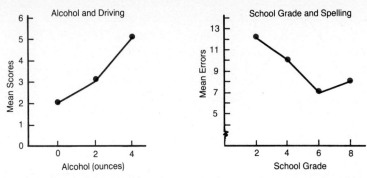

Figure 13.5 Graphic representation of the results of two hypothetical studies analyzed in this chapter. Line graphs were used because the independent variable was measured on at least an interval scale.

The straight line connecting data points for the 2-ounce and 4-ounce conditions provides a best estimate of the mean for the missing 3-ounce group.

Figure 13.6 summarizes two other hypothetical studies. In the left panel of the figure are data from a study of weight loss in obese people as a function of the type of therapy received. The therapy was either a behavior modification program (BM), group therapy (GP), or a control group that was on a waiting list to begin treatment (CO). The right panel of Figure 13.6 provides a summary of a study relating memory errors to the location of brain damage (hypothetical brain areas A, B, and C).

Contrasting the format of Figures 13.5 and 13.6, we clearly see that one is a line graph and the other a bar graph. The reason for this difference is that the independent variables types of therapy and area of brain damage are both *qualitative* (nominal scale of measurement). With this type of variable there

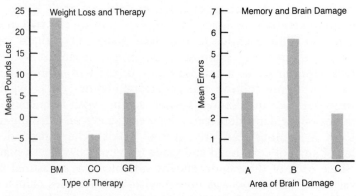

Figure 13.6 Graphic representation of two hypothetical studies not analyzed here. Bar graphs were used because the independent variable was measured on a nominal scale. Rank ordering of the groups on the X-axis is arbitrary.

is no measurement basis for placing the groups in any particular order on the X-axis. In Figure 13.6 they have simply been placed in alphabetical order.

There is also no reason to attach meaning to the distance between groups along the axis. The distance between the data for the behavior modification group and the group therapy condition happens to be the same as the distance between the group therapy condition and the no-treatment controls. These distances have been made constant only for aesthetic reasons. Using vertical bars to represent qualitative independent variables helps to avoid inappropriate interpretations that should be reserved for variables measured on quantitative scales.

As a final note on the nature of the independent variable, you should not confuse the way scores get into groups (by random assignment versus classification) with the way the independent variable is measured. The difference between random assignment (manipulated variables) and classification (measured independent variables) has implications for whether the outcome will be interpreted in a cause-and-effect manner. In contrast, the difference between nominal and quantitative measurement of factors has implications for the way graphic summaries of the results are constructed.

To illustrate, the left panels of Figures 13.5 and 13.6 present data for manipulated variables, where subjects were randomly assigned to different amounts of alcohol (measured quantitatively) or to different types of therapy (nominal categories). In each case group differences in behavior could be interpreted as being caused by the differences in treatments.

In contrast, the right panel of Figures 13.5 and 13.6 present data for measured variables, where subjects were classified according to characteristics not under the control of the researcher. Both school grade (measured quantitatively) and area of brain damage (nominal categories) lead to conclusions with no statistical basis for inferring a cause-and-effect relationship.[4]

When dealing with classificatory independent variables such as these it is especially important to sample subjects randomly. Random selection gives statistical validity to the obtained probability value as well as facilitating interpretations about generality. If the subjects in the school grade and brain damage studies were randomly sampled, there would be a statistical basis to infer generality of the finding. If they were not randomly sampled, we could act as if the scores were independent and submit them to an analysis of variance. If H_0 were rejected, the likely inference would be that a systematic relationship between the independent and dependent variable had been observed. Arguments about generality would be based on nonstatistical criteria such as comparison with other studies on the topic.

---

[4]In this example we assumed that the subjects were humans who experienced some kind of accident resulting in brain injury. Thus, the area of the brain that was damaged was classificatory and not under the control of the researcher. If the subjects had been laboratory rats, the area of brain damage could have been a manipulated variable. That is, the rats could have been randomly assigned to groups that received damage in target areas of interest.

SUMMARY

The analysis of variance (ANOVA) is one of the most widely used statistical procedures in behavioral research. In this chapter we examined the use of ANOVA in studies where a single factor (independent variable) has more than two levels (values or categories of the independent variable). The null hypothesis tested with ANOVA is that there is no difference among the population means. The alternative hypothesis is that not all means are equal.

The null hypothesis is tested with a ratio of two variances called the F-ratio: $F = MS_b/MS_w$. Sometimes the ratio is described as treatment variance/error variance. The numerator of this ratio represents the variance associated with k group means and has $k - 1$ degrees of freedom. The denominator of the ratio represents the pooled variability of individual scores about the means of their respective groups. Its degrees of freedom are found by adding the degrees of freedom from the separate groups; for samples of equal size, $df_w = k(n - 1)$. When the obtained value of F is larger than the critical value found in the F-table, we reject the null hypothesis and accept the alternative hypothesis.

In addition to statistical significance, we often want to know about the strength of the relationship between the independent and dependent variables. In the context of ANOVA this value can be obtained with either the correlation ratio, eta squared (η^2), or the ratio omega squared (ω^2). These measures quantify the percentage of variation in behavior scores that is accounted for by the differences in groups (treatments or category membership).

The analysis of variance is a robust procedure, meaning that assumptions underlying its use can be violated to some degree without severely altering the meaning of the analysis. In general, statistical strengths and weaknesses of the F-ratio are the same as those of the t-ratio discussed earlier.

The analysis of variance is used in research where the number of levels of a factor may become large. As this number increases, it becomes increasingly likely that a graphic figure will be used to communicate the results. When the independent variable is measured on at least an interval scale, either a line graph or a bar graph can be used to display group means. When the variable is categorical (nominal measurement) only a bar graph should be used.

KEY WORDS

factor	grand mean (*GM*)
levels of a factor	*F*-ratio
manipulated factor	*F*-distribution
measured factor	percentage of variation

within-group variation	eta squared (η^2)
error variance	omega squared (ω^2)
between-group variation	robust test
explained variance	line graph
mean square (*MS*)	bar graph
grand total (*G*)	

PROBLEMS

1 Why is use of ANOVA preferred to a series of *t*-tests?

2 Hospital records were used to estimate the relationship between age at first pregnancy and total number of pregnancies. Sixty cases were sampled from the records
of 1216 women over 35 years who had had a hysterectomy in the last five years.
Stratified random sampling was used to obtain 20 cases in each of three age groups.
Groups were defined in terms of age at first pregnancy, 15 to 17 years, 18 to 20
years, and 21 to 23 years. The mean total pregnancies for three age groups were
$\overline{X}_{15-17} = 4.8$, $\overline{X}_{18-20} = 3.6$, $\overline{X}_{21-23} = 2.2$. An ANOVA indicated a statistically significant relationship between these variables: $F(2,57) = 4.66$, $p < .05$.
  (a) What variable was treated as a "factor" in this study?
  (b) Was the factor manipulated or classificatory?
  (c) What are the levels of this factor?
  (d) What was the dependent variable?
  (e) Does this study provide a statistical basis to argue for a causal relationship be-
      tween these variables? Why or why not?
  (f) Does this study provide a statistical basis to argue for generality of the results?
      Why or why not?

3 Calculate the degrees of freedom for $MS_{between}$ and MS_{within} for each of the following
research designs:
  (a) $k = 3$, $n_1 = 6$, $n_2 = n_3 = 8$ ($N = 22$).
  (b) $k = 5$, $n = 12$ ($N = 60$).

4 For each of the following cases, determine the minimal value of F needed to reject
the null hypothesis (F_{crit}):
  (a) $k = 3$, $n_1 = 6$, $n_2 = n_3 = 8$, $\alpha = .05$.
  (b) $k = 4$, $n = 16$, $\alpha = .01$.

5 Psychology students ($N = 21$) were asked to make confidence ratings about statistical findings knowing only the alpha level used in rejecting the null hypothesis. A
set of eight alpha values ranging from .001 to .20 were presented in one of three
orders: A = .001 to .20, B = .20 to .001, and C = a random order. The rating scale
ranged from a maximum of 5 (extremely confident that a systematic event was
observed) to zero (no confidence that the event was systematic). The following confidence ratings for $p = .001$ were obtained:

Order A	Order B	Order C
4	4	4
3	5	3
4	5	4
2	4	5
4	5	5
4	5	3
3	5	4

(a) What variable was treated as a factor in this study?
(b) Carry out ANOVA on these data and report the F value.
(c) Do these data allow you to reject H_0 at $\alpha = .05$? At $\alpha = .01$?
(d) What are the values of η^2 and ω^2?

6 Draw a graphic figure of the outcome of the study in problem 5. Why did you choose to draw a line graph or a bar graph?

7 Assume that two psychologists announced a program that would help with weight loss. They advertise that anyone who is at least 50 pounds overweight is eligible. Twenty people who fit this description sign up for treatment, but only 12 can be dealt with at one time. One therapist wants to use behavior modification (BM), and the second therapist wants to use group therapy (GP). Twelve patients are randomly assigned to one or another of these treatments, and the remaining 8 are placed on a waiting list and serve as a control group (CO). All 20 patients are weighed at the outset and again after six months of treatment in these conditions. The following mean pounds lost in six months were recorded:

Description of weight-loss study

Treatment	BM	GP	CO
$\overline{X}_j$	11.2	7.6	2.5
s_j^2	9.3	10.4	8.6
n_j	6	6	8

(a) Provide an ANOVA summary table for these data. [Hint 1: To obtain SS_b with the computational formula, you need group sums that can be obtained from computing $\overline{X}_j(n_j)$ for each group. Hint 2: For SS_w you need SS_{wj} for each group. This value can be obtained from $s_j^2(n_j - 1)$ for each group.]
(b) Do the data lead you to reject or fail to reject the null hypothesis?
(c) What percentage of the variation in the weight-loss scores can be accounted for by the difference in treatments?
(d) From the method used here, what can be said about the generality of the observed relationship?
(e) From the method used here, what can be said about the cause of the observed relationship?

8 A group of 11 patients was randomly divided into three groups that received different treatments. They generated the following scores:

Treatment A: 3, 4, 3, 6
Treatment B: 7, 10, 6, 4
Treatment C: 15, 9, 41

(a) Compute an F-test of the difference between means and make a statistical decision about the outcome.

(b) If you have access to the computer program NPSTAT, complete the following exercise. Compute a randomization test to see if the scores are independent of their random assignment to groups and make a statistical decision about the outcome.

(c) Compare the results of these two analyses and suggest a likely reason for the difference.

9 A group of ten subjects was randomly divided into three groups that received different treatments. They generated the following scores:

Treatment A: 1, 5, 3
Treatment B: 5, 6, 8, 9
Treatment C: 8, 9, 12

(a) Compute an F-test of the difference between means and make a statistical decision about the outcome.

(b) If you have access to the computer program NPSTAT, complete the following exercise. Compute a randomization test to see if the scores are independent of their random assignment to groups and make a statistical decision about the outcome.

(c) Compare the results of these two analyses and suggest a likely reason for the difference.

Chapter
14

Multiple Comparisons

14.1   INTRODUCTION

Chapter 13 showed that one-factor ANOVA can be used to test the null hypothesis that two or more means are equal. If this hypothesis is rejected, you can accept the alternative hypothesis that not all means are equal. Accepting this nonspecific or omnibus alternative hypothesis does not, however, specify which means differ. Rather, it indicates only that at least one difference between two means or among some combination of means is significant at the selected criterion such as $\alpha = .05$. Is this omnibus alternative hypothesis of much interest to you?

Frequently, when the analysis of variance is used with three or more means, the omnibus alternative hypothesis does *not* provide sufficient information. Rather, information about more specific hypotheses is usually preferred. Consider the example in Chapter 13 dealing with the relationship between driving scores and the amount of alcohol consumed. The ANOVA indicated a significant relationship: $F(2,12) = 9.14$, $p < .01$. We might consider this outcome to indicate that the mean from the no-alcohol control group ($\overline{X} = 2.20$ errors) is significantly lower than the mean for the 4-ounce group ($\overline{X} = 5.17$ errors). But how does the 2-ounce group ($\overline{X} = 3.25$ errors) compare with the other two means? Is the mean for this group significantly different from either of the others? From both? From neither? The analysis of variance does not answer these questions directly. The techniques that do answer these questions are called multiple comparison procedures, and to discuss them it is necessary first to define some basic distinctions central to their proper use.

14.2   BASIC DISTINCTIONS

Per Comparison Versus Experimentwise Error Rate

An advantage of ANOVA over a series of *t*-tests is that it yields a known Type I error probability. An advantage of the procedures discussed in this chapter is that they take into account factors influencing the probability of a Type I error while making more specific comparisons than the omnibus ANOVA.

When only one comparison is made, the probability of a Type I error when H_0 is true is the stated significance level adopted by the researcher (e.g., $\alpha = .05$). A researcher making two or more comparisons may decide to use a Type I error of .05 for each individual comparison. If so, the error rate for the study is referred to as a **per comparison error** rate, α_{PC}.

PER COMPARISON ERROR: The probability of a Type I error selected by the researcher for an individual comparison.

One problem with a series of comparisons (e.g., t-tests) each using .05 is that the researcher takes multiple opportunities to reject the null hypotheses. When each test has the same criterion, the probability of making at least one Type I error among the entire set of comparisons is not simply α. Rather, it is greater than .05 if .05 is used for each individual comparison.

With a collection of comparisons, the researcher has a choice of setting the error rate at the level of each individual comparison (per comparison rate) or setting the rate for the collection as a whole. Frequently, with multiple comparison procedures, the rate for a collection of comparisons is set so that the sum of Type I errors is .05 or some other value selected by the researcher. The probability of a Type I error estimated in this way is referred to as the **experimentwise error** rate, α_{EW}.

EXPERIMENTWISE ERROR: The probability of at least one Type I error when two or more comparisons are made.

When dealing with small values of α, the experimentwise rate can be estimated by multiplying the per comparison error rate by the number of comparisons performed, c. Thus, if α_{PC} is .05 for each of three comparisons, the value of α_{EW} is estimated by $c\,(\alpha_{PC}) = 3(.05) = .15$. This Type I error level clearly exceeds the conventional probability of a Type I error, and the researcher may wish to set the α for individual comparisons at a lower rate so that $c(\alpha_{PC})$ is not greater than .05. For example, if α for individual comparisons is .01 and there are three comparisons, the experimentwise rate is $3(.01) = .03$ for the set of comparisons.

Planned Versus Unplanned Comparisons

When there are several possible comparisons that might be made, it is unlikely that all comparisons are of interest to the researcher. More likely, a subset of comparisons will be used. The subset might contain only two comparisons that are of special interest to the researcher before the data are collected. These comparisons are referred to as **planned (a priori) comparisons.** There are two important points to remember about planned comparisons. First, they may be made *without* a preliminary omnibus test of the null hypothesis with ANOVA. Second, the experimentwise error rate takes into account only the number of comparisons actually planned and made.

In one sense, the rationale for these comparisons is similar to that for directional alternative hypotheses. In earlier chapters it was pointed out that in a one- or two-sample test the region of rejection is larger for a directional (specific) than a nondirectional (general) alternative hypothesis. Thus, a weaker outcome (e.g., smaller value of t) leads to rejection of H_0 when we can justify a specific alternative. Similarly, the decision to make specific multiple tests with more than two groups must be justified before the data are collected. When this justification is given, we receive a little statistical credit for asking a more specific question and we use a less stringent criterion.

PLANNED (A PRIORI) COMPARISONS: Tests between sample means that are justified before the data are collected.

Inspection of the data frequently raises questions about hypotheses that were not considered before the data were collected. Methods used to test these hypotheses are referred to as **post hoc (unplanned) comparisons.** Post hoc tests are carried out only after the data have been inspected and the null hypothesis has been rejected by a statistical test. Furthermore, even though a small number of post hoc comparisons may actually be tested, α_{EW} takes into account all possible comparisons. For example, tests comparing *all* pairs of means use an adjusted critical value that is valid for the entire collection of potential pairwise tests as a whole.

POST HOC (UNPLANNED) COMPARISONS: Tests between sample means that were not planned before the data were collected.

14.3 TUKEY'S POST HOC TEST

Although there are several methods available for making unplanned comparisons, we will mention only Tukey's Honestly Significant Difference (HSD) test. Tukey's test has been chosen because it is widely used and among the least controversial multiple comparison procedures.

This test allows for a comparison of all possible pairs of means and ensures that the experimentwise error is maintained at the chosen level. It is carried out only after an analysis of variance (ANOVA) produces a significant *F*-ratio. In general, Tukey's HSD test involves three steps: (1) List the differences between all possible pairs of obtained means, (2) compute the value of HSD as follows, and (3) compare HSD with each obtained pair difference.

Data to illustrate the use of Tukey's HSD test are taken from Chapter 13. Recall the example in which spelling scores were obtained from children in grades 2, 4, 6, and 8. The ANOVA summary of these data is given in Table 13.6, and the null hypothesis was rejected: $F(3,20) = 7.36$, $p < .05$ $(MS_w = 3.75)$. The means of the four samples have been arranged for multiple comparison analysis in Table 14.1. This table gives all possible differences between the pairs of these four means.

The task is to find which of the differences in Table 14.1 are sufficiently large to be called significant at a given experimentwise error level. To do so we need to know (1) α_{EW}, (2) the number of groups, (3) the number of scores

Table 14.1 DIFFERENCES IN MEAN SPELLING ERRORS
FOR CHILDREN IN GRADES 2, 4, 6, AND 8
(The Means Are Arranged in Order of Value
from Smallest to Largest.)

	$\overline{X}_6$	$\overline{X}_8$	$\overline{X}_4$	$\overline{X}_2$
$\overline{X}_6 = 7.33$	—	.84	2.67	4.84
$\overline{X}_8 = 8.17$		—	1.83	4.00
$\overline{X}_4 = 10.00$			—	2.17
$\overline{X}_2 = 12.17$				—

in each group, and (4) the MS_{within} from the ANOVA carried out before the HSD analysis. This information will be used to compute HSD as defined in Formula 14.1.

$$\text{HSD} = q_{(\alpha_{EW}, df, k)} \sqrt{\frac{MS_{within}}{n}} \qquad (14.1)$$

Where q = a value of the studentized range statistic from Table H in Appendix III

α_{EW} = probability of experimentwise Type I error

df = degrees of freedom for MS_{within}

k = number of groups

n = number of subjects in each group

For this example, let $\alpha_{EW} = .05$. The value of q for specific values of α, df, and k is found in Table H in Appendix III. The table is entered by using the degrees of freedom for MS_{within} (df_{within}) and the number of groups, k. In this example, the appropriate row entry is determined by $df_{within} = 20$, and the column entry is determined by $k = 4$. Thus, we find that the critical table value for $q_{(\alpha, df, k)}$ is 3.96. Substitute the value of $q = 3.96$ and $MS_{within} = 3.75$ (from Table 13.5) into Formula 14.1 to find the value of HSD for these data:

$$\text{HSD} = 3.96 \sqrt{\frac{3.75}{6}} = 3.96(.791) = 3.13$$

Now compare the HSD value of 3.13 to each difference between means listed in Table 14.1. Only two of the differences, 4.84 and 4.00, are larger than this critical value, so only those two differences are considered to be statistically significant at $\alpha = .05$. In a research report this outcome could be given in a sentence, for example, "The mean spelling errors for children in grade 2 ($\overline{X} = 12.17$) was greater than the errors made by children in grades 6

$(\overline{X} = 8.17)$ and 8 $(\overline{X} = 7.33)$, and all other differences were not significant, $p < .05$, Tukey's test."

It is instructive to compare these results from Tukey's HSD test using α_{EW} with a series of t-tests using α_{PC}. With both procedures the two largest mean differences (4.84 and 4.00) are identified as statistically significant. The next largest difference $(\overline{X}_4 - \overline{X}_6 = 10.00 - 7.33 = 2.67)$ is significant by the t-test—$t(10) = 2.33$, $p < .05$—but not by Tukey's HSD test.

To summarize, there are three steps in making comparisons with Tukey's HSD test:

1. Make a table of differences between all pairs of means.
2. Compute HSD with Formula 14.1.
3. Compare the value of HSD with each of the differences.

Any difference greater than HSD is declared to be significant at the Type I error level you have adopted. Remember that the HSD test sets the experimentwise error according to *all* possible pairwise comparisons even though fewer comparisons may be of interest.

HSD with Unequal *n*

Although our example of Tukey's HSD test involves samples of equal size, the test may also be used when samples are of moderately different sizes. To do so it is necessary to replace the sample size n in Formula 14.1 with the *harmonic mean*, $\overline{n}_h$, of the sample sizes by using Formula 14.2. In Formula 14.2, k is the number of groups and n_k is the number of subjects in the kth group:

$$\overline{n}_h = \frac{k}{(1/n_1) + (1/n_2) + \ldots + (1/n_k)} \tag{14.2}$$

Consider, for example, the study in Chapter 13 in which 15 people were given one of three amounts of alcohol before taking a driving test. There were five people in the no-alcohol control group $(n_0 = 5)$, four in the group receiving 2 ounces $(n_2 = 4)$, and six in the group receiving 4 ounces $(n_4 = 6)$. Using Formula 14.2, we find that the harmonic mean of these three sample sizes is 4.86. If we were actually to compare these three means with the HSD test, 4.86 would be used as the value of n in Formula 14.1.

$$\overline{n}_h = \frac{3}{1/5 + 1/4 + 1/6} = 4.86$$

14.4 PLANNED COMPARISONS

In many research contexts at least one subset of comparisons is planned. The remainder of this chapter focuses on the procedures appropriate to such situations.

Formal Definition of Comparisons

Any given comparison (C_i) may be defined as a combination of all the k means in a set, where each mean is multiplied by some weight, w_i. The weights are selected according to the hypothesis to be tested, with the restriction given in Formula 14.3 that the sum of the weights must equal zero. For example, to compare one group mean with another the weight applied to one mean could be $+1$ ($w_1 = +1$), and the weight applied to the second mean could be -1 ($w_2 = -1$). These weights satisfy the restriction that the sum of the weights must be zero: $w_1 + w_2 = (+1) + (-1) = 0$.

$$\Sigma w_i = 0 \text{ for any given } C_i \tag{14.3}$$

The null hypothesis about a single comparison such as $\mu_1 = \mu_2$ can be stated in alternative ways without changing the essential meaning of the comparison:

$$H_0: (\mu_1 = \mu_2) = (\mu_1 - \mu_2 = 0)$$

When each mean is given a weight and the sum of the weights is zero, the hypothesis can be rewritten as follows:

$$H_0: \mu_1(w_1) + \mu_2(w_2) = 0$$
$$H_0: \mu_1(1) + \mu_2(-1) = 0$$

When you multiply the means by weights that sum to zero, the expression is functionally equal to the difference between means. The comparison is just expressed as the sum of weighted means.

The advantage of using weights is that they provide a single system for constructing comparisons no matter how simple or complex they are. (They also provide a convenient way of computing sums of squares in testing the significance of each comparison.) All groups in the study can be included in each comparison without changing the hypothesis about only two groups. For example, you might have a study with two treatment groups and a control group, and one comparison of interest is the difference in the treatment means. By assigning the control group a weight of zero, we acknowledge the existence of a mean that is momentarily excluded from analysis. Assigning the third group a weight of zero, we have

$$H_0: \mu_1(1) + \mu_2(-1) + \mu_3(0) = 0$$

With three means we can express a comparison in the following form:

$$C_i = \mu_1 w_1 + \mu_2 w_2 + \mu_3 w_3$$

In terms of unbiased estimators we have

$$C'_i = \overline{X}_1 w_1 + \overline{X}_2 w_2 + \overline{X}_3 w_3$$

Pairwise and Complex Comparisons

In the example with alcohol consumption and driving behavior, the sum of three weighted means leads to six possible comparisons, which are listed below. Three of them involve pairs of means $(C_1 - C_3)$ and are called *pairwise* comparisons. The three others $(C_4 - C_6)$ involve comparing the average of one or more groups with an average of one or more different groups. For example, you might test the average of all treatment groups (2 ounces and 4 ounces of alcohol) against the mean of the no-treatment controls (0 alcohol). These are called *complex* comparisons.

$$C_1: \mu_1(1) + \mu_2(-1) + \mu_3(0) \quad \text{pairwise}$$
$$C_2: \mu_1(1) + \mu_2(0) + \mu_3(-1) \quad \text{pairwise}$$
$$C_3: \mu_1(0) + \mu_2(1) + \mu_3(-1) \quad \text{pairwise}$$
$$C_4: [(\mu_1 + \mu_2)/2] - \mu_3 \quad \text{complex}$$
$$C_5: [(\mu_2 + \mu_3)/2] - \mu_1 \quad \text{complex}$$
$$C_6: [(\mu_1 + \mu_3)/2] - \mu_2 \quad \text{complex}$$

It should be clear that with samples of equal size, averaging two means is the same as multiplying each mean by one-half and adding the results. For example,

$$[(\mu_1 + \mu_2)/2 - \mu_3] = [\mu_1(1/2) + \mu_2(1/2) + \mu_3(-1)]$$

Similarly with four groups, averaging three means is the same as multiplying three means by the weight of one-third and adding the results:

$$[(\mu_1 + \mu_2 + \mu_3)/3 - \mu_4] = [\mu_1(1/3) + \mu_2(1/3) + \mu_3(1/3) + \mu_4(-1)]$$

14.5 PLANNED COMPARISONS AS *t*-TESTS

Earlier it was mentioned that ANOVA is more appropriate than a series of *t*-tests. We now illustrate that *t*-tests are useful in dealing with several groups *if* two conditions are satisfied. Specifically, the denominator of the *t*-ratio is based on the MS_w from ANOVA, and α_{EW} is used instead of α_{PC}.

This type of *t*-test is often referred to as Dunn's test, after O. J. Dunn (1961). It is also called the *Bonferroni t* after a mathematical notion known as Bonferroni's inequality, which is the basis for calculating α_{EW}. Use of Dunn's test or the Bonferroni *t* does *not* require a prior significant overall *F*-ratio. It does, however, require the comparisons to be planned before the data are collected.[1]

One feature common to the comparison procedures discussed in this chapter is that they use the mean square within (MS_w) from ANOVA as an estimate of the population error. This point is illustrated in alternative for-

[1]When *t*-tests are used with MS_w in the denominator and α_{PC}, they are sometimes called Fisher's least significant difference (LSD) tests. LSD tests require rejection of the omnibus alternative hypothesis by ANOVA before they are performed. Preliminary analysis by ANOVA is not required for planned comparisons with α_{EW}.

mulas for the t-ratio. The pooled variance estimate based on two groups in Formula 11.11, s_p^2, is replaced by MS_w based on k groups in Formula 14.4.

$$t(df) = \frac{\overline{X}_1 - \overline{X}_2}{\sqrt{s_p^2(1/n_1 + 1/n_2)}} \qquad (11.11)$$

$$t(df) = \frac{\overline{X}_1(w_1) + \overline{X}_2(w_2) + \ldots \overline{X}_k(w_k)}{\sqrt{MS_w\left(\dfrac{w_1^2}{n_1} + \dfrac{w_2^2}{n_2} + \ldots + \dfrac{w_k^2}{n_k}\right)}} \qquad (14.4)$$

Furthermore, the difference between two means in Formula 11.11 is changed in Formula 14.4 to the sum of weighted means. In a study with only two group means, the values of t from Formulas 11.11 and 14.4 are the same. With $k = 2$ groups, the value of df is also the same ($df = n_1 + n_2 - 2$). With more than two groups the degrees of freedom associated with the t value from Formula 14.4 is df_w, the value associated with the MS_w in ANOVA.

Formula 14.4 may be used when samples are of either equal or unequal size. When the k samples are all of equal size, Formula 14.4 can be simplified, as shown in Formula 14.5. If the comparison is pairwise, with the nonzero weights equal to $+1$ and -1, $\Sigma w_i^2 = (+1^2) + (-1^2) = 2$. This computation makes the denominator of Formula 14.5 $\sqrt{MS_w(2/n)}$.

$$t(df) = \frac{\overline{X}_1(w_1) + \overline{X}_2(w_2) + \ldots + \overline{X}_k(w_k)}{\sqrt{MS_w\dfrac{\Sigma w_i^2}{n}}} \qquad (14.5)$$

Dunn's test is computed with Formulas 14.4 or 14.5, but the obtained value of t is evaluated by referring to Dunn's values in Table I in Appendix III. To control α_{EW}, the critical values in Table I increase as the number of comparisons increase. The greater the number of comparisons being made, the larger is the critical value of t.

You can compare Dunn's test with a conventional t-test by contrasting Dunn's critical values in Table I in Appendix III with the critical per comparison values of t in the standard t-table, Table D. With $df = 12$, $c = 2$ comparisons, and a nondirectional (two-tailed) test, the critical value in Table D is 2.179 but the critical value in Table I is 2.553. With the same value of df but four comparisons ($c = 4$), the critical value of the standard t is still 2.179 but the value for Dunn's test is increased to 2.924.

An Example

To illustrate the use of Dunn's test, we make two comparisons among mean spelling errors from the data in Table 14.1. One reasonable comparison that can be made is that between the mean errors of the two younger groups (grades 2 and 4) and the mean of the two older groups (grades 6 and 8). We make this complex comparison to test the hypothesis that the sum of these weighted means is zero; that is, there is no significant difference between the average of the children in grades 2 and 4 compared with the average of the children in grades 6 and 8.

$$H_0: \mu_2(1/2) + \mu_4(1/2) + \mu_6(-1/2) + \mu_8(-1/2) = 0$$

Using obtained sample means to estimate the population values of each group, we have

$$H_0: 12.17(1/2) + 10.00(1/2) + 7.33(-1/2) + 8.17(-1/2) = 0$$

This hypothesis can be tested with Formula 14.5, with the following numerator:

$$\text{numerator} = 12.17(1/2) + 10.00(1/2) + 7.33(-1/2) + 8.17(-1/2)$$

$$= 11.085 - 7.75 = \underline{3.335}$$

Using Formula 14.5 and $MS_w = 3.75$, the denominator becomes

$$\sqrt{3.75\left(\frac{1/4 + 1/4 + 1/4 + 1/4}{6}\right)} = \sqrt{3.75(.167)} = \underline{.791}$$

Therefore we have the following t-ratio with $df = 20$ from the overall ANOVA of all four groups:

$$t(20) = \frac{3.335}{.791} = 4.216$$

For the second comparison we can compare the mean errors from the children in grade 4 with the average of the children in the two higher grades.

$$\text{numerator} = 12.17(0) + 10.00(1) + 7.33(-1/2) + 8.17(-1/2)$$

$$= 10.00 - 7.75 = 2.25$$

Using Formula 14.5 and $MS_w = 3.75$, the denominator becomes

$$\sqrt{3.75\left(\frac{0 + 1 + 1/4 + 1/4}{6}\right)} = \sqrt{3.75(.250)} = .968$$

In this comparison we have the following t-ratio with $df = 20$, as in the first comparison:

$$t(20) = \frac{2.250}{.968} = 2.324$$

We can now evaluate Dunn's t statistic by using the critical value in Table I in Appendix III. Inspection of the table shows that the critical value of t for $df = 20$ is 2.417, with $\alpha = .05$ and a nondirectional alternative hypothesis. Under these conditions and $c = 2$ comparisons, each observed t must be equal to or larger than 2.417 for a comparison to be declared significant.

Therefore our first comparison with $t = 4.216$ leads to rejection of the null hypothesis that the mean of the two lower grade groups is equal to the mean of the two higher grade groups.

t(critical)   = 2.417

t(observed) = 4.216

Decision: Reject H_0

The second comparison with t = 2.324 does not lead to the rejection of the hypothesis that the mean of grade 4 children is equal to the mean of the two higher level groups:

t(critical)   = 2.417

t(observed)= 2.324

Decision: Fail to reject H_0

It should be noted that a different combination of statistical decisions would have been made if these two comparisons had been made without the Bonferroni adjustment of Type I error. Table D in Appendix III is used to evaluate t-tests made with a per comparison error rate. Under the conditions of this example (df = 20, α = .05, and a nondirectional alternative hypothesis), the critical value of t is 2.086. Thus, with a per comparison error rate, both of our comparisons of spelling errors would have been declared significant. With the experimentwise error rate of Dunn's test, only one of the two comparisons is significant.

In summary, we have discussed two multiple comparison procedures. Tukey's test is appropriate for making unplanned pairwise comparisons. Dunn's test, or the Bonferroni t, is appropriate when a planned subset of all comparisons is made, where the subset may include pairwise comparisons, complex ones, or some combination of both types.

14.6   PLANNED ORTHOGONAL COMPARISONS

Orthogonal Versus Nonorthogonal Comparisons

A potential problem in making multiple tests is that some comparisons may not be independent of other comparisons. If a test involving a particular group mean results in a Type I error, a second test involving that same mean is especially likely to produce another Type I error. The problem is less pronounced when comparisons are *orthogonal*, or statistically independent of each other. That is, the outcome of one test provides no information about how other tests might turn out. Two comparisons are statistically independent if knowing the statistical significance of one does not tell you about the statistical significance of the other.

Consider the example in which a researcher compares $\overline{X}_1$ with $\overline{X}_2$ and then compares $\overline{X}_1$ with $\overline{X}_3$. Since the tests used $\overline{X}_1$ twice in exactly the same way, these two comparisons are not statistically independent. For example, knowing the outcome of the comparison between $\overline{X}_1$ and $\overline{X}_2$ may provide information about whether the comparison between $\overline{X}_1$ and $\overline{X}_3$ is likely to be significant.

Two orthogonal comparisons can be made with three means, but only if one of the comparisons involves generating a new mean by combining two or more group means. If the first comparison involves $\overline{X}_1 - \overline{X}_2$, the second comparison would involve the average of these groups compared with the third group mean: $[(\overline{X}_1 + \overline{X}_2)/2] - \overline{X}_3$. Of course these comparisons may be written as the sum of weighted means:

$$C_1' = \overline{X}_1(1) + \overline{X}_2(-1) + \overline{X}_3(0)$$
$$C_2' = \overline{X}_1(1/2) + \overline{X}_2(1/2) + \overline{X}_3(-1)$$

By convention, when comparisons are both planned and orthogonal, most researchers do not adjust the Type I error for multiple tests.

An Example

Suppose that you wished to study obese people who wanted to lose weight. If you had 21 applicants for weight-loss therapy you might randomly assign 7 of them to a behavior modification program (condition BM) and 7 to a group therapy program (condition GP). The other applicants could be placed on a waiting list and serve as a no-treatment control (condition CO). The dependent variable, weight loss, could be determined from the difference in weight of each subject when entering these conditions and his or her weight six months later. The descriptive statistics and ANOVA summary table for this hypothetical study are given in Table 14.2.

Table 14.2 ANALYSIS OF VARIANCE FOR WEIGHT-LOSS DATA (IN POUNDS)

Statistics	BM	GP	CO		
$\overline{X}$	8.29	6.14	2.14		
Variance	4.57	10.48	5.14		
n	7	7	7		

Source	SS	df	MS	F^*	η^2
Between	136.10	2	68.05	10.11	.5291
Within	121.14	18	6.73		
Total	257.24	20			

$^*F_{(2,18)\text{crit}} = 3.55$.

What comparisons are likely to be of interest? Justification for making specific comparisons derives from the purpose of the study, and this purpose is generally reflected in the nature of the treatment conditions. In our example there are two treatment groups and a control group. It is unlikely that the two treatment conditions would have been included in the study if the researcher was not interested in comparing them. The null hypothesis about the two treatments can be expressed as follows:

$$H_0: \mu_{BM}(1) + \mu_{GP}(-1) + \mu_{CO}(0) = 0$$

Given that the researcher wishes to compare the effectiveness of these two treatments, what other hypothesis might be of interest? Consider that the control group must serve some purpose. Most likely, it serves as a baseline to determine whether some treatment is better than no treatment. That is, weight loss in the two treatment conditions taken together may differ from the weight loss in the no-treatment control. The null hypothesis about the relation of the two treatments to the control group can be expressed as follows:

$$H_0: \mu_{BM}(1/2) + \mu_{GP}(1/2) + \mu_{CO}(-1) = 0$$

Thus, we plan to make two orthogonal comparisons with these three means. In one comparison the two treatment groups are compared, and in the other the average of the treatment groups is compared with the control group. It is no accident that two comparisons are being made with three groups. In general, the number of orthogonal comparisons is equal to the number of degrees of freedom associated with between-group sum of squares. That is, for any set of k groups, $k - 1$ orthogonal comparisons may be made. In this example with $k = 3$, we have $3 - 1$, or 2, orthogonal comparisons.

Now we can apply weights to the sample means as suggested by these hypotheses. To help with this task, a comparison matrix can be generated, as shown in Table 14.3. Weights are assigned to each treatment mean (from Table 14.2) based on the hypotheses of interest to the researcher. In Table 14.3 the weights given in comparison 1 lead to a comparison of the mean of the behavior modification group (1) with the mean for the group therapy subjects (-1), and the mean of the controls is functionally ignored (0).

The weights in comparison 2 allow the average of the two treatment means to be compared to the mean of the control group. The weights of 1/2 and -1 were selected for two reasons. First the weights must sum to zero. Second, the intention of the comparison is to average the first two means

Table 14.3 A COMPARISON MATRIX INDICATING THE VALUES OF WEIGHTS TO BE APPLIED TO EACH MEAN

Comparison	$\overline{X}_{BM}$	$\overline{X}_{GP}$	$\overline{X}_{CO}$	Σw
C_1	+1	−1	0	0
C_2	+1/2	+1/2	−1	0

before comparing them to the third. A little arithmetic shows that $(\overline{X}_1 + \overline{X}_2)/2 = \overline{X}_1(1/2) + \overline{X}_2(1/2)$.

C_1': $8.29(1) + 6.14(-1) + 2.14(0)$

C_2': $8.29(1/2) + 6.14(1/2) + 2.14(-1)$

Checking Orthogonality

Before we proceed to test formally the significance of these two comparisons, it is useful to confirm that they are in fact orthogonal. Recall from Chapter 6 that the numerator of the Pearson correlation coefficient between variables X and Y is a sum of products. When the value of the sum of products is zero, the Pearson r is zero and the variables X and Y are said to be unrelated or independent. The same logic is involved when assessing the relationship between two comparisons. If the sum of the products of the weights in the comparisons is zero, the comparisons are statistically independent. That is, two comparisons are defined as orthogonal if the sum of the *products* of the weights equals zero:

$$\Sigma(w_i)(w_j) = 0 \qquad (14.6)$$

The orthogonality of the two comparisons in the weight-loss study can be assessed by using Formula 14.6 to combine the weights given in Table 14.3. To illustrate the use of Formula 14.6, first multiply the two weights assigned to the behavior modification group: $(1)(1/2) = 1/2$. Then do the same for each of the other groups. Finally, add the three resulting products $(1/2, -1/2, 0)$.

$(C_1'w_{BM})(C_2'w_{BM}) + (C_1'w_{GP})(C_2'w_{GP}) + (C_1'w_{CO})(C_2'w_{CO}) = 0$

$(1)(1/2) \qquad\qquad + (-1)(1/2) \qquad\qquad + (0)(-1) \qquad\qquad = 0$

$(1/2) \qquad\qquad\quad + (-1/2) \qquad\qquad\qquad + (0) \qquad\qquad\quad = 0$

Since the sum of the products of the weights is zero, we can proceed to assess the significance of the comparisons without concern about the lack of independence.

Testing the Significance of Orthogonal Comparisons

Given samples of equal size, the statistical significance of comparisons can be assessed by computing the sum of squares for each comparison, SS_{C_i}, with Formula 14.7.

$$SS_{C_i} = \frac{n(\Sigma\overline{X}_j w_i)^2}{\Sigma w_j^2}$$

$$= \frac{n[\overline{X}_1(w_1) + \ldots + \overline{X}_k(w_k)]^2}{w_1^2 + \ldots + w_k^2} \qquad (14.7)$$

By applying Formula 14.7 to the data from the weight-loss study, we obtain the following sum of squares for each planned comparison:

$$SS_{C_1} = \frac{7[8.29(1) + 6.14(-1) + 2.14(0)]^2}{(1)^2 + (-1)^2 + (0)^2} = \frac{32.15}{2} = \underline{16.07}$$

$$SS_{C_2} = \frac{7[8.29(1/2) + 6.14(1/2) + 2.14(-1)]^2}{(1/2)^2 + (1/2)^2 + (-1)^2} = \frac{180.04}{1.5} = \underline{120.03}$$

It is useful to treat these sums of squares as components of the $SS_{between}$ in the analysis of variance. Doing so makes it easy to see how comparisons are related to ANOVA and why they will be tested with an F-ratio.

$$SS_b = SS_{C_1} + SS_{C_2}$$

$$136.10 = 16.07 + 120.03$$

As illustrated in Figure 14.1, the procedure involves partitioning the SS_b into two orthogonal comparisons, each with $df = 1$. Again, there is one comparison allowed for each df associated with the $SS_{between}$ ($df_b = k - 1$).

To summarize, in setting up orthogonal comparisons we have conformed to the following three constraints:

1. $\Sigma w_i = 0$ for any given C_i.
2. $\Sigma(w_i)(w_j) = 0$.
3. Number of comparisons = df for SS_b (i.e., $k - 1$).

Once the sums of squares and their degrees of freedom have been obtained, the remainder of the analysis follows the same steps used in computing the F-ratio in one-factor ANOVA. The SS values arc divided by their df values to obtain mean squares for each comparison. Then a ratio of $MS_{comparison}$ to MS_{within} gives an F-ratio.

$$F_{comparison} = \frac{MS_{comparison}}{MS_{within}}$$

Although the omnibus test is not necessary, we might note that the obtained F value in Table 14.2 is larger than the critical value in Table G in Appendix III. Thus, H_0 can be rejected and the omnibus alternative accepted:

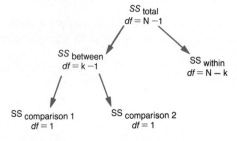

Figure 14.1 Flow chart showing how the SS_{total} and its degrees of freedom are partitioned in the analysis of variance and the analysis or orthogonal comparisons.

Table 14.4 THE RELATIONSHIP BETWEEN ONE-FACTOR
ANOVA AND TWO ORTHOGONAL COMPARISONS
ON WEIGHT-LOSS DATA

Source	SS	df	MS	F*	η^2
Between	136.10	2	68.05	10.11	.5291
Comparison 1	16.07	1	16.07	2.39	.0625
Comparison 2	120.03	1	120.03	17.84	.4666
Within	121.14	18	6.73		
Total	257.24	20			

*$F_{(1,18)_{crit}} = 4.41$.

$F_{(2,18)} = 10.11$, $p < .05$. More to the point, we need the value of MS_{within} to test the significance of the comparisons. Often, as when data are in a computer file, the easiest way to obtain MS_{within} is to carry out the ANOVA

As shown in Table 14.4, the test of comparison 1 is not significant (we cannot reject H_0 at $\alpha = .05$): $F_{(1,18)} = 2.39$, $p > .05$. This outcome may be interpreted to mean that the behavior modification and group therapy treatments had similar effects on the dependent variable of weight loss. On the other hand, comparison 2 is significant: $F_{(1,18)} = 17.84$, $p < .01$. This outcome suggests that being in treatment leads to more weight loss than being in a control group waiting for treatment.

14.7 PERCENTAGE OF VARIATION

Recall the argument in Chapters 11 and 13 that a statistical test rarely provides sufficient information to evaluate a research outcome. In addition to a probability value, we need some index of the strength of the relationship between the independent variable and the dependent variable. In Chapter 11, when $k = 2$, we used the point-biserial correlation:

$$r_{pb}^2(100) = \% \text{ of variation explained}$$

In Chapter 13, when $k > 2$ we used eta squared, η^2:

$$\eta^2 = \frac{SS_{between}}{SS_{total}} \text{ and } \eta^2(100) = \% \text{ of variation explained}$$

When examining orthogonal comparisons, η^2 can be partitioned into the amounts of variation in the sample explained by each separate comparison.[2]

---

[2]Eta squared cannot be partitioned unambiguously with nonindependent comparisons.

$$C_i\% = \frac{SS_{\text{comparison}}}{SS_{\text{total}}}(100) = \% \text{ of variation explained by } C_i \qquad (14.8)$$

Applying Formula 14.8 to our weight-loss data, we find that the percentage of total variation in the sample that is accounted for by comparison 1 is

$$C_1\% = \frac{16.07}{257.24}(100) = 6.25$$

and the percentage accounted for by comparison 2 is

$$C_2\% = \frac{120.03}{257.24}(100) = 46.66$$

If the researcher wishes to estimate the strength of the relationship in the population, omega squared (ω^2) can be computed:

$$\omega^2 = \frac{SS_{\text{comparison}} - (k-1)MS_{\text{within}}}{SS_{\text{total}} + MS_{\text{within}}} \qquad (14.9)$$

For our analysis in Table 14.4, we have the following value of ω^2 (100) for comparison 2:

$$\omega_2{}^2(100) = \frac{120.03 - (3-1)(6.73)}{257.24 + 6.73}(100) = 40.37$$

ANOVA and Regression

You might ask *how* the correlation ratio, η^2, describes the strength of the relationship between group membership and the behavior of interest. This relationship is easiest to see when the entire problem is recast as a regression analysis. This transformation has been done for our weight-loss data and summarized in Table 14.5.

In Table 14.5 the raw data for the 21 subjects have been listed in the column headed Y (the dependent variable). The weights used in making two orthogonal comparisons have been listed in columns marked X_1 for comparison 1 and X_2 for comparison 2. Previously these weights were applied to means, but in this regression analysis we apply them to individual scores.

The three columns of data $(X_1, X_2,$ and $Y)$ can be correlated, yielding three correlation coefficients, $r_{X_1X_2}$, r_{X_1Y}, and r_{X_2Y}. Each of these correlations has a specific meaning. For example, the correlation between the comparison weights in column X_1 and the behavior scores in column Y estimates the strength of the relationship between this comparison and weight loss: $r = .25$. When this correlation is converted to a percentage of variation, we find that $r^2(100) = 6.25$. In other words, 6.25 percent of the variation in the weight scores is accounted for by the difference between the two treatments.

Table 14.5 REGRESSION ANALYSIS OF WEIGHT-LOSS DATA

Group	Subject	X_1	X_2	Y	
BM	1	1	.5	8	
BM	2	1	.5	5	$r_{X_1.X_2} = 0$
BM	3	1	.5	7	
BM	4	1	.5	11	$r_{X_1.Y} = .250$
BM	5	1	.5	8	
BM	6	1	.5	11	$r_{X_2.Y} = .683$
BM	7	1	.5	8	$C_1\% = .250^2(100) = 6.25$
GP	8	-1	.5	3	
GP	9	-1	.5	6	$C_2\% = .683^2(100) = 46.66$
GP	10	-1	.5	4	
GP	11	-1	.5	8	$\eta^2(100) = C_1\% + C_2\%$
GP	12	-1	.5	3	
GP	13	-1	.5	7	$= 6.25 + 46.66$
GP	14	-1	.5	12	
CO	15	0	-1	4	$= 52.91$
CO	16	0	-1	1	
CO	17	0	-1	4	
CO	18	0	-1	0	
CO	19	0	-1	2	
CO	20	0	-1	-1*	
CO	21	0	-1	5	

*A weight loss of -1 pound equals a gain of 1 pound.

Using the same kind of arithmetic, we find that 46.66 percent of the variation is accounted for by the treatment versus no-treatment comparison in comparison 2. As shown in Table 14.4, these are the same values of $C_i\%$ found when we divided $SS_{comparison}$ by SS_{total} with Formula 14.8.

What about the correlation between the two sets of comparison weights? You should know the value of that correlation without making any computations because the weights were purposely selected so that the two comparisons would be independent. When two variables are independent, their correlation has a value of zero. Computing this correlation, $r_{X_1X_2}$, simply verifies that the weights were properly selected in the first place; that is, $r_{X_1X_2} = 0$.

Through this type of analysis we are able to see that analysis of variance and regression analysis can provide the same information about a set of data. The percentage of variation in behavior scores that is explained by group membership can be computed by taking a ratio of two sums of squares derived from ANOVA. It can also be obtained by directly correlating comparison weights with behavior scores and taking $r^2(100)$. Even though the topics of regression (Chapter 7) and ANOVA (Chapter 13) have been presented in different chapters, the two procedures are closely related.

14.8   QUANTITATIVE FACTORS AND TREND ANALYSIS

Factors like the amount of alcohol consumed or grade level in school are usually measured quantitatively on an interval or ratio scale of measurement. This procedure results in levels of a factor that are ordered, and the distances between ordered levels have quantitative meaning. One consequence is that we can make a specialized set of comparisons with a different meaning from the types of comparisons previously discussed. With a quantitatively measured factor we can meaningfully ask about the *shape* of the relationship between the independent and dependent variables. That is, we may not be interested in the treatment versus control comparisons discussed so far. Rather, we might ask if the overall relationship among three or more levels of the factor has a particular shape.

This sort of analysis is generally referred to as *trend analysis.* The typical question asked of trend analysis is whether the variables are related in a *linear* (straight line) or *curvilinear* (e.g., quadratic) fashion. Functions representing linear and nonlinear trends are given in Figure 14.2. When there are four or more levels of a factor, the researcher can assess even higher-order components of trend (cubic, quartic, quintic, etc.). Fortunately, most applications of trend analysis in behavioral research result in a significant proportion of the variation in scores being accounted for by either a **linear trend** or a **quadratic trend.** Thus, we rarely need to examine higher-order trends.

LINEAR TREND: A relationship among means that is best described by the equation for a straight line.

QUADRATIC TREND: A relationship among means that is best described by the equation for a line that has only one point of inflection (change of direction).

To illustrate, we can use the data from the problem relating the number of spelling errors to grade in school. The means for these data are plotted in Figure 14.3. We might ask whether the four means from grades 2, 4, 6, and 8

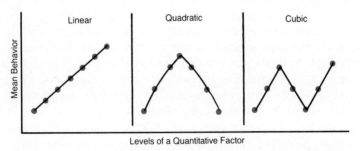

Figure 14.2 Representative trends in data. These are idealized cases of linear, quadratic, and cubic trends.

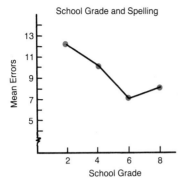

Figure 14.3 Hypothetical mean spelling errors from children in four school grades.

come closer to falling on a straight line (linear relationship) or a curved line (e.g., a quadratic relationship).

A precise way to carry out an analysis of trends is to compute a special set of orthogonal comparisons. Each component of trend is an independent estimate of the best-fitting line that describes the relationship between quantitative independent and dependent variables. The analysis is carried out in the same general way that other orthogonal comparisons are made. Specifically, the $SS_{between}$ is partitioned into components, each having 1 degree of freedom. With k groups, $k - 1$ orthogonal components of trend may be computed.

Generally, the only problem to be dealt with in computing trend analysis is selection of weights, w_i, for making the comparisons. Fortunately, researchers in many disciplines are interested in describing trends, and a table of weights is widely available. A portion of this table is provided in Table 14.6.

Use of the weights in Table 14.6 for trend analysis assumes both that the sample sizes are equal and that there are equal distances between levels of

Table 14.6 COMPARISON WEIGHTS FOR COMPUTATION OF TREND ANALYSIS

k	Comparison			Weights			Σw^2
3	Linear	-1	0	1			2
	Quadratic	1	-2	1			6
4	Linear	-3	-1	1	3		20
	Quadratic	1	-1	-1	1		4
	Cubic	-1	3	-3	1		20
5	Linear	-2	-1	0	1	2	10
	Quadratic	2	-1	-2	-1	2	14
	Cubic	-1	2	0	-2	1	10
	Quartic	1	-4	6	-4	1	60

Table 14.7   SPELLING ERRORS AND COMPARISON
WEIGHTS FOR TREND ANALYSIS

Grade level	2	4	6	8
Mean errors	12.17	10.00	7.33	8.17
$C1$: Linear	−3	−1	1	3
$C2$: Quadratic	1	−1	−1	1
$C3$: Cubic	−1	3	−3	1

the factor. An example of unequal distances would arise from testing children in grades 3, 4, 6, and 9. Clearly, the distance between 3 and 4 is not equal to the distance between 6 and 9. Trend analysis may be carried out with unequal sample sizes and unequal distances between levels of the factor, but not with the weights provided here (see, e.g., an article by Gaito, 1965). In practice this analysis is best accomplished with a computer program such as SPSS^{x} or BMD.

As an example of trend analysis, we have taken the mean spelling errors from 24 children in grades 2, 4, 6, and 8. These means and the corresponding weights are summarized in Table 14.7. Using Formula 14.7, we partitioned the $SS_{between}$ into three orthogonal trend components: SS_{linear}, $SS_{quadratic}$, and SS_{cubic}. For example, the SS_{linear} was computed as follows:

$$SS_{linear} = \frac{6[12.17(-3) + 10.00(-1) + 7.33(1) + 8.17(3)]^2}{(-3)^2 + (-1)^2 + (1)^2 + (3)^2} = 64.56$$

The results of these computations are summarized in Table 14.8, where you will find that the data are best described by a linear trend: $F(1,20) = 17.21$, $p < .01$. Neither the quadratic nor cubic comparisons are significant: $p > .05$ in each case.

The η^2 column in Table 14.8 shows that the variation in spelling errors accounted for by different grade levels is mostly associated with a straight line relating these two variables. The linear comparison accounts for about 41 percent of the explained variation. The quadratic and cubic trends account only for a combined total of 11.60 percent of the variation. In reporting the outcome from nonsignificant higher-order trends, it is common to simply pool them together as "nonlinear."

$$\eta^2 = r^2_{linear} + r^2_{quadratic} + r^2_{cubic}$$
$$= 40.88 + \quad 8.56 \quad + \quad 3.04$$
$$\eta^2 = r^2_{linear} + r^2_{nonlinear}$$
$$= 40.88 + \quad 11.60$$

From this example you can see that when there are more than two groups, η^2 contains variations from at least two r^2 values; one is the linear

Table 14.8 **TREND ANALYSIS ON SPELLING ERRORS**

Source	SS	df	MS	F*	η^2
Between	82.83	3	27.61	7.36	.5248
Linear	64.53	1	64.53	17.21	.4088
Quadratic	13.50	1	13.50	3.60	.0856
Cubic	4.80	1	4.80	1.28	.0304
Within	75.00	20	3.75		
Total	157.83	23			

*$F_{(1,20)\text{crit}} = 4.35$.

component of the relationship and one is the nonlinear component. Thus, when k is greater than 2, any single r^2 value will be less than η^2.

When $k = 2$, $r^2 = \eta^2$.

When $k > 2$, $r^2 \le \eta^2$.

When $k > 2$, $r^2_{C_1} + \ldots + r^2_{C_{k-1}} = \eta^2$.

14.9 INTERPRETING COMPARISONS

It should be clear that having a quantitatively measured factor does not demand trend analysis. The set of comparisons that is made depends on the questions of interest to the researcher. For example, for the factor grade in school the researcher might have justification for comparing the average errors of grades 2 and 4 with the average from grades 6 and 8. If a hypothesis about this comparison was considered to be more important than a hypothesis about the general shape of the relationship, trend analysis would not be carried out.

In general, there is more than one set of orthogonal comparisons that can be made for any factor with more than two levels. Table 14.9 lists three sets of weights that might be used in a study having four groups. The sets have been listed twice to emphasize that the absolute value of the weights is arbitrary. The comparisons in the left column include fractions, and those on the right are restricted to whole numbers. Some workers feel that whole numbers are easier to work with, but others prefer using fractions because they more obviously indicate that subsets of groups are being averaged. The answers are the same in each case.

You should try to imagine research situations in which each of these sets might be appropriate. For example, set I might be used if there were two treatment groups and two control groups. Comparison C_3 takes the average of the means from two treatment groups $(\overline{X}_1$ and $\overline{X}_2)$ and compares it with the average of the two control groups $(\overline{X}_3$ and $\overline{X}_4)$. Can you describe the purpose of the other two comparisons, C_1 and C_2, in this set?

In Table 14.9, the comparison matrix labeled "Set III" is of special interest. Since it forms the focus of the material presented in Chapter 15 we illustrate the use of these comparisons for one hypothetical study.

Suppose that a researcher is interested in the effects of motivational variables on the behavior of laboratory rats. One factor that might be chosen for study is the type of deprivation, such as food deprivation versus water deprivation. A second possible factor is the amount of deprivation measured in hours (e.g., 12 hours versus 24 hours). If each level of one factor is paired with each level of the second factor, we have the four treatment conditions summarized in Table 14.10. Before being tested, some rats would be deprived of food for 12 hours and others would be deprived for 24 hours. Still other rats would be deprived of water for either 12 or 24 hours before testing.

As indicated in Table 14.10, you should try to figure out what psychological meaning would be associated with each of the three comparisons, C_1, C_1, and C_3. First, consider comparison 1. According to the weights listed in the table, the average of the two food-deprived groups is to be compared with the average of the two water-deprived groups. Thus, this comparison tests the overall effect of type of deprivation. Similarly, comparison 2 compares the average of the two groups subjected to 12 hours of deprivation with the average of the groups having 24 hours of deprivation. This comparison tests the overall effect of the amount of deprivation. Finally, comparison 3 tests the joint effects of these two factors, the type and amount of deprivation. Comparisons testing the joint effect of two or more factors are referred

Table 14.9 THREE SETS OF ORTHOGONAL COMPARISONS FOR $k = 4$ SAMPLES OF DATA WITH $k - 1$ COMPARISONS IN EACH SET (Those Sets Using Fractions Are Equal to Those Using Whole Numbers.)

Set I		$\overline{X}_1$	$\overline{X}_2$	$\overline{X}_3$	$\overline{X}_4$	$\overline{X}_1$	$\overline{X}_2$	$\overline{X}_3$	$\overline{X}_4$
	C_1	1	−1	0	0	1	−1	0	0
	C_2	0	0	1	−1	0	0	1	−1
	C_3	1/2	1/2	−1/2	−1/2	1	1	−1	−1
Set II									
	C_1	−1	1/3	1/3	1/3	−3	1	1	1
	C_2	0	−1	1/2	1/2	0	−2	1	1
	C_3	0	0	−1	1	0	0	−1	1
Set III									
	C_1	1/2	1/2	−1/2	−1/2	1	1	−1	−1
	C_2	1/2	−1/2	1/2	−1/2	1	−1	1	−1
	C_3	1/2	−1/2	−1/2	1/2	1	−1	−1	1

Table 14.10 A RESEARCH DESIGN WITH TWO FACTORS,
           TYPE OF DEPRIVATION AND AMOUNT OF
           DEPRIVATION (HOURS), AND FOUR GROUP MEANS

Type of Deprivation	Food		Water	
Amount of Deprivation	12	24	12	24
Sample Means	$\overline{X}_1$	$\overline{X}_2$	$\overline{X}_3$	$\overline{X}_4$
Meaning of C_1?	1/2	1/2	$-1/2$	$-1/2$
Meaning of C_2?	1/2	$-1/2$	1/2	$-1/2$
Meaning of C_3?	1/2	$-1/2$	$-1/2$	1/2

to as *interactions*. In the next chapter, significant attention will be paid to the computation, graphing, and interpretation of interaction effects.

SUMMARY

Rejecting the null hypothesis with one-factor ANOVA permits acceptance of an omnibus alternative hypothesis that rarely provides sufficient details for a researcher. Therefore, additional comparisons are made to spell out more fully the relationships among means. For a given problem, one of two approaches to making comparisons is likely to be used.

Unplanned comparisons are made only if the overall null hypothesis has been rejected (e.g., by an *F*-test). Tukey's HSD test is often used to make all pairwise comparisons. It tests the significance of differences between each mean and every other mean and offers protection against inflating the probability of a Type I error.

Planned comparisons may be made without a preliminary *F*-test, but adjustment of Type I error for the several comparisons is recommended. This computation is often made with Dunn's test, using the Bonferroni procedure. The Type I error desired for the experiment as a whole (α_{EW}) is divided by the number of comparisons made to obtain the error used for each comparison.

Researchers frequently make sets of comparisons that are both planned and orthogonal (statistically independent). These comparisons are defined as a combination of all sample means such that each mean is multiplied by some weight and the weights sum to zero. Two comparisons are orthogonal when the sum of the products of their weights is zero. Means that are excluded from a given comparison are assigned a weight of zero. The weights are chosen to test specific hypotheses of interest to the researcher, and $k - 1$ orthogonal comparisons may be made in a given study.

Certain general types of research problems are so common that special names have been given to the orthogonal comparisons tested in these situations. One is trend analysis, where the names of comparisons refer to the shape of the function that best summarizes the relation between quantitative independent and dependent variables (e.g., linear or quadratic). Another case occurs when two different factors are assessed in a single study. The comparison testing joint effects of the factors is called an interaction. Comparisons of this type are the focal point of Chapter 15.

KEY WORDS

omnibus alternative hypothesis

per comparison error

experimentwise error

post hoc (unplanned) comparisons

planned (a priori) comparisons

pairwise comparison

complex comparison

Tukey's HSD test

Dunn's test

Bonferroni t

orthogonal comparison

$SS_{comparison}$

$F_{comparison}$

linear trend

quadratic trend

PROBLEMS

1 From among three means in a study, you compare the largest mean with the smallest mean. Is the probability of a Type I error equal to, greater than, or smaller than the per comparison error rate?

2 Assume that you have carried out a study with three samples of ten subjects to test an omnibus alternative hypothesis and found the following three means: $\overline{X}_1 = 5.00$, $\overline{X}_2 = 10.00$, $\overline{X}_3 = 15.00$. The ANOVA indicates that the null hypothesis should be rejected: $F(2,27) = 3.62$, $p < .05$, $MS_w = 69.06$. Explore the nature of this outcome with Tukey's HSD test.
(a) Which means are significantly different at $\alpha = .05$?
(b) Which means are significantly different at $\alpha = .01$?

3 A developmental psychologist wanted to investigate whether young children can be trained to do Piagetian conservation tasks. Eighty four-year-olds who could not conserve were randomly divided into four groups of 20, two groups that received training and two control groups. Both trained groups were given 30 minutes of training followed by an immediate test on ten conservation tasks and then trained and tested again two weeks later. One control group was tested twice (separated by two weeks) and the other control group was tested once. The dependent variable was the percentage correct on the final test (or the only test for the control group that received one test session).

The mean percentage correct for trained group 1 = 45 percent, trained group 2 = 34 percent, two-test controls = 18 percent, and one-test controls = 5 percent. The MS_w from ANOVA was 250. Carry out three planned comparisons by using Dunn's test with $\alpha = .05$. Comparison 1 is between the two trained groups. Comparison 2 is between the two control groups. Comparison 3 compares the average of the two trained groups with the average of the two control groups.

(a) What is the obtained value of t for each of these comparisons?

(b) What is the critical value of t from Dunn's test?

(c) For which comparison(s) can the null hypothesis be rejected in favor of the non-directional alternative?

(d) What would be concluded if the difference between the two control groups was statistically significant?

(e) Which of these three comparisons are not orthogonal?

4 Assume that the information in Problem 2 came from a study in which the reported number of friends was recorded for three groups of preschoolers. One group attended a "relaxed" preschool ($\overline{X}_R = 15.00$ friends), a second group attended a "strict" preschool ($\overline{X}_S = 11.00$), and the third group did not attend any preschool ($\overline{X}_N = 5.00$).

(a) Set up a comparison matrix for making two planned orthogonal comparisons and justify your choice of comparisons (e.g., What is the purpose of each of them?).

(b) Test the significance of the two comparisons and describe the results of each in a sentence.

(c) Use η^2 to determine what percentage of total variation is accounted for by each comparison. (Hint: To obtain the required SS values you will need to reproduce the complete ANOVA summary table. The SS_b can be obtained by converting the means to sums and using Formula 13.7.)

5 Assume that the information in Problem 2 came from a study in which secretaries were given different amounts of time to learn a new word processing procedure. After one, two, or three weeks of practice they were given a test that measured the number of minutes required to type a business report without errors. The group with one week of practice took 15 minutes ($\overline{X}_1 = 15.00$), and the other groups took less time ($\overline{X}_2 = 11.00$ and $\overline{X}_3 = 5.00$) to produce an errorless report.

(a) Set up a comparison matrix for making linear and quadratic trend comparisons.

(b) Test the significance of the two comparisons and describe the results of each in a sentence.

(c) Use ω^2 to determine what percentage of total variation is accounted for by each comparison. (Hint: Use the information from Problem 4c and Formula 14.7.)

Chapter 15

Analysis of Variance: Two or More Factors

15.1   INTRODUCTION

In Chapters 13 and 14 we discussed analysis of variance procedures for comparing the means of two or more levels of a *single* factor or independent variable. In practice, however, behavioral researchers recognize that many phenomena do not depend on a single variable but instead are influenced simultaneously by many variables. In this chapter we extend our discussion of the analysis of variance to cover comparisons among means that reflect the combined influence of two or more factors.

Consider research on modeling, in which a child views another person (the model) interacting with a room full of toys. The room contains one toy of special interest, a Bobo doll (a plastic air-filled doll with a weight in its base). Eight-year-old children individually view the model treating the Bobo doll in either a "friendly" or an "aggressive" fashion. Then the child is given the opportunity to play with the doll. The researcher wishes to determine whether children will treat the doll in a manner consistent with that of the model. In other words, will children who observed an aggressive model make more aggressive responses to the doll than children who observed a friendly model. Aggressive behavior is measured by the number of times the subject punches or kicks the doll in a fixed period of time like 30 minutes.

This example illustrates a one-factor independent samples design investigating the effect of a single independent variable (action of model) with two levels (friendly and aggressive) on the dependent variable of aggressiveness (punching and kicking). Suppose that we expand the design to investigate whether action-of-model effects are the same for models of different ages. We could do so by randomly assigning half the subjects to view a model who is four years younger than themselves and half to view a model who is four years older. This procedure results in the *two-factor* design illustrated in Table 15.1.

In Table 15.1 the levels of the action-of-model factor (friendly or aggressive) are listed across the top, and the levels of the age-of-model factor (youn-

Table 15.1   ARRANGEMENT OF 16 SUBJECTS INTO FOUR GROUPS BY AGE OF MODEL AND ACTION OF MODEL

Factors ⟶		Action of model		Row total
↓ Levels →		Aggressive	Friendly	
Age of model	Younger	4	4	8
	Older	4	4	8
	Column total	8	8	16

ger or older) are listed down the left-hand side. Each combination of one level of one factor with one level of another factor constitutes a **cell** of the research design. The numbers in each cell correspond to the number of subjects included in each combination of levels of the factors. For example, four subjects observed a younger model (age 4) react in a friendly fashion and four saw this model act in an aggressive manner. Similarly, four subjects observed an older model (age 12) act in a friendly way and four observed an aggressive older model. The column totals refer to the number of subjects included in each level of the action-of-model factor (eight friendly and eight aggressive), and the row totals refer to the number of subjects included in the age-of-model factor (eight subjects viewed a younger model and eight viewed an older model).

CELL: A specific combination of one level of a factor with one level of every other factor.

Experimental designs in which the levels of every factor are combined with the levels of every other factor are called **factorial designs.** Different types of factorial designs are labeled under a system that describes the number of factors and the number of levels of each factor included in the design. For example, the simplest factorial design has two factors, each having two levels. It is described as a 2 X 2 factorial design, where the letter *X* is read "by" (as in "2 by 2"). Each number denotes a different factor, and the value of each number refers to the number of levels of the factor. A two-factor design with three levels of one factor and four levels of the other factor would be referred to as a 3 X 4 factorial design.

FACTORIAL DESIGN: Research design in which the levels of every factor are combined with the levels of every other factor.

Designs that include more than two factors can be represented by expressions that include more numbers. For example, if we were to expand the present example to include subjects of two different ages (e.g., age levels 8 and 12 years), we would have a three-factor design described as a 2 (age of model) X 2 (action of model) X 2 (age of subject) factorial design. In this chapter we will simplify matters by focusing on two-factor designs. Furthermore, we will consider only designs in which the numbers of scores in each cell are equal. Unequal cell sizes introduce statistical complexities that are beyond the scope of this book.[1]

---

[1]The advanced student will find a systematic treatment of the effects of unequal samples in factorial design in articles by Mulligan, Wong, and Thompson (1987) and Spinner and Gabriel (1981).

Advantages of Factorial Designs

You might wonder why we do not investigate the effects of two factors by carrying out two separate one-factor studies. There is, in fact, nothing to stop us from doing so, but combining two one-factor studies into a single factorial study has several advantages.

Economy   One advantage of factorial designs is that they require fewer subjects to obtain the same information with the same degree of statistical power as separate one-factor designs. In the study illustrated in Table 15.1, the effect of both the action-of-model factor and the age-of-model factor are tested with 8 subjects per group. Since each subject is included simultaneously in one level of each of the two factors, both of these effects are tested with the same group of 16 subjects. To carry out two separate one-factor studies, each having 8 subjects per group, we would need to test 16 subjects per study, for a total of 32 subjects.

Control   Sometimes a researcher suspects that a factor is correlated with a particular dependent variable. If left uncontrolled, the factor can cloud our ability to identify and interpret the effects of other variables that may be of greater interest. For example, if the design illustrated in Table 15.1 were treated as a one-factor study of the effect of action of model, variation in aggressiveness scores associated with age of model would be treated as error variance and would be included in the within-groups variance estimate (MS_w) used to test the hypothesis about action-of-model effects. By including age of model as a factor, its effects are controlled by removing them from MS_w. This removal can reduce error variance and provide a more powerful test of the action-of-model effect.

Interaction   The major advantage of factorial designs is that they permit researchers to investigate the interaction between two or more independent variables. An interaction is the combined or joint effect of two or more factors on a dependent variable. The nature of the **interaction effect** is determined by the extent that the effect of one factor differs across levels of other factors. For example, the effect of a model's actions on a subject could depend on whether the model was younger or older than the subject. If the model was younger than the subject, the model's actions might not have much effect on the subject's behavior. Alternatively, if the model were older, the model's actions could have a strong effect on the subject's behavior. The potential for assessing such a result would be lost if action of model and age of model were investigated with separate one-factor research designs. We have much more to say about interactions later in this chapter.

INTERACTION EFFECT: The extent to which the effect of one independent variable (factor) varies across the levels of a second independent variable.

Generalizability The effect of one factor is generalizable to the extent that its effect is the same across levels of other factors. This result is reflected by a nonsignificant interaction effect. When the effect of one factor is not generalizable, its effect is different across different levels of the other factor. This aspect is reflected by a significant interaction effect. If, for example, the effect of action of model on aggressiveness were the same for young and old models, the interaction effect would not be significant. In comparison, if the effect of action of model were substantially different for young and old models, the interaction between these factors would be statistically significant. We would then say that the action-of-model effect does not generalize to both ages.

Consider what would happen if action of model and age of model interacted significantly and a one-factor study of action of model were carried out with a mixed group of older and younger models. In this situation the differential effects of action of model on younger and older models could mask each other to the extent that the results might indicate no action of model effect at all. At the very least, a significant action of model effect would be ambiguous. Its magnitude and nature would not apply exactly to older or younger models.

15.2 GENERAL LOGIC OF THE ANALYSIS

Recall from our discussion of one-factor ANOVA that the total variation in a dependent variable can be partitioned into two components, variation *within* levels of an independent variable (within-group variation) and variation *between* levels of an independent variable (between-group variation). When the null hypothesis (H_0) is true, both sources of variation estimate the same population variance (error variance) and the ratio of these variance estimates is approximately equal to 1.00. When H_0 is not true, within-group variation still estimates error variance but between-group variation estimates variance due to both error and factor effects (i.e., manipulated treatments or measured traits). Thus, when H_0 is not true, the ratio of between-group variance to within-group variance will be substantially larger than 1.00. The general rationale for analyzing two-factor designs is a direct extension of the rationale for analyzing one-factor designs.

Partitioning the Sum of Squares$_{total}$

The total variation in the scores can again be partitioned into two components: within-group variation and between-group variation. Within-group variation is expressed as the deviation of the individual scores, X, from the mean of the cell to which the scores belong, $\overline{X}_{cell}$. This within-group variation reflects error variation both when H_0 is true and when H_0 is not true because subjects within a cell are all in the same treatment/trait combination of conditions. That is, individuals within a cell cannot possibly differ because of action-of-model or age-of-model effects because they represent the same action and age conditions.

The between-group variation is expressed as the deviation of cell means, $\overline{X}_{cell}$, from the grand mean, GM $(\overline{X}_{cell} - GM)$. Therefore, in the context of factorial designs, between-group variation is called *between-cell variation*. This variation also reflects error variance when H_0 is true. When H_0 is not true it reflects error variance plus variance due to the effect of factors being studied (e.g., age of model and action of model).

The value of SS_{cell} does not indicate to what extent each factor is uniquely responsible for the overall between-cell variation. The means could vary because of action-of-model effects on aggressiveness, age-of-model effects on aggressiveness, or the joint effect of action and age on aggressiveness. Therefore, to determine the nature of between-cell variation, it must be partitioned into three independent components reflecting (1) variation unique to action-of-model effects, (2) variation unique to age-of-model effects, and (3) variation unique to the joint effects of these two factors. This partitioning of between-cell variation is outlined in Figure 15.1.

First consider variation unique to action-of-model differences. It is based on the deviations of the means for each action level from the GM while ignoring (i.e., averaging over) the presence of age-of-model differences. In Table 15.2 this estimate is based on the deviations of the *marginal* means for aggressive (10.12) and for friendly (9.88) conditions from the grand mean (10.00). These means come from all the data in each column and their deviations from GM are referred to as the **column main effect** (c). In the context of a particular study, the column main effect is labeled according to the factor name represented by the column means.

MAIN EFFECT: The effect of one factor averaged across levels of other factors.

In the present example, the column main effect is called the action-of-model main effect. If the column factor has no effect, the column means will be equal to each other and equal to the grand mean (since GM is the average of the column means). Therefore, the H_0 for the column main effect can be stated in the following two ways:

$$H_0: \mu_{c_1} = \mu_{c_2} = \ldots = \mu_{c_k}$$
$$H_0: \text{All } (\mu_c - \mu_G) = 0$$

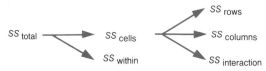

Figure 15.1 Outline of the way that the sum of squares total is partitioned in a two-factor ANOVA.

Table 15.2   MEAN NUMBER OF AGGRESSIVE ACTS IN FOUR GROUPS ACCORDING TO AGE OF MODEL AND ACTION OF MODEL

| | | Action of model | | Row means |
		Aggressive	Friendly	
Age of model	Younger	7.75	10.00	8.88
	Older	12.50	9.75	11.12
Column means		10.12	9.88	10.00

For our particular example, the null hypothesis is

H_0: $\mu_{\text{aggressive}} = \mu_{\text{friendly}}$

H_0: $(\mu_{\text{aggressive}} - \mu_G) = (\mu_{\text{friendly}} - \mu_G) = 0$

When H_0 is true, the interpretation of the column main effect is exactly the same as the overall between-group variation in the one-factor ANOVA. That is, it estimates the same population variance (error variance) as within-group variance, and the ratio of the two estimates is expected to be approximately 1.00. When H_0 is not true, the column main effect estimates error variance *plus* variance specific to the effect of the column factor (in this case action of model), and the ratio of the two variance estimates is expected to be much greater than 1.00.

A second component of between-cells variation is variation unique to the age-of-model effect. This component is based on deviations of the mean for each level of age of model from the grand mean while it ignores (averages over) the presence of action differences. In the present example it is based on deviations of the marginal means for the younger-model condition (8.88) and for the older-model condition (11.12) from the grand mean (10.00). These deviations can be referred to as the **row main effect** (r), or in this example, the age-of-model main effect. The null hypothesis for the row main effect is

H_0: $\mu_{r_1} = \mu_{r_2} = \ldots = \mu_{r_k}$

H_0: All $(\mu_r - \mu_G) = 0$

For our particular example, the null hypothesis is

H_0: $\mu_{\text{aggressive}} = \mu_{\text{friendly}}$

H_0: $(\mu_{\text{aggressive}} - \mu_G) = (\mu_{\text{friendly}} - \mu_G) = 0$

As in the case for the column main effect, variance due to the row main effect is an estimate of error when H_0 is true, and the ratio of that variance to within-group variance is expected to be about 1.00. When H_0 is not true, the ratio is generally expected to be greater than 1.00 because of effects due to the row factor (age of model in this case).

The third unique component of between-cell variation is the variation due to the interaction of action-of-model and age-of-model effects. This component is based on the deviations of each cell mean from the grand mean, adjusted for the main effects of action of model and age of model. That is, the interaction is based on subtracting the grand mean from each cell mean and then subtracting from that quantity the corresponding row and column main effects. In symbols, for any cell the row-by-column interaction effect (rc) is computed from the following deviations:

$$rc_{cell} = (\mu_{cell} - \mu_G) - (\mu_{col} - \mu_G) - (\mu_{row} - \mu_G)$$

With a little algebraic manipulation, this expression equals the following:

$$rc_{cell} = \mu_{cell} - \mu_{col} - \mu_{row} + \mu_G$$

In our example, for subjects who saw an aggressive model who was younger, the interaction effect is $(7.75 - 8.88 - 10.12 + 10.00) = -1.25$. The null hypothesis for the interaction effect is

$$H_0: \text{All } (\mu_{rc} - \mu_r - \mu_C + \mu_G) = 0$$

The variance due to the interaction effect is an estimate of error variance when H_0 is true. When H_0 is false, the interaction consists of error variance plus variance due to the joint effects of the two factors that cannot be accounted for by the main effects of those factors.

Having discussed the deviations on which main effects and the interaction effect are based, and the rationale for testing hypotheses about them, we now turn to the procedures used for computing ANOVA with a two-factor research design.

A Computational Example

As was the case for one-factor ANOVA, computations for two-factor ANOVA are more easily carried out by using group totals rather than group means. We introduce computational formulas with the data listed in Table 15.3. These data are hypothetical individual scores for the study involving the factors of age of model and action of model.

A convenient first step in the analysis is to treat the four groups as coming from a one-factor design, allowing easy computation of SS_t and SS_w, as in Chapter 13. The SS_b is also computed as in Chapter 13, but in the context of a two-factor design we call it SS_{cell}. Thus, we begin analysis of the two-factor design by using exactly the same computational formulas used to analyze a one-factor design.

The computational formula for the total sum of squares is

$$SS_t = \Sigma X^2 - \frac{G^2}{N} \tag{15.1}$$

Table 15.3 NUMBER OF AGGRESSIVE ACTS FOR 16 SUBJECTS
ARRANGED IN A 2 X 2 FACTORIAL DESIGN

Actions:	Aggressive		Friendly		
Age:	Younger	Older	Younger	Older	
	8	13	10	9	
	8	12	9	10	
	9	14	10	9	
	6	11	11	11	
T_j	31	50	40	39	$G = 160$
$\bar{X}_j$	7.75	12.50	10.00	9.75	$GM = 10.00$
ΣX^2_j	245	630	402	383	$\Sigma X^2 = 1660$

		Action of model		Row
		Aggressive	Friendly	total
Age of model	Younger	31	40	71
	Older	50	39	89
	Column total	81	79	160

From Table 15.3 we see that the sum of all squared raw scores, ΣX^2, is 1660 and that the grand total, G, is 160. The total number of scores in the study is $N = 16$. Thus, for this example,

$$SS_t = 1660 - \frac{160^2}{16} = 1660 - 1600$$

$$= \underline{60.00}$$

The computational formula for between-cell variation of the scores is given in Formula 15.2:

$$SS_{cell} = \frac{\Sigma T_j^2}{n_j} - \frac{G^2}{N} \tag{15.2}$$

Table 15.3 gives the four cell totals, T_j, each based on $n = 4$ scores per cell. Using these quantities in Formula 15.2, we have the following:

$$SS_{cell} = \frac{31^2 + 50^2 + 40^2 + 39^2}{4} - \frac{160^2}{16}$$

$$= 1645.50 - 1600$$

$$= \underline{45.50}$$

The within-group variation can be found by computing the sum of squares within each of the four groups and adding the results:

$$SS_w = SS_{w_1} + SS_{w_2} + \ldots + SS_{w_k}$$

where $SS_{wj} = \Sigma(X - \overline{X}_j)^2 = \Sigma X_j^2 - \dfrac{T_j^2}{n_j}$

$$SS_{w_1} = 245 - 31^2/4 = 245 - 240.25 = 4.75$$

$$SS_{w_2} = 630 - 50^2/4 = 630 - 625 = 5.00$$

$$SS_{w_3} = 402 - 40^2/4 = 402 - 400 = 2.00$$

$$SS_{w_4} = 383 - 39^2/4 = 383 - 380.25 = 2.75$$

$$SS_w = 4.75 + 5.00\ + 2.00 + 2.75\ \ = \underline{14.50}$$

This value can also be found by subtracting the sum of squares for cells from the total sum of squares:

$$SS_w = SS_t - SS_{cell}$$

$$= 60.00 - 45.50 \tag{15.3}$$

$$= \underline{14.50}$$

With these values we can build the summary table shown in the left panel of Table 15.4. It is not necessary to complete the analysis of these quantities because we are not testing an omnibus alternative hypothesis about cell means. Remember, the cell means carry information about main effects and the interaction. We wish to test specific hypotheses about the unique effects of each factor and their interaction. That is, we wish to test hypotheses about the sources of variation shown in the right panel of Table 15.4. The reason for computing SS_{cell} is that it is useful in computing the sum of squares for interaction. The reason for computing SS_w is that we use it to estimate the error variance needed to test all hypotheses in the factorial design.

Table 15.4 PARTITIONING THE SS_t FOR A ONE-WAY ANOVA AND FOR A 2 X 2 FACTORIAL ANOVA

One Way			Factorial		
Source	SS	df	Source	SS	df
			Row effect	?	1
Cells	45.40	3	Column effect	?	1
			Interaction	?	1
Within	14.50	12	Within	14.50	12
Total	60.00	15	Total	60.00	15

The second step in two-factor analysis is to partition the SS_{cell} to obtain the sum of squares for each main effect and the interaction effect. At the same time we will partition the df_{cell} to arrive at variance estimates of these effects. One of the easiest ways to partition SS_{cell} is to arrange the group totals, T_{ji}, into a 2 X 2 table, as shown in the lower part of Table 15.3. The marginal values from this table can then be used for computing the sum of squares for the main effects. For example, to obtain the sum of squares associated with age of model, we use the marginal row totals, T_r, of 71 and 89. To obtain the sum of squares for action of model, we use the marginal column totals, T_c, 81 and 79.

The computational formula for the row (age-of-model) comparison is given in Formula 15.4

$$SS_r = \frac{\Sigma T_r^2}{nc} - \frac{G^2}{N} \tag{15.4}$$

where nc is the number of scores in a row.

You should notice that the row totals are divided by the number of scores contributing to each total. This value is determined by the product of two numbers, n, the number of scores in each cell, and c, the number of levels of the column factor. In this example there are four subjects per cell and the column factor has two levels, giving $4(2) = 8$ scores contributing to each row total. Therefore, the sum of squares for rows is given by

$$SS_r = \frac{71^2 + 89^2}{8} - \frac{160^2}{16} = 1620.25 - 1600$$

$$= \underline{20.25}$$

The computational formula for the column (action-of-model) comparison is given in Formula 15.5.

$$SS_c = \frac{\Sigma T_c^2}{nr} - \frac{G^2}{N} \tag{15.5}$$

where nr is the number of scores in a column (i.e., n is the number of scores per cell and r is the number of rows).

$$SS_c = \frac{81^2 + 79^2}{8} = \frac{160^2}{16} = 1600.25 - 1600$$

$$= \underline{.25}$$

Finally, the computational formula for the row-by-column interaction is given in Formula 15.6:

$$SS_{rc} = \frac{\Sigma T_j^2}{n} - \frac{\Sigma T_r^2}{nc} - \frac{\Sigma T_c^2}{nr} + \frac{G^2}{N} \tag{15.6}$$

Each of the four terms in Formula 15.6 can be found in at least one of the earlier formulas (15.1–15.5) so there is no need to point out any new terms. For the present example, the sum of squares for the interaction is

$$SS_{rc} = 1645.50 - 1620.25 - 1600.25 + 1600.00$$

$$= \underline{25.00}$$

An even easier way of obtaining SS_{rc} is to subtract the value of SS_r and SS_c from the between-cell sum of squares, SS_{cell}. This procedure is shown in Formula 15.7 and clearly indicates that an interaction represents that portion of the between-cell variability that remains after accounting for the main effects.

$$SS_{rc} = SS_{cell} - SS_r - SS_c$$

$$= 45.50 - 20.25 - .25 \qquad (15.7)$$

$$= \underline{25.00}$$

Degrees of Freedom

Table 15.5 lists the sums of squares along with their respective degrees of freedom. The row and column degrees of freedom are computed in a manner comparable to one-factor ANOVA. Specifically, *df* for a main effect is the number of levels of the factor minus 1. For the row factor it is the number of rows minus 1 $(r - 1)$ and for the column factor it is the number of columns minus 1 $(c - 1)$. The degrees of freedom for the interaction sum of squares, df_{rc}, can be obtained by subtracting the row and column *df* values from the df_{cell}.

$$df_{rc} = df_{cell} - df_r - df_c$$

$$= (k - 1) - (r - 1) - (c - 1)$$

$$= (4 - 1) - (2 - 1) - (2 - 1) = 1$$

Table 15.5 THE ANOVA SUMMARY TABLE FOR A 2 X 2 FACTORIAL ANALYSIS OF NUMBER OF AGGRESSIVE BEHAVIORS

Source		SS	df	MS	F	η^2
Age	(Rows)	20.25	1	20.25	16.76	.3375
Action	(Columns)	.25	1	.25	.21	.0042
Interaction	(R X C)	25.00	1	25.00	20.69	.4168
Within	(Error)	14.50	12	1.21		
Total		60.00	15			

The value of df_{rc} can also be obtained from the product of the main effect degrees of freedom:

$$df_{rc} = (r - 1)(c - 1)$$

$$= (2 - 1)(2 - 1) = 1(1) = 1$$

Finally, the degrees of freedom for the within-cell variation (error) is equal to the degrees of freedom for each cell $(n - 1)$ summed across all of the cells. When there are equal numbers of subjects per cell, df_w can be found by multiplying the df for each cell by the total number of cells in the design. The total number of cells is obtained by taking the product of the number of levels of each factor: rc. In the present example there are two levels of each factor, for a total of $2(2) = 4$ cells. Therefore,

$$df_w = rc(n - 1)$$

$$= 2(2)(3) = 12$$

Mean Squares and F-ratios

Once the values of the sum of squares and degrees of freedom are known, the mean squares (variance estimates) and F-ratios can be computed by using the same procedure as in one-way ANOVA. The mean square for each effect is found by dividing the sum of squares values by their corresponding df. The F-ratios are computed by dividing the MS values for each effect by MS_w. In general,

$$F = \frac{MS_{effect}}{MS_w}$$

We evaluate the F-ratios in Table 15.5 by consulting Table G in Appendix III, with $\alpha = .05$ for 1 and 12 degrees of freedom. According to Table G, the minimum value of F required to reject H_0 is 4.75. For our example, $MS_{age} = 20.25$ and $MS_w = 1.21$, so $F_{age} = 20.25/1.21 = 16.76$. This observed value is greater than the critical table value, so we find that age of model has a significant effect on aggressiveness, $F(1,12) = 16.76$, $p < .01$.

$F(\text{critical}) = 4.75$

$F(\text{observed}) = 16.76$

Decision: Reject H_0

Because the subjects were randomly assigned to the different age-of-model conditions, we can interpret the difference in means $(11.12 - 8.88)$ as being caused by the different treatments. Even though factorial ANOVA is a test based on random *sampling*, when subjects are randomly *assigned* to levels of one or more factors, we generally interpret the result of the test as a good approximation of the result that would have been produced with a randomization test. Of course, if the subjects had been randomly sampled from a specified population, we would also have a statistical basis to infer that the causal result could be generalized to that particular population.

The effect of action of model is tested in a similar way. As shown in Table 15.5, this effect has 1 and 12 degrees of freedom and an *F*-ratio of .21. Therefore, we fail to reject the null hypothesis about this main effect, $p > .05$.

F(critical) = 4.75

F(observed) = .21

Decision: Fail to reject H_0

As seen in Table 15.2, the *F*-ratio for the interaction between these factors is 20.69 with 1 and 12 degrees of freedom. This observed ratio is greater than the critical table value and allows rejection of the null hypothesis, $F(1,12) = 20.69$, $p < .01$.

F(critical) = 4.75

F(observed) = 20.69

Decision: Reject H_0

15.3   INTERPRETATION OF INTERACTION IN A TWO-FACTOR DESIGN

As a general rule it is wise to begin the interpretation of the results from a two-factor design by starting with the interaction, if it is significant, because the nature of the interaction will qualify the interpretation of the main effects. Frequently, detailed examination of the interaction leaves little to say about the main effects of the variables involved in that interaction. When an interaction is not significant, the meaning of the significant main effects may be interpreted directly.

Graphing Interactions

A useful starting point in interpretation of a significant interaction is to generate a graphic figure of the means. An example is given in Figure 15.2, which shows the significant interaction between age of model and action of model resulting from the analysis of the aggression scores in Table 15.3.

The same data have been plotted twice in Figure 15.2 to illustrate that either independent variable may be plotted along the X-axis. Although the researcher may plot the data either way, in some cases one plot lends itself to a different emphasis of interpretation than the other plot. The plot in the left panel of Figure 15.2 has age of model on the X-axis. This plot emphasizes that subjects are more likely to act aggressively after watching aggressive

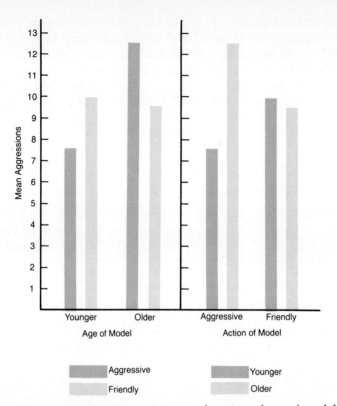

Figure 15.2 Mean aggressions as a function of age of model and action of model plotted with age of model on the X-axis (left panel) and with action of model on the X-axis (right panel).

behavior, but only when the model is older. When the model is younger, subjects are more likely to act aggressively after watching friendly behavior. The plot in the right panel of Figure 15.2 indicates that subjects are more likely to act aggressively after watching an older model than after watching a younger model, but only when the models are aggressive. When the model is friendly, subjects act aggressively to about the same extent, regardless of the age of the models. If age of model is the major factor of interest, the right panel would be reported because it emphasizes that there is an age of model effect for aggressive actions but not for friendly actions.

Figure 15.2 was constructed as a bar graph because both of the independent variables were measured on a qualitative scale. The width of the bars and the distance between bars is arbitrary. As you will recall from Chapter 13, when a factor is measured on an interval or ratio scale, a line graph may be used instead of a bar graph. In a line graph both the ordering of the values along the X-axis and the distance between these values have quantitative meaning.

Verbal Interpretations of Interaction

There are three common ways to describe verbally the relationships revealed in a graphic figure of an interaction.

Independence Versus Dependence   The effects of two (or more) factors on behavior are said to be *independent* when the interaction between these factors is *not* significant. In this case you can interpret the effects of any given main effect without considering the presence of other independent variables in the design. Each factor is considered to affect the behavior being measured independently. When an interaction is not significant, it gives generality to the interpretation of the main effects.

In our example, we might have had a significant effect of age of model and a nonsignificant interaction between the factors. In that case it would have been possible to say that the effect of age of model was independent of action of model.

For our example, the interaction was significant. Therefore, the effects of the two factors are *dependent* on each other. The age-of-model effect must be qualified by specifying the nature of this effect for each level of the action-of-model variable. It would not be appropriate to interpret only the main effect. As shown in Figure 15.2, the effect of action of model was different when the models were younger than when they were older. Thus, we cannot generalize the age-of-model effect to each action group.

Difference Between Differences   Instead of using the terms independent and dependent, interpretation of an interaction can focus directly on the differences between means. For example, we can point out that for younger models the average friendly versus aggressive difference was -2.25 aggressions ($7.75 - 10.00 = -2.25$). When the model was older, the average aggressive-friendly effect was 2.75 aggressions ($12.50 - 9.75 = 2.75$). The fact that the interaction is significant means that there is a significant difference between these two differences. That is, the difference $2.75 - (-2.25) = 5.00$ is significantly different from zero. The larger the value of the difference between differences, the more likely it is that the interaction will be significant.

Additive Versus Nonadditive Effects   If the interaction had not been significant, changing the values of action of model would have led to relatively uniform increases in aggression for each age group. Then we could say that there is an *additive* relationship between the factors. Each change in the value of action of model would add a constant increment to the performance of each age condition. Thus, one way to state that an interaction is not significant is to say that there is an additive relationship between the factors.

For the interaction plotted in Figure 15.2 we find that a change from friendly to aggressive models led to a large increase in aggressive responses with an older model but to a decrease in aggression with a younger model. It appears that changing levels of the action-of-model variable does not have a uniform effect on the two age-of-model conditions. Changing the level of action of model led to differential changes in aggression for younger (decrement) and older (increment) model conditions. We can say, therefore, that there is a *nonadditive* relationship between the two factors in their effect on aggressive behavior.

To summarize, when an interaction is *not* significant, the effects of two factors on behavior are independent, the difference between differences is small, and the relationship between factors is additive. When an interaction *is* significant, the effects of the two factors on behavior are dependent on one another, the difference between differences is large, and the relationship between factors is nonadditive.

15.4   PERCENTAGE OF VARIATION

The methods of estimating the percentage of total variation accounted for by effects in a factorial design are basically the same as in a one-factor design. Table 15.5 gives eta squared (η^2). The η^2 values for each effect (main effects and interaction effect) are computed by dividing the SS_{effect} by the SS_{total}. For our example we have age of model (R) with r levels and action of model (C) with c levels.

$$\eta_R{}^2 = \frac{SS_R}{SS_{total}} = \frac{20.25}{60.00} = .338$$

$$\eta_C{}^2 = \frac{SS_C}{SS_{total}} = \frac{.25}{60.00} = .004$$

$$\eta_{RC}{}^2 = \frac{SS_{RC}}{SS_{total}} = \frac{25.00}{60.00} = .417$$

In this way we found that approximately 34 percent of the total variation in aggression scores is accounted for by the effect of age of model. Similarly, less than 1 percent of the variation is accounted for by action of model, and about 42 percent is accounted for by the interaction between age of model and action of model.

As with one-factor ANOVA, a population estimate of explained variation can be computed by using the statistic omega squared, ω^2.

$$\omega_R{}^2 = \frac{SS_R - (r - 1)MS_w}{SS_{total} + MS_w} = \frac{20.25 - (1)1.21}{60.00 + 1.21} = .311$$

$$\omega_C{}^2 = \frac{SS_C - (c - 1)MS_w}{SS_{total} + MS_w} = \frac{.25 - (1)1.21}{60.00 + 1.21} = .016$$

$$\omega_{RC}{}^2 = \frac{SS_{RC} - (r - 1)(c - 1)MS_w}{SS_{total} + MS_w} = \frac{25.00 - (1)(1)1.21}{60.00 + 1.21} = .389$$

15.5 A SECOND EXAMPLE: THE 2 X 3 CASE

Consider the weight-loss study examined in Chapter 14. You may recall that we had two treatment conditions for obese people who wanted to lose weight, behavior modification treatment (BM) and group therapy treatment (GP). (For this example we will not deal with the control group that was on a waiting list to begin treatment.) It is possible that the effect of the treatments on weight loss is a function not only of the type of therapy but also of other factors, such as the amount of money the clients paid for each treatment session. Perhaps people who spend larger amounts pay more attention to what happens during the sessions in order to "get their money's worth." If this is true, differences in weight loss that are associated with different therapies might depend on how much money clients pay.

Table 15.6 gives the number of pounds lost over six months in our hypothetical study in which the effect of these therapies was compared for clients who paid $10, $20, or $30 per session. The major computations required to produce an ANOVA summary are included in this table. In this example, 30 people were randomly assigned to the six treatment conditions or cells of the research design. For instance, 5 people received group therapy

Table 15.6 **NUMBER OF POUNDS LOST IN SIX MONTHS**

Amount:	$10		$20		$30		
Therapy:	BM	GP	BM	GP	BM	GP	
	6	1	8	3	9	10	
	11	0	10	7	13	9	
	10	5	7	5	7	13	
	12	3	12	7	13	11	
	11	5	11	8	10	13	
T_j	50	14	48	30	52	56	$G = 250$
ΣX_j^2	522	60	478	196	568	640	$\Sigma X^2 = 2464$

$$SS_t = 2464 - \frac{250^2}{30} = 2464 - 2083.33$$

$$= \underline{380.67}$$

$$SS_{cell} = \frac{50^2 + 14^2 + \ldots + 56^2}{5} - \frac{250^2}{30} = 2348 - 2083.33$$

$$= \underline{264.67}$$

$$SS_w = SS_t - SS_{cell}$$

$$= 380.67 - 264.67$$

$$= \underline{116.00}$$

and paid $10 per session, 5 different people received group therapy and paid $20 per session, and so on.

The lower part of Table 15.6 shows that we begin the data analysis by computing the three basic sum of squares: SS_{total}, SS_{cell}, and SS_{within}. The SS_{cell} is then partitioned into the variation associated with each main effect and the interaction. This partitioning is illustrated in Table 15.7. First the cell sums are organized into rows and columns. The choice of which factor is treated as the row or column factor is arbitrary. Then the marginal values of the matrix are used to compute the sum of squares for the main effects. As shown at the foot of Table 15.7, these sum of squares are subtracted from the between-cells sum of squares to obtain the interaction sum of squares.

Finally, all the required sum of squares are listed in Table 15.8 along with their degrees of freedom. From these values the mean squares (MS) and F-ratios are obtained. As shown in Table 15.8, all three effects, both main effects and the interaction effect, are statistically significant with these data. More detailed analysis of these significant outcomes begins with the examination of the nature of the significant interaction.

Figure 15.3 shows a plot of data from the experiment on the effects of the type of therapy and the amount paid. In the left panel of Figure 15.3 the quantitative variable "Amount Paid" has been placed on the X-axis and the

Table 15.7 **TOTAL POUNDS LOST IN SIX MONTHS**

		Amount paid per session			Row total
		$10	$20	$30	
Type of therapy	BM	50	48	52	150
	GP	14	30	56	100
Column total		64	78	108	250

$$SS_r = \frac{150^2 + 100^2}{15} - \frac{250^2}{30} = \underline{83.33}$$

$$SS_c = \frac{64^2 + 78^2 + 108^2}{10} - \frac{250^2}{30} = \underline{101.07}$$

$$SS_{rc} = SS_{cell} - SS_r - SS_c$$

$$= 264.67 - 83.33 - 101.07$$

$$= \underline{80.27}$$

Table 15.8   ANOVA SUMMARY TABLE FOR POUNDS LOST DATA

Source	SS	df	MS	F	η^2
Amount (A)	101.07	2	50.53	10.46	.2655
Therapy (T)	83.33	1	83.33	17.24	.2189
A X T	80.27	2	40.13	8.30	.2109
Within	116.00	24	4.83		
Total	380.67	29			

means plotted as a line graph. The same data have been plotted in the right panel of this figure as a bar graph, with "Type of Therapy" on the X-axis. In both cases you can see that with behavior modification therapy the effect of amount paid was relatively small. Alternatively, amount paid had a more substantial effect on the pounds lost in the group therapy condition. The effect of amount paid depends on which therapy is given. Thus, we cannot generalize the amount paid effect to each therapy.

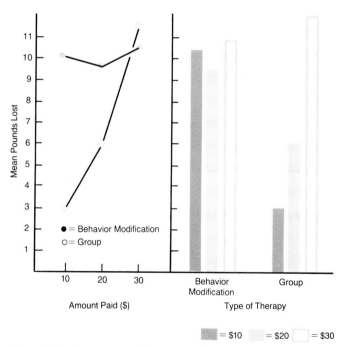

Figure 15.3   Mean pounds lost as a function of type of therapy and amount paid plotted with amount paid on the X-axis (left panel) and type of therapy on the X-axis (right panel).

15.6 SIMPLE EFFECTS: STATISTICAL PROBES OF INTERACTIONS

Our analysis of the significant interaction in the weight-loss study used verbal description of a graphic figure. Many researchers supplement such an analysis with more precise and quantitative analysis, called *simple effects*. A simple effect is the analysis of a given variable at one level of a second variable. In our weight-loss example we can examine the effects of amount paid within each type of therapy condition.

Analysis of simple effects will provide a more precise statement of the verbal analysis that "with behavior modification therapy the effect of amount paid was relatively small." If this verbal analysis is accurate, the simple effect for amount paid among behavior modification subjects should be nonsignificant. By the same kind of argument, to assess the simple effect of amount paid among group therapy subjects, we focus on the total pounds lost in these three specific groups. If amount paid has a substantial effect on pounds lost, this simple effect should be statistically significant. The relevant cell totals are found in Table 15.7.

Using the general row and column notation, we examine the column effect (amount paid) at level one of the row factor (behavior modification). We calculate a sum of squares for this particular simple effect: SS_c at r_1.

$$SS_c \text{ at } r_1 = \frac{\Sigma T_c^2 \text{ at } r_1}{n} - \frac{(\Sigma T_{r_1})^2}{nc}$$

Substituting the total from behavior modification cases, we have

$$SS_c \text{ at } r_1 = \frac{50^2 + 48^2 + 52^2}{5} - \frac{150^2}{15} = 1.60$$

$$MS_c \text{ at } r_1 = SS/df = 1.60/2 = .80$$

The value of MS_c at r_1 is evaluated by dividing by an estimate of error. The best estimate of error is the pooled error term from ANOVA, MS_w. As shown in Table 15.8, MS_w for this example is 5.05.

$$F_c \text{ at } r_1(2,24) = \frac{.80}{4.83} = \underline{.16}$$

We can also examine the effect of amount paid among only the group therapy subjects in row two of Table 15.7.

$$SS_c \text{ at } r_2 = \frac{\Sigma T_c^2 \text{ at } r_2}{n} - \frac{(\Sigma T_{r_2})^2}{nc}$$

Substituting the data for group therapy, we have

$$SS_c \text{ at } r_2 = \frac{14^2 + 30^2 + 56^2}{5} - \frac{100^2}{15} = 179.73$$

$$MS_c \text{ at } r_2 = SS/df = 179.73/2 = 89.87$$

$$F_c \text{ at } r_2 = \frac{89.87}{4.83} = \underline{18.61}$$

To check on the accuracy of computations, it may be noted that the sum of the $SS_{\text{interaction}}$ effect and the SS_{main} effect equals (within rounding error) the sum of the simple effects. For our analysis of the interaction between type of therapy (T) and amount paid (A) we have the following:

$$SS_{rc} + SS_c = SS_c \text{ at } r_1 + SS_c \text{ at } r_2$$

$$SS_{TA} + SS_T = SS_A \text{ at BM} + SS_A \text{ at GP}$$

$$80.27 + 101.07 = 1.60 + 179.73$$

$$181.34 \approx 181.33$$

In this set of data the analysis of simple effects supports the conclusions derived by inspection of Figure 15.3. The amount-paid variable had no significant effect on the pounds lost when studied with behavior modification, $F < 1$, but it did have a significant effect when studied with group therapy subjects, $F(2,24) = 17.80$, $p < .01$.

The probabilities of Type I errors associated with these simple effects are clearly not near the critical value of .05. If, however, the outcomes had been less clear-cut, the researcher would probably use an experimentwise error rate. Given that $\alpha = .05$ for the test of the interaction, $\alpha/c = .05/2 = .025$ could have been used for each of the two simple effects.

Additional analysis of data in a factorial design can be carried out by using the multiple comparison techniques given in Chapter 14. For example, Tukey's HSD test might be applied to test the amount-paid effect, using all pairwise comparisons within the group therapy condition. Similarly, if the interaction were not significant, either Tukey's HSD test or other multiple comparisons could be applied to analyze the main effect means of any factor having more than two levels. In all cases MS_w is the error term.

15.7   STATISTICAL ASSUMPTIONS

In applying factorial analysis of variance to a set of data, the same assumptions must be met as when using ANOVA with a single factor. We assume that the populations of scores associated with each condition are normally distributed and that they have equal variances. As long as the scores are independent (e.g., through random sampling), the assumptions need not be satisfied perfectly. A dependent variable that has a more or less symmetrical and unimodal distribution generally will yield a valid F-ratio. Similarly, the variances need not be precisely equal because the F-ratio is a robust statistic. As long as the sample sizes are equal, the F-ratio is usually valid when variances are unequal up to about a four-to-one ratio, and often beyond.

Problems of appropriate interpretation may result when available subjects are tested instead of randomly selected samples. For many purposes the best way to obtain a sample is to use some form of random sampling, but in practice random samples can be difficult to obtain. In such cases we use the *F*-ratio derived from the random sampling model to obtain an estimate of the statistical result that would have been obtained with a randomization test. (The randomization test for factorial designs is discussed by Edgington, 1987, but its treatment is beyond the scope of this book.)

For the obtained probability to have statistical meaning when random sampling is not carried out, it is important to have random assignment of subjects to conditions. When neither random sampling nor random assignment is actually used, the resulting probability values should be interpreted cautiously. In such cases interpreting probability values from statistical tests is often more a matter of faith than statistics. The researcher might infer that a systematic outcome has been observed, but there would be no statistical basis for either generality or causal inference. This is another case in which replication of the study is especially important.

15.8 ALTERNATE INTERPRETATIONS OF TWO-FACTOR DESIGNS

In this section we present two different approaches to the analysis of data in a factorial design that do not require Formulas 15.1 through 15.7. In one approach we treat the data by regression analysis, in which sums of squares are computed with correlations. In the other approach we treat the main effects and the interaction effect as a set of three planned comparisons. Brief examination of these alternate methods should help in understanding the nature of the *F*-ratio for each effect. Both of these methods utilize the fact that each effect in a factorial analysis of variance is an independent source of variation.

We can treat each effect tested in factorial ANOVA as having two possible outcomes. It is either significant (reject H_0) or nonsignificant (fail to reject H_0). Thus, in a two-factor design with three effects, there are $2^3 = 8$ possible combinations of significant and nonsignificant results. These range from the case in which none of the three effects is significant to the case in which all three effects are significant. This variety of outcomes is possible because each effect is statistically independent of all other effects. The main effect of age of model, for example, can be significant or not significant regardless of the status of the main effect of action of model or the interaction between these factors.

When two variables are independent, the correlation between them is zero. In the study on aggression, being in the younger or older age-of-model condition was not independent of whether a model was aggressive or friendly. In this case, knowing that a subject observed a younger model did not permit accurate prediction that the person performed one type of action or the other.

If the age-of-model factor has no significant effect, there will be a negligible correlation between aggression scores and being in the younger or older condition. Knowing that a person observed a younger or older model will not tell you about the size of his or her aggression score. When the effect of the factor is significant, there will be a substantial correlation between conditions and aggression scores. Knowing their condition tells you something about their behavior score.

Regression Analysis

Our first alternative approach involves treating the analysis of scores as a regression problem. This analysis is outlined in Table 15.9, where you can see that in columns X_1, X_2, and X_3 weights (coding variables) have been paired with behavior scores (the column headed Y). The values of the weights were chosen to reflect the comparisons made in ANOVA. The column headed X_1 corresponds to the row or age-of-model main effect. The scores for each person in the younger condition were paired with weights of 1, and those for each person in the older condition were paired with weights of -1. When these weights are correlated with the behavior scores, the resulting value of

Table 15.9 REGRESSION ANALYSIS OF AGGRESSION DATA FROM A 2 X 2 FACTORIAL DESIGN GIVING PERCENTAGE OF VARIATION VALUES FROM r^2 VALUES

Subject number	Model Age	Model Action	X_1	X_2	X_3	Y
1	younger	aggressive	1	1	1	8
2	younger	aggressive	1	1	1	8
3	younger	aggressive	1	1	1	9
4	younger	aggressive	1	1	1	6
5	younger	friendly	1	−1	−1	10
6	younger	friendly	1	−1	−1	9
7	younger	friendly	1	−1	−1	10
8	younger	friendly	1	−1	−1	11
9	older	aggressive	−1	1	−1	13
10	older	aggressive	−1	1	−1	12
11	older	aggressive	−1	1	−1	14
12	older	aggressive	−1	1	−1	11
13	older	friendly	−1	−1	1	9
14	older	friendly	−1	−1	1	10
15	older	friendly	−1	−1	1	9
16	older	friendly	−1	−1	1	11

Correlation Matrix

	X_1	X_2	X_3	Y	$r^2(100)$
X_1	1.000	0.000	0.000	−.5809	33.74
X_2		1.000	0.000	.0645	.42
X_3			1.000	−.6455	41.67
Y				1.0000	

$r^2(100)$ yields the same percentage of variation accounted for as was obtained by forming a ratio of the sum of squares values in Table 15.5 (within rounding error).

$$\% \text{ of variation} = \frac{SS_{age}}{SS_{total}}(100) = \frac{20.25}{60.00}(100) = 33.75\%$$

$$= r_{X_1Y}^2(100) = -.5809^2(100) = 33.74\%$$

In a similar way, the weights in the column headed X_2 represent the comparison between aggressive or friendly conditions. Those in the column headed X_3 represent the comparison made in the interaction between these factors. The correlations between comparison weights (X_1, X_2, X_3) and the dependent variable (Y) are given at the foot of Table 15.9. The percentage of variation values, $r^2(100)$, can be used to obtain the sums of squares for the main effects and interaction. When the total sum of squares from ANOVA is multiplied by the percentage of variation accounted for by an effect, the result is the sum of squares for that effect.

$$SS_{age} = SS_{total}(r_{X_1Y})^2 = 60(.3374) = 20.25$$

$$SS_{action} = SS_{total}(r_{X_2Y})^2 = 60(.0042) = .25$$

$$SS_{age \times action} = SS_{total}(r_{X_3Y})^2 = 60(.4167) = 25.00$$

At the foot of Table 15.9 you should notice that the correlations between the three X variables are all zero. These values emphasize the fact that the main effects and interaction effects tested in factorial ANOVA are statistically independent of each other. Each one of the effects may be significant or nonsignificant regardless of the values of the other effects in the analysis.

Planned Comparisons

Another way of conceptualizing a two-factor ANOVA is to consider the effects to be a set of three planned orthogonal comparisons. Computation of F-ratios for the main effects and interactions involves making comparisons in the fashion outlined in Chapter 14.[2] As in the regression approach, weights

---

[2]Using ANOVA to assess the effects of two or more independent variables in factorial ANOVA raises concern about Type I error rate when making these planned orthogonal comparisons. The common practice with factorial ANOVA is to assess the main effect of each variable and their interaction in a series of comparisons, where each comparison uses the per comparison rate (e.g., .05). Some researchers, however, adjust the rate to take into account the number of comparisons. They might, for example, use the Bonferroni procedure discussed in Chapter 14. With two main effects and one interaction, the experimentwise error rate could be set at .05 and individual comparisons would be declared significant only at $\alpha/c = .05/3 = .0167$. See, for example, Keselman and Keselman (1987).

such as $+1$ and -1 are used. Unlike the regression approach, these weights, w_i, will be multiplied by each sample mean by using Formula 14.5:

$$SS_{Ci} = \frac{n[(w_1)\overline{X}_1 + \ldots + (w_k)\overline{X}_k]^2}{w_1^2 + \ldots + w_k^2} \tag{14.5}$$

In Chapter 14 we discussed three constraints that characterize these comparisons.

1. The weights for each comparison are selected so that the sum of the weights is zero.

   $\Sigma w_i = 0$ for any given C_i

2. Two comparisons are orthogonal if the sum of the products of their weights is zero.

   $\Sigma(w_i)(w_j) = 0$

3. The number of orthogonal comparisons in a given set is determined by the number of cells, k.

   number of comparisons $= df$ for SS_{cell} (i.e., $k - 1$)

Table 15.10 shows three sets of weights that, when applied to four means, lead to three sums of squares. These are the SS values corresponding to the two main effects and the interaction effect for our experiment. By applying Formula 14.5 to the example means from the age-of-model study, we obtain the following sums of squares for each planned comparison:

$$SS_{Cr} = \frac{4[(1)7.75 + (-1)12.50 + (1)10.00 + (-1)9.75]^2}{(1)^2 + (1)^2 + (-1)^2 + (-1)^2} = \frac{81}{4} = 20.25$$

$$SS_{Cc} = \frac{4[(1)7.75 + (1)12.50 + (-1)10.00 + (-1)9.75]^2}{(1)^2 + (-1)^2 + (1)^2 + (-1)^2} = \frac{1.0}{4} = .25$$

$$SS_{Crc} = \frac{4[(1)7.75 + (-1)12.50 + (-1)10.00 + (1)9.75]^2}{(1)^2 + (-1)^2 + (-1)^2 + (1)^2} = \frac{100}{4} = 25.00$$

Table 15.10 **A COMPARISON MATRIX INDICATING THE VALUES OF WEIGHTS TO BE APPLIED TO EACH MEAN**

Action of model:	Aggressive		Friendly	
Age of model:	Younger	Older	Younger	Older
Means	7.75	12.50	10.00	9.75
C_1 (rows)	$+1$	-1	$+1$	-1
C_2 (columns)	$+1$	$+1$	-1	-1
C_3 (interaction)	$+1$	-1	-1	$+1$

When these sums of squares are compared with those in Table 15.5, it is easy to see that the main effects and the interaction effect in a factorial design are really specific cases of planned orthogonal comparisons.

15.9   FACTORIAL DESIGNS WITH MORE THAN TWO FACTORS

It is common to find research designs with more than two factors. In particular, designs with three or four factors are often seen in the research literature, although designs with more than four factors are rare.

The analysis of variance for research designs with more than two factors is a straightforward extension of the ANOVA for two-factor designs. The only difference is that there are more hypotheses to test. In general, we can test hypotheses concerning the main effects of each factor included in the design, as well as the interaction between every combination of two factors, three factors, and so on. For example, in a three-factor design we can test hypotheses concerning the main effects of factor A, factor B, and factor C. In addition, we can test three two-factor interactions (AB, AC, and BC) and a three-factor interaction (ABC). If the design has four factors, we can test four main effects (A, B, C, D), six two-factor interactions (AB, AC, AD, BC, BD, CD), four three-factor interactions (ABC, ABD, ACD, BCD), and one four-factor interaction (ABCD).

As long as the research design involves independent groups of subjects in every combination of levels of the factors, the procedures for analyzing the variance of multifactor designs are essentially the same as those discussed in this chapter. We do not go into the specific computations required to carry out ANOVA on designs with more than two factors. Conceptually, they are no more difficult than computations associated with two-factor designs; there are simply more of them.

SUMMARY

A factorial design is one that combines two or more independent variables in a single study. Because they require fewer subjects, factorial designs are more economical than separate single-factor designs that provide the same information. Moreover, factorial designs provide information beyond that obtained in single-factor studies, namely, information about the joint effects of two or more independent variables.

In this chapter we focused primarily on the simplest factorial design, in which independent groups of subjects served in each combination of levels of two factors. The analysis involves partitioning total variation into four unique sources: (1) variation unique to the row factor, called the row main effect; (2) variation unique to the column factor, called the column main effect; (3) variation unique to the joint effect of the factors, called the interaction; and (4) error variation. Null hypotheses for the two main effects and the interaction effect are tested by forming a ratio of variance for each effect to the error variance, producing *F*-ratios. When the observed value of these *F*-ratios exceeds the tabled value of *F*, the respective null hypotheses are rejected. In addition to considering whether a particular *F*-ratio is significant or not, another important piece of information is the proportion of variation accounted for by that effect. Two useful measures of proportion of variation accounted for are eta squared (η^2) and omega squared (ω^2).

The most important new concept introduced in this chapter is interaction. A significant interaction between two factors indicates that their effects are dependent because the effect of one factor depends on the particular level of the other factor. Another way of describing interaction relates to differences between differences. When the nature of the differences among levels of one factor differs across levels of a second factor, we say that the factors interact in their effect on the dependent variable. Interaction also can be described as a nonadditive relationship between two factors. A nonadditive relationship means that at different levels of one factor the effect of the second factor is not constant.

When interactions are significant they should be graphed to help assess their meaning. They should also be statistically probed by analysis of simple effects. This computation involves analyzing the effect of one factor at each level of the other factor.

Factorial ANOVA can be conceptualized in several related ways. Traditionally it is conceptualized as a technique for comparing means that reflect differences due to a factor or combination of factors. However, factorial ANOVA can also be conceptualized within the framework of linear regression. This approach focuses on the extent to which factors and combinations of factors are correlated with a dependent variable. Finally, the main effects and interaction effect(s) in a factorial design can be treated as a set of planned orthogonal comparisons.

KEY WORDS

cell	independence of factors
factorial design	difference between differences
main effect	additive relationship
interaction effect	simple effects

PROBLEMS

1 One of the advantages of factorial designs is that they provide a type of information not directly available in designs with only one factor.
   (a) What direct information is unique to factorial designs?
   (b) What are the other advantages of factorial designs?

2 Suppose that you randomly sampled eight university students to take part in a reading experiment. The sentences to be read were presented one word at a time on a microcomputer. After the sentence appeared, the students were asked whether a particular word was in that sentence. The students were randomly divided into two groups that received the stimulus sentences at either a slow rate (160 milliseconds per word) or a fast rate (80 milliseconds per word). Half of the students in each of these groups were randomly assigned to a group receiving feedback (correct or incorrect) after their responses or one receiving no feedback. The total correct responses for 50 stimulus sentences are

Rate of Presentation:	Slow		Fast	
Feedback:	Yes	No	Yes	No
	42	33	26	31
	40	34	29	27

(a) Build an ANOVA summary table and evaluate the results of the analysis of two main effects and an interaction (let $\alpha = .05$).
(b) Give a verbal description of the major features of these results.

The following problems (3–5) refer to Problem 2:

3 How would you describe this research design (e.g., 2 X 2, 2 X 3, 3 X 3)?

4 If you discovered that the first subject in each cell of this design was male and the second subject was female, what would prevent you from further analysis of these data that included the original factors and added sex of subject as a factor?

5 To what extent can statistically based inferences be derived in this problem?
(a) Comment on generality inference.
(b) Comment on causal inference.

6 Assume that you have a 2 X 2 factorial design in which one factor is the age of subjects (20 years or 60 years) and the other factor is amount of alcohol consumed before taking a test (0 ounces or 6 ounces).
(a) Name the effect(s) that have the greatest chance of being declared statistically significant in the outcome given in the graphic figure. (There are eight alternatives: no effects, age effect, alcohol effect, interaction effect, age and alcohol, age and interaction, alcohol and interaction, and all three effects.)

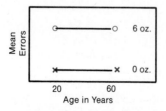

(b) Make up some hypothetical means (not individual scores) for each of the four groups in the age and alcohol study and plot them in a figure. Select mean values so that only the interaction appears to be statistically significant.

(c) Repeat Problem b above but alter the means so that both the age effect and the interaction appear to be significant.

7 Consider a 2 (age of model) X 2 (action of model) X 4 (age of subject) factorial design with $n = 4$ subjects per cell. Make a partial ANOVA summary table for this design listing (a) the sources of variation that would be computed and (b) the degrees of freedom for each of the sources, including the error term.

8 Complete the following summary table for a factorial design involving factors A and B.

Source	SS	df	MS	F
A		2		
B	45	3		
A X B	60			
Within	336			
Total	441	179		

Problems 9–12 refer to the following table for a factorial design involving factors A and B.

Source	SS	df	MS	F
A	25	1	25	10
B	20	2	10	4
A X B	20	2	10	4
Within	135	54	2.5	
Total	200	59		

9 How many levels of each factor are there?

10 How many scores are there in this study? Into how many independent groups are the scores divided? How many subjects are in each group (assume equal division)?

11 What proportion of variation
(a) Is associated with factor A?
(b) Is associated with the interaction between factors A and B?
(c) Is unexplained?

12 Explicitly state the null and alternative hypotheses for each effect in this design
(a) When the random sampling model is assumed appropriate.
(b) When the random assignment model is assumed appropriate.

Chapter 16

Analysis of Variance: Repeated Measures

16.1   INTRODUCTION

Two kinds of analysis of variance have been described so far. Both versions are appropriate for studies in which each subject participates in a single condition or, in the case of a factorial design, a single combination of conditions. There are instances, however, in which it is beneficial, even necessary, to have each subject take part in *all* conditions that are being studied. In these cases a third kind of analysis of variance can be used. This analysis represents an extension of the dependent samples *t*-test and is applicable for cases in which there are two or more levels of the independent variable.

For example, in longitudinal studies of development individual subjects are studied over long time periods, and a measurement of the dependent variable is taken on a number of different occasions. The different conditions in the study would be the different ages at which the subjects are tested. For example, if one wanted to find out whether intelligence declines in old age, one might administer an intelligence test to each member of a sample at three different times in his or her life (e.g., at ages 50, 60, and 70).

Even when the question being asked by a researcher does not demand that each subject be tested under all levels of the independent variable, it often is a good idea to conduct a study in this way. For a given sample of subjects, greater power in the analysis of variance usually can be achieved by testing each subject in all conditions rather than randomly assigning them to different conditions. A similar point concerning *t*-tests was made in Chapter 12.

16.2   DESIGN ISSUES

A major issue in designing a study and selecting an appropriate statistical analysis is whether each subject takes part in just one or all conditions in the study. Studies in which subjects participate in only one condition are called independent sample or *between subjects* designs. The term *between subjects* refers to the fact that because different subjects are present in each condition, differences between condition means are due to differences between scores obtained by different subjects.

When a study is set up so that each subject is measured under all conditions, the design may be referred to by any one of a number of different terms, including dependent samples, repeated measures, or within subjects. *Repeated measures* indicates that each subject is measured more than one time. The term *within subjects* emphasizes the idea that because each subject has a score in each condition, differences in condition means are the result of changes within each subject's behavior across the conditions. Later in this chapter we show how this aspect of the design makes the repeated measures ANOVA so powerful.

Applications of Repeated Measures Designs

The repeated measures design typically is used in one of three different situations, and the same analysis of variance can be applied to each. One case involves studies in which subjects are measured a number of times under the same circumstances. The objective of these studies is to assess the change in scores as a result of the passage of time (as in the longitudinal study mentioned earlier) or as a result of learning. In learning studies, each measurement is called a *trial,* and the researcher is interested in finding out whether scores change over trials.

For instance, a researcher interested in brain structures and learning might want to find out whether rats are able to learn to negotiate a maze after some structure in their brain has been removed. After the required surgical procedure, each animal is given a series of opportunities (trials) to move through the maze and receive a food reward at the end. Evidence of learning the maze would be obtained if the time taken to complete the maze decreased over trials.

A second application of the repeated measures design involves testing subjects under different treatments. In a study of attitude change, for example, the subjects' attitudes toward some issue might be assessed by a questionnaire before (pretest) and again after (posttest) the presentation of persuasive material. In this case a dependent samples *t*-test or a repeated measures ANOVA could be used, and both would yield the same result. As a second example consider a hypothetical study of the influence of emotional state on memory. Subjects might be asked to read and then recall a story under three different conditions. In one condition the subjects are placed in a sad mood right after reading the story by having them think of a sad personal event. Then they attempt to recall the story. In another condition a happy mood is induced in the same subjects by having them think of a happy event, and in a third condition the subjects experience a neutral mood by thinking about an emotionally neutral event.

A difficulty with the use of repeated measures when studying the effects of different treatments is that each subject must experience the treatments in some specific order. This requirement allows the possibility that a subject's score under one condition might be influenced by previous testing under some other condition. For example, in the mood and memory study, story recall scores might improve with more testing. If all subjects received the mood conditions in the same order, it would not be possible to tell whether the differences in condition means were due to different moods or to **order effects.**

ORDER EFFECTS: The effect of earlier testing of subjects on later testing of the same subjects.

Problems caused by order effects can be addressed by having different subjects experience the treatments in different orders. This step can be accomplished by using a random order for each subject or a procedure known as **counterbalancing.** This procedure involves establishing a number of possible orders of conditions such that across all the orderings each condition appears in each sequential position. For example, in the emotion and memory study, three orderings might be (1) happy, sad, neutral; (2) sad, neutral, happy; and (3) neutral, happy, sad. An equal number of subjects is then assigned to each ordering of conditions.

COUNTERBALANCING: The order in which treatment conditions are experienced is varied across subjects so that each treatment is experienced in each ordinal position by a different set of subjects.

A third application of the repeated measures design is to situations in which counterbalancing is not an adequate solution to the problem of order effects. A researcher may choose to use the **matched groups design,** in which different subjects are assigned to each condition but assignment is not completely random. Instead, groups of subjects are formed such that the subjects in each group are matched according to some variable. There are as many subjects in each group as there are conditions in the experiment. Then one member of each group is assigned to each condition in the study. The variable used in forming the matched groups is related to the dependent variable used in the study.

For example, the emotion and memory study could be done in this way. All subjects might be given a preliminary story recall test. Based on their scores, the subjects are arranged in groups of three. The first group consists of the subjects with the three highest scores on the preliminary test, the second set has the next three highest-scoring subjects, and so on. Then one subject in each set is randomly assigned to each of the conditions in the study: happy, sad, or neutral. In analyzing the data, however, the scores from the three subjects in a set are treated as though they came from the same subject. An example of this procedure is shown in Box 16.1.

MATCHED GROUPS DESIGN: Groups of subjects are matched on a variable related to the dependent variable; then one subject from each group is assigned randomly to one of the conditions in the study.

16.3   GENERAL LOGIC OF THE ANALYSIS

As in the independent samples ANOVA, the null hypothesis in a repeated measures study is that the means of the populations represented by the conditions in the study are the same:

H_0: $\mu_1 = \mu_2 = \ldots = \mu_k$

Similarly, the alternative hypothesis is that not all means are the same. The

Box 16.1   # Example of the Matched Groups Assignment Procedure

Suppose that 12 subjects are to take part in the hypothetical emotion and memory study described in the text. The subjects are to be organized into matched groups of three according to scores on a preliminary story recall test given under neutral conditions. Then one subject from each matched group will be randomly assigned to one of the conditions in the study: happy, sad, or neutral.

Step 1: Administer the preliminary story recall test.

Subject identification	Number of ideas recalled on pretest
S1	18
S2	13
S3	22
S4	12
S5	10
S6	11
S7	20
S8	19
S9	17
S10	16
S11	20
S12	18

Step 2: Form matched groups based on preliminary test scores. The first group consists of the highest three scores, the second group has the next highest three scores, and so on.

Group number	Subject identification			Pretest scores			Mean pretest score
1	S3	S7	S11	22	20	20	20.67
2	S8	S1	S12	19	18	18	18.33
3	S9	S10	S2	17	16	13	15.33
4	S4	S6	S5	12	11	10	11.00

Step 3: Randomly assign one member of each group to each condition.

Condition	Subject identification				Pretest scores				Mean pretest score
Happy	S3	S8	S9	S5	22	19	17	10	17.00
Sad	S11	S1	S10	S4	20	18	16	12	16.50
Neutral	S7	S12	S2	S6	20	18	13	11	15.50

essential difference between the independent samples and repeated measures ANOVAs has to do with what causes the differences between the condition means. In the independent samples ANOVA, differences between the condition means were attributed to treatment effects, if any, and differences between the subjects who were randomly assigned to those conditions. In the repeated measures design, however, each subject is tested in each condition, so the conditions do not differ with respect to the subjects assigned to them. Therefore, in the repeated measures design, if condition means differ, it is not because there are different subjects in each condition.

Variability Among Condition Means

What *does* cause sample means to differ in the repeated measures design? One obvious possibility is that a subject's behavior varies from one condition to the next because there are treatment effects.

It also is possible for there to be differences between condition means in the repeated measures design even when there are no treatment effects. Some variability in condition means will result from random error in measuring the same subjects multiple times. Recall from Chapter 2 that if a test is not perfectly reliable, some amount of random error will be part of each person's score. When that person is tested again, a different amount of random error may be present and a different score will result even though the true score is not at all influenced by the condition in which the subject is tested.

There are two sources, then, that contribute to differences between condition means in a repeated measures design. One is random error in measuring subjects multiple times, and the other is true differences between population means (i.e., treatment effects). We can test for differences in population means by comparing the variability in sample means to a pure estimate of random error that occurs when measuring subjects multiple times. If variability in sample means is about the same as the estimate of random error, there is no evidence for differences between population means.

Estimation of Error

Random error in measurement can be assessed in terms of the consistency of a subject's score, relative to scores obtained by other subjects, across multiple measurements. For example, suppose that we have four subjects who are measured twice each on some variable, as would occur in a repeated measures study with two conditions. If H_0 is true and if there is no measurement error, each subject would obtain the same score both times and his or her score relative to the other subjects would be unchanged. This result is shown in Figure 16.1(a), where each subject's scores are plotted and connected by a straight line.[1] Some subjects obtain higher scores than others, but their relative position is the same on both measurements. If H_0 is not true, but still there is no measurement error, the subjects' scores remain stable, *relative to one another*, as shown in Figure 16.1(b). Notice that we assume that the independent variable has the same effect on each subject.

However, neither of these situations is likely to occur because almost always we are faced with some measurement error. This error leads to some inconsistency in a subject's score, relative to other subjects. We show this result in Figure 16.1(c), where we assume that H_0 is true but a small amount of inconsistency in the subjects' scores has been produced by measurement error. In Figure 16.1(d) an even greater amount of measurement error is apparent. With more measurement error, then, there will be more inconsistencies in subjects' scores, relative to other subjects.

The inconsistency of subjects' scores across conditions is analogous to the interaction between independent variables discussed in Chapter 15. In that case an interaction was conceptualized in terms of the influence of one factor changing as a function of the level of the other factor. A similar situation occurs in a single-factor repeated measures design. In this case, however, we see the effect of the independent variable changing as a function of which subject is measured. Therefore, the inconsistency in subjects' scores across conditions is an interaction between subjects and conditions. The greater the interaction, the greater the error in measurement.

Suppose we consider the scores in Figure 16.1(c) and those in Figure 16.1(d) as two different populations. We use these two small populations to demonstrate how measurement error influences differences between sample means in a repeated measures study. Consider first Figure 16.1(c). Suppose we were to draw a random sample of two subjects from this population. Table 16.1 shows all possible samples of size two that could be drawn without replacement from this population, the condition means for each sample, and the difference between the condition means. The second part of Table 16.1

---

[1]In this chapter we plot individual subject scores as single points and connect them with straight lines even though the independent variable is not measured on an interval scale. Although this technique differs from those we introduced for plotting condition means, it is justified when plotting individual subject scores because it makes obvious the presence of inconsistencies in the scores.

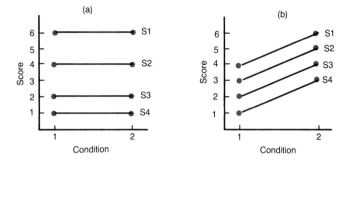

Figure 16.1 Hypothetical scores of subjects measured on some variable under two different conditions. Only in (b) is there a difference between condition means, and only in (c) and (d) is there measurement error.

Table 16.1   DIFFERENCES BETWEEN CONDITION MEANS WITHIN ALL POSSIBLE SAMPLES OF SIZE TWO

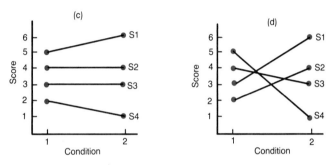

		Source population: Figure 16.1(c)					Source population: Figure 16.1(d)		
Subjects		$\overline{X}_1$	$\overline{X}_2$	$\overline{X}_1 - \overline{X}_2$	Subjects		$\overline{X}_1$	$\overline{X}_2$	$\overline{X}_1 - \overline{X}_2$
S1	S2	4.5	5.0	−0.5	S1	S2	2.5	5.0	−2.5
S1	S3	4.0	4.5	−0.5	S1	S3	3.5	4.5	−1.0
S1	S4	3.5	3.5	0.0	S1	S4	4.0	3.5	0.5
S2	S3	3.5	3.5	0.0	S2	S3	3.0	3.5	0.5
S2	S4	3.0	2.5	0.5	S2	S4	3.5	2.5	1.0
S3	S4	2.5	2.0	0.5	S3	S4	4.5	2.0	2.5

shows the results of using this procedure with the data in Figure 16.1(d). You can see that there is much greater potential for larger differences between condition means in the second case, where there is greater measurement error. But in both cases condition means in the populations do not differ (H_0 is true), so any difference between condition means produced by the random samples is due to error.

The amount of inconsistency in subjects' scores across conditions, then, serves as an estimate of measurement error. In the repeated measures ANOVA, variability among condition means is compared to this estimate of error by forming an F-ratio. When H_0 is true, measurement error is the only source contributing to variability in condition means, so we would expect variability among condition means to be about equal to the measure of error. This result would produce an F-ratio of approximately 1. If the F-ratio is much larger than 1, we have reason to reject the null hypothesis. We then can claim that some of the variability among condition means is due to differences in population means.

16.4   COMPUTATION OF THE ANALYSIS

In the repeated measures ANOVA, total variability represents the average squared deviation between each subject's score in each condition and the grand mean. The sum of these squared deviations can be expressed in the form used for the two previous kinds of ANOVA:

$$SS_{total} = \Sigma(X - GM)^2$$

Sources of Variability

There are three sources of variability that contribute to the deviation of an individual score, X, from the grand mean. One is the overall level of performance of the subject who produced the score. A score is likely to be higher than the grand mean if it comes from a subject who generally obtains high scores. The second source of variability among individual scores is the influence of the independent variable. If the score is obtained in a condition that generally yields very low scores, the score will probably be lower than the grand mean. The third source of variability is the interaction between subjects and conditions. In this case particular combinations of subject and condition may lead to large deviations from the grand mean. For any raw score, X, its deviation from the grand mean can be expressed as a combination of these three sources of variability. To show how this computation can be done we first explain how to compute each of the three sources.

Overall performance of an individual subject is defined as the subject's mean score, $\overline{X}_i$, computed by adding the score obtained in each condition and then dividing by the number of conditions. By taking the subject's mean across all conditions, we obtain the best available pooled estimate of the subject's true score. Variability among subjects' mean scores is computed by finding the sum of squared deviations of these means from the grand mean, then multiplying by the number of conditions in the study, k.

$$SS_{\text{subjects}} = k\Sigma(\overline{X}_i - GM)^2$$

The term SS_{subjects} represents an estimate of differences between subjects.

The second source of variability is the influence of the independent variable on the scores. A score's square deviation from the grand mean may be large or small depending on whether the condition in which the score is obtained influences the dependent variable. The influence of the independent variable is measured by variability among condition means, just as in the independent samples ANOVA. Once again we let $\overline{X}_j$ represent condition means, with the subscript j used to distinguish condition from subject means. The sum of squared deviations of condition means from the grand mean is

$$SS_{\text{conditions}} = n\Sigma(\overline{X}_j - GM)^2$$

where n is the number of subjects in the study. The term $SS_{\text{conditions}}$ provides an estimate of variability among raw scores that is due to treatment effects and measurement error.

The third source of variability is the interaction between conditions and subjects. It is the estimate of raw score measurement error. For a single score, we can express the interaction as the deviation of the score from the grand mean, with the effects of (1) the subject's overall level of performance and (2) the condition subtracted out.

$$\text{interaction} = \text{total} \quad - \text{subjects} \quad - \text{conditions}$$
$$= (X - GM) - (\overline{X}_i - GM) - (\overline{X}_j - GM)$$
$$= X - \overline{X}_i \quad - \overline{X}_j + GM$$

Next we square and sum these deviations across all scores to obtain the sum of squares for the interaction:

$$SS_{\text{conditions} \times \text{subjects}} = \Sigma(X - \overline{X}_i - \overline{X}_j + GM)^2$$

Computational Formulas

The computational formulas for sums of squares that we are about to present can be used in place of the definitional formulas just given. As usual, they will produce the same results as the definitional formulas except that less rounding error is likely to be involved. Consider a set of data obtained from six subjects who took part in the hypothetical emotion and memory study described earlier. Each subject was tested in each condition, and the scores are presented in Table 16.2. The values in the column labeled T_i represent the total of all scores for each subject. The values in the row labeled T_j are the total of all scores in each condition.

We use an abbreviated subscript for each of the sum of squares sources, as was done in the last three chapters. The total sum of squares for repeated

Table 16.2   RAW DATA FROM A STUDY OF EMOTION AND MEMORY

Subject number	Condition			T_i	$\overline{X}_i$
	Happy	Sad	Neutral		
1	6	5	5	16	5.33
2	7	4	6	17	5.67
3	5	2	3	10	3.33
4	4	3	4	11	3.67
5	8	6	9	23	7.67
6	9	7	8	24	8.00
T_i	39	27	35	101 = G	
$\overline{X}_i$	6.50	4.50	5.83	ΣX^2 = 641	

measures ANOVA, SS_t, has the same form as in the independent samples ANOVA.

$$SS_t = \Sigma X^2 - \frac{G^2}{N} \tag{16.1}$$

From Table 16.2 we see that the sum of all squared raw scores is 641 and the grand total is 101. The number of scores in the entire study, N, is 18—three for each of the six subjects. Using Formula 16.1 for this example gives,

$$SS_t = 641 - \frac{101^2}{18} = 641 - 566.72 = 74.28$$

The total number of degrees of freedom is $N - 1$, as in the independent samples ANOVA. In our example, $df_t = 18 - 1 = 17$.

The computational formula for variability between subjects is

$$SS_s = \frac{\Sigma T_i^2}{k} - \frac{G^2}{N} \tag{16.2}$$

Applying Formula 16.2 to the example in Table 16.2, we have

$$SS_s = \frac{16^2 + 17^2 + 10^2 + 11^2 + 23^2 + 24^2}{3} - \frac{101^2}{18} = 623.67 - 566.72$$
$$= 56.95$$

The degrees of freedom are $n - 1$ because in estimating variability between subjects, 1 degree of freedom is lost in first estimating the grand mean from which deviations of subject means are computed. In the example we have $df_s = 6 - 1 = 5$. No mean square is computed for this source because it does not participate in the F-ratio.

The sum of squared deviations of condition means can be computed with Formula 16.3.

$$SS_c = \frac{\Sigma T_j^2}{n} - \frac{G^2}{N} \qquad (16.3)$$

In this formula note the distinction between n, which refers to the number of subjects, and N, which represents the total number of scores in the study. For the example in Table 16.2 we have

$$SS_c = \frac{39^2 + 27^2 + 35^2}{6} - \frac{101^2}{18} = 579.17 - 566.72 = 12.45$$

The degrees of freedom for conditions is $k - 1$, as in the independent samples ANOVA. In the example, $df_c = 3 - 1 = 2$. The mean square for conditions is computed by taking SS_c/df_c, and it is the numerator for the F-ratio. It represents an estimate of variability due to differences between population means (if any exist) and measurement error. For the example, $MS_c = 12.45/2 = 6.22$.

Finally, we have Formula 16.4 for computing the interaction of conditions and subjects:

$$SS_{cs} = \Sigma X^2 - \frac{\Sigma T_i^2}{k} - \frac{\Sigma T_j^2}{n} + \frac{G^2}{N} \qquad (16.4)$$

When applying this formula the intermediate results of computing other sums of squares can be used. Each one of the four terms of this formula can be found in at least one of the three earlier formulas, so there is no need to compute any new terms.

$$SS_{cs} = \Sigma X^2 - \frac{\Sigma T_i^2}{k} - \frac{\Sigma T_j^2}{n} + \frac{G^2}{N}$$

$$= 641 - 623.67 - 579.17 + 566.72 = 4.88$$

The degrees of freedom for the interaction is the product of the degrees of freedom for the two "main effects," just as in the independent groups factorial ANOVA. We have $df_{cs} = (k - 1)(n - 1)$. In the example, $df_{cs} = (3 - 1)(6 - 1) = 10$. The mean square for the interaction represents an estimate of measurement error and is the denominator in the F-ratio. In the example, $MS_{cs} = 4.88/10 = 0.49$, so the F-ratio is

$$F = \frac{MS_c}{MS_{cs}} = \frac{6.22}{0.49} = 12.69$$

The analysis of variance applied to the example data is summarized in Table 16.3. The F-ratio obtained in the example can be tested for significance by using Table G in Appendix III. This F has 2 and 10 degrees of freedom, and Table G indicates that the critical F value for $\alpha = .05$ is 4.10. The obtained F is larger than this value so we can reject the null hypothesis and claim that mood influences the amount of story content that can be recalled.

Table 16.3 ANOVA SUMMARY TABLE FOR
             DATA IN TABLE 16.2

Source	SS	df	MS	F
Subjects	56.95	5	—	—
Conditions	12.45	2	6.22	12.69
C X S	4.88	10	0.49	
Total	74.28	17		

F(critical) = 4.10

F(observed) = 12.69

Decision: Reject H_0

Percentage of Variation

The significance of the F-ratio determines our decision about whether a relationship between the independent and dependent variables exists in the entire population from which the subjects in the study were sampled. When a significant relationship is found, it is also useful to obtain an estimate of the strength of the relationship. In repeated measures designs, a procedure similar to the computation of η^2 in the independent samples ANOVA can be used. For repeated measures the percentage of variation in scores due to effects of the independent variable can be expressed as

$$\text{percentage of variation} = \frac{SS_c}{SS_c + SS_{cs}}(100) \tag{16.5}$$

Formula 16.5 is similar to η^2 as computed for the independent samples ANOVA, except that the denominator is not SS_t. Instead, the denominator consists of two of the three sources that make up SS_t. The third source, SS_s, does not contribute to estimates of either measurement error or effects of the independent variable, and it is treated as an extraneous source of variability. In the example from Table 16.2, the percentage of variation due to effects of the independent variable is

$$\frac{12.45}{12.45 + 4.88}(100) = 71.84\%$$

An additional numerical example of the repeated measures ANOVA is provided in Box 16.2.

Estimation of Error Revisited

In Section 16.3 we explained how the interaction between conditions and subjects allowed us to estimate the error associated with measuring each sub-

Box 16.2 **Familiarity and Humor**

A social psychologist is interested in whether children's judgments about the humor of a cartoon change if they are exposed repeatedly to the cartoon. The null hypothesis is that humor judgments are not affected by repeated exposure. The null hypothesis is tested by having a random sample of children from a local elementary school rate the humor of a set of cartoons on a seven-point scale. A higher rating indicates a higher amount of humor. One week after the first session the children are asked to rate the same cartoons a second time. After another week this procedure is repeated, making a total of three rating sessions. Thus, each subject is tested under three conditions, representing the first, second, or third exposure to the cartoons. Each subject's score in a condition is that subject's mean rating for all cartoons. The scores for each subject follow, along with a repeated measures ANOVA.

		Exposure		
Subject	First	Second	Third	T_i
1	6	5	2	13
2	5	5	4	14
3	5	6	3	14
4	6	5	4	15
5	7	3	3	13
6	4	2	1	7
7	4	4	1	9
8	5	7	2	14
T_j	42	37	20	99 = G

$$\Sigma X^2 = 477$$

$$SS_t = 477 - \frac{99^2}{24} = 477 - 408.375 = 68.625$$

$$SS_s = \frac{13^2 + 14^2 + \ldots + 14^2}{3} - \frac{99^2}{24} = 427 - 408.375 = 18.625$$

$$SS_c = \frac{42^2 + 37^2 + 20^2}{8} - \frac{99^2}{24} = 441.625 - 408.375 = 33.25$$

$$SS_{cs} = 477 - 427 - 441.625 + 408.375 = 16.75$$

Source	SS	df	MS	F
Subjects	18.625	7	—	—
Conditions	33.250	2	16.62	13.85
C X S	16.750	14	1.20	
Total	68.625	23		

With $\alpha = .05$, the observed results allow rejection of H_0.

F(critical) = 3.74

F(observed) = 13.85

Decision: Reject H_0

The percentage of variation in ratings that is accounted for by the effect of repeated exposure is

$$\frac{33.25}{33.25 + 16.75}(100) = 66.5\%$$

ject multiple times. We showed that with greater inconsistency in the subjects' scores across conditions, there was greater potential for condition means to vary even when H_0 is true. Now that the computation of the repeated measures ANOVA has been introduced, we provide a computational demonstration of how inconsistency in patterns of scores influences the F-ratio.

In Figure 16.2(a) we have plotted the raw data from Table 16.2. Notice that the pattern of scores across conditions is quite consistent and that the condition means differ. Indeed, the ANOVA results in Table 16.3 indicate that there was a reliable effect of mood on memory.

Now suppose that the variability of condition means was just as large as the data in Table 16.2 indicate but that the pattern of scores across conditions was not so consistent from subject to subject. In Table 16.4 we show another set of hypothetical raw data, a rearrangement of the scores in Table 16.2. Rearrangement was achieved by reassigning scores *within a condition*. Although the condition means are unchanged, there is far less consistency in the patterns of scores for the individual subjects. This fact is apparent in the plot of the raw data shown in Figure 16.2(b).

The repeated measures ANOVA of the revised data is summarized in Table 16.5. Comparing this summary table with that in Table 16.3 reveals a number of important facts. The value of SS_t has not changed because exactly the same scores are present in both sets of data. The SS_c has not changed

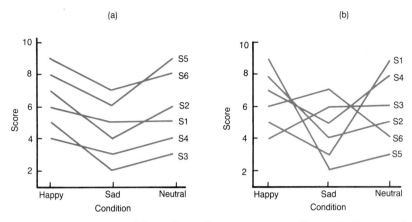

Figure 16.2 Two sets of hypothetical scores on a recall test. Differences between condition means are the same in cases (a) and (b), but condition effects are much more consistent in (a).

because the condition means are the same. But there is a decrease in the amount of variability in subject means, as indicated by the smaller SS_s value in Table 16.5. Further, the amount of variability due to error (interaction between conditions and subjects) is much larger in the analysis of the revised data. This result is consistent with the patterns shown in Figure 16.2. Consequently, the increased error estimate, MS_{cs}, produces a smaller F-ratio, which in this case is not significant with $\alpha = .05$.

$$F(\text{critical}) = 4.10$$

$$F(\text{observed}) = 1.12$$

Decision: Fail to reject H_0

Table 16.4 **REARRANGEMENT OF DATA FROM TABLE 16.2**

Subject number	Condition			T_i	$\bar{X}_i$
	Happy	Sad	Neutral		
1	5	3	9	17	5.67
2	8	4	5	17	5.67
3	4	6	6	16	5.33
4	7	5	8	20	6.67
5	9	2	3	14	4.67
6	6	7	4	17	5.67
T_j	39	27	35	101 = G	
$\bar{X}_j$	6.50	4.50	5.83	ΣX^2 = 641	

Table 16.5 ANOVA SUMMARY TABLE FOR
DATA IN TABLE 16.4

Source	SS	df	MS	F
Subjects	6.28	5	—	—
Conditions	12.44	2	6.22	1.12
C X S	55.56	10	5.56	
Total	74.28	17		

Comparison with Independent Samples ANOVA

At the beginning of this chapter we indicated that the repeated measures ANOVA generally is more powerful than the independent samples version. The key to the difference in power is in the error term used in the two ANOVAs. Remember that for the independent samples case, different subjects are used in each condition. Under H_0, then, the condition means differ because of differences between subjects. This variability is the SS_w term in the independent samples ANOVA. For the repeated measures ANOVA, however, each subject appears in all conditions, so none of the variability in condition means can be due to differences between subjects. Therefore, differences between subjects are excluded from the calculation of the error term in the repeated measures ANOVA.

The difference in error terms used for the two types of ANOVA can be illustrated by treating the data in Table 16.2 as though they were obtained with an independent samples design. For now, assume that six *different* subjects were tested in each emotional condition. The resulting ANOVA summary table is shown in Table 16.6.

$F(\text{critical}) = 3.68$

$F(\text{observed}) = 1.51$

Decision: Fail to reject H_0

Compare this summary table with the one for the repeated measures AN-

Table 16.6 INDEPENDENT SAMPLES ANOVA
SUMMARY TABLE FOR
DATA IN TABLE 16.2

Source	SS	df	MS	F
Between	12.44	2	6.22	1.51
Within	61.84	15	4.12	
Total	74.28	17		

OVA in Table 16.3. Notice that the variability in condition means (SS_b in Table 16.6 and SS_c in Table 16.3) is the same in the two cases but that the error term is less in the repeated measures case. This result occurs because variability due to differences between subjects (SS_s) has been excluded from the computation of SS_{cs}. You can see that although variability among condition means is the same in the two versions of ANOVA, differences in the error terms produce different statistical decisions in these two examples— rejection of H_0 in the repeated measures case but not in the independent samples case.

16.5   ASSUMPTIONS

In applying the repeated measures ANOVA to a set of data, a number of assumptions must be made. As with the independent samples ANOVA, we assume that subjects have been independently sampled from some population and that the populations of scores associated with the different conditions are normally distributed and of equal variance. An additional assumption is required when there are more than two conditions in the study. The assumption is based on the variance of difference scores for each pair of conditions. For example, with three conditions there are three possible pairs: conditions 1 and 2, 1 and 3, and 2 and 3. For each pair of conditions a difference score can be computed for each subject.

Huynh and Feldt (1970) have shown that when a repeated measures ANOVA is applied, it must be assumed that in the population the variance of difference scores is the same for each pair of conditions. This is known as the assumption of *sphericity*. In Table 16.7 we present two hypothetical sets of data with four subjects tested in each of three conditions. In each case we have computed the variance of difference scores for each possible pair of conditions. Notice that in the first case these variances are quite different, whereas in the second case they are very similar. Because researchers almost always work with samples, we would not expect the variances of difference scores to be identical, but they should be similar.

The reason for the sphericity assumption is based on the nature of the error term. The error term is a measure of the interaction between conditions and subjects. When there are more than two conditions, the interaction may be stronger between one pair of conditions than another. For example, in Figure 16.3(a) we have plotted the first data set from Table 16.7. We see that very little interaction is apparent across the first two conditions. But if we compare conditions two and three, or one and three, we see a strong interaction—which can be expressed by computing the variance of difference scores in each pair of conditions.

When there is a stronger interaction across two conditions, the variance of difference scores is larger. This result can be seen by comparing relevant sections of Figure 16.3(a) with difference score variances in Table 16.7. Figure 16.3(b) shows the plot of the second set of data from Table 16.7, in which

Table 16.7   TWO SETS OF RAW DATA, DIFFERENCE SCORES, AND VARIANCES OF
DIFFERENCE SCORES

(a)

Raw data

Subject	Condition			Subject	Condition		
	1	2	3		1	2	3
1	9	8	5	1	9	7	5
2	8	7	9	2	8	5	8
3	5	5	2	3	5	7	6
4	2	1	6	4	2	1	2

Difference scores

Subject	Condition pair			Subject	Condition pair		
	1–2	1–3	2–3		1–2	1–3	2–3
1	1	4	3	1	2	4	2
2	1	−1	−2	2	3	0	−3
3	0	3	3	3	−2	−1	1
4	1	−4	5	4	1	0	−1
s^2	0.25	13.67	8.92	s^2	4.67	4.92	4.92

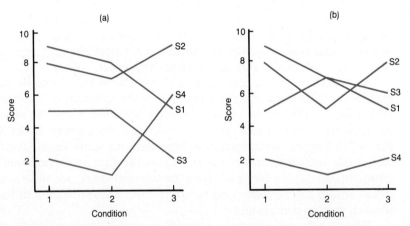

Figure 16.3 Hypothetical scores from two repeated measures studies with three conditions. In (a) the size of the interaction between subjects and conditions varies widely between each pair of conditions. In (b) the size of the interaction is more consistent for each pair of conditions.

there is greater similarity among the variance of difference scores. Notice that in this case the degree of interaction between subjects and conditions is similar for each pair of conditions.

Sphericity is required because the error term in the repeated measures ANOVA is an estimate of the consistency of patterns of scores across conditions in the population. Each pair of conditions in a repeated measures design is an estimate of that consistency, and these estimates are pooled in the calculation of the error term. Dissimilarity among the error estimates that are pooled will produce an inaccurate estimate of the error term.

Violation of Assumptions

In earlier chapters we stated that the independent samples ANOVA is robust with respect to violations of assumptions of normal distribution of scores and homogeneity of variance. The repeated measures ANOVA, however, is not robust with respect to violation of homogeneity of variances within conditions or violation of sphericity.

When either of these assumptions is violated it usually turns out that the probability of obtaining large F-ratios is greater than indicated by tabled values of F. Consequently, the critical F-ratios obtained from tables like Table G in Appendix III are too *small*. For example, when assumptions are violated, the tabled F value for $\alpha = .05$ actually represents an α value larger than .05, perhaps as much as .08 (Collier, Baker, Mandeville, & Hayes, 1967). Using tabled values of critical F-ratios when homogeneity of variance or sphericity assumptions have been violated usually will increase the likelihood of making a Type I error.

Testing for violation of the sphericity assumption is complex. Some computerized statistical packages compute this test for the repeated measures ANOVA, but a description of it is beyond the scope of this book. In the absence of a means to compute a test of the sphericity assumption, it is safe to act as though that assumption has *not* been met.

There are a number of possible approaches to interpreting a repeated measures F-ratio in cases where violation of sphericity is suspected. One possibility is to use the tabled F values as usual (Keppel, 1982). The rationale is that using tabled F values when in violation of the sphericity assumption will increase the probability of a Type I error by only two or three percentage points. Many researchers are willing to be convinced by findings that are significant even when $\alpha = .07$ or .08. Furthermore, in many research reports, obtained F-ratios are much larger than the tabled critical value, so even if the true critical F-ratio were somewhat larger than the tabled value, the observed results would still make rejection of the null hypothesis valid.

An alternative approach is to compute the repeated measures ANOVA as usual but to select a critical F-ratio that is based on adjusted degrees of freedom. Greenhouse and Geisser (1959) have suggested that one could adjust the degrees of freedom according to the seriousness of the violation of the sphericity assumption. Again, computation of this correction is beyond the scope of this book, although Greenhouse and Geisser also proposed an approach that is simpler but sacrifices power. One can use a critical F-ratio based on 1 and $n - 1$ degrees of freedom to obtain a test of the observed F-ratio even under serious violation of the sphericity assumption. Normally, the critical F-ratio would be based on $k - 1$ and $(k - 1)(n - 1)$ degrees of freedom, so this Greenhouse-Geisser procedure involves smaller df and, therefore, a larger critical F-ratio. A larger critical F-ratio means that a larger treatment effect is needed to reject H_0, so there is less power but also less chance of a Type I error. In our study of emotion and memory, the Greenhouse-Geisser procedure would produce 1 and 5 degrees of freedom, for a critical F-ratio of 6.61 with $\alpha = .05$. The observed F-ratio is larger than this critical value, so we would still be able to reject H_0 even with this less powerful test.

$$F(\text{critical}) = 6.61$$

$$F(\text{observed}) = 12.69$$

Decision: Reject H_0

16.6   MULTIPLE COMPARISONS

When a significant F-ratio is obtained in a repeated measures ANOVA, the researcher can reject the null hypothesis that the population means are all equal. But if there are more than two conditions in the study, the researcher does not yet know which means differ significantly from one another. With some modification the multiple comparison techniques discussed in Chapter 14 for independent samples designs can be applied to repeated measures data as well. We briefly show how to make all possible (post hoc) pairwise comparisons and how to make planned pairwise comparisons.

Post Hoc Comparisons

A modified version of the Tukey HSD test can be used in repeated measures studies after a significant F-ratio has been obtained. The procedure allows all pairs of means to be compared while maintaining experimentwise α at a fixed level. The modification involves the error term and is a result of concern with the possible violation of the assumption of sphericity.

Rather than using the MS_{cs} error term in computing the HSD test for each pair of means, experts recommend using a different error term for each comparison (e.g., Keppel, 1982). The error term MS_{cs_i} for a particular comparison is computed with Formula 16.4 for SS_{cs}, but it includes data from only those two conditions whose means are included in the comparison. Except for this change, the Tukey HSD test is computed just as in Chapter 14.

$$\text{HSD} = q_{\alpha, df, k} \sqrt{\frac{MS_{cs_i}}{n}} \tag{16.6}$$

The degrees of freedom refer to df_{cs_i}, the degrees of freedom for the error term in comparison i. The degrees of freedom for a comparison's error term will be $(k - 1)(n - 1)$ or just $n - 1$ because there are only two conditions per comparison $(k = 2)$. The term n is the number of subjects in the study.

We can apply this test to the hypothetical data from the emotion and memory study shown in Table 16.2. The analysis of variance, summarized in Table 16.3, produced a significant F-ratio, so Tukey's HSD test can be used to find which pairs of means are significantly different with experimentwise $\alpha = .05$. The difference between each pair of means and the associated MS_{cs_i} for each comparison is shown in Table 16.8. Each MS_{cs_i} term was computed by obtaining SS_{cs_i} with Formula 16.4 and scores from the two conditions being compared. Then SS_{cs_i} was divided by df_{cs_i} to obtain MS_{cs_i}. The next step is to find the value of the q statistic from Table H in Appendix III. For each comparison $df = 5$ and $k = 3$, so the appropriate value of q according to Table H is 4.60. A unique value of HSD must be found for each comparison because each one has its own MS_{cs_i}. In our hypothetical example, error terms for two of the three happen to be the same. Using Formula 16.6, the value of HSD for the comparison of the sad and neutral conditions is

$$\text{HSD} = 4.60 \sqrt{\frac{0.53}{6}} = 1.37$$

Similarly, the HSD values for the comparisons of sad versus happy and neutral versus happy conditions, respectively, are

$$\text{HSD} = 4.60 \sqrt{\frac{0.40}{6}} = 1.19 \quad \text{and} \quad \text{HSD} = 4.60 \sqrt{\frac{0.53}{6}} = 1.37$$

We can see from Table 16.8 that for only one comparison (sad versus happy) do the means differ by at least the corresponding HSD value. We can conclude that the mean for the happy condition is significantly greater than the mean for the sad condition. The other two pairs of means are not significantly different: (1) the sad condition and the neutral condition and (2) the neutral condition and the happy condition.

Table 16.8   TABLE OF DIFFERENCES BETWEEN MEANS
             AND ASSOCIATED ERROR TERMS (MS_{cs_i})

		Sad	Neutral	Happy
Sad	$(\overline{X} = 4.50)$	—	1.33 $(MS_{cs_i} = .53)$	2.00 $(MS_{cs_i} = .40)$
Neutral	$(\overline{X} = 5.83)$		—	0.67 $(MS_{cs_i} = .53)$
Happy	$(\overline{X} = 6.50)$			—

Planned Comparisons

Testing planned pairwise comparisons in dependent samples designs can be done by using Dunn's test, which was discussed in Chapter 14. The application to the repeated measured case involves computing a dependent samples t-test for each pair of conditions and evaluating the obtained t by using Table I in Appendix III. The critical t-ratio from Table I is obtained from the number of planned comparisons and the degrees of freedom for each t-test: $n - 1$.

For example, suppose that two pairwise comparisons had been planned for the emotion and story recall study. Specifically, suppose we were primarily interested in performance when subjects are put into a sad mood. We might want to compare the sad condition with each of the other two conditions: sad versus neutral and sad versus happy. Data from Table 16.2 were used to perform a dependent samples t-test for each of these two comparisons. The obtained t-ratio for the sad versus neutral comparison was 3.16, and for the sad versus happy comparison, $t = 5.48$. According to Table I, for two comparisons and $df = 5$, the critical t-ratio for experimentwise $\alpha = .05$ is 3.16. For both comparisons the observed t-ratio is greater than or equal to the critical t, so both are significant by Dunn's test. We can conclude that story recall is more accurate when subjects are in either a happy or a neutral mood rather than a sad mood.

When we applied the Tukey HSD test to these same data, however, the sad versus neutral comparison was not significant. You should recall from Chapter 14 that the Tukey HSD test is less powerful than Dunn's test because in the latter case comparisons are planned and restricted to only some of the possible comparisons that could be made. On the other hand, the advantage of the Tukey HSD test is that any pairwise comparisons can be conducted without having planned them ahead of time.

16.7   RANDOM ASSIGNMENT MODEL

The repeated measures ANOVA and the assumptions on which it is based are derived from the random sampling model. Thus, the analysis is intended for use in cases in which subjects have been randomly sampled from a particular population. As we have pointed out in earlier chapters, it often is the case that analyses based on the random sampling model are applied even when subjects have not been randomly sampled. As in the cases we discussed earlier, this procedure can be justified for the repeated measures ANOVA by treating results obtained from it as an approximation to the randomization test for repeated measures.

Using the repeated measures ANOVA as an approximation to the randomization test means that we are working with a different null hypothesis, which does not involve population means. Instead, the null hypothesis for the repeated measures randomization test is that a subject's scores are independent of the conditions under which they were obtained. Rejection of H_0 could not be generalized to some population on the basis of the outcome of the ANOVA. Without random sampling, inferences about treatment effects are restricted to the subjects included in the sample.

Use of the repeated measures ANOVA as an approximation to the randomization test is reasonable because it has been shown (e.g., Collier & Baker, 1966) that these two tests produce similar probability values and have similar levels of power. Alternatively, one could compute the randomization test instead of the repeated measures ANOVA. The former test might be used either because random sampling was not carried out or because other assumptions of the repeated measures ANOVA have been violated. The randomization test is completely free of assumptions of homogeneity of variance and sphericity, so using this test solves the problem of violating such assumptions.

The repeated measures randomization test is performed just as described in Chapter 9, except that two or more conditions may be involved. The different possible outcomes of the study are formed by considering all possible assignments of an individual subject's scores to the various conditions. The number of possible arrangements of data in a repeated measures design with k conditions and n subjects is $(k!)^n$. When more than two conditions are involved, the measure of differences between conditions is taken as $\Sigma(T_j^2/n)$, which is the first part of the computational formula for SS_c. The statistical package we have made available with this book, NPSTAT, can be used to conduct this kind of test. NPSTAT provides both a repeated measures ANOVA and a randomization test.

NPSTAT was used to compute the randomization test of the data from the emotion and memory study that appear in Table 16.2. There are a total of $(3!)^6 = 46,656$ possible arrangements of the data, but to save time NPSTAT was run on only 10,000, so an estimate of the exact probability was obtained. It was found that, under H_0, the estimated probability of the observed variability among condition means (or more extreme variability) was .00270. This probability estimate is very similar to the probability associated with the F-ratio obtained from the ANOVA, .00179. This is an example of how closely the randomization test and ANOVA can agree. Assuming that $\alpha = .05$, the randomization test allows rejection of the null hypothesis. We can conclude that for the subjects included in this study, recall is influenced by the subject's mood.

To explore the pattern of differences among conditions, we recommend using planned comparisons. A randomization test can be computed for each pair of conditions we wish to compare. The obtained probability is evaluated by using a correction to maintain experimentwise α (α_{EW}) at some specified value. The correction is similar to that used in Dunn's test. The α value for each comparison is set at α_{EW}/k, where k is the number of comparisons to be made. For example, if we wish to set α_{EW} at .05, the α for each of two planned comparisons would be $.05/2 = .025$.

As an example of using planned comparisons with the randomization test, consider the data in Box 16.2 involving humor ratings. We ran NPSTAT with all three conditions and obtained an estimated probability, based on 10,000 randomly selected arrangements of the data, of .00120. This figure is reasonably close to the probability of .00047 associated with the F-ratio produced by the repeated measures ANOVA. Suppose that two comparisons had been planned, first versus second exposure and first versus third exposure. Assume that α_{EW} is set to .05, so each comparison has $\alpha = .05/2 = .025$. The randomization test of the first comparison produced an exact probability of .5000, based on all of the 256 possible arrangements of the data. The second comparison produced an exact probability of .0078. Therefore, only the comparison of the first versus the third ratings yielded a significant difference. We can conclude that for subjects in this study the third exposure to a cartoon produces lower humor ratings than the first exposure.

SUMMARY

The repeated measures design involves testing each subject in each condition of the study. This design calls for far fewer subjects than an independent samples design, but it also raises the problem that the order in which conditions are experienced might alter their influence on the subjects' scores. This problem can be reduced by having different subjects experience the conditions in different orders, either through a random order for each subject or through counterbalancing, which ensures that each condition is experienced in each sequential position by a subset of the subjects.

The repeated measures design allows a researcher to observe the effects of conditions *within* each subject. The differences between condition means are due to the possible influence of treatments on individual subjects and to measurement error associated with measuring a subject multiple times. Measurement error influences the degree of consistency of the pattern of subjects' scores across conditions. It is estimated by the interaction between conditions and subjects in the repeated measures ANOVA and is the denominator in the F-ratio. The large differences often observed between subjects are not included in the error term, making the repeated measures ANOVA more powerful in most instances than the independent samples ANOVA. Multiple comparisons between all pairs of conditions or planned pairwise comparisons can be carried out to specify the pattern of differences between condition means.

The repeated measures ANOVA is based on the assumptions of independent selection of subjects from a population and the normality and homogeneity of variance in the populations of scores. In addition, it is assumed that variances of difference scores are homogeneous across pairs of conditions (the sphericity assumption). Violations of the assumptions of homogeneity of variance or sphericity can lead to increased probability of a Type I error. This is not a serious problem in cases where large F-ratios are obtained or when the Greenhouse-Geisser procedure is used and produces a significant result.

In cases where subjects are not randomly sampled, the significance of the obtained F-ratio can be considered an estimate of the result of a randomization test for a relationship between the independent and dependent variables. An advantage to computing the randomization test instead of the repeated measures ANOVA is that the former is not based on any assumptions of homogeneity of variance or sphericity and is especially useful when these assumptions are violated.

KEY WORDS

between subjects	counterbalancing
repeated measures	matched groups design
within subjects	measurement error
trial	difference score variances
order effects	sphericity

PROBLEMS

1 In a repeated measures design why do differences between subjects not contribute to differences between condition means?

2 What four assumptions are made when applying the repeated measures ANOVA to data obtained from a sample of subjects?

3 What three solutions to the problem of violation of assumptions were proposed?

4 A researcher uses a repeated measures ANOVA to evaluate the results of an experiment. The obtained F-ratio is $F(3,24) = 3.74$.
   (a) How many conditions and subjects were there in the experiment?
   (b) What is the critical F-ratio in this case for $\alpha = .05$?
   (c) Do the observed results allow rejection of H_0?

5 A researcher computes a repeated measures ANOVA and obtains $F(2,38) = 5.20$.
   (a) Does the obtained F-ratio allow rejection of H_0 with $\alpha = .05$?
   (b) The researcher is concerned that the assumption of homogeneity of difference score variances has been violated and decides to use the Greenhouse-Geisser procedure. What are the degrees of freedom and critical F-ratio for this test? With $\alpha = .05$, does this test allow rejection of H_0?

6 A researcher wants to determine whether performance on a motor coordination task is influenced by level of arousal. A random sample of eight subjects is tested under each of three different levels of arousal: high, medium, and low. The raw data are these:

Subject	Arousal High	Medium	Low
1	19	17	15
2	4	7	2
3	6	12	11
4	5	15	13
5	7	12	12
6	11	18	2
7	5	12	8
8	2	14	9

(a) State the null and alternative hypotheses for this study.
(b) Carry out a repeated measures ANOVA with $\alpha = .05$ and determine whether the null hypothesis can be rejected. What do you conclude about the relationship between arousal and motor coordination on the basis of this study?
(c) Determine whether the observed F-ratio is significant with the Greenhouse-Geisser procedure.
(d) Compute the percentage of variability in motor coordination scores that is due to level of arousal.
(e) Carry out a Tukey HSD test of all pairwise comparisons with experimentwise $\alpha = .05$. Be sure to use a separate error term for each comparison.

7 Treat the data in problem 6 as though they had been obtained in an independent samples design, with eight different subjects randomly assigned to each of the three conditions. Carry out an independent samples ANOVA.
(a) Is the obtained F-ratio significant with $\alpha = .05$ in this analysis?
(b) Compare the obtained F-ratio with the F-ratio obtained in Problem 6 and explain why they differ.
(c) In the independent samples analysis what percentage of variability in motor coordination scores is accounted for by the arousal level? Compare this figure with the percentage of variability obtained in the repeated measures analysis in Problem 6 and explain why there is a difference.

8 A researcher wants to determine whether knowing the type of person who produced an adage influences how people judge its popularity. A long list of adages is obtained and presented in random order to each of six randomly sampled subjects. Each adage is attributed to one of three possible sources: a scientist, a politician, a writer, or a movie star. The selection of a source for each adage is made randomly for each subject, so that across the different subjects, each adage is attributed to different sources. Subjects judge the popularity of each adage by estimating how many times they believe they have heard the adage. Each subject's score in a condition is based on the mean estimate for adages attributed to that source, and these scores follow:

	Source			
Subject	Scientist	Politician	Writer	Movie Star
1	8	6	9	4
2	7	3	8	1
3	10	9	5	8
4	3	9	5	1
5	12	8	11	4
6	8	7	6	5

(a) What are the null and alternative hypotheses in this study?

(b) Why did the researcher use a different random assignment of the sources for the adages for each subject?

(c) Compute a repeated measures ANOVA and test the F-ratio for significance with $\alpha = .05$.

(d) What is the percentage of variability in popularity estimates that is accounted for by the source of the adage?

(e) Carry out a set of planned pairwise comparisons between the movie star condition and each of the other three conditions. Set experimentwise $\alpha = .05$.

(f) What do you conclude about the relationship between the source of an adage and its judged popularity?

9 Suppose that the data from Problem 8 had actually turned out as follows:

	Source			
Subject	Scientist	Politician	Writer	Movie Star
1	12	7	5	4
2	10	9	6	1
3	8	3	11	1
4	8	8	9	4
5	7	9	8	5
6	3	6	5	8

(a) Compute a repeated measures ANOVA and test the significance of the F-ratio with $\alpha = .05$.

(b) Compare the results of this test with the results of the test in Problem 8. Even though the means for the three conditions are the same in both studies, why are the results of the ANOVAs different? (Hint: For each study plot the raw data for each subject, as in Figure 16.2.)

10 Use NPSTAT to apply the repeated measures randomization test to the data in Problem 6. Select a reasonable value for the number of data arrangements to be

considered. Compare the obtained probability value with the probability value for the F-ratio from the repeated measures ANOVA that NPSTAT computes. Using NPSTAT, follow up with planned comparisons between the low arousal condition and each of the other two conditions. Set experimentwise $\alpha = .05$ for these comparisons. Which comparisons are significant?

11 Use NPSTAT to analyze the following data with a repeated measures randomization test involving at least 2000 arrangements of the data. Compare the probability values produced by the ANOVA and by the randomization test. By examining the raw data, find evidence that the assumption of homogeneity of difference score variances has been violated. What do you conclude about using randomization tests instead of ANOVA when this assumption is violated?

Subject	Condition			
	A	B	C	D
1	5	6	8	9
2	5	4	7	6
3	13	12	20	35

FIVE

Tests with Frequencies and Ranks

Most of the statistical tests we have discussed so far are called *parametric* tests because they are designed to evaluate hypotheses about specific population parameters. For example, the *t*-test or the analysis of variance are used to test such parametric hypotheses as

$H_0: \mu = a$ $\qquad\qquad\qquad\qquad$ $H_0: \rho = 0$

$H_0: \mu_1 = \mu_2$ $\qquad\qquad\qquad\quad$ $H_0: \rho = a$

$H_0: \mu_1 = \mu_2 = \mu_3$

To use parametric tests appropriatcly, several assumptions about population distributions and about characteristics of sample data should be met. The most common of these assumptions are

1. The population distributions from which samples are drawn are normal.
2. The population variances are equal.
3. The observations (or pairs of observations) are independent. This assumption is tied to random sampling from populations.
4. The data are measured on at least an interval scale.

Frequently, behavioral researchers are faced with research situations in which these assumptions are violated, and using a parametric test can lead to erroneous decisions regarding H_0. When this situation occurs the researcher can use one of the hypothesis-testing procedures collectively referred to as *nonparametric* or *distribution-free* tests.

As the name implies, nonparametric tests are not designed to test hypotheses about population parameters. Rather, they test *any* differences that might arise between sample distributions, be they differences in central tendency, variability, shape, or any other characteristic of a distribution. Thus, the null hypotheses for a nonparametric test could be stated as

H_0: distribution$_1$ = distribution$_2$

Another characteristic of nonparametric tests is that they are free of most of the restrictive assumptions concerning population distributions associated with parametric tests (hence the alternative name, distribution-free tests). For example, nonparametric tests do not assume that the population distributions from which samples are drawn are normal and have homogeneous variances.

Furthermore, many nonparametric tests do not require random sampling of observations. They do assume independence, but that assumption can be tied to the method of randomization (random assignment) rather than to random sampling. Decisions about H_0 are then made on the basis of probabilities derived from all possible randomizations of a particular group of N subjects to various treatment conditions. This characteristic implies not only that hypotheses tested by nonparametric tests are not concerned with population parameters but also that they need not be concerned with populations at all. Instead, the hypothesis can be stated simply in terms of whether chance or a treatment effect determined the arrangement of a particular set of data into treatment conditions. That is,

H_0: chance (no treatment effect)

H_1: treatment effect

Of course if random sampling were carried out, generalizing to populations would be possible, but the point is that with many nonparametric tests the validity of our decisions about H_0 need not be tied to random sampling.

We have already discussed several nonparametric tests in previous chapters, although we did not identify them as such at the time. They are the binomial test, the independent and dependent two-group randomization tests, and the independent and dependent k-samples randomization tests. All illustrate the characteristics of nonparametric tests because they do not assume random sampling from normal populations with homogeneous variances. Moreover, from the binomial test, which is appropriate for analyzing categorical (nominal) data having only two possible outcomes, you can see that not all nonparametric tests require interval-level data. In Chapter 17 we introduce the nonparametric test, *chi-square,* and related tests of association that are appropriate for analyzing categorical data in which two or more outcomes are possible. In Chapter 18 we present nonparametric tests that are appropriate for analyzing rank-ordered (ordinal) data.

Chapter 17

Chi-Square: Analysis of Frequencies

17.1   INTRODUCTION

Chi-square tests are used when data consist of frequency counts distributed across the levels of a categorical variable. For example, an introductory psychology class may consist of 96 males and 102 females. Here, the categorical variable is gender, the number of levels is two (male and female), and the frequencies are simply the numbers of students who are males (96) or females (102). Other categorical variables include college major (sciences, humanities, or social sciences), personality type (introverted or extroverted), and preferred leisure-time activity (watching television, reading, playing sports, or dabbling in the fine arts). In each of these examples the variables (e.g., college major) are measured as categories (e.g., sciences/humanities/social sciences), and the data consist of the frequency or number of individuals falling into each category. The nonparametric procedure most often used to test hypotheses with such data is the *chi-square test.*

There are two general types of hypotheses for which chi-square tests are used. One type involves comparing the sample frequency distribution of a *single* categorical variable with a predetermined or theoretical frequency distribution of that variable. One might test, for example, the hypothesis that obtained frequencies are distributed equally across the levels of a categorical variable, that the frequencies describe a normal distribution, or that a frequency distribution obtained from a particular sample is proportionally equivalent to the frequency distribution of a national norm group. Because the hypothesis in each of these examples concerns the match or *fit* between an obtained sample frequency distribution and a theoretically expected frequency distribution, the chi-square test used to evaluate such hypotheses is referred to as a **goodness-of-fit test.**

GOODNESS-OF-FIT TEST: A test of how well a sample distribution corresponds to some theoretical distribution.

The second type of hypothesis involves *two* categorical variables and examines the extent to which the frequency distribution of one categorical variable (e.g., college major) changes or stays the same across the levels of a second categorical variable (e.g., gender). In other words, this second type of hypothesis is concerned with whether or not the frequency distribution of one variable is dependent, or *contingent*, on another variable. The chi-square test is a **contingency test,** and the test used to analyze the contingency between two categorical variables is called the *chi-square test of independence* or the *chi-square test of homogeneity.*

CONTINGENCY TESTS: Tests of the independence of two categorical variables.

In sum, chi-square tests are used to evaluate hypotheses concerning categorical variables. Clues to the appropriateness of using a chi-square test include the following:

1. The variables under investigation are measured as discrete categories (e.g., personality type or treatment group).
2. The data consist of the frequency with which observations fall into each of the categories.
3. There is a hypothesis concerning whether the obtained frequencies of a categorical variable fit some theoretically expected pattern.
4. There is a hypothesis concerning whether the distributions of frequencies across levels of one categorical variable differ across levels of a second categorical variable.

17.2   THE CHI-SQUARE GOODNESS-OF-FIT TEST

A chi-square goodness-of-fit test is used to test the hypothesis that an obtained frequency distribution corresponds to some theoretical or expected frequency distribution. In this section we present two examples representing the most common ways in which expected frequency distributions are derived. The first example illustrates the goodness-of-fit test when expected frequencies are equal across categories. This situation arises when there is no a priori reason to expect any other form of frequency distribution. The second example illustrates using the goodness-of-fit test when a priori reasons do exist for expecting unequal frequencies. We spend extra time on our first example to illustrate several concepts and procedures common to all chi-square tests, be they goodness-of-fit tests, tests of independence, or tests of homogeneity.

Example 1

A college professor would like to determine if undergraduate students prefer essay exams, multiple-choice exams, or take-home exams. She randomly samples 120 students and finds that their responses to a forced-choice preference questionnaire distribute across the three categories of exam types as shown in Table 17.1. (A forced-choice questionnaire permits one and only one alternative to be chosen; in this case only one type of exam can be chosen as the preferred type.)

Table 17.1   OBTAINED FREQUENCIES FOR A χ^2 GOODNESS-OF-FIT TEST ON THE STUDENT EXAM–PREFERENCE EXAMPLE

	Exam type			
	Essay	Multiple choice	Take home	Total
Number of students choosing	25	40	55	120

In this example there is no a priori reason to expect the students to prefer one type of exam over another. Therefore, we expect the students to choose one of the three types of exams at random, and the null hypothesis is that one-third of the students should choose essay exams, one-third should choose multiple-choice exams, and one-third should choose take-home exams. The alternative hypothesis is that students are not equally likely to choose each type of exam. Stated more formally, the null and alternative hypotheses are

H_0: Students are equally likely to choose one of the three types of exams.

H_1: Students are not equally likely to choose one of the three types of exams.

Like all other statistical tests we have encountered, the expected values with which we compare our obtained data are derived from assuming the null hypothesis to be true. In this example, if H_0 is true the 120 students should be distributed equally across the three types of exams, and therefore, we would expect $1/3 \times 120 = 40$ students to choose each type. The issue then becomes "Does the distribution of obtained frequencies (25, 40, 55) match, or *fit*, the distribution of frequencies expected under the null hypothesis (40, 40, 40)?" If the two distributions match, we fail to reject the null hypothesis. If they do not match but differ more than would be expected by chance because of a random selection of exam types, we reject the null hypothesis and accept the alternative hypothesis. We proceed by following basically the same steps as those of other statistical tests:

1. Transform the data into a test statistic that quantifies in a single index the difference between observed and expected data.
2. Compare the obtained value of the test statistic to a sampling distribution of that statistic when H_0 is true.
3. If the obtained value falls in the critical region of the sampling distribution, reject H_0. Otherwise, H_0 cannot be rejected.

The Chi-Square Statistic—χ^2

The test statistic that quantifies the fit between observed and expected frequencies is the chi-square statistic (χ^2). Like the test of H_0 about means or correlation coefficients, the test of a null hypothesis about frequencies is based on examining the difference between an obtained sample value and an expected population value if H_0 is true. With categorical data, the difference of interest is the difference between obtained frequencies and expected frequencies, or in symbols,

$$(O - E)$$

where O = an obtained frequency

E = an expected frequency if H_0 is true

The chi-square statistic is based on this difference and is defined as

$$\chi^2 = \Sigma \frac{(O - E)^2}{E} \qquad (17.1)$$

An inspection of Formula 17.1 shows its appropriateness to the task of comparing obtained and expected frequencies. The numerator, $O - E$, directly measures the difference between the obtained frequencies and the frequencies hypothesized under H_0. Small values of $O - E$ will indicate a good fit, and large values will indicate a poor fit. These values are squared, $(O - E)^2$, because some differences are positive and some are negative. If they were summed without squaring they would produce a χ^2 value of zero regardless of the fit. The denominator, E, weights the size of the squared differences relative to the size of the expected frequencies. The reason for this weighting can be illustrated with a simple example. Suppose you enrolled in a seminar in which past enrollments lead you to expect a class size of 10 students. You would certainly notice and perhaps be rather disappointed if you arrived at the first meeting of the seminar to find 40 students crowding the classroom. In contrast, entering a lecture hall in which 340 students turned up to take a course that typically attracted 310 students would probably not make any impression on you. In both instances the difference between the obtained and the expected frequencies is 30, but in the seminar that difference is much more impressive than in the lecture hall.

The obtained and the expected frequencies are presented together in Table 17.2. The chi-square statistic is computed as

$$\chi^2 = \Sigma \frac{(O - E)^2}{E}$$

$$= \frac{(-15)^2}{40} + \frac{(0)^2}{40} + \frac{(15)^2}{40}$$

$$= 5.63 + 0 + 5.63$$

$$= 11.26$$

Although Formula 17.1 conceptualizes the chi-square statistic very well, Formula 17.2 makes computation easier

$$\chi^2 = \Sigma \frac{O^2}{E} - N \qquad (17.2)$$

Using this formula with our example data we find

$$\chi^2 = \frac{25^2}{40} + \frac{40^2}{40} + \frac{55^2}{40} - 120$$

$$= \frac{625}{40} + \frac{1600}{40} + \frac{3025}{40} - 120$$

$$= 15.63 + 40.00 + 75.63 - 120$$

Table 17.2 OBTAINED AND EXPECTED FREQUENCIES FOR THE STUDENT EXAM–
PREFERENCE EXAMPLE (Notice that the Expected Frequencies Are Equal
Across Categories.)

	Exam type			
	Essay	Multiple choice	Take home	Total
Observed frequency	25	40	55	120
Expected frequency	40	40	40	120
Observed − expected	− 15	0	15	

$$= 131.26 - 120$$

$$= 11.26$$

the same value found previously with Formula 17.1.

Now that we have calculated a value of χ^2, we need to know the probability of finding such a value if the obtained frequencies were in fact sampled from a population represented by the expected frequencies. In other words, we need to compare our calculated value to the sampling distribution of the chi-square statistic when H_0 is true.

The Chi-Square Sampling Distribution

The sampling distribution of the chi-square statistic is called the *chi-square distribution*. It consists of chi-square values for all possible random samples when H_0 is true. Like the sampling distributions of t and F, there is actually a family of chi-square distributions, each depending on the degrees of freedom associated with the sample data. In the case of the goodness-of-fit test, the degrees of freedom are $k - 1$, where k refers to the number of levels of the categorical variable. Once the frequencies of $k - 1$ levels of the variable are known, the frequency of the remaining level is determined because the sum of the k frequencies must equal N, the total frequency. For the current example there are three types of exams ($k = 3$) and, therefore, $3 - 1 = 2$ degrees of freedom. Once we know the number of students choosing any two types of exams (e.g., 65 students combined to choose essay and multiple-choice exams), the number of students choosing the remaining type of exam is known (e.g., $120 - 65 = 55$ students choose the take-home exam).

The sampling distribution of chi-square for 1, 2, 4, and 8 degrees of freedom are shown in Figure 17.1, along with critical values that bound the rejection region for $\alpha = .05$. Notice that all values of chi-square are positive, ranging from zero to infinity. Also, notice that for small degrees of freedom the sampling distribution of chi-square is positively skewed, but as the number of degrees of freedom increases, the distribution approaches symmetry.

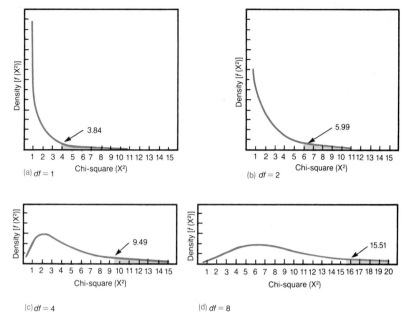

Figure 17.1 χ^2 distributions for 1, 2, 4, and 8 degrees of freedom.

Finally, notice that the size of the critical value increases as the degrees of freedom increase. For example, the critical value at α equals .05 for 1 degree of freedom is 3.84, whereas for 4 degrees of freedom the critical value is 9.49.

In our example, $\chi^2 = 11.26$ on 2 degrees of freedom. Looking at Figure 17.1 you can see that the critical value of chi-square on 2 degrees of freedom is 5.99. Therefore, we can reject H_0 at the $\alpha = .05$ level and conclude that the three types of exams are not equally preferred. In a research report, the professor might state that "the student population is not evenly distributed on the type of exam they prefer to write, χ^2 (2, $N = 120$) $= 11.26$, $p < .05$. It appears as though essay exams are least often preferred and take-home exams are most often preferred."

$$\chi^2(\text{critical}) = 5.99$$

$$\chi^2(\text{obtained}) = 11.26$$

Decision: Reject H_0

Tabled Critical Values of the Chi-Square Distributions

Table H in Appendix III gives the critical values of chi-square for six selected α levels on 1 to 30 degrees of freedom. Turning for the moment to Table H, you will see that it is entered by locating the relevant degrees of freedom along the left-hand margin. Then, scanning from left to right, you will find the critical values associated with the alpha levels labeled at the top of the table. You will see, for example, that for 2 degrees of freedom the critical value at $\alpha = .05$ is 5.99, the same value found in Figure 17.1. Notice that at $\alpha = .005$, the critical value is 10.59, which is still smaller than the χ^2 value obtained in our example (11.26). Thus, for the current example, H_0 could have been rejected at the .005 level of significance.

Table H contains critical values for up to 30 degrees of freedom, which is sufficient for most research in the behavioral sciences. However, when the degrees of freedom associated with a chi-square test are more than 30, an alternative test statistic can be obtained by transforming chi-square to a z-value using Formula 17.3

$$z = 2\chi^2 - 2df - 1 \qquad (17.3)$$

This statistic has a sampling distribution that is approximately normal, and values of it can be referred to the standard normal distribution (Table B, Appendix III).

Having laid out the general procedures for the chi-square goodness-of-fit test, let us try one more example for practice. This time, however, the expected frequencies are not equal, as they were in the first example (i.e., 40, 40, 40).

Example 2

An educational psychologist randomly sampled 1000 parents from a community and sent them all questionnaires concerning the use of corporal punishment in the schools. The sample consisted of 280 parents (28 percent of the sample) with children in grades kindergarten through grade 3, 330 parents (33 percent) with children in grades 4 through 7, 150 parents (15 percent) with children in grades 8 and 9, and 240 parents (24 percent) with children in grades 10 through 12. Of the original 1000 parents sampled, 400 responded by completing the questionnaire. The distribution across children's grade level for the 400 parents who responded is shown in Table 17.3.

Does the psychologist have evidence to indicate that the parents who completed the questionnaire responded in a manner comparable to parents in the initial random sample? In other words, is the distribution across grade levels for the 400 parents who responded to the questionnaire proportionally the same as the distribution for the original 1000 parents sampled?

Table 17.3   OBTAINED FREQUENCIES FOR A χ^2 GOODNESS-OF-FIT TEST ON THE PARENT QUESTIONNAIRE DATA

	Grade level of children				
	K–3	4–7	8–9	10–12	Total
Number of parents responding	133	142	50	75	400

The first step in answering this question is to compute the expected frequencies under the null hypothesis that the respondents were in fact representative of the entire sample. If H_0 is true, the same percentages of parents having children at the various grade levels found in the original sample of 1000 parents should apply to the 400 respondents. Therefore, of the 400 respondents, 28 percent should have children in grades kindergarten through grade 3, 33 percent should have children in grades 4 through 7, and so on. Applying these percentages to the 400 parents who responded to the questionnaire, we find that the expected frequencies under the null hypothesis are

$0.28(400) = 112$, the expected frequency having children in grades K–3

$0.33(400) = 132$, the expected frequency having children in grades 4–7

$0.15(400) = 60$, the expected frequency having children in grades 8–9

$0.24(400) = 96$, the expected frequency having children in grades 10–12

Now the chi-square statistic can be used to determine whether the obtained frequencies (133, 142, 50, 75) fit the frequencies expected under H_0 (112, 132, 60, 96). The obtained and expected frequencies are combined in Table 17.4. The value of chi-square is

$$\chi^2 = \Sigma \frac{(O - E)^2}{E}$$

$$= \frac{21^2}{112} + \frac{10^2}{132} + \frac{-10}{60} + \frac{-21^2}{96}$$

$$= 3.94 + 0.76 + 1.67 + 4.59$$

$$= 10.96$$

Since there are four categories of grades, $df = 4 - 1 = 3$, and from Table H we find that H_0 can be rejected at the $\alpha = .025$ level of significance. Thus, our psychologist might write that "across grade levels the parents who re-

Table 17.4   OBTAINED AND EXPECTED FREQUENCIES FOR THE PARENT QUESTIONNAIRE EXAMPLE (Notice that the Expected Frequencies Are Unequal Across Categories.)

| | Grade level | | | | |
	K–3	4–7	8–9	10–12	Total
Observed frequency	133	142	50	75	400
Expected frequency	112	132	60	96	400
Observed − expected	21	10	−10	−21	

sponded are not representative of all parents in the community, χ^2 (3, N = 400) = 10.96, $p < .025$. Parents of children in elementary grades responded more, whereas parents of children in higher grades responded less than in the original random sample."

χ^2(critical) = 7.82

χ^2(obtained) = 10.96

Decision: Reject H_0

17.3   THE CHI-SQUARE ANALYSIS OF CONTINGENCY

Although chi-square is useful as a test of goodness-of-fit, it is more often used as a test of contingency between two categorical variables, that is, as a test of whether the frequency distribution of one categorical variable is contingent on (changes or stays the same) the levels of a second categorical variable. In the sections to follow we consider two types of contingency analysis: the chi-square test of independence and the chi-square test of homogeneity.[1]

17.4   THE CHI-SQUARE TEST OF INDEPENDENCE

The chi-square test of independence is used to determine whether two categorical variables, each measured on members of a *single* population, are independent of one another. If the two variables *are* independent, the frequency distribution of one variable will stay the same across levels of the second variable. If they are *not* independent, the frequency distribution of one variable will change across levels of the second variable.

To illustrate the chi-square test of independence, consider the following hypothetical study of personality development. According to Erik Erikson's theory of personality, young adults are in a stage of psychosocial development characterized by conflict over issues of intimacy. One's intimacy status can be described as isolated, pseudointimate, or intimate according to the following criteria:

Isolated individuals live in an interpersonal void with only casual acquaintances.

Pseudointimate individuals are involved in a relatively permanent sexual relationship that is defined more by shallow conventional roles than by sharing deep feelings and self-disclosure.

---

[1]Chi-square can be used as a goodness-of-fit test on contingency tables if a null hypothesis completely specifies the joint distribution between two categorical variables. However, complete specification of such joint distributions is rare in psychology, and chi-square is typically used to test independence or homogeneity.

Intimate individuals are committed to a permanent sexual relationship that is based on mutual self-disclosure and understanding.

One of the central tenets of Erikson's theory is that intimacy status during young adulthood should depend on how well psychosocial crises have been resolved in the past, in particular, on how well the identity crisis of adolescence has been resolved. Thus, individuals lower in identity status should more frequently be lower in intimacy status, whereas individuals higher in identity status should more frequently be higher in intimacy status. An individual's identity status can be described as diffuse, foreclosed, moratorium, or achieved according to the following criteria:

Diffuse individuals may or may not have seriously questioned their identity, but regardless, they are not particularly concerned over their lack of direction.

Foreclosed individuals have not really questioned their identity, but instead have made commitments to identities pressed on them by their parents.

Moratorium individuals are currently in crisis over their identity and have not yet made firm commitments.

Achieved individuals have passed through a period of self-exploration and have made self-chosen commitments.

Suppose a psychologist is interested in testing Erikson's theory about the relationship between identity and intimacy status. One hundred college students are randomly sampled and interviewed to determine their status on both variables. The data are organized into a *contingency table* (Table 17.5), which in this example is called a 3 × 4 contingency table to emphasize the fact that there are three levels of intimacy status and four levels of identity status. Each row of Table 17.5 represents a different level of the identity variable, and each column represents a different level of intimacy. The cells of Table 17.5 contain the observed frequencies with which individuals in the sample fall into a particular level on *each* variable. For example, 13 individuals are both diffuse and isolated, 9 are both diffuse and pseudointimate, and so on.

The row and column totals show the marginal frequency distributions of each variable considered independently. Looking at the row totals you can see that when intimacy status is ignored, 26 of 100 students (26 percent of the total sample) are diffuse, 33 percent are foreclosed, 17 percent are moratorium, and 24 percent are achieved. Similarly, ignoring identity status, we see that 27 percent of the individuals are isolated, 43 percent are pseudointimate, and 30 percent are intimate. These marginal distributions are important because they form the basis for computing the expected frequencies in each cell, a topic we return to shortly.

Looking at Table 17.5, we see that the distribution of intimacy status differs across the levels of identity status and vice versa. For example, of the

Table 17.5   OBTAINED FREQUENCIES FOR A χ^2 TEST OF INDEPENDENCE ON THE STUDENT INTIMACY AND IDENTITY STATUS DATA

		Intimacy status			
		Isolated	Pseudointimate	Intimate	Row total
	Diffuse	13	9	4	26
	Foreclosed	9	18	6	33
Identity status	Moratorium	3	8	6	17
	Achieved	2	8	14	24
	Column total	27	43	30	100

26 individuals with diffuse identities, half (13) were also isolated and only 4 had reached the highest level of intimacy. In contrast, nearly the opposite results were obtained for individuals with achieved identities: Of those 24 individuals, over half (14) had also reached the highest level of intimacy (i.e., 14 of 24) and only 2 were isolated. The null hypothesis is that the distribution of intimacy status is the same at each level of identity status. Alternatively, the null hypothesis is that the distribution of identity status is the same at each level of intimacy status. In the chi-square test of independence the null hypothesis is symmetrical, much as it was in correlation analysis— where it made no difference whether the null hypothesis referred to the correlation of variable *A* with variable *B* or of variable *B* with variable *A*.

The null hypothesis is tested by computing the same chi-square statistic we used to test goodness-of-fit and then comparing our obtained value to the same chi-square distribution. All that differs between the goodness-of-fit test and the test of independence is how the expected frequencies and the degrees of freedom are determined (and of course, the nature of H_0).

Expected Frequencies for the Chi-Square Test of Independence

In the goodness-of-fit test the expected frequencies are determined before collecting the data. For example, we can assume the laws of chance are operating and, therefore, that the expected frequencies are equal across categories; or expected frequencies may be determined a priori on theoretical grounds. In contrast, the expected frequencies for the test of independence are determined from the obtained data, or more specifically, from the marginal distributions of each variable (the row and column totals).

Consider again the column totals at the bottom of Table 17.5 (27, 43, 30). These totals represent the overall frequencies with which students fall into the various categories of intimacy status, regardless of their identity status.

If intimacy and identity are independent—if the null hypothesis is true—we would expect this pattern of frequencies to be proportionally the same for students with diffuse, foreclosed, moratorium, and achieved identity statuses alike. That is, if H_0 is true, out of any random sample of students we would expect

$$\frac{27}{100} = 27\% \text{ of students to be isolated}$$

$$\frac{43}{100} = 43\% \text{ of students to be pseudointimate}$$

$$\frac{30}{100} = 30\% \text{ of students to be intimate}$$

regardless of their identity status.

Therefore, if we apply these percentages to each of the row totals in Table 17.5 (26, 33, 17, and 24) we will arrive at the expected frequency distributions for each category of identity status. For example, if H_0 is true, the expected frequencies with which the 26 students having diffuse identities should fall into the intimacy status categories are

isolated:
27% of 26   or $.27 \times 26 = 7.02$

pseudointimate:
43% of 26   or $.43 \times 26 = 11.18$

intimate:
30% of 26   or $.30 \times 26 = 7.80$

By applying these same percentages (27, 43, 30) to each of the remaining row totals (33, 17, 24) the rest of the expected frequencies for the data in Table 17.5 can be computed. These expected frequencies are shown in Table 17.6. You should verify them by performing the appropriate calculations. You also should verify them by using the computational formula for expected values, presented next.

Consider once again how expected frequencies are calculated. Using as an example the students whose intimacy status is diffuse and whose identity status is isolated, recall that their expected frequency was found by taking 27 percent of 26. The 27 percent equals the *overall* percentage of students whose intimacy status is isolated, and it was obtained by dividing the total number of students with that status (the column total for the isolated category = 27) by the total number of students in the sample ($N = 100$). The 26 equals the total number of students whose identity status is diffuse, and it was found simply as the row total for the diffuse category. Thus, we can symbolize the entire operation as

$$\frac{27}{100} \times 26 = \frac{27 \times 26}{100} = \frac{\text{column total} \times \text{row total}}{\text{total } N}$$

Table 17.6   EXPECTED FREQUENCIES FOR THE STUDENT INTIMACY AND IDENTITY
STATUS DATA

		Intimacy status			
		Isolated	Pseudointimate	Intimate	Row total
	Diffuse	7.02	11.18	7.80	26
	Foreclosed	8.91	14.19	9.90	33
Identity status	Moratorium	4.59	7.31	5.10	17
	Achieved	6.48	10.32	7.20	24
	Column total	27	43	30	100

Use this simplified formula to calculate the expected frequencies for the remaining cells in Table 17.5. They should agree with the expected frequencies shown in Table 17.6.

Calculating Chi-Square for the Test of Independence

The calculation of chi-square for the test of independence is easy because it uses exactly the same formula that was used to calculate chi-square for the goodness-of-fit test:

$$\chi^2 = \Sigma \frac{(O - E)^2}{E}$$

Applying this formula to the obtained and expected frequencies in Tables 17.5 and 17.6, we obtain

$$\chi^2 = \frac{(13 - 7.02)^2}{7.02} + \frac{(9 - 11.18)^2}{11.18} + \frac{(4 - 7.80)^2}{7.80} + \ldots + \frac{(14 - 7.20)^2}{7.20}$$

$$= 5.09 + 0.43 + 1.85 + \ldots + 6.42$$

$$= 20.75$$

To use this value to evaluate H_0, we need to consult Table H in Appendix III, and to do that we must know the degrees of freedom.

Degrees of Freedom for the Test of Independence

For the chi-square test of independence we must estimate both the row frequencies *and* the column frequencies. Given that the row frequencies and the column frequencies must add up to N, we are only free to estimate one less than the number of categories in the row variable and one less than the number of categories in the column variable. If we let R stand for the number of categories in the row variable and C for the number of categories in the columns variable, there are $R - 1$ and $C - 1$ degrees of freedom associated with each, and these must be subtracted from the total degrees of freedom to arrive at the degrees of freedom for the contingency table.

$$df = df_{tot} - df_r - df_c$$

$$= RC - 1 - (R - 1) - (C - 1)$$

$$= (R - 1)(C - 1)$$

In our example there are four rows $(R = 4)$ and three columns $(C = 3)$. Therefore, the degrees of freedom are

$$df = (4 - 1)(3 - 1)$$

$$= 6$$

Entering Table H with 6 degrees of freedom, you can see that our obtained value of χ^2 (20.75) exceeds the critical value for $\alpha = .005$ (18.55), which means that H_0 should be rejected. The form of reporting chi-square for the test of independence is the same as for the goodness-of-fit test. For example, the psychologist might state, "There is a significant relationship between intimacy status and identity status, χ^2 (6, $N = 100$) = 20.75, $p < .005$. The likelihood of having achieved intimacy increases as identity status increases."

χ^2(critical) = 18.55

χ^2(obtained) = 20.75

Decision: Reject H_0

17.5   THE CHI-SQUARE TEST OF HOMOGENEITY

The procedures used to compute the chi-square test of homogeneity are identical to those used with the chi-square test of independence. In fact, there is only one important distinction between the two tests, and it involves differences in their respective sampling procedures. We turn to this distinction next.

Recall that for the test of independence a sample is randomly selected from a *single* population, and each individual in that sample is then classified on *two* categorical variables (e.g., identity status and intimacy status). The test then compares the frequency distribution of one of the variables across the levels of the other variable. Thus, the test of independence is a *single-sample test of contingency between two categorical variables*. Typically, researchers conducting such a single-sample study are not interested in distinguishing one variable as the predictor or independent variable and the other variable as the dependent variable. That is, they are not any more interested in comparing the distribution of variable A across levels of another variable B than they are in comparing the distribution of variable B across the levels of variable A. Thus, appropriate null hypotheses for the test of independence would be

1. H_0: In the population the distribution of variable A is proportionally equal at all levels of variable B.
2. H_0: In the population the distribution of variable B is proportionally equal at all levels of variable A.
3. H_0: In the population variables A and B are independent.

In contrast, for the test of homogeneity, samples are randomly selected from *two or more* populations (e.g., males and females) or are formed by randomly assigning individuals to two or more treatment groups, and each individual in each sample is then classified on a *single* categorical variable (e.g., intimacy status or pass or fail on an experimental test). The statistical test then compares the different samples with respect to how they are distributed across the levels of the measured categorical variable. Thus, the test of homogeneity is a *k-sample test of the equality of frequency distributions across a single categorical variable.* Researchers conducting this kind of study are specifically interested in comparing selected samples with respect to their frequency distributions. Therefore, the variable representing sample membership (e.g., gender or treatment group) is generally considered the predictor or independent variable, and the only reasonable null hypotheses for the test of homogeneity are

H_0: distribution$_{\text{pop1}}$ = distribution$_{\text{pop2}}$ = . . . = distribution$_{\text{pop}k}$

if samples are randomly selected from k populations, or

H_0: no treatment effect

if samples are formed by randomly assigning subjects to treatment groups.

The conceptual distinction between the test of independence and the test of homogeneity is relatively straightforward. However, recognizing whether your research represents an independence or a homogeneity problem can be difficult because in both cases your data will be cast into a contingency table and in both cases you will analyze the data with the chi-square statistic. Probably the easiest way to distinguish between the two types of problems is by considering the way in which the samples are drawn and recognizing the effect the sampling procedure has on marginal distributions (the row and column totals). In the test of independence, a single random sample is drawn and then subjects are classified on both variables. Therefore, the totals for both the rows and the columns will be known only *after* the data have been collected. In the test of homogeneity, two or more random samples of a specific size are selected by the researcher and then subjects are classified on only one variable. Thus, the frequencies of one of the marginal distributions will be known *before* the data have been collected (e.g., the row or column total that indicates the numbers of males and females or numbers of subjects in each treatment group).

To illustrate a research situation in which the chi-square test of homogeneity would be appropriate, consider the following example. Suppose that because of different socialization practices young women are expected to show higher levels of intimacy than are young men. Random samples of 50 male and 50 female college sophomores are selected and interviewed to determine their intimacy status. The results are presented in Table 17.7. Apparently females do show higher levels of intimacy than do males (22 of 50 females have achieved intimacy, whereas only 11 of 50 males are at that level). But is there statistical evidence that males and females in the populations differ overall in their intimacy status?

The chi-square test of homogeneity is appropriate in answering this question because a random sample of individuals from two populations (males and females) was selected and a single categorical variable (intimacy status) was measured. The null hypothesis is that males and females will show the same relative frequency distributions across the three levels of intimacy status.

$$H_0: \text{distribution}_{male} = \text{distribution}_{female}$$

Notice that the numbers of males and females were determined by the researcher (50 each, although sample sizes need not be equal), and as such the row totals were known before the data were collected. Had a random sample of 100 sophomores been selected and both their gender and their intimacy status measured *after* selection, neither the row nor the column totals would have been known a priori, and these data would have been better interpreted as a test of independence.

With this distinction in mind, the chi-square statistic is computed exactly as it was for the test of independence. Expected values are obtained for each cell as

$$\frac{\text{row total} \times \text{column total}}{\text{total } N}$$

Table 17.7 OBTAINED FREQUENCIES FOR THE χ^2 TEST OF HOMOGENEITY ON THE MALES' AND FEMALES' INTIMACY STATUS

| | Intimacy status | | | |
	Isolated	Pseudointimate	Intimate	Row total
Male	12	27	11	50
Female	8	20	22	50
Column total	20	47	33	100

Table 17.8   EXPECTED FREQUENCIES FOR THE MALES' AND
FEMALES' INTIMACY STATUS

| | Intimacy status | | | |
	Isolated	Pseudointimate	Intimate	Row total
Male	10.0	23.5	16.5	50
Female	10.0	23.5	16.5	50
Column total	20	47	33	100

For example, the expected number of isolated males is

$$\frac{50 \times 20}{100} = 10.0$$

and the expected values for all of the cells are presented in Table 17.8.

Applying Formula 17.1 to the obtained and expected frequencies in Tables 17.7 and 17.8, we find that the value of chi-square is

$$\chi^2 = \Sigma \frac{(O - E)^2}{E}$$

$$= \frac{(12 - 10)^2}{10} + \frac{(27 - 23.5)^2}{23.5} + \frac{(11 - 16.5)^2}{16.5} + \ldots + \frac{(22 - 16.5)^2}{16.5}$$

$$= .40 + .52 + 1.83 + .40 + .52 + 1.83$$

$$= 5.50$$

The critical value of χ^2 on $(2 - 1)(3 - 1) = 2$ degrees of freedom, $\alpha = .05$, is 5.99 (see Table H in Appendix III). Since our obtained χ^2 value of 5.50 is smaller than the critical value, we cannot reject the null hypothesis and perhaps would write "The distributions of intimacy status for males and females do not differ, χ^2 (2, $N = 100$) = 5.50, $p > .05$." Of course the probability of the obtained chi-square is so close to the conventional level for rejecting H_0 that we might append to our statement a sentence like "However, there is a tendency for females to show higher levels of intimacy than do males."

$\chi^2(\text{critical}) = 5.99$

$\chi^2(\text{obtained}) = 5.50$

Decision: Fail to reject H_0

In sum, although there is much in common between the chi-square test of independence and the chi-square test of homogeneity, there are some important distinctions. In practice the two tests differ in sampling procedures, in the status of one variable as the predictor or independent variable, and in the kinds of conclusions drawn. In the test of independence a single random sample is drawn, and the basic issue concerns whether there is a relationship between two variables in some population. In the test of homogeneity, k random samples are drawn, and the basic issue concerns whether the populations represented by those samples differ in their distributions across a categorical variable. Moreover, regardless of how subjects are selected, if the k samples represent randomly assigned treatment groups, the test of homogeneity permits conclusions regarding cause and effect.

17.6   STRENGTH OF RELATIONSHIP IN CONTINGENCY TABLES

The results of a chi-square test of contingency merely indicate whether or not there is a statistically reliable relationship between two categorical variables. As with all significance tests, a statistically significant relationship does not necessarily imply a strong relationship. It is desirable, therefore, to include in any analysis of contingency both a significance test *and* a measure of the strength of the relationship.

In previous chapters the strength of the relationship between variables was measured by using the Pearson r (r^2) or the correlation ratio (η^2). A statistic called *Cramer's phi* is used to measure the strength of the relationship in contingency analysis. Cramer's phi is defined as

$$\text{Cramer's } \phi = \sqrt{\frac{\chi^2}{N(k-1)}} \tag{17.4}$$

where k equals the smaller of R (the number of rows in the contingency table) or C (the number of columns), and either R or C if $R = C$. The value of Cramer's ϕ ranges from 0.0 to 1.0, with 0.0 indicating no relationship (completely independent) and 1.0 indicating a perfect relationship (completely dependent).

For the example relating intimacy status and identity status shown in Table 17.5, $\chi^2 = 20.75$, $k = 3$, and $N = 100$. Using Formula 17.4 we find

$$\text{Cramer's } \phi = \sqrt{\frac{20.75}{100(3-1)}}$$
$$= .32$$

This value is fairly small, indicating that the relationship between intimacy and identity status, although statistically significant, is not particularly strong. Notice that this value of Cramer's ϕ would be considered significantly different from zero because the chi-square value on which it is based is statistically significant. Indeed, one interpretation of chi-square tests of contingency tables is that they test the null hypothesis that in the population Cramer's ϕ equals zero.

It is not immediately apparent that Cramer's ϕ is a correlation-type measure. However, one can better appreciate that fact by recognizing that Cramer's ϕ is actually a generalization of the Pearson correlation between two dichotomous variables, ϕ. In Chapter 6 we calculated ϕ to test the null hypothesis of no relationship between family stability and subsequent ability to maintain an intimate relationship, and we found that $\phi = .20$. The data used in that example (Table 6.6) are recast into the 2 X 2 contingency table shown in the upper portion of Table 17.9. The expected frequencies are shown in the lower portion of Table 17.9. The chi-square value computed on Table 17.9 is $\chi^2 = .83$. Placing that value into Formula 17.4, we find

$$\text{Cramer's } \phi = \sqrt{\frac{.83}{20(2-1)}}$$

$$= \sqrt{.0415}$$

$$= .203$$

$$= \phi \text{ (within rounding error)}$$

Table 17.9 DATA FOR CALCULATING PHI FROM χ^2 (THESE DATA WERE ORIGINALLY PRESENTED IN TABLE 6.6.)

Obtained frequencies

	Subject divorced (0)	Subject not divorced (1)	Row total
Parents divorced (0)	5	5	10
Parents not divorced (1)	3	7	10
Column total	8	12	20

Expected frequencies

	Subject divorced (0)	Subject not divorced (1)	Row total
Parents divorced (0)	4	6	10
Parents not divorced (1)	4	6	10
Column total	8	12	20

$$\chi^2 = \frac{(5-4)^2}{4} + \frac{(5-6)^2}{6} + \frac{(3-4)^2}{4} + \frac{(7-6)^2}{6}$$

$$= .83$$

Notice that for a 2 X 2 table, the $k - 1$ term in Formula 17.4 always equals 1 and, therefore, can be removed from the formula when calculating ϕ. Thus, ϕ can be calculated directly by using the formula for the Pearson correlation or indirectly by first calculating chi-square and then transforming it with a simplified version of Formula 17.4:

$$\phi = \sqrt{\frac{\chi^2}{N}} \qquad (17.5)$$

We recommend using Formula 17.5 because it leads more easily to information concerning both the strength of the relationship and the statistical significance.

17.7 ASSUMPTIONS FOR CHI-SQUARE TESTS

As with most of the statistical tests presented so far, the appropriate use of the chi-square test requires several assumptions to be met:

1. Each observation is independent of every other observation, which means, for example, that each individual in a study can be classified into one and only one cell of a contingency table. This assumption is most commonly violated when individuals are repeatedly measured and their classifications entered into a table two or more times. The easiest check of this assumption is to ensure that the overall total from a contingency table (total N) equals the number of subjects in the study.

2. The categories must be *exhaustive.* That is, not only must every individual be classified into a category but also, overall, the categories must account for (exhaust) all of the individuals in a study. This assumption is most often violated when one of the levels of a variable is ignored. For example, if 20 of 50 subjects in a control group passed an experimental test, whereas 40 of 50 subjects in a treatment group passed the test, it would be incorrect to use χ^2 to compare only the subjects in the two groups who passed the test (20 versus 40) while ignoring those who failed the test (30 versus 10). The incorrect way to table the data would look like this:

	Control	Treatment	Total
Observed	20	40	60
Expected	30	30	60

whereas the correct way to table the data would look like this:

	Control	Treatment	Total
Pass	20	40	60
Fail	30	10	40
Total	50	50	100

Not taking the fail category into account in this example is paramount to translating erroneously a test of homogeneity into a goodness-of-fit test. Again, the easiest check on the assumption of exhaustive categories is to make sure the total N equals the number of subjects in the study.

3. Perhaps the most controversial assumption surrounding the use of chi-square tests concerns the size of the expected frequencies. The sampling distribution of the chi-square statistic is only approximated by the theoretical chi-square distribution, and this approximation is not very good with small expected frequencies, especially when degrees of freedom also are small (take note that we are discussing the size of expected frequencies here, *not* the size of obtained frequencies). The controversy revolves around deciding just how small is a small expected frequency. A position that is fairly widely accepted and not overly conservative is that with 1 degree of freedom, expected frequencies should be at least 5, otherwise chi-square tests should not be used; for 2 degrees of freedom all expected frequencies should be greater than 2; and with more than 3 degrees of freedom, expected frequencies can be as small as 1 as long as only a few are that small (e.g., one out of every five expected frequencies).

But what should be done when expected frequencies do not meet these recommended sizes? Some statisticians suggest that a correction should be applied to the formula for computing chi-square, but just as many argue against such a correction.[2] A better procedure when chi-square tests are not recommended is to avoid them entirely and use instead a test based on the randomization model.

---

[2]Some authors suggest using *Yates Correction for Continuity* on 2 X 2 contingency tables when expected frequencies are small. The correction amounts to subtracting .5 from the absolute value of the numerator of Formula 17.1 before squaring. However, just as many authors argue against the correction. We recommend using Fisher's exact test in this situation because it is not fraught with assumptions about expected frequencies and controversies about corrections. We have included Yates correction in NPSTAT for purposes of comparison with the uncorrected chi-square test and Fisher's exact test.

17.8   RANDOMIZATION APPROACH TO ANALYZING CONTINGENCY

In this section we illustrate a randomization test called *Fisher's exact test* for analyzing a 2 X 2 contingency table. Although randomization tests exist for analyzing larger contingency tables and for evaluating goodness-of-fit, they require staggering amounts of computation and will be omitted here. Besides, it is with 2 X 2 tables that chi-square assumptions are most commonly violated; they have the fewest degrees of freedom (1) and require the highest minimum expected frequencies of any size contingency table.

As with randomization tests discussed in previous chapters, the rationale underlying Fisher's exact tests differs from the rationale underlying random sampling tests. Specifically, with a chi-square test a table of frequencies is transformed into a chi-square value, and that value is referred to a theoretical sampling distribution based on an infinite number of possible outcomes when H_0 is true. In contrast, with Fisher's exact test, a table of frequencies is referred directly to a finite distribution based on all the possible ways the *observed* table of frequencies could have been arranged by chance alone. The exact probability of the obtained result occurring by chance (i.e., occurring when H_0 is true) is equal to the relative frequency of that result or one more extreme with respect to the total number of possible results. If the exact probability is less than $\alpha = .05$, the decision is to reject H_0. If the exact probability is greater than .05, we fail to reject H_0.

As an example, suppose a developmental psychologist were interested in whether adding information about normal infant development to standard prenatal classes would influence the extent to which mothers attributed intentionality to their infants' acts. Twenty expecting mothers were randomly assigned in equal numbers to one of two types of prenatal classes. One class was traditional (traditional group) and focused primarily on preparation for delivering the infant and subsequently providing for its physical care. The other class offered identical content plus some basic information about normal infant cognitive development (extra instruction group). After completing the classes all mothers were shown a film in which a mother was trying to bathe her 4-month-old infant. The infant, however, was not particularly happy about being bathed and over the course of the film became progressively more fussy. The more the mother persisted the more the infant resisted until finally the infant worked itself into a mild tantrum. The mothers were asked to indicate whether the 4-month-old was reacting impulsively to the bathing situation (reaction) or acting purposefully with the intention of communicating displeasure (intention). The data appear in Table 17.10, where it appears that mothers who took the traditional class attributed intentionality relatively more frequently than did mothers who took the extra information class.

If the expected frequencies were computed, you would see that two of them are less than 5 (we suggest that you do compute expected frequencies). Therefore, a chi-square test of homogeneity is inappropriate for these data. However, the exact probability of these results occurring when H_0 is true can

Table 17.10   OBTAINED FREQUENCIES FOR FISHER'S EXACT TEST ON MOTHERS'
ATTRIBUTION OF INTENTION

	Attribution		Row total
	Intention	Reaction	
Traditional	7	3	10
Extra information	2	8	10
Column total	9	11	20

be obtained by using Fisher's exact test. The rationale of the test on these data is as follows: This particular sample has a total of 20 individuals, 9 who attribute intention and 11 who attribute reaction to the infant's actions. If there is no real difference in the effects of the two types of classes, each individual would have shown the same attribution of the infant's actions regardless of which prenatal class she attended. Thus, if H_0 is true, the obtained arrangement of frequencies could have come about by chance simply as one of many possible random arrangements of 20 such individuals into two groups of 10. To test H_0 we need to find *all* such possible arrangements. Then we can compute the relative frequency of arrangements that are equal to or more extreme (more indicative of a difference between the two prenatal classes) than the obtained arrangement. That relative frequency would equal the probability under the null hypothesis of finding a difference in frequency distributions between the two prenatal classes at least as big as the obtained difference.

Carrying out the test reduces to computing the total number of arrangements of 20 individuals into two groups of 10, with the constraint that 9 of them respond one way and 11 respond another way. We could do this computation by creating every possible 2 X 2 table having row totals of 10 for each row and column totals of 9 for column 1 and 11 for column 2. The problem with this approach is that there are $20!/(10! \times 10!) = 92,378$ possible tables. Fortunately, R. A. Fisher developed a formula for directly computing the proportion of arrangements that would contain a particular observed set of frequencies. Using the letters shown in Table 17.11, that formula is

$$p = \frac{(A + B)!(C + D)!(A + C)!(B + D)!}{N!\,A!B!C!D!} \tag{17.6}$$

Applying Formula 17.6 to the data in Table 17.10, we find that the proportion of arrangements that would result in that particular observed set of frequencies is

$$p = \frac{10!10!9!11!}{20!7!3!2!8!}$$

$$= .0321$$

Table 17.11   EXAMPLE OF LABELS FOR COMPUTING FISHER'S EXACT TEST

	Response type		Row total
	Response *A*	Response *B*	
Group 1	*A*	*B*	*A + B*
Group 2	*C*	*D*	*C + D*
Column total	*A + C*	*B + D*	*N*

To find the probability of *at least* the obtained arrangement of frequencies, we need not only the probability just computed but also the probability of tables that are more indicative of a difference between the two prenatal classes. Two tables showing even more systematic differences between the two classes are shown in Table 17.12. The uppermost table was found by subtracting 1 from cells *B* and *C* and adding 1 to cells *A* and *D*. This procedure was continued to produce the lower table, and in general it continues by systematically rearranging the data (keeping the row and column totals constant) until one cell has a frequency of zero.

Applying Formula 17.6 to each of these tables we find

$$p = \frac{10!10!9!11!}{20!8!2!1!9!}$$

$$= .0027$$

Table 17.12   TABLES REPRESENTING GREATER DIFFERENCES
BETWEEN THE TWO PRENATAL CLASSES

	Attribution		Row total
	Intention	Reaction	
Traditional	8	2	10
Extra information	1	9	10
Column total	9	11	20

	Attribution		Row total
	Intention	Reaction	
Traditional	9	1	10
Extra information	0	10	10
Column total	9	11	20

and

$$p = \frac{10!\,10!\,9!\,11!}{20!\,9!\,1!\,0!\,10!}$$

$$= .00006$$

Thus, when H_0 is true, the probability of finding our obtained results or one more indicative of a difference between the two prenatal classes is

$$p = .0321 + .0027 + .00006$$

$$= .0349$$

This obtained critical value is smaller than $\alpha = .05$, so the null hypothesis of no difference between the two classes is rejected. (Note: This analysis was also performed and verified by using NPSTAT. We suggest you try it also.)

$p(\text{critical}) = .05$

$p(\text{observed}) = .0348$

Decision: Reject H_0

Such a result might be reported by saying, "The finding supports the notion that the type of prenatal training affects mothers' interpretation of infant behavior ($p < .04$, Fisher's exact test)." Notice that the Fisher exact test is one-tailed. Unless there is good reason for a one-tailed test, the results produced by following the preceding computations should be doubled to arrive at a two-tailed probability. For the present example, the two-tailed probability is .0697, which would fail to reject H_0. Both one- and two-tailed probabilities of Fisher's exact test are shown when a 2 X 2 contingency table is analyzed using NPSTAT.

SUMMARY

In this chapter we discussed statistical inference with categorical variables by using the chi-square statistic. Three types of tests were included: the goodness-of-fit test, the test of independence, and the test of homogeneity. In each of these tests the chi-square statistic was used to evaluate the magnitude of discrepancy between the observed and expected frequencies.

The goodness-of-fit test is a single-sample test that compares the shape of an obtained frequency distribution with a theoretical frequency distribution. The test of independence is also a single-sample test, but it tests the null hypothesis that the frequency distribution of one categorical variable is the same across the levels of another categorical variable. The test of homogeneity is a k-sample test that compares the frequency distributions of several randomly selected or randomly assigned groups.

Two measures of association, phi and Cramer's phi, were introduced. They are used most often following a statistically significant chi-square value to evaluate the strength of the relationship between two categorical variables. Phi is useful only for measuring the strength of relationship in a 2 X 2 contingency table. Cramer's phi can be used on any size contingency table.

Several assumptions underlying the appropriate use of chi-square tests were discussed. When the assumption of minimum expected frequencies is not met, an exact probability test is more appropriate. An example of such a test was presented, namely, Fisher's exact test for evaluating 2 X 2 contingency tables.

KEY WORDS

parametric test	chi-square statistic (χ^2)
nonparametric test	chi-square distribution
distribution-free test	contingency table
chi-square test	test of independence
goodness-of-fit test	test of homogeneity
contingency tests	Cramer's phi (ϕ)
obtained frequency	Fisher's exact text
expected frequency	

PROBLEMS

Indicate whether statements 1 through 10 are true or false.

1 Chi-square tests can detect differences in distribution means.

2 Chi-square tests can detect differences in distribution variances.

3 In the chi-square goodness-of-fit test the expected frequencies are computed after collecting the data.

4 The larger the value of chi-square, the more likely H_0 will be rejected.

5 To compute a chi-square test of independence the number of rows in a contingency table must always equal the number of columns.

6 The number of degrees of freedom associated with a contingency table is equal to the number of rows times the number of columns.

7 The computations involved in the chi-square test of independence are the same as those involved in the chi-square test of homogeneity.

8 In conducting an analysis of contingency the obtained frequency of one or more of the cells can be less than 2.

9 The critical value for χ^2 with $\alpha = .05$ is 3.84.

10 In computing Fisher's exact test of a 2 X 2 contingency table, the expected frequency of one or more cells can be less than 5.

11 Explain the difference between the numbers analyzed with a chi-square test and the numbers analyzed with a t-test.

12 Define expected frequency. Describe three ways in which expected frequencies are derived.

13 Discuss the similarities and differences between the chi-square tests of independence and homogeneity.

14 Give three examples of null hypotheses that can be tested with chi-square tests.

15 Discuss the differences in rationale between chi-square tests of contingency in a 2 X 2 table and Fisher's exact test.

16 A professor is trying to determine the criteria that people use when choosing a course. A random sample of 100 students is drawn, and each student is asked to select from a list of alternatives the single factor he or she relies on most often in choosing a course. The data are

	Interest	Hearsay	Size of class	Total
Number of students choosing	40	40	20	100

Can the professor conclude that there is any specific factor that is most important for choosing courses? What assumption would have been violated if students could choose more than one alternative? How do you check this assumption?

17 The same professor then wonders if the factors considered in choosing courses are the same for freshmen, sophomores, juniors, and seniors in college. Another random sample of 100 students is chosen, but this time both their level of college seniority and the factor they rely on most in choosing courses are measured. The data are

	Interest	Hearsay	Class size	Row total
Freshmen	5	20	5	30
Sophomores	5	10	5	20
Juniors	10	5	5	20
Seniors	20	5	5	30
Column total	40	40	20	100

Can the professor conclude that the reason for choosing a course is independent of one's college seniority? How strong is the relationship? How can you tell that this is a test of independence? Is a chi-square test appropriate for these data? Give three reasons why or why not.

18 An educational psychologist is interested in whether a kindergarten teacher's perception of children's behavior agrees with the perceptions of the children's parents. The following data were obtained:

		Parents' perceptions			
		Friendly	Aggressive	Typical	Row total
	Friendly	7	2	5	14
Teacher's perception	Aggressive	3	11	10	24
	Typical	5	2	5	12
	Column total	15	15	20	50

Compute a chi-square test of independence to see if the teacher's perceptions agree with the parents' perceptions. How strong is the relationship? How can you tell that this is a test of independence? How might the study be altered to become a test of homogeneity comparing the teacher's and parents' perceptions of children? Create two sets of data for such a test, both of which show the same strength of relationship but only one of which produces a significant value of chi-square. How can you most easily affect the significance level?

19. The following data come from a study of the effect of head injury on the ability to solve a spatial discrimination problem:

	Solve problem	Do not solve problem	Row total
Head injured	1	6	7
Control group	5	2	7
Column total	6	8	14

What test should be used on these data? Why? Is there a significant difference between the two groups? Try carrying out the analysis by using the NPSTAT program.

Chapter 18

Rank Tests

18.1   INTRODUCTION

Occasionally researchers collect data with a scale of measurement that is clearly ordinal. An example would be ranking patients from lowest to highest according to how much improvement they showed following several sessions of psychotherapy. More often, however, ordinal data arise when scores are converted to ranks because the researcher is not convinced they meet the requirements of interval or ratio scales. When data either are measured directly as ranks or are converted to ranks they can be analyzed with a *nonparametric rank test.*

In this chapter we present four of the most commonly used rank tests. Their names are listed in Table 18.1 together with the experimental design to which each test applies. Also listed in Table 18.1 are the parametric and randomization tests that could be applied to each design should the conditions underlying their use be met. For purposes of comparison, we illustrate each rank test by using data from examples presented in previous chapters. Be forewarned, however, that the issue of which test to use for a particular design is not clear-cut. We touch on this issue as we discuss each rank test and consider in detail the relative merits of parametric and nonparametric tests at the end of this chapter.

18.2   RANKING SCORES

All of the tests presented in this chapter are based on sums of ranks. Therefore, scores that are not measured directly as ranks must first be transformed to ranks before the tests can be used. The procedures for transforming data into ranks vary according to the particular test, but basically they fall into two types.

One type of ranking procedure is essentially the same as that used in

Table 18.1   PARAMETRIC AND NONPARAMETRIC TESTS FOR FOUR RESEARCH DESIGNS

Design	Parametric test	Nonparametric test	
		Randomization test	Rank test
Two independent samples	*t*-test for two independent samples	Randomization test for two independent samples	Mann-Whitney test
Two dependent samples	*t*-test for two dependent samples	Randomization test for two dependent samples	Wilcoxon test
k independent samples	ANOVA for *k* independent samples	Randomization test for *k* independent samples	Kruskal-Wallis test
k dependent samples	ANOVA for *k* dependent samples	Randomization test for *k* dependent samples	Friedman test

Table 18.2   EXAMPLE OF RANK ORDERING OF SINGLE SCORES AND PAIRED SCORES

Original data	Ordered data	Rank-ordered data
30	20	1.0
70	30	2.0
105	40	3.0
45	45	4.0
295	55	5.5
55	55	5.5
200	60	7.0
60	65	8.0
80	70	9.5
70	70	9.5
145	80	11.0
20	105	12.0
55	145	13.0
65	200	14.0
40	295	15.0

Paired scores		Difference score	Ranked differences	Signed ranks
15	3	12	9.5	9.5
11	17	−6	5.0	−5.0
21	9	12	9.5	9.5
15	13	2	1.5	1.5
13	11	2	1.5	1.5
9	13	−4	3.0	−3.0
19	9	10	7.5	7.5
17	11	6	5.0	5.0
9	3	6	5.0	5.0
21	11	10	7.5	7.5

Chapter 6 with the Spearman rank correlation. This procedure is summarized as follows and illustrated in Table 18.2.

1. List all the original scores in order from smallest to largest.
2. Assign a rank (first, second, etc.) to each score in the ordered list.
3. When tied scores occur, compute the average of their ranks and assign that average to each score.

A second type of ranking, also illustrated in Table 18.2, is used when each individual in an experiment produces two scores and we want to rank the differences between each pair of scores. To transform paired scores into ranks,

1. Compute the difference between each pair of scores.
2. Rank order these differences without taking into consideration their

sign (i.e., positive or negative). Differences of zero are dropped from the analysis, and tied differences are given the average of their ranks.

3. Attach the sign of the difference to the rank of the difference.

Rank tests assume that variables have a continuous underlying distribution, which implies that tied scores should not exist. Of course, in practice ties occur frequently, and when many of them occur between two groups (ties within a group do not affect rank tests) some statisticians (e.g., Bradley, 1968) recommend that special correction procedures be applied. We discuss only "uncorrected" tests in this chapter, but we recommend consulting these sources before trying to analyze data in which there are few subjects and where more than 25 percent of the scores between groups are tied.

18.3   MANN-WHITNEY *U*-TEST FOR TWO INDEPENDENT SAMPLES

The Mann-Whitney *U*-test is used to compare two independent samples on a variable that is measured at the ordinal level. It is often recommended as the best nonparametric alternative to the independent samples *t*-test, although this is not true in all situations. The Mann-Whitney *U*-test is the best alternative to the *t*-test when the formal assumptions underlying the *t*-test are violated *and* the data are measured at the ordinal level. However, if the assumptions underlying the *t*-test are violated but the data are measured at the interval level, the best nonparametric alternative to the *t*-test is the independent samples randomization test discussed in Chapter 11.

The Mann-Whitney *U*-test evaluates a different, more general null hypothesis than does the independent samples *t*-test. It does not evaluate whether the means of two samples are identical but rather whether the distributions of two samples are identical. Thus, rejecting H_0 with a Mann-Whitney test implies only that the distributions differ in some way. If, however, the shape of the two distributions is similar, which is often the case in practice, the Mann-Whitney test evaluates whether the two samples have equal medians.

All of the tests presented in this chapter are known as *rank-randomization tests* because they apply to ranks and take as their null distribution all possible randomizations of the same sample of subjects among the different treatments. We examine in some detail how the Mann-Whitney *U*-test can be derived from randomization theory to illustrate procedures common to all rank tests.

Consider the following simple example. A therapist is interested in comparing two methods of reducing patients' phobic reactions. He randomly assigns six patients to two groups of three patients each. One group receives hypnotherapy three times a week for one month, and the other group receives systematic desensitization for the same period of time. At the end of treatment all subjects receive a standard test of phobic anxiety. The data for the two groups are

Hypnosis group: 7, 12, 18

Desensitization group: 20, 14, 24

The Mann-Whitney U-test begins by rank ordering all of the scores from the combined groups as follows:

7, 12, 14, 18, 20, 24

Next, a rank is assigned to each score such that the lowest score gets a rank of 1, the second lowest a rank of 2, and so on:

Score: 7, 12, 14, 18, 20, 24

Rank: 1, 2, 3, 4, 5, 6

Finally, the group membership corresponding to each ranked score is specified with an H to indicate individuals from the hypnosis group and a D to indicate individuals from the desensitization group. This final result is shown in Table 18.3.

At issue is deciding whether the obtained ordering of scores over the two groups is likely or unlikely to have occurred by chance because of random assignment. This is a familiar issue in hypothesis testing and amounts to deciding between

H_0: The obtained ordering is due to chance.

H_1: The obtained ordering is due to a treatment effect.

If H_0 were true and random assignment does account for the distributions of scores within each group, these distributions should be approximately the same. Therefore, combining the scores into a single ordered sequence should produce a distribution in which the scores from the two groups are evenly dispersed. In other words, scores from the hypnosis group should precede scores from the desensitization group about as often as scores from the desensitization group precede scores from the hypnosis group. For example,

H, D, H, D, H, D

On the other hand, if there were a treatment effect, the scores of each group should systematically cluster at opposite ends of the scale. For example,

H, H, H, D, D, D

or

D, D, D, H, H, H

Like all other statistical tests, the Mann-Whitney U-test proceeds through three steps:

Table 18.3 RANK ORDERING OF SCORES FROM LOWEST
TO HIGHEST FOR THE COMBINED HYPNOSIS
AND DESENSITIZATION GROUPS

Score	7	12	14	18	20	24
Rank	1	2	3	4	5	6
Group*	H	H	D	H	D	D

*H = hypnosis.
 D = desensitization.

Counting method of obtaining U_H and U_D

$$U_H = 3 + 3 + 2 = 8$$

$$U_D = 1 + 0 + 0 = 1$$

Using equations to obtain U_H and U_D

$$\Sigma R_H = 1 + 2 + 4 = 7$$

$$\Sigma R_D = 3 + 5 + 6 = 14$$

$$U_H = 3(3) + \frac{3(3 + 1)}{2} - 7 = 8$$

$$U_D = 3(3) + \frac{3(3 + 1)}{2} - 14 = 1$$

1. The data are transformed into a test statistic, in this case one that quantifies the degree to which the scores in two groups overlap (or conversely, are systematically separated into two distinct clusters).
2. The obtained value of the statistic is compared to a distribution of all possible values of the statistic when H_0 is true.
3. If the obtained value falls in the critical region of the distribution, reject H_0. Otherwise, fail to reject H_0.

The Mann-Whitney *U*-Statistic

The test statistic that quantifies the degree to which the scores in two groups overlap is the Mann-Whitney U-statistic. It is simply a measure of the total number of scores in one group that precede each of the scores in the other group. The U-statistic can be computed in two ways: (1) using a counting method or (2) using equations. Using the data from the phobia example, we illustrate the counting method first because it more concretely illustrates the nature of the U-statistic.

After arranging the scores in order (see Table 18.3), we can compute the U-statistic by assigning each score in the hypnosis group a point for every score in the desensitization group that it precedes. For example the first H-score (7) precedes three D-scores (14, 20, and 24) and therefore is assigned three points, for a value of 3. The second H-score (12) is also assigned a value of 3 because it also precedes three D-scores (14, 20, and 24). Finally, the third H-score (18) precedes two D-scores (20 and 24) and is assigned a value of 2. To compute U, you simply add up the total number of points that each H-score was assigned:

$$U_H = 3 + 3 + 2$$

$$= 8$$

Beginning the counting method with an H-score is arbitrary. We could have just as easily calculated U by beginning with a D-score. If you try counting the number of times in which the D-scores precede the H-scores you will find the following:

$$U_D = 1 + 0 + 0$$

$$= 1$$

Although computing both U_H and U_D is not necessary for hypothesis testing, we recommend it for two reasons. First, a simple check on your arithmetic can be obtained by noting that

$$U_H + U_D = n_H n_D \qquad (18.1)$$

where n_H = the sample size for the hypnosis group

n_D = the sample size for the desensitization group

For the present example, Formula 18.1 gives

$$8 + 1 = 3(3)$$

$$9 = 9$$

Second, by computing both U's, you can get a "feel" for your data with respect to the null hypothesis. That is, from our discussion of the U-test you should realize that if H_0 is true the scores in each group should precede each other equally often and the two U-statistics should be equal within chance differences. Thus, another way to conceive of the Mann-Whitney U-test is as a test of the null hypothesis that $U_{group1} = U_{group2}$.

Although the counting method illustrates the nature of the U-statistic, in practice it can be tedious, especially with large samples. Moreover, the counting method cannot easily be used when there are tied scores between groups. Fortunately, a formula for U has been developed that is simple to compute and has more general application. To use this formula, the data are combined and rank ordered as in Table 18.3. Then the sum of ranks, ΣR, is found for each separate group. In our example, for the hypnosis group,

$$\Sigma R_H = 1 + 2 + 4$$

$$= 7$$

and for the desensitization group,

$$\Sigma R_D = 3 + 5 + 6$$

$$= 14$$

From these sums of ranks, the U-statistic can be found for each group by using Formulas 18.2 and 18.3: For the hypnosis group,

$$U_H = n_H n_D + \frac{n_H(n_H + 1)}{2} - \Sigma R_H \qquad (18.2)$$

$$U_H = 3(3) + \frac{3(3 + 1)}{2} - 7$$

$$= 8$$

and for the desensitization group,

$$U_D = n_H n_D + \frac{n_D(n_D + 1)}{2} - \Sigma R_D \qquad (18.3)$$

$$U_D = 3(3) + \frac{3(3 + 1)}{2} - 14$$

$$= 1$$

As you can see, these are the same U values obtained earlier with the counting method. This will always be the case when there are no ties between groups.

At issue now is determining the probability of obtaining these U values if the data were in fact purely the result of chance factors. In other words, we need to compare our obtained values to the distribution of the U-statistic when H_0 is true.

The Null Distribution of U

The rationale for the distribution of U under H_0 is randomization. That is, it is a null distribution consisting of U values for all possible random arrangements of the observed sample into two groups of some specified size. For the current example the null distribution would consist of the $_6C_3 = 20$ different arrangements shown in Table 18.4. These arrangements are ordered from the outcome in which all the scores from the hypnosis group precede the scores from the desensitization group, to the outcome in which all the scores from the desensitization group precede the scores from the hypnosis group. Moving

Table 18.4   THE NULL DISTRIBUTION OF U FOR TWO
             GROUPS OF THREE SUBJECTS EACH

Arrangements		U_H	U_D	$p(U_D, U_H)$
HHH	DDD	9	0	.05
HHD	HDD	8	1	.05
HHD	DHD	7	2	
HDH	HDD	7	2	.10
HHD	DDH	6	3	
HDH	DHD	6	3	
DHH	HDD	6	3	.15
HDH	DDH	5	4	
HDD	HHD	5	4	
DHH	DHD	5	4	.15
HDD	HDH	4	5	
DHH	DDH	4	5	
DHD	HHD	4	5	.15
HDD	DHH	3	6	
DHD	HDH	3	6	
DDH	HHD	3	6	.15
DHD	DHH	2	7	
DDH	HDH	2	7	.10
DDH	DHH	1	8	.05
DDD	HHH	0	9	.05

toward the middle of the distribution from these two extremes, we see that the scores from the two groups become progressively more mixed.

Shown beside each arrangement listed in Table 18.4 are the corresponding U_H and U_D values. The exact probability of each pair of U values is equal to the relative frequency of each pair with respect to the total number of possible pairs of U values. For example, pair $U_H = 9$, $U_D = 0$ occurs only once (in arrangement 1) out of the 20 possible arrangements, and therefore,

$$p(U_H = 9, U_D = 0) = p(\text{arrangement 1})$$

$$= \frac{1}{20} = .05$$

Looking at another pair, $U_H = 3$, $U_D = 6$, you can see that these values occur three times out of the 20 possible arrangements (in arrangements 14, 15, and 16). Therefore,

$$p(U_H = 3, U_D = 6) = p(\text{arrangements 14, 15, or 16})$$

$$= \frac{3}{20} = .15$$

From the probabilities shown in Table 18.4 we can determine a region of rejection; it is all the extreme arrangements whose individual probabilities sum to a value equal to or less than α. For a nondirectional hypothesis this sum includes probabilities associated with arrangements that are extreme in both directions. From Table 18.4 you can see that summing the probabilities of the two most extreme arrangements (arrangements 1 and 20) produce

$$p(\text{arrangement 1 or 20}) = .05 + .05$$

$$= .10$$

Therefore, if $\alpha = .05$ it would be impossible to reject H_0 by using a nondirectional test even with the most extreme outcomes possible. Certainly our obtained arrangement does not fall in the region of rejection, and in fact the probability of that arrangement or one more extreme under H_0 is

$$p(U_H \leq 8, U_D \geq 1) + p(U_H \geq 1, U_D \leq 8) = p(\text{arrangements 1, 2, 19, or 20})$$

$$= .05 + .05 + .05 + .05$$

$$= .20$$

As seen in Table 18.4, the region of rejection for a directional test at $\alpha = .05$ consists only of either arrangement 1 or arrangement 20 (depending on the direction specified by the alternative hypothesis) because each of them has a probability of .05 (see Table 18.4). The exact directional probability of our obtained result if the alternative hypothesis stated that the hypnosis treatment should produce lower scores than the desensitization treatment is

$$p(U_H \leq 8, U_D \geq 1) = p(\text{arrangement 1 or 2})$$

$$= .05 + .05$$

$$= .10$$

Thus, neither a nondirectional nor a directional test leads us to reject the null hypothesis that our obtained result was due to random assignment alone. One reason is that the samples were small ($n_H = n_D = 3$), and as a result the power of the test is very low. Let us look now at an example in which the samples are larger.

This example was previously used in Chapter 11 to illustrate the t-test and the randomization test with independent samples. Sixteen students were randomly assigned into two groups of eight students each. One group studied a list of high-frequency words for one minute and the other group studied low-frequency words for one minute. Following the study period, all students wrote down all the words they could recall. The data (number of words correctly recalled) are reproduced in Table 18.5.

To obtain U values from these data, the scores are ordered from lowest to highest across the combined groups and then assigned ranks by using the method described earlier for dealing with tied ranks. These steps were carried out to produce Table 18.5. Next, the ranks of the scores in each groups are summed, and from these summed ranks, values of the U-statistic are computed for each group with Formulas 18.2 and 18.3. The sums of ranks are ΣR_L

Table 18.5   RANKING OF NUMBER OF CORRECT SCORES
FROM TWO INDEPENDENT SAMPLES GIVEN
A RECALL TEST AFTER STUDYING LIST OF
HIGH- OR LOW-FREQUENCY WORDS

High frequency			Low frequency		
Subject	Score	Rank	Subject	Score	Rank
1	13	15.0	9	10	9.0
2	9	5.5	10	9	5.5
3	12	14.0	11	8	2.5
4	14	16.0	12	10	9.0
5	10	9.0	13	11	12.0
6	11	12.0	14	8	2.5
7	9	5.5	15	9	5.5
8	11	12.0	16	6	1.0
	$\Sigma R_H = 89$			$\Sigma R_L = 47$	

$= 47$ and $\Sigma R_H = 89$. The U value for the low-frequency group is

$$U_L = n_L n_H + \frac{n_L(n_L + 1)}{2} - \Sigma R_L$$

$$= 8(8) + \frac{8(9)}{2} - 47$$

$$= 53$$

and for the high-frequency group is

$$U_H = n_L n_H + \frac{n_H(n_H + 1)}{2} - \Sigma R_H$$

$$= 8(8) + \frac{8(9)}{2} - 89$$

$$= 11$$

We can check our computations by noting that $U_L + U_H = 11 + 53 = 64$, which is equal to $n_L n_H = 8(8) = 64$.

To evaluate these U values with respect to H_0, we could produce a null distribution based on the $_{16}C_8 = 12{,}870$ possible randomizations of these ranked data.[1] However, Table I in Appendix III provides an easier way. It lists

---

[1] Recalling that nonparametric rank tests are rank randomization tests, an alternative method for carrying out the Mann-Whitney test and the other tests in this chapter is to transform data into ranks and enter them into NPSTAT. The randomization test output will then provide the appropriate exact probabilities.

nondirectional critical values of U for alpha equal to .10, .05, .02, and .01 (simply divide these values in half for the appropriate directional significance levels). You enter Table I by locating the row and column values corresponding to the sample sizes of the two groups. At the intersection of the appropriate row and column are two values of U. To be significant at a specified alpha level, the smaller obtained U value must be equal to or less than the smaller critical U value, and the larger obtained U value must be equal to or greater than the larger critical U value. In other words, if the obtained values of U fall between the two values presented in Table I, do not reject H_0. Otherwise reject H_0. For the current example, with $\alpha = .05$ and $n_L = n_H = 8$, the nondirectional critical U values are 13 and 51. Because the obtained U values, 11 and 53, fall outside these tabled values we reject H_0:

$$U(\text{critical}) = 13, 51$$

$$U(\text{obtained}) = 11, 53$$

Decision: Reject H_0

Notice that only one U value actually needs to be computed to use Table I. For example the obtained U value of 11 falls outside the critical values of 13 and 51, as does the obtained U value of 53, and in both cases we reject H_0. In fact the results of a Mann-Whitney U-test are usually reported by using only one (most often the smaller) U value. The results for the current example might be reported as "Students who studied high-frequency words showed better recall than students who studied low-frequency words (Mann-Whitney $U = 11$, $p < .05$)."

The Normal Approximation to the Mann-Whitney U-Test

Table I in Appendix III contains critical values for sample sizes of 20 or fewer subjects. When the larger of two samples is more than 20 and the two samples are not too discrepant in size, the null distribution of U can be closely approximated by a normal curve with a mean and standard deviation equal to

$$\mu_U = \frac{n_1 n_2}{2}$$

$$\sigma_U = \sqrt{\frac{n_1 n_2 (n_1 + n_2 + 1)}{12}}$$

where μ_U = the mean of U

σ_U = the standard deviation of U

n_1 = the sample size of one of the groups

n_2 = the sample size of the other group

Therefore, the Mann-Whitney U-test can be approximated by computing a z-statistic and referring the result to Table B in Appendix III. The z-statistic has the familiar form shown in Formula 18.4

$$z = \frac{U - \mu_U}{\sigma_U} \qquad (18.4)$$

in which U can be either the smaller or larger of the two obtained U values.

We demonstrate the normal approximation to the Mann-Whitney U-test by using the data from the word frequency example, although with such sample sizes Table I should be used. The mean and standard deviation for U are

$$\mu_U = \frac{8(8)}{2} = 32$$

$$\sigma_U = \sqrt{\frac{8 \times 8(8 + 8 + 1)}{12}} = 9.52$$

Using the obtained U value of 11, we find the corresponding z value to be

$$z = \frac{11 - 32}{9.52} = \frac{-21}{9.52}$$

$$= -2.21$$

From Table B in Appendix III the nondirectional critical value of z at $\alpha = .05$ is -1.96. Because the obtained z value of -2.21 is in the region of rejection, our decision is to reject H_0.

z(critical) $= -1.96$

z(obtained) $= -2.21$

Decision: Reject H_0

Strength of Relationship

The measure of the strength of relationship associated with the Mann-Whitney U-test is called the *Glass rank biserial correlation coefficient* (r_g). It is computed using Formula 18.5.

$$r_g = \frac{2(\overline{R}_1 - \overline{R}_2)}{N} \qquad (18.5)$$

where $\overline{R}_1$ = the mean of the ranks for one of the groups

$\overline{R}_2$ = the mean of the ranks for the other group

N = the total sample size

The Glass rank correlation ranges in value from -1.0 to 1.0. As with the Pearson r, larger values of r_g indicate a greater strength of relationship, although unlike the Pearson r, interpreting r_g directly in terms of the reduction in variance is not applicable. Computing r_g for the word frequency data, where $\overline{R}_H = 11.13$ and $\overline{R}_L = 5.88$, we find

$$r_g = \frac{2(11.13 - 5.88)}{16}$$

$$= .66$$

which indicates a fairly high association between the word frequency conditions and the recall scores.

18.4 WILCOXON TEST FOR TWO DEPENDENT SAMPLES

The Wilcoxon signed-rank test is used to compare two samples when the observations come from the same subjects or from matched subjects and the dependent variable is measured at the ordinal level. It is the rank test counterpart to the t- and randomization tests for two dependent samples.

Procedurally the Wilcoxon test is very straightforward, and conceptually it shares close ties with the Mann-Whitney test in that both are based on the idea of randomization. We begin by ranking the data according to the second procedure described in Section 18.2: The first step is to compute difference scores for all repeatedly measured individuals or for all matched pairs, taking care to include the sign of the difference and eliminating all differences with a value of zero. Next, these difference scores are rank ordered from the smallest difference to the largest difference in *absolute* magnitude (i.e., at this step take care *not* to include the sign of the difference), with ties handled in the usual manner. Finally, the signs of the original difference scores are reattached to the ranks for these differences. These steps were carried out in Table 18.6, which is a reproduction of the recall test data used in Chapter 11 to illustrate the dependent groups t-test. As a check on your arithmetic, note that

$$\Sigma R = \frac{N(N + 1)}{2} \tag{18.6}$$

where ΣR = the sum of the unsigned ranks

N = the number of nonzero ranked difference scores

For this example, Formula 18.6 gives

$$\Sigma R = \frac{8(8 + 1)}{2}$$

$$= 36$$

The null hypothesis is that the obtained set of signed ranks reflects chance because of random assignment of subjects to treatment orders, or in the case of a matched subjects design, to random assignment of members of

Table 18.6   RANKING OF SUBJECTS GIVEN A RECALL TEST AFTER STUDY
OF A LIST WITH BOTH HIGH-FREQUENCY WORDS AND
LOW-FREQUENCY WORDS

Subject	High frequency	Low frequency	Difference	Ranked difference	Signed ranks
1	4	3	+1	3.0	3.0
2	3	4	−1	3.0	−3.0
3	5	6	−1	3.0	−3.0
4	2	3	−1	3.0	−3.0
5	4	5	−1	3.0	−3.0
6	5	7	−2	6.0	−6.0
7	3	6	−3	7.5	−7.5
8	4	7	−3	7.5	−7.5
				$\Sigma R = 36$	$T = 3.0$

each matched pair to treatment groups. The alternative hypothesis is that the obtained set of signed ranks reflects a treatment effect.

H_0: The signed ranks reflect chance.

H_1: The signed ranks reflect a treatment effect.

If H_0 were true and the obtained differences between pairs of scores were due to chance, we would expect positive and negative differences to occur equally often. On the other hand, a treatment effect should elevate the scores of one group above those of the other group and produce difference scores that are systematically negative or positive.

The test statistic that captures the extent to which the positive and negative difference scores are evenly intermixed is the Wilcoxon T-statistic. To compute T you merely sum the negative ranks, then separately sum the positive ranks, and take as T the smaller of the two sums:

ΣR_n = the sum of the negative ranks

ΣR_p = the sum of the positive ranks

T = the smaller of ΣR_n and ΣR_p

For the data in Table 18.6

$\Sigma R_n = 33.0$

$\Sigma R_p = 3.0$

$T = 3.0$

The null distribution of T is based on all the possible 2^N sets of signed ranks that could be obtained by randomly assigning positive or negative signs to the N-ranked differences. Directional and nondirectional critical values from this distribution have been worked out by Wilcoxon and appear in Table J in Appendix III for $5 \geq N \leq 50$. You enter Table J by using N, which is the number of nonzero ranked differences. Across from each value of N are a series of critical values, one for each of the alpha levels listed. To reject H_0 the obtained T must be *less than* the critical value.

In the present example, the number of nonzero ranked differences is 8, and the obtained value of T is 3.0. Going to Table J, we find that the nondirectional critical value for $\alpha = .05$ when $N = 8$ is 3. Because the obtained T value of 3.0 is equal to the critical T we reject the null hypothesis.

T(critical) $= 3$

T(obtained) $= 3.0$

Decision: Reject H_0

The results of this analysis might be reported as "Students showed better recall of low-frequency words than of high-frequency words ($T = 3.0$, $N = 8$, $p < .05$)."

The Normal Approximation to the Wilcoxon Test

Like the Mann-Whitney U-statistic, the null distribution of T can be approximated by a normal distribution if N, the number of ranked differences, is large enough. Although Table J in Appendix III can be used with Ns up to 50, the normal approximation will be satisfactory if N is from 25 to 40, and very good beyond that. The mean and standard deviation of T are

$$\mu_T = \frac{N(N + 1)}{4}$$

$$\sigma_T = \sqrt{\frac{N(N + 1)(2N + 1)}{24}}$$

Formula 18.7 transforms an obtained T into a z-statistic.

$$z = \frac{T - u_T}{\sigma_T} \tag{18.7}$$

For the current example, $\mu_T = 17$, $\sigma_T = 7.14$, and

$$z = \frac{3 - 17}{7.14}$$

$$= -1.96$$

As always, the obtained z value will be compared to Table B in Appendix III to determine if H_0 can be rejected at specified alpha levels. With $\alpha = .05$, the nondirectional critical values of z are ± 1.96, and again, for this example we would reject H_0. Notice, however, that the sample size in this example warrants using Table J to determine a p value.

Strength of Relationship

A measure of the strength of the relationship for the Wilcoxon signed-ranks test is called the *matched-pairs rank biserial correlation coefficient*. The matched-pairs correlation, r_c, is computed by Formula 18.8.

$$r_c = \frac{4(T - \mu_T)}{N(N + 1)} \tag{18.8}$$

where N, T, and μ_T are as previously defined. The matched-pairs correlation is interpreted in the same way as the Glass rank biserial correlation.

18.5   KRUSKAL-WALLIS TEST FOR k INDEPENDENT SAMPLES

The rank tests presented so far are specifically suited to analyzing ordinal data from two-sample research designs. In this section and the one that follows we extend the arguments for the Mann-Whitney and Wilcoxon tests to situations involving ordinal data from K-sample research designs.

The Kruskal-Wallis test is a generalized version of the Mann-Whitney test and in that sense is the rank test counterpart of the analysis of variance and the randomization test for k independent samples. The Kruskal-Wallis test begins like the Mann-Whitney test by rank ordering all scores from smallest to largest without regard to group membership. Then, the ranks for individuals in each group are isolated and summed. These steps were carried out in Table 18.7 with data from the experiment investigating the effects of alcohol on driving performance, discussed in Chapter 13.

The null hypothesis is that the ranks were randomly assigned to groups. If H_0 is true, any differences in the sums of ranks among groups should be within chance limits. The alternative hypothesis is that any differences among summed ranks are due to treatment effects.

H_0: Group differences are due to chance.

H_1: Group differences are due to treatment.

The test statistic that evaluates these hypotheses is called the Kruskal-Wallis H-statistic and is computed as follows:

$$H = \left[\frac{12}{N(N + 1)} \right]\left[\Sigma\frac{T^2}{n} \right] - 3(N + 1) \tag{18.9}$$

where $\dfrac{T^2}{n} =$ the total of the ranks for a particular group squared divided by the number of subjects in that group

$N =$ the total number of subjects

$\Sigma =$ the sum across all groups

Applying this formula to the data in Table 18.7, we find

Table 18.7   RANKED DRIVING PERFORMANCE SCORES AFTER CONSUMING
DIFFERENT AMOUNTS OF ALCOHOL

	Amount of alcohol				
0 oz		2 oz		4 oz	
Score	Ranked score	Score	Ranked score	Score	Ranked score
1	1.0	2	3.0	3	6.5
2	3.0	3	6.5	4	10.0
2	3.0	4	10.0	5	12.0
3	6.5	4	10.0	6	13.5
3	6.5			6	13.5
				7	15.0
$T = 20.0$		$T = 29.5$		$T = 70.5$	

$$H = \left[\frac{12}{15(15 + 1)}\right]\left[\frac{20.0^2}{5} + \frac{29.5^2}{4} + \frac{70.5^2}{6}\right] - 3(15 + 1)$$

$$= 8.29$$

We could determine the probability of this H value under H_0 by repeatedly applying Formula 18.9 to all possible randomizations of the obtained data and calculating the relative frequency of H values at least as large as 8.29. Fortunately, there are easier ways. When there are fewer than six observations per group, critical values of H based on the randomization method can be found in tables supplied by Siegel and Castellan (1988). With large sample sizes the null distribution of H is closely approximated by the chi-square distribution on $k - 1$ degrees of freedom, so that Table H in Appendix III can be used to obtain critical values of H.

Chi-Square Approximation to the Kruskal-Wallis Test

In practice, studies usually include more than five subjects per group, so we will present only the chi-square method of evaluating H even though our hypothetical example would warrant using tables based on actual randomizations of the data. For a chi-square distribution with $k - 1 = 3 - 1 = 2$ degrees of freedom, and $\alpha = .05$, the critical value of H is 5.99. The obtained value of 8.74 exceeds the critical value, so we reject H_0.

$\chi^2(\text{critical}) = 5.99$

$\chi^2(\text{obtained}) = 8.29$

Decision: Reject H_0

An example of how this result would be reported is "There was a systematic relationship between the amount of alcohol consumed and the number of errors on a driving test, $H = 8.29$, $df = 2$, $p < .05$."

As with other k-sample tests, rejecting H_0 does not indicate the nature of the differences between groups but only that at least one of the groups differs in ranks from the remaining groups. One procedure for probing the nature of the relationship is to apply the Mann-Whitney test to all pairs of rank sums and setting the per comparison alpha level to $\alpha/2C$, where C equals the number of paired comparisons. For example, with three groups there are three possible paired tests, and the per comparison alpha would be $.05/(2)(3) = .0083$.

Strength of Relationship

The measure of the strength of relationship corresponding to the Kruskal-Wallis test is called *epsilon squared* $(E_R{}^2)$. It is interpreted analogously to eta squared and is computed using Formula 18.10 as follows:

$$E_R{}^2 = \frac{H - k + 1}{N - k} \tag{18.10}$$

using the same definitions of H, N, and k previously presented. For the current example,

$$E_R{}^2 = \frac{8.29 - 3 + 1}{15 - 3}$$

$$= .36$$

18.6   FRIEDMAN TEST FOR k DEPENDENT SAMPLES

The rank test counterpart of the analysis of variance and randomization tests for k dependent samples is called the Friedman test. It is appropriate when the same or matched individuals receive each of k treatments and are measured on an ordinal dependent variable.

Consider an experiment first discussed in Chapter 16 to illustrate the analysis of variance for k dependent samples. Six individuals read and then recalled each of three stories—a happy story, a sad story, and a neutral story. The data from this hypothetical study are repeated in the left portion of Table 18.8.

To compute the Friedman test we begin by rank ordering the scores for each individual or set of matched individuals *across* the treatments (i.e., the scores in each row are ranked). Tied scores are handled by averaging their ranks. Finally, the ranks within each treatment are summed (i.e., the ranks in each column are summed). These steps were carried out to produce the right portion of Table 18.8.

The null hypothesis is that the obtained ranks occurred by chance because of randomly assigning subjects to treatment orders or randomly assign-

Table 18.8   RANKED SCORES FROM THE HYPOTHETICAL STUDY OF EMOTION AND MEMORY

Subject	Condition scores			Condition ranks		
	Happy	Sad	Neutral	Happy	Sad	Neutral
1	6	5	5	3.0	1.5	1.5
2	7	4	6	3.0	1.0	2.0
3	5	2	3	3.0	1.0	2.0
4	4	3	4	2.5	1.0	2.5
5	8	6	9	2.0	1.0	3.0
6	9	7	8	3.0	1.0	2.0
				$T = 16.5$	6.5	13.0

ing matched subjects to treatments. The alternative hypothesis is that the obtained ranks are due to treatment effects.

H_0: Obtained ranks are due to chance.

H_1: Obtained ranks are due to treatment effects.

If H_0 were true, each of the possible randomization of ranks within rows should be equally likely, which implies that the sums of column ranks should be equal or should differ only by chance. If H_1 is true, there should be a pile up of low or high ranks in at least one of the groups, resulting in differences among column sums that are unlikely to occur by chance alone.

The test statistic that captures the extent to which column rank sums differ is called the Friedman F_r-statistic. It is computed using Formula 18.11 as follows:

$$F_r = \left[\frac{12}{nk(k+1)} \right] \left[\Sigma T^2 \right] - 3N(k+1) \tag{18.11}$$

where N = the total number of individuals in the experiment

k = the number of treatments

T = the sum of ranks for a particular group

Σ = the sum across all groups

Applying this formula to the data in Table 18.8 produces

$$F_r = \left[\frac{12}{6(3)(4)} \right] \left[16.5^2 + 6.5^2 + 13.0^2 \right] - 3(6)(4)$$

$$= \frac{12}{72} [483.5] - 72$$

$$= 8.58$$

Chi-Square Approximation to the Friedman Test

The null distribution of F_r under H_0 is distributed approximately as chi-square with $k - 1$ degrees of freedom. This approximation is best when $k \geq 3$ and $N \geq 10$; otherwise special tables based on all possible randomizations of the obtained data should be used (see Siegel & Castellan, 1988). For illustrative purposes we will compare our obtained F_r value to the critical value of chi-square found in Table H of Appendix III. At $\alpha = .05$ and $df = 2$, the critical value of χ^2 is 5.99, which is smaller than our obtained value. Therefore, our decision is to reject H_0.

$$\chi^2(\text{critical}) = 5.99$$

$$\chi^2(\text{obtained}) = 8.58$$

Decision: Reject H_0

This result might be reported as "The relationship between mood and recall was statistically significant: $F_r = 8.58$, $df = 2$, $p < .05$." Notice that additional analyses using Wilcoxon tests between pairs of treatments are needed to better understand the nature of the treatment effect. Each of these tests would be conducted at the $\alpha/2C$ level as described in the section on the Kruskal-Wallis test.

Strength of Relationship

The measure of the strength of the relationship for the Friedman test is *epsilon squared* (E_R^2). It is interpreted in the same way as epsilon squared for the Kruskal-Wallis test but is computed with Formula 18.12:

$$E_R^2 = \frac{F_r - (k + 1)}{Nk} \tag{18.12}$$

The value of E_R^2 for the current example is

$$E_R^2 = \frac{8.58 - (3 + 1)}{6(3)}$$

$$= .25$$

18.7   COMPARING PARAMETRIC AND NONPARAMETRIC TESTS

We have presented both parametric and nonparametric tests for most of the research designs covered in this text (see Table 18.1), and in several places we have made suggestions concerning which tests are most appropriate in a given research situation. In particular, we have focused on such issues as the scale of measurement (nominal, ordinal, or interval) and the type of random process (random assignment or random sampling) in determining our choice of statistical tests. In this section we expand some of our earlier points and add a few new ones to provide further direction in the use of parametric and nonparametric tests. To aid our discussion we concentrate on two points of comparison: power-efficiency and robustness.

Power-Efficiency

Recall that power is the probability of correctly rejecting a null hypothesis. Given two statistical tests that could be used to test the same null hypothesis (e.g., the Mann-Whitney U-test versus the independent samples t-test), **power-efficiency** is the ratio of the sample sizes that each test needs to achieve the same power. For example, if the t-test required a sample of 20 subjects to achieve power of .95, whereas the Mann-Whitney U-test required 25 subjects to achieve the same power, the power-efficiency of the Mann-Whitney test relative to the t-test would be

$$\frac{20}{25}(100) = 80\%$$

In general, the more subjects that a test needs to attain the same power as an alternative test, the lower is its power-efficiency.

POWER-EFFICIENCY: The ratio of the sample sizes from two tests required to achieve the same power.

When nonparametric rank tests are compared with their parametric counterparts in situations in which the parametric assumptions apply, the rank tests have less than 100 percent power-efficiency. Such findings are often construed as evidence for using parametric tests whenever possible. However, two points can be directed against this conclusion. First, the reason that nonparametric rank tests have less than 100 percent power-efficiency is because they are rank tests, *not* because they are nonparametric tests. In other words, their lower power-efficiency is a result of throwing away information by using a lower scale of measurement (ordinal versus interval), rather than a result of some inherent inferiority of nonparametric procedures. Randomization tests preserve the interval quality of the data, and when they are used in situations where parametric assumptions apply, their power-efficiency is 100 percent. Thus, although one would be ill advised to perform a rank test on data that are truly interval, nothing would be lost relative to a parametric test if a randomization test were used. Of course, if the data were truly ordinal, nonparametric rank tests would be the best choice.

Robustness

The first point relates to the power-efficiency of nonparametric rank tests being less than 100 percent *when the parametric assumptions apply*. At issue with the second point is the relative performance of parametric and rank tests when the parametric assumptions *do not* apply. This issue touches on the idea of robustness, discussed in previous chapters. To reiterate, parametric tests are robust for moderate departures from normality and homogeneity of variance. In such situations parametric tests may still be more powerful than rank tests, although again the reason is related to scale of measurement, not to parametric versus nonparametric methods per se. If moderate departures from normality and homogeneity of variance occur, and the dependent variable is measured on an interval scale, either parametric tests or randomization tests are recommended.

For situations in which departures from the parametric assumptions of normality and homogeneity of variance are considerable, the power-efficiency of nonparametric tests can be greater than 100 percent, meaning that nonparametric tests can be more powerful than parametric tests. For example, if 5 to 10 percent of the scores in one tail of a population distribution are extreme scores (outliers), nonparametric tests, even nonparametric rank tests, can be more powerful than parametric tests. Thus, when departure from parametric assumptions is considerable, nonparametric tests are recommended. Whether to use randomization or rank tests in such situations depends on the scale of measurement.

Although parametric tests are robust with respect to departures from normality and homogeneity of variance, they are not robust when the assumption of independent observations is violated. This assumption is typically tied to random sampling and is essential for determining the sampling distributions underlying all of the parametric procedures discussed in this text. When nonindependence occurs, these sampling distributions and the p values obtained from them may be invalid, leading to very serious errors in parametric inference. Thus, in the absence of random sampling, statistical inferences about population parameters may be meaningless and should not be carried out.

In contrast, nonparametric statistical inference is valid in the absence of random sampling. Nonparametric tests are not designed to make inferences from sample statistics to population parameters but instead to test whether the scores from *any* sample, however obtained, are independent of some grouping variable (e.g., a treatment variable). Accordingly, nonparametric p values are obtained from the data at hand rather than from theoretical distributions based on all possible random samples. These features make nonparametric tests ideal for analyzing research that does not involve random sampling. Of course, merely using nonparametric procedures does not mean that one is magically transported to a position in which statistical inference about populations is valid. Such inference is always dangerous without random sampling. It does mean that one can make valid inferences about causality (with respect to randomly assigned treatments) or independence (with respect to trait variables) for the particular sample that generated the data. Fortunately, such inferences are the primary aim of much behavioral research, which brings us to a final point.

Most behavioral research does not actually involve random sampling, which is appropriate because most behavioral research is not aimed at making inferences about the values of population parameters. Rather, it is interested primarily in description or in making inferences about treatment effects. True, there is often at least an implicit attempt to generalize obtained treatment effects to individuals who are similar to the tested sample. But this is quite different from making inferences about specific values of population parameters.

Given these aims and the rarity of random sampling, one would expect most of this research to employ nonparametric statistical procedures. Yet parametric tests such as *t*-tests and ANOVA are used far more commonly than nonparametric tests. This use might suggest that the bulk of behavioral research is invalid, but fortunately this is not the case. The reason is that parametric tests can be valid in such circumstances inasmuch as they provide valid estimates of the results of nonparametric tests.

Consider the following example. A convenience sample is formed into two groups by random assignment, and each group receives a different treatment before being measured on some interval-level dependent variable. We could analyze such a design with an independent two-group randomization test. This test would involve deriving a null distribution based on all possible arrangements of the data into two groups, finding the difference between the means of the two groups for every arrangement, and then seeing if the obtained difference falls in the region of rejection. Alternatively, we could compute a *t*-statistic for all possible arrangements to produce a null distribution of *t* values, and then see if the *t* value generated from the obtained data falls in the region of rejection of that distribution. Both procedures will lead to exactly the same result. Moreover, it turns out that for sample sizes of 20 or more the null distribution of *t* values is closely approximated by the theoretical sampling distribution of *t*. We could, therefore, compute a *t*-test on the obtained data, refer the resulting value to the theoretical *t*-distribution, and obtain a valid estimate of the *p* value that would be obtained from the randomization procedure. In this context, the *t*-test is being used in a manner akin to using normal curve approximations to estimate the results of rank tests. And there are many other situations (e.g., some ANOVA designs) in which theoretical sampling distributions provide good estimates of the results of nonparametric tests. In all such cases, however, although theoretical sampling distributions are used, they are used to evaluate treatment effects rather than to make inferences about population parameters.

Thus, in many situations in which random sampling is not used, valid *p* values can be obtained either directly, by using nonparametric tests, or indirectly, by using estimates from tests typically associated with parametric inference. Still, one might wonder why approximation procedures are used so much more often than nonparametric procedures. There are several reasons. First, the computations involved in *t*-tests, ANOVA, and the like are more widely known, easier to carry out, and better understood than are the computations involved in nonparametric tests. Second, parametric tests are more widely available in popular statistical packages such as SPSS than are nonparametric tests. Finally, some aspects of complex experimental designs, for example, higher-order interactions in factorial designs, are not easily handled by nonparametric procedures, or at least the way in which they should be handled is not always agreed on. In contrast, parametric procedures are applicable to even the most complex designs, and the ways in which they should be used are universally accepted. However, a word of caution: There is a price tag on using parametric tests in situations in which a nonparametric approach would be appropriate but a suitable nonparametric test is not available. In such situations, the result produced by the parametric test obviously cannot be validated against the result produced by a nonparametric test. Consequently, the validity of statistical inference is on shakier ground compared to situations in which the results of parametric and nonparametric tests are known to agree.

SUMMARY

This chapter presented several rank tests suitable for analyzing ordinal-level data. The Mann-Whitney U-test for analyzing ranked data from two independent samples was presented first and discussed most thoroughly. In that discussion we illustrated the randomization (i.e., nonparametric) approach to analyzing ranked data in some detail because it forms the basic rationale underlying all rank tests. Following the Mann-Whitney test, rank tests for analyzing two-group dependent sample designs (the Wilcoxon test), k-group independent sample designs (the Kruskal-Wallis test), and k-group dependent sample designs (the Friedman test) were presented.

For the Mann-Whitney and Wilcoxon tests we presented both the randomization method and the normal approximation method of obtaining p values. We pointed out that the randomization method also could be used with k-sample designs, but we only presented chi-square approximation tests. Also, we presented strength of association measures for each rank test.

Finally, we discussed bases for choosing between parametric and nonparametric statistical tests. In particular we focused on the issues of power-efficiency and robustness, where power-efficiency is the relative sample size required by two tests to achieve equal power, and robustness reflects the performance of a statistical test when its assumptions are violated. In general, we recommended using rank tests only when data are clearly ordinal. With interval data, parametric tests are the only tests available if the object of a study is to estimate parameters. However, if the object is to evaluate treatment or trait effects, either randomization tests or parametric tests are appropriate.

KEY WORDS

ranks	Mann-Whitney U-test
tied ranks	Glass rank biserial correlation
rank tests	Wilcoxon signed-rank test

matched-pairs rank correlation

Kruskal-Wallis *H*-test

epsilon squared

Friedman test

power-efficiency

PROBLEMS

1 What is the difference between a randomization test and a rank test? How are they similar?

2 How do the null hypotheses differ between rank tests and parametric tests?

3 How do parametric tests, randomization tests, and rank tests compare in terms of power efficiency?

4 A researcher believed that children would learn to read better in a computer-assisted program than in a standard reading program. Twenty children were randomly assigned to learn reading by the computer-assisted program or by the standard program. At the end of each program each child was tested on a standardized reading test. The scores were

Computer Program	Standard Program
13	15
12	7
12	9
10	14
11	7
16	4
9	18
19	8
9	8
8	7

(a) What rank test would be appropriate for analyzing these data? How would NPSTAT be used to analyze these data? Try using NPSTAT with 2000 permutations.

(b) Is the computer program superior to the standard program?

(c) What is the strength of relationship between program type and reading scores?

5 Nine physicians were asked to rate two films in terms of their effectiveness in communicating information about AIDS (Acquired Immune Deficiency Syndrome). The rating scale ranged from one to ten and the data were as follows:

Physician	Program I	Program II
1	6	6
2	7	8
3	8	7
4	10	6
5	10	8

6	8	6
7	8	10
8	6	3
9	7	2

(a) What rank test would be appropriate for analyzing these data? How would NPSTAT be used to analyze these data? Try using NPSTAT and compare the result with the rank test procedure.

(b) Is one program superior to the other?

(c) What is the strength of relationship between program type and rated effectiveness?

6 A psychologist wanted to test the effects of type of exercise on perceived self-esteem. Twelve subjects were randomly assigned to three types of workouts to be completed three times per week: aerobic, anaerobic, and a combination of the two. After two months of exercising a self-esteem inventory was administered and produced the following data?

Aerobic	Anaerobic	Combination
20	15	23
19	16	21
22	12	27
17	9	19

(a) What rank test should be used to analyze these data? How would NPSTAT be used to analyze these data? Try using NPSTAT.

(b) Is there a significant relationship between exercise type and self-esteem? What is the nature of the relationship?

(c) What is the strength of the relationship between exercise type and self-esteem?

7 A social psychologist was interested in the relationship between physical attractiveness and attributed intelligence. To assess this relationship, 10 subjects were presented with pictures of 12 people. Of the 12 pictures 4 had been reliably judged as very attractive, 4 as moderately attractive and 4 as unattractive. Each subject rated the intelligence of all 12 pictures on a scale of one to ten. The average of each subject for each class of attractiveness follows:

Subject	Attractive	Moderate	Unattractive
1	7	4	3
2	6	5	2
3	9	6	1
4	8	5	6
5	5	7	4
6	6	4	9
7	8	5	2

8	4	6	2
9	9	3	7
10	7	4	5

(a) Which rank test should you use to analyze these data? How would NPSTAT be used to analyze these data? Try using NPSTAT.
(b) Is perceived intelligence related to attractiveness? What is the nature of this relationship?
(c) What is the strength of the relationship?

Mathematics Review

In this section we provide a review of some basic principles of mathematics. The purpose of this review is to reacquaint you with the standard mathematical symbols used in the book and with the principles of algebra we use in our explanations of statistical concepts. In addition, we have included a brief section on rules of summation to help prepare you for the formulas we introduce. At the end of the review there are exercises you can work on to test and practice your knowledge of these concepts. Answers to the exercises are provided at the end of this section.

I   MATHEMATICAL SYMBOLS

Following are some of the most important symbols we use in the book. For each symbol we provide an explanation of its function and a number of examples of its use. In most instances we include one or more general examples that use letters to represent unspecified values, rather than specific numbers.

Symbol and Examples	Explanation
$=$	is equal to
$a = a$	a is equal to a
$a = b$	a is equal to b
$6 = 2 + 4$	6 is equal to $2 + 4$
$\neq$	is not equal to
$a \neq b$	a is not equal to b
$4 \neq 2$	4 is not equal to 2
$<$	is less than
$a < b$	a is less than b
$5 < 9$	5 is less than 9
$>$	is greater than
$a > b$	a is greater than b
$12 > 3$	12 is greater than 3
$\leq$	is less than or equal to
$a \leq b$	a is less than or equal to b
$7 \leq 10$	7 is less than or equal to 10
$\geq$	is greater than or equal to
$a \geq b$	a is greater than or equal to b
$4 \geq 1$	4 is greater than or equal to 1
$8 < a < 12$	a is greater than 8 and less than 12
$4 \leq a \leq 7$	a is greater than or equal to 4 and less than or equal to 7
$|a|$	absolute value of a (ignore the positive or negative sign of a)
$|+2|$	absolute value of $+2$, which is 2
$|-5|$	absolute value of -5, which is 5
$a! = a(a-1)(a-2)\ldots$	*factorial* of a: obtained by multiplying a
$4! = 4(3)(2)(1)$	series of integers ranging from a down to 1
$\quad = 24$	
a/b	in a fraction or ratio: upper part (a) is called the *numerator*; lower part (b) is called the *denominator*
$a/b,\ b/a$	*reciprocal* of a fraction: produced by
$3/4,\ 4/3$	reversing the position of the numerator and
$5,\ 1/5$	denominator
$\sqrt{a}$	*square root* of a
$\sqrt{4} = 2,\ 2(2) = 4$	square root of 4
$\sqrt{25} = 5,\ 5(5) = 25$	square root of 25

II ALGEBRA

In this part we review some basic operations of algebra, then use some of these operations to show how equations can be manipulated to solve for an unknown value.

Basic Operations

Operation	Explanation

$a + (-b) = a - b$
$5 + (-2) = 5 - 2 = 3$

Addition of a negative number is equivalent to subtracting its absolute value.

$a - (-b) = a + b$
$8 - (-5) = 8 + 5 = 13$

Subtraction of a negative number is equivalent to adding its absolute value.

$a(-b) = -(ab)$
$6(-2) = -12$

Multiplication of numbers with opposite signs produces a negative result.

$-a(-b) = ab$
$-4(-3) = 12$

Multiplication of two negative numbers produces a positive result.

$-a/b = -(a/b)$
$-3/5 = -(3/5)$

Division involving numerator and denominator with opposite signs produces a negative result.

$-a/-b = a/b$
$-4/-2 = 4/2 = 2$

Division involving a negative numerator and a negative denominator produces a positive result.

$$\frac{a/b}{c/d} = \frac{a}{b}\frac{d}{c} = \frac{ad}{bc}$$
$$\frac{3/5}{2/9} = \frac{3}{5}\frac{9}{2} = \frac{27}{10}$$

Division by some number is equivalent to multiplication by the reciprocal of that number.

$a + b + c = b + c + a$
$5 + 2 + 8 = 8 + 5 + 2 = 15$
$3 - 5 + 11 = 11 - 5 + 3 = 9$

The order in which numbers are added or subtracted does not matter.

$a \times b \times c = b \times a \times c$
$3 \times 2 \times 5 = 5 \times 2 \times 3 = 30$

The order in which numbers are multiplied does not matter.

$(6 + 2) \times 2 = 8 \times 2 = 16$
$9 - (4 \times 3) = 9 - 12 = -3$
$(6 \div 3) \div 4 = 2 \div 4 = 1/2$
$8 \div (2 + 2) = 8 \div 4 = 2$

Operations within parentheses are to be carried out first.

$6 \times 2 + 4 = 12 + 4 = 16$
$5 + 3 \times 8 = 5 + 24 = 29$
$4 - 6 \times 2 = 4 - 12 = -8$
$8 \div 4 + 3 = 2 + 3 = 5$

When multiple operations are specified and no parentheses are present, multiplication and division are carried out before addition and subtraction.

$$\frac{a}{c} + \frac{b}{c} = \frac{a + b}{c}$$
$$\frac{6}{8} - \frac{2}{8} = \frac{6 - 2}{8} = \frac{4}{8}$$

When adding or subtracting fractions the numerators may be combined if the fractions have the same denominator.

$$\frac{a}{b} \times \frac{c}{d} = \frac{ac}{bd}$$
$$\frac{6}{9} \times \frac{2}{3} = \frac{6(2)}{9(3)} = \frac{12}{27}$$

Multiplication of two fractions is equivalent to multiplication of the two numerators divided by the multiplication of the two denominators.

$$\frac{\cancel{a}}{b} \times \frac{c}{\cancel{a}} = \frac{c}{b}$$

$$\frac{1\cancel{3}}{4\cancel{8}} \times \frac{12}{1\cancel{3}} = \frac{1}{4}$$

$$\frac{6}{3\cancel{9}} \times \frac{1\cancel{3}}{5} = \frac{2\cancel{6}}{1\cancel{3}\,(5)} = \frac{2}{5}$$

When multiplying fractions that have identical values in the numerator and denominator, the identical values may be *cancelled.*

$5/8 = .625$
$.625 \times 100 = 62.5\%$

Conversion of a fraction or proportion to a percentage involves multiplication by 100.

$a^2 = a(a)$
$a^3 = a(a)(a)$
$5^2 = 5(5) = 25$
$3^3 = 3(3)(3) = 27$

A number raised to a power *(exponent)* is equivalent to multiplying that number by itself as many times as specified by the exponent.

$a^2 a^4 = a^{2+4} = a^6$
$4^3 4^2 = 4^{3+2} = 4^5$
$\qquad\quad = 1024$

Multiplication of a number raised to an exponent by the same number raised to an exponent is equivalent to the number raised to the sum of the two exponents.

$$\frac{a^4}{a^2} = a^{4-2} = a^2$$

$$\frac{2^5}{2^2} = 2^{5-2} = 2^3 = 8$$

Division of a number raised to an exponent by the same number raised to an exponent is equivalent to the number raised to the difference between the exponents.

$\sqrt{a}\sqrt{b} = \sqrt{ab}$
$\sqrt{6}\sqrt{3} = \sqrt{18}$

Multiplication of the square roots of numbers is equivalent to the square root of the multiplication of the numbers.

$ab + ac + ad = a(b + c + d)$
$a + a + a + a = a(1 + 1 + 1 + 1)$
$\qquad\qquad\quad = a(4)$
$3(2) + 3(3) = 3(2 + 3)$
$4 + 4 + 4 = 4(1 + 1 + 1)$
$\qquad\qquad = 4(3)$

Factoring involves reducing an expression to its simplest components. When multiplied together these components produce the original expression. Note that this means adding a number to itself *n* times is equivalent to multiplying that number by *n*.

$a(b + c + d) = ab + ac + ad$
$5(2 + 7) = 5(2) + 5(7)$
$(a + b)^2 = (a + b)(a + b)$
$\qquad\quad = a^2 + 2ab + b^2$
$(a - b)^2 = (a - b)(a - b)$
$\qquad\quad = a^2 - 2ab + b^2$

Expansion of an expression is the reverse of factoring.

Solving Equations for One Unknown

The object of solving an equation for an unknown is to isolate the unknown value (usually represented in the equation by a letter, such as X) on one side of the equation. The other side of the equation is reduced to its simplest form. Isolating the unknown on one side of the equation consists of applying an operation to the side of the equation that contains the unknown. The operations are selected so that all parts except the unknown will be cleared from that side of the equation. For the equation to remain true, however, whatever operation is applied to one side of the equation must also be applied to the other side. The following examples illustrate how this is accomplished.

Example	**Explanation**
$X + 4 = 6$ $X + 4 - 4 = 6 - 4$ $X = 2$	To clear the addition of a value to the unknown we subtract it from the unknown. This operation must be applied to each side of the equation.
$X - 9 = 12$ $X - 9 + 9 = 12 + 9$ $X = 21$	To clear the subtraction of a value from the unknown, we add it to the unknown.
$X(6) = 14$ $\dfrac{X(6)}{6} = \dfrac{14}{6}$ $X = 7/3$	To clear multiplication by a value, we divide each side of the equation by that value.
$\dfrac{X}{8} = 2$ $\dfrac{X}{8}(8) = 2(8)$ $X = 16$	To clear division by a value, we multiply each side of the equation by that value.
$\dfrac{7}{X} = 5$ $\dfrac{7}{X}(X) = 5(X)$ $7 = 5(X)$ $\dfrac{7}{5} = \dfrac{5(X)}{5}$ $7/5 = X$	When the unknown is in the denominator of a fraction, we multiply both sides of the equation by that denominator to put the unknown into a numerator.
$\dfrac{5}{(X + 2)} = 4$ $\dfrac{5}{(X + 2)}(X + 2) = 4(X + 2)$ $5 = 4(X + 2)$ $\dfrac{5}{4} = \dfrac{X + 2}{4}$ $(5/4) - 2 = X + 2 - 2$ $(5/4) - 2 = X$ $-\dfrac{3}{4} = X$	With a more complicated expression, proceed with each simplification step in turn.
$3X + 17 = 25$ $3X = 25 - 17$ $3X = 8$ $X = 8/3$ $(6 + X)4 = 12$ $(6 + X) = 3$ $X = 3 - 6$ $X = -3$	In general, first clear addition and subtraction of values that are not inside parentheses with the unknown. Then clear division and multiplication of values. Finally, clear the terms appearing inside parentheses with the unknown.

III RULES OF SUMMATION

Many of the formulas presented in this book involve the summation of numbers, such as raw scores. To express these formulas in a general form, we use the Greek letter Σ to represent the operation of summation. We use letters such as X to represent the numbers that are being summed. The expression ΣX is to be interpreted as an instruction to sum the set of scores represented by X. For example, suppose we have a collection of six scores: 3, 5, 6, 6, 7, and 9. If we use X to represent this collection of scores, the formula ΣX is to be interpreted as $3 + 5 + 6 + 6 + 7 + 9$. For many of the formulas, however, something more complicated than summing a set of raw scores is involved. For this reason, it is important to be familiar with some of the rules involving summation. As we introduce these rules, you will notice that in many cases they are identical to rules of addition reviewed earlier. This should come as no surprise because summation expressed with Σ is, after all, just addition.

Summation of a Constant

On some occasions the numbers being added together are all the same—which is referred to as summation of a *constant*. If we allow the letter k, for instance, to refer to the value of each of the numbers being added, we have Σk. This expression represents the following summation operation: $k + k + k + \ldots + k$. That is, k is being added to itself n times, where n is the number of ks in the set. As you may recall from our review of basic algebra operations, this is equivalent to multiplying the constant by n. In general, then, we have

$$\Sigma k = nk$$

For example, suppose we have a set of five numbers, all equal to a constant value, 3. In this case $\Sigma k = 5(3) = 15$.

Multiplication by a Constant

Some formulas call for each member of a set of scores to be multiplied by a constant; then these products are to be summed. In general, this operation may be expressed as follows, with X representing the set of scores and k representing the constant:

$$\Sigma kX$$

This is equivalent to multiplying the sum of the scores by the constant:

$$\Sigma kX = k\Sigma X$$

This rule of summation is just the application of *factoring*, discussed earlier in the review of basic algebra operations. For example, suppose we have a set of four scores, 5, 8, 9, and 11, and a constant 2. Multiplying each score by the constant and summing we have

$$\Sigma kX = 2(5) + 2(8) + 2(9) + 2(11) = 10 + 16 + 18 + 22 = 66$$
$$k\Sigma X = 2(5 + 8 + 9 + 11) = 2(33) = 66$$

Order of Operations

The review of basic algebra operations included the rule that the order in which a series of numbers is summed does not matter—the same answer will result. Suppose we have a set of numbers and the task is to add a constant to each one, then sum the results. This could be expressed as follows:

$$\Sigma(X + k)$$

This is equivalent to first summing the scores, then summing the constant to itself n times, then adding the two results:

$$\Sigma X + \Sigma k$$

For example, with the scores 3, 5, and 6, and the constant 7, we have

$$\Sigma(X + k) = (3 + 7) + (5 + 7) + (6 + 7) = 10 + 12 + 13 = 35$$

$$\Sigma X + \Sigma k = (3 + 5 + 6) + (7 + 7 + 7) = 14 + 21 = 35$$

This rule will hold even if a constant is subtracted from each score

$$\Sigma(X - k) = \Sigma X - \Sigma k$$

or if a different number, represented here by Y, is added to or subtracted from each score

$$\Sigma(X + Y) = \Sigma X + \Sigma Y$$

As an example of the latter case, consider a set of scores, 3, 4, and 8, represented by X, and a second set of scores, 5, 9, and 12, represented by Y. The task is to sum the first score in each set, the second score in each set, and the third score in each set, then to sum these results:

$$\Sigma(X + Y) = (3 + 5) + (4 + 9) + (8 + 12) = 8 + 13 + 20 = 41$$

$$\Sigma X + \Sigma Y = (3 + 4 + 8) + (5 + 9 + 12) = 15 + 26 = 41$$

Similarly, suppose that the task were to subtract the Y score from the X score in each pair:

$$\Sigma(X - Y) = \Sigma X - \Sigma Y$$

$$\Sigma(X - Y) = (3 - 5) + (4 - 9) + (8 - 12) = -2 + (-5) + (-4) = -11$$

$$\Sigma X - \Sigma Y = (3 + 4 + 8) - (5 + 9 + 12) = 15 - 26 = -11$$

Finally, summation formulas obey the rule that multiplication and division are to be done before addition and subtraction unless otherwise specified by parentheses. For example, suppose that each score is to be squared (multiplied by itself) before being summed. This is expressed as

$$\Sigma X^2$$

and is *different* from squaring the sum of the scores,

$$(\Sigma X)^2$$

in which summation is specified by parentheses as the first operation. For example, suppose we have the scores 2, 4, and 5. The sum of the squared scores is

$$\Sigma X^2 = 2^2 + 4^2 + 5^2 = 4 + 16 + 25 = 45$$

but the square of the sum of the scores is

$$(\Sigma X)^2 = (2 + 4 + 5)^2 = 121$$

IV EXERCISES

a. True or false

1. $6 = 6$ **2.** $4 = 5 + 1$ **3.** $7 \neq 4$ **4.** $18 < 9 + 8$ **5.** $12 \geq 7$
6. $17 \neq 5 + 7$ **7.** $8 > 7$ **8.** $17 \leq 17$ **9.** $6 \leq 11 \leq 15$ **10.** $5 < 2 + 3$

b. Compute

11. $|-2| = ?$ **12.** $|6| = ?$ **13.** $6! = ?$ **14.** $3! = ?$
15. $\sqrt{16} = ?$ **16.** $\sqrt{100} = ?$ **17.** $5 - (-4) = ?$ **18.** $-4 + (-2) = ?$
19. $8(-2) = ?$ **20.** $-7 - (-5) = ?$ **21.** $-7(4) = ?$ **22.** $-2(-5) = ?$
23. $-6/4 = ?$ **24.** $7/-3 = ?$ **25.** $-5/-2 = ?$ **26.** $\dfrac{4/5}{7/8} = ?$
27. $6 + 4 - 8 = ?$ **28.** $4 - 8 + 6 = ?$ **29.** $3 \times 2 \times 5 = ?$ **30.** $5 \times 2 \times 3 = ?$
31. $6 \div 3 + 2 = ?$ **32.** $(4 + 2) \times 3 = ?$ **33.** $5 + 2 \div 2 = ?$ **34.** $8 \div 4 \div 2 = ?$
35. $8 \div (4 \div 2) = ?$ **36.** $4/5 + 7/5 = ?$ **37.** $2/3 + 7/8 = ?$ **38.** $2/5 \times 3/7 = ?$

c. Simplify by cancelling

39. $\dfrac{a}{bc} \times \dfrac{c}{da}$ **40.** $7/10 \times 5/8$

d. Convert to a percentage

41. $5/7$ **42.** $12/27$

e. Compute

43. $7^2 = ?$ **44.** $5^3 = ?$ **45.** $2^3 2^4 = ?$ **46.** $5^4/5^3 = ?$ **47.** $\sqrt{5}\,\sqrt{20} = ?$

f. Factor

48. $7(2) + 5(2)$ **49.** $4(-3) + 4(2)$ **50.** $3X + X$

g. Expand

51. $4(3 - 8 + 2)$ **52.** $(X + Y)^2$ **53.** $(X - Y)^2$

h. Solve for X

54. $7X = 4$ **55.** $X + 2 = 4$ **56.** $5/(X + 3) = 7$ **57.** $4(X - 3) = 16$
58. $2X^2 = 6$

g. Summation

59. For $k = 3$ and X scores of 1, 2, and 5, compute the following:
(a) Σk **(b)** ΣkX **(c)** $\Sigma(X + k)$ **(d)** $\Sigma(X - k)$ **(e)** ΣX^2
(f) $(\Sigma X)^2$ **(g)** $\Sigma(X - k)^2$

60. For the following pairs of X and Y scores compute (a) $\Sigma(X - Y)$ and (b) $\Sigma(X + Y)$:

X	Y
4	7
5	2
3	1
6	5

h. Answers to exercises

1. T **2.** F **3.** T **4.** F **5.** T **6.** T **7.** T **8.** T **9.** T **10.** F **11.** 2 **12.** 6 **13.** 720 **14.** 6 **15.** 4
16. 10 **17.** 9 **18.** -6 **19.** -16 **20.** -2 **21.** -28 **22.** 10 **23.** -1.5 **24.** -2.33 **25.** 2.5
26. 32/35 or 0.91 **27.** 2 **28.** 2 **29.** 30 **30.** 30 **31.** 4 **32.** 18 **33.** 6 **34.** 1 **35.** 4 **36.** 11/5
37. 37/24 **38.** 6/35 **39.** $1/bd$ **40.** 7/16 **41.** 71.4% **42.** 44.4% **43.** 49 **44.** 125 **45.** 2^7 or 128
46. 5^1 or 5 **47.** $\sqrt{100}$ or 10 **48.** $2(7 + 5)$ **49.** $4(-3 + 2)$ **50.** X(4) **51.** $4(3) + 4(-8) + 4(2)$
52. $X^2 + 2XY + Y^2$ **53.** $X^2 - 2XY + Y^2$ **54.** 4/7 **55.** 2 **56.** $-16/7$ **57.** 7 **58.** $\sqrt{3}$
59. (a) 9 (b) 24 (c) 17 (d) -1 (e) 30 (f) 64 (g) 9 **60.** (a) 3 (b) 33

Appendix
II

Solutions to Problems

CHAPTER 1

1. Examples include various forms of public media such as newspapers, television, and radio.
2. (a) descriptive
   (b) inferential
   (c) inferential
   (d) descriptive
3. The population consists of the subscribers to the magazine, and the sample consists of the 500 subscribers who were randomly selected. If only some of the contacted subscribers respond we cannot consider the respondents a random sample from the original population of all subscribers because decisions about whether or not to respond to the survey probably were not made randomly. Those who respond to the questionnaire may systematically differ from those

who did not respond. The obtained sample could be considered a random sample of the population of magazine subscribers who would be willing to respond to the questionnaire.

4. An example is a study in which a sample of subjects is measured on two variables, such as intelligence and creativity, and the researcher is interested in whether or not the scores on the two variables are related (e.g., a person who is highly intelligent is also very creative).

5. An example is a study in which some subjects are randomly assigned to a condition in which they are exposed to a persuasive argument and other subjects are assigned to a condition in which no argument is presented. Then all subjects are measured with respect to their attitudes toward an issue relevant to the persuasive argument. The purpose of the study is to determine whether exposure to the persuasive argument influences attitudes.

6. Any example must include a sample that has been randomly drawn from a population. For instance, opinion-poll workers contact randomly selected individuals to obtain their opinions on some subject (e.g., political campaigns, television programs) and make inferences about the population based on those people included in the sample.

7. On the basis of inferential statistics, results could be generalized only to the students in the section from which the random sample was drawn. One might argue that the results also could be generalized to all introductory psychology students because students in the three sections are generally similar.

8. Follow the example in Box 1.6. Because there are three conditions let three single digits be associated with each condition (e.g., 1, 2, and 3 for condition A; 4, 5, and 6 for condition B; 7, 8, and 9 for condition C) and ignore the remaining digit (i.e., zero).

9. Choose the starting point following the directions given in Box 1.6. Select single-digit numbers or three-digit numbers, beginning at the starting point.

10. For the study in Box 1.3 the conceptual hypothesis was that listening to relaxing music would more effectively induce the relaxation necessary for the relief of headache pain than would a biofeedback procedure. The statistical hypothesis was that the number of reported headaches would be fewer for subjects who receive relaxation training with music than for those trained with biofeedback. The statistical conclusion was that subjects in the group reported fewer headaches than subjects in the biofeedback group. The conceptual conclusion was that music provided a more effective means of relaxation than biofeedback. For the study in Box 1.5 the conceptual hypothesis was that high-quality day care would lead to higher intellectual achievement than standard day care. The statistical hypothesis was that children assigned to the high-quality day-care program would obtain higher scores on an IQ and an intellectual achievement test than children assigned to regular day-care programs. The statistical conclusion was that higher scores were obtained by children assigned to high-quality day care. The conceptual conclusion was that high-quality day care produced higher intellectual achievement than standard day care.

CHAPTER 2

1. (a) variable (b) constant
   (c) constant (d) variable
2. (a) IQ is one way of measuring intelligence.
   (b) Both are concepts.
   (c) GPA is one way of measuring academic ability.
   (d) Both are measures of performance.
3. (a) concept (b) concept (c) measure
   (d) concept (e) measure (f) measure
   (g) measure (h) concept (i) concept
4. (a) scores on the reading test
   (b) the type of reading method (whole word or phonics)
   (c) manipulated by random assignment
5. (a) reported handedness (self-report)
   (b) reaction time scores
   (c) measured (self-report)
6. (a) interval-ratio (b) nominal
   (c) ordinal (d) interval-ratio
   (e) ordinal
7. The number of chairs is discrete and seconds is continuous.
8. (a) .665 to .675 (b) 81.5 to 82.5
9. (a) 2.05 (b) 200.00 (c) 4.98
   (d) 1.00 (e) 37.67 (f) 16.62
10. (a.) Rifles B and C both perform in a reliable way.
    (b.) Only rifle B gives a valid performance.
11. You cannot have high validity without first having high reliability. You can have high reliability with low validity when scores are consistent but lack intended meaning.

CHAPTER 3

1. grouped and cumulative frequency distribution

(a)

Class Interval	f	Cum. f	Cum. %
39–41	1	32	100.0
36–38	8	31	96.9
33–35	8	23	71.9
30–32	7	15	46.8
27–29	2	8	25.0
24–26	2	6	18.8
21–23	2	4	12.5
18–20	1	2	6.2
15–17	1	1	3.1

(b) 9 intervals **(c)** negatively skewed
2. See column 4 in table for problem 1.
3. **(a)** This is an ordinal scale but the data can be treated for some purposes as if they are from an interval scale.

(b) Frequency Table

Category Name	Frequency of Occurrence
A	11
B	25
C	50
D	25
E	11

(c) The distribution is roughly normal in shape.
4. The term *bar graph* refers to any of several more specific types of bar figures regardless of the width of the bars or the distance between them. With a qualitative variable on the X-axis, the bars should be separated by an arbitrary distance. With a quantitative variable on the X-axis, a particular type of bar graph called a frequency polygon is used. In that case, the successive bars are adjacent; they touch each other.
5. stem-and-leaf display

    3.   55666677889
    3*   001112233444
    2.   699
    2*   14
    1.   69
    1*

6. **(a)** $X = 30$; $PR = 28.125$.   **(b)** $X = 36$; $PR = 78.125$.
7. **(a)** $PR = 90$; $X = 37.40$.   **(b)** $PR = 40$; $X = 31.433$.
8. Percentiles are ordinal data.

CHAPTER 4

1. Mean $= 4.85$, median $= 5$, and mode $= 5$.
2.

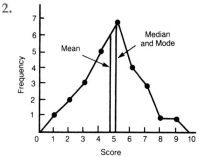

3. Mean = 4.77, median = 4, and mode = 3.

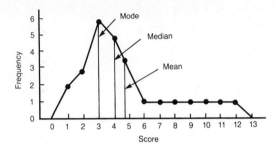

The measures of central tendency are more similar for the first data set because that distribution is more nearly symmetric than the second data set.

4. **(a)** Mean = 7 and median = 8.
   (b) 0
   (c) 64 and 69; the sum of squared deviations is smaller when based on the mean.

5. Set A: Range = 15, variance = 21.60, and s = 4.65.
   Set B: Range = 15, variance = 33.87, and s = 5.82.
   The variance and standard deviation are more sensitive to the difference in variability.

6. Your results depend on which numbers are randomly selected, but you are likely to observe that the mean value of the range changes more than the mean value of the variance as you go from samples of size 4 to samples of size 10.

7. By the definitional formula, with 8.83 as the mean, the variance is 16.57. By the computational formula, the variance is 16.57. The answers are the same to two decimal places of accuracy. If more places of accuracy are used, rounding error may produce a slight discrepancy.

8. Mean = 104 and s = 3.03. Only one score (108) is more than 1 standard deviation (3.03 points) above the mean. Four scores (102, 103, 104, and 107) are no more than 1 standard deviation away from the mean.

9. All scores would be the same.

10. Mean = 8 and s = 4. The constant should be 8, which is the mean of the original scores. The transformed scores are 2, −5, 5, 1, −3. The standard deviation for the transformed scores is 4, which is the same as for the original scores. Divide each transformed score by the constant 4 (the standard deviation) to obtain a new set of scores with a standard deviation of 1.

CHAPTER 5

1. Mean = 8 and s = 1.79. The z-scores would be −1.12, −.56, 0, .56, 1.12, 1.68, and 2.23, for raw scores of 6, 7, 8, 9, 10, 11, and 12, respectively. Mean z-score = 0.00 and s = 1.00.

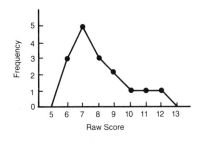

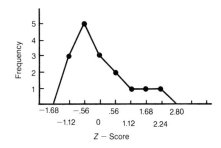

2. **(a)** 7.4 **(b)** 23 **(c)** 56 **(d)** 23.6 **(e)** 14.6 **(f)** 35
3. 6.25
4. **(a)** 43.33 **(b)** 50.00 **(c)** 60.00 **(d)** 37.78 **(e)** 65.56
5. .16
6. Mean = 44; s = 6.
7. 78.23; 72.57; 44.80; 57.12
8. **(a)** .0062 **(b)** 81 people **(c)** 78.88% **(d)** 23
9.

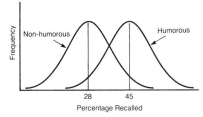

    (a) 92.22% **(b)** 4.46% **(c)** Humorous commercials would be preferable because they are better remembered.
10. 26.92; 33.70; 20.68
11. 2.94–7.86; 1.56–9.24; the student's score is extreme relative to scores obtained by other class members and it is consistent with his original argument.

CHAPTER 6

1. F	2. F	3. T	4. T	5. T
6. T	7. F	8. F	9. T	10. T

11. A scatterplot is a graphic display of a bivariate distribution.

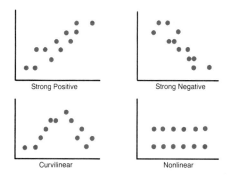

12. If the sign of the correlation coefficient is positive, it indicates that as scores on one variable increase so do the corresponding scores on a second variable. If the sign is negative, high scores on one variable tend to be accompanied by low scores on the second variable and vice versa. The size of the correlation coefficient refers to its numerical value. It ranges from negative 1 (-1.0) to positive 1 (1.0), the former indicating a perfect negative relationship, and the latter, a perfect positive relationship. A correlation of zero indicates no *linear* relationship (there could be strong curvilinear relationship). Remember, high values in either the negative or the positive direction indicate strong linear relationships; negative numbers *do not* mean weak relationships.

13. Restricting the range of one or both variables typically reduces the size of the correlation coefficient (an exception arises when restricted ranges reduce a curvilinear relationship to a linear one). In contrast, using only extreme groups tends to inflate the correlation coefficient.

14. **(a)** The Pearson correlation is appropriate for correlating two interval level variables.

   (b) The point-biserial correlation is appropriate for correlating a dichotomous variable with an interval variable.

   (c) The phi coefficient is appropriate for correlating two dichotomous variables.

   (d) The Spearman correlation is appropriate for correlating two ordinal variables.

15. A bivariate relationship holds when conditional distributions differ—that is, when some aspect (e.g., the mean) of the distribution of one variable differs at different values of a second variable. For the correlation coefficient to index appropriately a bivariate relationship, the conditional mean must differ *and* fall approximately in a straight line.

16.

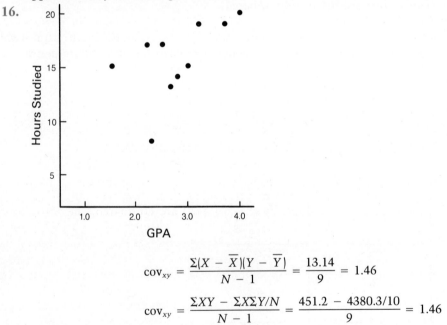

$$\text{cov}_{xy} = \frac{\Sigma(X - \overline{X})(Y - \overline{Y})}{N - 1} = \frac{13.14}{9} = 1.46$$

$$\text{cov}_{xy} = \frac{\Sigma XY - \Sigma X \Sigma Y/N}{N - 1} = \frac{451.2 - 4380.3/10}{9} = 1.46$$

$$r_{xy} = \frac{\Sigma z_x z_y}{N-1} = \frac{5.07}{9} = 0.56$$

$$r_{xy} = \frac{N\Sigma XY - \Sigma X\Sigma Y}{\sqrt{[N\Sigma X^2 - (\Sigma X)^2][N\Sigma Y^2 - (\Sigma Y)^2]}}$$

$$= \frac{10(451.2) - 4380.3}{\sqrt{[10(2579.0) - 24649][10(82.69) - 778.41]}}$$

$$= \frac{131.7}{\sqrt{55327.1}} = 0.56$$

There does appear to be a linear relationship between hours studied and GPA. However, this correlation (.56) is probably smaller than the correlation in the general population. The subjects were a random sample of college students, who probably represent a restricted range of variability in GPA, study hours, or both. This reduced variation should attenuate the population correlation.

17.
Hours	GPA
1.0	3.0
4.5	7.0
4.5	1.0
3.0	6.0
8.5	8.0
2.0	5.0
6.5	2.0
6.5	4.0
10.0	10.0
8.5	9.0

The value of r_s is 0.59

18. With the five students who studied the least coded as 0 and the five who studied the most coded as 1, the point-biserial correlation is 0.47. The sign merely reflects how the groups were coded. In this example the sign could be negative simply by reversing the coding scheme so that 1 = students who studied the least and 0 = students who studied the most.

19.
	Memory	IQ	Impression
Drug	$r_{pb} = .39$	$r_{pb} = 0.0$	phi = .30
Memory		$r = .60$	$r_{pb} = .01$
IQ			$r_{pb} = -.43$

20. The modest correlation between drug type and memory performance indicates that subjects who took the experimental drug tended (on the average) to score higher on memory performance than did subjects who took the placebo. Notice that although memory performance and IQ are correlated, the zero correlation between drug treatment and IQ means that the relationship between drug and memory variables could not have been due to different average IQs in the two drug treatment groups. Also, more subjects who took the experimental drug reported that their memory had improved, and again this relationship cannot have been due to different average IQs (in spite of the correlation between IQ and impression) because drug and IQ are not correlated. Finally, one's impression of memory improvement is unrelated to actual memory performance.

CHAPTER 7

1.	F	6.	T
2.	F	7.	T
3.	T	8.	F
4.	T	9.	T
5.	F	10.	T

11. **(a)**

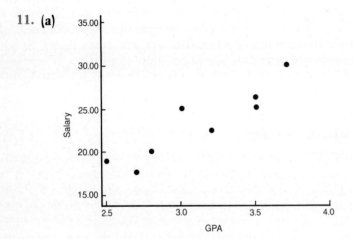

(b)

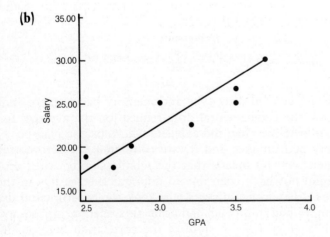

(c) Regression coefficients: $a = -5.76$; $b = 9.12$.

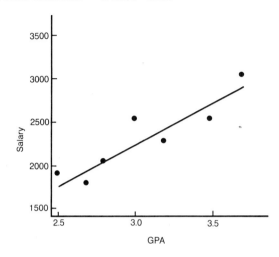

Regression Coefficients: $a = -576.50$; $b = 912.13$

(d)

GPA	Predicted Score
2.9	20.69
3.3	24.33
3.6	27.07

(e)

GPA (X)	Salary (Y)	Estimate (Y')	Error (Y − Y')
2.5	18	17.04	.96
2.7	17	18.86	−1.86
2.8	26	19.97	.23
3.0	24	21.60	2.40
3.2	22	23.42	−1.42
3.5	26	26.16	−0.16
3.5	24	26.16	−2.16
3.7	30	27.98	2.02

(f) $SS_Y = 129.878$; $SS_{Y'} = 108.886$; $SS_{Y-Y'} \approx 20.989$.
(g) $s_{Y-Y'}{}^2 = 3.507$; $s_{Y-Y'} = 1.87$.
(h) $r^2 = .838$; $1 - r^2 = .162$.

CHAPTER 8

1. b, c, and e
2. a, b, and d
3. n = number of trials; r = number of trials that produce the outcome of interest; p = probability of a trial producing the outcome of interest; q = probability of a trial not producing the outcome of interest.
4. **(a)** .75   **(b)** .25   **(c)** .07   **(d)** .80   **(e)** .13   **(f)** .04   **(g)** .51

5. **(a)** .50, .60 **(b)** .10, .14 **(c)** .16, .16 **(d)** .02, .02
6. **(a)** .25, .25 **(b)** .05, .07 **(c)** .0004, .0004
7. .4737; in 1000 plays 474 wins are expected; the result would be a net loss of $52. $474 won; $(1000 - 474) \$1 = \$526$ lost
8. 495; .00024; .1188; .1934
9. .0312
10. **(a)** .2051; .1201 **(b)** .1445; .1050
11. .5; .0228; .0456

CHAPTER 9

1. to determine whether observed results were produced by chance factors or by a systematic relationship between variables
2. Reject the null hypothesis.
3. Fail to reject the null hypothesis.
4. .95
5. **(a)** 15 **(b)** 0–5 and 15–20
6. **(a)** H_0: The ride (first or second) chosen by the subject is independent of the suspension system used on that ride. H_1: The ride chosen by the subject is more likely to have used the new rather than the old suspension system. **(b)** 26 or more subjects choosing the ride with the new suspension system **(c)** If 30 people preferred the ride with the new system, H_0 would be rejected; but if 25 preferred the ride with the new system, H_0 would not be rejected.
7. **(a)** H_0: The amount of verbalization is independent of whether the subject received behavior modification training. **(b)** H_1: The amount of verbalization is not independent of whether the subject received behavior modification training.
    (c)

$\overline{X}_1 - \overline{X}_2$	f	p	cum p
−2.50	1	.10	.10
−1.67	1	.10	.20
−0.83	2	.20	.40
0.00	2	.20	—
0.83	2	.20	.40
1.67	1	.10	.20
2.50	1	.10	.10

   (d) There is no region of rejection because even the most extreme result possible has a probability greater than .05.
   (e) H_0 could not be rejected on the basis of this study because even the most extreme outcome is more probable than .05. The researcher would have to set α to at least .10 in order to reject H_0.
8. **(a)** H_0: Frequency of reported headaches is independent of whether relaxation training included music. H_1: Reported headaches will be reduced by including music with relaxation training. **(b)** 2.4 to 2.8 **(c)** The observed difference be-

tween means, 2.4, is in the region of rejection, so the null hypothesis can be rejected. We conclude that including music with relaxation training reduces the number of reported headaches.

9. (a) H_0: The amount recalled is independent of the mood in which the subject is placed. H_1: The amount recalled is affected by the mood in which a subject is placed.   (b) The alternative hypothesis is nondirectional, so there are two regions of rejection, 1.857 to 2.143 and -1.857 to -2.143.   (c) The observed difference between means, 1.571, does not fall in either region, so the null hypothesis would not be rejected. We conclude that this experiment provides no evidence for the claim that amount recalled is influenced by mood.

CHAPTER 10

1. (a) Random sampling permits assessment of an obtained outcome with a "normal curve" statistic such as z or t.   (b) The results may be generalized to the specific population that was sampled.

2. Random assignment is used more often than random sampling, and *in theory* random sampling is needed to satisfy the assumption of independence that underlies z- and t-tests.

3. Sampling with restriction permits a better approximation to a representative sample with fewer subjects than needed with simple random sampling; an example is stratified sampling, in which cases are randomly drawn from each of two or more strata such as age groups or income groups.

4. Without random sampling the probability value resulting from a z- or t-test has unknown validity and the results are specific to the sample that was assessed.

5. The sample is random by definition of the method used to obtain it. It may not be representative with respect to numbers of each gender, but that is the chance you take with a simple random sample. If equal gender representation is considered important, then you should stratify, sampling an equal number within each gender category.

6. (a) ± 1.96 (b) ± 2.575

7. (a) $+1.65$ (b) $+2.326$

8. Both values are .025.

9. (a) H_0: $\mu = 5$ (b) H_1: $\mu < 5$
   (c) $\overline{X} = 3.0$; $s^2 = 18/7 = 2.57$; $s_{\overline{X}} = \sqrt{2.57}/\sqrt{8} = .567$

   $$t(7) = \frac{3.0 - 5.0}{.567} = -3.527$$

   (d) Reject H_0. She will not give the examination.

10. (a) $t(8) = -5/3.333 = 1.50$; fail to reject H_0.
    (b) $t(24) = -5/2.000 = 2.50$; reject H_0.
    (c) Given constant mean and variance, it is easier to obtain statistical significance with larger samples than smaller ones.

11. (a) .68   (b) .90   (c) .99   (d) .50

12. **(a)** 95 percent confidence interval is 106.5 ± 1.65, or 104.85 to 108.15.
    (b) 99 percent confidence interval is 106.5 ± 2.24, or 104.26 to 108.74.
13. **(a)** 95 percent confidence interval is -0.26 to .077.
    99 percent confidence interval is -0.44 to 0.84.
    (b) 95 percent confidence interval is -0.83 to -0.37.
    99 percent confidence interval is -0.86 to -0.25.
    (c) 95 percent confidence interval is 0.02 to 0.26.
    99 percent confidence interval is -0.01 to 0.29.
14. All values less than 92.51 and greater than 107.49 would be rejected under the null hypothesis.

CHAPTER 11

1. **(a)** H_0: $\mu_{males} = \mu_{females}$; H_1: $\mu_{males} > \mu_{females}$.
   (b) $t(21) = \dfrac{8.22 - 6.31}{\sqrt{\dfrac{9(3.23)^2 + 12(2.86)^2}{10 + 13 - 2}\left(\dfrac{1}{10} + \dfrac{1}{13}\right)}} = \dfrac{1.91}{1.27} = 1.50$

   Fail to reject H_0.
   (c) The sample can be looked at as a convenience (or available) sample of past, present, and future clients of that counselor. (The alternative is to consider the 23 clients the entire population of the counselor and find σ^2 by SS/N instead of finding s^2 by $SS/n - 1$.)
   (d) **(i)** Fail to reject H_0; infer that the two groups are not significantly different. **(ii)** There is no *statistical* basis for making any inference about generality. **(iii)** There is no statistical basis for making any inference about the cause of the nonsignificant relationship.
2. **(a)** H_0: $\mu_{forward} = \mu_{backward}$; H_1: $\mu_{forward} \neq \mu_{backward}$.
   (b) $t(10) = \dfrac{11.00 - 8.00}{.966} = 3.10$
   (c) $p < .05$ (two-tailed); reject H_0.
   (d) On the basis of random assignment, your best inference about the observed difference in mean number correct is that it was caused by the forward versus backward practice.
   (e) There is no statistical basis for making any generality inference. It can be concluded that there is a systematic difference in the behavior of these specific subjects when given these treatments.
3. Although a critic might question whether the observed difference would generalize to other samples, there is little doubt that a systematic finding was observed between the means, $t(10) = 3.10$, $p < .05$, and the group difference accounts for 49 percent of the variation in the number correct scores.
4. $t(9) = \dfrac{-1.800}{1.153} = -1.56$; $p > .15$; fail to reject H_0.

5. **(a)** $t(5) = \dfrac{3.000}{.577} = 5.20$; $p < .01$; reject H_0.

   (b) This is a matched-groups design (one type of dependent samples design).

   (c) The t ratio in problem 5 is larger because the correlation between paired scores was subtracted from the denominator of the ratio.

   (d) Compute $r^2(100)$ for each problem. In problem 2, $3.10^2/(3.10^2 + 10) = .490$ so 49% of the variation is accounted for. In problem 5, $5.20^2/(5.20^2 + 5) = .844$ so 84.4% of the variation is accounted for.

6. **(a)** Based on prior data, H_1 is directional.

   (b) Outcome is not significant for alpha $= .05$ or less.

   (c) Using Formula 11.16, for $t(120) = 2.00$, $r = .18$, and for $t(18) = 1.60$, $r = .35$.

   (d) Although the study with $t = 2.00$ is statistically significant ($p < .05$), the relationship is relatively weak: $r = 18$. The nonsignificant replication ($p > .05$) shows a stronger relationship: $r = .35$.

7. It is assumed that the scores have been randomly *sampled* from specific populations. Using the test without random sampling is justified because under most circumstances the resulting probability value is a good estimate of the value that would have been obtained with the theoretically more appropriate randomization test.

8. **(a)** $t(7) = .073$; fail to reject H_0.

   (b) $p(\text{randomization test}) = 1/84 = .012$; reject H_0.

   (c) Comparison of outcomes: This study has unequal group sizes and unequal variances (s_b^2 is 94 times larger than s_a^2), and the larger variance is in the smaller group. Since t is known to be biased under these circumstances, the randomization test provides a better test of H_0.

9. **(a)** $t(5) = 3.10$; $p < .05$; reject H_0.

   (b) $p(\text{randomization test}) = 4/64 = .0625$; fail to reject H_0.

   (c) The nondirectional (two-tailed) outcomes lead to different statistical decisions. If the researcher is testing a directional (one-tailed) alternative hypothesis, both tests lead to the same decision. It appears that either more scores or a more extreme difference between means is needed to reject H_0 with a randomization test of a nondirectional alternative hypothesis.

CHAPTER 12

1. One is more likely to compute power when a finding is not significant. In this case the goal is to find out whether the study had reasonable power to detect the effect.

2. **(a)** and **(c)**

3. effect size, the nature of the alternative hypothesis, α, sample size, and variability of scores

4. .83; 48

5. .05(60) $= 3$

6. .29(60) $= 17$

7. (a)

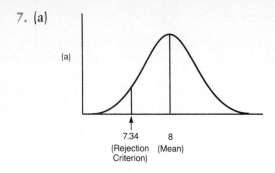

(a)

7.34   8
(Rejection (Mean)
Criterion)

(b) and (c)

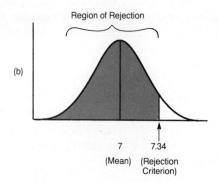

Region of Rejection

(b)

7   7.34
(Mean)   (Rejection
Criterion)

The area in the region of rejection = .8023; the remaining area = .1977. The probability of a Type II error = .1977. (d) .9909 using the normal distribution, or .99 using Table F in Appendix III.

8. (a) .22   (b) 77   (c) .70   (d) 67
9. (a) A directional alternative hypothesis would be warranted in this case and using it will make for a more powerful test. Using an α value of .05 is accepted practice. Equal numbers of subjects should be assigned to each condition to maximize power. Previous research suggests that the assumed values for σ and γ are appropriate. (b) .85, with harmonic mean of sample sizes = 27.9 (c) With ρ = .2, power = .94; with ρ = .5, power = .99; and with ρ = 0, power = .87. With larger values of ρ, power is greater.
10. .17, .74, and .98, for small, medium, and large effect sizes, respectively
11. .94; .82
12. .75; .20; 401
13. (a) .80 (b) The study had sufficient power to detect a large effect, but the observed difference was not significant. We can conclude that there is not a large effect. (c) The power of the study to detect a small effect was less than .17, so its failure to find a significant difference probably was a Type II error. A small effect may exist.

CHAPTER 13

1. Analysis of variance is preferred because you can estimate whether at least two means are not equal and do so with a known probability of a Type I error.
2. (a) age at first pregnancy
   (b) classificatory
   (c) first pregnancy at ages 15–17 years, 18–20 years, and 21–23 years
   (d) total number of pregnancies
   (e) No; random assignment of women to ages could not be performed.
   (f) Yes; stratified random sampling was carried out.
3. (a) $df_b = 3 - 1 = 2$; $df_w = (6 - 1) + (8 - 1) + (8 - 1) = 19$
   (b) $df_b = 5 - 1 = 4$; $df_w = 5(12 - 1) = 55$
4. (a) $F_{crit}(2,19) = 3.52$.
   (b) $F_{crit}(3,60) = 4.13$.
5. (a) Factor = order of presentation of alpha values.
   (b)

Source	SS	df	MS	F	η^2
Between	5.81	2	2.90	5.71	.3886
Within	9.14	18	.51		
Total	14.95	20			

   (c) For $\alpha = .05$, yes, $F(crit) = 3.55$.
   For $\alpha = .01$, no, $F(crit) = 6.01$.

6.

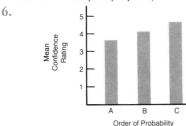

A bar graph is appropriate because the levels of the factor (Orders A, B, and C) are measured on a nominal scale.

7. (a)

Source	SS	df	MS	F	η^2
Between	267.41	2	133.70	14.31	.628
Within	158.70	17	9.34		
Total	426.11	19			

   (b) Reject H_0 at alpha = .01.
   (c) Eta^2(100) = 62.8.

(d) Since subjects were volunteers who were not randomly sampled, there is no statistical basis to infer generality.

(e) Since random assignment was used, observed differences in sample means were probably *caused* by differences in treatments.

8. (a) $F(2,8) = 3.94$; $p = .064$; fail to reject H_0.

(b) p(randomization test) $= 80/11550 = .007$; reject H_0.

(c) Comparison of outcomes: This study has unequal group sizes and unequal variances (s_c^2 is 145 times larger than s_a^2), and the larger variance is in the smaller group. Since F is known to be biased under these circumstances, the randomization test provides a better test of H_0.

9. (a) $F(2,7) = 8.89$; $p = .012$; reject H_0.

(b) p(randomization test) $= 38/4200 = .009$; reject H_0.

(c) Comparison of outcomes: Although this study has moderately unequal sample sizes, the largest variance is not in the smallest group, and the variances are homogeneous (nearly equal). Therefore ANOVA provides a good estimate of the exact probability from the randomization test.

CHAPTER 14

1. The true alpha is *greater than* the stated alpha. This is because you implicitly make at least three comparisons when you select the most extreme means to compare after inspecting the data.

2. (a) $q = 3.51$; $\sqrt{MS_W/n} = 2.628$; $HSD = 9.224$.
Thus, all differences equal to or larger than 9.224 are significant at $\alpha = .05$.

(b) With $q = 4.5$, $HSD = 11.826$. No pairwise differences are significant in this data set with $\alpha = .01$.

3. (a) Comparison 1: $t(76) = (45 - 34)/5 = 2.2$.
Comparison 2: $t(76) = (18 - 5)/5 = 2.6$.
Comparison 3: $t(76) = (39.5 - 11.5)/3.54 = 7.92$.

(b) With $df = 60$, the critical value of t is 2.456.

(c) For comparison 1, fail to reject H_0. For both of the other comparisons, H_0 may be rejected at $\alpha = .05$.

(d) Practice alone (without specific training) leads to improved performance.

(e) None; all three comparisons are orthogonal.

4. (a)

Comp.	Preschool Experience		
	None	Strict	Relaxed
1	0	−1	1
2	−2	1	1

Comparison 1 tests the hypothesis that there is no difference in the number of friends between subjects in the strict and relaxed programs. Comparison 2 tests the hypothesis that there is no difference in the number of friends between the no-program control group and the average of the two treatment groups.

(b) For comparison 1, $SS_{C_1} = 80$ and $F(1,27) = 1.16$; $p > .05$. For comparison 2, $SS_{C_2} = 426.67$ and $F(1,27) = 6.18$; $p < .05$. Conclusion: The mean number of friends in the strict group (11.00) and relaxed group (15.00) were not significantly different, but the average of these groups (13.00) is greater than the mean of the no-treatment controls (5.00).

(c)

Source	SS	df	MS	F	η^2
Between	506.67	2	253.33	3.67	.2137
Within	1864.62	27	69.06		
Total	2371.29	29			

$F_{crit}(2,27) = 3.35$

5. (a)

	Weeks of Practice		
Comps	1	2	3
C_1	−1	0	1
C_2	1	−2	1

(b) $SS_{linear} = 500$ and $SS_{quadratic} = 6.67$. The F-ratio for linear trend is $500/69.06 = 7.24$, and the F-ratio for quadratic trend is $6.67/69.06 = .096$. The F_{crit} with 1 and 27 df is 4.21. Thus, there is a significant linear trend in this data set and the quadratic component of trend is not significant.

(c) Omega-squared for the linear component of trend $= 14.83$.
Omega-squared for the quadratic component $= .04$.

CHAPTER 15

1. **(a)** The unique contribution of factorial designs is the interaction(s) between factors.
   (b) Other advantages are economy of subjects, control of nuisance factors, and generalizability of main effect results across levels of other factors.
2. **(a)** ANOVA summary table for 2×2 analysis of the number correct in the reading of sentences that were presented at two rates, with and without feedback.

Source	SS	df	MS	F	$p <$	η^2
Rate (slow/fast)	162.00	1	162.00	43.20	.01	.687
Feedback (yes/no)	18.00	1	18.00	4.80	n.s.	.076
Rate × feedback	40.50	1	40.50	10.80	.05	.171
Error	15.00	4	3.75			
Total	235.50	7				

(b) Although slow presentation leads to better performance than fast presentation $(p < .01)$, inspection of the significant interaction $(p < .05)$ suggests that a combination of slow rate and feedback yields a better performance than any of the other three treatments. Simple effects could be used to explore this notion.

3. This is a 2×2 (2 by 2) factorial design.

4. You would have only one score per cell, which prevents direct calculation of within-group variation. You must have at least two scores per cell to obtain MS_w directly.

5. (a) Through random sampling there is a statistical basis to generalize these results to the particular population of university students that was sampled.

   (b) Through random assignment of subjects to treatments the differences in treatments are the most likely cause of the observed differences in mean performance.

6. (a) Only the alcohol main effect is likely to be significant. The age main effect is not likely to be significant because the average of the two 20-year groups is the same as the average of the two 60-year groups. There is no interaction because the difference between alcohol groups is the same size at each level of age.

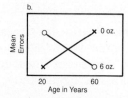
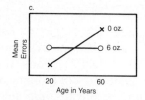

7. Sources of variation and degrees of freedom for a $2 \times 2 \times 4$ factorial design with $n = 4$ cases per cell

Source	df	(Computation)
Age of model (AgeM)	1	(2-1)
Action of model (ActM)	1	(2-1)
Age of subject (AgeS)	3	(4-1)
AgeM × ActM	1	(2-1)(2-1)
AgeM × AgeS	3	(2-1)(4-1)
ActM × AgeS	3	(2-1)(4-1)
AgeM × ActM × AgeS	3	(2-1)(2-1)(4-1)
Error (within)	48	[(2)(2)(4)](4-1)
Total	63	[(2)(2)(4)(4)] − 1

8.

Source	SS	df	MS	F
A	20	2	10	5.0
B	45	3	15	7.5
A × B	60	· 6	10	5.0
Within	336	168	2	
Total	461	179		

9. There are two levels of factor A and 3 levels of factor B.
10. There were 60 scores in this study, divided into 6 groups of 10 scores each.
11. (a) $\eta^2 = .125$; $\omega^2 = .111$
    (b) $\eta^2 = .100$; $\omega^2 = .074$
    (c) Either 67.5 percent or 74.1 percent of the variation is unexplained (depending on the method used to calculate variation accounted for, either η^2 or ω^2).
12. For the random sampling model:

The A main effect: H_0: $\mu_A - \mu_G = 0$.
                       H_1: Not all $\mu_A - \mu_G = 0$.
The B main effect: H_0: $\mu_B - \mu_G = 0$.
                       H_1: Not all $\mu_B - \mu_G = 0$.
The AB interaction: H_0: $\mu_{AB} - \mu_A - \mu_B + \mu_G = 0$.
                       H_1: Not all $\mu_{AB} - \mu_A - \mu_B + \mu_G = 0$.

For the random assignment model:

A effect: H_0: Obtained differences are due to chance (values of scores are independent of group membership).
                       H_1: Obtained differences are due to factor A (values of scores are not independent of group membership).
B main effect: H_0: Obtained differences are due to chance.
                       H_1: Obtained differences are due to factor B.
AB interaction: H_0: Obtained differences are due to chance.
                       H_1: Obtained differences are due to the interaction between factors A and B.

CHAPTER 16

1. Each subject is tested in each condition, so all condition means are based on the same subjects.
2. (a) Subjects are independently (e.g., randomly) sampled from a population, (b) scores in the populations represented by different conditions are normally distributed and (c) have equal variance, and (d) the populations of scores have equal variance of difference scores for each possible pair of conditions (sphericity).
3. Use tabled F values as usual in the belief that alpha changes vary little under violation of assumptions. Use a critical F value based on adjusted degrees of freedom. Use a randomization test.
4. (a) 4 conditions, 9 subjects   (b) $F_{crit} = 3.01$.   (c) Reject the null hypothesis.
5. (a) Reject the null hypothesis.   (b) $df = 1,19$; $F_{crit} = 4.38$; reject the null hypothesis.
6. (a) H_0: $\mu_1 = \mu_2 = \mu_3$; H_1: Not all population means are equal.   (b) $F_{crit} = 3.74$; $F_{obs} = 5.80$; reject H_0. Motor coordination is optimal under a moderate level of arousal and is suboptimal at low or high levels of arousal.   (c) $df = 1,7$; $F_{crit} = 5.59$; reject H_0.   (d) 45.3%

(e)
Comparison	$\overline{X}_i - \overline{X}_j$	MS_{cs}	HSD	Significant?
Med. vs. high	6.00	9.14	4.45	Yes
Low vs. high	1.62	17.99	6.24	No
Med. vs. low	4.38	12.71	5.24	No

7. **(a)** $F_{crit} = 3.47$; $F_{obs} = 3.60$; reject H_0.   **(b)** The F-ratio for the independent samples design is smaller because MS_w includes variability due to differences between subjects. In the repeated measures design this variability is not included in calculations of F.   **(c)** 25.5%. This value is less than in the repeated measures design because in the independent samples design, variability due to differences between subjects contributes to variability among condition means and thus is included in the computation of the percentage of the variability accounted for.

8. **(a)** H_0: $\mu_1 = \mu_2 = \mu_3 = \mu_4$; H_1: Not all population means are equal.   **(b)** To prevent confounding of source and adage; if the same attribution assignments were used for each subject and differences between sources were found, it would not be possible to determine whether those differences were due to the effect of source or to differences between adages.   **(c)** $F_{crit} = 3.29$; $F_{obs} = 3.94$; reject H_0.   **(d)** 44.1%   **(e)** With experimentwise $\alpha = .05$, three comparisons, and $df = 5$ for the error term, t_{crit} for Dunn's test is 3.35. The t_{obs} values for the comparison of the movie star condition against the scientist, politician, and writer conditions, respectively, are 4.25, 3.03, and 2.21. Only the comparison between the scientist and movie star conditions is significant.   **(f)** Judged popularity of adages is higher when attributed to scientists than when attributed to movie stars.

9. **(a)** $F_{crit} = 3.29$; $F_{obs} = 2.48$; fail to reject H_0.   **(b)** Even though condition means are the same as in problem 8, the null hypothesis cannot be rejected in this case because the effect of the independent variable within subjects is much less consistent. Therefore the error term in the F-ratio is larger than in problem 8.

10. When you run NPSTAT on this data set you should obtain a p value of approximately .015 for the randomization test and a p value of .0146 for the ANOVA. These two values are in very good agreement. With experimentwise $\alpha = .05$ and two comparisons, per comparison $\alpha = .05/2 = .025$. Using NPSTAT, the randomization test comparing low vs. high yields $p = .484$, and the test comparing low vs. medium yields $p = .016$. Only the low vs. medium comparison is significant $(p < .025)$.

11. Applying NPSTAT to this data set should produce $p = .234$ for the ANOVA and $p = .03$ (approximately) for the randomization test. Evidence for violation of the assumption of sphericity is found by comparing variability of difference scores based on conditions A and B, which is quite small, with any other pair of conditions (e.g., B and D). This example demonstrates that at least in some cases where there is violation of the sphericity assumption, the randomization test will produce a significant result although ANOVA will not.

CHAPTER 17

1. F	2. F	3. F	4. T	5. F
6. F	7. T	8. T	9. F	10. T

11. Chi-square tests are used to analyze frequencies, whereas t-tests are used to analyze scores.

12. An expected frequency is the frequency one expects to result if H_0 is true. Expected frequencies can be derived a priori as (a) frequencies expected by chance or (b) frequencies expected on theoretical grounds. Expected frequencies can also be derived from the obtained data.

13. The chi-square tests of independence and homogeneity are identical in computational procedures. They are different, however, in their respective sampling procedures and in the conclusions drawn from each. Specifically, for the chi-square test of independence, a single sample is randomly selected from a single population and each individual is classified on two variables. In contrast, for the chi-square test of homogeneity, samples are drawn from two or more populations and are classified on a single variable. The conclusion arrived at from the test of independence concerns a possible relationship between two variables, whereas the conclusion arrived at from the test of homogeneity concerns population differences or causal inference.

14. H_0: Obtained frequencies are equally distributed across categories.
    H_0: Variable 1 and variable 2 are independent.
    H_0: There is no treatment effect.

15. For a chi-square test of contingency, the rationale involves transforming a table of frequencies into a chi-square value and referring that value to a theoretical sampling distribution based on an infinite number of possible outcomes when H_0 is true. For Fisher's exact test, the rationale involves referring a table of frequencies to a finite distribution based on all the possible ways the observed table of frequencies could have been arranged by chance alone.

16. χ^2(critical) = 5.99
    χ^2(observed) = 8.08
    Decision: Reject H_0.
    The professor can conclude that interest and heresay are more important than the size of the class for determining what courses students will choose; the assumptions of independence; by ensuring that the overall total from the table is equal to the number of subjects in the study.

17. χ^2(critical) = 12.59
    χ^2(observed) = 22.92
    Decision: Reject H_0.
    The professor can conclude that interest appears to be more important for more senior students, whereas heresay may be more important for less senior students. The strength of relationship, as measured by Cramer's phi, is .34. This is a test of independence because a single random sample of students was selected and then measured on the two variables of college level and criteria for choosing a course. Yes, a chi-square test is appropriate because each individual is classified into one and only one cell, the categories are exhaustive, and the size of the expected frequencies is appropriate.

18. χ^2(critical) = 9.49
    χ^2(observed) = 8.82
    Decision: Fail to reject H_0.
    The chi-square test indicates that parental and teacher perceptions are independent, they do not agree. The strength of the relationship, as measured by

Cramer's phi, is .30. This is a test of independence because a single sample of children was drawn and two variables measured (parental and teacher perceptions); notice that both row and column totals would *not* be known prior to data collection. To become a test of homogeneity, random samples of parents and teachers, each of known size, would be selected and queried about their perceptions of children.

	Perception Friendly	Perception Aggressive	Typical	Row Total
Parents	14	24	12	50
Teachers	15	15	20	50
Column Total	29	39	32	100

χ^2(critical) = 5.99 $\qquad$ χ^2(obtained) = 4.11

Decision: Fail to reject H_0. $\qquad$ Cramer's phi = .20

	Perception Friendly	Perception Aggressive	Typical	Row Total
Parents	28	48	24	100
Teachers	30	30	40	100
Column Total	58	78	64	200

χ^2(critical) = 5.99 $\qquad$ χ^2(obtained) = 8.22

Decision: Reject H_0. $\qquad$ Cramer's phi = .20

The significance level is most easily altered by changing the sample size.

19. Fisher's exact test should be used because the degrees of freedom are 1 and the expected values are less than 5. The two-tailed Fisher's exact probability is .10, indicating that the two groups do not differ. However, a one-tailed test, which might be reasonable for this example, yields a probability of .05, indicating that the two groups do differ when using that criterion.

CHAPTER 18

1. Randomization tests assume interval data and are usually carried out with obtained scores. Rank tests assume ordinal data and are usually carried out on scores that have been transformed to ranks. The tests are similar in that both derive probability values from a null distribution consisting of all possible random arrangements of observed data (either scores or ranks).

2. The null hypothesis for rank tests concerns the equality of sample distributions and thus is more general than the null hypothesis for parametric tests, which concerns the equality of specific population parameters of distributions (e.g., population means).

3. When parametric assumptions hold, parametric tests and randomization tests have the same power efficiency, and rank tests have lower power efficiency than either of the others. When parametric assumptions do not hold, randomization tests and rank tests can have greater power efficiency than parametric tests and can differ between themselves depending on the scale of measurement.

4. **(a)** The Mann-Whitney U test would be most appropriate. NPSTAT may be used to transform scores to ranks and to perform an independent two-group randomization test on the ranks. The result of this analysis is an estimated probability (based on 2000 permutations) of .0495 (directional) and .098 (nondirectional). Notice that your answer may differ slightly because only 2000 permutations, rather than all possible permutations, were used to calculate the probability value.

   (b) The researcher predicts that the computer program is superior, implying a directional test. The Mann-Whitney U is 28 or 72, which are between the directional critical values of 27 and 73 for $\alpha = .05$, indicating that the researcher cannot support the prediction (notice the difference between the results obtained by using Table H in Appendix III and the results obtained by actually carrying out the rank-randomization test).

   (c) The strength of relationship, as measured by the squared Glass rank biserial correlation coefficient, is $.44^2 = .19$.

5. **(a)** The Wilcoxon signed-rank test is most appropriate. NPSTAT may be used to transform scores to ranks and perform a dependent two-group randomization test on the ranks. The result of this analysis is an exact probability of .05 (directional) and .10 (nondirectional).

   (b) No directional hypothesis is specified, so a nondirectional test is called for. The observed Wilcoxon T is 5.5, which is greater than the nondirectional critical value of 3.0 for $\alpha = .05$ (notice that the value of n is 8 because one of the pairs had a difference of zero). Thus, the evidence does not suggest that one program is judged superior to the other.

   (c) The strength of relationship, as measured by the squared matched-pairs rank biserial correlation coefficient, is $-0.69^2 = .48$.

6. **(a)** The Kruskal-Wallis test is most appropriate. NPSTAT may be used to transform scores to ranks and perform an independent k-group randomization test (with $k = 3$). The result is an exact probability of .0028.

   (b) No directional hypothesis is specified, so a nondirectional test is called for. The observed Kruskal-Wallis H is 8.16, which has a probability of .017, assuming a chi-square distribution with $df = 2$. It appears as if the aerobic and combination conditions lead to greater self-esteem than the anaerobic condition.

   (c) The strength of relationship, as measured by epsilon squared, is .46.

7. **(a)** The Friedman test is most appropriate. NPSTAT may be used to transform scores to ranks and perform a dependent k-group randomization test (with $k = 3$). The result of this analysis is an estimated probability value (based on 2000 permutations) of .021.

   (b) The Friedman F_r statistic is 7.8, which has a probability value of .02, assuming a chi-square distribution with 2 degrees of freedom. Thus, perceived intelligence seems to be related to attractiveness. Specifically, perceived intelligence increases as attractiveness increases.

   (c) The strength of relationship as measured by epsilon squared is .13.

Appendix
III

Statistical Tables

Table A RANDOM NUMBERS

11 30 62 18 79	52 49 93 15 62	36 28 22 77 08	53 47 81 99 01	37 68 22 59 39
84 99 44 18 62	75 10 14 59 07	48 49 35 91 89	76 90 80 68 81	45 16 15 84 99
02 52 84 85 14	86 59 01 47 93	96 24 56 66 21	39 31 58 20 29	62 62 64 62 78
15 41 49 96 41	90 07 74 83 34	95 46 58 34 55	26 14 67 92 43	50 78 46 39 43
78 90 92 21 13	24 44 45 88 10	51 18 50 01 61	52 49 94 08 56	70 67 25 29 19
05 92 61 31 44	14 70 44 88 02	04 73 38 86 95	72 97 38 80 79	59 62 89 21 86
42 00 75 83 42	45 17 49 36 25	64 48 91 71 58	08 47 90 19 23	06 88 90 56 60
34 24 74 09 44	47 84 73 01 75	07 02 22 66 84	92 81 98 07 16	59 06 86 02 81
71 53 34 08 70	06 86 84 97 09	61 77 52 68 24	28 12 85 18 49	16 44 97 15 54
34 33 59 67 08	67 90 15 36 13	75 98 91 58 08	04 37 46 19 28	52 78 01 19 18
31 68 92 30 13	60 89 92 27 26	09 10 32 72 54	78 45 77 47 42	96 05 96 48 38
05 39 79 52 96	05 09 92 92 51	14 02 86 02 07	52 93 21 38 92	62 70 66 77 59
50 68 07 58 06	59 38 83 75 29	54 80 47 33 25	68 31 27 44 50	63 78 72 56 16
72 53 58 74 14	82 15 51 39 06	91 38 88 69 04	99 70 76 09 09	32 90 88 44 82
95 88 85 74 53	49 15 08 01 10	32 79 56 29 65	10 85 39 38 67	91 03 70 50 88
83 44 22 82 65	01 14 01 04 83	20 14 94 58 05	28 75 27 24 29	62 19 46 10 26
42 73 42 80 05	25 85 73 51 37	08 36 74 30 75	57 89 24 68 90	69 10 88 34 42
08 71 40 60 47	74 62 01 33 17	58 45 60 53 48	10 29 32 43 15	14 76 55 57 59
22 51 39 10 17	44 74 40 77 32	40 39 12 21 48	24 79 68 03 21	62 23 11 19 44
32 21 24 15 60	05 31 38 54 96	96 84 52 96 68	67 97 52 44 91	63 75 95 17 50
21 47 96 61 08	19 58 47 18 75	42 48 24 46 83	68 04 88 65 02	76 58 10 08 06
83 15 58 41 69	43 25 72 53 45	27 66 75 58 78	37 24 08 33 75	01 40 80 07 37
09 02 41 07 61	58 85 98 31 78	34 67 50 32 06	79 25 87 45 39	50 70 56 11 41
28 55 99 10 29	76 10 70 45 33	95 86 72 49 38	84 58 33 34 23	71 64 58 16 85
79 05 74 75 66	69 12 96 42 01	38 53 30 51 57	10 04 54 85 83	65 41 31 37 58
47 24 58 53 70	66 24 90 33 53	15 41 19 15 11	77 63 79 63 33	13 09 64 07 19
74 54 44 27 95	28 62 50 42 40	99 02 95 34 37	08 13 63 77 58	10 52 78 59 64
58 38 95 08 22	08 64 86 14 77	44 14 02 79 41	04 12 00 14 28	58 62 73 95 63
59 23 88 94 95	08 01 77 64 79	92 62 69 23 78	76 47 35 85 78	30 35 70 55 35
05 15 40 25 25	84 98 85 34 45	76 61 70 73 07	72 17 19 93 27	41 06 86 91 53
68 90 13 35 33	54 36 34 59 99	52 23 45 51 82	65 06 29 68 24	76 34 38 54 66
87 38 29 69 04	73 33 35 65 58	39 60 26 79 31	73 61 76 23 83	21 33 34 66 21
54 64 88 67 81	33 48 88 84 29	55 22 70 67 22	58 54 05 22 47	82 16 91 13 58
43 74 77 73 57	47 25 28 37 65	07 48 76 95 61	85 96 11 66 81	23 46 72 35 89
77 10 92 10 42	75 79 11 43 28	99 07 54 82 64	40 31 22 06 78	18 21 63 11 26
44 42 50 40 18	66 55 49 88 80	67 57 67 06 43	42 79 40 47 76	52 95 80 55 42
77 96 30 40 65	09 84 20 37 92	42 93 32 81 38	09 16 84 98 42	40 58 42 86 88
75 33 13 42 80	52 69 59 00 05	15 22 42 77 15	00 37 59 39 42	26 27 90 26 33
71 57 04 75 55	54 72 91 78 83	28 78 24 91 30	95 42 26 23 04	59 89 66 79 81
36 44 85 28 66	59 07 47 90 43	08 15 33 36 38	69 72 13 03 01	10 88 51 55 92

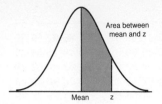
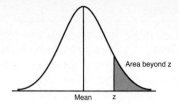

Table B AREAS UNDER THE NORMAL CURVE

Only positive z-score values are shown because the normal distribution is symmetrical. Areas for positive z-scores are identical to those for positive z-scores.

z	Area Between z and Mean	Area Beyond z	z	Area Between z and Mean	Area Beyond z	z	Area Between z and Mean	Area Beyond z
0.00	0.0000	0.5000	0.33	0.1293	0.3707	0.66	0.2454	0.2546
0.01	0.0040	0.4960	0.34	0.1331	0.3669	0.67	0.2486	0.2514
0.02	0.0080	0.4920	0.35	0.1368	0.3632	0.68	0.2517	0.2483
0.03	0.0120	0.4880	0.36	0.1406	0.3594	0.69	0.2549	0.2451
0.04	0.0160	0.4840	0.37	0.1443	0.3557	0.70	0.2580	0.2420
0.05	0.0199	0.4801	0.38	0.1480	0.3520	0.71	0.2611	0.2389
0.06	0.0239	0.4761	0.39	0.1517	0.3483	0.72	0.2642	0.2358
0.07	0.0279	0.4721	0.40	0.1554	0.3446	0.73	0.2673	0.2327
0.08	0.0319	0.4681	0.41	0.1591	0.3409	0.74	0.2704	0.2296
0.09	0.0359	0.4641	0.42	0.1628	0.3372	0.75	0.2734	0.2266
0.10	0.0398	0.4602	0.43	0.1664	0.3336	0.76	0.2764	0.2236
0.11	0.0438	0.4562	0.44	0.1700	0.3300	0.77	0.2794	0.2206
0.12	0.0478	0.4522	0.45	0.1736	0.3264	0.78	0.2823	0.2177
0.13	0.0517	0.4483	0.46	0.1772	0.3228	0.79	0.2852	0.2148
0.14	0.0557	0.4443	0.47	0.1808	0.3192	0.80	0.2881	0.2119
0.15	0.0596	0.4404	0.48	0.1844	0.3156	0.81	0.2910	0.2090
0.16	0.0636	0.4364	0.49	0.1879	0.3121	0.82	0.2939	0.2061
0.17	0.0675	0.4325	0.50	0.1915	0.3085	0.83	0.2967	0.2033
0.18	0.0714	0.4286	0.51	0.1950	0.3050	0.84	0.2995	0.2005
0.19	0.0753	0.4247	0.52	0.1985	0.3015	0.85	0.3023	0.1977
0.20	0.0793	0.4207	0.53	0.2019	0.2981	0.86	0.3051	0.1949
0.21	0.0832	0.4168	0.54	0.2054	0.2946	0.87	0.3078	0.1922
0.22	0.0871	0.4129	0.55	0.2088	0.2912	0.88	0.3106	0.1894
0.23	0.0910	0.4090	0.56	0.2123	0.2877	0.89	0.3133	0.1867
0.24	0.0948	0.4052	0.57	0.2157	0.2843	0.90	0.3159	0.1841
0.25	0.0987	0.4013	0.58	0.2190	0.2810	0.91	0.3186	0.1814
0.26	0.1026	0.3974	0.59	0.2224	0.2776	0.92	0.3212	0.1788
0.27	0.1064	0.3936	0.60	0.2257	0.2743	0.93	0.3238	0.1762
0.28	0.1103	0.3897	0.61	0.2291	0.2709	0.94	0.3264	0.1736
0.29	0.1141	0.3859	0.62	0.2324	0.2676	0.95	0.3289	0.1711
0.30	0.1179	0.3821	0.63	0.2357	0.2643	0.96	0.3315	0.1685
0.31	0.1217	0.3783	0.64	0.2389	0.2611	0.97	0.3340	0.1660
0.32	0.1255	0.3745	0.65	0.2422	0.2578	0.98	0.3365	0.1635

Table B *(continued)*

z	Area Between z and Mean	Area Beyond z	z	Area Between z and Mean	Area Beyond z	z	Area Between z and Mean	Area Beyond z
0.99	0.3389	0.1611	1.42	0.4222	0.0778	1.85	0.4678	0.0322
1.00	0.3413	0.1587	1.43	0.4236	0.0764	1.86	0.4686	0.0314
1.01	0.3438	0.1562	1.44	0.4251	0.0749	1.87	0.4693	0.0307
1.02	0.3461	0.1539	1.45	0.4265	0.0735	1.88	0.4699	0.0301
1.03	0.3485	0.1515	1.46	0.4279	0.0721	1.89	0.4706	0.0294
1.04	0.3508	0.1492	1.47	0.4292	0.0708	1.90	0.4713	0.0287
1.05	0.3531	0.1469	1.48	0.4306	0.0694	1.91	0.4719	0.0281
1.06	0.3554	0.1446	1.49	0.4319	0.0681	1.92	0.4726	0.0274
1.07	0.3577	0.1423	1.50	0.4332	0.0668	1.93	0.4732	0.0268
1.08	0.3599	0.1401	1.51	0.4345	0.0655	1.94	0.4738	0.0262
1.09	0.3621	0.1379	1.52	0.4357	0.0643	1.95	0.4744	0.0256
1.10	0.3643	0.1357	1.53	0.4370	0.0630	1.96	0.4750	0.0250
1.11	0.3665	0.1335	1.54	0.4382	0.0618	1.97	0.4756	0.0244
1.12	0.3686	0.1314	1.55	0.4394	0.0606	1.98	0.4761	0.0239
1.13	0.3708	0.1292	1.56	0.4406	0.0594	1.99	0.4767	0.0233
1.14	0.3729	0.1271	1.57	0.4418	0.0582	2.00	0.4772	0.0228
1.15	0.3749	0.1251	1.58	0.4429	0.0571	2.01	0.4778	0.0222
1.16	0.3770	0.1230	1.59	0.4441	0.0559	2.02	0.4783	0.0217
1.17	0.3790	0.1210	1.60	0.4452	0.0548	2.03	0.4788	0.0212
1.18	0.3810	0.1190	1.61	0.4463	0.0537	2.04	0.4793	0.0207
1.19	0.3830	0.1170	1.62	0.4474	0.0526	2.05	0.4798	0.0202
1.20	0.3849	0.1151	1.63	0.4484	0.0516	2.06	0.4803	0.0197
1.21	0.3869	0.1131	1.64	0.4495	0.0505	2.07	0.4808	0.0192
1.22	0.3888	0.1112	1.65	0.4505	0.0495	2.08	0.4812	0.0188
1.23	0.3906	0.1094	1.66	0.4515	0.0485	2.09	0.4817	0.0183
1.24	0.3925	0.1075	1.67	0.4525	0.0475	2.10	0.4821	0.0179
1.25	0.3943	0.1057	1.68	0.4535	0.0465	2.11	0.4826	0.0174
1.26	0.3962	0.1038	1.69	0.4545	0.0455	2.12	0.4830	0.0170
1.27	0.3980	0.1020	1.70	0.4554	0.0446	2.13	0.4834	0.0166
1.28	0.3997	0.1003	1.71	0.4564	0.0436	2.14	0.4838	0.0162
1.29	0.4015	0.0985	1.72	0.4573	0.0427	2.15	0.4842	0.0158
1.30	0.4032	0.0968	1.73	0.4582	0.0418	2.16	0.4846	0.0154
1.31	0.4049	0.0951	1.74	0.4591	0.0409	2.17	0.4850	0.0150
1.32	0.4066	0.0934	1.75	0.4599	0.0401	2.18	0.4854	0.0146
1.33	0.4082	0.0918	1.76	0.4608	0.0392	2.19	0.4857	0.0143
1.34	0.4099	0.0901	1.77	0.4616	0.0384	2.20	0.4861	0.0139
1.35	0.4115	0.0885	1.78	0.4625	0.0375	2.21	0.4864	0.0136
1.36	0.4131	0.0869	1.79	0.4633	0.0367	2.22	0.4868	0.0132
1.37	0.4147	0.0853	1.80	0.4641	0.0359	2.23	0.4871	0.0129
1.38	0.4162	0.0838	1.81	0.4648	0.0352	2.24	0.4875	0.0125
1.39	0.4177	0.0823	1.82	0.4656	0.0344	2.25	0.4878	0.0122
1.40	0.4192	0.0808	1.83	0.4664	0.0336	2.26	0.4881	0.0119
1.41	0.4207	0.0793	1.84	0.4671	0.0329	2.27	0.4884	0.0116

Table B *(continued)*

z	Area Between z and Mean	Area Beyond z	z	Area Between z and Mean	Area Beyond z	z	Area Between z and Mean	Area Beyond z
2.28	0.4887	0.0113	2.64	0.4959	0.0041	3.00	0.4986	0.0014
2.29	0.4890	0.0110	2.65	0.4960	0.0040	3.01	0.4987	0.0013
2.30	0.4893	0.0107	2.66	0.4961	0.0039	3.02	0.4987	0.0013
2.31	0.4896	0.0104	2.67	0.4962	0.0038	3.03	0.4988	0.0012
2.32	0.4898	0.0102	2.68	0.4963	0.0037	3.04	0.4988	0.0012
2.33	0.4901	0.0099	2.69	0.4964	0.0036	3.05	0.4989	0.0011
2.34	0.4904	0.0096	2.70	0.4965	0.0035	3.06	0.4989	0.0011
2.35	0.4906	0.0094	2.71	0.4966	0.0034	3.07	0.4989	0.0011
2.36	0.4909	0.0091	2.72	0.4967	0.0033	3.08	0.4990	0.0010
2.37	0.4911	0.0089	2.73	0.4968	0.0032	3.09	0.4990	0.0010
2.38	0.4913	0.0087	2.74	0.4969	0.0031	3.10	0.4990	0.0010
2.39	0.4916	0.0084	2.75	0.4970	0.0030	3.11	0.4991	0.0009
2.40	0.4918	0.0082	2.76	0.4971	0.0029	3.12	0.4991	0.0009
2.41	0.4920	0.0080	2.77	0.4972	0.0028	3.13	0.4991	0.0009
2.42	0.4922	0.0078	2.78	0.4973	0.0027	3.14	0.4992	0.0008
2.43	0.4924	0.0076	2.79	0.4974	0.0026	3.15	0.4992	0.0008
2.44	0.4927	0.0073	2.80	0.4974	0.0026	3.16	0.4992	0.0008
2.45	0.4929	0.0071	2.81	0.4975	0.0025	3.17	0.4992	0.0008
2.46	0.4931	0.0069	2.82	0.4976	0.0024	3.18	0.4993	0.0007
2.47	0.4932	0.0068	2.83	0.4977	0.0023	3.19	0.4993	0.0007
2.48	0.4934	0.0066	2.84	0.4977	0.0023	3.20	0.4993	0.0007
2.49	0.4936	0.0064	2.85	0.4978	0.0022	3.21	0.4993	0.0007
2.50	0.4938	0.0062	2.86	0.4979	0.0021	3.22	0.4994	0.0006
2.51	0.4940	0.0060	2.87	0.4979	0.0021	3.23	0.4994	0.0006
2.52	0.4941	0.0059	2.88	0.4980	0.0020	3.24	0.4994	0.0006
2.53	0.4943	0.0057	2.89	0.4981	0.0019	3.25	0.4994	0.0006
2.54	0.4945	0.0055	2.90	0.4981	0.0019	3.30	0.4995	0.0005
2.55	0.4946	0.0054	2.91	0.4982	0.0018	3.35	0.4996	0.0004
2.56	0.4948	0.0052	2.92	0.4982	0.0018	3.40	0.4997	0.0003
2.57	0.4949	0.0051	2.93	0.4983	0.0017	3.45	0.4997	0.0003
2.58	0.4951	0.0049	2.94	0.4984	0.0016	3.50	0.4998	0.0002
2.59	0.4952	0.0048	2.95	0.4984	0.0016	3.60	0.4998	0.0002
2.60	0.4953	0.0047	2.96	0.4985	0.0015	3.70	0.4999	0.0001
2.61	0.4955	0.0045	2.97	0.4985	0.0015	3.80	0.4999	0.0001
2.62	0.4956	0.0044	2.98	0.4986	0.0014	3.90	0.49995	0.00005
2.63	0.4957	0.0043	2.99	0.4986	0.0014	4.00	0.49997	0.00003

Table C **BINOMIAL DISTRIBUTION**
Binomial Probabilities when a Total of *N* Cases Are Tested and *r* Outcomes Are of One
Type. The Chance Probability for Any Single Event is $p = .50$.

r/N	5	6	7	8	9	10	11	12	13	14
0	.0312	.0156	.0078	.0039	.0020	.0010	.0005	.0002	.0001	.0001
1	.1562	.0938	.0547	.0312	.0176	.0098	.0054	.0029	.0016	.0009
2	.3125	.2344	.1641	.1094	.0703	.0439	.0269	.0161	.0095	.0056
3	.3125	.3125	.2734	.2188	.1641	.1172	.0806	.0537	.0349	.0222
4	.1562	.2344	.2734	.2734	.2461	.2051	.1611	.1208	.0873	.0611
5	.0312	.0938	.1641	.2188	.2461	.2461	.2256	.1934	.1572	.1222
6		.0156	.0547	.1094	.1641	.2051	.2256	.2256	.2095	.1833
7			.0078	.0312	.0703	.1172	.1611	.1934	.2095	.2095
8				.0039	.0176	.0439	.0806	.1208	.1572	.1833
9					.0020	.0098	.0269	.0537	.0873	.1222
10						.0010	.0054	.0161	.0349	.0611
11							.0005	.0029	.0095	.0222
12								.0002	.0016	.0056
13									.0001	.0009
14										.0001

r/N	15	16	17	18	19	20	21	22	23	24
0	.0000	.0000	.0000	.0000	.0000	.0000	.0000	.0000	.0000	.0000
1	.0005	.0002	.0001	.0001	.0000	.0000	.0000	.0000	.0000	.0000
2	.0032	.0018	.0010	.0006	.0003	.0002	.0001	.0001	.0000	.0000
3	.0139	.0085	.0052	.0031	.0018	.0011	.0006	.0004	.0002	.0001
4	.0417	.0278	.0182	.0117	.0074	.0046	.0029	.0017	.0011	.0006
5	.0916	.0667	.0472	.0327	.0222	.0148	.0097	.0063	.0040	.0025
6	.1527	.1222	.0944	.0708	.0518	.0370	.0259	.0178	.0120	.0080
7	.1964	.1746	.1484	.1214	.0962	.0739	.0554	.0407	.0292	.0206
8	.1964	.1964	.1885	.1669	.1442	.1201	.0970	.0762	.0585	.0438
9	.1527	.1746	.1885	.1855	.1762	.1602	.1402	.1186	.0974	.0779
10	.0916	.1222	.1484	.1669	.1762	.1762	.1682	.1542	.1364	.1169
11	.0417	.0667	.0944	.1214	.1442	.1602	.1682	.1682	.1612	.1488
12	.0139	.0278	.0472	.0708	.0961	.1201	.1402	.1542	.1612	.1612
13	.0032	.0085	.0182	.0327	.0518	.0739	.0970	.1186	.1364	.1488
14	.0005	.0018	.0052	.0117	.0222	.0370	.0554	.0762	.0974	.1169
15	.0000	.0002	.0010	.0031	.0074	.0148	.0259	.0407	.0585	.0779
16		.0000	.0001	.0006	.0018	.0046	.0097	.0178	.0292	.0438
17			.0000	.0001	.0003	.0011	.0029	.0063	.0120	.0206
18				.0000	.0000	.0002	.0006	.0017	.0040	.0080
19					.0000	.0000	.0001	.0004	.0011	.0025
20						.0000	.0000	.0001	.0002	.0006
21							.0000	.0000	.0000	.0001
22								.0000	.0000	.0000
23									.0000	.0000
24										.0000

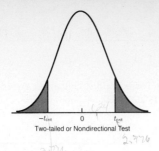

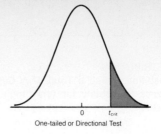

Two-tailed or Nondirectional Test   One-tailed or Directional Test

Table D CRITICAL VALUES OF t

	Area in both tails					
	.50	.20	.10	.05	.02	.01
	Area in one tail					
df	.25	.10	.05	.025	.01	.005
1	1.000	3.078	6.314	12.706	31.821	63.657
2	0.816	1.886	2.920	4.303	6.965	9.925
3	0.765	1.638	2.353	3.182	4.541	5.841
4	0.741	1.533	2.132	2.776	3.747	4.604
5	0.727	1.476	2.015	2.571	3.365	4.032
6	0.718	1.440	1.943	2.447	3.143	3.707
7	0.711	1.415	1.895	2.365	2.998	3.499
8	0.706	1.397	1.860	2.306	2.896	3.355
9	0.703	1.383	1.833	2.262	2.821	3.250
10	0.700	1.372	1.812	2.228	2.764	3.169
11	0.697	1.363	1.796	2.201	2.718	3.106
12	0.695	1.356	1.782	2.179	2.681	3.055
13	0.694	1.350	1.771	2.160	2.650	3.012
14	0.692	1.345	1.761	2.145	2.624	2.977
15	0.691	1.341	1.753	2.132	2.602	2.947
16	0.690	1.337	1.746	2.120	2.583	2.921
17	0.689	1.333	1.740	2.110	2.567	2.898
18	0.688	1.330	1.734	2.101	2.552	2.878
19	0.688	1.328	1.729	2.093	2.539	2.861
20	0.687	1.325	1.725	2.086	2.528	2.845
21	0.686	1.323	1.721	2.080	2.518	2.831
22	0.686	1.321	1.717	2.074	2.508	2.819
23	0.685	1.319	1.714	2.069	2.500	2.807
24	0.685	1.318	1.711	2.064	2.492	2.797
25	0.684	1.316	1.708	2.060	2.485	2.787
26	0.684	1.315	1.706	2.056	2.479	2.779
27	0.684	1.314	1.703	2.052	2.473	2.771
28	0.683	1.313	1.701	2.048	2.467	2.763
29	0.683	1.311	1.699	2.045	2.462	2.756
30	0.683	1.310	1.697	2.042	2.457	2.750
40	0.681	1.303	1.684	2.021	2.423	2.704
60	0.679	1.296	1.671	2.000	2.390	2.660
120	0.677	1.289	1.658	1.980	2.358	2.617
∞	0.674	1.282	1.645	1.960	2.326	2.576

Taken from Table III of Fisher & Yates: *Statistical Tables for Biological, Agricultural and Medical Research,* Longman Group UK Ltd. London, 1974 (previously published by Oliver & Boyd Ltd., Edinburgh), and by permission of the authors and publishers.

Table E FISHER'S r- TO z-TRANSFORMATION

r	.000	.002	.004	.006	.008	r	.000	.002	.004	.006	.008
			r (3rd decimal)						*r* (3rd decimal)		
.00	.0000	.0020	.0040	.0060	.0080	50	.5493	.5520	.5547	.5573	.5600
1	.0100	.0120	.0140	.0160	.0180	1	.5627	.5654	.5682	.5709	.5736
2	.0200	.0220	.0240	.0260	.0280	2	.5763	.5791	.5818	.5846	.5874
3	.0300	.0320	.0340	.0360	.0380	3	.5901	.5929	.5957	.5985	.6013
4	.0400	.0420	.0440	.0460	.0480	4	.6042	.6070	.6098	.6127	.6155
.05	.0500	.0520	.0541	.0561	.0581	.55	.6184	.6213	.6241	.6270	.6299
6	.0601	.0621	.0641	.0661	.0681	6	.6328	.6358	.6387	.6416	.6446
7	.0701	.0721	.0741	.0761	.0782	7	.6475	.6505	.6535	.6565	.6595
8	.0802	.0822	.0842	.0862	.0882	8	.6625	.6655	.6685	.6716	.6746
9	.0902	.0923	.0943	.0963	.0983	9	.6777	.6807	.6838	.6869	.6900
.10	.1003	.1024	.1044	.1064	.1084	.60	.6931	.6963	.6994	.7026	.7057
1	.1104	.1125	.1145	.1165	.1186	1	.7089	.7121	.7153	.7185	.7218
2	.1206	.1226	.1246	.1267	.1287	2	.7250	.7283	.7315	.7348	.7381
3	.1307	.1328	.1348	.1368	.1389	3	.7414	.7447	.7481	.7514	.7548
4	.1409	.1430	.1450	.1471	.1491	4	.7582	.7616	.7650	.7684	.7718
.15	.1511	.1532	.1552	.1573	.1593	.65	.7753	.7788	.7823	.7858	.7893
6	.1614	.1634	.1655	.1676	.1696	6	.7928	.7964	.7999	.8035	.8071
7	.1717	.1737	.1758	.1779	.1799	7	.8107	.8144	.8180	.8217	.8254
8	.1820	.1841	.1861	.1882	.1903	8	.8291	.8328	.8366	.8404	.8441
9	.1923	.1944	.1965	.1986	.2007	9	.8480	.8518	.8556	.8595	.8634
.20	.2027	.2048	.2069	.2090	.2111	.70	.8673	.8712	.8752	.8792	.8832
1	.2132	.2153	.2174	.2195	.2216	1	.8872	.8912	.8953	.8994	.9035
2	.2237	.2258	.2279	.2300	.2321	2	.9076	.9118	.9160	.9202	.9245
3	.2342	.2363	.2384	.2405	.2427	3	.9287	.9330	.9373	.9417	.9461
4	.2448	.2469	.2490	.2512	.2533	4	.9505	.9549	.9594	.9639	.9684
.25	.2554	.2575	.2597	.2618	.2640	.75	0.973	0.978	0.982	0.987	0.991
6	.2661	.2683	.2704	.2726	.2747	6	0.996	1.001	1.006	1.011	1.015
7	.2769	.2790	.2812	.2833	.2855	7	1.020	1.025	1.030	1.035	1.040
8	.2877	.2899	.2920	.2942	.2964	8	1.045	1.050	1.056	1.061	1.066
9	.2986	.3008	.3029	.3051	.3073	9	1.071	1.077	1.082	1.088	1.093
.30	.3095	.3117	.3139	.3161	.3183	.80	1.099	1.104	1.110	1.116	1.121
1	.3205	.3228	.3250	.3272	.3294	1	1.127	1.133	1.139	1.145	1.151
2	.3316	.3339	.3361	.3383	.3406	2	1.157	1.163	1.169	1.175	1.182
3	.3428	.3451	.3473	.3496	.3518	3	1.188	1.195	1.201	1.208	1.214
4	.3541	.3564	.3586	.3609	.3632	4	1.221	1.228	1.235	1.242	1.249
.35	.3654	.3677	.3700	.3723	.3746	.85	1.256	1.263	1.271	1.278	1.286
6	.3769	.3792	.3815	.3838	.3861	6	1.293	1.301	1.309	1.317	1.325
7	.3884	.3907	.3931	.3954	.3977	7	1.333	1.341	1.350	1.358	1.367
8	.4001	.4024	.4047	.4071	.4094	8	1.376	1.385	1.394	1.403	1.412
9	.4118	.4142	.4165	.4189	.4213	9	1.422	1.432	1.442	1.452	1.462
.40	.4236	.4260	.4284	.4308	.4332	.90	1.472	1.483	1.494	1.505	1.516
1	.4356	.4380	.4404	.4428	.4453	1	1.528	1.539	1.551	1.564	1.576
2	.4477	.4501	.4526	.4550	.4574	2	1.589	1.602	1.616	1.630	1.644
3	.4599	.4624	.4648	.4673	.4698	3	1.658	1.673	1.689	1.705	1.721
4	.4722	.4747	.4772	.4797	.4822	4	1.738	1.756	1.774	1.792	1.812
.45	.4847	.4872	.4897	.4922	.4948	.95	1.832	1.853	1.874	1.897	1.921
6	.4973	.4999	.5024	.5049	.5075	6	1.946	1.972	2.000	2.029	2.060
7	.5101	.5126	.5152	.5178	.5204	7	2.092	2.127	2.165	2.205	2.249
8	.5230	.5256	.5282	.5308	.5334	8	2.298	2.351	2.410	2.477	2.555
9	.5361	.5387	.5413	.5440	.5466	9	2.647	2.759	2.903	2.106	2.453
r	.000	.002	.004	.006	.008	r	.000	.002	.004	.006	.008
			r (3rd decimal)						*r* (3rd decimal)		

E. S. Pearson and H. O. Hartley, eds., *Biometrika Tables for Statisticians,* Vol. 1, 3d ed., New York, Cambridge University Press, 1966. By permission of the Biometrika Trustees.

Table F   POWER AS A FUNCTION OF
STATISTICAL EFFECT SIZE (δ) AND
TYPE I ERROR PROBABILITY (α)

	Alpha for a directional H_1			
	.05	.025	.01	.005
δ	Alpha for a nondirectional H_1			
	.10	.05	.02	.01
1.00	0.26	0.17	0.09	0.06
1.10	0.29	0.20	0.11	0.07
1.20	0.33	0.22	0.13	0.08
1.30	0.37	0.26	0.15	0.10
1.40	0.40	0.29	0.18	0.12
1.50	0.44	0.32	0.20	0.14
1.60	0.48	0.36	0.23	0.17
1.70	0.52	0.40	0.27	0.19
1.80	0.56	0.44	0.30	0.22
1.90	0.60	0.48	0.34	0.25
2.00	0.64	0.52	0.37	0.28
2.10	0.68	0.56	0.41	0.32
2.20	0.71	0.60	0.45	0.35
2.30	0.74	0.63	0.49	0.39
2.40	0.78	0.67	0.53	0.43
2.50	0.80	0.71	0.57	0.47
2.60	0.83	0.74	0.61	0.51
2.70	0.85	0.77	0.65	0.55
2.80	0.88	0.80	0.68	0.59
2.90	0.90	0.83	0.72	0.63
3.00	0.91	0.85	0.75	0.66
3.10	0.93	0.87	0.78	0.70
3.20	0.94	0.89	0.81	0.73
3.30	0.95	0.91	0.84	0.77
3.40	0.96	0.93	0.86	0.80
3.50	0.97	0.94	0.88	0.82
3.60	0.98	0.95	0.90	0.85
3.70	0.98	0.96	0.92	0.87
3.80	0.98	0.97	0.93	0.89
3.90	0.99	0.97	0.94	0.91
4.00	0.99	0.98	0.95	0.92
4.10	0.99	0.98	0.96	0.94
4.20	—	0.99	0.97	0.95
4.30	—	0.99	0.98	0.96
4.40	—	0.99	0.98	0.97
4.50	—	0.99	0.99	0.97
4.60	—	—	0.99	0.98
4.70	—	—	0.99	0.98
4.80	—	—	0.99	0.99
4.90	—	—	—	0.99
5.00	—	—	—	0.99

Reprinted with permission from D. C. Howell, © 1985, *Fundamental Statistics for the Behavioral Sciences*, Boston: PWS-KENT Publishing Co.

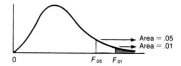

Area = .05
Area = .01

0      $F_{.05}$ $F_{.01}$

Table G   CRITICAL VALUES OF *F*

Each specific *F* distribution must be identified by the number of degrees of freedom in both the numerator and the denominator. If the observed *F* is larger than the table value, then $p < .05$ (light print) or $p < .01$ (dark print).

Degrees of Freedom: Denominator	Degrees of Freedom: Numerator														
	1	2	3	4	5	6	7	8	9	10	11	12	14	16	20
1	161	200	216	225	230	234	237	239	241	242	243	244	245	246	248
	4,052	**4,999**	**5,403**	**5,625**	**5,764**	**5,859**	**5,928**	**5,981**	**6,022**	**6,056**	**6,082**	**6,106**	**6,142**	**6,169**	**6,208**
2	18.51	19.00	19.16	19.25	19.30	19.33	19.36	19.37	19.38	19.39	19.40	19.41	19.42	19.43	19.44
	98.49	**99.00**	**99.17**	**99.25**	**99.30**	**99.33**	**99.34**	**99.36**	**99.38**	**99.40**	**99.41**	**99.42**	**99.43**	**99.44**	**99.45**
3	10.13	9.55	9.28	9.12	9.01	8.94	8.88	8.84	8.81	8.78	8.76	8.74	8.71	8.69	8.66
	34.12	**30.82**	**29.46**	**28.71**	**28.24**	**27.91**	**27.67**	**27.49**	**27.34**	**27.23**	**27.13**	**27.05**	**26.92**	**26.83**	**26.69**
4	7.71	6.94	6.59	6.39	6.26	6.16	6.09	6.04	6.00	5.96	5.93	5.91	5.87	5.84	5.80
	21.20	**18.00**	**16.69**	**15.98**	**15.52**	**15.21**	**14.98**	**14.80**	**14.66**	**14.54**	**14.45**	**14.37**	**14.24**	**14.15**	**14.02**
5	6.61	5.79	5.41	5.19	5.05	4.95	4.88	4.82	.478	4.74	4.70	4.68	4.64	4.60	4.56
	16.26	**13.27**	**12.06**	**11.39**	**10.97**	**10.67**	**10.45**	**10.27**	**10.15**	**10.05**	**9.96**	**9.89**	**9.77**	**9.68**	**9.55**
6	5.99	5.14	4.76	4.53	4.39	4.28	4.21	4.15	4.10	4.06	4.03	4.00	3.96	3.92	3.87
	13.74	**10.92**	**9.78**	**9.15**	**8.75**	**8.47**	**8.26**	**8.10**	**7.98**	**7.87**	**7.79**	**7.72**	**7.60**	**7.52**	**7.39**
7	5.59	4.47	4.35	4.12	3.97	3.87	3.79	3.73	3.68	3.63	3.60	3.57	3.52	3.49	3.44
	12.25	**9.55**	**8.45**	**7.85**	**7.46**	**7.19**	**7.00**	**6.84**	**6.71**	**6.62**	**6.54**	**6.47**	**6.35**	**6.27**	**6.15**
8	5.32	4.46	4.07	3.84	3.69	3.58	3.50	3.44	3.39	3.34	3.31	3.28	3.23	3.20	3.15
	11.26	**8.65**	**7.59**	**7.01**	**6.63**	**6.37**	**6.19**	**6.03**	**5.91**	**5.82**	**5.74**	**5.67**	**5.56**	**5.48**	**5.36**
9	5.12	4.26	3.86	3.63	3.48	3.37	3.29	3.23	3.18	3.13	3.10	3.07	3.02	2.98	2.93
	10.56	**8.02**	**6.99**	**6.42**	**6.06**	**5.80**	**5.62**	**5.47**	**5.35**	**5.26**	**5.18**	**5.11**	**5.00**	**4.92**	**4.80**

Reprinted by permission from *Statistical Methods*, 7th ed., George W. Snedecor and William G. Cochran, © 1980 by Iowa State University Press, Ames, Iowa, 50010.

Table G (continued)

Degrees of Freedom: Denominator	\multicolumn{15}{c}{Degrees of Freedom: Numerator}
	1	2	3	4	5	6	7	8	9	10	11	12	14	16	20
10	4.96	4.10	3.71	3.48	3.33	3.22	3.14	3.07	3.02	2.97	2.94	2.91	2.86	2.82	2.77
	10.04	7.56	6.55	5.99	5.64	5.39	5.21	5.06	4.95	4.85	4.78	4.71	4.60	4.52	4.41
11	4.84	3.98	3.59	3.36	3.20	3.09	3.01	2.95	2.90	2.86	2.82	2.79	2.74	2.70	2.65
	9.65	7.20	6.22	5.67	5.32	5.07	4.88	4.74	4.63	4.54	4.46	4.40	4.29	4.21	4.10
12	4.75	3.88	3.49	3.26	3.11	3.00	2.92	2.85	2.80	2.76	2.72	2.69	2.64	2.60	2.54
	9.33	6.93	5.95	5.41	5.06	4.82	4.65	4.50	4.39	4.30	4.22	4.16	4.05	3.98	3.86
13	4.67	3.80	3.41	3.18	3.02	2.92	2.84	2.77	2.72	2.67	2.63	2.60	2.55	2.51	2.46
	9.07	6.70	5.74	5.20	4.86	4.62	4.64	4.30	4.19	4.10	4.02	3.96	3.85	3.78	3.67
14	4.60	3.74	3.34	3.11	2.96	2.85	2.77	2.70	2.65	2.60	2.56	2.53	2.48	2.44	2.39
	8.86	6.51	5.56	5.03	4.69	4.46	4.28	4.14	4.03	3.94	3.86	3.80	3.70	3.62	3.51
15	4.54	3.68	3.29	3.06	2.90	2.79	2.70	2.64	2.59	2.55	2.51	2.48	2.43	2.39	2.33
	8.68	6.36	5.42	4.89	4.56	4.32	4.14	4.00	3.89	3.80	3.73	3.67	3.56	3.48	3.36
16	4.49	3.63	3.24	3.01	2.85	2.74	2.66	2.59	2.54	2.49	2.45	2.42	2.37	2.33	2.28
	8.53	6.23	5.29	4.77	4.44	4.20	4.03	3.89	3.78	3.69	3.61	3.55	3.45	3.37	3.25
17	4.45	3.59	3.20	2.96	2.81	2.70	2.62	2.55	2.50	2.45	2.41	2.38	2.33	2.29	2.23
	8.40	6.11	5.18	4.67	4.34	4.10	3.93	3.79	3.68	3.59	3.52	3.45	3.35	3.27	3.16
18	4.41	3.55	3.16	2.93	2.77	2.66	2.58	2.51	2.46	2.41	2.37	2.34	2.29	2.25	2.19
	8.28	6.01	5.09	4.58	4.25	4.01	3.85	3.71	3.60	3.51	3.44	3.37	3.27	3.19	3.07
19	4.38	3.52	3.13	2.90	2.74	2.63	2.55	2.48	2.43	2.38	2.34	2.31	2.26	2.21	2.15
	8.18	5.93	5.01	4.50	4.17	3.94	3.77	3.63	3.52	3.43	3.36	3.30	3.19	3.12	3.00
20	4.35	3.49	3.10	2.87	2.71	2.60	2.52	2.45	2.40	2.35	2.31	2.28	2.23	2.18	2.12
	8.10	5.85	4.94	4.43	4.10	3.87	3.71	3.56	3.45	3.37	3.30	3.23	3.13	3.05	2.94
21	4.32	3.47	3.07	2.84	2.68	2.57	2.49	2.42	2.37	2.32	2.28	2.25	2.20	2.15	2.09
	8.02	5.78	4.87	4.37	4.04	3.81	3.65	3.51	3.40	3.31	3.24	3.17	3.07	2.99	2.88
22	4.30	3.44	3.05	2.82	2.66	2.55	2.47	2.40	2.35	2.30	2.26	2.23	2.18	2.13	2.07
	7.94	5.72	4.82	4.31	3.99	3.76	3.59	3.45	3.35	3.26	3.18	3.12	3.02	2.94	2.83
23	4.28	3.42	3.03	2.80	2.64	2.53	2.45	2.38	2.32	2.28	2.24	2.20	2.14	2.10	2.04
	7.88	5.66	4.76	4.26	3.94	3.71	3.54	3.41	3.30	3.21	3.14	3.07	2.97	2.89	2.78
24	4.26	3.40	3.01	2.78	2.62	2.51	2.43	2.36	2.30	2.26	2.22	2.18	2.13	2.09	2.02
	7.82	5.61	4.72	4.22	3.90	3.67	3.50	3.36	3.25	3.17	3.09	3.03	2.93	2.85	2.74
25	4.24	3.38	2.99	2.76	2.60	2.49	2.41	2.34	2.28	2.24	2.20	2.16	2.11	2.06	2.00
	7.77	5.57	4.68	4.18	3.86	3.63	3.46	3.32	3.21	3.13	3.05	2.99	2.89	2.81	2.70
26	4.22	3.37	2.98	2.74	2.59	2.47	2.39	2.32	2.27	2.22	2.18	2.15	2.10	2.05	1.99
	7.72	5.53	4.64	4.14	3.82	3.59	3.42	3.29	3.17	3.09	3.02	2.96	2.86	2.77	2.66
27	4.21	3.35	2.96	2.73	2.57	2.46	2.37	2.30	2.25	2.20	2.16	2.13	2.08	2.03	1.97
	7.68	5.49	4.60	4.11	3.79	3.56	3.39	3.26	3.14	3.06	2.98	2.93	2.83	2.74	2.63
28	4.20	3.34	2.95	2.71	2.56	2.44	2.36	2.29	2.24	2.19	2.15	2.12	2.06	2.02	1.96
	7.64	5.45	4.57	4.07	3.76	3.53	3.36	3.23	3.11	3.03	2.95	2.90	2.80	2.71	2.60
29	4.18	3.33	2.93	2.70	2.54	2.43	2.35	2.28	2.22	2.18	2.14	2.10	2.05	2.00	1.94
	7.60	5.42	4.54	4.04	3.73	3.50	3.33	3.20	3.08	3.00	2.92	2.87	2.77	2.68	2.57
30	4.17	3.32	2.92	2.69	2.53	2.42	2.34	2.27	2.21	2.16	2.12	2.09	2.04	1.99	1.93
	7.56	5.39	4.51	4.02	3.70	3.47	3.30	3.17	3.06	2.98	2.90	2.84	2.74	2.66	2.55
32	4.15	3.30	2.90	2.67	2.51	2.40	2.32	2.25	2.19	2.14	2.10	2.07	2.02	1.97	1.91
	7.50	5.34	4.46	3.97	3.66	3.42	3.25	3.12	3.01	2.94	2.86	2.80	2.70	2.62	2.51
34	4.13	3.28	2.88	2.65	2.49	2.38	2.30	2.23	2.17	2.12	2.08	2.05	2.00	1.95	1.89
	7.44	5.29	4.42	3.93	3.61	3.38	3.21	3.08	2.97	2.89	2.82	2.76	2.66	2.58	2.47

Table G *(continued)*

Degrees of Freedom: Denominator	Degrees of Freedom: Numerator														
	1	2	3	4	5	6	7	8	9	10	11	12	14	16	20
36	4.11	3.26	2.86	2.63	2.48	2.36	2.28	2.21	2.15	2.10	2.06	2.03	1.98	1.93	1.87
	7.39	**5.25**	**4.38**	**3.89**	**3.58**	**3.35**	**3.18**	**3.04**	**2.94**	**2.86**	**2.78**	**2.72**	**2.62**	**2.54**	**2.43**
38	4.10	3.25	2.85	2.62	2.46	2.35	2.26	2.19	2.14	2.09	2.05	2.02	1.96	1.92	1.85
	7.35	**5.21**	**4.34**	**3.86**	**3.54**	**3.32**	**3.15**	**3.02**	**2.91**	**2.82**	**2.75**	**2.69**	**2.59**	**2.51**	**2.40**
40	4.08	3.23	2.84	2.61	2.45	2.34	2.25	2.18	2.12	2.07	2.04	2.00	1.95	1.90	1.84
	7.31	**5.18**	**4.31**	**3.83**	**3.51**	**3.29**	**3.12**	**2.99**	**2.88**	**2.80**	**2.73**	**2.66**	**2.56**	**2.49**	**2.37**
42	4.07	3.22	2.83	2.59	2.44	2.32	2.24	2.17	2.11	2.06	2.02	1.99	1.94	1.89	1.82
	7.27	**5.15**	**4.29**	**3.80**	**3.49**	**3.26**	**3.10**	**2.96**	**2.86**	**2.77**	**2.70**	**2.64**	**2.54**	**2.46**	**2.35**
44	4.06	3.21	2.82	2.58	2.43	2.31	2.23	2.16	2.10	2.05	2.01	1.98	1.92	1.88	1.81
	7.24	**5.12**	**4.26**	**3.78**	**3.46**	**3.24**	**3.07**	**2.94**	**2.84**	**2.75**	**2.68**	**2.62**	**2.52**	**2.44**	**2.32**
46	4.05	3.20	2.81	2.57	2.42	2.30	2.22	2.14	2.09	2.04	2.00	1.97	1.91	1.87	1.80
	7.21	**5.10**	**4.24**	**3.76**	**3.44**	**3.22**	**3.05**	**2.92**	**2.82**	**2.73**	**2.66**	**2.60**	**2.50**	**2.42**	**2.30**
48	4.04	3.19	2.80	2.56	2.41	2.30	2.21	2.14	2.08	2.03	1.99	1.96	1.90	1.86	1.79
	7.19	**5.08**	**4.22**	**3.74**	**3.42**	**3.20**	**3.04**	**2.90**	**2.80**	**2.71**	**2.64**	**2.58**	**2.48**	**2.40**	**2.28**
50	4.03	3.18	2.79	2.56	2.40	2.29	2.20	2.13	2.07	2.02	1.98	1.95	1.90	1.85	1.78
	7.17	**5.06**	**4.20**	**3.72**	**3.41**	**3.18**	**3.02**	**2.88**	**2.78**	**2.70**	**2.62**	**2.56**	**2.46**	**2.39**	**2.26**
55	4.02	3.17	2.78	2.54	2.38	2.27	2.18	2.11	2.05	2.00	1.97	1.93	1.88	1.83	1.76
	7.12	**5.01**	**4.16**	**3.36**	**3.37**	**3.15**	**2.98**	**2.85**	**2.75**	**2.66**	**2.59**	**2.53**	**2.43**	**2.35**	**2.23**
60	4.00	3.15	2.76	2.52	2.37	2.25	2.17	2.10	2.04	1.99	1.95	1.92	1.86	1.81	1.75
	7.08	**4.98**	**4.13**	**3.65**	**3.34**	**3.12**	**2.95**	**2.82**	**2.72**	**2.63**	**2.56**	**2.50**	**2.40**	**2.32**	**2.20**
65	3.99	3.14	2.75	2.51	2.36	2.24	2.15	2.08	2.02	1.98	1.94	1.90	1.85	1.80	1.73
	7.04	**4.95**	**4.10**	**3.62**	**3.31**	**3.09**	**2.93**	**2.79**	**2.70**	**2.61**	**2.54**	**2.47**	**2.37**	**2.30**	**2.18**
70	3.98	3.13	2.74	2.50	2.35	2.23	2.14	2.07	2.01	1.97	1.93	1.89	1.84	1.79	1.72
	7.01	**4.92**	**4.08**	**3.60**	**3.29**	**3.07**	**2.91**	**2.77**	**2.67**	**2.59**	**2.51**	**2.45**	**2.35**	**2.28**	**2.15**
80	3.96	3.11	2.72	2.48	2.33	2.21	2.12	2.05	1.99	1.95	1.91	1.88	1.82	1.77	1.70
	6.96	**4.88**	**4.04**	**3.56**	**3.25**	**3.04**	**2.87**	**2.74**	**2.64**	**2.55**	**2.48**	**2.41**	**2.32**	**2.24**	**2.11**
100	3.94	3.09	2.70	2.46	2.30	2.19	2.10	2.03	1.97	1.92	1.88	1.85	1.79	1.75	1.68
	6.90	**4.82**	**3.98**	**3.51**	**3.20**	**2.99**	**2.82**	**2.69**	**2.59**	**2.51**	**2.43**	**2.36**	**2.26**	**2.19**	**2.06**
125	3.92	3.07	2.68	2.44	2.29	2.17	2.08	2.01	1.95	1.90	1.86	1.83	1.77	1.72	1.65
	6.84	**4.78**	**3.94**	**3.47**	**3.17**	**2.95**	**2.79**	**2.65**	**2.56**	**2.47**	**2.40**	**2.33**	**2.23**	**2.15**	**2.03**
150	3.91	3.06	2.67	2.43	2.27	2.16	2.07	2.01	1.95	1.89	1.85	1.82	1.76	1.71	1.64
	6.81	**4.75**	**3.91**	**3.44**	**3.14**	**2.92**	**2.76**	**2.62**	**2.53**	**2.44**	**2.37**	**2.30**	**2.20**	**2.12**	**2.00**
200	3.89	3.04	2.65	2.41	2.26	2.14	2.05	1.98	1.92	1.87	1.83	1.80	1.74	1.69	1.62
	6.76	**4.71**	**3.88**	**3.41**	**3.11**	**2.90**	**2.73**	**2.60**	**2.50**	**2.41**	**2.34**	**2.28**	**2.17**	**2.09**	**1.97**
400	3.86	3.02	2.62	2.39	2.23	2.12	2.03	1.96	1.90	1.85	1.81	1.78	1.72	1.67	1.60
	6.70	**4.66**	**3.83**	**3.36**	**3.06**	**2.85**	**2.69**	**2.55**	**2.46**	**2.37**	**2.29**	**2.23**	**2.12**	**2.04**	**1.92**
1000	3.85	3.00	2.61	2.38	2.22	2.10	2.02	1.95	1.89	!.84	1.80	1.76	1.70	1.65	1.58
	6.66	**4.62**	**3.80**	**3.34**	**3.04**	**2.82**	**2.66**	**2.53**	**2.43**	**2.34**	**2.26**	**2.20**	**2.09**	**2.01**	**1.89**
∞	3.84	2.99	2.60	2.37	2.21	2.09	2.01	1.94	1.88	1.83	1.79	1.75	1.69	1.64	1.57
	6.64	**4.60**	**3.78**	**3.32**	**3.02**	**2.80**	**2.64**	**2.51**	**2.41**	**2.32**	**2.24**	**2.18**	**2.07**	**1.99**	**1.87**

Table H CRITICAL VALUES OF THE STUDENTIZED RANGE STATISTIC

df_w	α	\multicolumn{9}{c}{k = number of groups}
		2	3	4	5	6	7	8	9	10
5	.05	3.64	4.60	5.22	5.67	6.03	6.33	6.58	6.80	6.99
	.01	5.70	6.98	7.80	8.42	8.91	9.32	9.67	9.97	10.24
6	.05	3.46	4.34	4.90	5.30	5.63	5.90	6.12	6.32	6.49
	.01	5.24	6.33	7.03	7.56	7.97	8.32	8.61	8.87	9.10
7	.05	3.34	4.16	4.68	5.06	5.36	5.61	5.82	6.00	6.16
	.01	4.95	5.92	6.54	7.01	7.37	7.68	7.94	8.17	8.37
8	.05	3.26	4.04	4.53	4.89	5.17	5.40	5.60	5.77	5.92
	.01	4.75	5.64	6.20	6.62	6.96	7.24	7.47	7.68	7.86
9	.05	3.20	3.95	4.41	4.76	5.02	5.24	5.43	5.59	5.74
	.01	4.60	5.43	5.96	6.35	6.66	6.91	7.13	7.33	7.49
10	.05	3.15	3.88	4.33	4.65	4.91	5.12	5.30	5.46	5.60
	.01	4.48	5.27	5.77	6.14	6.43	6.67	6.87	7.05	7.21
11	.05	3.11	3.82	4.26	4.57	4.82	5.03	5.20	5.35	5.49
	.01	4.39	5.15	5.62	5.97	6.25	6.48	6.67	6.84	6.99
12	.05	3.08	3.77	4.20	4.51	4.75	4.95	5.12	5.27	5.39
	.01	4.32	5.05	5.50	5.84	6.10	6.32	6.51	6.67	6.81
13	.05	3.06	3.73	4.15	4.45	4.69	4.88	5.05	5.19	5.32
	.01	4.26	4.96	5.40	5.73	5.98	6.19	6.37	6.53	6.67
14	.05	3.03	3.70	4.11	4.41	4.64	4.83	4.99	5.13	5.25
	.01	4.21	4.89	5.32	5.63	5.88	6.08	6.26	6.41	6.54
15	.05	3.01	3.67	4.08	4.37	4.59	4.78	4.94	5.08	5.20
	.01	4.17	4.84	5.25	5.56	5.80	5.99	6.16	6.31	6.44
16	.05	3.00	3.65	4.05	4.33	4.56	4.74	4.90	5.03	5.15
	.01	4.13	4.79	5.19	5.49	5.72	5.92	6.08	6.22	6.35
17	.05	2.98	3.63	4.02	4.30	4.52	4.70	4.86	4.99	5.11
	.01	4.10	4.74	5.14	5.43	5.66	5.85	6.01	6.15	6.27
18	.05	2.97	3.61	4.00	4.28	4.49	4.67	4.82	4.96	5.07
	.01	4.07	4.70	5.09	5.38	5.60	5.79	5.94	6.08	6.20
19	.05	2.96	3.59	3.98	4.25	4.47	4.65	4.79	4.92	5.04
	.01	4.05	4.67	5.05	5.33	5.55	5.73	5.89	6.02	6.14

Table H *(continued)*

df_w	α	\(k = \) number of groups								
		2	3	4	5	6	7	8	9	10
20	.05	2.95	3.58	3.96	4.23	4.45	4.62	4.77	4.90	5.01
	.01	4.02	4.64	5.02	5.29	5.51	5.69	5.84	5.97	6.09
24	.05	2.92	3.53	3.90	4.17	4.37	4.54	4.68	4.81	4.92
	.01	3.96	4.55	4.91	5.17	5.37	5.54	5.69	5.81	5.92
30	.05	2.89	3.49	3.85	4.10	4.30	4.46	4.60	4.72	4.82
	.01	3.89	4.45	4.80	5.05	5.24	5.40	5.54	5.65	5.76
40	.05	2.86	3.44	3.79	4.04	4.23	4.39	4.52	4.63	4.73
	.01	3.82	4.37	4.70	4.93	5.11	5.26	5.39	5.50	5.60
60	.05	2.83	3.40	3.74	3.98	4.16	4.31	4.44	4.55	4.65
	.01	3.76	4.28	4.59	4.82	4.99	5.13	5.25	5.36	5.45
120	.05	2.80	3.36	3.68	3.92	4.10	4.24	4.36	4.47	4.56
	.01	3.70	4.20	4.50	4.71	4.87	5.01	5.12	5.21	5.30
∞	.05	2.77	3.31	3.63	3.86	4.03	4.17	4.29	4.39	4.47
	.01	3.64	4.12	4.40	4.60	4.76	4.88	4.99	5.08	5.16

Table I **DUNN'S CRITICAL VALUES FOR BONFERRONI** *t*
These are nondirectional alphas. For directional tests, the correct alpha value is
one-half of the tabled alpha value.

df	α_{EW}	2	3	4	5	6	7	8	9	10
					Number of Comparisons (*C*)					
2	.10	4.243	5.243	6.081	6.816	7.480	8.090	8.656	9.188	9.691
	.05	6.164	7.582	8.774	9.823	10.769	11.639	12.449	13.208	13.927
	.01	14.071	17.248	19.925	22.282	24.413	26.372	28.196	29.908	31.528
3	.10	3.149	3.690	4.115	4.471	4.780	5.055	5.304	5.532	5.744
	.05	4.156	4.826	5.355	5.799	6.185	6.529	6.842	7.128	7.394
	.01	7.447	8.565	9.453	10.201	10.853	11.436	11.966	12.453	12.904
4	.10	2.751	3.150	3.452	3.669	3.909	4.093	4.257	4.406	4.542
	.05	3.481	3.941	4.290	4.577	4.822	5.036	5.228	5.402	5.562
	.01	5.594	6.248	6.751	7.166	7.520	7.832	8.112	8.367	8.600
5	.10	2.549	2.882	3.129	3.327	3.493	3.638	3.765	3.880	3.985
	.05	3.152	3.518	3.791	4.012	4.197	4.358	4.501	4.630	4.747
	.01	4.771	5.243	5.599	5.888	6.133	6.346	6.535	6.706	6.862
6	.10	2.428	2.723	2.939	3.110	3.253	3.376	3.484	3.580	3.668
	.05	2.959	3.274	3.505	3.690	3.845	3.978	4.095	4.200	4.296
	.01	4.315	4.695	4.977	5.203	5.394	5.559	5.704	5.835	5.954
7	.10	2.347	2.618	2.814	2.969	3.097	3.206	3.302	3.388	3.465
	.05	2.832	3.115	3.321	3.484	3.620	3.736	3.838	3.929	4.011
	.01	4.027	4.353	4.591	4.782	4.941	5.078	5.198	5.306	5.404
8	.10	2.289	2.544	2.726	2.869	2.987	3.088	3.176	3.254	3.324
	.05	2.743	3.005	3.193	3.342	3.464	3.569	3.661	3.743	3.816
	.01	3.831	4.120	4.331	4.498	4.637	4.756	4.860	4.953	5.038
9	.10	2.246	2.488	2.661	2.796	2.907	3.001	3.083	3.155	3.221
	.05	2.677	2.923	3.099	3.237	3.351	3.448	3.532	3.607	3.675
	.01	3.688	3.952	4.143	4.294	4.419	4.526	4.619	4.703	4.778
10	.10	2.213	2.446	2.611	2.739	2.845	2.934	3.012	3.080	3.142
	.05	2.626	2.860	3.027	3.157	3.264	3.355	3.434	3.505	3.568
	.01	3.580	3.825	4.002	4.141	2.256	4.354	4.439	4.515	4.584
11	.10	2.186	2.412	2.571	2.695	2.796	2.881	2.955	3.021	3.079
	.05	2.586	2.811	2.970	3.094	3.196	3.283	3.358	3.424	3.484
	.01	3.495	3.726	3.892	4.022	4.129	4.221	4.300	4.371	4.434
12	.10	2.164	2.384	2.539	2.658	2.756	2.838	2.910	2.973	3.029
	.05	2.553	2.770	2.924	3.044	3.141	3.224	3.296	3.359	3.416
	.01	3.427	3.647	3.804	3.927	4.029	4.114	4.189	4.256	4.315

Table I (cont.)

| df | α_{EW} | \multicolumn{9}{c}{Number of Comparisons (C)} |
		2	3	4	5	6	7	8	9	10
13	.10	2.146	2.361	2.512	2.628	2.723	2.803	2.872	2.933	2.988
	.05	2.526	2.737	2.886	3.002	3.096	3.176	3.245	3.306	3.361
	.01	3.371	3.582	3.733	3.850	3.946	4.028	4.099	4.162	4.218
14	.10	2.131	2.342	2.489	2.603	2.696	2.774	2.841	2.900	2.953
	.05	2.503	2.709	2.854	2.967	3.058	3.135	3.202	3.261	3.314
	.01	3.324	3.528	3.673	3.785	3.878	3.956	4.024	4.084	4.138
15	.10	2.118	2.325	2.470	2.582	2.672	2.748	2.814	2.872	2.924
	.05	2.483	2.685	2.827	2.937	3.026	3.101	3.166	3.224	3.275
	.01	3.285	3.482	3.622	3.731	3.820	3.895	3.961	4.019	4.071
16	.10	2.106	2.311	2.453	2.563	2.652	2.726	2.791	2.848	2.898
	.05	2.467	2.665	2.804	2.911	2.998	3.072	3.135	3.191	3.241
	.01	3.251	3.443	3.579	3.684	3.771	3.844	3.907	3.963	4.013
18	.10	2.088	2.287	2.426	2.532	2.619	2.691	2.753	2.808	2.857
	.05	2.439	2.631	2.766	2.869	2.953	3.024	3.085	3.138	3.186
	.01	3.195	3.379	3.508	3.609	3.691	3.760	3.820	3.872	3.920
20	.10	2.073	2.269	2.405	2.508	2.593	2.663	2.724	2.777	2.824
	.05	2.417	2.605	2.736	2.836	2.918	2.986	3.045	3.097	3.143
	.01	3.152	3.329	3.454	3.550	3.629	3.695	3.752	3.802	3.848
25	.10	2.047	2.236	2.367	2.466	2.547	2.614	2.672	2.722	2.767
	.05	2.379	2.558	2.683	2.779	2.856	2.921	2.976	3.025	3.069
	.01	3.077	3.243	3.359	3.449	3.521	3.583	3.635	3.682	3.723
30	.10	2.030	2.215	2.342	2.439	2.517	2.582	2.638	2.687	2.731
	.05	2.354	2.528	2.649	2.742	2.816	2.878	2.932	2.979	3.021
	.01	3.029	3.188	3.298	3.384	3.453	3.511	3.561	3.605	3.644
40	.10	2.009	2.189	2.312	2.406	2.481	2.544	2.597	2.644	2.686
	.05	2.323	2.492	2.608	2.696	2.768	2.827	2.878	2.923	2.963
	.01	2.970	3.121	3.225	3.305	3.370	3.425	3.472	3.513	3.549
60	.10	1.989	2.163	2.283	2.373	2.446	2.506	2.558	2.603	2.643
	.05	2.294	2.456	2.568	2.653	2.721	2.777	2.826	2.869	2.906
	.01	2.914	3.056	3.155	3.230	3.291	3.342	3.386	3.425	3.459
120	.10	1.968	2.138	2.254	2.342	2.411	2.469	2.519	2.562	2.600
	.05	2.265	2.422	2.529	2.610	2.675	2.729	2.776	2.816	2.852
	.01	2.859	2.994	3.087	3.158	3.215	3.263	3.304	3.340	3.372
∞	.10	1.949	2.114	2.226	2.311	2.378	2.434	2.482	2.523	2.560
	.05	2.237	2.388	2.491	2.569	2.631	2.683	2.727	2.766	2.800
	.01	2.806	2.934	3.022	3.089	3.143	3.186	3.226	3.260	3.289

This table is taken from Games (1977), reproduced with permission of the editor of the *Journal of the American Statistical Association*.

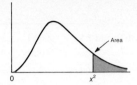

Table J CRITICAL VALUES OF THE CHI-SQUARE DISTRIBUTION

The degrees of freedom for each chi-square distribution appear in column 1. The heading of each column gives the proportion of the area under the curve which falls above the tabled value of chi-square.

Degrees of freedom df	$p = .99$	.98	.95	.90	.80	.70
1	.000157	.000628	.00393	.0158	.0642	.148
2	.0201	.0404	.103	.211	.446	.713
3	.115	.185	.352	.584	1.005	1.424
4	.297	.429	.711	1.064	1.649	2.195
5	.554	.752	1.145	1.610	2.343	3.000
6	.872	1.134	1.635	2.204	3.070	3.828
7	1.239	1.564	2.167	2.833	3.822	4.671
8	1.646	2.032	2.733	3.490	4.594	5.527
9	2.088	2.532	3.325	4.168	5.380	6.393
10	2.558	3.059	3.940	4.865	6.179	7.267
11	3.053	3.609	4.575	5.578	6.989	8.148
12	3.571	4.178	5.226	6.304	7.807	9.034
13	4.107	4.765	5.892	7.042	8.634	9.926
14	4.660	5.368	6.571	7.790	9.467	10.821
15	5.229	5.985	7.261	8.547	10.307	11.721
16	5.812	6.614	7.962	9.312	11.152	12.624
17	6.408	7.255	8.672	10.085	12.002	13.531
18	7.015	7.906	9.390	10.865	12.857	14.440
19	7.633	8.567	10.117	11.651	13.716	15.352
20	8.260	9.237	10.851	12.443	14.578	16.266
21	8.897	9.915	11.591	13.240	15.445	17.182
22	9.542	10.600	12.338	14.041	16.314	18.101
23	10.196	11.293	13.091	14.848	17.187	19.021
24	10.856	11.992	13.848	15.659	18.062	19.943
25	11.524	12.697	14.611	16.473	18.940	20.867
26	12.198	13.409	15.379	17.292	19.820	21.792
27	12.879	14.125	16.151	18.114	20.703	22.719
28	13.565	14.847	16.928	18.939	21.588	23.647
29	14.256	15.574	17.708	19.768	22.475	24.577
30	14.953	16.306	18.493	20.599	23.364	25.508

Taken from Table IV of Fisher and Yates, *Statistical Tables for Biological, Agricultural and Medical Research,* published by Longman Group UK Ltd. London (previously published by Oliver and Boyd Ltd., Edinburgh) and by permission of the authors and publishers.

Table J *(continued)*

.50	.30	.20	.10	.05	.02	.01
.455	1.074	1.642	2.706	3.841	5.412	6.635
1.386	2.408	3.219	4.605	5.991	7.824	9.210
2.366	3.665	4.642	6.251	7.815	9.837	11.341
3.357	4.878	5.989	7.779	9.488	11.668	13.277
4.351	6.064	7.289	9.236	11.070	13.388	15.086
5.348	7.231	8.558	10.645	12.592	15.033	16.812
6.346	8.383	9.803	12.017	14.067	16.622	18.475
7.344	9.524	11.030	13.362	15.507	18.168	20.090
8.343	10.656	12.242	14.684	16.919	19.679	21.666
9.342	11.781	13.442	15.987	18.307	21.161	23.209
10.341	12.899	14.631	17.275	19.675	22.618	24.725
11.340	14.011	15.812	18.549	21.026	24.054	26.217
12.340	15.119	16.985	19.812	22.362	25.472	27.688
13.339	16.222	18.151	21.064	23.685	26.873	29.141
14.339	17.322	19.311	22.307	24.996	28.259	30.578
15.338	18.418	20.465	23.542	26.296	29.633	32.000
16.338	19.511	21.615	24.769	27.587	30.995	33.409
17.338	20.601	22.760	25.989	28.869	32.346	34.805
18.338	21.689	23.900	27.204	30.144	33.687	36.191
19.337	22.775	25.038	28.412	31.410	35.020	37.566
20.337	23.858	26.171	29.615	32.671	36.343	38.932
21.337	24.939	27.301	30.813	33.924	37.659	40.289
22.337	26.018	28.429	32.007	35.172	38.968	41.638
23.337	27.096	29.553	33.196	36.415	40.270	42.980
24.337	28.172	30.675	34.382	37.652	41.566	44.314
25.336	29.246	31.795	35.563	38.885	42.856	45.642
26.336	30.319	32.912	36.741	40.113	44.140	46.963
27.336	31.391	34.027	37.916	41.337	45.419	48.278
28.336	32.461	35.139	39.087	42.557	46.693	49.588
29.336	33.530	36.250	40.256	43.773	47.962	50.892

Table K **CRITICAL VALUES OF THE MANN-WHITNEY** *U*
For a Directional Test at .05 or a Nondirectional Test at .10 (underlined)

(Each cell: upper value = directional .05; lower *italic* value = nondirectional .10)

n_B \ n_A	1	2	3	4	5	6	7	8	9	10	11	12	13	14	15	16	17	18	19	20
1	—	—	—	—	—	—	—	—	—	—	—	—	—	—	—	—	—	—	0 *19*	0 *20*
2	—	—	—	—	0 *10*	0 *12*	0 *14*	1 *15*	1 *17*	1 *19*	1 *21*	2 *22*	2 *24*	2 *26*	3 *27*	3 *29*	3 *31*	4 *32*	4 *34*	4 *36*
3	—	—	0 *9*	0 *12*	1 *14*	2 *16*	2 *19*	3 *21*	3 *24*	4 *26*	5 *28*	5 *31*	6 *33*	7 *35*	7 *38*	8 *40*	9 *42*	9 *45*	10 *47*	11 *49*
4	—	—	0 *12*	1 *15*	2 *18*	3 *21*	4 *24*	5 *27*	6 *30*	7 *33*	8 *36*	9 *39*	10 *42*	11 *45*	12 *48*	14 *50*	15 *53*	16 *56*	17 *59*	18 *62*
5	—	0 *10*	1 *14*	2 *18*	4 *21*	5 *25*	6 *29*	8 *32*	9 *36*	11 *39*	12 *43*	13 *47*	15 *50*	16 *54*	18 *57*	19 *61*	20 *65*	22 *68*	23 *72*	25 *75*
6	—	0 *12*	2 *16*	3 *21*	5 *25*	7 *29*	8 *34*	10 *38*	12 *42*	14 *46*	16 *50*	17 *55*	19 *59*	21 *63*	23 *67*	25 *71*	26 *76*	28 *80*	30 *84*	32 *88*
7	—	0 *14*	2 *19*	4 *24*	6 *29*	8 *34*	11 *38*	13 *43*	15 *48*	17 *53*	19 *58*	21 *63*	24 *67*	26 *72*	28 *77*	30 *82*	33 *86*	35 *91*	37 *96*	39 *101*
8	—	1 *15*	3 *21*	5 *27*	8 *32*	10 *38*	13 *43*	15 *49*	18 *54*	20 *60*	23 *65*	26 *70*	28 *76*	31 *81*	33 *87*	36 *92*	39 *97*	41 *103*	44 *108*	47 *113*
9	—	1 *17*	3 *24*	6 *30*	9 *36*	12 *42*	15 *48*	18 *54*	21 *60*	24 *66*	27 *72*	30 *78*	33 *84*	36 *90*	39 *96*	42 *102*	45 *108*	48 *114*	51 *120*	54 *126*
10	—	1 *19*	4 *26*	7 *33*	11 *39*	14 *46*	17 *53*	20 *60*	24 *66*	27 *73*	31 *79*	34 *86*	37 *93*	41 *99*	44 *106*	48 *112*	51 *119*	55 *125*	58 *132*	62 *138*
11	—	1 *21*	5 *28*	8 *36*	12 *43*	16 *50*	19 *58*	23 *65*	27 *72*	31 *79*	34 *87*	38 *94*	42 *101*	46 *108*	50 *115*	54 *122*	57 *130*	61 *137*	65 *144*	69 *151*
12	—	2 *22*	5 *31*	9 *39*	13 *47*	17 *55*	21 *63*	26 *70*	30 *78*	34 *86*	38 *94*	42 *102*	47 *109*	51 *117*	55 *125*	60 *132*	64 *140*	68 *148*	72 *156*	77 *163*
13	—	2 *24*	6 *33*	10 *42*	15 *50*	19 *59*	24 *67*	28 *76*	33 *84*	37 *93*	42 *101*	47 *109*	51 *118*	56 *126*	61 *134*	65 *143*	70 *151*	75 *159*	80 *167*	84 *176*
14	—	2 *26*	7 *35*	11 *45*	16 *54*	21 *63*	26 *72*	31 *81*	36 *90*	41 *99*	46 *108*	51 *117*	56 *126*	61 *135*	66 *144*	71 *153*	77 *161*	82 *170*	87 *179*	92 *188*
15	—	3 *27*	7 *38*	12 *48*	18 *57*	23 *67*	28 *77*	33 *87*	39 *96*	44 *106*	50 *115*	55 *125*	61 *134*	66 *144*	72 *153*	77 *163*	83 *172*	88 *182*	94 *191*	100 *200*
16	—	3 *29*	8 *40*	14 *50*	19 *61*	25 *71*	30 *82*	36 *92*	42 *102*	48 *112*	54 *122*	60 *132*	65 *143*	71 *153*	77 *163*	83 *173*	89 *183*	95 *193*	101 *203*	107 *213*
17	—	3 *31*	9 *42*	15 *53*	20 *65*	26 *76*	33 *86*	39 *97*	45 *108*	51 *119*	57 *130*	64 *140*	70 *151*	77 *161*	83 *172*	89 *183*	96 *193*	102 *204*	109 *214*	115 *225*
18	—	4 *32*	9 *45*	16 *56*	22 *68*	28 *80*	35 *91*	41 *103*	48 *114*	55 *123*	61 *137*	68 *148*	75 *159*	82 *170*	88 *182*	95 *193*	102 *204*	109 *215*	116 *226*	123 *237*
19	0 *19*	4 *34*	10 *47*	17 *59*	23 *72*	30 *84*	37 *96*	44 *108*	51 *120*	58 *132*	65 *144*	72 *156*	80 *167*	87 *179*	94 *191*	101 *203*	109 *214*	116 *226*	123 *238*	130 *250*
20	0 *20*	4 *36*	11 *49*	18 *62*	25 *75*	32 *88*	39 *101*	47 *113*	54 *126*	62 *138*	69 *151*	77 *163*	84 *176*	92 *188*	100 *200*	107 *213*	115 *225*	123 *237*	130 *250*	138 *262*

(Dashes in the body of the table indicate that no decision is possible at the stated level of significance.)

From D. Auble, Extended Tables for the Mann-Whitney Statistic, Tables 2, 3, 5, and 7, *Bulletin of the Institute of Educational Research*, vol. 1, no. 2, Indiana University. Reprinted with permission of the author and publisher.

Table K (*cont*)
For a Directional Test at .025 or a Nondirectional Test at .05 (underlined)

The upper (italicized) value in each cell is the nondirectional (underlined) critical value. Dashes indicate that no decision is possible.

n_B \ n_A	1	2	3	4	5	6	7	8	9	10	11	12	13	14	15	16	17	18	19	20
1	—	—	—	—	—	—	—	—	—	—	—	—	—	—	—	—	—	—	—	—
2	—	—	—	—	—	—	—	0	0	0	0	1	1	1	1	1	2	2	2	2
								16	*18*	*20*	*22*	*23*	*25*	*27*	*29*	*31*	*32*	*34*	*36*	*38*
3	—	—	—	—	0	1	1	2	2	3	3	4	4	5	5	6	6	7	7	8
					15	*17*	*20*	*22*	*25*	*27*	*30*	*32*	*35*	*37*	*40*	*42*	*45*	*47*	*50*	*52*
4	—	—	—	0	1	2	3	4	4	5	6	7	8	9	10	11	11	12	13	13
				16	*19*	*22*	*25*	*28*	*32*	*35*	*38*	*41*	*44*	*47*	*50*	*53*	*57*	*60*	*63*	*67*
5	—	—	0	1	2	3	5	6	7	8	9	11	12	13	14	15	17	18	19	20
			15	*19*	*23*	*27*	*30*	*34*	*38*	*42*	*46*	*49*	*53*	*57*	*61*	*65*	*68*	*72*	*76*	*80*
6	—	—	1	2	3	5	6	8	10	11	13	14	16	17	19	21	22	24	25	27
			17	*22*	*27*	*31*	*36*	*40*	*44*	*49*	*53*	*58*	*62*	*67*	*71*	*75*	*80*	*84*	*89*	*93*
7	—	—	1	3	5	6	8	10	12	14	16	18	20	22	24	26	28	30	32	34
			20	*25*	*30*	*36*	*41*	*46*	*51*	*56*	*61*	*66*	*71*	*76*	*81*	*86*	*91*	*96*	*101*	*106*
8	—	0	2	4	6	8	10	13	15	17	19	22	24	26	29	31	34	36	38	41
		16	*22*	*28*	*34*	*40*	*46*	*51*	*57*	*63*	*69*	*74*	*80*	*86*	*91*	*97*	*102*	*108*	*114*	*119*
9	—	0	2	4	7	10	12	15	17	20	23	26	28	31	34	37	39	42	45	48
		18	*25*	*32*	*38*	*44*	*51*	*57*	*64*	*70*	*76*	*82*	*89*	*95*	*101*	*107*	*114*	*120*	*126*	*132*
10	—	0	3	5	8	11	14	17	20	23	26	29	33	36	39	42	45	48	52	55
		20	*27*	*35*	*42*	*49*	*56*	*63*	*70*	*77*	*84*	*91*	*97*	*104*	*111*	*118*	*125*	*132*	*138*	*145*
11	—	0	3	6	9	13	16	19	23	26	30	33	37	40	44	47	51	55	58	62
		22	*30*	*38*	*46*	*53*	*61*	*69*	*76*	*84*	*91*	*99*	*106*	*114*	*121*	*129*	*136*	*143*	*151*	*158*
12	—	1	4	7	11	14	18	22	26	29	33	37	41	45	49	53	57	61	65	69
		23	*32*	*41*	*49*	*58*	*66*	*74*	*82*	*91*	*99*	*107*	*115*	*123*	*131*	*139*	*147*	*155*	*163*	*171*
13	—	1	4	8	12	16	20	24	28	33	37	41	45	50	54	59	63	67	72	76
		25	*35*	*44*	*53*	*62*	*71*	*80*	*89*	*97*	*106*	*115*	*124*	*132*	*141*	*149*	*158*	*167*	*175*	*184*
14	—	1	5	9	13	17	22	26	31	36	40	45	50	55	59	64	67	74	78	83
		27	*37*	*47*	*57*	*67*	*76*	*86*	*95*	*104*	*114*	*123*	*132*	*141*	*151*	*160*	*171*	*178*	*188*	*197*
15	—	1	5	10	14	19	24	29	34	39	44	49	54	59	64	70	75	80	85	90
		29	*40*	*50*	*61*	*71*	*81*	*91*	*101*	*111*	*121*	*131*	*141*	*151*	*161*	*170*	*180*	*190*	*200*	*210*
16	—	1	6	11	15	21	26	31	37	42	47	53	59	64	70	75	81	86	92	98
		31	*42*	*53*	*65*	*75*	*86*	*97*	*107*	*118*	*129*	*139*	*149*	*160*	*170*	*181*	*191*	*202*	*212*	*222*
17	—	2	6	11	17	22	28	34	39	45	51	57	63	67	75	81	87	93	99	105
		32	*45*	*57*	*68*	*80*	*91*	*102*	*114*	*125*	*136*	*147*	*158*	*171*	*180*	*191*	*202*	*213*	*224*	*235*
18	—	2	7	12	18	24	30	36	42	48	55	61	67	74	80	86	93	99	106	112
		34	*47*	*60*	*72*	*84*	*96*	*108*	*120*	*132*	*143*	*155*	*167*	*178*	*190*	*202*	*213*	*225*	*236*	*248*
19	—	2	7	13	19	25	32	38	45	52	58	65	72	78	85	92	99	106	113	119
		36	*50*	*63*	*76*	*89*	*101*	*114*	*126*	*138*	*151*	*163*	*175*	*188*	*200*	*212*	*224*	*236*	*248*	*261*
20	—	2	8	13	20	27	34	41	48	55	62	69	76	83	90	98	105	112	119	127
		38	*52*	*67*	*80*	*93*	*106*	*119*	*132*	*145*	*158*	*171*	*184*	*197*	*210*	*222*	*235*	*248*	*261*	*273*

(Dashes in the body of the table indicate that no decision is possible at the stated level of significance.)

Table K (*cont*)
For a Directional Test at .01 or a Nondirectional Test at .02 (underlined)

n_B \ n_A	1	2	3	4	5	6	7	8	9	10	11	12	13	14	15	16	17	18	19	20
1	—	—	—	—	—	—	—	—	—	—	—	—	—	—	—	—	—	—	—	—
2	—	—	—	—	—	—	—	—	—	—	—	—	0	0	0	0	0	0	1	1
													26	28	30	32	34	36	37	39
3	—	—	—	—	—	—	0	0	1	1	1	2	2	2	3	3	4	4	4	5
							21	24	26	29	32	34	37	40	42	45	47	50	52	55
4	—	—	—	—	0	1	1	2	3	3	4	5	5	6	7	7	8	9	9	10
					20	23	27	30	33	37	40	43	47	50	53	57	60	63	67	70
5	—	—	—	0	1	2	3	4	5	6	7	8	9	10	11	12	13	14	15	16
				20	24	28	32	36	40	44	48	52	56	60	64	68	72	76	80	84
6	—	—	—	1	2	3	4	6	7	8	9	11	12	13	15	16	18	19	20	22
				23	28	33	38	42	47	52	57	61	66	71	75	80	84	89	94	93
7	—	—	0	1	3	4	6	7	9	11	12	14	16	17	19	21	23	24	26	28
			21	27	32	38	43	49	54	59	65	70	75	81	86	91	96	102	107	112
8	—	—	0	2	4	6	7	9	11	13	15	17	20	22	24	26	28	30	32	34
			24	30	36	42	49	55	61	67	73	79	84	90	96	102	108	114	120	126
9	—	—	1	3	5	7	9	11	14	16	18	21	23	26	28	31	33	36	38	40
			26	33	40	47	54	61	67	74	81	87	94	100	107	113	120	126	133	140
10	—	—	1	3	6	8	11	13	16	19	22	24	27	30	33	36	38	41	44	47
			29	37	44	52	59	67	74	81	88	96	103	110	117	124	132	139	146	153
11	—	—	1	4	7	9	12	15	18	22	25	28	31	34	37	41	44	47	50	53
			32	40	48	57	65	73	81	88	96	104	112	120	128	135	143	151	159	167
12	—	—	2	5	8	11	14	17	21	24	28	31	35	38	42	46	49	53	56	60
			34	43	52	61	70	79	87	96	104	113	121	130	138	146	155	163	172	180
13	—	0	2	5	9	12	16	20	23	27	31	35	39	43	47	51	55	59	63	67
		26	37	47	56	66	75	84	94	103	112	121	130	139	148	157	166	175	184	193
14	—	0	2	6	10	13	17	22	26	30	34	38	43	47	51	56	60	65	69	73
		28	40	50	60	71	81	90	100	110	120	130	139	149	159	168	178	187	197	207
15	—	0	3	7	11	15	19	24	28	33	37	42	47	51	56	61	66	70	75	80
		30	42	53	64	75	86	96	107	117	128	138	148	159	169	179	189	200	210	220
16	—	0	3	7	12	16	21	26	31	36	41	46	51	56	61	66	71	76	82	87
		32	45	57	68	80	91	102	113	124	135	146	157	168	179	190	201	212	222	233
17	—	0	4	8	13	18	23	28	33	38	44	49	55	60	66	71	77	82	88	93
		34	47	60	72	84	96	108	120	132	143	155	166	178	189	201	212	224	234	247
18	—	0	4	9	14	19	24	30	36	41	47	53	59	65	70	76	82	88	94	100
		36	50	63	76	89	102	114	126	139	151	163	175	187	200	212	224	236	248	260
19	—	1	4	9	15	20	26	32	38	44	50	56	63	69	75	82	88	94	101	107
		37	53	67	80	94	107	120	133	146	159	172	184	197	210	222	235	248	260	273
20	—	1	5	10	16	22	28	34	40	47	53	60	67	73	80	87	93	100	107	114
		39	55	70	84	98	112	126	140	153	167	180	193	207	220	233	247	260	273	286

(Dashes in the body of the table indicate that no decision is possible at the stated level of significance.)

Table K (cont)

For a Directional Test at .005 or a Nondirectional Test at .01 (underlined)

Each cell shows the critical value (top) and its underlined complement (bottom, shown in italics). Dashes indicate no decision is possible.

n_B \ n_A	1	2	3	4	5	6	7	8	9	10	11	12	13	14	15	16	17	18	19	20
1	—	—	—	—	—	—	—	—	—	—	—	—	—	—	—	—	—	—	—	—
2	—	—	—	—	—	—	—	—	—	—	—	—	—	—	—	—	—	—	0 / _38_	0 / _40_
3	—	—	—	—	—	—	—	—	0 / _27_	0 / _30_	0 / _33_	1 / _35_	1 / _38_	1 / _41_	2 / _43_	2 / _46_	2 / _49_	2 / _52_	3 / _54_	3 / _57_
4	—	—	—	—	—	0 / _24_	0 / _28_	1 / _31_	1 / _35_	2 / _38_	2 / _42_	3 / _45_	3 / _49_	4 / _52_	5 / _55_	5 / _59_	6 / _62_	6 / _66_	7 / _69_	8 / _72_
5	—	—	—	—	0 / _25_	1 / _29_	1 / _34_	2 / _38_	3 / _42_	4 / _46_	5 / _50_	6 / _54_	7 / _58_	7 / _63_	8 / _67_	9 / _71_	10 / _75_	11 / _79_	12 / _83_	13 / _87_
6	—	—	—	0 / _24_	1 / _29_	2 / _34_	3 / _39_	4 / _44_	5 / _49_	6 / _54_	7 / _59_	9 / _63_	10 / _68_	11 / _73_	12 / _78_	13 / _83_	15 / _87_	16 / _92_	17 / _97_	18 / _102_
7	—	—	—	0 / _28_	1 / _34_	3 / _39_	4 / _45_	6 / _50_	7 / _56_	9 / _61_	10 / _67_	12 / _72_	13 / _78_	15 / _83_	16 / _89_	18 / _94_	19 / _100_	21 / _105_	22 / _111_	24 / _116_
8	—	—	—	1 / _31_	2 / _38_	4 / _44_	6 / _50_	7 / _57_	9 / _63_	11 / _69_	13 / _75_	15 / _81_	17 / _87_	18 / _94_	20 / _100_	22 / _106_	24 / _112_	26 / _118_	28 / _124_	30 / _130_
9	—	—	0 / _27_	1 / _35_	3 / _42_	5 / _49_	7 / _56_	9 / _63_	11 / _70_	13 / _77_	16 / _83_	18 / _90_	20 / _97_	22 / _104_	24 / _111_	27 / _117_	29 / _124_	31 / _131_	33 / _138_	36 / _144_
10	—	—	0 / _30_	2 / _38_	4 / _46_	6 / _54_	9 / _61_	11 / _69_	13 / _77_	16 / _84_	18 / _92_	21 / _99_	24 / _106_	26 / _114_	29 / _121_	31 / _129_	34 / _136_	37 / _143_	39 / _151_	42 / _158_
11	—	—	0 / _33_	2 / _42_	5 / _50_	7 / _59_	10 / _67_	13 / _75_	16 / _83_	18 / _92_	21 / _100_	24 / _108_	27 / _116_	30 / _124_	33 / _132_	36 / _140_	39 / _148_	42 / _156_	45 / _164_	48 / _172_
12	—	—	1 / _35_	3 / _45_	6 / _54_	9 / _63_	12 / _72_	15 / _81_	18 / _90_	21 / _99_	24 / _108_	27 / _117_	31 / _125_	34 / _134_	37 / _143_	41 / _151_	44 / _160_	47 / _169_	51 / _177_	54 / _186_
13	—	—	1 / _38_	3 / _49_	7 / _58_	10 / _68_	13 / _78_	17 / _87_	20 / _97_	24 / _106_	27 / _116_	31 / _125_	34 / _135_	38 / _144_	42 / _153_	45 / _163_	49 / _172_	53 / _181_	56 / _191_	60 / _200_
14	—	—	1 / _41_	4 / _52_	7 / _63_	11 / _73_	15 / _83_	18 / _94_	22 / _104_	26 / _114_	30 / _124_	34 / _134_	38 / _144_	42 / _154_	46 / _164_	50 / _174_	54 / _184_	58 / _194_	63 / _203_	67 / _213_
15	—	—	2 / _43_	5 / _55_	8 / _67_	12 / _78_	16 / _89_	20 / _100_	24 / _111_	29 / _121_	33 / _132_	37 / _143_	42 / _153_	46 / _164_	51 / _174_	55 / _185_	60 / _195_	64 / _206_	69 / _216_	73 / _227_
16	—	—	2 / _46_	5 / _59_	9 / _71_	13 / _83_	18 / _94_	22 / _106_	27 / _117_	31 / _129_	36 / _140_	41 / _151_	45 / _163_	50 / _174_	55 / _185_	60 / _196_	65 / _207_	70 / _218_	74 / _230_	79 / _241_
17	—	—	2 / _49_	6 / _62_	10 / _75_	15 / _87_	19 / _100_	24 / _112_	29 / _124_	34 / _136_	39 / _148_	44 / _160_	49 / _172_	54 / _184_	60 / _195_	65 / _207_	70 / _219_	75 / _231_	81 / _242_	86 / _254_
18	—	—	2 / _52_	6 / _66_	11 / _79_	16 / _92_	21 / _105_	26 / _118_	31 / _131_	37 / _143_	42 / _156_	47 / _169_	53 / _181_	58 / _194_	64 / _206_	70 / _218_	75 / _231_	81 / _243_	87 / _255_	92 / _268_
19	—	0 / _38_	3 / _54_	7 / _69_	12 / _83_	17 / _97_	22 / _111_	28 / _124_	33 / _138_	39 / _151_	45 / _164_	51 / _177_	56 / _191_	63 / _203_	69 / _216_	74 / _230_	81 / _242_	87 / _255_	93 / _268_	99 / _281_
20	—	0 / _40_	3 / _57_	8 / _72_	13 / _87_	18 / _102_	24 / _116_	30 / _130_	36 / _144_	42 / _158_	48 / _172_	54 / _186_	60 / _200_	67 / _213_	73 / _227_	79 / _241_	86 / _254_	92 / _268_	99 / _281_	105 / _295_

(Dashes in the body of the table indicate that no decision is possible at the stated level of significance.)

Table L **CRITICAL VALUES OF THE WILCOXON *T***

For a given N (the number of pairs of scores minus the pairs having zero differences), reject H_0 if the observed value is *less than or equal to* the table value for the appropriate level of significance.

	Level of significance for a directional test					Level of significance for a directional test			
	.05	.025	.01	.005		.05	.025	.01	.005
	Level of significance for a nondirectional test					Level of significance for a nondirectional test			
N	.10	.05	.02	.01	N	.10	.05	.02	.01
5	0	—	—	—	28	130	116	101	91
6	2	0	—	—	29	140	126	110	100
7	3	2	0	—	30	151	137	120	109
8	5	3	1	0	31	163	147	130	118
9	8	5	3	1	32	175	159	140	128
10	10	8	5	3	33	187	170	151	138
11	13	10	7	5	34	200	182	162	148
12	17	13	9	7	35	213	195	173	159
13	21	17	12	9	36	227	208	185	171
14	25	21	15	12	37	241	221	198	182
15	30	25	19	15	38	256	235	211	194
16	35	29	23	19	39	271	249	224	207
17	41	34	27	23	40	286	264	238	220
18	47	40	32	27	41	302	279	252	233
19	53	46	37	32	42	319	294	266	247
20	60	52	43	37	43	336	310	281	261
21	67	58	49	42	44	353	327	296	276
22	75	65	55	48	45	371	343	312	291
23	83	73	62	54	46	389	361	328	307
24	91	81	69	61	47	407	378	345	322
25	100	89	76	68	48	426	396	362	339
26	110	98	84	75	49	446	415	379	355
27	119	107	92	83	50	466	434	397	373

R. E. Kirk (1984), *Elementary Statistics,* 2nd ed., California, Brooks/Cole. Reprinted with permission of the author and publisher.

References

Agnew, N. Mck., & Pike, S. W. (1978). *The science game* (2nd ed.). Englewood Cliffs, NJ: Prentice-Hall.

Anderson, N. H. (1961). Scales and statistics: Parametric and nonparametric. *Psychological Bulletin, 58*, 305–315.

Bell, E. T. (1937). Gauss: The prince of mathematics. In J. R. Newman (Ed.), *The world of mathematics*, vol. 1 (pp. 295–299). New York: Simon & Schuster.

Beyer, E. T. (1964). *Handbook of tables for probability and statistics*. Cleveland: Chemical Rubber Co.

Binder, A. (1984). Restrictions on statistics imposed by method of measurement: Some reality, much mythology. *Journal of Criminal Justice, 12*, 467–481.

Boik, R. J. (1987). The Fisher-Pitman permutation test: A non-robust alternative to the normal theory F when variances are heterogeneous. *British Journal of Mathematical and Statistical Psychology, 40*, 26–42.

Boneau, C. A. (1960). The effects of violations of assumptions on the t-test. *Psychological Bulletin, 57*(1), 49–64.

Bradley, J. V. (1968). *Distribution-free statistical tests*. Englewood Cliffs, NJ: Prentice-Hall.

Cochran, W. G. (1977). *Sampling Techniques* (3rd ed.). New York: Wiley.

Cohen, J. (1977). *Statistical power analysis for the behavioral sciences*. New York: Academic Press.

Collier, R. O., Jr., & Baker, F. B. (1966). Some Monte Carlo results on the power of the F-test under permutation in the simple randomized block design. *Biometrika, 53*, 199–203.

Collier, R. O., Jr., Baker, F. B., Mandeville, G. K., & Hayes, T. F. (1967). Estimates of test size for several test procedures based on conventional variance ratios in the repeated measures design. *Psychometrika, 32*, 399–353.

Dunn, O. J. (1961). Multiple comparisons among means. *Journal of the American Statistical Association, 56*, 52–64.

Edgington, R. S. (1987). *Randomization tests* (2nd ed.). New York: Marcell Dekker.

Feinstein, A. R. (1985). *Clinical epidemiology* (pp. 398–399). Philadelphia: W. J. Saunders.

Gaito, J. (1965). Unequal intervals and unequal *n* in trend analyses. *Psychological Bulletin, 63*, 125–127.

Gaito, J. (1986). Some issues in the measurement-statistics controversy. *Canadian Psychology, 27*, 63–68.

Galton, F. (1889). *Natural inheritance,* (p. 66). London: Macmillan.

Games, P. (1977). An improved *t* table for simultaneous control on *g* contrasts. *Journal of the American Statistical Association, 72*, 531–534.

Greenhouse, S. W., & Geisser, S. (1959). On methods in the analysis of profile data. *Psychometrika, 24*, 95–112.

Gregg, V. H., Montgomery, D., & Castaño, D. (1980). Recall of common and uncommon words from pure and mixed lists. *Journal of Verbal Learning and Verbal Behavior, 5*, 351–360.

Grice, G. R. (1966). Dependence of empirical laws upon the source of variation. *Psychological Bulletin, 66*, 488–493.

Hays, W. L. (1963). *Statistics for psychologists.* New York: Holt, Rinehart and Winston.

Huynh, H., & Feldt, L. S. (1970). Conditions under which mean square ratios in repeated measures designs have exact *F*-distributions. *Journal of the American Statistical Association, 65*, 1582–1589.

Johnson, R. C., McClearn, G. E., Yuen, S., Nagoshi, C. T., Ahern, F. M., & Cole, R. E. (1985). Galton's data a century later. *American Psychologist, 40*, 875–892.

Keppel, G. (1982). *Design and analysis: A researcher's handbook.* Englewood Cliffs, NJ: Prentice-Hall.

Keselman, H. J., & Keselman, J. C. (1987). Type I error control and the power to detect factorial effects. *British Journal of Mathematical and Statistical Psychology, 40*, 196–208.

Kish, L. (1965). *Survey sampling.* New York: Wiley.

Lord, F. M. (1953). On the statistical treatment of football numbers. *American Psychologist, 8*, 750–751.

McHugh, R. B. (1963). Comment on "scales and statistics: parametric and nonparametric." *Psychological Bulletin, 60*,350–355.

May, R. B., Cuddy, L. J., & Norton, J. M. (1979). Temporal contrast and the word frequency effect. *Canadian Journal of Psychology, 33*, 141–147.

May, R. B., Masson, M. E. J., & Hunter, M. A. (1989). Randomization tests: Viable alternatives to normal curve tests. *Behavior Research Methods, Instruments, and Computers, 21*, 482–483.

Mees, C. E. K. (1934). Scientific thought and social reconstruction. *Sigma Xi Quarterly, 22*, 13–24.

Mook, D. G. (1983). In defense of external invalidity. *American Psychologist, 38*, 379–387.

Mulligan, G. W., Wong, D. S., and Thompson, P. A. (1987). Robustness properties of nonorthogonal analysis of variance. *Psychological Bulletin, 101,* 464–470.

Pagano, R. R. (1986). *Understanding statistics in the behavioral sciences* (2nd ed.). St. Paul: West Publishing.

Publication Manual of the American Psychological Association. (3rd ed.) (1983). Washington DC: American Psychological Association.

Ramsey, P. H. (1980). Exact type 1 error rates for robustness of Student's *t* test with unequal variances. *Journal of Educational Statistics, 5,* 337–349.

Siegel, S., & Castellan, N. J., Jr. (1988). *Nonparametric statistics for the behavioral sciences* (2nd ed.). New York: McGraw-Hill.

Spinner, B., & Gabriel, R. M. (1981). Factorial analysis of variance with unequal cell frequencies. *Canadian Psychology, 22,* 260–270.

Stevens, S. S. (1951). Mathematics, measurement and psychophysics. In S. S. Stevens (Ed.), *Handbook of experimental psychology* (pp. 1–49). New York: Wiley.

Tukey, J. W. (1977). *Exploratory data analysis.* Reading, MA: Addison-Wesley.

Index

Normal Approximation of the Binomial

$$z = \frac{r_{RL} - np}{\sqrt{npq}} \qquad (8.6)$$

z Statistic for a Single Sample Mean

$$z_{\bar{x}} = \frac{\bar{X} - \mu}{\sigma_{\bar{x}}} \quad \text{where } \sigma_{\bar{x}} = \sigma/\sqrt{n} \qquad (10.2)$$

t Statistic for a Single Sample Mean

$$t = \frac{\bar{X} - \mu}{s_{\bar{x}}} \quad df = n - 1 \qquad (10.4)$$

t Ratio for a Single Correlation

$$t = \frac{r}{s_r} \quad \text{where } s_r = \sqrt{\frac{1 - r^2}{n - 2}} \qquad (10.6)$$

Pooled Variance for Independent Samples

$$s_p^2 = \frac{SS_1 + SS_2}{df_1 + df_2} = \frac{SS_1 + SS_2}{(n_1 - 1) + (n_2 - 1)} = \frac{SS_1 + SS_2}{n_1 + n_2 - 2} \qquad (11.7)$$

t Ratio for Two Independent Samples

$$t = \frac{\bar{X}_1 - \bar{X}_2}{\sqrt{s_p^2 \left(\frac{1}{n_1} + \frac{1}{n_2} \right)}} \quad df = n_1 + n_2 - 2 \qquad (11.11)$$

t Ratio for Two Dependent Samples

$$t(df) = \frac{\bar{X}_1 - \bar{X}_2}{s_{\bar{D}}} = \frac{\bar{D}}{s_{\bar{D}}} \quad df = n - 1 \qquad (11.13)$$

$$\text{where } s_{\bar{D}} = \frac{s_{\bar{D}}}{\sqrt{n}} = \sqrt{\frac{SS_D}{n(n - 1)}}$$

Anova for One Independent Factor

$$SS_{total} = \Sigma(X - GM)^2 = \Sigma X^2 - \frac{G^2}{N} \qquad (13.4)$$

$$SS_{within} = SS_{w1} + SS_{w2} + \ldots + SS_{wk} \qquad (13.6)$$

$$\text{where } SS_{wj} = \Sigma X^2 - \frac{T_j^2}{n_j}$$

$$SS_{between} = \Sigma n_j(\bar{X}_j - GM)^2 = \Sigma \frac{T_j^2}{n_j} - \frac{G^2}{N} \qquad (13.7)$$

$$F = \frac{MS_{between}}{MS_{within}}$$